*Equity and Justice
in Social Behavior*

Equity and Justice
in Social Behavior

Edited by

JERALD GREENBERG
Faculty of Management Sciences
The Ohio State University
Columbus, Ohio

RONALD L. COHEN
Social Science Division
Bennington College
Bennington, Vermont

With a Foreword by George C. Homans

ACADEMIC PRESS   1982
A Subsidiary of Harcourt Brace Jovanovich, Publishers
New York   London
Paris San Diego San Francisco São Paulo Sydney Tokyo Toronto

ACADEMIC PRESS, INC.
111 Fifth Avenue, New York, New York 10003

United Kingdom Edition published by
ACADEMIC PRESS, INC. (LONDON) LTD.
24/28 Oval Road, London NW1 7DX

Library of Congress Cataloging in Publication Data
Main entry under title:

Equity and justice in social behavior.

Includes bibliographies and index.
1. Social psychology. 2. Social justice.
3. Justice. 4. Interpersonal relations. I. Greenberg,
Jerald. II. Cohen, Ronald L.
HM251.E68   303.3'72   82-1602
ISBN 0-12-299580-5   AACR2

PRINTED IN THE

82 83 84 85   9

Contents

chapter 3

Justice and the Awareness of Social Entities   77

DANIEL M. WEGNER

chapter 4

Perceiving Justice: An Attributional Perspective   119

RONALD L. COHEN

chapter 5

Equity in Attitude Formation and Change   161

ICEK AJZEN

chapter 6

Effects of Conformity Pressure on Justice Behavior   187

VERNON L. ALLEN

chapter 7

Moral Evaluation in Intimate Relationships   217

WILLIAM AUSTIN AND JOYCE TOBIASEN

chapter 8

Prosocial Behavior, Equity, and Justice   261

DENNIS KREBS

chapter 9

Aggression and Inequity   309

EDWARD DONNERSTEIN AND ELAINE HATFIELD

Contributors

Numbers in parentheses indicate the pages on which the authors' contributions begin.

ICEK AJZEN (161), Department of Psychology, University of Massachusetts, Amherst, Massachusetts 01003

VERNON L. ALLEN (187), Department of Psychology, University of Wisconsin—Madison, Madison, Wisconsin 53706

WILLIAM AUSTIN (217), Department of Behavioral Medicine and Psychiatry, University of Virginia Medical Center, Charlottesville, Virginia 22908

RONALD L. COHEN (1, 119, 437), Social Science Division, Bennington College, Bennington, Vermont 05201

KAY DEAUX (43), Department of Psychological Sciences, Purdue University, West Lafayette, Indiana 47907

EDWARD DONNERSTEIN* (309), Department of Psychology, University of Wisconsin—Madison, Madison, Wisconsin 53706

JERALD GREENBERG (1, 389, 437), Faculty of Management Sciences, Ohio State University, Columbus, Ohio 43210

ELAINE HATFIELD (309), Department of Psychology, University of Hawaii at Manoa, Honolulu, Hawaii 96822

LINDA J. KEIL (337), Department of Psychology, University of California, Santa Barbara, Santa Barbara, California 93106

Present address: Communication Arts, University of Wisconsin—Madison, Madison, Wisconsin 53706.

DENNIS KREBS (261), Department of Psychology, Simon Fraser University, Burnaby, British Columbia, Canada V5A 1S6

BRENDA MAJOR (43), Department of Psychology, State University of New York at Buffalo, Buffalo, New York 14226

CHARLES G. McCLINTOCK (337), Department of Psychology, University of California, Santa Barbara, Santa Barbara, California 93106

JOYCE TOBIASEN† (217), Department of Psychology, University of Virginia, Charlottesville, Virginia 22901

DANIEL M. WEGNER (77), Department of Psychology, Trinity University, San Antonio, Texas 78284

†*Present address:* Department of Pediatrics, University of Kansas Medical Center, Kansas City, Kansas 66103.

Foreword

The office on an introduction to a volume of papers by different authors with somewhat different backgrounds and points of view, even though they are all writing about the same general subject, is to point out to the readers, who are usually not as well versed in the subject as are the authors, salient issues, especially important discussions, possible misunderstandings, and, if it is necessary, mistakes. The purpose of an introduction is to guide the readers.

The first point to be made about this book is that its authors are social psychologists. Yet social scientists of all fields, and philosophers too, have studied "equity and justice in social behavior," and all human beings at one time or another have taken an intense interest in the subject. The social psychologists have no monopoly on it, and the present authors often refer, quite properly, to the work of scholars in other fields.

The second point is that, as so often occurs in the social sciences, the words used in discussing the subject are many, sometimes redundant, and often confusing. Over and over again in this book, readers will encounter such words as *justice, equity* and *fairness,* and some of the authors treat them as if they referred to different things. In their most general sense they do not. The special senses are the ones that make trouble.

Take *equity,* for example, a word that social psychologists introduced only recently into the discussion of justice. In its general sense it does mean *justice,* but unfortunately it had long ago acquired a special meaning in law. In medieval England, when the common law offered no remedies or what were perceived to be, by some higher standard, unfair remedies for certain injuries, the sufferers might petition the king for special treatment. These petitions went to the court of the Lord Chancellor (Chancery) for action. Chancery was supposed to reach its decisions according to the principles of equity. In time its rules and procedures became just as complicated as those of the common law and by "higher standards" just as inequitable. But for centuries the English operated under a dual legal system, that of law *and* equity. Chapter 10 of this volume recognizes the fact. Those of us who feel tender toward the history of law would have preferred that the social psychologists had not introduced the word *equity*.

Aristotle, who in the *Nichomachean Ethics* wrote the earliest treatise on justice, used the Greek equivalent of that word and not the equivalent of equity. He distinguished among various different kinds of justice, such as *retributive justice*, justice in compensation for, and punishment of, injuries; and *distributive justice*, justice in the distribution of goods and services. In this volume, it is almost always distributive justice that the authors are talking about, and my feeling is that it ought to be called that rather than *equity*. Unfortunately *equity* has the advantage of being a much shorter word. Nor do the authors have much to say about a third kind of justice, *procedural justice*. It is subsidiary to the other two, for it is concerned with the processes of decision that will or will not result in just retributions or distributions.

There are three main rules of distributive justice. They are often in competition with one another, and which one people will apply or what compromise they will reach between them depends on the persons and goods concerned and on other circumstances. The first rule is distribution according to *need:* Of two or more persons who need a good in short supply, the one who needs it most should get it. People are most likely to apply this rule to others who do not have the resources to meet their needs for themselves. Thus a parent will buy a pair of glasses for that one of his young children who needs them; or a charitable organization, including the government, provides relief for the indigent poor.

The second rule is the one that Aristotle was most interested in, as are the social psychologists now. The rule says that, as between at least two persons or groups who are directly or indirectly in a relation of exchange with one another, the one who has contributed more of a given good, or contributed a more valuable good, should also receive more in return. A more valuable good is generally one that, in comparison with another, is in short supply relative to demand. For Aristotle the rule is not only normative—the way people ought to behave—but also substantive—the way many people do behave or try to behave. Since his time, there has been more agreement that people do behave in this way than that they ought to.

The rule is full of possible ambiguities. The authors of this book, for instance, do not seem to realize that there are at least two different kinds of *contributions:* first, those that a person contributes immediately, such as the work done in performing a task; and second, those that have been acquired from past history or even from being the kind of person he or she is. Among this second group are such things as seniority, sex, race, and ethnic group. After all, it was not so long ago that women were paid less than men for doing the same work—a violation of the rule unless one believes that women were less well able to carry out the work than men. In applying this rule, people usually bring in both kinds of contribution.

Many of the authors state this rule, as indeed Aristotle himself did, as one of proportionality: The proportion that one person's or group's contribution bears to another's should equal the proportion the former's reward bears to the latter's. But *proportion* here is used in a very loose way. It cannot be cardinal, as there are usually no ways of measuring both proportions with mathematical accuracy. At best, the proportionality is ordinal or that of rank-order. With this warning, it is reasonable to call this the proportionality rule.

Every application of the proportionality rule requires a comparison between the contributions and rewards of one person or group with those of another, sometimes even of the same group at different times. Accordingly, the question always arises which person or group is chosen for comparison and why. This question relates the theory of distributive justice to that of reference groups. And some of the earliest modern studies of distributive justice spoke instead of *relative deprivation* (Merton & Kitt, 1950). Relative deprivation means exactly the same thing as distributive *in*justice. We do not need both terms.

Finally, this rule of distributive justice is one aspect of what has been called the theory of social exchange. (See, especially, Chapter 10 in this volume.) The rule may be applied to at least two different conditions of exchange: first, when one person or group is directly exchanging goods and services with another; and second, when at least two groups are each exchanging goods and services with a third party but still comparing one another's contributions and rewards. The third party is often called the allocator, although he may have little power to allocate. A typical example is two different groups working for the same company. The company allocates to each its work and its wages, and the two compare their wage differentials with their work differentials. Many of the early field studies of distributive justice were made in such situations. Luckily, the proportionality rule of distributive justice applies in the same way to the two conditions of exchange. The difference lies not in the rule but in the ease with which injustices can be corrected.

Besides the rules of need and proportionality, the third rule of distributive justice is that of *equality:* All persons, or at least all persons of a certain class, should be rewarded equally. Like the others, the rule is in competition with them and is often ambiguous. For instance, if two persons or groups have been equally rewarded but have made equal contributions, this does not violate the proportionality rule but rather follows directly from it. We apply the proportionality rule in this way when we say that, because we are all equal as American citizens, we are all entitled to "equal justice under law." The equality rule becomes a distinct rule only when persons make contributions of different value but nevertheless are rewarded equally. Throughout history people have put this rule forward, but perhaps they have done so more often in recent times than in the past. People like the Marxists, who have supported it most strongly in theory, have, however, been the slowest to try to put it into effect when they have had the power to do so. Consider the Soviet Union! It is doubtful that the rule can ever be applied across the board, that people can receive equal shares of every kind of reward. The rule works best when it is applied to rewards like civil rights, and that is just where democracies have tried to apply it. I believe it works least well when it is applied to such matters as industrial production. No one aspect of social behavior, including distributive justice, is without links to the others. If one industrial group performs a more skilled job than another but the two are paid equally, the motivation of the former and thus its productivity may well decline. But the company and even the nation may need the productivity. Still, equality of reward can certainly be achieved in some areas, and it may be that inequality can, without deleterious side effects, be lessened in others.

The history of mankind has always been crammed with furious disputes about distributive justice. Aristotle argued that disputes were less likely to arise over the rules themselves than over the ways they ought to be applied. History seems to bear him out. Given that the rules are accepted, which of them should apply under what conditions? How should compromises between them be worked out? Under what conditions should certain kinds of contributions or rewards count as relevant to questions of justice? The answers given to these questions have varied from place to place and from time to time. We have seen them vary even within our own time. And some of the studies in this book show that individuals answer them differently at different ages. By the same token, if a distribution once considered unfair can be maintained, perhaps by the superior power of the beneficiaries of injustice, for a long enough time, even its original victims may come to accept it as legitimate. The members of a group or a group of groups are more apt to reach consensus that a particular distribution is fair, the more similar they are in their present situation and in their past experiences, for then they will also be more similar in what they expect. Finally, there are some situations in which people treat questions of justice as irrelevant, as when we say, "All's fair in love and war."

The various chapters of this book provide answers to many of these questions and to many others that may be raised about the applications of the rules of distributive justice. But with the exception of some references to the theories of the philosophers Rawls and Nozick (see, especially, Chapter 1), the authors do not try to deal with the ways in which people ought to resolve the issues but with how they actually do so. Their work is substantive not normative.

In the tradition of social psychology, the authors take the evidence largely from experiments made on subjects enticed into university laboratories and not from studies of "real-life" situations carried on by observation or interview. Only Chapters 7, 10, and 11 pay much heed to studies of the latter kind, although they were the starting points for the modern rebirth of the study of distributive justice.

Now laboratory and experimental studies must be handled with care. Often the investigators can carry them out rather rapidly; there are also many investigators, and as a result the number of experimental studies carried out seems to have increased exponentially over the last 30 years. No one can acquire thorough knowledge of all of them. They cannot be fully reported even in a volume such as this one, and what is left out may be just what made the difference to the results. It is often difficult to motivate the subjects of an experiment as strongly as they are motivated in real life, because it usually costs money to produce strong motivation, and the research budget cannot bear the expense. The result is that the behavior of the subjects is often much more random that it usually is in real life. In an experiment reported in Chapter 5, "college students read a description of a three-person group that had earned $3.30 for its work on an experimental task, and one of the group members was asked to distribute the reward." The members of the group, including the allocator, contributed unequally to the task. If the allocator distributed the reward equally, he would earn only $1.10, and this amount, in my experience, means little or nothing to college students. Not even the whole amount, $3.30, means much. Only if the payoff had been $330.00 would the members have even begun to be adequately motivated. But amounts like these make applications for research grants sound too costly.

Again, many social psychological experiments on distributive justice are "one shot" affairs. The subjects treated justly and those treated unjustly may meet only once, if at all. The victims, for instance, may only be *told* that some other group has exploited them. Yet in real life it takes successive meetings of the same persons or groups to bring out some of the fundamental features of distributive justice. Only then can the victims task the beneficiaries with their behavior and, if these be feasible, threaten and carry out reprisals. The knowledge that the victims may carry out reprisals may lead the beneficiaries to treat them less unjustly in the first place or make good their injustice more rapidly later. In real life when two persons exchange goods for money in a market at what they both know is the going market price, no question of injustice usually arises. But then in the classical market there is no guarantee that a particular buyer and a particular seller will ever meet again. This need not prevent the parties from complaining that "the market system" as a whole produces an unjust distribution. But generally it takes repeated exchanges between the same persons or groups to produce complaints about, and reactions to, injustice.

These questions about experimental studies of social behavior and their relation to "real life" imply that, if a reader of this book encounters experimental results that seem to run counter to common sense or to disprove hypotheses well established on other grounds, he or she will do well to scrutinize in detail the conditions under which the experiments were carried out, if necessary, by going back to the original research reports.

Some of the authors also deal with phenomena closely related to distributive justice, such as power and status. They have rather little to say about power, but Chapter 11 deals at some length with the relations between distributive justice and status congruence. A state of distributive justice is also a state of congruence, although each may have different effects on behavior.

One of my purposes, seldom achieved, is to reduce redundancy in the concepts and propositions of social science. Chapter 10 makes reference to Thibaut and Kelley's (1959) concept, *the comparison level for alternatives.* This concept is identical with the concept of *cost* in the sense of the value of the result of an alternative action foregone in performing a different action (Homans, 1974, p. 119). We do not need both concepts. And the *expectancy* × *value* theory of behavior (Tolman, 1932) cited in Chapter 11 is identical with what I have called the *rationality proposition* (Homans, 1974, p. 43). It is a fundamental proposition of decision theory: Of at least two alternative actions open to an individual, a person is apt to perform that one for which the perceived value of the expected result of the action, multiplied by the expected probability that the action will be successful in bringing about that result, is the higher.

Finally, many of the authors rightly deal with the responses both beneficiaries and victims make to distributive injustice. Here I should like to correct what I believe to be a mistake. The authors of both Chapters 5 and 11 assert that "equity theory" derives from "balance theory." Although the two theories have points in common, the statement is incorrect. It is incorrect historically, since Aristotle laid down the main principles of distributive justice at least two millenia before Festinger (1957) and Heider (1958) began to develop "balance theory."

It is also incorrect intellectually. The theory of distributive justice derives from what is sometimes called the frustration–aggression proposition in behavioral psychology, when it is applied to social exchange. The proposition states that, if a person (or indeed a member of other species of higher animal) does not get what he has come to expect in the way of reward for a particular action, he will become angry. In his anger, he will find the results of aggressive behavior toward the perceived cause of the frustration to be rewarding, and thus becomes more likely to perform the aggression. What the person expects is determined by his past experience. In the present case the question then becomes: What does a person expect in social exchange with another? I shall not go into the detailed explanation, but in ordinary exchanges unaffected by rules of distributive justice, the person who controls and is willing to part with the more valuable good will be able to get a more valuable good in return from the other or others. By the same token the person who controls the less valuable good will receive the less valuable return. The former has the superior bargaining power—and almost all forms of power can be brought under this rubric. The value of a good is largely determined by its scarcity in relation to the demand for it. Thus he who contributes most to the exchange gets most of it. But this is the proportionality rule of distributive justice. And since persons from an early age encounter this kind of situation over and over again, the result comes to be what they expect in the way of the distribution of goods, and indeed what their elders teach them they ought to expect. Accordingly, by the frustration–aggression proposition, they are apt to take action calculated to restore distributive justice and also to take aggressive action against its producer and/or beneficiary. In fact the latter action may contribute to the former, because aggression, if the threat of it is credible, is something its target may wish to avoid. None of this has anything to do with "balance theory." (See Homans, 1974, pp. 249-250.)

Of course, the victim may have learned that aggression may hurt him more than it does the perpetrator of injustice: The latter may be able to give at least as good as he gets. Then the victim may learn to displace his aggression on some less dangerous target or concoct a rationalization that he deserved his injustice after all. And since distributive justice is a matter of expectations, and expectations depend on actual experience, which changes with time, the distribution originally perceived as unjust may eventually become accepted as the very reverse.

With this guidance and these warnings, this volume is highly recommended. The person who studies it carefully will indeed learn much about distributive justice in social behavior.

George C. Homans
Harvard University

REFERENCES

Festinger, L. *A theory of cognitive dissonance.* Evanston, Ill.: Row, Peterson, 1957.

Heider, F. *The psychology of interpersonal relations.* New York: Wiley, 1958.

Homans, G. *Social behavior: Its elementary forms* (Rev. ed.). New York: Harcourt Brace Jovanovich, 1974.

Merton, R., & Kitt. A. Contributions to the theory of reference group behavior. In R. Merton & P. Lazarsfeld (Eds.), *Continuities in social research: Studies in the scope and method of "The American Soldier."* Glencoe, Ill.: The Free Press, 1950.

Thibaut, J., & Kelley, H. *The social psychology of groups.* New York: Wiley, 1959.

Tolman, E. *Purposive behavior in animals and men.* New York: Appleton-Century-Crofts, 1932.

Preface

Justice is a fundamental theme in social life. Certainly, the theme of justice underlies the claims of legitimacy made by a society's social and political institutions. When those claims begin to lose their force, institutional and societal change is likely to follow. At the same time, one need look no further than daily social interaction to appreciate the pervasiveness of the concern for and the impact of the theme of justice. Although there may be differences in response to them, there is a universal appreciation for the appeals made for "fair treatment," "fair play," and "a fair day's pay for a fair day's work."

The present volume is designed to assess critically the extent of current social psychological knowledge relevant to justice. We have not attempted to do this to advance any particular theoretical position. Instead, we have tried to compile contributions that show how the broad concept of justice pervades the core literature of social psychology and how concepts, theories, and research findings from this literature bear on several theoretical formulations of justice. Our goal is to advance an understanding of social and interpersonal justice that transcends any one "equity" theory. By showing how the justice theme is involved in a vast array of social behaviors, we intend not only to demonstrate the breadth of justice concepts per se, but also to highlight a wealth of critical issues that may have otherwise escaped attention.

Unlike those investigating more unified bodies of literature, the justice researcher does not have the luxury of limiting his or her background research to any one field. The ubiquity of the justice concept makes it one that pervades all aspects of social psychological inquiry. In preparing this volume, we have charged our contributors with the responsibility of uncovering and examining some of the interconnections between justice and various domains of social behavior. In so doing, we believe we have prepared a volume that will assist students of social and interpersonal justice in gaining a better understanding of how work in various areas of social behavior may be relevant to their own efforts. At the same time, we hope to have shown how work in various fields can be better understood by recourse to concepts and research from the field of justice.

A word about organization. In our introductory chapter we summarize the major justice theories and identify some of the focal issues with which they are concerned. This chapter provides some of the necessary theoretical background for much of the material that follows. The chapters are roughly organized around the traditional distinction between social phenomena analyzed in terms of individual processes (Chapters 2 through 5), and those conceptualized as collective phenomena (Chapters 6 through 11). The contribution by Major and Deaux (Chapter 2) analyzes the various individual difference variables known to affect adherence to social justice norms, and reactions to justice norm violations. Although they show us that justice is in the eyes of the beholder, Chapter 3 by Wegner makes it clear that many of the same cognitive processes operate in all persons' judgments about justice. His argument that perceptions of justice depend on the social entities in focal awareness ties in with Cohen's analysis of the role of attribution in justice (Chapter 4). Cohen explains how the perceived causes of injustice affect attempts to seek redress, and how actors and observers diverge in their perspectives about justice. The manner in which these perceptions affect attitudes toward others and how inequity is involved in attitude formation and change is then taken up by Ajzen in Chapter 5.

Justice as a collective social phenomenon is the central theme of the next six chapters. As a normative standard, the pressure to conform to others' notions about justice can be quite strong, as Allen contends (Chapter 6). Justice standards also come into play in intimate relationships, where, as Austin and Tobiasen note in Chapter 7, the fair exchange of resources may be considered a contributor to the success of a relationship. In Chapter 8, Krebs takes up the related issue of justice in prosocial behavior by discussing such topics as the distributive justice of sharing and helping to redress inequity. Such redress often takes the form of aggression; and, in their contribution, Donnerstein and Hatfield analyze the factors affecting the tendency for inequitable situations to elicit aggressive behavior (Chapter 9). Such behaviors may not become manifest in view of the justice standard in guiding social exchange, as

McClintock and Keil document in Chapter 10. However, Greenberg (Chapter 11) notes that, although individuals in groups and organizations may often attempt to avoid unjust situations, such situations are inevitable and elicit a host of strategies for coping with them.

Finally, our closing chapter ties together the varied perspectives taken throughout the book by noting some of the common themes. Here, we consider the normative and instrumental interpretations that have been offered to explain justice behavior (Chapter 12).

To give our contributors the freedom needed to provide the most insightful analyses, we imposed few restrictions on the level of their writing or their conceptualizations. The result is a work intended primarily for professional and graduate-level audiences.

Our contributions to this volume, and our responsibilities for it, are equal; the order in which our names are listed as editors was determined at random.

Acknowledgments

The efforts of our contributors have not only made this volume possible, but working with them has broadened our own thinking considerably. We are indebted to them for their careful consideration of our editorial suggestions, for their patience, and for their fine scholarly work. A note of grateful appreciation is also extended to Phil Brickman for suggesting that we collaborate on this project. We are grateful as well to our current institutions for providing much in the way of intellectual and financial support. The Departments of Psychology at Case Western Reserve University and Tulane University, as well as a Fulbright research grant, also provided support at various stages of this project. Special thanks go to our families, who have shared our ups and downs at every stage of our work. Thanks especially to Carolyn and to Judy, and to Becky, Jessie, and Hannah Cohen. Finally, we must give special acknowledgment to the staff at Academic Press for their steadfast support, advice, and encouragement.

*Equity and Justice
in Social Behavior*

chapter 1

The Justice Concept
in Social Psychology

RONALD L. COHEN
JERALD GREENBERG

Whether or not it is "the first virtue of social institutions, as truth is of systems of thought [Rawls, 1971, p. 3]," justice has been a fundamental theme in the history of thought and in the practice of political and social institutions. During the past two decades, this theme has become the focus of a large and growing number of social psychologists. The purpose of this chapter is to trace the development of the concept of justice as it has emerged in social psychological theory and research. Toward this end, we will devote some attention to several landmarks in the development of the concept in philosophy, and to the social and disciplinary context in which work in social psychology has developed.

This chapter will discuss the major theoretical conceptions of justice in social psychology. We will begin by noting the early work in social psychology, specifically the statements by Homans (1961), Blau (1964), and Adams (1965), which shaped much of the work that followed. We will then turn to the more recent theoretical statements derived from the research activity of the 1960s and the 1970s. Finally, we will discuss a set of issues that we consider to be most important in underlying past work and in establishing the outlines of an agenda for the future. Before beginning, though, several notes of clarification are in order.

At the core of the concept of justice lies the notion of an allotment of goods or conditions to recipient units; and, in the case of distributive justice, the notion of comparative allotment (cf. Frankena, 1962). We will devote attention primarily to distributive justice, which we conceive as involving the application of a normative rule to the allocation of resources to recipients. That which is allocated may vary from material

1

EQUITY AND JUSTICE
IN SOCIAL BEHAVIOR

goods of all sorts to social goods such as status, as well as to social opportunities and conditions. Recipients may be individual persons, but they
may also be small groups or social organizations varying in size and
complexity.

Although many complex issues are related to this conception, we want
to be clear from the outset that our primary focus is distributive justice,
and not other closely related concepts, unless otherwise specified (e.g.,
the discussion of procedural justice in Section IV.A.). Furthermore,
because there has been considerable confusion in the social psychological
literature on the meaning of "equity," we will restrict our use of that
concept to particular theoretical statements that adopt it (e.g., Adams,
1965; Walster, Berscheid, & Walster, 1973) and to one normative principle of distributive justice: that which prescribes an allocation based on
recipient units' contributions to a socially defined goal or product.

I. INTRODUCTION

A. Philosophical Discussions

Philosophers writing on justice have addressed two different kinds of
issues. The first involves the definition of the concept of justice and what
it could be argued to entail. Perelman (1963) describes this as an attempt
to establish the *formal principles* of justice. Formal principles include
those such as "giving each his or her due," or "treating like cases or
persons similarly." Whereas such principles define the broad domain of
justice, they do not provide the specific principles necessary for a determination of justice. Thus, the second issue involves attempts to establish
material principles of justice, specifications of the conditions that must be
met if justice is to exist. Material principles often appear in the form, "to
each according to his or her merit," or "contribution," or "ability." Material principles specify which characteristics of human beings are to be
treated as relevant to a determination of justice, and which, irrelevant.
Thus, as Frankena writes:

> Human beings are alike and unlike in all sorts of respects. Not all of their
> similarities and differences are important or even relevant to the question of
> how they are to be treated, and not just any manner of treatment may be
> assigned to just any class of cases. Consistency [of treatment, a formal princi-
> ple] is a requirement of justice, not merely a "hobgoblin of little minds"; but it
> is not enough, it is not the whole of justice.... We must also have some
> *material* principles of distribution, principles that tell us something more
> about the content of our rules, more about the similarities and differences

that are to be regarded as relevant [Frankena, 1976, p. 94; emphasis in original; copyright 1976 by University of Notre Dame Press, Notre Dame, Indiana].

We will discuss several classical and contemporary philosophical statements on justice. For the most part, those we have chosen to discuss argue for different material principles of justice, accepting the same formal principles. We will attempt no more here than to indicate the major themes in these statements, themes that are particularly important for a social psychological understanding of justice.[1]

1. ARISTOTLE

In Book V of the *Nichomachean Ethics,* Aristotle distinguishes distributive justice, "that which is manifested in distributions of honour or money or the things that fall to be divided among those who have a share in the constitution [Ross, 1925; Book V, p. 1130]," from rectificatory justice, the restoration of a previous relationship between individuals disturbed by a wrongful act. Distributive justice involves two persons and a division of objects between them. A good is distributed justly when the distribution satisfies the principle of proportionate equality; this is Aristotle's primary formal principle of justice.[2]

The relevant quality according to which goods are justly distributed equally is "merit." Thus, because not all persons have equal merit, proportionate equality in no way requires that all have equal shares. Furthermore, the definition of "merit" is problematic, "for all men agree that what is just in distribution must be according to merit in some sense, though they do not all specify the same sort of merit, but democrats identify it with the status of freeman, supporters of oligarchy with wealth (or noble birth), and supporters of aristocracy with excellence [Ross, 1925; Book V, p. 1131]."

Aristotle also points out that justice "in exchange" is often confused with both distributive and rectificatory justice. Because distributive justice depends on the "merit" of the parties concerned and rectificatory justice depends on the assessment of a wrongful gain or loss determined

---

[1]We have omitted discussions of many philosophical statements that may be relevant in some contexts. Among the most important of these omissions are probably Plato's *Republic,* Hume's *A Treatise of Human Nature* (1739/1928), and Kant's *Metaphysicl Elements of Justice* (1794/1965). Collections of useful critical discussions can be found in Brandt (1962), Friedrich and Chapman (1963), and Rescher (1967).

[2]A recent discussion of Aristotle's theory of justice, and a critique of the use to which it has been put by political philosphers (e.g., Rawls, 1971, and Nozick, 1974) appears in Winthrop (1978).

by a third-party magistrate, justice "in exchange" has its own meaning. Justice in "mutual" exchange consists of a reciprocal proportionate equality. Such an exchange is just because proportionate equality obtains between the value of the goods held by two individuals and reciprocal exchange occurs. Money, or some other common scale of value, establishes the rate at which the good offered by one party equals the good offered by the other. Justice in exchange, then, is equated with "going" rates of exchange between goods. This identity reappears in Hobbes's discussion of justice, to which we now turn.[3]

2. HOBBES

Hobbes includes a theory of justice in his attempt to describe the set of "immutable and eternal" Natural Laws necessary as preconditions for social order. Justice, the Third Law of Nature, is nothing other than the keeping of valid agreements: "When a covenant is made, then to break it is *unjust;* and the definition of INJUSTICE is no other than the *not performance of covenant.* And whatsoever is not unjust, is *just* [Hobbes, 1651/1947; Chapter 15, p. 94; emphasis in original]."

For Aristotle's distinction between rectificatory and distributive justice, Hobbes has only contempt: "as if it were injustice to sell dearer than we buy; or to give more to a man than he merits [Hobbes, 1651/1947; Chapter 15, p. 98]." In the end, Aristotle's position depends on criteria of merit based on birth, status, or family, criteria independent of the thing distributed or transferred. Hobbes will not admit the relevance of such distinctions. Therefore, the value of all things contracted for is determined not by the status of the contractors, but by their "appetite," and therefore "the just value, is that which they be contented to give [p. 98]." Demonstrated most clearly here is the difference between a conception of justice based on status (Aristotle) and one based on contract (Hobbes), each in its turn a reflection of the society in which it was produced (cf. Bedau, 1971; Macpherson, 1962). This variability is itself a focus of each of the next two statements to be examined, those of Mill and Marx.

3. MILL

In his classic utilitarian theory of justice, J. S. Mill (1861/1940) describes five modes of action in which injustice can be identified. These involve violations of legal rights, of moral rights, of deserving, of faith based on mutual agreement, and of impartiality. In each case, injustice involves a claim, a wrong done by failure to satisfy the claim, and an

---

[3]The distinction between "going" and "fair" rates of exchange is taken up explicitly by Blau (1964). (See the discussion in Section II.B.)

identifiable individual wronged by the failure. In addition, the "sentiment of justice," the desire expressed in the attempt to correct wrongs or to prevent their occurrence, is the result of individual or socially sympathetic self-interest.

Mill responds to criticism of the uncertainty of the utilitarian standard, the greatest good for the greatest number, with a similar claim about justice : "Not only have different nations and individuals different notions of justice, but in the mind of one and the same individual, justice is not some one rule, principle, or maxim, but many, which do not coincide in their dictates [Mill, 1861/1940, p.51]." In choosing among these principles, an individual will be guided either by some "extraneous standard" or by personal predilection. Thus, no one justice standard can be universally applicable. Only the principle of utility can provide a basis for decision, and this principle provides Mill with his conception of justice: proportionate equality of treatment based on desert, modified by recognized social expediency, which limits the exercise of the right to equal treatment.

4. MARX

A common interpretation of Marx's work is that it expressed a protest against the injustices of capitalism. However, Marx attacked the demand for a "fair distribution of the proceeds of labor" in his *Critique of the Gotha Program:* "Do not the bourgeois assert that the present–day distribution is fair? And is it not, the only 'fair' distribution on the basis of the present–day mode of production? Are economic relations regulated by legal conceptions or do not, on the contrary, legal regulations arise from economic ones [Marx, 1875; quoted in Tucker, 1978, p. 528]?"

In addition, Marx's discussion of the exploitation of labor expresses his view of the inappropriateness of "justice" as a standard against which to evaluate capitalism. Even though the exchange value of a day's labor extracted by the capitalist is greater than the value for the laborer, the difference being "surplus value," this transaction is not unjust: "So much the better for the purchaser [of labor], but it is nowise an injustice to the seller [Marx, 1867/1929; quoted in Tucker, 1963, p. 315]." Thus the only applicable standard of justice is the one inherent in the relevant economic system. Each mode of production has its own mode of distribution and its own normative standards of justice.

This interpretation of Marx's position on distributive justice, presented initially by Tucker (1963) and extended by Wood (1972), has not gone unchallenged (e.g., Allen, 1974; McBride, 1975). However, a pursuit of this controversy would take us too far afield. Suffice it to say that Marx raises three crucial issues that are relevant here. First, the very concept of justice may be relevant only to social relations in certain kinds of historical societies. Second, material principles of justice may be directly related to, a direct consequence of, and no more than a justificatory reflection of, specific societies. Thus, to criticize one distribution as unjust in terms of material principles appropriate to another type of society, is improper and meaningless. Finally, a related but distinct issue: To treat the distribution of goods and services independently of the social organization of production is both foolish and insulting; foolish, because distributions and the norms to which they are attached are direct consequences of the organization of production; and insulting, because it suggests treating consumption rather than productive activity as the most basic human need.

5. RAWLS

In a work that has rekindled significant debate on justice in philosophy and in related disciplines in the social sciences, Rawls (1971) provides a sophisticated contractarian approach to justice. Rawls's construction has individuals meeting in an "original position" behind a "veil of ignorance" to select principles of justice to apply to basic political and social institutions. The conditions set for this agreement are as follows: The principles agreed to must be general, and publicly known, and they must constitute a final choice such that future conformity to them is part of the agreement. In addition, the principles must be consistent with our considered judgments about what constitutes justice in particular situations. Individuals in this position are to be rationally self-interested, but mutually disinterested, and they are to operate without knowledge of their place in society (class position and social status) or their natural assets and liabilities (such as intelligence).

These constraints and conditions give Rawls reason to argue that whatever emerges from such a position will be just: "The guiding idea is that the principles of justice for the basic structure of society are the object of the original agreement. They are the principles that free and rational persons concerned to further their own interests would accept in an initial position of equality as defining the fundamental terms of their association [Rawls, 1971, p. 11]." Beyond his concern with justice as fairness, Rawls believes that individuals so described, operating under the specified constraints, would select two material principles of justice. The first would guarantee to each person equal right to the "most extensive system of equal basic liberties compatible with a similar system of liberty to all [p. 302]." The second principle would require that all social and economic inequalities meet two conditions: (1) that they are arranged to the greatest benefit of the least advantaged members of society; and (2) that they are attached to positions accessible to all persons "under conditions of fair equality of opportunity [p. 302]." These principles would be lexically ordered, such that the first would have to be fully satisfied before the second came into play.

6. NOZICK

Whereas critical reactions to Rawls abound (e.g., Daniels, 1975; Wolff, 1977), Nozick's (1974) "entitlement" theory of justice is one of the few that attempts to provide both a critique and an alternative. Nozick distinguishes between historical principles of justice, which evaluate the justice of a distribution in terms of the procedures that brought it about, and "current time-slice" principles, which evaluate according to judgments in terms of some structural principles of just distribution. Historical theories, of which his own is one example, are seen as superior because they take past relevant circumstances into account: "Historical principles of justice hold that past circumstances or actions of people can create differential entitlements or differential deserts to things [p. 155]."

In contrast to nonhistorical principles, which may infringe on individual liberties,[4] Nozick offers his entitlement theory of justice: "A distribution is just if everyone is entitled to the holdings they possess under the distribution [1974, p. 151]." Any distribution is just if it is the result of any admixture of three basic processes: (1) "first moves" according to the principle of "justice in acquisition"; (2) subsequent moves according to the principle of "justice in transfer"; and (3) rearrangements according to the principle of "rectification of injustice in holdings." Such injustices are said to arise as the result of violations of the first two principles. Although Nozick admits that to produce a specific theory would require specifying the three principles of justice in holdings, he does not go beyond a discussion of Locke's principle of justice in acquisition.[5]

7. SUMMARY

We have tried to describe the basic themes underlying several important classical and contemporary philosophical statements on justice. An understanding of these themes is important, both to establish a historical framework and continuity for our present concerns, and to point to sources for their future development.

---

[4]Nozick makes this argument by way of his famous "Wilt Chamberlain" example in a section entitled "How liberty upsets patterns." Both the argument and the example have been challenged; see G. A. Cohen (1978) and Held (1976).

[5]Held (1976) takes the view that Nozick unjustly "wraps himself in the mantle of Locke" on property, liberty, and rights, and that to the extent that he does so, "he may be guilty of what he takes to be a most serious offense: unjustified appropriation [p. 169]."

Aristotle first provided distinctions among justice in exchange, distributive justice, and rectificatory justice, and he described the most widely accepted formal principle of justice: proportionate equality. "Merit" provided the dimension along which equal treatment was to be administered, but the definition of merit is problematic. Hobbes saw no reason for a conception of justice independent of the terms established by individuals in freely established covenants. This provided the framework for all subsequent contractarian positions. Mill outlined a utilitarian position, conceiving of justice as equal treatment accorded each individual as a matter of right. Varying definitions of justice required arbitration in practice by the standard of the greatest good for the greatest number. Marx suggested that both formal and material justice principles were tied to specific types of societies, and thus to judge one society, or relations within it, by the justice principles derived from another was meaningless. Furthermore, Marx suggested that a focus on distributive justice artificially and incorrectly divorced the spheres of production and distribution, and denied the foremost of all human characteristics, productive labor, for what was only apparent, consumption.

Much of the current philosophical debate turns on interpretations of Rawls and Nozick. Rawls's contractarianism establishes the two principles of equal liberty and justifiable inequalities most beneficial to the least advantaged. These principles emerge from a decision reached by self-interested individuals searching for principles to govern their future association in ignorance of the places they would occupy in it. Nozick rejects ahistorical principles of distributive justice as denying the freedom of individuals to enter associations on any terms they choose. The justice of a distribution at any time is solely a function of the extent to which individuals deserve what they hold through gift, voluntary labor, or transfer from another.

B. Historical Overview of Work in Social Psychology

Homans first introduced the concept of distributive justice into the social psychological literature in the first edition of his *Social Behavior* (1961). Whereas earlier statements, such as those involving a comparison-level standard of individual deserving (Thibaut & Kelley, 1959), can be directly linked to justice, it was with Homans's work that the concept of justice became a focus in its own right. Shortly thereafter, Blau (1964) discussed the role of justice in his exchange theory, and Adams (1965) began a research program that culminated in his statement of a theory of inequity.

These early discussions drew on and extended earlier work in a number of traditions, including exchange theory, social comparison theory, and dissonance theory (cf. Crosby, 1976; Pettigrew, 1967). These traditions have continued to shape theory and research following the formative statements of Homans, Blau, and Adams, although their influence can be seen both in extensions and refinements, and in critiques. For example, with the publication of Adams's early research on responses to inequity, Berger and his colleagues began to develop a critique of the exchange foundations of the early justice statements (e.g., Anderson, Berger, Zelditch, & Cohen, 1969; Anderson & Shelly, 1970, 1971; Zelditch, Berger, Anderson, & Cohen, 1970). These criticisms culminated in a competing theoretical statement, the status–value formulation (Berger, Zelditch, Anderson, & Cohen, 1972) that has itself generated some research (e.g., Cook, 1975; Donnenwerth & Törnblom, 1975; Parcel & Cook, 1977) as well as a theoretical extension (Törnblom, 1977). Most recently, Jasso (1978, 1980) has attempted a theoretical integration of these two traditions.

With respect to the social comparison foundations of the original statements, both Goodman (1974) and Austin (1977) have tried to bring the problem of comparison choice into sharper focus for statements on justice. In spite of these efforts, this problem remains a significant one for future research.

Finally, although the motivational emphasis and assumptions contained in dissonance theory and originally incorporated into Adams's theoretical statement (1965) remain central for Walster's extension of equity theory (Walster *et al.*, 1973; Walster, Walster, & Berscheid, 1978), there has also been a significant trend away from a motivational and toward a cognitive emphasis in work on justice. This can be seen in several developments, including the introduction of cognitive models of justice decisions and judgments (e.g., Anderson, 1974, 1976; Cohen, 1978; Farkas & Anderson, 1979; Leventhal, 1976b), attempts to demonstrate the consensual nature of justice judgments (e.g., Hamilton & Rytina, 1980; Jasso, 1978; Jasso & Rossi, 1977), the development of arguments against the drive-reduction approach to inequity (e.g., Greenberg, 1979; in press), and attempts to integrate the work on attribution and justice (e.g., Cohen, Chapter 4, this volume; Kidd & Utne, 1978; Utne & Kidd, 1980). Finally, significant strides have been made in trying to distinguish justice as a goal from justice as a strategy (e.g., Greenberg, Chapter 11, this volume; McClintock & Keil, Chapter 10, this volume; Van Avermaet, McClintock, & Moscowitz, 1978).

Research on justice can be grouped into categories that have both substantive and historical dimensions. First, prior to the initial theoretical statements by Homans, Blau, and Adams, work on coalitions, status congruence, and relative deprivation focused attention on issues closely related to justice.[6] Immediately after the publication of Adams's research and theoretical statement, a great deal of research in its mold was undertaken in simulated industrial settings (reviews are available in Goodman & Friedman, 1971; Greenberg, Chapter 11, this volume; Mowday, 1979; Pritchard, 1969). Much of this work adopted the outline of Adams's (1965) theoretical formulation and focused on individual responses to unjust rates of pay.

Shortly after this, Leventhal began conducting research that reversed this emphasis. Rather than looking at responses to fixed, unjust outcomes, Leventhal investigated the principles employed by individuals in allocating outcomes among recipients, sometimes including themselves (e.g., Leventhal & Lane, 1970). Although some of this research was tied less directly to industrial settings, much of it still employed direct measures of work productivity and monetary outcomes. As a consequence of this work (reviewed in Leventhal, 1976a), aspects of the initial theoretical formulations began to be questioned (e.g., Deutsch, 1975; Leventhal, 1976b, 1980; Mikula, 1980b; Mikula & Schwinger, 1978; Sampson, 1975).

While research proceeded on responses to unjust receipts and on receipt allocations, two additional developments occurred. First, Lerner began his systematic examination of observers' reactions to victims of accidental fates (e.g., Lerner & Simmons, 1966), which led to the "just world" hypothesis and additional research on its applicability (Lerner & Miller, 1978; Lerner, Miller, & Holmes, 1976). In addition, and partially in response to a similar interest in reactions to accident victims (Walster, 1966), Walster and her colleagues began to apply the logic of Adams's (1965) theory of justice as equity to interpersonal attraction. This led to an extended statement of equity theory (Walster *et al.*, 1973; Walster *et al.*,1978) and to an explicit attempt to broaden its range of applicability.

Today, research continues to develop along the various lines described here. In addition, links with other substantive areas in social psychology are now being explored more systematically. The remaining chapters in this volume, and the appearance of other volumes describing research on justice (e.g., Folger, in press; Lerner & Lerner, 1981; Mikula, 1980a) testify to the continuing interest in this area. Finally, research and theory are now beginning to cross disciplinary boundaries, an issue that we will address in our concluding remarks.

---

[6]Early research on coalitions was reviewed by Gamson (1964). Early work on status congruence and relative deprivation was reviewed by Sampson (1969) and Pettigrew (1967), respectively.

II. INITIAL THEORETICAL STATEMENTS IN SOCIAL PSYCHOLOGY

A. Homans

George Homans introduced the concept of distributive justice in his exchange theory of social behavior (1961, 1974). The fundamental "rule of distributive justice" states that an individual in an exchange relationship with another has two expectations: (1) that the rewards of each will be proportional to the costs of each; and (2) that net rewards, or profits, will be proportional to investments. In addition, when each of two individuals is being rewarded by a third party, each will expect the allocator to maintain this same relationship between the recipients in the division of rewards. Homans believes that the notion of proportionality[7] between investment and profit that underlies this rule is universal, but that differences among individuals, societies, and times arise because of differences as to what legitimately constitutes investments, rewards, and costs, and how these things are to be ranked.

Homans identifies three sources for the proportionality belief: (1) direct tuition resulting in specific links between investment and profit; (2) experiences with the "natural environment"; and (3) experience in exchange. As a consequence of these experiences, individuals come to develop probabilistic expectations that the links between investments and profits will continue to hold in the future. In time, these probabilities become normative expectations: "Precedents are always turning into rights [Homans, 1961, p. 73]." One important consequence of this is that a reward once experienced as unjust may, by repeated occurrences, come to be experienced as just (Homans, 1974, p. 263).

When an individual does not receive the outcome she or he feels is deserved, the individual is likely to display "emotional behavior": anger, if the actual receipt is less valuable than that expected; and, although this is less likely, guilt, if the actual receipt is more valuable than that expected. The differential threshold for the experiences of guilt and anger is clearly a consequence of self-interest. Guilt is less often experienced, and less often the basis for future action, as the beneficiaries "often manage to discover good reasons why they are not profiteers at all, but only getting what they deserve [Homans, 1974, p. 265]."

Although it is possible to examine an individual in isolation, as if he or she were comparing actual current receipts to those of some unspecified

---

[7] Homans's discussion seems to suggest a proportionality that implies cardinal measures, but later he clarifies that and refers to ordinal proportionality (1961, p. 242; 1974, p. 248).

"other," Homans prefers to focus on a direct exchange relation where each party is both giving and receiving reward from the other. In this direct exchange relation, the relevant question for each individual is whether the reward received from the other, less the cost paid in getting it, was as much as expected, and therefore, as much as the individual deserved. One reason to focus on direct exchanges is that individuals are more likely to compare themselves with others who are close and similar than with those who are distant and dissimilar.

Although the rule of distributive justice is thought to operate both in direct exchanges and in third–party allocation situations, the distinction between the two is important. An individual who perceives herself or himself to be unjustly treated, that is, receiving less than deserved, will feel anger and display aggressive behavior toward "the source or beneficiary of the injustice [Homans, 1974, p. 257]." In direct exchanges, source and beneficiary are identical, whereas in third-party exchanges, the exchange partner is the beneficiary and the third party, the source.

The distinction is important for another reason. Although Homans examines a third-party allocation primarily from the perspective of a recipient, it is also possible to examine it from the perspective of the allocator. Here, two additional questions emerge: (1) What is the impact of the rule of distributive justice on the allocator's parceling out of rewards?; and (2) What is the impact of the rule when the number of recipients exceeds two, both on the behavior of the allocator and on the more complex "exchanges" among recipients? These questions begin to be addressed systematically in the work of Leventhal (see Section III. C.).

Finally, for individuals to agree in their perceptions of justice, they must agree on three things: (1) the (proportionality) principle of distributive justice; (2) what legitimately constitutes rewards, investments, and contributions; and (3) how persons rank on each of these dimensions (Homans, 1974, p. 250). According to Homans, disagreements are much more likely to arise over the second and third issues, both of which are subject to many sources of variability, than over the first.

B. Blau

In his own statement on exchange, Blau (1964) discusses justice by pointing to the importance of expectations for the experience of satisfaction in social relationships. The expectations are based on past individual experience and on acquired reference standards, each of which results partly from benefits individuals have obtained in the past and partly from learning about the benefits received by others in comparable situations.

Blau distinguishes three types of expectations concerning social rewards. There is the "general" expectation an individual has concerning the total benefits he or she will obtain in all aspects of social life, the "particular" expectation an individual has concerning the rewards that associating with another particular individual would bring, and the "comparative" expectation, the "profits" an individual expects to achieve in social associations, that is, "their rewards minus their costs [Blau, 1964, p. 146]." It is these comparative expectations that are most important for Blau's discussion of justice.

Although particular expectations differ for different associates, comparative expectations constitute a common standard by which comparisons of the satisfactions provided by various associates can be made. Thus, comparative expectations are expectations of returns relative to investment, and they are "governed by social norms that define what fair rates of exchange are [Blau, 1964, p. 147]."

Blau distinguishes between the "going rate of exchange" between two social benefits, and the "fair rate of exchange." The going rate of exchange is determined roughly by the supply and demand for the two benefits; supply is inversely related, and demand directly related, to the actual (and hypothetical equilibrium) price for a benefit. However, this going rate of exchange is by no means identical with the "fair rate," which represents normative standards defining a just return for a particular service: "Common norms develop in societies that stipulate fair rates of exchange between social benefits and the returns individuals deserve for the investments made to provide those benefits. These normative standards . . . have their ultimate source in the society's need for this service and in the investments required to supply it. [Blau, 1964, p. 155]." Thus, Blau suggests that norms of fairness ultimately derive from demand (society's need for a service) and supply (investments needed to provide the service), but that at any time, a discrepancy may exist between the rate of exchange stipulated by these norms and the rate at which services are actually exchanged.

Both the going and the fair rates of exchange create expectations, but expectations of different kinds. The going rate creates expectations that certain returns will be received for certain services, and that certain investments are required to supply those services. Such expectations have only a probabilistic quality; they are "merely anticipations that influence conduct [Blau, 1964, p. 156]." The fair rate of exchange creates expectations of investment–return links that are moral, violations of which evoke social disapproval.

When the demand for a service declines, those who have had to invest, to commit themselves to provide it, are caught in a squeeze. The going rate of exchange for the service has declined, and the fair rate has not yet adjusted. During the interim, those caught in the squeeze receive unjust returns for their investments. The human cost of this situation helps to readjust occupational supply and demand, and is expressed in clear-cut terms: "Their inability to obtain a fair deal in terms of social norms owing to forces beyond their control is a punishing experience, to which they are likely to react with bitterness and perhaps belligerence [Blau, 1964, p. 162]."

Blau explicitly describes the sources of fair exchange norms in the society's need for a service, and in the investments needed to supply it. The function of these norms is thought to be the integration of consumption needs to production capacities, brought about by advertising and providing incentives for individuals to make investments. Thus, it might be said that, whereas Blau draws clear links to the functions specific forms of the principle of distributive justice have for the society at large, Homans focuses more sharply on the source of the "underlying" principle itself in microlevel exchange processes.

C. Adams

Unlike the work of Homans and Blau, J. Stacy Adams's theory of inequity (1963, 1965) purports to focus primarily on the "causes and consequences of the absence of equity in human exchange relationships [1965, p. 276]." Adams draws explicitly on Homans's concept of distributive justice, and on previous work on relative deprivation (Stouffer, Suchman, DeVinney, Star, & Williams, 1949), social comparison (Festinger, 1954), and cognitive dissonance theory (Festinger, 1957).

The major structural components of the theory are "inputs" and "outcomes". Inputs are described as what a person "perceives as his contributions to the exchange, for which he expects a just return [Adams, 1965, p. 277]." Adams sees inputs as identical to Homans's "investments," among which he includes such factors as training, seniority, and effort. Outcomes are described as an individual's receipts from the exchange and can include such factors as pay and intrinsic satisfaction. To function as inputs or outcomes in any particular situation, such factors must be "recognized" by their possessor and considered "relevant" to the exchange. Adams admits the difficulty of distinguishing between inputs and outcomes and sees them as independent only in the conceptual sense.

In the course of direct exchange with another, or when person and other are corecipients in a direct exchange with a third party, persons compare their own and the other's inputs and outcomes. Inequity is said to exist whenever an actor "perceives that the ratio of his outcomes to inputs and the ratio of Other's outcomes to Other's inputs are unequal [Adams, 1965, p. 280]." The result of perceived inequity is tension, which exists in proportion to the magnitude of inequity, and which motivates individuals to reduce it. Adams uses the terms "equity" and "inequity" as equivalent to "justice" and "injustice," a practice that has produced some confusion and considerable discussion of the most basic form of "the" rule of distributive justice (see Section IV.C.).

Based on cognitive dissonance theory, Adams proposes six different modes of inequity resolution. Specifically, individuals experiencing an inequity may reduce it by: (1) altering their inputs; (2) altering their outcomes; (3) cognitively distorting their inputs or outcomes; (4) leaving the field; (5) acting on the object of comparison by altering or cognitively distorting the other's inputs or outcomes; or (6) changing the object of comparison. Although all these modes of inequity reduction may be available to a person, Adams notes that it is doubtful that they are all equally likely *psychologically*. He proposes six "admittedly, fairly crude" and undeveloped propositions concerning the relative likelihood of each, and some conditions under which they may occur (Adams, 1965, p. 296).

The majority of studies examining responses to experienced inequity have taken Adams's lead by focusing on alteration of inputs as the primary mode of inequity reduction. In the prototypical study, subjects are led to believe that they are either overpaid or underpaid for their work, and are found to respond by raising or lowering, respectively, their productivity (e.g., Adams & Rosenbaum, 1962). Although several critical reviews of this body of literature have appeared (e.g., Goodman & Friedman, 1971; Mowday, 1979; Pritchard, 1969), the theory appears to be capable of handling many of the methodological and conceptual questions raised (see Greenberg, Chapter 11, this volume).

Despite such an optimistic assessment, Adams and Freedman (1976), in their revisitation of equity theory, point to four questions that still require research attention. These involve: (1) the nature of the phenomenological experience of inequity; (2) the instrumental use of inequity; (3) the interactive dynamics of inequity reduction; and (4) the quantification of inequity. These questions have begun and will continue to stimulate a good deal of additional research, both by those who accept and by those who seriously challenge the fundamental dimensions of Adams's theory of inequity.

D. Summary

All three initial statements were developed in the context of social exchange approaches to social behavior (see, however, McClintock & Keil, Chapter 10, this volume). Homans and Adams specifically emphasize the role that experience in direct exchange has on establishing standards of just receipts, whereas Blau focuses more attention on the role of preexisting social norms of just receipt for investment. Whatever the source of these standards, individuals develop expectations about the consequences they ought to obtain in various circumstances. Whether these expectations are general or specific to the situation, individuals evaluate their current levels of receipts by comparing them to the standard defined as "deserved."

Experienced discrepancies between expected–deserved and actual receipts are psychologically discomforting, and they motivate some cognitive or behavioral response. This response may be self- or other-directed, where the "other" may be a partner in exchange, the source of the discrepancy, or, in cases of direct exchange, both. Responses may include altered expectations, comparison standards, beliefs or attitudes, or overt behavior.

The focus of all three statements is the relative experience of individual satisfaction. Because of the nature of the comparison involved, the experience is described in terms of "deserving." In direct exchange, the individual's perception that he or she has received less than deserved is likely to accompany the perception that the exchange partner received more than deserved. Although reference is made to the third party who dispenses receipts to two distinct others, emphasis is on the experience of a single recipient. Thus, these statements focus on situations in which immediate self-interest ought to be prevalent: Expectations of deserving and reactions to receipts are not solely a consequence of discrepancies between actual and deserved levels, but also a consequence of other factors bearing on self-interest. This is one issue on which critics of these formulations have focused much attention (see Sections III.C.; III.E.; and IV.C.).

III. RECENT THEORETICAL STATEMENTS IN SOCIAL PSYCHOLOGY

The work of Homans, Blau, and Adams provided the impetus for a large volume of research in the 1960s and the 1970s. It also provided the context within which subsequent theoretical statements have developed. We turn now to examination of these more recent formulations.

A. Walster, Berscheid, and Walster

Walster and her colleagues (Walster *et. al.*, 1973; Walster *et. al.*, 1978) developed their version of an "equity theory" in the hopes of providing the outlines of a general social psychological theory. Their formulation is meant to draw on and integrate the insights of a number of other statements, including psychoanalytic theory, cognitive consistency theory, exchange theory, and reinforcement theory. Although its intended scope is broad, the authors have described the major purpose of their work as an attempt to predict when individuals will perceive themselves to be unjustly treated and how they will react to that perception.

The theory retains most of the basic features of Adams's (1965) theory but also extends and explicates that formulation in many ways. The nucleus of the theory consists of four interlocking propositions: (1) Individuals will try to maximize their outcomes; (2) groups evolve definitions of equity and sanction group members on the basis of those definitions; (3) inequity leads to psychological distress proportional to the size of the inequity; and (4) such distress will lead to attempts to eliminate it by restoring equity (Walster *et al.*, 1978).

With its focus on explaining perceived justice for the individual in relationships with others, and with its motivational emphasis, Walster and her colleagues maintain some basic features of each of the earlier theories. However, they also extend this approach in three different ways. First, the arithmetic equation offered by Adams could not accommodate negative values for inputs or outcomes; attempts to include them in Adams's initial formulation led to counterintuitive predictions. Without essentially altering Adams's conceptual definitions of inputs and outcomes, Walster and her colleagues offered an equation similar in structure but one that incorporates both negative and positive values. Since the initial publication of the reformulation, significant objections have been raised to it as well, and a controversy has emerged over the form of the equation that most accurately describes an equity principle and the implicit assumptions concerning the combination of input information (e.g., Farkas & Anderson, 1979; Harris, 1976; Moschetti, 1979; Romer, 1977; Samuel, 1978). Although significant problems remain, these developments are responsive to an early call by Adams (1965, p. 297), repeated in his literature review a decade later (Adams & Freedman, 1976, pp. 52–55), for work on the quantification of experienced inequity.

Second, Walster and her colleagues attempt a broadly based distinction between two basically different equity-restoration techniques: restoration of "actual equity," and restoration of "psychological equity." The first involves actual modifications of the person's own, or the partner's, relative gains from the relationship, whereas the second involves cognitive distortions of reality. Restorations of actual equity are described as attempts at "compensation" when undertaken by the individual advantaged by the inequity, and perhaps when undertaken by third-party observers;[8] when undertaken by the disadvantaged, they are called "re-

---

[8]The discussion of "third parties" is limited to a consideration of "exploitative exchange" in which one person takes more than he or she deserves at the direct expense of

taliation." Attempts to restore psychological equity are described as "justifications" no matter who undertakes them, although it is clear that the
consequences of this technique differ for different actors. Because of the
first proposition concerning outcome maximization, those advantaged by
the inequity are postulated to prefer psychological justification, whereas
the disadvantaged are postulated to prefer actual equity restoration.

Finally, Walster and her colleagues extend the range of phenomena
to which their equity theory is applicable. Most of the research related to
Adams's (1965) theory of inequity involved monetary outcomes and
work inputs in work settings. In addition to these kinds of settings,
Walster *et al.*'s extended equity theory tries to explain perceptions of
justice and reactions to injustice in exploitative relationships between a
harm-doer and a victim, helping relationships between a philanthropist
and a recipient, and intimate relationships. Although the distinctions
among these types of relationships are not always clear and specification
of inputs and outcomes in such relationships remains a problem, the
results of numerous studies in each area are consistent with the predictions made by this extended equity theory (see Walster *et al.*, 1978).

Walster and her colleagues echo the explicit view of Homans (1961),
only implicit in Adams (1965), that the proportional equality principle
they term equity is the most fundamental principle of justice. Research
appearing to indicate support for the existence and importance of other
justice principles is interpreted by reconceptualizing the nature of the
inputs thought to be relevant to actors in the situation. Although at one
point they define inputs in terms of contributions (Walster *et al.*, 1978, p.
12), it is not clear whether any conceivable characteristic of a participant
in a relationship could be considered an input, or whether, as Homans
has suggested (1976, pp. 237–238), certain characteristics may combine
to make justice considerations irrelevant. It is not clear at this point
whether Walster *et al.*'s reinterpretation of all other justice principles as
variations on proportional equality is, as Sampson (1975) suggests, a
move toward unwise parsimony, or a significant theoretical advance (see
Section IV. C. 3.).

B. Lerner

Two early studies concerned with reactions to recipients of accidental
outcomes (Lerner, 1965; Walster, 1966) were the first empirical demon-

---

another (1978, p. 21). Only when discussing Austin's concept of equity–with–the–world
(see Austin & Walster, 1975) do the authors approach a more systematic consideration of
the distinction between source and beneficiary of inequity.

strations of what Lerner came to call the "belief in a just world." According to the hypothesis developed on the basis of this and much subsequent research, people need to believe that the world they inhabit is one in which people generally get what they deserve (Lerner & Miller, 1978). This often, although not always, seems to include the belief that people deserve what they get. Central to the hypothesis, and to Lerner's discussion of justice, is the concept of deserving, which relates a person and his or her outcomes. A person is said to have deserved an outcome to the extent that he or she has met the socially defined preconditions for obtaining it.

Individuals become committed to the ideas of deserving and justice, for the self and for others, as a consequence of universal aspects of development in childhood. For children who are both motivated to act and able to act effectively in their environments, the prospect of immediate gratification is gradually replaced by the promise of delayed gratification. This shift leads to the development of a "psychology of entitlement"; cognitive expectancies become replaced by normative expectations of what "ought" to happen. Lerner suggests that it is with regard to the nonhuman, impersonal environmental transactions that such a sequence is initially likely to emerge, and that human mediation may often prevent a psychology of entitlement from developing by inconsistent or arbitrary reactions to a child's behavior. Thus, he believes that his perspective does not depend on socialization agents to inculcate rules of deserving in their most basic form.

According to Lerner, the concept of justice requires the introduction of a "humanlike figure" into a situation. Not all discrepancies between actual and deserved outcomes are experienced as injustices. Only when this discrepancy is seen to be the consequence of an identifiable, humanlike cause is it likely to be experienced as an injustice (Lerner et al., 1976). The identifiable cause of an justice is usually another person, but it may also be identified as a societal agency or an abstract social process such as progress or social change. The two most noteworthy exceptions here are discrepancies between received and deserved outcomes that are not experienced as injustices because they are "caused" by the person himself or herself, or by accidental factors.

Lerner believes there is a direct relationship between a person's commitment to deserving his or her own outcomes, what he calls the "personal contract," and the extent to which others are able to receive the outcomes they deserve. When others do not receive what they deserve, the situation represents a threat to the individual's own personal contract. In addition, Lerner suggests that individuals express interest in justice for others because they recognize possible conflicts of interest among persons. This recognition, plus the recognition that otherwise unobtainable outcomes can be secured through cooperation, lead people to realize that rules must be developed to distribute generally desired resources.

Lerner identifies several forms of justice, defined as "rules for determining how the desired pool of resources are to be deserved [1974, p. 333]." Several of these rules are specified: (1) *competition*—contestants' performances decide who is deserving; (2) *parity*—each person deserves the same outcome regardless of any differences among them; (3) *equity*—each person's share is proportional to his or her investments or costs; and (4) *Marxian justice*—resources are allocated according to needs, regardless of individual contributions.

No single justice rule is thought to be appropriate for the variety of situations in which considerations of justice will appear. Attraction among friends, for example, is likely to elicit the justice rule of equality, whereas the Marxian justice of need is likely to predominate when people have an empathetic identification with one another. The equity rule is likely to predominate in exchanges between people who have no particular regard for each other, such as individuals in a marketplace. A final form, the justice of rules or laws, is likely to appear where participants are strangers or contestants with a clear conflict of interest (Lerner, 1974, pp. 336–339).

Lerner categorizes the forms of justice in terms of the relationships among participants in social structures defined by these forms. The determinants of the forms vary along two dimensions: (1) *perceived relationship* (identity—perception of other as self; unit—perception of similarity or belonging with other; nonunit—perception of conflicting interests and personal differences); and (2) *object of perception* (person or position). The type of situation in which a person perceives himself or herself to be located elicits the form of justice applied. Therefore, the individual can cope with potential internal conflict by altering his or her perception of the situation (Lerner *et al.*, 1976).

Research related to Lerner's just world hypothesis typically involves reactions to an individual suffering through no apparent "fault" of his or her own (e.g., Lerner & Simmons, 1966). Lerner argues that if the perceiver is unable to relieve the suffering directly, the victim is often derogated to bring that person's fate and character into balance. Subsequent research has revealed several factors that limit the appearance of the effect (e.g., if the victim can be seen to have behaved in a way to cause the suffering, derogation may not occur because "no injustice has occurred"; Lerner & Miller, 1978). Within these limitations, the effect has been replicated in diverse settings (Lerner & Miller, 1978). In addition, initial research on the relationship between the forms of justice and the perceived relationship among participants is supportive of Lerner's suggestions (e.g., Carles & Carver, 1979).

Lerner's work ties justice to fundamental and universal experiences in early development. These experiences are thought to establish a groundwork for strong commitment to a need to see one's own, and others', outcomes, both positive and negative, as deserved. The nature of the desired outcome is determined by the situation in which the recipient is located and the rule of justice appropriate to that situation.

C. Leventhal

Whereas most of the early research stimulated by Adams's (1965) theory of inequity focused on reactions to unjust outcomes (see Section II. C.), another body of research has emerged that focuses on the allocation of outcomes among two or more recipients. Leventhal has contributed much of this research (reviewed in Leventhal, 1976a), and on the basis of that work, developed a critique of equity theory and his own model of justice judgments (Leventhal, 1976b, 1980).

Leventhal (1976b, 1980) has identified three major problems with equity theory. First, equity theory recognizes the relevance of only one justice rule, the "contributions rule," whereas it is clear that people often employ other rules, such as equality and need. Second, equity theory ignores procedural justice, the perceived justice of the procedures by which distributive decisions are made. Leventhal feels that individuals readily evaluate the justice of procedural components, several of which he identifies explicitly, and that such evaluations affect perceptions of the justice of the outcome distribution (1976b). Finally, equity theory overemphasizes the importance of perceived justice as a determinant of behavior. According to Leventhal, there are many situations in which little thought is given to questions of justice, and even where it is an issue, a person's justice judgments are unlikely to be thorough or precise.

In his review of allocation research, Leventhal (1976a) points to the importance of various allocation norms that specify criteria by which distributions of outcomes are defined as just. Leventhal suggests that the impact of any allocation norm (for example, the contributions, equality, or needs norm) does *not* rest solely upon the allocator's desire for justice as an end in itself, but also upon the predictability that any norm allows and on the expected benefits associated with a particular norm. Thus, an equitable allocation might indicate the allocator's preference for justice and what his or her perception of it entails, but it might also indicate a desire to maximize productivity or stimulate future performance. The questions Leventhal raises about allocation behavior are the same ones previous theorists raised earlier about research on reactions to "unjust outcomes" (e.g., Goodman & Friedman, 1971; Pritchard, 1969; Weick, 1966), namely: (1) What do these reactions reveal about the nature of perceived justice?; and (2) how important is perceived justice in these situations, as opposed to other concerns?

As a result of his critique of equity theory and his interpretation of allocation research, Leventhal (1976b) offered a model of justice judgments to explain perceptions of justice. Individuals are thought to apply different rules of just distribution selectively in time and space. The justice-judgment model posits a four-stage sequence whereby an individual evaluates the justice of his or her own, or another's, outcomes. The individual (1) decides which justice rules are applicable and how much weight to accord to each; (2) estimates the amount and type of outcome the recipient deserves based on each rule; (3) combines the outcomes deserved on the basis of each rule into a final estimate; and (4) evaluates the justice of the actual outcome by comparing the actual to the deserved outcome.

The justice-judgment sequence must be activated if it is to influence perception and behavior. Activation may occur if the person occupies a role whose primary function is to evaluate deservingness or adjudicate conflict, when there is reason to believe a justice rule has been violated, or when there has been a sudden change in recipients' outcomes. Once the sequence has been activated, an individual may take any one of several steps to maintain or to restore actual outcomes to their deserved levels. The options available are essentially those outlined by Adams (1965) and by Walster *et al.* (1973), but with one major difference. Leventhal specifically emphasizes the possibility that an individual may not try to maintain or restore actual outcomes to their deserved levels. This is a possibility when the recipient is personally unimportant to the judge, when the judge believes nothing can be done to change the situation, when the necessary actions are too costly, or when the size of the perceived injustice is small (Leventhal, 1976b).

Leventhal has attempted to break away from equity theory by stressing the fundamental importance of several norms of distributive justice operative in different situations. Much of his own research (e.g., Leventhal, Michaels, & Sanford, 1972) and research inspired by it (e.g., Kahn, 1972) provides evidence of allocations that bear variable resemblance to what appeared to be clear-cut predictions from equity theory. Leventhal shifted the focus of research on justice toward allocation and the role of the allocator, and raised fundamental questions about the allocator's role in matters of distributive justice.

D. Berger, Zelditch, Anderson, and Cohen

Although there are substantial areas of disagreement among the authors of the various positions just described, none have seriously challenged Homans's original position that distributive justice is both a basic component and a basic consequence of a social exchange process. However, the status-value formulation, developed by Berger and his colleagues (Berger *et al.*, 1972) does just that. Rather than question the importance of justice considerations, or the relative importance of different allocation norms, Berger *et al.* return to a question implicit in the earliest statements: What is the nature of the standard against which an individual compares his or her own outcomes? They see the purpose of a theory of distributive justice no differently than those whose work is based primarily on exchange. That is, they propose to focus on reactions to violations of normative expectations concerning the allocation of socially valued rewards, violations that are likely to produce strain and some pressure toward change. What is different is the process by which meaning is thought to be given to rewards and expectations formed about their allocation apart from interpersonal comparisons.

Berger and his colleagues agree with exchange theorists (e.g., Blau, 1964; Homans, 1961) that the deprivations involved in injustice are clearly relative. However, they feel that strictly "local" comparisons, in which a specific individual compares himself or herself to another specific individual, are insufficient to produce a distributive justice process. Rather, these comparisons produce a process they refer to as *anomie*, where the individual has no social standard in terms of which to evaluate his or her own outcome. Thus, exchange formulations confuse unjust with anomic states. In addition, they may also: (1) misclassify just and unjust states; (2) fail to distinguish between individual and collective injustice; and (3) fail to distinguish between an unjust outcome for the self and an unjust outcome for the other.

To remedy these difficulties, the status-value formulation explicitly introduces the concept of "referential" comparison, whereby an individual compares himself or herself with a generalized other, such as an occupational grouping or class. This standard provides the social definition of rewards that exchange formulations are thought to lack. The relationship between the actual allocation of rewards[9] and the expected

---

[9]Berger *et al.* (1972) prefer the concept "goal object" to "reward" for three reasons: (1) they want to incorporate both positive and negative values; (2) they want to exclude psychological notions such as reinforcement from their theory of status value; and (3) "reward" connotes direct gratification for the person, whereas they mean to emphasize the "status," or "honorific" significance of the goal object.

allocation of rewards, determined by reference to the referential comparison standard, suggests that either distributive justice or injustice is perceived to exist, and if injustice, the type of injustice perceived. *Distributive justice* is defined as the coincidence of actual and expected allocations, and *type of imbalance* (injustice) is defined as the total relationship between each individual's expected and actual reward state for the social system as a whole; thus, there may be self-imbalance, other-imbalance, or collective-imbalance.

Berger and his colleagues claim that this formulation accomplishes what exchange formulations cannot. It enables one to distinguish clearly between overreward and underreward, and to distinguish both clearly from justice by comparison with the referential structure. Furthermore, one can distinguish collective from individual injustice, the first defined as the coincidence of expected and actual allocations, the second as the relationship between any single individual's actual and expected reward. Finally, when only one member of a social system is in an imbalanced condition, only that member has an unjust reward; thus, self-injustice and other-injustice can be distinguished.

The status-value formulation raises several issues central to an understanding of distributive justice. Three of the most important of these concern: (1) the definition and relevance of different comparison standards; (2) the differential importance of valued objects and their distribution; and (3) the possibility of different types of justice and injustice. Empirical research and theoretical extensions stimulated by the formulation (e.g., Cook, 1975; Donnenwerth & Törnblom, 1975; Parcel & Cook, 1977; Törnblom, 1977) indeed suggest the possibility that exchange formulations may require either significant modification or, as Berger *et al.* suggest, even outright rejection if these issues are to be confronted successfully. Another possibility, that an adequate statement on justice requires elements essential to each orientation, is suggested in the final formulation to be presented here, the recent work of Jasso.

E. Jasso

Although early theoretical and empirical work often made reference to societal-wide distributions of goods and their relationship to justice, that link usually did not become the object of direct attention itself. However, in their work on the perceived justice of the distribution of earned income, Rossi and his colleagues (e.g., Alves & Rossi, 1978; Jasso & Rossi, 1977) demonstrated the relevance of both need and merit criteria of justice held consensually and largely independent of respondents' demographic characteristics. On the basis of this research, Jasso (1978, 1980) has developed what she calls a "new" theory of distributive justice that attempts to integrate the exchange and status-value formulations.

Jasso believes that the ratio definition of proportionate equality adopted by Homans (1961, 1974) and those she sees following in his path (e.g., Adams, 1965; Walster *et al.*, 1973) is intuitively appealing as a conception of justice. However, she also agrees with Berger and his colleagues (1972) that this orientation has two flaws. It is unable to specify the kind of injustice resulting from proportionate inequality; nor does it recognize the possibility that both individuals in an exchange may be unjustly rewarded. She also sees promise in the Berger *et al.* model (1972) of justice as the difference between an actor's actual outcomes and the outcomes received by a counterpart in a "referential structure." However, the status-value formulation can neither specify an injustice evaluation in a quantitatively meaningful way nor incorporate the intuitive appeal of the idea that unjust underreward is experienced and resented more deeply than unjust overreward.

As a major part of her "new" and comprehensive theory of distributive justice, Jasso proposes what she calls a "universal law of Justice Evaluation: justice evaluation varies as the logarithm of the ratio of the actual share of the good to the perceived just share [1980, p. 3]." Although developed initially in her work on perceived justice in distributions of earned income (Jasso & Rossi, 1977), the new theory generalizes to justice evaluations of all distributed goods. The focus of the theory is an individual's evaluation of the justice of his or her own share of a good, not an evaluation of others' shares.

An individual evaluates the justice of his or her actual holding of goods first by taking a ratio of the actual to the just holding, what Jasso calls the "Comparison Ratio." For quality goods, "nonadditive, nontransferable personal attributes such as beauty, intelligence, or social honor [1980, p. 4]," this comparison consists of a ratio of actual to just *rank*. For quantity goods such as wealth, the comparison is the ratio of actual to just *amounts*. After taking the ratio of actual to just holdings, the individual then evaluates the comparison by a function that can be represented as the logarithm of the "Comparison Ratio." The justice of the comparison can then be represented in justice units, where zero represents justice, a negative value represents unjust underreward, and a positive value represents unjust overreward.

Jasso also focuses attention on the social collectivity characterized by the distribution of justice "sentiments" characteristic of its members.

Various parameters of this distribution of justice sentiments are hypothesized to vary with important features of social aggregates, including political instability, social discontent, and revolutionary conflict.

Jasso's theory is complex and wide-ranging. It attempts to explain an extremely broad range of phenomena, both at the individual and at the social level, through specifying a fully testable and fully mathematical theory that treats the sense of justice as a crucial determinant of important phenomena. Although it obviously cannot be adequately summarized here, and although tests of its major hypotheses remain to be conducted, it is important to take cognizance of it for two major reasons. First, it demonstrates the possibility of integrating a focus on, and an explanation of, justice at the individual and collective levels. This possibility appears as an often stated but rarely addressed goal in most statements on justice. Second, it suggests ways in which an integration of two dominant trends in basic conceptions of justice at the microlevel might be achieved.

IV. SOME FOCAL ISSUES

Preceeding sections of this chapter should indicate that currently available statements on justice leave many important questions unaddressed or incompletely answered. The remaining chapters in this volume point to many of the issues raised by examining the relationship between the accumulated theory and research on justice and several traditional areas of social psychological inquiry. What we hope to do in this section is to identify a number of issues crucial to the development of work on justice in the hopes of bringing to the fore some current controversies, criticism, and work that needs to be undertaken.

A. Procedural and Distributive Justice

Although little explicit attention was devoted to procedural justice in the first decade of work following publication of Homans's initial statement (1961), many current formulations of distributive justice caution that an understanding of procedural justice is critically important (e.g., Deutsch, 1975; Leventhal, 1976b). This concern is expressed both as a desire to understand procedural justice in its own right, and as a desire to understand the role that procedural factors play in distributive justice. We will focus on the latter.

Although these warnings have intuitive appeal, and although initial research on procedural justice is indeed promising (e.g., Folger, 1977;

Folger, Rosenfield, Grove, & Corkran, 1979; Thibaut & Walker, 1975), we believe that significant future advances in understanding will require considerable conceptual clarification. For example, in the most complete social psychological analysis of procedural justice to date, Thibaut and Walker (1975) identify the key requirement of procedural justice as "an optimal distribution of control [p. 2]." Accordingly, a decision-making procedure is just to the extent that control over the outcome decision is distributed optimally, and presumably justly, among those whose outcomes are dependent upon it. Difficulties also attend the operationalization of procedural justice in research, where the procedural element identified, the ability to express an opinion concerning the final distribution, is itself distributed equally among recipients (e.g., Folger, 1977; Folger et al., 1979).

Nozick (1974; see Section I. A. 6.) claims that justice is purely procedural, although he begs crucial questions about the content of just procedures and the substance of previous distributions. However, he does raise what we take to be the basic question here: How do the procedures that eventuate in outcome distributions affect perceptions of distributive justice? There is evidence to indicate that the manner by which the outcomes of an individual are altered affects perceived justice, whether from the standpoint of a recipient or a nonrecipient observer (e.g., Brickman & Bryan, 1975, 1976; Folger, 1977; Folger et al., 1979). Beyond the necessary conceptual clarification, what is needed is more work on identifying the important dimensions of decision-making procedures that affect perceptions of justice. Glimmerings of what these dimensions might be have been suggested recently by Leventhal (1980).

Whatever the current conceptual problems, attempts to distinguish procedural justice from distributive justice have pointed to several issues that promise to receive continued research attention. One of these concerns the distinction between allocation decisions made collectively by recipients and those made by an allocator who is not also a recipient. Burnstein and Katz (1972) suggest that it is difficult to infer anything unequivocal about perceptions of distributive justice when an allocation decision is made collectively by recipients; a particular distribution may be agreed to merely because it is "conspicuous," a "compelling focus for agreement," rather than just. However, the fact that recipients themselves, and not a distinctly separate allocator, have a determinant "voice" in the decision may lead recipients to see any distribution that emerges as just. This is the basis of the suggestion made by Thibaut and Walker (1975) for changes in methods of dispute resolution, as well as the basis for Rawls's (1971) position of justice as fairness (see Section I. A. 5.).

Finally, the concept of procedural justice points to the importance of temporal factors in justice. It calls attention to a distinct preallocation period when methods of assessing recipients' characteristics may become matters of dispute, and it suggests the importance of prior outcome distributions as a standard against which the justice of present distributions is evaluated (cf. deCarufel, 1979; deCarufel & Schopler, 1979).

B. Justice at Different Levels of Analysis

Most of the social psychological work on distributive justice has focused on the justice of a single recipient's outcome or on the justice of a distribution among a very small number of recipients, usually two. Several commentators (e.g., Brickman, Folger, Goode, & Schul, 1981; Cohen, 1979; Eckhoff, 1974) have pointed to the importance of the size of the recipient class as a variable in its own right. Since individuals seem quite willing to evaluate and are often very interested in the justice of distributions among very large classes of recipients (e.g., Brickman *et al.*, 1981; Rainwater, 1974; Thurow, 1973), it is important to elevate our knowledge of justice in these situations. An examination of the processes thought to govern justice perceptions suggests that such knowledge is severely limited.

With the individual's outcome as the focal point, analyses point to the importance of intrapersonal comparisons (cf. Brickman & Campbell, 1971) or social comparisons (cf. Crosby, 1976) that provide standards against which the individual's outcome is evaluated. The concept of distributive justice is then seen to provide the rule by which the justice of the outcome is evaluated, whether the standard is local or referential. A similar analysis is provided for the study of justice in distributions between two recipients. In exchange formulations (e.g., Homans, 1961), each individual provides a standard for the other, whereas the status-value formulation (Berger *et al.*, 1972) stresses the standard provided by a generalized other in a referential structure.

Complex models of decision making have been presented as descriptions of the process by which individuals judge the justice of an individual's outcome (e.g., Leventhal, 1976b) or a division between two recipients (e.g., Anderson, 1976). These models may work well in predicting perceived justice for one or two recipients, but it seems unlikely that they will apply when the size of the recipient class increases. At the very least, ordinal rankings are likely to replace ratio comparisons of outcomes. Recipient characteristics may even be ignored completely, and individuals may well make judgments about distributive justice based on characteristics of the outcome distribution alone. This argument from complexity also suggests the primary importance of distribution rules from which departures are easily recognizable, such as equality of outcome. Rather than proceeding from possible cognitive limitations of the judges (cf. Hook & Cook, 1979), we are suggesting that certain distribution rules may be particularly relevant when the size and complexity of the recipient class itself markedly increases.

Finally, recognition of the levels issue directs attention to three additional questions. First it is important to understand how the individual circumscribes the class of recipients, including some and excluding others. Second, not only may the size of the recipient class be important, so too may be the nature of the recipient unit. Most work has focused on the individual person, and we need to know the conditions under which other units (e.g., small groups, racial, sexual, class groupings, nation-states) are seen as recipient units and whether what we now know about justice is applicable. Third, the recognition of both individual and collective units of receipt raises the possibility of conflict between justice conceived at different levels. Thus, justice can be seen to involve not only competing claims among units at the same level of analysis, but conflict over which recipient level to consider relevant. As these questions emerge, recent work on group categorization and awareness must be exploited for the light it may shed on justice (e.g., Hamilton, 1979; Tajfel, 1978).

C. Competing Norms of Justice

In the final quarter of the twentieth century in the United States, equal distributions seem to be considered just when considering the distribution of votes to citizens, the distribution of chances for military induction to men, the distribution of educational opportunity to ethnic and racial groups, and the distribution of parental affection among children in the nuclear family. Need seems to be the preferred basis when considering the distribution of medical care, and some aspects of economic welfare. Finally, merit seems preferred when speaking of wages for jobs, grades for academic performance, and publication space for articles submitted to professional journals. In all these cases, of course, these indicate major trends, and often trends only at the level of verbal endorsement.

Assuming there is sufficient underlying similarity in these examples, what inferences can be drawn from them? Do they demonstrate the existence of several fundamentally different norms of distributive justice? Does the application of these norms depend on the nature of the outcomes distributed, the size of the recipient class, the nature of the relationship between allocator and recipients? Or can one conclude that behind the apparent variability there lies a common thread that defines the essential nature of distributive justice, in effect Aristotle's conception of proportionate equality?

Representatives of both views can be found in the social psychological literature. Walster *et al.* (1978) argue that proportionate equality is the fundamental principle. Situations where other principles appear to have an effect are incompletely specified, as on closer examination, an "input-like" variable can be shown to be present. Where equal outcomes are thought to be just, there is no need to point to an equality norm of justice, only to recognize that the relevant input for recipients is equal. Just and equal protection before the law, equal opportunity, and equal suffrage apply in situations where all recipients "possess equal humanity" and thus all deserve equal outcomes (Walster & Walster, 1975; see also Homans, 1976).

However, several theorists suggest that merit, equality, and need describe fundamentally different principles of justice. Sampson (1975), for example, suggests that conceiving of equality as a special case of equity (merit) is a fundamental error: "Social psychologists often have erroneously assumed that an equity principle is either the only solution to the distributive problem that ever existed, or, as the most preferred solution in the contemporary Western world, must therefore characterize a fundamental quality of human psychological functioning [Sampson, 1975, p. 49]." Sampson is joined by a host of other theorists (e.g., Deutsch, 1975; Lamm, Kayser, & Schwinger, in press; Lerner, 1975, 1977; Leventhal, 1976b; Mikula, 1980b; Pepitone, 1976; Rescher, 1967; Schwinger, 1980) who point to situational and cultural as well as historical, variability in the use of different justice principles.

What are the crucial issues here? First, there appears to be more controversy about the status of the equality principle than about any other. This is reflected both in allocation research (Leventhal, 1976a), and in the philosophical literature, where continual references are made to the close relationship between justice and equality (e.g., Bedau, 1971; Eckhoff, 1974; Oppenheim, 1980; Vlastos, 1962; Williams, 1962).

Second, it seems important to recall the distinction between formal and material principles of justice (see Section I.). Frankena (1962) suggests a principle of consistency underlying all formal principles of justice, a consistency very closely related to equality. Consistent treatment across persons suggests the application of the same set of rules to each and all, thus equality of treatment. In this sense, then, equality could be described as the most basic formal principle of justice. However, this formal principle, although prescribing equality of outcomes of a sort, also leaves open the possibility of substantial inequalitites in outcomes of other kinds. Here, one sees replicated the basic dimensions of attempts to distinguish procedural from distributive justice.

Equality seems to be the most basic principle because some cognate of it is a constituent part of any *formal* principle of justice. As a material principle, equality would require equal shares in the distribution of outcomes. It is important to note that equality as a formal principle may be consistent with various inequalities in outcome distributions. Thus Coleman (1974) speaks of Rawls's theory as an attempt to present a case for justified inequalities. If individual persons are the relevant recipient unit, the application of equality as a formal principle might require different outcomes for the same individual over time and across situations (according to age, for example).

Which of the various principles of justice is more fundamental? Such a question is most likely unanswerable, perhaps even unproductive. How many different principles are there? This, too, seems unanswerable (see Reis, 1979, who has distinguished 17 different principles). Two different questions appear to be more reasonable to pose, and more likely to be productive. The first focuses on an attempt to identify the situational, dispositional, and structural, as well as the historical, factors that affect adherence to and application of different principles of justice. A second question concerns the possible consequences of such adherence. If it were possible to describe fundamentally different principles, what consequences, other than the differing distributions, would follow adherence to them? How do endorsements of the merit (equity) principle, defined as proportionate equality based on contribution, or endorsements of the principles of need or equality interact with other concerns? Recognizing that distributions of both natural and social characteristics are among the most fundamental dimensions of human societies, how does the concern expressed over the justice of these distributions interact with concerns such as efficiency, power, or productivity? It is these questions to which we turn now.

D. Justice and Other Concerns

1. EFFICIENCY

Theorists such as Sampson (1969), for small groups, and Okun (1975), for society as a whole, have pointed to the potential conflict between productive efficiency and justice. Both argue that a system's efficiency at any time depends on the distribution of scarce and valued resources among potentially productive units. Both argue also that the incentive and disincentive effects of different amounts and distributions of resources influences the system's efficiency by affecting the ability and willingness of human producers to work.

Distributions of outcomes can be seen partially as responses to the past, particularly to those recipient characteristics that provide the groundwork for different principles of justice, and partially as anticipations of the future. In addition to the evidence that both allocators and recipients respond to distributions in terms of how just they appear to be, there is also evidence that allocators employ specific techniques of outcome administration based on their beliefs about the instrumental effects of varying amounts, histories, and distributions of outcome (e.g., Greenberg & Leventhal, 1976; Leventhal, 1976a, 1976b; Rothbart, 1968).

If standards of justice and efficiency are at least conceptually distinct, then distributions meant to satisfy them may well conflict. The "most efficient" distribution might be extremely unjust, and a completely just distribution might be moderately, or even extremely, inefficient (Greenberg, 1981). The relationship between efficiency and justice is often described as a "tradeoff" (Okun, 1975), in which attempts to move in the direction of one invariably mean moving away from the other. Inequalities that might initially seem unjust are tolerated if they seem to benefit less advantaged members of society, the so-called trickle-down effect (cf. Rawls).

There is already some evidence that individuals tolerate such inequalities if they believe they are necessary to maintain productive efficiency or increase growth (e.g., Cavala & Wildavsky, 1970; Cohen, 1974; Hirschman, 1973; Rainwater, 1974). There are also hints in some of these data (e.g., Cohen, 1974) that these beliefs not only produce a tolerance for unjust inequalities but also begin to make them appear to be just. This suggests the importance of investigating the relationship between beliefs about the existence of outcome distributions, on the one hand, and evaluations of those distributions, on the other hand (cf. Furby, 1979).

2. POWER

Closely related to these considerations is the relationship between justice and power. Perceptions of justice serve to legitimize a society's structure of power. Several theorists, from very different perspectives (e.g., Homans, 1976; Marx, 1875, in Tucker, 1978; Walster & Walster, 1975) have suggested that both perceptions of justice and predominant principles of justice may be little more than reflections of a distribution of power. If this is the case, however, there are at least two important questions that arise: (1) how can one explain the emergence of alternative perceptions of justice?; and (2) if predominant principles of justice work primarily to the advantage of the powerful, why do the less powerful often endorse them?

The first question suggests a focus on situations where predominant conceptions of justice change. Moore (1978) suggests that revolutions are just such situations, where shifts in the conceptions of justice that legitimize power differences provide the groundwork for revolutionary movements designed to alter the structure of power. Research on so-called revolutionary coalitions (Webster & Smith, 1978) points to the importance of recipients' beliefs in the legitimacy of the allocator's right to dispense outcomes in maintaining then-current power relationships, as well as the consequences of decreased legitimacy. The formation of such coalitions also would seem to require the emergence of a perception of common fate and collective consciousness. Recent stimulating work on forms of group awareness and identification would be important sources of ideas here (e.g., Billig, 1976; Gurin, Miller, & Gurin, 1980; Tajfel, 1978).

The second question suggests a close examination of the endorsements given by those low in the distribution of outcomes. These endorsements may only be verbal, as public adherence to alternative principles or perceptions of justice may be perceived to be, and may actually be, severely sanctioned. Furthermore, the power to sanction is also in the hands of those likely to be high in the distribution of outcomes (cf. Gartrell, 1979a). However, public endorsements may be coincident with private beliefs. In most social psychological statements on justice, this coincidence is thought to result from the internalization of normative standards. The relative role of external and internal sanctioning forces in the development and maintenance of justice perceptions, particularly among those for whom self-interest might suggest a challenge to prevailing perceptions, remains an important area for future work.

3. PRODUCTION

Most work on justice focuses primarily on matters of distribution and not at all on the production of those outcomes whose distribution is at issue. It is not necessary to agree that the organization of production determines distribution and justice principles to pose questions about the relationship between production and distributive justice. We can raise only a few here.

Some critics of the separate examination of production and distribution claim that many of the goods whose distribution is to be evaluated are already "linked" to individuals when these goods first appear on the scene. Thus, any question about their distribution actually becomes a matter of *redistribution* (e.g., Nozick, 1974). This view suggests the importance of conceptions of ownership and property, which we are only beginning to understand (e.g., Furby, 1978; Moessinger, 1975), as well as the importance of concepts of "rectification" of injustice (cf. Phillips, 1980). Some preliminary evidence (e.g., Furby, 1979; Horowitz, 1977; Tannenbaum, Kavcic, Rosner, Vianello, & Wieser, 1974) suggests that variations in conceptions of possession and in control over the production process may be related to perceptions of justice, but the nature and the extent of this relationship requires clarification and further work.

Experimental work on distributive justice, particularly the work involving allocations, often distorts aspects of the relationship between production and distribution. Perhaps most importantly, the highly complex and social nature of work in many real-life settings is obscured when allocators and recipients are presented with clear-cut, individualized information on the work produced by each person. The clarity of the distinction among individuals masks the complex interdependencies of many work settings where the disentangling of individual contributions would be a problem in itself. This suggests the importance of examining the impact of varying levels of clarity and perceived legitimacy of information individualizing potential recipients on their perceptions of justice.

Finally, one might ask whether the nature of the work performed in the social organization of production is related to perceptions of justice. The "work" performed by subjects in much allocation research is uninteresting and repetitive. These characteristics may contribute to the external validity of the research, given the nature of the work settings to which it is often applied, where repetition over long periods of time may be extremely alienating. Future work might address the impact of variations in the intrinsic satisfaction associated with different types of work (cf. Lepper & Greene, 1978) on distributive justice.

V. CONCLUSION

Social psychological work on justice is essentially a product of the past two decades. Serious gaps in research and significant conceptual problems remain to be addressed, and many questions only implicit in the early work need to be posed more clearly. Still, the theoretical statements we have discussed here and the large research literature they have stimulated have begun to provide the groundwork for an understanding of some of the most fundamental dimensions of social life. We have attempted in this chapter to point out some of the accomplishments of the major social psychological statements on justice, and to identify some of the major tasks for the immediate future.

The interest expressed by social psychologists in justice has coincided with increased interest among those working in other social scientific disciplines. The major works in political philosophy by Rawls (1971) and Nozick (1974) have already produced a sizable critical literature (e.g., Daniels, 1975) and are likely to continue to do so. In addition, major works in other disciplines have focused on the concept of justice and the major distributional issues to which it is linked (e.g., Bowles & Gintis, 1976; Gartrell, 1979b; Jencks, Smith, Acland, Bane, Cohen, Gintis, Heyns, & Michaelson, 1972; Levine & Bane, 1975; Moore, 1978; Rainwater, 1974; Thurow, 1973, 1975, 1980). As work in other disciplines develops, it will provide a source of important stimulation for future work in social psychology, and, no doubt, the reverse will also be true.

Much of the reawakened interest in justice has no doubt to do with the tumultuous political events of the 1960s, both domestic and international. Issues raised by many of these events are likely to increase in importance in the final two decades of the twentieth century; interest in and work on justice is therefore likely to increase. Revolutionary change, all forms of discrimination and collective conflict (racial, sexual, class, and international), policy questions concerning the creation and allocation of increasingly sophisticated technology and natural resources to meet human needs (cf. Calabresi & Bobbitt, 1978; Greenberg, 1981), all of these issues are likely to become more important in the future. As they do, justice is likely to become even a more central focus for social and political events, and for members of societies in which these events occur. Social psychologists will be subject to the influence of these developments, both in their everyday lives and in their work.

REFERENCES

Adams, J. S. Toward an understanding of inequity. *Journal of Abnormal and Social Psychology*, 1963, *67*, 422–436.

Adams, J. S. Inequity in social exchange. In L. Berkowitz (Ed.), *Advances in experimental social psychology* (Vol. 2). New York: Academic Press, 1965.

Adams, J. S., & Freedman, S. Equity theory revisited: Comments and annotated bibliography. In L. Berkowitz & E. Walster (Eds.), *Advances in experimental social psychology* (Vol. 9). New York: Academic Press, 1976.

Adams, J. S., & Rosenbaum, W. B. The relationship of worker productivity to cognitive dissonance about wage inequities. *Journal of Applied Psychology*, 1962, *46*, 161–164.

Allen, D. P. H. Is Marxism a philosophy? *Journal of Philosophy*, 1974, *71*, 601–612.

Alves, W. M., & Rossi, P. H. Who should get what? Fairness judgments of the distribution of earnings. *American Journal of Sociology*, 1978, *84*, 541–564.

Anderson, B., Berger, J., Zelditch, M., & Cohen, B. P. Reactions to inequity. *Acta Sociologica*, 1969, *12*, 1-12.

Anderson, B., & Shelly, R. K. Reactions to inequity II: A replication of the Adams experiment and a theoretical formulation. *Acta Sociologica*, 1970, *13*, 1-10.

Anderson, B., & Shelley, R. K. Reactions to inequity III: Inequity and social influence. *Acta Sociologica*, 1971, *14*, 236-244.

Anderson, N. H. Cognitive algebra: Integration theory applied to social attribution. In L. Berkowitz (Ed.), *Advances in experimental social psychology* (Vol. 7). New York: Academic Press, 1974.

Anderson, N. H. Equity judgments as information integration. *Journal of Personality and Social Psychology*, 1976, *33*, 291-299.

Austin, W. Equity theory and social comparison processes. In J. Suls & R. Miller (Eds.), *Social comparison theory*. Washington: Hemisphere, 1977.

Austin, W., & Walster, E. Equity with the world: Transrelational effects of equity and inequity. *Sociometry*, 1975, *38*, 474-496.

Bedau, H. A. *Justice and equality*. Englewood Cliffs, N.J.: Prentice-Hall, 1971.

Berger, J., Zelditch, M., Anderson, B., & Cohen, B. P. Structural aspects of distributive justice: A status-value formulation. In J. Berger, M. Zelditch, & B. Anderson (Eds.), *Sociological theories in progress* (Vol. 2). Boston: Houghton Mifflin, 1972.

Billig, M. *Social psychology and intergroup relations*. London: Academic Press, 1976.

Blau, P. M. *Exchange and power in social life*. New York: Wiley, 1964.

Bowles, S., & Gintis, H. *Schooling in capitalist America: Educational reform and the contradictions of economic life*. New York: Basic Books, 1976.

Brandt, R. B. (Ed.). *Social justice*. Englewood Cliffs, N.J.: Prentice-Hall, 1962.

Brickman, P., & Bryan, J. H. Moral judgment of theft, charity, and third-party transfers that increase or decrease equality. *Journal of Personality and Social Psychology*, 1975, *31*, 156-161.

Brickman, P., & Bryan, J. H. Equity versus equality as factors in children's moral judgments of thefts, charity, and third-party transfers. *Journal of Personality and Social Psychology*, 1976, *34*, 757-761.

Brickman, P., & Campbell, D. T. Hedonic relativism and planning the good society. In M. H. Appley (Ed.), *Adaptation level theory*. New York: Academic Press, 1971.

Brickman, P., Folger, R., Goode, E., & Schul, Y. Micro and macro justice. In M. J. Lerner & S. Lerner (Eds.), *The justice motive in social behavior*. New York: Plenum, 1981.

Burnstein, E., & Katz, S. Group decisions involving equitable and optimal distributions of status. In C. G. McClintock (Ed.), *Experimental social psychology*. New York: Holt, Rinehart and Winston, 1972.

Calabresi, G., & Bobbitt, P. *Tragic choices*. New York: Norton, 1978.

Carles, E. M., & Carver, C. S. Effects of person salience versus role salience on reward allocation in the dyad. *Journal of Personality and Social Psychology*, 1979, *37*, 2071-2080.

Cavala, B., & Wildavsky, A. The political feasibility of income by right. *Public Policy*, 1970, *18*, 321-354.

Cohen, R. L. Mastery and justice in laboratory dyads: A revision and extension of equity theory. *Journal of Personality and Social Psychology*, 1974, *29*, 464-474.

Cohen, R. L. *Toward an integration of equity and attribution perspectives on conceptions of distributive justice*. Unpublished manuscript, Bennington College, 1978.

Cohen, R. L. On the distinction between individual deserving and distributive justice. *Journal for the Theory of Social Behaviour*, 1979, *9*, 167-185.

Cohen, G. A. Robert Nozick and Wilt Chamberlain: How patterns preserve liberty. In J. Arthur & W. H. Shaw (Eds.), *Justice and economic distribution*. Englewood Cliffs, N.J.: Prentice-Hall, 1978.

Coleman, J. S. Inequality, sociology, and moral philosophy: A review essay. *American Journal of Sociology,* 1974, *80,* 739-764.

Cook, K. S. Expectations, evaluations, and equity. *American Sociological Review,* 1975, *40,* 372-388.

Crosby, F. A model of egoistical relative deprivation. *Psychological Review,* 1976, *83,* 85-113.

Daniels, N. (Ed.). *Reading Rawls: Critical studies of "A theory of justice."* New York: Basic Books, 1975.

deCarufel, A. Factors affecting the evaluation of improvement: The role of normative standards and allocator resources. *Journal of Personality and Social Psychology,* 1979, *37,* 847-857.

deCarufel, A., & Schopler, J. Evaluation of outcome improvement resulting from threats and appeals. *Journal of Personality and Social Psychology,* 1979, *37,* 662-673.

Deutsch, M. Equity, equality, and need: What determines which value will be used as the basis for distributive justice? *Journal of Social Issues,* 1975, *31,* 137-150.

Donnenwerth, G. V., & Törnblom, K. Y. Reactions to three types of distributive injustice. *Human Relations,* 1975, *28,* 407-430.

Eckhoff, T. *Justice: Its determinants in social interaction.* Rotterdam: Rotterdam University Press, 1974.

Farkas, A. J., & Anderson, N. H. Multidimensional input in equity theory. *Journal of Personality and Social Psychology,* 1979, *37,* 879-896.

Festinger, L. A theory of social comparison processes. *Human Relations,* 1954, *7,* 117-140.

Festinger, L. *A theory of cognitive dissonance.* Evanston, Ill.: Row, Peterson, 1957.

Folger, R. Distributive and procedural justice: Combined impact of "voice" and improvement on experienced inequity. *Journal of Personality and Social Psychology,* 1977, *35,* 108-119.

Folger, R. (Ed.). *The sense of injustice: Social psychological perspectives.* New York: Plenum, in press.

Folger, R., Rosenfield, D., Grove, J., & Corkran, L. Effects of "voice" and peer opinions on responses to inequity. *Journal of Personality and Social Psychology,* 1979, *37,* 2253-2261.

Frankena, W. K. The concept of social justice. In R. B. Brandt (Ed.), *Social justice.* Englewood Cliffs, N.J.: Prentice-Hall, 1962.

Frankena, W. K. Some beliefs about justice. In K. E. Goodpaster (Ed.), *Perspectives on morality.* Notre Dame, Ind.: University of Notre Dame Press, 1976.

Friedrich, C. J., & Chapman, J. W. (Eds.), *NOMOS VI: Justice.* New York: Atherton, 1963.

Furby, L. Possessions: Toward a theory of their meaning and function throughout the life cycle. In P. B. Baltes (Ed.), *Life-span development and behavior* (Vol. 1). New York: Academic Press, 1978.

Furby, L. Inequalities in personal possessions: Explanations for and judgments about unequal distributions. *Human Development,* 1979, *22,* 180-202.

Gamson, W. A. Experimental studies of coalition formation. In L. Berkowitz (Ed.), *Advances in experimental social psychology* (Vol. 1). New York: Academic Press, 1964.

Gartrell, C. D. *How valid are experimental studies of equity theory?* Unpublished manuscript, University of Georgia, 1979. (a)

Gartrell, C. D. *The scope of wage comparisons: Insights from institutional labor economics.* Unpublished manuscript, University of Georgia, 1979. (b)

Goodman, P. S. An examination of referents used in the evaluation of pay. *Organizational Behavior and Human Performance,* 1974, *12,* 170-195.

Goodman, P. S., & Friedman, A. An examination of Adams' theory of inequity. *Administrative Science Quarterly,* 1971, *16,* 271-288.

Greenberg, J. Justice perceived versus justice enacted. In J. Greenberg (Chair), *Recent*

38   RONALD L. COHEN AND JERALD GREENBERG

developments in interpersonal justice theory and research. Symposium presented at the meeting of the American Psychological Association, New York, September 1979.

Greenberg, J. The justice of distributing scarce and abundant resources. In M. J. Lerner & S. Lerner (Eds.), *The justice motive in social behavior.* New York: Plenum, 1981.

Greenberg, J. On the apocryphal nature of inequity distress. In R. Folger (Ed.), *The sense of injustice: Social psychological perspectives.* New York: Plenum, in press.

Greenberg, J., & Leventhal, G. S. Equity and the use of overreward to motivate performance. *Journal of Personality and Social Psychology,* 1976, *34,* 179–190.

Gurin, P., Miller, A. H., & Gurin, G. Stratum identification and consciousness. *Social Psychology Quarterly,* 1980, *43,* 30–47.

Hamilton, D. L. A cognitive–attributional analysis of stereotyping. In L. Berkowitz (Ed.), *Advances in experimental social psychology* (Vol. 12). New York: Academic Press, 1979.

Hamilton, V. L., & Rytina, S. Social consensus on norms of justice: Should the punishment fit the crime? *American Journal of Sociology,* 1980, *85,* 1117–1144.

Harris, R. J. Handling negative inputs: On the plausible equity formulae. *Journal of Experimental Social Psychology,* 1976, *12,* 194–209.

Held, V. John Locke on Robert Nozick. *Social Research,* 1976, *43,* 169–195.

Hirschman, A. O. The changing tolerance for income inequality in the course of economic development. *Quarterly Journal of Economics,* 1973, *87,* 544–566.

Hobbes, T. *Leviathan* (M. Oakeshott, Ed.). Oxford: Basil Blackwell, 1947. (Originally published, 1651.)

Homans, G. C. *Social behavior: Its elementary forms.* New York: Harcourt Brace & World, 1961.

Homans, G. C. *Social behavior: Its elementary forms* (Rev. ed.). New York: Harcourt Brace Jovanovich, 1974.

Homans, G. C. Commentary. In L. Berkowitz & E. Walster (Eds.), *Advances in experimental social psychology* (Vol. 9). New York: Academic Press, 1976.

Hook J. G., & Cook, T. D. Equity theory and the cognitive ability of children. *Psychological Bulletin,* 1979, *86,* 429–445.

Horowitz, I. L. (Ed.). *Equity, income, and policy: Comparative studies in three worlds of development.* New York: Praeger, 1977.

Hume, D. A treatise of human nature. (L. A. Selby-Bigge, Ed.). Oxford: Clarendon Press, 1928. (Originally published, 1739).

Jasso, G. On the justice of earnings: A new specification of the justice evaluation function. *American Journal of Sociology,* 1978, *83,* 1398–1419.

Jasso, G. A new theory of distributive justice. *American Sociological Review,* 1980, *45,* 3–32.

Jasso, G., & Rossi, P. H. Distributive justice and earned income. *American Sociological Review,* 1977, *42,* 639–651.

Jencks, C., Smith, M., Acland, H., Bane, M. J., Cohen, D., Gintis, H., Heyns, R., & Michelson, S. *Inequality: A reassessment of the effects of family and schooling in America.* New York: Basic Books, 1972.

Kahn, A. Reactions to generosity or stinginess from an intelligent or stupid work partner: A test of equity theory in a direct exchange relationship. *Journal of Personality and Social Psychology,* 1972, *21,* 116–123.

Kant, I. *The metaphysical elements of justice* (J. Ladd, Introduction and trans.). Indianapolis: Bobbs-Merrill, 1965. (Originally published, 1791.)

Kidd, R. F., & Utne, M. K. Reactions to inequity: A perspective on the role of attributions. *Law and Human Behavior,* 1978, *2,* 301–312.

Lamm, H., Kayser, E., & Schwinger, T. Justice norms and other determinants of allocation and negotiation behavior. In M. Irle (Ed.), *Decision making: Social psychological and socioeconomic analyses.* New York: de Gruyter, in press.

Lepper, M. L., & Greene, D. *The hidden costs of reward*. Hillsdale, N.J.: Erlbaum, 1978.

Lerner, M. J. Evaluation of performance as a function of performer's reward and attractiveness. *Journal of Personality and Social Psychology*, 1965, *1*, 355–360.

Lerner, M. J. Social psychology of justice and interpersonal attraction. In T. Huston (Ed.), *Foundations of interpersonal attraction*. New York: Academic Press, 1974.

Lerner, M. J. The justice motive in social behavior: An introduction. *Journal of Social Issues*, 1975, *31*, 1–19.

Lerner, M. J. The justice motive: Some hypotheses as to its origins and forms. *Journal of Personality*, 1977, *45*, 1–52.

Lerner, M. J., & Lerner, S. (Eds.). *The justice motive in social behavior*. New York: Plenum, Press, 1981.

Lerner, M. J., & Miller, D. T. Just world research and the attribution process: Looking back and ahead. *Psychological Bulletin*, 1978, *85*, 1030–1051.

Lerner, M. J., Miller, D. T., & Holmes, J. G. Deserving and the emergence of forms of justice. In L. Berkowitz & E. Walster (Eds.), *Advances in experimental social psychology* (Vol. 9). New York: Academic Press, 1976.

Lerner, M. J., & Simmons, C. H. Observers' reaction to the "innocent victim": Compassion or rejection? *Journal of Personality and Social Psychology*, 1966, *4*, 203–210.

Leventhal, G. S. The distribution of rewards and resources in groups and organizations. In L. Berkowitz & E. Walster (Eds.), *Advances in experimental social psychology* (Vol. 9). New York: Academic Press, 1976. (a)

Leventhal, G. S. Fairness in social relationships. In J. Thibaut, J. Spence, & R. Carson (Eds.), *Contemporary topics in social psychology*. Morristown, N.J.: General Learning Press, 1976. (b)

Leventhal, G. S. What should be done with equity theory? In K. Gergen, M. Greenberg, & R. Willis (Eds.), *Social exchange theory*. New York: Plenum, 1980.

Leventhal, G. S., & Lane, D. W. Sex, age, and equity behavior. *Journal of Personality and Social Psychology*, 1970, *15*, 312–316.

Leventhal, G. S., Michaels, J. W., & Sanford, C. Inequity and interpersonal conflict: Reward allocation and secrecy about reward as methods of preventing conflict. *Journal of Personality and Social Psychology*, 1972, *23*, 88–102.

Levine, D. M., & Bane, M. J. (Eds.). *The "Inequality" controversy: Schooling and distributive justice*. New York: Basic Books, 1975.

Macpherson, C. B. *The political theory of possessive individualism*. London: Oxford University Press, 1962.

Marx, K. *Capital: A critique of political economy*. (Translated from the fourth German edition by E. Paul & C. Paul.) New York: International Publishers, 1929.

Marx, K. Critique of the Gotha Program. In R. C. Tucker (Ed.), *The Marx-Engels reader* (2nd ed.). New York, Norton, 1978. (Originally published, 1875.)

McBride, W. L. The concept of justice in Marx, Engels, and others. *Ethics*, 1975, *85*, 204–218.

Mikula, G. (Ed.). *Justice and social interaction*. New York: Springer-Verlag, 1980. (a)

Mikula, G. On the role of justice in allocation decisions. In G. Mikula (Ed.), *Justice in social interaction*. New York: Springer-Verlag, 1980. (b)

Mikula, G., & Schwinger, T. Intermember relations and reward allocation: Theoretical considerations of affects. In H. Brandstatter, J. H. Davis, & H. Schuler (Eds.), *Dynamics of group decisions*. Beverley Hills: Sage, 1978.

Mill, J. S. *Utilitarianism, liberty, and responsive government*. London: J. M. Dent, 1940. (Originally published, 1861.)

Moessinger, P. Developmental study of fair division and property. *European Journal of Social Psychology*, 1975, *5*, 385–394.

Moore, B. *Injustice: The social bases of obedience and revolt.* White Plains, N.Y.: M. E. Sharpe, 1978.

Moschetti, G. J. Calculating equity: Ordinal and ratio criteria. *Social Psychology Quarterly,* 1979, *42,* 172–176.

Mowday, R. T. Equity theory predictions of behavior in organizations. In R. M. Steers & L. W. Porter (Eds.), *Motivation and work behavior* (2nd ed.). New York: McGraw-Hill, 1979.

Nozick, R. *Anarchy, state, and utopia.* New York: Basic Books, 1974.

Okun, A. M. *Equality and efficiency: The big tradeoff.* Washington: The Brookings Institution, 1975.

Oppenheim, F. E. Egalitarian rules of distribution. *Ethics,* 1980, *90,* 164–179.

Parcel, T. L., & Cook, K. S. Status characteristics, reward allocation, and equity. *Sociometry,* 1977, *40,* 311–324.

Pepitone, A. Toward a normative and comparative biocultural social psychology. *Journal of Personality and Social Psychology,* 1976, *34,* 641–653.

Perelman, C. *The idea of justice and the problem of argument.* London: Routledge & Kegan Paul, 1963.

Pettigrew, T. F. Social evaluation theory. In D. Levine (Ed.), *Nebraska symposium on motivation.* Lincoln: University of Nebraska Press, 1967.

Phillips, D. L. *Equality, justice, and rectification: An explorative study in normative sociology.* London: Academic Press, 1980.

Pritchard, R. D. Equity theory: A review and critique. *Organizational Behavior and Human Performance,* 1969, *4,* 176–211.

Rainwater, L. *What money buys.* New York: Basic Books, 1974.

Rawls, J. *A theory of justice.* Cambridge: Harvard University Press, 1971.

Reis, H. T. Theories of interpersonal justice: From exploration through assimilation to accommodation. In J. Greenberg (Chair), *Recent developments in interpersonal justice theory and research.* Symposium presented at the meeting of the American Psychological Association, New York, September 1979.

Rescher, N. *Distributive justice.* Indianapolis: Bobbs-Merrill, 1967.

Romer, D. Limitations in the equity theory approach: Toward a resolution of the "negative-inputs" controversy. *Personality and Social Psychology Bulletin,* 1977, *3,* 228–231.

Ross, W. D. (Ed.), *The Oxford translation of Aristotle, Vol. IX: The Nichomachean Ethics.* London: Oxford University Press, 1925.

Rothbart, M. Effects of motivation, equity, and compliance on the use of reward and punishment. *Journal of Personality and Social Psychology,* 1968, *9,* 353–362.

Sampson, E. E. Studies of status congruence. In L. Berkowitz (Ed.), *Advances in experimental social psychology* (Vol. 4). New York: Academic Press, 1969.

Sampson, E. E. On justice as equality. *Journal of Social Issues,* 1975, *31,* 45–64.

Samuel, W. Toward a simple but useful equity theory: A comment on the Romer article. *Personality and Social Psychology Bulletin,* 1978, *4,* 135–138.

Schwinger, T. Just allocations of goods: Decisions among three principles. In G. Mikula (Ed.), *Justice and social interaction.* New York: Springer-Verlag, 1980.

Stouffer, S. A., Suchman, E. A., DeVinney, L. C., Star, S. A., & Williams, R. M., Jr. *The American soldier* (Vol. 1). *Adjustment during army life.* Princeton: Princeton University Press, 1949.

Tajfel, H. (Ed.). *Differentiation between social groups: Studies in the social psychology of intergroup relations.* London: Academic Press, 1978.

Tannenbaum, A. S., Kavcic, B., Rosner, M., Vianello, M., & Wieser, G. *Hierarchy in organizations.* San Francisco: Jossey-Bass, 1974.

Thibaut, J., & Kelley, H. H. *The social psychology of groups.* New York: Wiley, 1959.

Thibaut, J., & Walker, L. *Procedural justice.* Hillsdale, N.J.: Erlbaum, 1975.

Thurow, L. C. Toward a definition of economic justice. *The Public Interest*, 1973, *31*, 56–80.

Thurow, L. C. *Generating inequality.* New York: Basic Books, 1975.

Thurow, L. C. *Toward the zero-sum society.* New York: Basic Books, 1980.

Törnblom, K. Y. Distributive justice: Typology and propositions. *Human Relations*, 1977, *30*, 1–24.

Tucker, R. C. (Ed.). *The Marx-Engels reader* (2nd ed.). New York: Norton, 1978.

Tucker, R. C. Marx and distributive justice. In C. J. Friedrichs & J. W. Chapman (Eds.), *NOMOS VI: Justice.* New York: Atherton, 1963.

Utne, M. K., & Kidd, R. F. Attribution and equity. In G. Mikula (Ed.), *Justice and social interaction.* New York: Springer-Verlag, 1980.

Van Avermaet, E., McClintock, C. G., & Moscowitz, J. Alternative approaches to equity: Dissonance reduction, pro-social motivation, and strategic accommodation. *European Journal of Social Psychology*, 1978, *8*, 419–437.

Vlastos, G. Justice and equality. In R. B. Brandt (Ed.), *Social justice.* Englewood Cliffs, N.J.: Prentice-Hall, 1962.

Walster, E. Assignment of responsibility for an accident. *Journal of Personality and Social Psychology*, 1966, *3*, 73–79.

Walster, E., Berscheid, E., & Walster, G. W. New directions in equity research. *Journal of Personality and Social Psychology*, 1973, *25*, 151–176.

Walster, E., & Walster, G. W. Equity and social justice. *Journal of Social Issues*, 1975, *31*, 21–43.

Walster, E., Walster, G. W., & Berscheid, E. *Equity: Theory and research.* Boston: Allyn & Bacon, 1978.

Webster, M., & Smith, L. R. F. Justice and revolutionary coalitions: A test of two theories. *American Journal of Sociology*, 1978, *84*, 267–292.

Weick, K. The concept of equity in the perception of pay. *Administrative Science Quarterly*, 1966, *11*, 414–439.

Williams, B. A. O. The idea of equality. In P. Laslett & W. G. Runciman (Eds.), *Philosophy, politics, and society* (Series II). London: Basil Blackwell, 1962.

Winthrop, D. Aristotle and theories of justice. *American Political Science Review*, 1978, *72*, 1201–1216.

Wolff, R. P. *Understanding Rawls.* Princeton: Princeton University Press, 1977.

Wood, A. W. The Marxian critique of justice. *Philosophy and Public Affairs*, 1972, *1*, 244–282.

Zelditch, M., Berger, J., Anderson, B., & Cohen, B. P. Equitable comparisons. *Pacific Sociological Review*, 1970, *13*, 19–26.

chapter 2

Individual Differences in Justice Behavior

BRENDA MAJOR
KAY DEAUX

I. INTRODUCTION

Although the concept of justice may be universal, the principles by which just outcomes are determined vary greatly. "An eye for an eye" coexists with "turning the other cheek." National and religious groups differ in their endorsement of these principles. At another level, individuals vary in the principles that they apply and in their reactions to the decisions of others.

This chapter is concerned with individual differences in two general areas of justice behavior: reward distributions and reactions to injustice. *Reward distribution* as used here refers to how people decide what is a "fair" allocation of resources, either to others, to themselves, or among themselves and others. The area broadly termed *reactions to injustice* is concerned with how a person reacts when he or she is treated unfairly by another. In this latter case, it is worth noting that our concern is with individual differences in the reaction of the victim or recipient of injustice. Individual differences among those who perpetrate injustice on others or among observers' reactions to injustice are not discussed.

Numerous writers have discussed the variety of justice rules that may exist (Deutsch, 1975; Hook & Cook, 1979; Leventhal, 1976a; Reis, 1979; Sampson, 1969). Equity, equality, reciprocity, self-interest, and need are only a few of those that have been mentioned. By far the most frequently discussed and heavily researched rule of justice is equity. Based on the assumption that "people will try to maximize their outcomes [Walster,

43

Walster, & Berscheid, 1978]," equity theory tries to resolve how people reconcile their self-interests with the need to maintain social relationships and preserve social order (Adams, 1965; Homans, 1961; Walster, Berscheid, & Walster, 1973; Walster, et al., 1978). With respect to reward distribution, equity theory postulates that outcomes (rewards) are allocated to persons on the basis of their recognized and relevant inputs (contributions) to some task or relationship, relative to the inputs of others. The greater a person's contributions, the greater the rewards (e.g., pay, status) he or she should receive. Equity theory further predicts that a person's satisfaction with an outcome is dependent upon whether or not that outcome is perceived as equitable. Presumably, both the perception of underreward and overreward results in feelings of distress, in the form of anger in the former case and guilt in the latter case. Thus, equity theory makes specific predictions for both reward distribution and reactions to injustice.

What equity theory and other justice theories have generally failed to address, however, is the issue of individual differences in justice behavior. Neither Adams's (1965) original conceptualization of inequity theory nor more recent formulations of the theory (e.g., Walster et al., 1978) have presented a framework to explain how individual differences might affect justice decisions and reactions to injustice. Consistent with, and perhaps as a consequence of, this lack of a theoretical framework, relatively little empirical research has addressed this issue. The work that does exist has been somewhat "scattershot," more opportunistic than systematic in most cases. By far the most frequently studied individual difference variables have been the easily obtained demographic variables, namely sex, age, and to a much lesser extent, nationality. Far less attention has been paid to psychological variables.

Due to the diversity of this research and to the lack of a theoretical framework, we will begin by reviewing the existent literature, looking first at the impact of demographic factors and then at the impact of psychological variables on justice behavior. Within each of these sections, we will first review individual differences in reward distribution, followed by a review of reactions to injustice. We will then consider possible explanations of individual differences. Finally, we will conclude with an assessment of the present situation and some prescriptions for future research.

To organize the diverse literature on individual differences in justice behavior, we have categorized existent research according to the paradigm used. Within the are of reward distribution, several distinct paradigms can be identified. One approach can be termed *allocations to others only* (cf. Leventhal, Michaels, & Sanford, 1972). In this situation, the focus is on the individual's allocation to other persons who differ in their performance inputs. The allocator does not share in the reward. In a second approach, *allocations to self only* (cf. Callahan-Levy & Messé, 1979), an individual allocates reward to herself or himself after performing a task, and no others are involved. A third research paradigm is *allocations to self and others* (cf. Leventhal & Lane, 1970). Typically, the subject works with another person on some mutual task, with payment contingent upon their joint performance. False performance feedback from the experimenter indicates that one of the coworkers was the superior performer and one was the inferior performer. Subjects are then assigned the task of allocating reward between themselves and their coworker. A fourth research paradigm is *group allocations to self and other* (cf. Vinacke, 1959, 1972), in which several people work or compete with each other on a task and the group decides how much reward each participant should receive. Subjects share in both the allocation and receipt of rewards and there is a high degree of interaction among participants.

Several research paradigms also can be identified in research on reactions to injustice. In the most frequently used approach, *reactions to an unjust experimenter-employer,* subjects are hired to perform a task and are either overpaid, underpaid, or equitably paid by the experimenter in relation to others. The dependent variable usually is the quantity or quality of work produced by the subject (cf. Adams, 1965). A second approach considers *reactions to an unjust partner* (cf. Kahn, 1972). In this case, the subject works with a partner on two tasks. On the first task, the partner makes reward allocations and either overpays, underpays, or equitably pays the subject. The major dependent variables are the subjects' subsequent reward allocations to their partners and themselves on the second task and their evaluations of their partners. A third research approach is *reactions to an unjust game.* In this situation, two people play a game that is set up so that one person arbitrarily and consistently makes much more, much less, or an amount equal to that of the other person. The major variable of interest is whether or not the players remain in the game or opt for a less profitable but more equal strategy (cf. Schmitt & Marwell, 1972), or use some other strategy to minimize differences between them (cf. Marwell, Ratcliff, & Schmitt, 1969).

As will be apparent in the following review, attention to the specific research paradigm is important. The impact of certain individual difference variables (e.g., subject's sex) on justice behavior can vary markedly as a function of the particular approach.

II. SEX DIFFERENCES IN JUSTICE BEHAVIOR

The individual difference variable that has received the most attention in justice research is sex of subject. In part, this attention is due to
the obvious ease of obtaining and "measuring" this variable. A second
reason for this attention, however, is more theoretical in nature. Early
research revealed frequent differences between men's and women's behavior, particularly in the area of reward distribution. Women, it was
observed, often did not conform to equity theory predictions. Partially as
a result of these findings, justice theory has been broadened beyond the
concept of a single rule of equity (cf. Kahn, 1979).

A. Sex Differences in Reward Distribution

1. ALLOCATIONS TO OTHERS ONLY

In the majority of studies using this paradigm, men and women show
no differences in their allocations to others when they do not expect to
interact with the recipients (Baker, 1974, Experiment 2; Greenberg,
1978a; Leventhal *et al.;* Leventhal, Weiss, & Buttrick, 1973; Leventhal &
Whiteside, 1973). Both women and men reward better performers with
higher amounts of reward and poorer performers with lower amounts
of reward. Women and men also do not differ in their allocations to
another when the other's performance inputs are unspecified
(Callahan-Levy & Messé, 1979, Experiment 1).

Similarly, men and women do not differ in their allocations when
future interaction with the recipients is definitely expected (Austin &
McGinn, 1977). Both prefer equitable allocations when they expect to
interact with a higher input person and equal allocations when they
expect to interact with a lower input person. Sex differences do emerge,
however, when allocators are unsure whether or not they will interact
with same-sex recipients (Austin & McGinn, 1977). In this situation, men
use equitable allocations with male recipients, whereas women use a
compromise between equity and equality with female recipients.

In summary, few sex differences are found when women and men
allocate rewards to others and are not involved as corecipients. The few
differences obtained appear to be due to the specific nature of the instructions (Leventhal, 1973), to ambiguity concerning whether or not the
allocator will interact with the recipients in the future (Austin & McGinn,
1977), or to confounding of sex of allocator with sex of recipient (Austin
& McGinn, 1977).

2. ALLOCATIONS TO SELF ONLY

Only one experiment has examined allocations to self only. Callahan-Levy and Messé (1979, Experiment 1) asked men and women to work on an essay-writing task for a specified period of time. No performance feedback was provided, and thus "inputs" should have been perceived as relatively equal. At the end of the time period, half of the subjects were asked to pay privately only themselves, whereas the other half of the subjects were asked to pay privately one of the other subjects in the group (either a male or a female, exact identity unknown). Females not only paid themselves less money than the males paid themselves, but they also reported that less money was "fair" pay for their work than did the males. In addition, females paid themselves less than other people paid females.

3. INDIVIDUAL ALLOCATIONS TO SELF AND OTHERS

Experiments using this paradigm have consistently demonstrated that whether the allocators' inputs are equal to, higher than, or less than their partners', women take less of the reward for themselves than do men in a similar position. When their performance is superior to that of their coworkers, women tend to split rewards equally between themselves and their coworker, whereas men split rewards equitably (in proportion to merit); when their performance is inferior to their coworker's, both sexes follow the equity rule, but women take less for themselves than do men (e.g., Leventhal & Anderson, 1970; Leventhal & Lane, 1970; Mikula, 1974). Furthermore, women take less reward for themselves than do men, even when their inputs and that of the coworker are equal (Lane & Messé, 1971, Experiment 1), or unspecified, and thus presumably equal (e.g., Katz & Messé, 1973). These patterns can be moderated, however, by several situational factors.

One such factor is the sex of the coworker(s). The majority of studies of self–other allocations have examined same-sex rather than mixed-sex pairs or groups. As a result, it is generally unclear whether observed sex differences are due to the sex of the allocator or to the sex of the recipient(s). However, Messé and Callahan-Levy (1979), who examined mixed-sex as well as same-sex pairs, report that sex differences are a function of both sex of subject and sex of recipient. They found that women were more generous toward their partners whether those partners were male or female. Men, however, varied their allocations as a function of their partner's sex; they were more generous toward a female than toward a male partner. Callahan-Levy and Messé (1979,

Experiment 1) found that both sexes were more generous toward a female than a male recipient.

Kahn, Nelson, and Gaeddert (1980, Experiment 1) investigated reward allocations to self and others in mixed-sex and same-sex triads. Subjects worked with two other coworkers; they were led to believe that one of the coworkers did much better than the subject and one did much worse. Each subject made reward allocations for himself or herself and the other two coworkers. No sex differences in allocations were found. Instead, effects for sex composition of the group appeared. Equitable allocations were preferred by both women and men when the group was composed of one or two men (besides the subject), whereas equal allocations were preferred when the group was composed of two females (besides the subject). These studies suggest that the sex of the other people involved in the experiment is one cue people use in deciding what is "fair" in a relationship. It appears that both sexes assume that women prefer more equal divisions of rewards between themselves and others than men do, and that it is appropriate to be more generous toward women than toward men.

A second factor that affects men's and women's allocations is task familiarity, or the sex-linkage of the task. Reis and Jackson (1981, Experiment 1), varied sex of allocator, sex of recipient, and sex-linkage of task (i.e., recognition of masculine or feminine items), using a procedure similar to that used in most self–other allocation experiments. All subjects were led to believe that he or she was the superior performer. On same-sex tasks, both men and women allocated rewards equitably with a same-sex partner and equally with an opposite sex partner. On opposite-sex tasks, men distributed the reward equitably, whereas women divided equally, regardless of the partner's sex. Thus, on a masculine task, the typical pattern of sex differences was observed: Males allocated rewards equitably when paired with other males and equally when paired with females; females allocated equally regardless of their partner's sex. On feminine tasks, however, both sexes allocated equitably to a same-sex partner.

The influence of a third factor, salience of self-presentational concerns, on the self–other allocations of men and women is suggested in a series of studies by Kidder, Bellettirie, and Cohn (1977). In their first study, women and men were asked to indicate privately their preference for course credit allocations between themselves and classmates with whom they had worked. Women preferred giving each person the exact amount of credit he or she had earned, whereas men were almost equally divided between giving their coworkers either an amount of credit equal to their own or giving each coworker the exact amount he or she had earned. Thus, women preferred equity whereas men were divided between equity and equality. One problem with this study, however, was that women had also completed more of the work than had men.

Two further experiments (Kidder *et al.*, 1977, Experiments 2,3) varied whether men and women allocated hypothetical extra credit points to themselves and a coworker with inferior performance in public (allocations would be discussed with both the experimenter and the coworker) or in private (the subject's allocations would not be identifiable to either the experimenter or to the coworker). Women and men reversed their allocations in the public and private conditions. Women allocated rewards relatively equally in public and equitably in private, whereas men allocated rewards equitably in public and more equally in private. Kidder *et al.* (1977) accounted for these findings by proposing that women and men fulfill traditional role expectations in the public condition and are "released" from these normative expectations in the private condition.

In summary, sex differences often emerge when allocators are also recipients of their allocations. In general, whether their inputs are equal to, higher than, or less than their partner's, female allocators take less for themselves than male allocators do. Particularly when their inputs are superior to a partner's, women's behavior does not conform to predictions from equity theory. These patterns can be modified, however, by situational factors such as sex of coworker, sex-linkage of task, and salience of self-presentational concerns.

4. GROUP ALLOCATIONS TO SELF AND OTHERS

Experiments by Vinacke and his colleagues (e.g., Amidjaja & Vinacke, 1965; Bond & Vinacke, 1961; Vinacke, 1959, 1972; Vinacke, Cherulnik & Lichtman, 1970; Vinacke & Gullickson, 1964; Vinacke, Mogy, Powers, Langan, & Beck, 1974) on coalition formation exemplify group allocations to self and others. Vinacke's experiments typically involve three people playing a series of board games. In any game, any two people, or all three of them, can join forces to try to win control of the winner's prize. Prior to the start of each game, power weights, or chances to win on that game, are assigned arbitrarily to the players. The major dependent variables are the outcomes of the pregame bargaining process: whether no coalitions, two-party coalitions or triple alliances are formed, and how the reward (usually points) is divided among the players. For purposes of evaluating these experiments within a justice framework, the initial power weights assigned to the players can be considered inputs (cf. Gamson, 1964), and the relevant outcomes are the partner's shares of the coalition prize.

Men and women show some similarities in their approaches to this situation. Both follow a general strategy in which the two weaker players ally against the stronger player when this is possible, and both sexes engage in few triple alliances when one person is all-powerful. However, women and men also display a variety of differences in this situation. Compared to males, females more often arrive at triple alliances, or arrive at no coalition at all, are more likely to form coalitions when none is necessary (e.g., when one member is all-powerful), are more likely to arrive at even divisions of the prize among coalition members, and are more likely to engage in altruistic offers in which one player suggests that the other players ally to her own disadvantage (Vinacke, 1959). In general, women are more likely to prefer an equal division of the reward among the players, whereas men are more apt to allocate the prize in proportion to the initial power weights.

Changing the nature of the situation from a board game to a political negotiation exercise does not alter these patterns (Vinacke, 1972). Male groups respond to differences in power relationships by consistently deciding upon unequal (rewards proportional to power) allocations. Females react less to the power variations; they typically choose not to divide the rewards at all, or if they do, divide them equally. Further research (Uesugi & Vinacke, 1963) has shown that altering the game to one presumably more feminine in nature increases the incidence of typically female strategies for both sexes, but particularly for women. Thus, sex differences are still observed.

Vinacke's results have been verified in a more recent coalition formation study by Wahba (1972), who found that both females and males divided rewards equally in coalitions among equals. When initial resources were unequal, however, females preferred equality of outcomes, whereas males preferred equality of gains after repayment of initial resources (a compromise between an equitable and equal allocation strategy).

Kahn et al. (1980, Experiment 2) have conducted the only study that examines sex differences in group allocations following differential task performance. Subjects participated in mixed-sex triads on a task designated as either masculine or feminine. After performing the task, each member was told that he or she had achieved high, moderate, or low performance on the task. The group then was given 5 min to discuss how they would divide the reward among themselves. Surprisingly, the pattern of allocations did not vary as a function of the number of men or women in the group, how well or how poorly the women and men in the group had performed, or the sex-typing of the task. An equal division of the money was preferred by 82% of the groups, an equitable division by 10% of the groups, and some other division by 8% of the groups. Kahn *et al.* suggested that the high preference for equality exhibited by all groups, regardless of sex composition, may have been due to the highly interpersonal nature of the situation. Furthermore, participants in this experiment were not playing a game, and the situation was not explicitly competitive, thus the salience of the equity norm may have been reduced (Deutsch, 1975). Alternatively, participants required to allocate money in this complex, multirecipient, differential performance situation may have preferred equal allocations primarily because of their greater cognitive simplicity relative to other justice rules (Harris & Joyce, 1980; Leventhal, 1976b).

In summary, results of coalition formation studies indicate that when presented with arbitrary power differences in a game setting, women prefer to divide the prize equally. Men are more likely to divide the prize in proportion to their initial power advantages. In nongame group allocation settings where differential inputs are performance-based, however, both sexes appear to prefer an equal division of the reward among group members.

5. GENERAL SUMMARY AND COMMENTARY

Sex differences in reward distribution occur primarily when the allocator is also a recipient of his or her allocations. That is, women and men typically allocate rewards similarly to others but differently to themselves. In general, women allocate less reward to themselves than do men. These effects are particularly noticeable when women's inputs are greater than their partner's. In this situation, women appear to follow a norm of equality, whereas men appear to follow a norm of equity. A variety of situational factors may moderate sex differences in reward distribution, however. These include such factors as sex of coworkers, type of task, and salience of self-presentational concerns. One problem with almost all of the experiments investigating allocations to self and others, whether these allocations have been made individually or in groups, is that the allocations are zero-sum. That is, the experiments have been designed so that allocations to the self are contingent on allocations to others. Thus, it is generally impossible to determine in these experiments whether women, in comparison with men, are allocating less reward to themselves or more rewards to their partners. Those experiments that have separated these allocations suggest that women allocate less reward to themselves than men do, but allocate rewards similarly to others.

B. Sex Differences in Reactions to Injustice

1. REACTIONS TO AN UNJUST EXPERIMENTER–EMPLOYER

Experimental studies of reactions to an unjust experimenter–employer yield little evidence of sex differences. As Kahn, O'Leary, Krulewitz, and Lamm (1980) have observed, sex differences have generally not been an issue for research using this approach. Most studies use males only, and those that use both sexes typically combine the results. There are some exceptions. Lawler (1968) and Deci, Reis, Johnston, and Smith(1977) found no differences in the performances of both women and men following inequitable outcomes. Garland (1973) found that men and women did not differ in their performances when they were underpaid, but women reacted less strongly than did men to being overpaid.

Following predictions from equity theory, one might expect that field research investigating sex differences in job and pay satisfaction would find striking sex differences. That is, women should be less satisfied than men with their pay and their jobs because women are generally concentrated in lower paying, lower prestige, and lower power jobs and are often paid less than men are for identical work (Levitan, Quinn, & Staines, 1971). This inequitable situation is one that should arouse feelings of being "underrewarded" relative to others, and that should result in feelings of dissatisfaction and anger.

Investigations of sex differences in job and pay satisfaction, however, reveal no such pattern. An early review of studies comparing males' and females' job satisfaction (Herzberg, Mausner, Peterson, & Capwell, 1957) reported conflicting and inconsistent findings. Some studies found that females were more satisfied with their jobs, others found that males were more satisfied, and still others found no sex differences in job satisfaction. Results of more recent investigations also have been inconsistent (e.g., Bartol & Wortman, 1975; Hulin & Smith, 1964; Smith, Scott, & Hulin, 1977), a situation that has been attributed (Hulin & Smith, 1964) to the failure of researchers to control for the numerous job characteristics that typically covary with sex (e.g., age, education, organizational tenure, and tenure in present position).

Sauser and York (1978) have addressed this problem directly in a study of male and female government employees' satisfaction with five facets of their jobs: (1) pay; (2) promotion policies; (3) coworkers; (4) immediate supervision; and (5) the work itself. An initial analysis ignoring covariate variables revealed a sex difference in overall job satisfaction, with males being significantly more satisfied with promotions and work than were females. An analysis of covariance controlling for pay grade, education, age, tenure in the organization, tenure in the present position, and four cross-product variables, however, revealed a striking reversal of this effect. Greater male job satisfaction was no longer in evidence but one highly significant sex difference remained—women were more satisfied with their pay than were men.

2. REACTIONS TO AN UNJUST PARTNER

Results of two studies using this approach suggest that males react more strongly to being treated unfairly by a partner than do females. Kahn (1972) found that when the subject and partner had equal inputs and the partner overpaid or equitably (in this case, equally) paid the subject, men and women did not differ in their subsequent reward allocations to the partner or evaluations of the partner. When the subject was underpaid by the partner, however, men felt more strongly than did women that the partner kept too much money, and men kept more reward for themselves and gave less to their partners on the second task. Similar results were obtained in a complex study by Blumstein and Weinstein (1969). After being inequitably treated by a partner in such a way that the subject was underbenefited, men tended to redress the injustice more than did women. Men tended to take more credit for themselves and give less to a partner on a subsequent task.

3. REACTIONS TO AN UNJUST GAME

Three studies have investigated sex differences using this approach. Schmitt and Marwell (1972) had two people participate in a cooperative task that arbitrarily produced unequal outcomes. More female than male pairs withdrew from this task, opting instead for an individual task that produced equal outcomes but was "economically irrational" in that it resulted in less money for both partners. Similar results were obtained by Marwell et al. (1969). When subjects participated in a game in which one person was behind at the beginning of the game, more female than male pairs played the game to minimize differences between the partners. Radinsky (1969) found that females were more likely than were males to make choices that ensured equality between themselves and another in an experimental game.

4. GENERAL SUMMARY AND COMMENTARY

In summary, experiments on reactions to injustice suggest that sex differences are a function of the particular situational context. Men and women react similarly when they are treated inequitably by an experimenter–employer in a laboratory situation. Field studies of sex differences in job satisfaction, however, suggest that women may be more tolerant of being underbenefited than are men. Similarly, women react less negatively than men do when they are treated unjustly by a partner. In contrast, women react more negatively than men do when they find themselves in a game that is arbitrarily unjust to one partner.

Self-presentation strategies may account for differences observed in women's and men's reactions to being treated unfairly by a person (experimenter, employer, or partner) as opposed to being treated unfairly by a game. That is, sex differences may be due to the *means* of injustice reduction available to people in these situations. For example, in experiments investigating reactions to an unjust partner, the only means of reducing the injustice is to retaliate, either by attitude or behavior, against the partner. This could be seen as an act of aggression, a behavior that is considered socially inappropriate for women in our society and one that women in these experiments may have been unwilling to display in front of an experimenter or another subject. In contrast, a different means of injustice reduction is available in studies of reactions to an unjust game—changing the game or altering one's strategy within the game. This may not be construed as an aggressive act, and in fact, may be perceived as the "nice" thing to do. Thus, women and men may be responding to impression management concerns when they react to injustice.

Alternatively, women and men may react to different types of injustice. Homans (1976) comments that, in many cases of competition, especially games, people raise the question of fairness, not over the outcomes of the competition, but over the procedures by which the result was reached—the competition itself must be fair. He further notes that in some conditions at least some people will consider procedural justice irrelevant (e.g., "All's fair in love and war."). Research on reactions to inequity suggests that women may be more concerned about issues of procedural justice (fairness of the process whereby outcomes are allocated), whereas men may be more concerned about issues of distributive justice (outcome fairness; see Folger, 1977, for a discussion of these two types of justice). Further research is needed to explore this possibility.

III. OTHER DEMOGRAPHIC VARIABLES: AGE AND NATIONALITY

Consideration of demographic variables other than sex has been limited. Age differences have commanded the most attention, and a small set of studies has dealt with nationality differences. Fewer research paradigms have been used to study these variables, hence our discussion will be based on the two more general categories of reward distribution and reactions to injustice.

A. Developmental Patterns of Justice Behavior

1. REWARD DISTRIBUTION

A recent comprehensive review by Hook and Cook (1979) conveniently summarizes this area. In analyzing studies of reward allocation behavior by individuals aged 3 years to adult (primarily studies in which allocations were made to both self and other), Hook and Cook (1979) convincingly argue that principles of reward allocation shift systematically with increasing age, beginning with a principle of self-interest and moving to a principle of proportional equity. Prior to the age of 6, children appear to use either self-interest or equality as the basis of reward allocation. It should be noted that neither of these principles requires a consideration of input variables; instead, reward alone can be considered in arriving at an allocation decision.

The shift from equality to equity apparently happens at around 6 years of age. One might speculate that at this age children begin to recognize inputs, and to perceive different inputs as relevant. Hook and Cook (1979) make a distinction between ordinal and proportional equity. In the former case, reward allocation reflects a rank order from the work dimension to the reward dimension, but the outcome is not directly proportional to inputs. Proportional equity (in which rewards are directly proportional to work) is not used until the child is approximately 13 years of age. The authors suggest that the proportionality concept required for equitable allocation may develop simultaneously with, or as a consequence of, the logico-mathematical proportionality concept. Referring to data of Piaget and others, Hook and Cook present a convincing case that the two variants of proportionality are indeed parallel, and hence suggest that the "norm" of equity requires a certain stage of cognitive development to be evidenced. This later stage may not reflect any substantial shifts in what inputs are perceived and/or recognized as important, however. Rather, the major difference may simply be an increasing sophistication in the ability to calculate inputs and outcomes.

Gunzburger, Wegner, and Anooshian (1977) suggested that reward allocation behavior should be related to developmental changes in moral reasoning. In lieu of a developmental study, however, the authors studied male high school students who scored at different stages on Kohlberg's (1971) measure of moral development. Subjects asked to distribute rewards among themselves and three other group members did vary their allocation as a function of moral developmental stage. An equality decision rule, although evident at all stages, was never the dominant response. With higher levels of moral development, social responsibility (defined as allocation both on the basis of actual and of intended inputs) became the more prominent decision rule. To the extent that Kohlberg's stages covary with age, these results suggest a basis for interpreting age differences in justice behavior.

2. REACTIONS TO INJUSTICE

Relatively less attention has been paid to developmental differences in reactions to injustice. With reference to the amount of distress that a person experiences in response to inequity, for example, Hook and Cook correctly observe that "almost all tests of equity leave this discomfort unmeasured and thus assumed [1979, p. 431]." A few studies have focused on behavioral responses to inequity, primarily grouped under the label of self-reinforcing behavior. Masters (1968, 1969), for example, observed the behavior of nursery school children ranging in age from 4 to 6 years who were given more, less, or the same number of tokens as was a partner. Children given a low payment were considerably more apt to show self-reinforcement when given the opportunity than were children who had been paid the same or considerably more than the partner. Unfortunately, no studies are available using this paradigm with other age groups.

B. Nationality Differences

The economic systems of nations are often based on radically different principles, exemplified perhaps in a contrast between socialist and capitalist societies. It would thus be reasonable to expect that such national norms might influence individual reward decisions. Indeed, Moscovici (1972) has argued that the basic tenets of equity theory are very Western, and more specifically American, and may have little application in other societies. Consistent with this view, Gergen, Morse, and Gergen (1980) concluded from their review of cross-cultural research on justice behavior that North Americans may be more prone to distribute rewards equitably than are Europeans and to prefer that their own outcomes match their inputs. Contrary to Moscovici (1972), however, Gergen et al. suggest that these national differences may be due more to different economic conditions than to cultural differences.

A number of investigators, primarily in the sociological tradition, have considered nationality differences in the judgment of fairness. Robinson and Bell (1978), for example, compared general attitudes toward equality in citizens of the United States and of England. Egalitarian values were linked to education in England but not in the United States; in the United States, but not in England, younger people were more apt to be egalitarian in their beliefs. In both societies, there was wide acceptance of inequality, but the basis for the acceptance differed: Belief in a just society was influential in England, whereas a belief in monetary success was more important in the United States. In these and other studies in this tradition, however, the concern is with observer judgments. Hence their findings, although interesting, lie outside the boundaries of the present chapter.

1. REWARD DISTRIBUTION

With respect to reward allocation, Mikula (1972, cited in Gergen *et al.*, 1980) varied the relative task performance of pairs of Austrian servicemen and found that, when the relative performance of the two members was highly discrepant, Austrians divided the monetary reward equally; when their relative performance was only slightly discrepant, an equitable distribution was preferred. In a later study, Mikula (1974) compared reward allocations of Austrian students with those of American students who were studying in Austria. Although his results indicated that American men were more apt to use an equality rule than were Austrian men, he questioned the representativeness of the United States sample. Mikula observed that the American students studying abroad may have felt a high degree of intergroup solidarity, and he noted the divergence of his results from those of Leventhal and Lane (1970) who studied a United States-based sample using similar procedures. When Austrian students' allocations were compared with those of the American students studied by Leventhal and Lane (1970), Austrians divided equally more than did Americans.

Nationality differences also have been observed in preferences for various distributions of rewards. Kahn, Lamm, and Nelson (1977) conducted separate studies of American and German students' preferences for various types of *allocators*. American students showed a stronger preference for a generous allocator—one who allocated equitably when his or her inputs were low and equally when his or her inputs were high—than did German students. German students tended to see a generous allocator as less potent than a stingy allocator.

Weick, Bougon, and Maruyama (1976) compared preferences for various forms of equity and inequity of Dutch students to those of American students studied by Weick and Nesset (1968). Subjects were asked to make choices between pairs of situations that varied in the extent to which three types of equity or inequity were present: one's *own equity* (own inputs and outcomes both high or both low) or inequity, *other equity* (other person's inputs and outcomes both high or both low) or inequity, and *comparison equity* (the ratio of inputs to outcomes was the same for both self and other) or inequity. Both the American and Dutch populations preferred a situation of comparison equity or other equity more than one of own equity. Additionally, subjects of both nationalities strongly preferred a situation involving low inputs and high outcomes for both self and other over any other type of situation. Some differences between the two populations also were observed. In particular, the Dutch generally preferred situations involving high inputs for the self, regardless of outcomes, whereas Americans generally preferred high outcomes for the self, regardless of inputs. Furthermore, although both populations preferred comparison equity over other forms of equity, the Dutch were less concerned with this than were Americans. Weick *et al.* (1976) explained these differences by referring to cultural factors in the Netherlands that differ from those in the United States, such as a high valuation of independence, the use of the family rather than coworkers as a predominant reference group, and a Calvinistic heritage that promotes the doctrine that high inputs are good and outcomes are irrelevant.

2. REACTIONS TO INJUSTICE

Several researchers have examined nationality differences in reactions to injustice. Gergen *et al.* (1980) concluded from their review of studies of reactions to overpayment that, contrary to North American samples, Europeans do not work harder when they are overpaid than when they are equitably paid. An experiment by Feldman (1968) further suggests that Americans may be more concerned about restoring equity than are Europeans. When cashiers in pastry shops in Paris, Athens, and Boston were overpaid for purchases, slightly less than half of the cashiers in Paris and Athens returned the overpayment, whereas 82% of the Americans did so. Gergen *et al.* (1980) suggest that these findings may be due to relative economic resources in these countries. The more limited a person's resources, the better able he or she may be to accept positive inequity.

Pepitone and his colleagues (Pepitone *et al.*, 1970) compared the responses of United States and Italian subjects in a prisoner's dilemma game after the experimenter had awarded money either on the basis of an aptitude test (equity) or arbitrarily (inequity). United States students who were awarded money on the basis of alleged ability subsequently behaved in a manner that continued to reflect the apparent disparity between the two players. When money was awarded arbitrarily, the United States students attempted to restore equity. Italian students, in contrast, attempted to restore equity no matter what was the previous basis for reward. The authors suggest that the Italian subjects may have disbelieved the experimenter's decisions regarding merit—in other words, disputed the difference in input—and consequently attempted to restore justice by equalizing outcomes. Gergen, Morse, and Bode (1974) compared the same two national groups and found no significant differences in cognitive responses to injustice.

In summary, although a variety of observations and analyses suggest national differences in justice behavior, research on actual behavioral differences is as yet too sparse for strong conclusions to be made. Research suggests that North Americans may be more concerned with equity than are other nationalities studied, but the reasons for this are not clear. This difference may be due to philosophical cultural differences, as Moscovici (1972) suggests, or to differing economic conditions, as Gergen *et al.* (1980) suggest. Research on justice behavior in non-Western countries is clearly needed. Given the considerable implications of differing justice systems for international harmony, it seems important to pursue this area of research further.

IV. PERSONALITY VARIABLES AND JUSTICE BEHAVIOR

Despite the frequent discussions of various justice rules, there have been relatively few attempts to assess personality differences in the adherence to these various rules. Furthermore, some of these attempts, reflecting an unfortuante tendency in much personality research, have haphazardly assessed individuals on a number of traits and attempted to find correlations. Other work, however, has been more thoughtful in its approach, specifically selecting variables that logically could be expected to relate to justice behavior. We will emphasize work in this latter category.

A. The Protestant Ethic

The Protestant Ethic Scale (PE), devised by Mirels and Garrett (1971) attempts to operationalize the ideas of Max Weber (1904–1905/1958). Accordingly, the scale assesses the ideals of asceticism, industriousness, and individuality. Sample items include the following: "People who don't succeed in life are just plain lazy"; "People who fail at a job have usually not tried hard enough"; and "I feel uneasy when there is little work for me to do." Studies indicate that the Protestant Ethic is a multidimensional concept and correlates with a number of other variables, including authoritarianism, belief in internal control, and a preference for occupations that require a concrete, pragmatic approach to work (MacDonald, 1971, 1972; Mirels & Garrett, 1971; Waters, Baltis, & Waters, 1975). More relevant to justice behavior are the findings that people scoring high on the scale tend to place a lower value on equality (MacDonald, 1972) and believe that people, rather than the system, are the source of injustice (MacDonald, 1971).

Studies using the PE Scale have been concerned primarily with reward allocation, and more specifically, with allocations to others. Garrett (1973), for example, found that high PE subjects rewarded performers in proportion to their contribution to a task, whereas low PE subjects followed an equality rule. Looking more closely at the nature of the input variables, Greenberg (1979) manipulated information about the quantity and the duration of a worker's performance. High PE subjects playing the role of a supervisor rewarded in proportion to both dimensions. Low PE subjects, in contrast, rewarded only according to the duration of performance (either 1 or 2 days of work) and ignored the differences in performance quantity per day. Speculating that these differences might reflect differential sensitivity of high and low PE persons to types of input—specifically internal versus external factors—Greenberg (1979) proceeded to specifically vary the nature of inputs, using the four categories of attributions suggested by Weiner, Frieze, Kukla, Reed, Rest, and Rosenbaum (1971). Subjects were told that Worker A produced more than Worker B, either because A had more ability, exerted more effort, had an easier task, or was lucky, and were asked to judge how fair it would be to pay Worker A more than Worker B. High PE persons regarded the decision as fair when internal factors (ability or effort) were causal, and unfair if external factors (task or luck) were causal. Low PE persons regarded the decision as somewhat unfair when internal factors were causal, and were neutral about the decision when external factors were ascribed.

Allocations to self and other in a competitive context have been considered by Greenberg (1978b). High PE subjects showed adherence to an equity rule when the competition was fair, whereas low PE subjects followed an equality rule. However, when the experimenter described the competition as unfair, as a result of answers provided to one of the partners, high PE subjects attempted to redress the balance by keeping less reward if they won and taking more reward if they lost. Low PE subjects continued to follow an equality rule under the same circumstances. If we view this latter condition as a study of responses to injustice, we can infer that the high PE person is more sensitive to the nature of inputs in determining that injustice has occurred.

In summary, studies of reward allocation behavior using the Protestant Ethic Scale point to the importance of perceived inputs. The high PE person, who by definition has endorsed items that emphasize the value of hard work and individual effort, in turn weights those factors as important inputs in the justice equation. The low PE person does not endorse those items nor does he or she consider those factors as relevant inputs. Such patterns underline the importance of carefully analyzing the links between a general personality variable and a specific allocation paradigm.

B. Other Personality Variables

Scattered throughout the literature are a number of studies that report relationships between various personality dimensions and justice behaviors. Blumstein and Weinstein (1969), for example, looked at the relationship between Machiavellianism (Mach), need for approval, and responses to inequitable claims by a partner. Low Mach subjects appeared to follow the principles of equity, whereas high Mach subjects were more apt to take advantage of a person who had previously benefited them. Concurrently, subjects low in need for approval followed equity principles, whereas subjects high in need for approval generally claimed less credit for themselves. In both cases, we may infer that different self-presentational concerns and/or goals for the interaction may have been operating for the two types of people, leading them to emphasize different outcomes.

Lawler and O'Gara (1967), in a study of work performance following either equitable payment or underpayment, included the California Personality Inventory as an assessment of individual differences. Across the combined conditions, these authors reported that subjects who were low on subscale measures of poise, ascendancy, and self-assurance were high in productivity. At the same time, individuals high in maturity and responsibility were likely to show higher *quality* in their work performance. These results suggest that individual differences may exist in the valence of various outcomes.

Many other personality variables might be considered for their potential linkage to justice behaviors. Self-concept or self-esteem, for example, might be thought to relate to an individual's responses to injustice. The difficulty with this suggestion, and perhaps a reason that no tests of this fairly obvious hypothesis have been reported, relates to the generality of most self-concept measures. Most studies of reward allocation and reactions to injustice have used quite specific tasks that may or may not relate to an individual's global self-concept. To find a relationship, we suspect that either one would have to define self-esteem quite specifically, in terms of specific task expectancies, or use a multiple act criterion in which a variety of injustice situations was included.

Another likely candidate, in view of the frequently reported sex differences in justice behavior, is some measure of psychological masculinity and femininity. A few attempts in this direction have been reported (Bowden & Zanna, 1978; Watts, Messé, & Vallacher, in press). Progress in this area, however, is probably contingent on a more systematic analysis of the justice behaviors themselves, and a theoretical rationale for the relationship between masculinity, femininity, and the behaviors of interest.

In summary, the contribution of personality variables to an understanding of justice behavior has been limited. More so than in the case of demographic variables, where accident and ex post facto explanations frequently serve each other reasonably well, psychological constructs demand a more thoughtful approach. A clearer understanding of justice behaviors should facilitate progress in this area.

V. EXPLAINING INDIVIDUAL DIFFERENCES IN JUSTICE BEHAVIOR

A number of explanations have been offered to account for individual differences in justice behavior. Most of these explanations rely on assumed differences in one of the following three factors: (1) norms; (2) interaction orientations or objectives; and (3) cognitive processes, such as differences in the perceptions of inputs and attributions for performance. Data relevant to each of these explanations will be discussed.

A. Normative Explanations

Several theorists have proposed that individual differences in justice behavior are due to adherence to different justice norms. Leventhal (1976a) and Sampson (1975), for example, have suggested that sex differences in justice behavior are due to the fact that women operate by a norm of equality whereas men operate by a norm of equity. Similarly, it has been suggested that persons scoring high on the PE Scale adhere to a norm of equity, whereas those scoring low on the scale adhere to a norm of equality. Differences between nationality groups have also been linked to different norms or principles of justice (Robinson & Bell, 1978).

Normative explanations present several problems, however. First, norms have generally served as after-the-fact explanations for aggregate data and have been remarkably nonpredictive. In addition, there appears to be a "norm" for almost every type of allocation pattern. Reis (1979) for example, identified 17 different distributive justice norms. Thus every different behavior pattern conceivably could be attributed to the use of a different norm.

Second, we could expect that a person who adheres to a certain norm would rely on this norm across a variety of situations. The data do not support this expectation. For example, persons who score high on the PE Scale do not always follow an equity rule but vary their allocation patterns as a function of the characteristics of the inputs. Similarly, the literature on male–female differences shows cases where women adhere to equality and men to equity, but many other instances where the differences are nonexistent or even reversed.

In summary, the proposal that individual differences in justice behavior are a result of adherence to different norms does not adequately account for existing data. A more individualized analysis of normative beliefs might hold more promise—but only if situational parameters were incorporated into the analysis.

B. Interaction Orientation Explanations

Perhaps the most frequently used explanation for individual differences in justice behavior, particularly sex differences, is that people differ in their interaction orientations or objectives. Numerous writers (e.g., Deaux, 1976; Kahn et al., 1980; Leventhal, 1973; Sampson, 1975; Vinacke, 1959) have proposed that sex differences in justice behavior are due to the fact that women are more oriented toward the interpersonal aspects of a relationship, seeking to establish or maintain friendly relations with their partners, whereas men are more focused on the task, seeking to solve the problem, assert their status over their partners, or maximize their own gain.

There is ample evidence that the nature of an interaction or relationship affects justice decisions (cf. Leventhal, 1976a). Cooperative relationships tend to increase the frequency of equality-oriented allocations, whereas competitive relationships tend to increase the frequency of equity-oriented allocations. Similarly, the degree of liking or acquaintanceship among participants affects justice behavior. Relative to pairs of strangers, pairs of friends prefer to divide rewards more evenly if the divider is the superior performer (Mikula, 1974), are more likely to try to benefit the other even at their own expense (Morgan & Sawyer, 1967), and are more likely to prefer that a favor freely offered not be immediately paid back in kind (Mills & Clark, in press). In general, equal allocations are preferred when the objective is to foster and to maintain harmonious social relationships (Deutsch, 1975; Gamson, 1964; Leventhal, 1976a; Sampson, 1975), maintain status equilibrium (Kahn, 1972; Sampson, 1975), avoid interpersonal strain and increase group solidarity (Bales, 1950), or minimize conflict (Leventhal et al., 1972). In contrast, equitable allocations generally are preferred when the goal is to increase economic productivity (Deutsch, 1975), foster high levels of task performance (Leventhal, 1976a), create status hierarchies (Sampson, 1975), or to maximize one's own gain (Sampson, 1975).

Specific evidence for sex differences in interaction orientations is mixed. Messé and Callahan-Levy (1979), hypothesizing that women would be more affected than men by explicit communication from their partners concerning reward allocation, obtained only partial support for their hypothesis. Male allocators generally were unaffected by their partner's explicit expectations for equity or equality; female allocators were affected, but only when the partner was male. Austin and McGinn (1977) found that men reported being more concerned with the interpersonal *costs* of their allocation decisions (e.g., avoiding conflict), whereas women were more concerned with the interpersonal *rewards* of their decisions (e.g., promoting friendliness). This study suggests that both sexes are responsive to the interpersonal consequences of their justice behavior, but that the reasons for behaving in a particular way may be different for women than for men.

Two recent experiments clarify how different interaction orientations can mediate sex differences in self–other allocations. Drawing upon theorizing by Lerner (1977), Carles and Carver (1979) hypothesized that equality should be preferred when the other is seen as a person similar to oneself (person-salient), whereas equity should be preferred when the other is seen as a functionary in a role (role-salient). Allocations made by women supported these predictions. Men, however, made allocations equitably in the person-salient conditions, and more evenly in the role-salient conditions. Subsequent manipulation checks showed that both sexes allocated more money to themselves when they perceived the other as a competitor. A sex difference existed in the perceptions, however, with men perceiving the other as more of a competitor in the person-salient condition, whereas women saw more competitiveness in the role-salient condition. Greenberg (1978c) found that both male and female allocators divided rewards equally with a lower-input partner when he or she was perceived as having attitudes similar to their own, and equitably when he or she was seen as having dissimilar attitudes. When the partner's similarity was unknown, however, women divided equally whereas men allocated a reward midway between the similar and dissimilar condition amounts. These experiments are provocative in that they suggest men and women may be perceiving the other very differently in the typical self–other allocation experiment, and that these perceptions may mediate differences in allocations.

The proposition that women and men differ in their interaction orientations and/or objectives accounts well for many sex differences observed in self–other allocations, although its use has been primarily post hoc rather than predictive. Other demographic variables have not been approached using this framework. Relatively few studies have pre-selected people on the basis of some measure of interaction orientation and assessed their justice behavior, and the results of these studies are inconclusive.

In summary, the interaction explanation is suggestive but not conclusive. Better methods of assessing an individual's orientation are necessary to pursue this explanation, together with an analysis of situations that might elicit various orientations. One important limitation of the interaction hypothesis, however, is that it applies only to the interactive situation. Allocation behavior when the "other" is not salient or is nonexistent cannot be predicted by this hypothesis. Yet sex differences, so frequently interpreted through the use of interaction explanations, are observed in allocations to self only and in studies of pay satisfaction.

C. Cognitive Explanations

A third explanation for individual differences in justice behavior, broadly termed the cognitive explanation, has received much less attention than the normative and interpersonal orientation explanations. However, several authors (e.g., Deaux, 1976; Greenberg, 1978b, 1979; Wittig, Marks, & Jones, 1981) have suggested that individual differences in certain cognitive processes may intervene between "inputs" (e.g., work) and "outcomes" (e.g., reward) to alter the extent to which the input–outcome ratio is perceived as fair.

There are a number of cognitive steps between inputs and outcomes where individual differences may occur. We shall discuss five pos-

sibilities: (1) perceptions of inputs; (2) performance evaluations; (3) attributions for performance; (4) outcome (reward) expectancies; and (5)
perceptions of outcomes.

1. INDIVIDUAL DIFFERENCES IN
PERCEPTIONS OF INPUTS

Adams (1965) emphasized that inputs "are *as perceived by their contributor* [p. 277, italics in original]," and do not necessarily correspond to
how others perceive them. He distinguished between two characteristics
of inputs, recognition and relevance. To be considered as an input, an
attribute must be recognized and it must be perceived as relevant to the
exchange by the possessor. It seems useful to us to add a third characteristic, namely, the perceived value or importance. Thus it is proposed
that individual differences in the extent to which inputs are *recognized,
perceived as relevant,* and *valued* may mediate individual differences in
justice behavior.

Some evidence for this proposition exists. Hook and Cook (1979)
have suggested that younger children may not recognize inputs and
hence allocate on the basis of outcome alone. Greenberg's (1978b, 1979)
research shows that an individual's score on the Protestant Ethic Scale
relates to the importance and relevance placed on inputs such as effort
and in turn affects allocation behavior. Similarly, Larwood, Levine,
Shaw, and Hurwitz (1979) observed that people using an equity rule
cited ability as an important input whereas those following an equality
rule viewed time and effort as important. Gunzburger *et al.*'s (1977)
research on moral reasoning and distributive justice further suggests
that reward allocations change as *intended* as well as *actual* inputs are
recognized and considered relevant.

Women and men may also differ in the extent to which they perceive
certain inputs as relevant and valuable. For example, women may place a
lower value on their time and effort than do men. Pilot work by Major
and Adams (1980) found that, relative to men, women were willing to
work longer hours to achieve the same rewards. Specifically, women
reported that they were willing to spend more time to earn either $50 or
a course grade of A than men were, even though money was somewhat
less important to the women. These results suggest that sex differences
in the value placed on work-related inputs such as time may mediate sex
differences in the perceived fairness of a given input–outcome ratio.

2. INDIVIDUAL DIFFERENCES IN
PERFORMANCE EVALUATIONS

A second cognitive step in justice behavior is the evaluations that
people make of their performances. Numerous studies of reward alloca-

tion have shown that people whose performance is objectively inferior to a partner's will take less reward for themselves than they will give to their partners. Individuals may differ, however, in their *subjective* evaluations of their performances, regardless of the objective criteria supplied, and these differences may mediate differences in justice behavior. For example, a large body of research indicates that women place a lower evaluation on the quality of their work than men do when external feedback is unavailable or is ambiguous (cf. Lenney, 1977 for a review), even if the performance is not objectively different. Sex differences in performance evaluations generally do not occur, however, when clear feedback on task performance is provided (Lenney, 1977).

Several experiments have explored the possibility that sex differences in subjective performance estimates may mediate differences in allocations to self and others. Leventhal and Lane (1970) found that women who were the superior performers in a dyad attributed a lower level of performance to themselves than did men who were the superior performers, but no sex differences in attributed level of performance were observed for the inferior performers. Several other researchers (Kahn, 1972; Kahn *et al.*, 1980; Reis & Jackson, 1981) found no sex differences in perceived ability, effort, or quality of performance, although sex differences in allocations were obtained. In all of these experiments, however, explicit performance feedback with respect to both the subject's and the coworker's performance was provided. Thus, evaluations of performance quality served more as a manipulation check than as a subjective assessment of performance.

Callahan-Levy and Messé (1979) provided no performance feedback and found that women paid themselves less money than men did after working on a task. The role that performance evaluations might have played in producing this effect is unclear, as these subjects were not asked to evaluate the quality of their performances. (Data collected on separate samples of subjects, however, indicated that, in contrast to many studies, women and men did not evaluate their own performance differently on this task, but women in general were expected to do better on the task than were men.) Thus, although sex differences in performance evaluations in the absence of clear feedback are well documented, there is no clear evidence that these evaluations account for differences in reward allocations and pay satisfaction.

3. INDIVIDUAL DIFFERENCES IN PERFORMANCE ATTRIBUTIONS

A third factor that may be relevant to justice behavior is the attributions that people make for their own performance. For example, women, relative to men, tend to make more external attributions for their success and internal attributions for their failure (Deaux & Farris, 1977; Feather & Simon, 1975). These attributions may mediate the perceived fairness of various allocation rules. Equity may be seen as an unfair allocation rule if the perceived cause of success or failure is external to the individual (e.g., good or bad luck, an easier or more difficult task), but may be seen as a fair allocation rule if the perceived cause of success or failure is internal to the individual (e.g., high or low ability, high or low effort). Thus, people who tend to attribute their success to external factors and their failure to internal factors (as women are apt to do), may allocate rewards equally when they are the superior performers and equitably when they are the inferior performers. This is the pattern that women tend to follow when they divide rewards between themselves and coworkers.

Several experiments have demonstrated that performance attributions provided by the experimenter can affect allocation behavior (Cohen, 1974; Greenberg, 1978b, 1979, 1980; Wittig et al., 1981). Researchers who have measured men's and women's own attributions for their performances (e.g., Greenberg, 1978c; Kahn et al., 1980; Reis & Jackson, 1981), however, have found no sex differences in attributions even though sex differences in allocations were observed. Given other evidence for attribution differences, this lack of a relationship is somewhat puzzling.

4. INDIVIDUAL DIFFERENCES IN REWARD EXPECTANCIES

Another possible mediator of individual differences in reward allocations and pay satisfaction is differential expectations concerning appropriate reward. In his formulation of inequity theory, Adams (1965) discussed the importance of expectancies in determining satisfaction with an outcome. In particular, he reviewed the concept of relative deprivation, noting that "felt injustice is a response to a *discrepancy* between what is perceived to be and what is perceived should be [p. 272, original italics]." Thus, someone with high expectancies may be more dissatisfied with a given outcome than someone else with lower expectancies might be with the same outcome. Reward expectancies may be derived from prior experience or from comparison with a relevant other. Unfortunately, the influence of prior experience and the issue of whom one chooses as a comparison other have been relatively ignored in justice research.

It has been suggested that women may expect less monetary reward for their work than men do (Chesler & Goodman, 1976; Mednick & Tangri, 1972), perhaps because of their history of wage discrimination. Evidence does show that women report being more satisfied with lower pay (Sauser & York, 1978) and regard less money as fairer than do men (Callahan-Levy & Messé, 1979; Major, Gagnon, & McFarlin, 1981). Expanding on this view, Callahan-Levy and Messé (1979) have proposed that women may have a "weaker sense of their own equity"; that is, women may perceive less of a connection between their work and monetary rewards than do men. In addition to reward expectancies, this proposal might suggest differences in the judged appropriateness of reward for a given amount of work, or in the value placed on reward.

5. INDIVIDUAL DIFFERENCES IN PERCEPTIONS OF OUTCOMES

Adams (1965) noted that outcomes are *as perceived,* and that they, as well as inputs, should be characterized in terms of recognition and relevance. Again, we think it useful to add the characteristic of value, or importance, to Adams's formulation. There are often a number of potential outcomes in an exchange: Some of these may be tangible, such as money, whereas others may be less tangible, such as being liked or making a good impression. Individual differences in the perceived relevance and value of various outcomes may mediate individual differences in justice behavior.

There is some evidence that women place a lower value on money as a reward than men do (Kahn, 1972; Major & Adams, 1980; Morgan & Sawyer, 1967). However, even though money has been used as a reward in the majority of allocation studies, differences in the value of money do not appear to account for observed sex differences, as similar allocation patterns are found when nonmonetary rewards are used (Callahan-Levy & Messé, 1979, Experiment 2; Major & Adams, 1980; Vinacke, 1959).

Kahn *et al.* (1980) suggest that social approval may be a more salient reward for women than it is for men. Although sex differences in sensitivity to social approval have not been found in children (Maccoby & Jacklin, 1974), such differences may occur in adults (Stein & Bailey, 1973). Personality measures that tap these motives may prove to be useful in predicting justice behavior, as the work of Blumstein and Weinstein (1969) suggests.

It is apparent that this model subsumes the "interpersonal orientation" explanation by clarifying the importance of outcome valence in justice decisions. This analysis suggests that it is important to identify the possible outcomes in an exchange, and to assess their relevance and importance to individuals. The reliance of most research on monetary rewards and allocations may have needlessly restricted our understanding of individual difference parameters.

A cognitive approach to individual differences in justice behavior is admittedly more complex than either the normative or the interaction orientation approach. Furthermore, the extent to which any of the five factors that we identified mediate individual justice behavior, alone or in combination, remains to be tested. Yet, in our minds, this multifaceted approach offers more promise than either of the "simple and sovereign" models to understanding the seemingly complex interaction of personality and situation in justice behavior.

VI. CONCLUSIONS AND PROSPECTS

Although there is no shortage of empirical work on the issues of individual differences in justice behavior, theoretical work has been rather limited. The two dominant explanations—norms and interaction orientations—have been based primarily on ex post facto reasoning and, for the most part, have been restricted in their application to demographic variables. As a result, our understanding of the role of individual differences in justice behavior is at a rudimentary stage. To correct this situation, a number of strategies seem to be appropriate.

1. More attention must be paid to the processes that mediate justice behavior. In much of the research, a tendency has been evident to consider input and outcome very globally and to pay little attention to the cognitive processes that may intervene. This general criticism suggests a number of approaches. Farkas and Anderson (1979), for example, have questioned the basis by which inputs are combined, arguing against the frequent assumption that multidimensional input is integrated into a single deservingness factor to determine outcome. The work of Foa and his colleagues (Donnenwerth & Foa, 1974; Foa, 1971; Foa & Foa, 1974; Turner, Foa, & Foa, 1971) specifies a variety of resources that may be involved in an exchange, and suggests a number of particular combinations that may be used. The general cognitive explanation that we have discussed also offers one approach to understanding justice behavior. Each of these strategies, and others that may be conceived, point to the importance of a more detailed analysis of the processes intervening between input and outcome.

2. Far more ingenuity needs to be shown in the development of appropriate paradigms. Since the inception of equity theory, the

performance–pay connection has been the predominant focus, and other types of exchanges have not been examined extensively. Furthermore, these allocation studies themselves have generally been restricted to a zero-sum situation, which may force certain types of allocation behaviors and preclude others. Little attention has been paid to any longer-term exchanges where various inputs and outcomes might be combined in complex fashion; rather, the one-shot study has dominated here as in so many other areas.

3. The research reviewed here, and indeed much of the research in the field, focuses on outcome justice. The equally, or perhaps more important topic of procedural justice has been studied much less often. Yet for many people, the procedures may be more important than the outcome, and this distinction might well prove to be an important individual difference variable.

4. Situational factors are undoubtedly an important influence on justice behavior. Numerous studies attest to that statement. Yet because the work on situations has been relatively unsystematic in its own right, an understanding of the role of individual difference factors may also have been impeded. In other words, we doubt that there are any individual difference variables that will predict justice behavior regardless of the situation. Consequently, if it is true that there are no main effects, then work must be done on both sides of the equation: both the personality variable and the situational variable must be linked by a logical theoretical network. Such efforts will necessarily take us beyond our present reliance on demographic variables and toward a more psychologically oriented model of individual differences.

REFERENCES

Adams, J. S. Inequity in social exchange. In L. Berkowitz (Ed.), *Advances in experimental social psychology* (Vol. 2). New York: Academic Press, 1965.

Amidjaja, I. R., & Vinacke, W. E. Achievement, nurturance, and competition in male and female triads. *Journal of Personality and Social Psychology*, 1965, *2*, 447–451.

Austin, W., & McGinn, N. C. Sex differences in choice of distribution rules. *Journal of Personality*, 1977, *45*, 379–394.

Baker, K. Experimental analysis of third-party justice behavior. *Journal of Personality and Social Psychology*, 1974, *30*, 307–316.

Bales, R. F. *Interaction process analysis.* Cambridge, Mass.: Addison-Wesley, 1950.

Bartol, K. M., & Wortman, M. S. Male vs. female leaders: Effects on perceived leader behavior and satisfaction in a hospital. *Personnel Psychology*, 1975, *28*, 533–547.

Blumstein, P. W., & Weinstein, E. A. The redress of distributive justice. *American Journal of Sociology*, 1969, *74*, 408–418.

Bond, J. R., & Vinacke, W. E. Coalitions in mixed-sex triads. *Sociometry*, 1961, *24*, 61–75.

Bowden, M., & Zanna, M. P. *Perceived relationship, sex-role orientation, and gender differences in reward allocation.* Paper presented at the meeting of the American Psychological Association, Toronto, 1978.

Callahan-Levy, C. M., & Messé, L. A. Sex differences in the allocation of pay. *Journal of Personality and Social Psychology,* 1979, *37,* 433–446.

Carles, E. M., & Carver, C. S. Effects of person salience versus role salience on reward allocations in a dyad. *Journal of Personality and Social Psychology,* 1979, *37,* 2071–2080.

Chesler, P., & Goodman, E. J. *Women, money and power.* New York: Morrow, 1976.

Cohen, R. L., Mastery and justice in laboratory dyads: A revision and extension of equity theory. *Journal of Personality and Social Psychology,* 1974, *29,* 464–474.

Deaux, K. *The behavior of women and men.* Monterey, Calif.: Brooks/Cole, 1976.

Deaux, K., & Farris, E. Attributing causes for one's own performance: The effects of sex, norms and outcome. *Journal of Research in Personality,* 1977, *11,* 59–72.

Deci, E. L. Intrinsic motivation, extrinsic reinforcement, and inequity. *Journal of Personality and Social Psychology,* 1972, *22,* 113–120.

Deci, E. L., Reis, H. T., Johnston, E. J., & Smith, R. Toward reconciling equity theory and insufficient justification. *Personality and Social Psychology Bulletin,* 1977, *3,* 224–227.

Deutsch, M. Equity, equality and need: What determines which value will be used as the basis of distributive justice? *Journal of Social Issues,* 1975, *31,* 137–149.

Donnenwerth, G. V., & Foa, V. G. Effect of resource class on retaliation to injustice in interpersonal exchange. *Journal of Personality and Social Psychology,* 1974, *29,* 785–793.

Farkas, A. J., & Anderson, N. H. Multidimensional input in equity theory. *Journal of Personality and Social Psychology,* 1979, *37,* 879–896.

Feather, N. T. Effects of prior success and failure on expectations of success and subsequent performance. *Journal of Personality and Social Psychology,* 1966, *3,* 287–298.

Feather, N. T., & Simon, J. G. Reactions to male and female success and failure in sex-linked occupations: Impressions of personality, causal attributions, and perceived likelihood of different consequences. *Journal of Personality and Social Psychology,* 1975, *31,* 20–31.

Feldman, R. E. Response to compatriot and foreigner who seek assistance. *Journal of Personality and Social Psychology,* 1968, *10,* 203–214.

Foa, V. G. Interpersonal and economic resources. *Science,* 1971, *171,* 345–351.

Foa, V. G., & Foa, E. B. *Societal structures of the mind.* Springfield, Ill.: Charles C Thomas, 1974.

Folger, R. Distributive and procedural justice: Combined impact of "voice" and improvement on experienced inequity. *Journal of Personality and Social Psychology,* 1977, *35,* 108–119.

Gamson, W. A. Experimental studies on coalition formation. In L. Berkowitz (Ed.), *Advances in experimental social psychology* (Vol. 1). New York: Academic Press, 1964.

Garland, H. The effects of piece-rate underpayment and overpayment on job performance: A test of equity theory with a new induction procedure. *Journal of Applied Social Psychology,* 1973, *3,* 325–334.

Garrett, J. B. Effects of Protestant ethic endorsement upon equity behavior. In L. Messé (Chair), *Individual differences in equity behavior.* Symposium presented at meeting of the American Psychological Association, Montreal, August 1973.

Gergen, K. J., Morse, S. J., & Bode, K. A. Overpaid or underworked? Cognitive and behavioral reactions to inequitable rewards. *Journal of Applied Social Psychology,* 1974, *4,* 259–174.

Gergen, K. J., Morse, S. J., & Gergen, M. M. Behavior exchange in a cross-cultural perspective. In H. C. Triandis and R. W. Breslin (Eds.), *Handbook of cross-cultural psychology*, (Vol. 5). Boston, Mass.: Allyn & Bacon, 1980.

Greenberg, J. Equity, motivation, and effects of past reward on allocation decisions. *Personality and Social Psychology Bulletin*, 1978, *4*, 131-134. (a)

Greenberg, J. Equity, equality, and the protestant ethic: Allocating rewards following fair and unfair competition. *Journal of Experimental Social Psychology*, 1978, *14*, 217-226. (b)

Greenberg, J. Allocator-recipient similarity and the equitable division of reward. *Social Psychology*, 1978, *41*, 337-341. (c)

Greenberg, J. Protestant ethic endorsement and the fairness of equity inputs. *Journal of Research in Personality*, 1979, *13*, 81-90.

Greenberg, J. Attentional focus and locus of performance causality as determinants of equity behavior. *Journal of Personality and Social Psychology*, 1980, *38*, 579-588.

Gunzburger, W. W., Wegner, D. M., & Anooshian, L. Moral judgment and distributive justice. *Human Development*, 1977, *20*, 160-170.

Harris, R. J., & Joyce, M. A. What's fair? It depends on how you phrase the question. *Journal of Personality and Social Psychology*, 1980, *38*, 165-179.

Herzberg, F., Mausner, B., Peterson, R. A., & Capwell, D. F. *Job attitudes: Review of research and opinion*. Pittsburgh: Psychological Service of Pittsburgh, 1957.

Homans, G. C. *Social behavior: Its elementary forms*. New York: Harcourt Brace & World, 1961.

Homans, G. C. Commentary. In L. Berkowitz & E. Walster (Eds.), *Advances in experimental social psychology* (Vol. 9). New York: Academic Press, 1976.

Hook, J. G., & Cook, T. D. Equity theory and the cognitive ability of children. *Psychological Bulletin*, 1979, *86*, 429-445.

Hulin, C. L., & Smith, P. C. Sex differences in job satisfaction. *Journal of Applied Psychology*, 1964, *48*, 88-92.

Kahn, A. Reactions to generosity or stinginess from an intelligent or stupid work partner. *Journal of Personality and Social Psychology*, 1972, *21*, 116-123.

Kahn, A. From theories of equity to theories of justice: An example of demasculinization in social psychology. *SASP Newsletter*, 1979, *5*, 12-13.

Kahn, A., Lamm, H., & Nelson, R. E. Preferences for an equal or equitable allocator. *Journal of Personality and Social Psychology*, 1977, *35*, 837-844.

Kahn, A., Nelson, R. E., & Gaeddert, W. P. Sex of subject and sex composition of the group as determinants of reward allocations. *Journal of Personality and Social Psychology*, 1980, *38*, 737-750.

Kahn, A., O'Leary, V., Krulewitz, J. E., & Lamm, H. Equity and equality: Male and female means to a just end. *Basic and Applied Social Psychology*, 1980, *1*, 173-197.

Katz, M. G., & Messé, L. A. *A sex difference in the distribution of oversufficient rewards.* Paper presented at the meeting of the Midwestern Psychological Association, Chicago, May 1973.

Kidder, L. H., Bellettirie, G., & Cohn, E. S. Secret ambitions and public performances. *Journal of Experimental Social Psychology*, 1977, *13*, 70-80.

Kohlberg, L. From is to ought. In T. Mischel (Ed.), *Cognitive development and epistemology*. New York: Academic Press, 1971.

Lane, I. M., & Messé, L. A. Equity and the distribution of rewards. *Journal of Personality and Social Psychology*, 1971, *20*, 1-17.

Larwood, L., Levine, R., Shaw, R., & Hurwitz, S. Relation of objective and subjective inputs to exchange preference for equity or equality reward allocation. *Organizational Behavior and Human Performance*, 1979, *23*, 60-72.

Lawler, E. E. Effects of hourly overpayment on productivity and work quality. *Journal of Personality and Social Psychology*, 1968, *10*, 306–313.

Lawler, E. E., III, & O'Gara, P. W. Effects of inequity produced by underpayment on work output, work quality, and attitudes toward the work. *Journal of Applied Psychology*, 1967, *51*, 403–410.

Lenney, E. Women's self-confidence in achievement settings. *Psychological Bulletin*, 1977, *84*, 1–13.

Lerner, M. J. The justice motive: Some hypotheses as to its origins and forms. *Journal of Personality*, 1977, *45*, 1–52.

Leventhal, G. S. Reward allocation by males and females. In L. Messé (Chair), *Individual differences in equity behavior*. Symposium presented at the meeting of the American Psychological Association, Montreal, August, 1973.

Leventhal, G. S. The distribution of rewards and resources in groups and organizations. In L. Berkowitz & E. Walster (Eds.), *Advances in experimental social psychology* (Vol. 9). New York: Academic Press, 1976. (a)

Leventhal, G. S. Fairness in social relationships. In J. W. Thibaut, J. T. Spence, & R. C. Carson (Eds.), *Contemporary topics in social psychology*. Morristown, N. J.: General Learning Press, 1976. (b)

Leventhal, G. S., & Anderson, D. Self-interest and the maintenance of equity. *Journal of Personality and Social Psychology*, 1970, *15*, 57–62.

Leventhal, G. S., & Lane, D. W. Sex, age, and equity behavior. *Journal of Personality and Social Psychology*, 1970, *15*, 312–316.

Leventhal, G. S., Michaels, J. W., & Sanford, C. Inequity and personal conflict: Reward allocation and secrecy about reward as methods of preventing conflict. *Journal of Personality and Social Psychology*, 1972, *23*, 88–102.

Leventhal, G. S., Weiss, T., & Buttrick, R. Attribution of value, equity, and the prevention of waste in reward allocation. *Journal of Personality and Social Psychology*, 1973, *27*, 276–286.

Leventhal, G. S., & Whiteside, H. D. Equity and the use of reward to elicit high performance. *Journal of Personality and Social Psychology*, 1973, *25*, 75–83.

Levitan, T., Quinn, R. P., & Staines, G. L. Sex discrimination against the American working woman. *American Behavioral Scientist*, 1971, *15*, 237–254.

Maccoby, E. E., & Jacklin, C. N. *The psychology of sex difference*. Stanford, Calif.: Stanford University Press, 1974.

MacDonald, A. P., Jr. Correlates of the ethics of personal conscience and the ethics of social responsibility. *Journal of Consulting and Clinical Psychology*, 1971, *37*, 443.

MacDonald, A. P., Jr. More on the protestant ethic. *Journal of Consulting and Clinical Psychology*, 1972, *39*, 116–122.

Major, B., & Adams, J. *Effects of reward type and allocation decision on distributive justice*. Paper presented at the meeting of the American Psychological Association, Montreal, September, 1980.

Major, B., Gagnon, D., & McFarlin, D. The impact of social comparison information on sex differences in self pay. Unpublished manuscript. State University of New York at Buffalo, 1981.

Marwell, G., Ratcliff, K., & Schmitt, D. R. Minimizing differences in a maximizing difference game. *Journal of Personality and Social Psychology*, 1969, *12*, 158–163.

Masters, J. C. Effects of social comparison upon subsequent self-reinforcement behavior in children. *Journal of Personality and Social Psychology*, 1968, *10*, 391–401.

Masters, J. S. Social comparison, self-reinforcement, and the value of a reinforcer. *Child Development*, 1969, *40*, 1027–1038.

Mednick, M. S., & Tangri, S. S. New social psychological perspectives on women. *Journal of Social Issues*, 1972, *28*, 1-16.

Messé, L. A., & Callahan-Levy, C. Sex and message effects in reward allocation behavior. *Academic Psychology Bulletin*, 1979, *1*, 129-133.

Mikula, G. Nationality, performance, and sex as determinants of reward allocation. *Journal of Personality and Social Psychology*, 1974, *29*, 435-440.

Mills, J., & Clark, M. S. Exchange and communal relationships. In E. Hatfield (Ed.), *Love, sex, and the marketplace*. In press.

Mirels, H. L., & Garrett, J. B. The protestant ethic as a personality variable. *Journal of Consulting and Clinical Psychology*, 1971, *36*, 40-44.

Morgan, W. R., & Sawyer, J. Bargaining expectations and the preference for equality over equity. *Journal of Personality and Social Psychology*, 1967, *6*, 139-149.

Moscovici, S. Society and theory in social psychology. In J. Israel & H. Tajfel (Eds.), *The context of social psychology: A critical assessment*. New York: Academic Press, 1972.

Pepitone, A., Maderna, A., Caporicci, E., Tiberi, E., Iacono, G., diMajo, G., Perfetto, M., Aspera, A., Villone, G., Fua, G., & Tonucci, F. Justice in choice behavior: A cross-cultural analysis. *International Journal of Psychology*, 1970, *5*, 1-10.

Radinsky, T. L. Equity and inequality as a source of reward and punishment. *Psychonomic Science*, 1969, *15*, 293-295.

Reis, H. T. Theories of interpersonal justice: From exploration through assimilation to accommodation. In J. Greenberg (Chair), *Recent developments in interpersonal justice theory and research*. Symposium presented at the meeting of the American Psychological Association, New York, September, 1979.

Reis, H. T., & Jackson, L. Sex differences in reward allocation: Subjects, partners, and tasks. *Journal of Personality and Social Psychology*, 1981, *40*, 465-478.

Robinson, R. V., & Bell, W. Equality, success, and social justice in England and the United States. *American Sociological Review*, 1978, *43*, 125-143.

Sampson, E. E. Studies of status congruence. In L. Berkowitz (Ed.), *Advances in experimental social psychology* (Vol. 4). New York: Academic Press, 1969.

Sampson, E. E. Justice as equality. *Journal of Social Issues*, 1975, *31*, 45-61.

Sauser, W. I., & York, M. Sex differences in job satisfaction: A reexamination. *Personnel Psychology*, 1978, *31*, 537-547.

Schmitt, D. R., & Marwell, G. Withdrawal and reward reallocation as responses to inequity. *Journal of Experimental Social Psychology*, 1972, *8*, 207-221.

Smith, F. J., Scott, K. D., & Hulin, C. L. Trends in job-related attitudes of managerial and professional employees. *Academy of Management Journal*, 1977, *20*, 454-460.

Stein, A. H., & Bailey, M. M. The socialization of achievement motivation in females. *Psychological Bulletin*, 1973, *80*, 345-366.

Turner, J. L., Foa, E. B., & Foa, V. G. Interpersonal reinforcers: Classification, interrelationship, and some differential properties. *Journal of Personality and Social Psychology*, 1971, *19*, 168-180.

Uesugi, T. K., & Vinacke, W. E. Strategy in a feminine game. *Sociometry*, 1963, *26*, 75-88.

Vinacke, W. E. Sex roles in a three-person game. *Sociometry*, 1959, *22*, 343-360.

Vinacke, W. E. Negotiations and decisions in a politics game. In B. Lieberman (Ed.), *Social choice*. New York and London: Gordon & Breach, 1972.

Vinacke, W. E., Cherulnik, P. D., & Lichtman, C. M. Strategy in intratriad and intertriad interaction. *Journal of Social Psychology*, 1970, **81**, 183-198.

Vinacke, W. E., & Gullickson, G. R. Age and sex differences in the formation of coalitions. *Child Development*, 1964, *35*, 1217-1231.

Vinacke, W. E., Mogy, R., Powers, W., Langan, C., & Beck, R. Accommodative strategy and communication in a three-person matrix game. *Journal of Personality and Social Psychology*, 1974, *29*, 509–525.

Wahba, M. A. Preferences among alternative forms of equity: The apportionment of coalition reward in the males and females. *Journal of Social Psychology*, 1972, *87*, 107–115.

Walster, E., Berscheid, E., & Walster, G. W. New directions in equity research. *Journal of Personality and Social Psychology*, 1973, *25*, 151–176.

Walster, E., Walster, G. W., & Berscheid, E. *Equity: Theory and research.* Boston: Allyn & Bacon, 1978.

Waters, L. K., Baltis, N., & Waters, C. W. Protestant ethic attitudes among college students. *Educational and Psychological Measurement*, 1975, *35*, 447–450.

Watts, B., Messé, L. A., & Vallacher, R. R. Toward understanding sex differences in pay allocation: Agency, communion, and reward distribution behavior. *Sex Roles*, in press.

Weber, M. [*The protestant ethic and the spirit of capitalism*] (T. Parsons, trans.). New York: Scribner's, 1958. (Originally published, 1904–1905.)

Weick, K. E., & Nesset, B. Preferences among forms of equity. *Organizational Behavior and Human Performance*, 1968, *3*, 400–416.

Weick, K. E., Bougon, M. G., & Maruyama, G. The equity context. *Organizational Behavior and Human Performance*, 1976, *15*, 32–65.

Weiner, B., Frieze, I., Kukla, A., Reed, L., Rest, S., & Rosenbaum, R. M. Perceiving the causes of success and failure. In E. E. Jones, D. E. Kanouse, H. H. Kelley, R. E. Nisbett, S. Valins, & B. Weiner (Eds.), *Attribution: Perceiving the causes of behavior*. Morristown, N. J.: General Learning Press, 1971.

Wittig, M. A., Marks, G., & Jones, G. A. Luck versus effort attributions: Effect on reward allocations to self and other. *Personality and Social Psychology Bulletin*, 1981, *7*, 71–78.

chapter 3

Justice and the Awareness of Social Entities[1]

DANIEL M. WEGNER

Justice is, for the most part, what we think it is. Although thinking may seem to take a back seat to emotion in the turmoil of reactions to injustice, or to simple habit in the everyday enactment of just behavior, it is nevertheless true that features of our social environment can be partitioned as "just" or "unjust" only because we can think about them. With this idea as the guiding assumption, this chapter introduces a distinction between two principal ways in which the social world impinges on the person's thoughts. First, just as the person might look *at* a distant light, the person may be *focally aware* of a social entity such as a person or a group. Second, just as the person might look *through* a telescope at the light, the person may be *tacitly aware* of social entities. This distinction makes it possible to characterize the person's social awareness both in terms of what is focal (what social object is being thought about) and in terms of what is tacit (what social perspective is being used). The chapter offers an analysis of the consequences for justice that are observed when people think about others, themselves, and groups in these different ways.

I. TACIT AND FOCAL AWARENESS

One of the most remarkable features of human thought is that we know more than we can tell. This idea has reverberated through the

[1]The preparation of this chapter and of the research reported in Section IV. B. was supported in part by NSF Grant BNS 78-26380 and by a grant from the Trinity University Faculty Research and Development Council.

77

EQUITY AND JUSTICE
IN SOCIAL BEHAVIOR

history of philosophy and psychology—from the Kantian a priori to the Freudian unconscious—and serves in modern psychology as the foundation of the study of cognition (Franks, 1974; Turvey, 1974). In this view, the reported contents of conscious experience are the product of a variety of knowledge structures and cognitive processes, only some of which themselves may be reported. The larger portion of what we know remains hidden, inaccessible to conscious awareness and inspection. This hidden knowledge, however, is responsible for the appearance of what we *can* tell (Shallice, 1978). Just as creative insights appear in consciousness without an accompanying understanding of the processes by which they arose, the more mundane contents of everyday phenomenal experience appear—constituted, organized, and portrayed in awareness by an underlying body of cognitive process and structure.

This dichotomy—between conscious thoughts and the "deeper" cognitive processes that produce them—is reflected in two broad literatures in the field of cognitive social psychology. The impact of conscious thought has been studied in terms of "awareness" (Duval & Wicklund, 1972), "focalization" (Duval & Hensley, 1976), "mindfulness" (Langer, 1978), "salience and attention" (Taylor & Fiske, 1978), "time and thought" (Tesser, 1978), and so forth. The operation of the underlying structures of thought, in turn, has been identified in terms of "schemas" (Neisser, 1976; Taylor & Crocker, 1981; Tesser, 1978), "construct systems" (Kelly, 1955), "implicit theories" (Wegner & Vallacher, 1977), "frames" (Minsky, 1975), "inferential sets" (Jones & Thibaut, 1958), and so on. It is with a view toward illuminating the fundamental interconnectedness of these two quite different mental systems that, in the present analysis, they are considered in terms of a special duality—*focal awareness* and *tacit awareness*.

A. An Instructive Metaphor

The concepts of focal and tacit awareness are perhaps most clearly grasped by means of a metaphor offered by Polanyi (1966). The metaphor consists of a person examining a cave with a stick. The cave is totally dark, and the person holds the stick in hand, using it to tap along the floor and walls. The peculiar aspect of this performance is that, although the sensation of the stick in hand may be noticeable at the beginning of the exploration, the way in which it touches the palm, moves against the fingers, and so on, very quickly drops from conscious awareness. Instead, one feels the point of the stick touching the walls, tapping the floor, slipping on water, pushing into earth, and otherwise sensing the cave. The awareness *of* the stick itself is changed upon repeated use to an awareness *of* the cave as experienced *through* the stick. The person who is using the stick as a sentient extension of the self, in terms of the present vocabulary, is focally aware of the cave and tacitly aware of the stick.

Three useful observations become available in further reflection on the metaphor. First, consider what would happen if different kinds of sticks were used. What if one employed a short stick, a rubber stick, or a sticky stick? To the person who had an opportunity to examine the particular stick being employed, these deviations from the standard household stick might not make much difference. But if the explorer were only tacitly aware of the stick, having never been allowed to manipulate the stick and understand its character, then the properties of each nonstandard stick would contribute to judgments of what the *cave* was like. The short stick would mean a larger cave, the rubber stick would find the cave especially spongy and giving, and the sticky stick would reveal a sticky cave. At the extreme, a stick with several bowling balls attached to the point might not find the cave at all. In short, then, the entities of which one is tacitly aware are wholly responsible for the appearance of focal entities.

The second observation suggested by the metaphor is a relatively simple one, but it is crucial for a correct understanding of tacit and focal awareness. Imagine that in the cave, one is very carefully poking the stick at every point along a wall. Intricate fissures are discovered, dangerous outcroppings become known, and as an even more intriguing feature of the wall is being explored, one steps past a drop-off and falls into a pond. For the lack of a few taps on the floor, an important feature of the environment has been missed. The moral here is obvious: One understands only that which is brought to focal awareness by way of tacit awareness. Those objects or events that are linked to the person by means of some tacit entity are given focal awareness, and in this way, are identified as entities themselves, are comprehended, and so are made the potential targets of evaluation and action.

The third observation provides the bridge between this metaphor and thought in general. Consider now what happens when one does not have a stick and explores the cave with one's hand alone. Extending the reasoning behind the original definitions, it seems that one must be tacitly aware of one's hand to be focally aware of the cave. As a generalization of this idea, Polanyi (1969) suggests that focal awareness of objects is produced by tacit awareness of the body; we become aware *of* objects only by being aware *through* the sense receptors and interpretation systems of the body. The stick, as a tacit extension of the body, serves as a concrete example of a multiplicity of potential tacit extensions. These range from other concrete objects used as tools for the direction of focal awareness to the more abstract systems of cognition and perception by which the mind directs focal awareness in the same way.

B. The Tacit-Focal Function

The translation of this metaphor into a useful model of social cognition begins with the realization that awareness of the social environment has a directed, vector-like quality. One does not merely perceive or attend to aspects of the social environment; rather, such focal awareness is always directed through a tacit awareness system in which focal entities are given their identifiability, meaning, and value. So, for a conscious thought or percept to occur, there must exist a tacit awareness system through which it may be brought into focal awareness. This characterization of the production of consciousness can be summarized in this way: *Tacit awareness supplies the dimensions and metrics by which entities given focal awareness are constituted, comprehended, and evaluated.* This general rule may be called the tacit–focal function.

Interpreted at a basic level, this function merely asserts that one must know both what is tacit and what is focal for the nature of a percept to be specified. In the *constitution* of entities, tacit awareness lets us become focally aware of "things"; the flow of experience is partitioned into units, identifiable as separate from the remaining body of experience. Actions and events are constituted from the temporal flow (Newtson, 1976), people and groups are constituted as entities from the field of social experience (Heider, 1958), and more generally, things are constituted through the differentiation and integration of experience (Wegner & Vallacher, 1977). For anything like this to occur, the experience must be given focal awareness. Phenomenologists such as Schutz (1967) have long recognized that conscious awareness of experience leads to "objectification" in this way, but have not appreciated the role of tacit awareness in the process. Quite simply, it is tacit awareness that provides the specifications whereby constitution is carried out. The constitution of focal entities occurs when tacit awareness suggests what should and should not be included in the definition of each entity.

Focal and tacit awareness are similarly interdependent in the *comprehension* of experience. Entities that appear in focal awareness are comprehended in the sense that they are located in a tacit mental system of other entities; they may be categorized, given a dimensional representation, placed in a semantic network, or simply imaged. In any of these mental systems, the focal entity becomes linked with other entities and is thereby given meaning in relation to them (Wegner, 1977). So, situations that are lent focal awareness have more compelling implications for our behavior (Langer, 1978); emotions to which our focal awareness is drawn are felt more strongly (Scheier & Carver, 1977); the agents we pay special attention are seen to have greater causal efficacy (Duval & Hensley, 1976). These effects occur not only because of the presence of focal awareness, but also because of the specific tacit systems that are engaged. Just as the sentence context within which a word is perceived may determine the word's meaning, the particular tacit system that serves as a link to focal awareness determines the nature of the comprehended focal entity.

The most critical aspect of comprehension is *evaluation,* and it is affected by the tacit–focal function in a similar way. First, the dimensions, standards, or values by which an entity is evaluated are components of the tacit system; for this reason, the contents of tacit awareness will determine whether any focal entity is seen as good or bad. Second, the extent to which an entity is subject to *any* evaluation suggested by the tacit system is dependent on the extent to which the entity is given focal awareness. Focal awareness of oneself, for instance, seems necessary for the onset of self-evaluation (Duval & Wicklund, 1972). And more generally, Tesser (1978) has shown that thinking carefully (and hence, focally) about anything tends to polarize one's attitudes toward that topic of thought.

To summarize these ideas about the tacit–focal function, it is helpful to return to the cave for some illumination. Suppose that one is poking the stick at a particular spot on the floor. The tacit–focal function says that the spot will be constituted ("here's something"), comprehended ("this seems to be a drop-off"), and evaluated ("I'd rather not be put on the spot, thanks"). And, because of the interdependence of tacit and focal awareness suggested by the function, it can also be said that (a) the particular focal spot is known (constituted, etc.), whereas other (nonfocal) spots are not known; and (b) the particular tacit stick determines how the spot is known, in a way that other tacit sticks might not. In short, every act of cognition is specifiable in terms of two features: What is tacit and what is focal.

C. The Awareness of Social Entities

The tacit–focal function provides an appealing way of expressing how people are represented in our thoughts. To begin with, it seems obvious that people—specific others, groups, and even oneself—can be objects of focal awareness. We can think about these entities, categorize and evaluate them, and otherwise consider them in consciousness. A more subtle but equally important idea is that we may be tacitly aware of such social entities. That one may be tacitly aware of oneself, of course, follows from Polanyi's (1969) observation that one can only see the world (or the cave) *through* oneself. But in a wide range of instances of social cognition, it seems we also use cognitive constructions of other people and groups in this way. When our attention is directed toward the sky by a crowd looking upward, for example, or when our attention is moved to a stubborn soft-drink machine by a person doing battle with it, we are using knowledge of these people as an instrument that guides our focal awareness beyond the people themselves to their situations. In this sense, we may be tacitly aware of others.

This line of reasoning suggests that a useful analysis of social cognition can be made by considering separately each of the major ways in which a person may be aware of a social entity (cf. Wegner & Giuliano, 1982). An outline of these forms of social awareness, partitioned in terms of tacit versus focal awareness of self, of a specific other, and of a group, is presented in Table 3.1. Each of these forms of social awareness may be considered a "state" of the person's awareness because each portrays the particular form that cognitive processing may take for an instance of social cognitive activity of indeterminate duration. Each is also viewable as an extension of the tacit self; because one invariably takes one's own perspective as the starting point for any other form of awareness, the self is always in the most basic tacit position across the forms of awareness.

As will be seen in upcoming sections of this chapter, these forms of awareness hold certain features in common with conceptions introduced in both the early and recent history of social psychology. Tacit self awareness, for example, is similar in some aspects to the "natural attitude" of phenomenology (e.g., Schutz, 1967) and to Duval and

Table 3.1
Forms of Social Awareness

Awareness form	Position of social entity	
	Tacit	Focal
Tacit self awareness	Self	Self's situation
Focal self awareness	Self	Self
Tacit other awareness	Self, other	Other's situation
Focal other awareness	Self	Other
Tacit group awareness	Self, group	Group's situation
Focal group awareness	Self	Group

Wicklund's (1972) "subjective self awareness." Focal self awareness, in turn, may be seen as a variant on Duval and Wicklund's "objective self awareness" and on the several early phenomenological and symbolic interactionist treatments of the reflective "social self" (Cooley, 1902; Mead, 1934; Schutz, 1967). Continuing through the tabled awareness forms, it can be noted that tacit other awareness corresponds in some ways with "empathy" (e.g., Stotland, 1969), "role-taking" (Flavell, Botkin, Fry, Wright, & Jarvis, 1968), and the phenomenal state of "intersubjectivity" (Schutz, 1967), whereas focal other awareness is reminiscent of Heider's (1958) suggestions regarding the state of mind necessary for the construction of people as phenomenal objects. Finally, the forms of group awareness can be seen together in Cooley's (1902) ideas about "we-feeling," and are differentiated into both focal and tacit forms in Holzner's (1978) arguments on the phenomenal representation of groups as objects versus subjects. Although a knowledge of this rich history is helpful for understanding the forms of social awareness, it is not crucial, as the key aspects of all of these traditions appear to be well characterized by the tacit–focal function.

These six forms of the awareness of social entities are only the elements of an even more complex system. It can be suggested, for example, that one could be tacitly aware of a group while holding a particular person in focal awareness; this sort of thing could occur when, for example, one's carload of compatriots is delayed on the way to an important event by a heedless, foot-shuffling pedestrian. Alternatively, one might be focally aware of oneself through tacit awareness of a specific other; the state of consciousness that ensues when one commits an indelicacy under the gaze of a haughty waiter is an example. This soon-dizzying array of combinations is limited in two ways. First, there are rules of combination that indicate which forms of awareness are "grammatical."[2] Second, there is the even more severe pragmatic limitation of the capacity of the human mind for tacit extension. Because one does not make many sensible judgments when asked to take a perspective on a perspective on a perspective on an object, it seems reasonable to assume that this limitation is quite stringent. Although the entire set of combined awareness forms that may exist under these limitations are of potential interest, the elemental forms presented in the table are of prime interest, and therefore they will be considered in greatest depth.

[2]The combination rules may be specified in this way: (a) Any form of social awareness consists of a string; (b) the string begins with tacit awareness of self; (c) the string continues with tacit awareness of an ordered array of social entities numbering zero or more; and (d) the string ends with focal awareness of a single entity or with focal awareness of the situation of the most recent entity in tacit awareness.

D. Awareness and Justice

It is the general thesis of this chapter that a perceiver's form of awareness determines what is seen as just. In this regard, the present view shares certain assumptions with previous treatments of justice as a system of social cognition (e.g., Kohlberg, 1969; Lerner, Miller, & Holmes, 1976; Selman & Damon, 1975) and social evaluation (e.g., Feinberg, 1970; Pettigrew, 1967; Wegner & Vallacher, 1977). That justice is dependent on what one understands about a social exchange, that it operates on a complex set of variables only some of which are seen as relevant to any particular exchange, and that it results both in the evaluation of persons and in the evaluation of their situations, for instance, are propositions derivable from these writings. The special contribution of the present approach is the tacit–focal function.

The tacit–focal function specifies that tacit awareness supplies the dimensions on which evaluation is accomplished, whereas focal awareness contains the target of the evaluation. When questions of justice, fairness, or deserving are posed, it is likely that they will be answered by a perceiver only by reference to the immediately available contents of these two systems. If one is tacitly aware of another person, for instance, and is asked what this person deserves, the person's situation is focal and it is the situation that will be evaluated; this evaluation will be carried out on the basis of dimensions supplied by tacit awareness of the person. If one is focally aware of the person, however, and the question of deserving is raised, then the person will be evaluated with respect to dimensions supplied by the self's tacit system. The rule underlying this case can be extended from other awareness to self-awareness and group awareness as well. In each case, tacit awareness of a social entity (self, other, or group) leads to an evaluation of the entity's situation, while focal awareness of the entity leads to an evaluation of the entity. These different kinds of evaluation contribute to decisions about what is just in different ways.

Tacit awareness of a social entity (self, other, or group) produces an orientation toward the needs of the entity; the entity's situation is evaluated in focal awareness in terms of its provision of those needs. This proposition acknowledges that the tacit evaluation system held by any social entity is likely to evaluate focal contents in terms of their hedonic consequences for the tacit entity. When in a state of tacit self awareness, for instance, one inspects the focal environment with a view toward the satisfaction of simple self-interest; focal entities are good or bad only when they are good or bad for self. When tacit awareness of others or of groups is overlaid on tacit self awareness, the focal situations of these entities are evaluated with respect to their satisfaction of the needs and interests of the tacit other or group. A concern for one's social responsibility (Berkowitz, 1972) or for the allocation of resources according to need (Lerner, 1975; Leventhal, 1976) is likely to be felt. In sum, to the degree that tacit awareness of a social entity is engaged, what the entity *deserves* is calculated according to what the entity *wants*.

Focal awareness of a social entity (self, other, or group) produces an orientation toward the evaluation of the entity; the entity is evaluated in focal awareness in terms of standards that serve the interests of the tacit system that is engaged. This principle reiterates the tacit–focal function, but in such a way that a second major relationship between awareness forms and justice can be discerned. The idea that social entities may be evaluated in focal awareness with respect to their adherence to standards that are in the interest of (tacit) others allows for the operation of a contribution rule in the judgment of what is fair. The broad precept that "you get what you pay for," as embodied in exchange rules such as the personal contract and social contract (Lerner, 1975), the equity norm (Walster, Berscheid, & Walster, 1973), the reciprocity norm (Gouldner, 1960), or the contribution rule (Leventhal, 1976), becomes available as a means of calculating deserving when social entities occupy focal awareness because the interests of most tacit entities are met by the regular application of such a rule. In sum, to the degree that focal awareness of a social entity is engaged, what the entity *deserves* is calculated according to what the entity *earns*.

These two propositions, one relating tacit awareness to a need rule and the other linking focal awareness with a contribution rule, provide a useful way of representing much of what is known about the interface of justice and social cognition. The idea that different distribution tactics may be used in different interpersonal settings, a common one in justice theory (Lerner *et al.*, 1976; Leventhal, 1976), is captured by these propositions when it is recognized that different interpersonal settings may instigate different predominant awareness forms. The ascription of variations in justice strategies to developmental changes or individual differences (Gunzburger, Wegner, & Anooshian, 1977), in turn, may be traced to variations in the propensity or capacity to adopt the different awareness forms. In the following sections, both situational and individual difference determinants of specific awareness forms are mapped in greater detail, and the evidence on the proposed relationship between each awareness form and justice is explored.

II. AWARENESS OF THE OTHER

The observation that others may be comprehended not only as objects in the world but also as subjects through which the world may be viewed is an old one in social theory (Cooley, 1902; Mead, 1934; Schutz, 1967). The features of this distinction emphasized in such early treatments remain essentially intact when they are formalized in terms of the tacit–focal function. Focal other awareness corresponds to viewing the particular other as a social object or entity; the other is focalized as a means of understanding his or her status as a responsible human agent who has potential impact on the tacit self. Tacit other awareness, in contrast, corresponds to seeing the other's environment from the perspective of a tacit cognitive construction of the other's subjective stance; the other's situation is focalized as a means of understanding his or her actions, motives, and goals.

A. Focal Other Awareness

1. DETERMINANTS

The tendency to hold others in focal awareness is a pervasive one in mental life. In the stream of an observer's experience, another person appears as a stricture or "bottleneck" in the flow; prior events act as causes in changing the person, and then in complex and often unanticipated ways, the person acts as an "origin" of further changes and events in the environment (Heider, 1944). For this reason, and because the behaviors of others may often have hedonic consequences for the observer, others are constituted in the observer's focal awareness as meaningful entities that may be judged, compared, categorized, and evaluated. Focal other awareness, like the "value maintenance set" described by Jones and Thibaut (1958), is aroused by the perceiver's needs to understand and control the impingements of the social world on the self.

In large part, the study of person perception in social psychology is the study of how persons are perceived in focal other awareness. When observers report on the traits of a person, evaluate the person, judge the person's physical or mental qualities, or otherwise ascribe properties to the person as an entity, focal awareness of the person is necessary. The other is seen as an entity whose features and attributes are (at least for the moment) static and identifiable, and to whom responsibility for behavior and events may be directly attributed. This close correspondence between focal other awareness and personal attribution of causality to the other is the basis for an important general rule. Because focal other awareness is the necessary precursor to such personal attribution, it can be said that many of the determinants of personal attribution may operate as such only because of their impact on focal other awareness.

Examining previous research and theory with this rule in mind, a range of variables can be isolated that are likely instigators of focal other awareness. Personal attributions often result, for example, when the observer lacks knowledge of the other's situation (Kelley, 1967), when the other is perceptually salient (McArthur & Post, 1977; Taylor & Fiske, 1978), when the other is seen as very unlike the self (Ross, Greene, & House, 1977), or when the other's actions have hedonic relevance for self (Jones & Davis, 1965). Although attribution theory has not provided any framework within which all of these determinants might find unitary representation, the tacit–focal function makes their internal coherence quite clear. It is reasonable that focal other awareness (and hence, personal attribution) should occur (*a*) when the other is difficult to know tacitly because his or her situation is unknown; (*b*) when the other's status as an object of perception and conscious thought is made salient; (*c*) when the other is seen as sufficiently different from self that tacit awareness of the other is precluded; and (*d*) when the other is highly relevant to the well-being of the tacit self. In broad outline, then, these are the properties of interpersonal settings that introduce focal other awareness.

2. CONSEQUENCES FOR PERSON EVALUATION AND ATTITUDE INFERENCE

According to the justice propositions developed earlier (Section I. D.), the evaluation of the other that occurs in focal other-awareness is carried out with reference to rules or standards of social exchange fairness. A focal other who makes an input appropriate to the level of outcome that is received will be evaluated positively, whereas one who obtains outcomes disproportionately higher or lower than inputs will be evaluated negatively. Because most social psychological studies of person perception are conducted under conditions likely to induce focal other awareness in observers, it is not surprising to find that results consistent with these predictions have been reported frequently in the person perception and justice literature (see, e.g., reviews by Austin, Walster, & Utne, 1976; Leventhal, 1976.)[3]

Perhaps the best known illustration of the impact of focal other awareness on justice and evaluation is the "just world phenomenon" (Lerner, 1971; Lerner & Miller, 1978; Lerner & Simmons, 1966). This phenomenon was observed when Lerner and Simmons (1966) asked

[3]The highly selective citation of such research in this section is undertaken because for the particular studies cited, there exists complementary research demonstrating how observers' evaluations and inferences change when they are tacitly aware of others. These studies are taken up in Section II. B. 2.

observer–subjects to give their evaluations of a target person who underwent a series of painful electric shocks. As compared to evaluations of a person who did not receive shocks, these evaluations were decidedly negative. Because such derogation of the victim does not obtain when the victim is given proper monetary compensation for the pain and suffering (Lerner, 1971), it appears that negative evaluation during focal other awareness occurred only when the other received the shocks in an *unfair* exchange. When a balance between input (shock reception) and outcome (monetary compensation) was maintained, evaluations of the victim were no longer negative and even became slightly positive.

That the evaluation of focal others becomes negative not only when they are victims of unfair exchanges, but also when they benefit from such interactions is shown in an experiment by Alexander and Knight (1971). These researchers conducted an observer simulation of the classic cognitive dissonance experiment by Festinger and Carlsmith (1959). Observer–subjects listened to an audio tape of an actor–subject who agreed to perform a task in exchange for money. The task varied in pleasantness for different observers; for some, the actor was heard to perform the relatively pleasant task of telling the truth (i.e., advocating participation in the experiment when he believed the experiment was fun), whereas for others, the actor was heard to perform the unpleasant task of lying (i.e., advocating participation in the experiment when he believed it was boring). The monetary compensation given the actor also varied for different observers from a low of $1 to a high of $20.

It would be expected that under the prevailing state of focal other awareness, observers would evaluate positively the actor who did the unpleasant task for high compensation, as well as the actor who did the pleasant task for low compensation, because in both cases the actor engaged in a fair exchange with contribution proportional to compensation. This is indeed what was found, as those conditions representing the "reverse incentive" effect resulted in positive actor evaluation. The conditions representing "incentive" effects, in turn, would be expected to yield negative actor evaluations, and this also was found. When the actor performed an unpleasant task for low compensation, like the shock recipient in Lerner and Simmons's (1966) research, he was disliked. When the actor performed a pleasant task for high compensation, reaping an unfair benefit by obtaining positive outcomes at little expense, he was also disliked. In short, adherence to the contribution rule produced positive evaluations, whereas deviations from such a rule resulted in negative evaluations.

This reinterpretation of the Alexander and Knight data holds special

appeal because it suggests a new way to conceptualize the reverse incentive effect—the central phenomenon of dissonance, self-perception, and
intrinsic motivation research. The reverse incentive is portrayed in this
light as a justice phenomenon. The attitude inferences that observers
make in Bemian simulations (Bem, 1967, 1972) may simply be the result
of the expectation that a focal other will be fair. When the actor receives
a large amount of money for doing a task (e.g., $20), observers infer that
the actor's input must have been substantial and that the task was thus a
tedious one; when the actor receives little compensation for doing the
task (e.g., $1), observers infer that the task must have been an easy one
requiring little input. Attitude inferences observers make about the actor
reflect these justice considerations, and task enjoyment is found to be
related to incentive magnitude in a reverse manner.

Focal awareness of another person, as described here, is a state in
which observers evaluate the other according to a contribution rule of
social exchange, and make attitude inferences about the other on the
basis of that rule as well. The possibility that this inference structure
changes dramatically when tacit other awareness is adopted is the topic
of the next section.

B. Tacit Other Awareness

1. DETERMINANTS

Conceptualized as empathy (Hoffman, 1976; Wegner, 1980), role taking (Flavell *et al.*, 1968), or perspective taking (Selman, 1976; Selman &
Damon, 1975), tacit other awareness has been treated as a developmental variable in many previous frameworks. Though focal other awareness may also depend on cognitive abilities that mature with development, it is fair to say that tacit other awareness depends on a somewhat
more complex set of abilities and hence appears even later in development. The capacity to entertain thoughts about a situation from the tacit
viewpoint of another person may vary among individual adult observers,
then, as a result of differential levels of cognitive maturation. Even so, it
is likely that adults normally have the capacity for both tacit and focal
other awareness and that fluctuations between states are in large part
determined by situational variables.

The situational determinants of tacit other awareness can be identified broadly as the complements of factors that increase focal other
awareness. Tacit other awareness would be expected to ensue to the
extent that (*a*) the other's situation is clear and salient; (*b*) the other's
status as an object of perception and thought is not salient; (*c*) the other

is seen as similar to the self; and (d) the other's actions are not detrimental to the well-being of the tacit self. An increase in attribution of the other's behavior to situational factors—a central indicant of tacit other awareness—has been observed in a variety of studies manipulating one or more of these factors (e.g., Storms, 1973; Taylor & Fiske, 1975). Perhaps most commonly, however, researchers have manipulated this awareness form by taking advantage of observers' ability to secure conscious control of it in response to instructional sets. In some studies, observers have been told that they would shortly be taking the role of the actor themselves (e.g., Wolfson & Salancik, 1977); in others, they have been given direct instructions to empathize with the actor (e.g., Gould & Sigall, 1977; Regan & Totten, 1975; Stotland, 1969; Wegner & Finstuen, 1977); in yet others, they have been instructed to read a story from a particular person's point of view (e.g., Pichert & Anderson, 1977). The results of these manipulations generally seem to parallel those that would be expected to occur in response to the naturally occurring environmental influences previously listed.

2. CONSEQUENCES FOR SITUATION EVALUATION AND ATTITUDE INFERENCE

The initial consequence of tacit other awareness is that the other is *not* evaluated. The other is used merely as a cue to direct focal awareness toward his or her situation, and so the other escapes accountability for behavior and events. This point is well made in a study of the "just world" effect by Aderman, Brehm, and Katz (1974). These researchers gave empathy instructions to observers who then witnessed the experience of an innocent victim receiving shocks. Although subjects who were not given special instructions derogated the victim in this setting—replicating Lerner and Simmons's (1966) original demonstration—those subjects given empathy instructions did not engage in such derogation. Rather than condemning the victim for participating in an unjust exchange, they remained neutral. Such "leniency" has been found to characterize empathic observers in a number of other studies (e.g., Archer, Foushee, Davis, & Aderman, 1979), and may be considered a central property of tacit other awareness.

The state of tacit other awareness leads the observer to evaluate the other's situation with reference to the other's needs and goals. When an observer reads a story with the perspective of a particular person in mind, for example, the story information relevant to the person's goals is given greater attention and rehearsal for memory (Pichert & Anderson, 1977) and the person's feelings and need states are more often considered (Bower, 1978). Observers instructed to empathize with live or filmed others are also likely to attend to need states (Stotland, 1969) and situational factors (Regan & Totten, 1975). And it is well documented that tacit other awareness (induced through instructions or through manipulated perceptions of similarity) can increase an observer's behavioral responsiveness to the other's needs (Aderman & Berkowitz, 1970; Krebs, 1975). In tacit other awareness, justice is served when a "good" situation is encountered and the other's needs are thereby met; for this reason, tacit other awareness should often lead observers to opt for a need-based allocation of resources to the other.

Some further insight into the inference processes that accompany tacit other awareness can be gained by considering again the judgments observers make in the Bemian simulation of the Festinger and Carlsmith (1959) cognitive dissonance study (cf. Section II. A. 2.). If it is true that observers who adopt tacit other awareness of an actor forsake the social exchange evaluation of the actor for a need-based evaluation of the actor's situation, it is possible to predict that observers in such a state would make attitude inferences in line with an incentive effect. When these observers find that an actor obtains $20 for doing a task, as opposed to $1 for doing the task, they should infer that greater subjective need gratification has been achieved by the actor. Hence, when asked how much the actor liked the task, they should evaluate the task—a part of the actor's situation—as more positive with increasing amounts of money. Findings precisely in line with this expectation have been reported by Wegner and Finstuen (1977); observers given empathy instructions made inferences about actor enjoyment of the task that varied directly with incentive magnitude.

The summary implication of this discussion of focal and tacit other awareness is this: To the degree that one is focally aware of another, the other's joys are seen as paid for with sorrows and the other is disapproved if this is not so; but to the extent that one is tacitly aware of another, the other's joy is held as a goal and the other's situation is esteemed when this goal is fulfilled.

III. AWARENESS OF THE SELF

Like the forms of other awareness, the forms of self awareness are traceable to an array of early philosophical and psychological frameworks. But unlike other awareness, the topic of self awareness has achieved current prominence in a major social psychological theory—the theory of objective self awareness proposed by Duval and Wicklund (1972). These theorists suggest that individuals spend some moments in an outward-focused state of attention (subjective self awareness) and others in a reflective state (objective self awareness). During objective self-awareness, the individual becomes acutely aware of a salient discrepancy between behavior and a standard for behavior, and feels a negative or positive affective state as a result of the direction of this discrepancy (Wicklund, 1975). The implications of this motivational system for action are clear: If the discrepancy is positive, the person attempts to approach or remain in the state of objective self awareness, whereas if the discrepancy is negative, the person attempts either to avoid the self-focused state or to reduce the discrepancy through action or attitude change. These ideas have been supported by a sizable body of research (see reviews by Wicklund, 1979a,b; Wicklund & Frey, 1980), and are essentially compatible with the present analysis. In the main, the present concepts of focal and tacit self awareness can be equated with objective and subjective self awareness, respectively.

More than a simple renaming, this conceptualization of self awareness in terms of the tacit–focal function provides a useful supplement to the original theory in two ways. First, by considering subjective self awareness as a state in which the person is tacitly aware of self, it becomes possible to make suggestions about what may guide behavior in this state; although objective self awareness theory has little to say about this problem, the tacit–focal function offers the suggestion that self-interest should serve as the primary goad to action in tacit self awareness. Second, the present formulation also helps to clarify how the source of particular standards adhered to in the objective or focal self awareness state may be specified; quite simply, the tacit–focal function indicates that evaluation of self in focal self awareness takes place with regard to standards that serve the interest of whatever social entity is held in tacit awareness. This idea allows for the expansion of self awareness notions to include the processes of self-presentation and impression management. These amplifications of the conception of self awareness are taken up in turn in this section.

A. Tacit Self Awareness and Self-Interest

Tacit self awareness is the most basic form of social entity awareness in two senses. First, echoing the point made by Polanyi (1969), one is focally or tacitly aware of environmental objects, persons, or groups, only by being tacitly aware of oneself. Because this awareness form is the first knowledge system in a chain of systems that may have several links, it is always engaged as a prelude to the activation of the other systems,

and thus is basic in this structural sense. Only when tacit or focal awareness of some social entity serves the interests of the tacit self will another
form of awareness be assumed. The second way in which tacit self
awareness is fundamental becomes apparent in thinking about the maturation of the human being. Because self-reflection is not in the prov-
ince of very young children (Lewis & Brooks-Gunn, 1979; Selman,
1976), or for that matter of most animals (Gallup, 1977), the state of tacit
self awareness is closer to the biological givens of the organism and is
basic in a developmental sense.

Tacit self-awareness in its "pure" form—without tacit or focal awareness of other social entities appended—occurs when the individual
focuses on activities, tasks, or environmental objects. Performing a
repetitive or rhythmic task (Duval & Wicklund, 1973), for example, or
becoming involved in automatic (Kimble & Perlmuter, 1970) or over-
learned behavior (Langer, 1978; Wicklund & Frey, 1980) is likely to arouse
this awareness form. It is under these conditions that the person is most
likely to scan the environment and operate on it according to the dictates
of simple self-interest; those activities or objects that promise the
gratification of needs are approached, whereas those that threaten the
continued gratification of needs are avoided. This sort of situational
"guidance system" is evident even in animals and infants, and may occur
without any form of social self-reflection (cf. Vallacher, Wegner, &
Hoine, 1980).

It is during the state of tacit self awareness that the individual
evaluates the environment in terms of the self-satisfactions it may provide. So, like the attitude inferences that are made when one is tacitly
aware of another, the estimates of one's own attitude offered during tacit
self-awareness are likely to reflect the operation of an incentive effect.
Situations that hold appreciable rewards or satisfactions are valued,
whereas those that yield lower levels of reward are not. Evidence in favor
of this reasoning is available in several studies of the effect of monetary
compensation on task enjoyment. Experiments by Crano and Messé
(1970) and Rosenberg (1965), for example, both may be interpreted in
such terms. Subjects in these studies were asked to write a counterattitudinal essay in exchange for payment, and then were engaged for
some time in absorbing tasks that quite likely promoted tacit self
awareness (i.e., walking and drawing, respectively). Subjects' attitudes on
the essay topic reported following these activities were consistent with an
incentive interpretation; the more money they were paid, the more they
agreed with their essays. Because agreement with a self-generated essay
is a measure of the perceived enjoyment of writing it (Kruglanski, 1975),

both of these studies indicate that, among tacitly self aware subjects, increased levels of need satisfaction were linked to increments in task enjoyment.

The direct covariation of enjoyment with incentive in tacit self awareness holds implications for an array of justice-related behaviors. A person in this state would be more likely to follow the dictates of self-interest in allocating rewards among members of a group; and when performance is measured, a person aware of self in this way should work hard to the extent that rewards for self are in view. The everyday examples of persons who, momentarily or chronically, are too busy, too distracted, or too absorbed in their own pursuits to consider the fairness of their actions are many. Unbridled by concerns for others or for the evaluation of self, the person in tacit self awareness is inclined toward greed.

B. Focal Self Awareness and Justice

One may become focally aware of oneself in a variety of ways. Research in the objective self awareness tradition of Duval and Wicklund (1972) has most often induced this state in the experimental subject by exposing the subject to his or her own mirror image. But other self-focusing stimuli such as a camera (e.g., Vallacher, 1978), audience (e.g., Scheier, Fenigstein, & Buss, 1974), self-description task (e.g., Duval, Duval, & Neely, 1979), or playback of one's own tape-recorded voice (e.g., Gibbons & Wicklund, 1976) or video image (e.g., Duval & Hensley, 1976) have been used to invoke the state, and a measure of the dispositional propensity toward "private self-consciousness" (Fenigstein, Scheier, & Buss, 1975) has been devised that holds promise as a measure of the same construct (Carver & Scheier, 1978). The assumption underlying all of these strategies for manipulating self-focus is that when a person is reminded in some way about the status of self as an object of attention and evaluation, the person will come to consider the self as a focal object in other ways as well. The further proposition offered by the present analysis is that focal self awareness produced by these or other means in justice-relevant settings sets off an evaluation of self in terms of the contribution rule.

1. TASK ENJOYMENT AND SELF ATTRIBUTION OF ATTITUDE

To round out the discussion of task enjoyment and attitude inference that has been broached at several points previously, it can be proposed that the person in a state of focal self awareness will regularly calculate his or her own enjoyment of tasks in line with a reverse incentive effect. Because the self may be evaluated positively in this state only when one's contribution is proportional to one's compensation, it is likely that individuals given a certain level of compensation will compute the magnitude of their contribution to maintain a positive self-view. Given a large amount of money for doing a task or delivering an essay, the person in this state should infer that the task was difficult or that the essay was a lie and hence was difficult to deliver. Given little money for these tasks, the person in this state should assume that the task was easy or that the essay was consistent with his or her own attitudes.

Unfortunately, experimental evidence bearing on these propositions is sparse. Although Wicklund and Duval (1971, Experiment 2) found that subjects who were paid nothing for writing a counterattitudinal essay reported attitudes more in line with the essay when they were made self aware by means of a mirror, no reward magnitude variation was included in the experiment, so no conclusions regarding the proposed relation between focal self awareness and the reverse incentive effect can be drawn. It is possible to suggest, however, that many of the dissonance and self-perception studies that have yielded evidence of reverse incentive phenomena were conducted under conditions in which subjects were in the state of focal self awareness. The reverse incentive effect is most often observed when subjects are led to believe that they have complete choice in deciding whether or not to engage in the exchange of reward for work (see, e.g., Folger, Rosenfield, & Hays, 1978). When personal responsibility is accepted in this way, some reflection on self as a focal social entity is necessary (cf. Hampshire, 1960). So, it may be that the many instances of the overjustification or reverse incentive effect (see Lepper & Greene, 1978; Wicklund & Brehm, 1976) occur because responsibility acceptance invokes focal self awareness and its associated inference system based on the contribution rule.

2. PERFORMANCE AND REWARD ALLOCATION

Several studies have examined the connection between focal self awareness and justice very directly. Gibbons, Wicklund, Karylowski, Rosenfield, and Chase (1978, Experiment 5), for instance, arranged for subjects who had either been overpaid or equitably paid by an experimenter for doing a task to have a chance to compensate the experimenter by working for a longer time. Whereas subjects given no special treatment to induce focal self awareness did not engage in more work when they had been overpaid, subjects made self-attentive by means of a mirror did restore equity in this way. Parallel findings have been observed in a similar study by Reis and Burns (cited in Reis, 1978). When subjects were either equitably paid or overpaid to perform a proofreading task, overpaid subjects who did the task in the presence of a mirror completed more work than did those who performed the task without a mirror. At the same time, however, the mirror subjects also made more errors, suggesting that they were fervently trying to get more work done.

Reward allocation as a function of self-focused attention has been studied by Greenberg (1980). Subjects in this study were presented with the problem of allocating payment to themselves and another participant for performance on a task; performance was (ostensibly) either chance determined or contingent on the participants' behavior, and subjects were told that they performed better than, more poorly than, or the same as did their partners. While some subjects made their allocation decision in the presence of a mirror, others made the decision without this self-focusing device. In both mirror and no-mirror conditions, allocations made to self and other were essentially equal when performance was chance determined; but when performance differences reflected behavioral input differences between participants, subjects in both mirror and no-mirror conditions allocated reward according to equity. What is especially noteworthy about these results is that, in the latter conditions, mirror subjects were more equitable than were no-mirror subjects, apparently taking the differential levels of input more completely into account in their allocation decisions. This finding is accompanied by another interesting result: In answers to a postexperimental questionnaire, mirror subjects expressed greater concern than did no-mirror subjects about the appropriateness of their allocations.

Although the research on the connection between self-focused attention and justice is just beginning, it seems that there is already firm evidence indicating that self-focus results in behavior designed to adhere to a contribution or equity rule. Subjects made focally self aware through mirror presence increase their performance on tasks when this would serve equity and divide rewards between self and other in an equitable fashion as well. A special caveat should be noted here, though, in the service of completeness. The present framework coincides with Duval and Wicklund's theory in noting that a frequent and sometimes prepotent response to self-focused attention is flight from the self-focusing stimulus. Because the self-evaluation that ensues from failure to meet the equity standard is phenomenally aversive, individuals in a state of focal self awareness may often be guided by their tacit interest in avoiding such displeasure to escape from the self-focusing setting. This escape may disrupt or preclude attempts to be equitable.

C. Tacit Perspectives and Self-Presentation

A recurrent issue in writings on the self is the extent to which the self is a stable aspect of the person. The idea that the self is typically a mutable and transient reflection of the person's immediate social situation, although somewhat antithetical to theories of self-concept or self awareness, has gained currency in social psychological treatments of self-presentation (e.g., Arkin, 1980), impression management (e.g., Tedeschi & Linskold, 1976), and situated identities (e.g., Alexander & Knight, 1971). Each of these frameworks suggests that people may behave in social settings not to be consistent with an internalized set of values or standards—a "true" self—but rather to be consistent with the values or expectations of others.

As a psychological theory, this view is incomplete. It fails to specify any intrapersonal mechanism whereby the translation of others' expectancies, or even the social definition of the situation, might be conveyed into the individual's understanding and behavior. To some extent, this difficulty is remedied by the recent attempts of self awareness theorists to incorporate "fleeting," social standards into their representations of the self-awareness processes. Wicklund and Frey (1980), for instance, have argued that self-focus produces adherence to rules one has most recently acted upon, whereas Hull and Levy (1979) have proposed that self-attention may generally sensitize the person to self-relevant social cues. Within the tacit–focal framework, however, it is possible to provide a resolution of even greater parsimony. Both the stable and variable aspects of self-evaluation can be represented when it is recognized that a person may become focally aware of self either through the (stable) tacit self or through the (variable) tacit awareness of specific others or groups.

1. TACIT PERSPECTIVES ON THE FOCAL SELF

As a first step in considering the different tacit views from which the self may be focalized, it is useful to specify in some greater detail the nature of simple focal self awareness—the state in which the person regards the focal self from the perspective of the tacit self (see Table 3.1). The point to be made about this form of awareness, and to be generalized to the other forms of awareness, is that the individual in this state comes to view the self as a *person*. When the individual reflects on self as a nonsocial entity—by attending to cognitive activities (Flavell & Wellman, 1977), for example, or to physical sensations or bodily states (Pennebaker & Skelton, 1978)—particular aspects of the functioning of self may be focalized and processes of self-regulation may be engaged (Carver, 1979). But in these cases, the tacit perspective does not necessarily constitute the self as a person, a responsible human agent in the field of other social entities. It is only when the tacit self constitutes, comprehends, and evaluates the focal self as a person that considerations of fairness and equity are brought to the fore. Under these conditions, self-focused attention can be analyzed as a form of social entity awareness.

This argument holds certain key aspects in common with the early theoretical propositions of Cooley (1902) and Mead (1934). These theorists suggested that, in development, the individual moves beyond an egocentric perspective only by first taking the perspectives of others and thereby viewing the self as a focal object. As the result of taking many different perspectives on the focal self, then, the individual is said to develop a cognitive construction of the "generalized other" that is invoked later when self-reflection occurs without the presence of specific others. In essence, the function attributed to the generalized other by these theorists is the same function ascribed here to the tacit self. When the tacit self constitutes the focal self as a person, the concept of "person" serves to guide the evaluation of the focal self in terms of properties (e.g., fairness) that are relevant to the evaluation of persons in general. Just as the tacit self prescribes the evaluation of focal others in terms of their worth as persons, it employs a "person" template in assessing the properties of the focal self. When manipulations of self-focused attention highlight the uniquely "social" aspects of the person (e.g., the face in the mirror or video monitor, the voice, the fact that one is viewed by others, etc.), it can be expected that self-evaluation of exchange fairness will ensue.

In looking beyond the typical experimental manipulations of self-focus, it seems that there are many instances in which one's status as a social entity could be made salient in even more subtle ways. When one's behavior is known to others, for example, or when one's attitudes are made evident to them, an impetus toward viewing oneself as a responsible human agent could be experienced. In these cases, the direct attention of others toward oneself might not even be necessary to induce focal self awareness; knowledge that others might have occasion to turn their attention and evaluation toward oneself, one's attitudes, or one's behavior could produce tendencies to view the self focally. Knowledge of this kind usually serves as the central manipulation in studies of self-presentation.

2. DETERMINANTS AND CONSEQUENTS OF SELF-PRESENTATION

On encountering specific others or groups, a person's typical reaction is to focalize and evaluate them. But under certain conditions, this usual tendency is set aside and the person turns instead to a focal awareness of self with the specific social entity in a tacit position. This perspective on self would be taken when (a) the specific social entity is perceived as relevant to the well-being of the tacit self; (b) the specific entity's attention is or could be directed toward the self, the self's attitudes, or the self's behavior; (c) the specific social entity is seen as likely to evaluate the self as a person; and (d) self-regulation in accord with the interests of the specific entity could lead to the gratification of the tacit self. When these conditions are met and the person enters this form of awareness, self-evaluation will ensue in accord with dimensions derived from the perceived interests of the tacit social entity.

Now, in many cases of the presentation of self to others, one knows very little about what specific interests the others may have. The "best guess" in these cases would be to evaluate self on the basis of simple "personhood," opting then for a standard of equity. When this happens, there is little reason to differentiate this awareness form from focal self awareness through the tacit self. It is only when the tacit specific other's interests or desires are seen to deviate from a contribution or equity rule that it becomes particularly useful to speak of self-presentation or impression management. With very few exceptions, however, the past literature on these processes has failed to offer experimental subjects any special information about the concerns of those to whom their self-presentations will be made. As a rule, subjects are led to believe that their responses or self-reports in an experiment will either be *public* or *private*. In some studies, this variation has been achieved by giving subjects to understand that their responses would be monitored by someone (public) or not observed by anyone (private). In others, the "bogus pipeline" technique of Jones and Sigall (1971) has been used to accomplish a similar variation; some subjects' responses are simply recorded on a questionnaire (public), whereas others' responses are recorded while their physiological processes are ostensibly being checked by means of a "lie detector" (private). Presumably, the subject in this latter condition is motivated to report private or "true" responses by the possibility that deviations from these will be known by the polygraph operator. With both forms of the public–private manipulation, then, public conditions mean public to the experimenter, and subjects are left to guess what the experimenter's interests might be.

Under these conditions, subjects are presenting themselves to a specific other whose justice preferences are unknown. With this understanding in mind, it is possible to inspect the self-presentation literature with a particular expectation: Subjects in public conditions should adhere more closely to equity—the tacit self system's rule for focal self-evaluation. With measures ranging from self-reported guilt and unhappiness (Rivera & Tedeschi, 1976) to task performance and perceived task difficulty (Morse, Gruzen, & Reis, 1976) to reward allocation preference (Reis & Gruzen, 1976), this is exactly what has been found. Like the focal self awareness induced by a mirror, focal self awareness induced through the tacit awareness of specific others whose justice preferences are unknown leads to greater acceptance of the standard of equity.

It should be noted that the experiment by Reis and Gruzen (1976) included a condition in which subjects' allocations were to be made public to someone other than the experimenter—the group of coworkers to whom the subject was allocating funds. Here, an equality rule was followed. The appearance of this allocation tactic when one is made aware of one's membership in a group signals an important possibility that is considered in detail in the next section.

IV. AWARENESS OF THE GROUP

Because the idea of a group can exist in the minds of individuals, and because a group so conceptualized seems to have properties of human agency resembling those of an individual (Campbell, 1958; Heider, 1958), forms of group awareness can occur. One may be tacitly aware of a group, evaluating its situation in focal awareness with the group's common interest in view; or, one may be focally aware of a group, evaluating it with reference to the self's tacit system. These forms of awareness may be assumed with or without group membership. The groups of which one is aware in these ways need only be assemblies of individuals that are present in one's immediate environment, that are held in memory as a unit, or that are expected to operate as a single entity in the future.

A. Implications of Group Awareness

Since 1902, when Cooley supplied the label of "we-feeling" for the awareness that individuals may have of their group, a variety of theoretical perspectives have arisen that examine the individual's mental representation of groups (e.g., Schutz, 1967; Wilder, 1977, 1978). Paralleling this development, and beginning with the identification of "ethnocentrism" by Sumner (1906), several theories have also suggested that individuals may take different perspectives on groups—largely as a function of whether the individuals are group members or not (Holzner, 1978). The present analysis, guided in part by the formulation of Pennebaker, McElrea, and Skelton (1979), combines these two strains of theory by

suggesting that the individual's perception of a group may be represented in terms of the tacit–focal function.

The implications of this idea can be explored in two domains. First,
there are a number of ways in which the forms of group awareness may
be helpful in conceptualizing an individual's perceptions of what is just
or fair for the group as a unit. Second, because an individual's focal
awareness has only limited capacity (Shallice, 1978) and hence may not
accommodate both a group and its individual members at once, group
awareness has important implications for the individual's perceptions of
what is just within the group. These two sets of implications are taken up
in turn in this section.

1. JUSTICE FOR THE GROUP

Predictions about the influence of group awareness forms on an individual's perceptions of what the group deserves follow in a fairly
straightforward way from an application of the tacit–focal function.
Whether the individual is engaged as group member, or is merely watch-
ing from the outside, an initial requisite is that the group be seen as a
unitary social entity. This first step may follow on perceptions of intermember proximity, similarity, or attraction (Heider, 1958), may accrue
from knowledge of the group's common agency or common fate
(Campbell, 1958; Holzner, 1978), may be produced by the perceptual
salience of the particular grouping (McArthur & Post, 1977), or may
arise from any number of other variables that have the effect of introducing a social categorization (see, e.g., Gerard & Hoyt, 1974; Rabbie &
Horowitz, 1969). Groups comprehended as units may then be held in
either tacit or focal awareness.

Tacit group awareness results in "identification" with the group and
concern for its interests. The group's needs are used as a guide in
evaluating the group's situation, and as noted earlier (Section III. C. 2.),
the tacitly known group could provide standards for the evaluation of
the focal self. More generally, though, it can be argued that this awareness form should produce effects on the individual by operating much as
"reference groups" have been held to operate (see Merton & Kitt, 1950),
orienting the individual toward group goals. Focal group awareness, in
contrast, should lead the individual to conceptualize the group and to
evaluate it in terms of its fairness in exchanges with other entities. The
formation of a group stereotype and the development of prejudice, in this
light, are processes that occur when a group is held in focal awareness
and is seen as having some unfair advantage or disadvantage in exchange.

Concepts of group awareness are also helpful in understanding how attentional processes may guide group perception and behavior. Although in well-defined groups it is probably true that individuals most often hold their own group in tacit awareness and other groups in focal awareness, certain principles of attention could override this tendency. The figure–ground principle of Gestalt psychology (Koffka, 1935), for example, suggests that smaller entities are seen as figural or focal against the ground of larger entities. Smaller groups, therefore, may often be given focal awareness, whereas larger groups are not (see Duval & Siegel, 1978; Wegner & Schaefer, 1978). As a consequence, extreme evaluations of minority groups are more likely to be developed, both by members and nonmembers. Because the majority is seldom lent focal awareness, its adherence to fairness in exchange goes largely unchecked.

2. JUSTICE FOR THE GROUP MEMBER

An important set of predictions about justice within a group becomes apparent on considering the potential conflict between focal group awareness and focal awareness of individuals within the group. When a group member is focally aware of the group as a whole, the limited scope of focal consciousness precludes the possibility that the member will be able to hold self or any other particular member in focal awareness at the same time. This idea is compatible with theories of deindividuation that argue that an awareness of individuals is attenuated by group membership (Diener, 1979; Zimbardo, 1969), and is also consistent with Wilder's (1978) research showing reductions in responsibility attribution to individuals who are members of groups. The notion has been tested most directly, however, in an innovative study by Pennebaker, McElrea, and Skelton (1979). These researchers arranged for small groups of three or four previously unacquainted subjects to be made focally aware of their status as a social entity; each group met facing a large mirror in which all the members could be seen. When these subjects were asked to indicate their personal responsibility for a series of hypothetical events, they accepted less responsibility than did subjects who met in groups without the mirror. Individual subjects asked these questions in mirror and no-mirror conditions, however, replicated the earlier finding of Duval and Wicklund (1973); focal self awareness induced by the mirror increased subjects' acceptance of personal responsibility.

The reduction of personal responsibility felt by group members who are focally group aware may have an especially interesting consequence—a reduction in the concern for equity within the group. Because the focal awareness and evaluation of any individual group member is prevented, an *equality rule* is likely to prevail as the chosen allocation tactic. Such a rule should emerge as the "default option" in this case because it is the only adequate way to solve the problem of resource distribution when differentiation among recipients is impossible. The frequent appearance of equal distribution in cases when individuals anticipate interaction (e.g., Shapiro, 1975), are motivated to achieve group cohesiveness (e.g., Clark & Mills, 1979), or are unconcerned with fostering individual productivity (see Deutsch, 1975) can be explained with reference to group awareness in this way. In each of these circumstances, individual group members are focalizing the group as a unitary entity. This form of awareness places a strict limitation on the extent to which individual group members can be identified, differentiated, and ascribed portions of responsibility for a group product. Focal group awareness, then, acts as an opaque window through which only equality can be seen.

Focal group awareness may also be a *goal* of individuals, and this might affect internal reward allocation as well. Just as a person who has achieved some special success may approach self-focusing stimuli to experience the positive self-evaluation more deeply (Wicklund, 1975), individuals in particularly successful groups might try to maintain focal group awareness. Because any deviation from equality would have the effect of identifying individual members and interfering with focal group awareness, it would be expected that such successful groups would prefer equality quite strongly. Groups that have some failure or negative characteristic to dwell on in focal group awareness, in turn, should be inclined to avoid equality and instead single out individual members through equitable treatment. This analysis adds an interesting footnote to the recently burgeoning literature on equity within close relationships (e.g., Hatfield, Utne, & Traupman, 1979); to wit, when equity is an important issue in a close relationship, the relationship may not be that close after all. The avoidance of focal group awareness signaled by a concern for equity suggests that the group is evaluated negatively by its members.

B. Experimental Demonstrations

In contrast to the ideas of self awareness and other awareness, the concept of group awareness is not traceable to any large body of contemporary research in social psychology. For this reason, and because experiments on group awareness reveal the generality of the present analysis of awareness states in a way that other investigations do not, two experiments involving group awareness and justice by Giuliano and Wegner (1981) are presented in some detail here.

1. GIULIANO AND WEGNER (1981): EXPERIMENT 1

This study was designed as a preliminary test of the idea that focal group awareness produces adherence to an equality rule in allocations that are made within the group. The use of a paradigm similar to that of Pennebaker *et al.* (1979) made a test of the idea that focal self-awareness results in equity feasible as well. Subjects of both sexes were randomly assigned to the cells of a 2 (partner present versus partner absent) × 2 (mirror present versus mirror absent) design. In all cases, subjects were told that they would be working on an individual task for 30 min, that their partner (another subject) would be working on a similar task for 1 hr, and that they would be paid at the end of the session. Subjects completed the 30 min of work under one of the four conditions, and then were taken aside and asked to divide $3 in quarters as payment for themselves and their partners (who ostensibly continued working for the full 1 hr).

Focal self awareness was expected to be aroused in the partner absent–mirror present condition, as this is the usual manipulation of self-focus used in the Duval and Wicklund (1972) tradition. Focal group awareness was anticipated as a result of the partner present–mirror present condition; like the manipulation successfully employed by Pennebaker *et al.* (1979), the room arrangement in this condition allowed each subject to see both self and other in a large mirror placed on a table before them. The partner absent–mirror absent condition served as a comparison group in this design, as the arousal of neither focal self awareness nor focal group awareness was expected for subjects working alone without the mirror. Finally, a partner present–mirror absent condition was included to find out whether partner presence alone would produce effects more like those of self awareness or group awareness.

The amount of the $3 payment the subjects allocated to themselves under these conditions is shown in Table 3.2; it should be noted that a self-allocation of $1 would be an equitable response here, as subjects ostensibly worked for half the time that their partners did. In an analysis of variance, neither main effect was significant. Partner presence and mirror presence did not have the simple additive effect on adherence to equity that might be predicted on the basis of an "increased strength of self-focus" hypothesis. Instead, the interaction of partner presence and mirror presence was significant ($p < .02$); although the relevant individual comparisons did not all reach standard levels of significance, the discernible trend is for greater adherence to equity with either mirror *or* partner present. When both are present, and subjects can become focally aware of the dyad, greater self-allocation is the result.

Table 3.2
Self-Allocation as a Function of Mirror Presence and
Partner Presence[a]

	Mirror presence	
Partner presence	Absent	Present
Absent	1.48 (10)	1.23 (11)
Present	1.07 (10)	1.36 (11)

Source: From Giuliano and Wegner (1981). Experiment 1.
[a] Main entries represent means in dollars; parenthetical entries indicate number of subjects in group.

The increase in self-allocation under focal group awareness conditions in this study might be interpreted in two ways. An explanation that might well be proposed by deindividuation theorists such as Diener (1979) or Zimbardo (1969) would be that the awareness of one's group membership acts as a simple releaser of self-interest. The present analysis, in contrast, suggests a different alternative. In this view, the enhanced self-allocation in the comparison condition (partner absent–mirror absent) may indeed reflect self-interest, as it is likely that tacit self-awareness was predominant for subjects under such circumstances. But the higher self-allocation in the focal group awareness condition is interpretable as a movement toward equality. A decision on the relative validity of these interpretations cannot be made given the arrangements of this study. So, although these results signal the importance of a distinction between self-focus and group-focus, they are not conclusive regarding the differential impact of these states on distribution tactics.

2. GIULIANO AND WEGNER (1981): EXPERIMENT 2

This study was designed to provide more complete information on the justice preferences of individuals in states of focal self awareness and focal group awareness, and also to explore the operation of some new manipulations of these states. The basic paradigm was straightforward: After one subject had worked alone for 25 min, he or she was joined at a table by another subject; the two proceeded to work individually for 25 min on questionnaires designed to assess their levels of focal self awareness and focal group awareness, and then were given individual forms on which they were to indicate how the payment of $4.20 for the two of them should be divided. Forty-seven subjects of both sexes participated under these conditions, several of whom were tested with confederate partners when their subject partners failed to arrive. Of the total sample, 24 participated in the low-input condition (25 min) and 23 participated in the high input condition (50 min).

Two questionnaires were used to assess subjects' social awareness in the experimental setting. One of these consisted of five responsibility attribution items modeled after those of Duval and Wicklund (1973); in contrast to the Duval and Wicklund procedure, however, which called for the subject to consider a hypothetical incident (e.g., an auto accident) and to assign a percentage of responsibility to self versus other, the present items allowed subjects to assign responsibility to self, other or *group* (both self and other). It was expected that self-attribution of responsibility would serve as a measure of focal self awareness, whereas attribution of responsibility to the group would tap focal group awareness. Self-responsibility and group-responsibility indices were computed, therefore, as the sums of a subject's responses of each type for the five items.

The second questionnaire was developed as an extension of the work of Davis and Brock (1975); these researchers found that mirror subjects asked to guess pronouns in foreign language prose more often guessed *I* and *me* than did no-mirror subjects. For the present measure, then, subjects were given a set of 30 English sentences with a pronoun missing in each (cf. Wegner & Giuliano, 1980). A set of three plausible alternative pronouns was provided for each blank, one a first person singular (I, me, my), one a first person plural (we, us, our), and one a third person singular or plural (he, she, they, him, her, them, his, hers, theirs). When subjects chose pronouns under the instruction that the questionnaire was planned to assess "ambiguity and redundancy in language," it was expected that the number of first person singular choices and the number of first person plural choices would reflect, respectively, the predominance of thoughts about self and about group in focal awareness. Thus, self-pronoun and group-pronoun indices were computed as the sum of these respective choices for each subject.

Correlations among the four indices of self-awareness and group awareness are shown in Table 3.3. Because these indices show a reasonable level of reliability and convergent and divergent validity for measures in this initial stage of development, self-total and group-total indices were formed by summation of the standardized responsibility and pronoun measures for each subject; correlations with these measures are also shown in Table 3.3. Unfortunately, because self versus group choices were ipsative in both the pronoun and attribution measures, it is not clear whether the actual relationship between focal self awareness and focal group awareness is the strongly negative one suggested by the

Table 3.3

Correlations among Awareness Measures[a]

Awareness measure	1	2	3	4	5
1. Self-pronoun	(.64)				
2. Self-responsibility	.17	(.55)			
3. Self-total	.76	.77			
4. Group-pronoun	−.69	−.18	−.57	(.60)	
5. Group-responsibility	−.15	−.80	−.62	.16	(.68)
6. Group-total	−.56	−.63	−.78	.77	.76

Source: From Giuliano and Wegner (1981), Experiment 2.

[a] Parenthetical entries in diagonal are interitem reliabilities; $N = 47$.

−.78 correlation between the totals. This possibility should be kept in mind, however, in interpreting the subsequent analyses.

Table 3.4 displays mean self-allocations for the high and low input conditions when subjects are partitioned in two different ways. Analysis of variance on the upper half of the table revealed a significant interaction of focal self awareness (as assessed by a median split of subjects on the self-total index) and input ($p < .02$). The significant simple main effect of input for subjects high in focal self awareness ($p < .05$) indicates that this awareness form sensitized subjects to the input difference; greater reward was allocated to self when self made a larger contribution of time. For subjects low in focal self awareness, the simple main effect of input was not significant (or in the direction of equity).

When subjects are partitioned according to input and focal group

Table 3.4

Self-Allocation as a Function of Awareness Indices and Input[a]

	Input	
Awareness score	High	Low
	Self-total index of focal self awareness	
High	2.28 (10)	1.83 (13)
Low	2.18 (13)	2.29 (11)
	Group-total index of focal group awareness	
High	2.13 (14)	2.29 (9)
Low	2.37 (9)	1.89 (15)

Source: From Giuliano and Wegner (1981), Experiment 2.

[a] Main entries represent means in dollars; parenthetical entries indicate number of subjects in group.

awareness as shown in the lower half of Table 3.4, analysis of variance also indicated a significant interaction ($p < .01$). Here, a significant simple main effect for input exists only for subjects low in group awareness ($p < .01$); these subjects adhere to equity, whereas those high in group awareness show only a small difference between input conditions in a direction opposite that of equity. This striking disparity in the effects of group awareness versus self-awareness on allocation decisions is reflected as well in subjects' responses to a postexperimental questionnaire. Ratings of the importance of one's own time worked and partner's time worked to the allocation decision were positively correlated with focal self awareness measures but negatively correlated with focal group awareness measures.

The summary implications of these findings are twofold. First, as suggested by the justice propositions derived from the tacit–focal function, and as previously demonstrated in several other studies (see Section III. B. 2), focal self awareness leads individuals to allocate resources in line with the dictates of equity. This connection appeared in both of the present experiments, and so substantiates the tacit–focal analysis of self awareness phenomena. The second general conclusion to be drawn from this research is that focal group awareness leads individuals to distribute rewards equally within the group. Whereas the first experiment showed that focal group awareness releases individuals from the constraints of equity to pursue another allocation strategy, the second experiment revealed that the strategy of choice in focal group awareness is equality. So, even though equality is not explicitly represented as an allocation option in the basic justice derivations from the tacit–focal function, its presence can be interpreted in terms of social entity awareness nonetheless. By interfering with the individual's appreciation of separate group members' inputs, focal group awareness serves as an antecedent of equal distribution within the group.

V. CONCLUSIONS

When any fairly compact explanatory system is imposed on a preexisting body of knowledge, there is bound to be some strain. The present analysis, in showing how several major patterns of distributive justice (self-interest, equity, equality, and need) can be counted as consequences of a single principle (the tacit–focal function), may be particularly strenuous in this regard. As a way of easing this strain, it is helpful to conduct two quite different concluding exercises. First, a workable understanding of this system can be promoted by means of a general example. Second, an appreciation of the future directions of this line of inquiry can be achieved through the consideration of emerging questions.

A. A General Example

Suppose that three diners conclude their meal and are given a single check by the waiter. Diner A has partaken of a modest meal, Diner B has enjoyed a feast complete with several drinks served in coconuts with little umbrellas, and Diner C has contented himself with a cup of tea and a bun. Suppose further that it is incumbent on Diner A to assemble the payment for the meal. Now, if for whatever situational or dispositional reasons, Diner A were to assume each of the six major awareness forms in turn, what method of payment might he propose in each case?

In tacit self awareness, Diner A would be cheap. He might be inclined to wander away from the table, to wait for B or C to pick up the tab, or at best, to round his contribution down as far as possible. Given focal self awareness, in contrast, Diner A would be equitable. To be sure, he would insist on paying his share of the check exactly. He might also prefer equity in payments from B and C, asking B to contribute more to pay for the more substantial meal, and C to give less for his snack.[4] Given tacit other awareness of Diner B, A, as allocator, should be responsive to B's remarkable need for food, perhaps then "treating" him to the meal; similarly, tacit other awareness of Diner C could lead to a "treat" for him. Focal other awareness of B might make A particularly concerned with squeezing the correct large payment from him, while focal awareness of C should move A to make sure that C pays his correct small portion. Note that in these cases, A's tacit or focal awareness of a particular other has no necessary implication for justice among those of whom A is unaware.

The impact of the forms of group awareness on bill settling in this dining party would be determined by which particular diners comprised the group of which A was aware. Tacit group awareness of the entire group might lead A to suggest that they all skip the bill or at least stiff the waiter. Focal group awareness of the entire group, in turn, would lead A to call for equal payments from himself, B, and C; in addition, he might be concerned about the overall equity of the exchange between his

[4]This prediction is not firm, however. Although the justice propositions do suggest that equity should be followed in all transactions during focal self awareness, and although the research reviewed indicates that this is clearly the case in constant-sum allocations between self and one other person, studies have yet to be conducted showing how self-focus affects distribution among several others.

group and the restaurant. Should A become tacitly aware of a specific subgroup—say, B and C, or himself and C—then the needs of this subgroup would be emphasized at the expense of the other diner and perhaps the restaurant. And, if A were to become focally aware of such a subgroup, then the amount owed in common by the subgroup would be of prime interest.

This set of six awareness forms, then, certainly allows for a complex array of perceptions of what a just response to the dinner check might be. And, when it is recognized that several combining forms (e.g., A's tacit awareness of B during focal awareness of A and C) have their own additional implications for justice perceptions and behaviors, it becomes evident that there exists in this system sufficient complexity to account for even the most dazzling and apparently chaotic of natural allocation configurations. That this complexity can be reduced to the six elemental forms of social awareness, which in turn can be traced to a single cognitive rule about tacit and focal awareness, suggests that the study of justice as a system of social cognition may be quite useful.

B. Emerging Questions

In looking past this analysis to the aspects of social awareness that may be of future interest, several themes become prominent. At the outset, of course, it seems necessary to gather evidence on several of the basic connections between awareness forms and justice. In this chapter, a number of these connections were made on the basis of reinterpretations of research conducted by other investigators for other purposes, and some of the connections were suggested as theoretical conjectures alone. In service of plugging these holes, it seems that a more adequate and integrated understanding of techniques whereby awareness forms can be manipulated and measured is a necessary condition.

Another theme arising from this framework involves the motivational properties of the different awareness forms. It can be argued, for example, that both tacit and focal self awareness have a strong impact on the behavior of the individual; this is the message conveyed by Duval and Wicklund (1972). But to what degree do other awareness forms share this immediacy and activation potential? It seems that the forms of group awareness, for example, might be particularly likely to involve the individual in the same way that the forms of self awareness do—when the individual is a member of the group. Unlike other awareness, or the group awareness that occurs when one is not a member, awareness of one's own group would seem to be more personally and behaviorally relevant. Instead of detachment and cool calculation, this awareness form might engender affective and motivational reactions like those engaged by the awareness of self. The immediacy of awareness forms to behavior production systems, then, is another important area for study.

A third theme embedded in this analysis is the problem of meta-awareness. Is it possible for individuals regularly to know or to control their own states of social entity awareness? Although the successful use of simple instructional sets to vary subjects' forms of other awareness suggests that meta-awareness of these states is child's play, the finding that individuals cannot usually report their own level of self awareness (Wicklund, 1975) indicates otherwise. Because such meta-awareness could prove to be an essential tool in the enterprise of moral education, questions such as these need to be raised and answered.

A final theme of interest is the question of the transformation of knowledge structures that occurs when these structures are moved between tacit and focal awareness. An observer may judge a person to be "greedy," for example, when the person is in focal awareness; when the observer later becomes tacitly aware of the person (for whatever reason), does the earlier attribution of greed lead the observer to become extraordinarily attuned to the satisfaction of the person's needs? In a larger context, this question is one of the formation and interactive development of the tacit system and focal consciousness. Satisfactory answers to such questions would do much to further the understanding of the role of cognition in justice and social life.

ACKNOWLEDGMENTS

Many of the ideas reported here originated in discussions with Robin R. Vallacher; his special contribution to this chapter is gratefully acknowledged. Appreciation is also extended to Ruth Lytle and Sally Ober for serving as experimenters in the research reported in Section IV. B. 2., and to Toni Giuliano, Michael Martin, James Pennebaker, Jane Sell, Robin Vallacher, and Robert Wicklund for their helpful comments on an earlier draft of the chapter.

REFERENCES

Aderman, D., & Berkowitz, L. Observational set, empathy, and helping. *Journal of Personality and Social Psychology*, 1970, *14*, 141–148.

Aderman, D., Brehm, S. S., & Katz, L. B. Empathic observation of an innocent victim: The just world revisited. *Journal of Personality and Social Psychology*, 1974, *29*, 342–347.

Alexander, N. C., & Knight, G. W. Situated identities and social psychological experimentation. *Sociometry*, 1971, *34*, 65–82.

Archer, R. L., Foushee, H. C., Davis, M. H., & Aderman, D. Emotional empathy in a courtroom simulation: A person–situation interaction. *Journal of Applied Social Psychology*, 1979, *9*, 275–291.

Arkin, R. M. Self-presentation. In D. M. Wegner & R. R. Vallacher (Eds.), *The self in social psychology*. New York: Oxford, 1980.

Austin, W., Walster, E., & Utne, M. K. Equity and the law: The effects of a harm doer's "suffering in the act" on liking and assigned punishment. In L. Berkowitz & E. Walster (Eds.), *Advances in experimental social psychology* (Vol. 9). New York: Academic Press, 1976.

Bem, D. Self-perception: An alternative interpretation of cognitive dissonance phenomena. *Psychological Review*, 1967, *74*, 183–200.

Bem, D. Self-perception theory. In L. Berkowitz (Ed.), *Advances in experimental social psychology* (Vol. 6). New York: Academic Press, 1972.

Berkowitz, L. Social norms, feelings, and other factors affecting helping and altruism. In L. Berkowitz (Ed.), *Advances in experimental social psychology* (Vol. 6). New York: Academic Press, 1972.

Bower, G. H. Experiments on story comprehension and recall. *Discourse Processes*, 1978, *1*, 211–231.

Campbell, D. T. Common fate, similarity, and other indices of the status of aggregates of persons as social entities. *Behavioral Science*, 1958, *3*, 14–25.

Carver, C. S. A cybernetic model of self-attention processes. *Journal of Personality and Social Psychology*, 1979, *37*, 1251–1281.

Carver, C. S., & Scheier, M. F. Self-focusing effects of dispositional self-consciousness, mirror presence, and audience presence. *Journal of Personality and Social Psychology*, 1978, *36*, 324–332.

Clark, M. S., & Mills, J. Interpersonal attraction in exchange and communal relationships. *Journal of Personality and Social Psychology*, 1979, *37*, 12–24.

Cooley, C. H. *Human nature and the social order*. New York: Scribner, 1902.

Crano, W. D., & Messé, L. A. When does dissonance fail? The time dimension in attitude measurement. *Journal of Personality*, 1970, *38*, 493–508.

Davis, D., & Brock, T. C. Use of first person pronouns as a function of increased objective self-awareness and prior feedback. *Journal of Experimental Social Psychology*, 1975, *11*, 381–388.

Deutsch, M. Equity, equality, and need: What determines which value will be used as the basis of distributive justice? *Journal of Social Issues*, 1975, *31*, 137–149.

Diener, E. Deindividuation: The absence of self-awareness and self-regulation in group members. In P. Paulus (Ed.), *The psychology of group influence*. Hillsdale, N.J.: Erlbaum, 1979.

Duval, S., Duval, V. H., & Neely, R. Self-focus, felt responsibility, and helping behavior. *Journal of Personality and Social Psychology*, 1979, *37*, 1769–1778.

Duval, S., & Hensley, V. Extensions of objective self-awareness theory: The focus of attention–causal attribution hypothesis. In J. H. Harvey, W. J. Ickes, & R. F. Kidd (Eds.), *New directions in attribution research* (Vol. 1). Hillsdale, N.J.: Erlbaum, 1976.

Duval, S., & Siegel, K. *Some determinants of objective self-awareness: Quantitative novelty*. Paper presented at the meeting of the American Psychological Association, Toronto, September, 1978.

Duval, S., & Wicklund, R. A. *A theory of objective self-awareness*. New York: Academic Press, 1972.

Duval, S., & Wicklund, R. A. Effects of objective self awareness on the attribution of causality. *Journal of Experimental Social Psychology*, 1973, *9*, 17–31.

Feinberg, J. *Doing and deserving*. Princeton, N.J.: Princeton University Press, 1970.

Fenigstein, A., Scheier, M. F., & Buss, A. Public and private self-consciousness: Assessment and theory. *Journal of Consulting and Clinical Psychology*, 1975, *43*, 522–527.

Festinger, L., & Carlsmith, J. M. Cognitive consequences of forced compliance. *Journal of Abnormal and Social Psychology*, 1959, *58*, 203–210.

Flavell, J. H., Botkin, P., Fry, C., Wright, J., & Jarvis, P. *The development of role-taking and communication skills in children.* New York: Wiley, 1968.

Flavell, J. H., & Wellman, H. M. Metamemory. In R. V. Kail & J. W. Hagen (Eds.), *Perspectives on the development of memory and cognition.* Hillsdale, N.J.: Erlbaum, 1977.

Folger, R., Rosenfield, D., & Hays, R. Equity and intrinsic motivation: The role of choice. *Journal of Personality and Social Psychology*, 1978, *36*, 557–564.

Franks, J. J. Toward understanding understanding. In W. B. Weimer & D. S. Palermo (Eds.), *Cognition and the symbolic processes.* Hillsdale, N.J.: Erlbaum, 1974.

Gallup, G., Jr. Self-recognition in primates: A comparative approach to the bidirectional properties of consciousness. *American Psychologist*, 1977, *32*, 329–338.

Gerard, H. B., & Hoyt, M. F. Distinctiveness of social categorization and attitude toward ingroup members. *Journal of Personality and Social Psychology*, 1974, *29*, 836–842.

Gibbons, F. X., & Wicklund, R. A. Selective exposure to self. *Journal of Research in Personality*, 1976, *10*, 98–106.

Gibbons, F. X., Wicklund, R. A., Karylowski, I., Rosenfield, D., & Chase, T. C. *Altruistic responses to self-focused attention.* Unpublished manuscript, University of Texas at Austin, 1978.

Giuliano, T., & Wegner, D. M. Justice and social awareness. Presented at symposium: *Justice as a pervasive theme in social behavior.* American Psychological Association, Los Angeles, August, 1981.

Gould, R., & Sigall, H. The effects of empathy on outcome and attribution: An examination of the divergent perspectives hypothesis. *Journal of Experimental Social Psychology*, 1977, *13*, 480–491.

Gouldner, A. The norm of reciprocity: A preliminary statement. *American Sociological Review*, 1960, *25*, 161–178.

Greenberg, J. Attentional focus and locus of performance causality as determinants of equity behavior. *Journal of Personality and Social Psychology*, 1980, *38*, 579–585.

Gunzburger, D. W., Wegner, D. M., & Anooshian, L. Moral judgment and distributive justice. *Human Development*, 1977, *20*, 160–170.

Hampshire, S. *Thought and action.* New York: Viking, 1960.

Hatfield, E., Utne, M. K., & Traupman, J. Equity theory and intimate relationships. In R. L. Burgess & T. L. Huston (Eds.), *Social exchange in developing relationships.* New York: Academic Press, 1979.

Heider, F. Social perception and phenomenal causality. *Psychological Review*, 1944, *51*, 358–374.

Heider, F. *The psychology of interpersonal relations.* New York: Wiley, 1958.

Hoffman, M. L. Empathy, role taking, guilt, and the development of altruistic motives. In T. Lickona (Ed.), *Moral development and behavior.* New York: Holt, 1976.

Holzner, B. The construction of social actors: An essay on social identities. In T. Luckmann (Ed.), *Phenomenology and sociology.* New York: Penguin, 1978.

Hull, J. S., & Levy, A. S. The organizational functions of self: An alternative to the Duval and Wicklund model of self-awareness. *Journal of Personality and Social Psychology*, 1979, *37*, 756–768.

Jones, E. E., & Davis, K. E. From acts to dispositions: The attribution process in person perception. In L. Berkowitz (Ed.), *Advances in experimental social psychology* (Vol. 2). New York: Academic Press, 1965.

Jones, E. E., & Sigall, H. The bogus pipeline: A new paradigm for measuring attitude and affect. *Psychological Bulletin,* 1971, *76,* 245–254.

Jones, E. E., & Thibaut, J. W. Interaction goals as bases of inference in interpersonal perception. In R. Tagiuri & L. Petrullo (Eds.), *Person perception and interpersonal behavior.* Stanford, Calif.: Stanford University Press, 1958.

Kelley, H. H. Attribution in social psychology. *Nebraska Symposium on Motivation,* 1967, *15,* 192–238.

Kelly, G. A. *The psychology of personal constructs.* New York: Norton, 1955.

Kimble, G. A., & Perlmuter, L. C. The problem of volition. *Psychological Review,* 1970, *77,* 361–384.

Koffka, K. *Principles of gestalt psychology.* New York: Harcourt Brace, 1935.

Kohlberg, L. Stage and sequence: The cognitive–developmental approach to socialization. In D. Goslin (Ed.), *Handbook of socialization theory and research.* Chicago: Rand McNally, 1969.

Krebs, D. Empathy and altruism. *Journal of Personality and Social Psychology,* 1975, *32,* 1134–1146.

Kruglanski, A. W. The endogenous–exogenous partition in attribution theory. *Psychological Review,* 1975, *82,* 387–406.

Langer, E. J. Rethinking the role of thought in social interaction. In J. H. Harvey, W. J. Ickes, & R. F. Kidd (Eds.), *New directions in attribution research* (Vol. 2). Hillsdale, N.J.: Erlbaum, 1978.

Lepper, M. R., & Greene, D. (Eds.). *The hidden costs of reward.* Hillsdale, N.J.: Erlbaum, 1978.

Lerner, M. J. Observer's evaluation of a victim: Justice, guilt, and veridical perception. *Journal of Personality and Social Psychology,* 1971, *20,* 127–135.

Lerner, M. J. The justice motive in social behavior: An introduction. *Journal of Social Issues,* 1975, *31,* 1–20.

Lerner, M. J., & Miller, D. T. Just world research and the attribution process: Looking back and ahead. *Psychological Bulletin,* 1978, *85,* 1030–1051.

Lerner, M. J., Miller, D. T., & Holmes, J. G. Deserving and the emergence of forms of justice. In L. Berkowitz & E. Walster (Eds.), *Advances in experimental social psychology* (Vol. 9). New York: Academic Press, 1976.

Lerner, M. J., & Simmons, C. H. Observer's reaction to the "innocent victim": Compassion or rejection? *Journal of Personality and Social Psychology,* 1966, *4,* 203–210.

Leventhal, G. S. *Fairness in social relationships.* Morristown, N.J.: General Learning Press, 1976.

Lewis, M., & Brooks-Gunn, J. *Social cognition and the acquisition of self.* New York: Plenum, 1979.

McArthur, L. Z., & Post, D. L. Figural emphasis in person perception. *Journal of Experimental Social Psychology,* 1977, *13,* 520–535.

Mead, G. H. *Mind, self, and society.* Chicago: University of Chicago Press, 1934.

Merton, R. K., & Kitt, A. S. Contributions to the theory of reference group behavior. In R. K. Merton & P. F. Lazarsfeld (Eds.), *Studies in the scope and method of "The American Soldier."* Glencoe, Ill.: Free Press, 1950.

Minsky, M. A framework for representing knowledge. In P. H. Winston (Ed.), *The psychology of computer vision.* New York: McGraw-Hill, 1975.

Morse, S. J., Gruzen, J., & Reis, H. T. The nature of equity restoration: Some approval-seeking considerations. *Journal of Experimental Social Psychology,* 1976, *12,* 1–8.

Neisser, U. *Cognition and reality.* San Francisco: Freeman, 1976.

Newtson, D. Foundations of attribution: The perception of ongoing behavior. In J. H.

Harvey, W. J. Ickes, & R. F. Kidd (Eds.), *New directions in attribution research* (Vol. 1). Hillsdale, N.J.: Erlbaum, 1976.

Pennebaker, J. W., McElrea, C. E., & Skelton, J. A. Levels of selfhood: From me to us. Presented at symposium: *The self in social psychology.* American Psychological Association, New York, September, 1979.

Pennebaker, J. W., & Skelton, J. A. Psychological parameters of physical symptoms. *Personality and Social Psychology Bulletin,* 1978, *4,* 524–530.

Pettigrew, T. Social evaluation theory: Convergences and applications. *Nebraska Symposium on Motivation,* 1967, *15,* 241–311.

Pichert, J. W., & Anderson, R. C. Taking different perspectives on a story. *Journal of Educational Psychology,* 1977, *69,* 309–315.

Polanyi, M. *The tacit dimension.* Garden City, N.Y.: Doubleday, 1966.

Polanyi, M. *Knowing and being.* Chicago, Ill.: University of Chicago Press, 1969.

Rabbie, J. M., & Horowitz, M. Arousal of ingroup–outgroup bias by a chance win or loss. *Journal of Personality and Social Psychology,* 1969, *13,* 269–277.

Regan, D. T., & Totten, J. Empathy and attribution: Turning observers into actors. *Journal of Personality and Social Psychology,* 1975, *32,* 850–856.

Reis, H. T. Self-presentations of just social exchange. Presented at symposium: *Meaning of self-presentation in social interaction.* American Psychological Association, Toronto, August, 1978.

Reis, H. T., & Gruzen, J. On mediating equity, equality, and self-interest: The role of self-presentation in social exchange. *Journal of Experimental Social Psychology,* 1976, *12,* 487–503.

Rivera, A. N., & Tedeschi, J. T. Public versus private reactions to positive inequity. *Journal of Personality and Social Psychology,* 1976, *34,* 895–900.

Rosenberg, M. J. When dissonance fails: On eliminating evaluation apprehension from attitude measurement. *Journal of Personality and Social Psychology,* 1965, *1,* 28–42.

Ross, L., Greene, D., & House, P. The "false consensus effect": An egocentric bias in social perception and attribution processes. *Journal of Experimental Social Psychology,* 1977, *13,* 279–301.

Scheier, M. F., & Carver, C. S. Self-focused attention and the experience of emotion: Attraction, repulsion, elation, and depression. *Journal of Personality and Social Psychology,* 1977, *35,* 624–636.

Scheier, M. F., Fenigstein, A., & Buss, A. Self-awareness and physical aggression. *Journal of Experimental Social Psychology,* 1974, *10,* 264–273.

Schutz, A. [*The phenomenology of the social world*]. Evanston, Ill.: Northwestern University Press, 1967 (Originally published 1932).

Selman, R. L. Toward a structural analysis of developing interpersonal relations concepts. In A. D. Pick (Ed.), *Minnesota symposium on child psychology* (Vol. 10). Minneapolis: University of Minnesota Press, 1976.

Selman, R. L., & Damon, W. The necessity (but insufficiency) of social perspective taking for conceptions of justice at three early levels. In D. J. Depalma & J. M. Foley (Eds.), *Moral development: Current theory and research.* Hillsdale, N.J.: Erlbaum, 1975.

Shallice, T. The dominant action system: An information-processing approach to consciousness. In K. S. Pope & J. L. Singer (Eds.), *The stream of consciousness.* New York: Plenum, 1978.

Shapiro, E. G. Effects of expectations of future interaction on reward allocations in dyads: Equity or equality. *Journal of Personality and Social Psychology,* 1975, *31,* 873–880.

Storms, M. D. Videotape and the attribution process: Reversing actors' and observers' points of view. *Journal of Personality and Social Psychology,* 1973, *27,* 165–175.

116   DANIEL M. WEGNER

Stotland, E. Exploratory studies of empathy. In L. Berkowitz (Ed.), *Advances in experimental social psychology* (Vol. 4). New York: Academic Press, 1969.

Sumner, W. C. *Folkways.* Boston: Ginn, 1906.

Taylor, S. E. & Crocker, J. Schematic bases of social information processing. In E. T. Higgins, C. P. Herman, & M. P. Zanna (Eds.), *Social cognition: The Ontario Symposium* (Vol. 1). Hillsdale, N.J.: Erlbaum, 1981.

Taylor, S. E., & Fiske, S. T. Point of view and perceptions of causality. *Journal of Personality and Social Psychology,* 1975, *32,* 439–445.

Taylor, S. E., & Fiske, S. T. Salience, attention, and attribution: Top of the head phenomena. In L. Berkowitz (Ed.), *Advances in experimental social psychology* (Vol. 11). New York: Academic Press, 1978.

Tedeschi, J. T., & Linskold, S. *Social psychology: Interdependence, interaction, and influence.* New York: Wiley, 1976.

Tesser, A. Self-generated attitude change. In L. Berkowitz (Ed.), *Advances in experimental social psychology* (Vol. 11). New York: Academic Press, 1978.

Turvey, M. T. Constructive theory, perceptual systems, and tacit knowledge. In W. B. Weimer & D. S. Palermo (Eds.), *Cognition and the symbolic processes.* Hillsdale, N.J.: Erlbaum, 1974.

Vallacher, R. R. Objective self-awareness and the perception of others. *Personality and Social Psychology Bulletin,* 1978, *4,* 63–67.

Vallacher, R. R., Wegner, D. M., & Hoine, H. A postscript on application. In D. M. Wegner & R. R. Vallacher (Eds.), *The self in social psychology.* New York: Oxford, 1980.

Walster, E., Berscheid, E., & Walster, G. W. New directions in equity research. *Journal of Personality and Social Psychology,* 1973, *25,* 151–176.

Wegner, D. M. Attribute generality: The development and articulation of attributes in person perception. *Journal of Research in Personality,* 1977, *11,* 329–339.

Wegner, D. M. The self in prosocial action. In D. M. Wegner & R. R. Vallacher (Eds.), *The self in social psychology.* New York: Oxford, 1980.

Wegner, D. M., & Finstuen, K. Observers' focus of attention in the simulation of self-perception. *Journal of Personality and Social Psychology,* 1977, *35,* 56–62.

Wegner, D. M., & Giuliano, T. Arousal-induced attention to self. *Journal of Personality and Social Psychology,* 1980, *38,* 719–726.

Wegner, D. M., & Giuliano, T. The forms of social awareness. In W. J. Ickes & E. S. Knowles (Eds.), *Personality, roles, and social behavior.* New York: Springer-Verlag New York, 1982.

Wegner, D. M., & Schaefer, D. The concentration of responsibility: An objective self awareness analysis of group size effects in helping situations. *Journal of Personality and Social Psychology,* 1978, *36,* 147–155.

Wegner, D. M., & Vallacher, R. R. *Implicit psychology.* New York: Oxford, 1977.

Wicklund, R. A. Objective self awareness. In L. Berkowitz (Ed.), *Advances in experimental social psychology* (Vol. 8). New York: Academic Press, 1975.

Wicklund, R. A. The influence of self on human behavior. *American Scientist,* 1979, *67,* 187–193. (a)

Wicklund, R. A. Group contact and self-focused attention. In P. Paulus (Ed.), *The psychology of group influence.* Hillsdale, N.J.: Erlbaum, 1979. (b)

Wicklund, R. A., & Brehm, J. *Perspectives on cognitive dissonance.* Hillsdale, N.J.: Erlbaum, 1976.

Wicklund, R. A., & Duval, S. Opinion change and performance facilitation as a result of objective self awareness. *Journal of Experimental Social Psychology,* 1971, *7,* 319–342.

Wicklund, R. A., & Frey, D. Self awareness theory: When the self makes a difference. In

D. M. Wegner & R. R. Vallacher (Eds.), *The self in social psychology*. New York: Oxford 1980.

Wilder, D. A. Perception of groups, size of opposition, and social influence. *Journal of Experimental Social Psychology*, 1977, *13*, 253–268.

Wilder, D. A. Perceiving persons as a group: Effects on attributions of causality and beliefs. *Social Psychology*, 1978, *41*, 13–23.

Wolfson, M. R., & Salancik, G. R. Observer orientation and actor–observer differences in attributions for failure. *Journal of Experimental Social Psychology*, 1977, *13*, 441–451.

Zimbardo, P. G. The human choice: Individuation, reason, and order versus deindividuation, impulse, and chaos. *Nebraska Symposium on Motivation*, 1969, *17*, 237–307.

chapter 4

Perceiving Justice: An Attributional Perspective

RONALD L. COHEN

I. INTRODUCTION

Perceptions of justice are based fundamentally on attributions of cause and responsibility. Whether one focuses on the person on the street, the subject in a research setting, the social theorist, or the philosopher, justice perceptions are grounded in these attributions. Their crucial importance can be observed by noting the following: (1) differences between individuals' perceptions of justice are based on differing attributions of cause and responsibility (attributional conflicts); (2) an individual's perception of justice will change as a consequence of changes in these attributions; and (3) individuals asked to describe and explain their justice perceptions search for attributional information and base their explanations on appeals to such information.

Homans (1976) states that for observers to agree on a perception of justice, they must agree on three things: the rule of justice, the legitimacy of the kinds of recipient characteristics and receipts to be taken into account in applying that rule, and the assessments of those characteristics and receipts.[1] He also suggests that disagreements are less likely to arise over the rule than over the legitimacy and assessment issues. My

---

[1]Homans (1976) focuses on distributive justice and argues that there is only one relevant rule, proportionality between characteristics and outcomes. There is serious disagreement over both the interpretation of proportionality (see Harris, 1976; Moschetti, 1979) and the status of other conceivable rules of justice, such as equality and needs (e.g., Deutsch, 1975; Leventhal, 1976b; Sampson, 1969, 1975; Walster, Walster, & Berscheid, 1978).

119

argument in this chapter is that individuals must also agree on the cause and responsibility to be assigned for the characteristics of recipient units. One might see this as an attempt to integrate Homans's emphasis on legitimacy and assessment, or in terms of Adams's (1965) concept of the *relevance* of inputs (see also Kayser & Lamm, 1980a). For individuals' perceptions of justice to agree, they must agree on causal and responsibility attributions. Conversely, the source of much disagreement about, and conflict over, issues of justice resides in differing attributions.

Social psychological work on justice has been hampered by many conceptual difficulties, two of which will be addressed here by reference to work on attribution. Both difficulties center on a specification of the boundaries of a relevant recipient class for issues of justice (cf. Eckhoff, 1974), one in terms of the size of the class, the other, its composition. Thus, work on justice has not systematically distinguished situations in which there is only one recipient from those in which there are more than one. A great deal of research on justice suggests, however, that justice is perceived differently in these two situations (cf. Cohen, 1979). The attribution literature points to differences in the types of attribution principles applied to situations involving single and multiple observations. This work may be crucial for an understanding of how justice perceptions vary as a consequence of the size of the recipient class. In addition, work on justice has not focused sufficient attention on distinguishing situations in which the perceiver is a direct recipient of outcomes from those in which he or she is merely a judge or observer. Attributional work on divergent perspectives and on cognitive and motivational biases can contribute to an understanding of the role the perceiver's direct "stake" or "interest" as a recipient has in his or her perceptions of justice.

My strategy in this chapter is as follows. Because of my claim that attributions of cause and attributions of responsibility are crucial, I will present a brief discussion of previous work on each and the relationship between the two. That discussion will be used as the basis for a focus on three different areas in which attributions may be crucial for an understanding of justice.

II. ATTRIBUTIONS OF CAUSE AND RESPONSIBILITY

A. Introduction

The crucial importance of causal and responsibility attributions for perceptions of justice can be demonstrated in three ways. First, by examining recent discussions of responsibility attribution, a conceptual link can be demonstrated between responsibility and justice. Second, social psychological statements on justice often include assumptions, usually implicit, about individuals' attributions of responsibility and cause. Finally, two recent and prominent philosophies of justice (Nozick, 1974; Rawls, 1971) try to make clear and explicit what a comprehensive perception of justice involves. These statements appear to involve beliefs about the causes of, and responsibilities for, allotments and human characteristics relevant to those allotments. I turn now to an examination of each.

B. Basic Issues

Responsibility refers most generally to "liability for sanctions based on a rule [Hamilton, 1978, p. 316]." Heider's (1958) initial discussion of responsibility attribution does not clearly define responsibility, but it does suggest a focus both on liability for blame or punishment, and on eligibility for praise and reward. Heider distinguishes five different levels of responsibility (association, commission, foreseeability, intention, and justification) that vary in the perceived balance of personal and environmental forces (1958, pp. 113–114). Attributions of personal responsibility to an actor increase as one moves from association through intention, and then decrease at the level of justification. Subsequent research has demonstrated that both characteristics of the perceiver (e.g., level of cognitive development) and characteristics of the stimulus situation influence attributions of responsibility (e.g., Brewer, 1977; Fincham & Jaspars, 1979; Fishbein & Ajzen, 1973; Harris, 1977; Sedlak, 1979; Shaw & Sulzer, 1964).

Heider's discussion was important not only for its suggestions concerning attributional development (see also Piaget, 1965) but also for the light it shed on the various meanings of "responsibility" in ordinary language. Most important for present purposes are the distinctions among responsibility as effective cause, responsibility as legal accountability, and responsibility as liability for moral sanction (cf. Shaver, 1975). Many of the studies of responsibility for accidents, beginning with the work by Walster (1966), failed to specify the meaning of responsibility that subjects were to adopt. Such imprecision no doubt contributed to the confusing and contradictory results obtained in much of this work (cf. Vidmar & Crinklaw, 1974; Wortman, 1976). Unfortunate though this lack of precision may be, it does inadvertently demonstrate the close conceptual linkages between "cause" and "responsibility."

Responsibility as moral accountability is the meaning most often used in work in this area (Shaver, 1975, p. 103) and is implied in Heider's discussion of moral judgments as "oughts." *Oughts* are conceived as impersonal standards that are consensually validated and cross-situationally consistent. Thus, such judgments of moral responsibility are judgments of characteristics or behavior in terms of standards that share the two primary characteristics of external attributions, consistency and consensus. Oughts are perceived as characteristics of the external world rather than as subjective judgments (cf. Kelley, 1971; Ross & DiTecco, 1975).

The fact that ought standards are usually perceived as externally determined raises some interesting questions for the perception of personal responsibility. Conformity to such standards will be seen as the result of external forces, and thus attributions will minimize the role of internal cause and personal responsibility. This may result in an asymmetry in the assignment of credit and blame. Close conformity to external standards may be attributed to external factors, and thus little praised. Deviance from these standards is more likely to be attributed to an internal cause, more likely to be perceived as something for which the individual is personally responsible, and thus more likely to elicit blame than conformity elicits praise (cf. Hamilton, 1978; Turner, 1968, 1978).

Two cautionary notes must be entered here. First, the relationships described here refer to general trends. There is research demonstrating differences in attributions of responsibility by individuals at different stages of cognitive and moral development (e.g., Harris, 1977; Sedlak, 1979). Different developmentally based understandings of the obligations involved in conceptions of responsibility may alter their relationship to perceptions of justice (e.g., Damon, 1977; Kohlberg, 1964, 1976; Weiner & Peter, 1973).

Second, the Heiderian-based treatment of oughts as external forces has recently been challenged in a provocative statement by Hamilton (1978). She identifies social *roles* as the most important normative context within which responsibility attributions and evaluations are made. Such a view emphasizes the importance of different kinds of obligations attaching to roles differently situated in the social structure, and the importance of oughts that are neither external nor internal, but internalized. Future work on responsibility attribution will need to incorporate variations in the role location of the actor and the understanding of those role obligations by the observer (see Section III. D. 4. for a slightly different attempt to conceptualize roles in an attributional context).

Attributions of responsibility seem to be based most fundamentally on an assessment of the extent of the actor's effective causal contribution in terms of what the observer believes the actor should (ought to) have done or been. Almost all the empirical work in this area deals with a single observer making responsibility attributions with regard to a *single actor* for behavior or characteristics thought to be liable for *negative sanctions*. One might reasonably ask if conceptual and empirical work done to date has implications for three related problems: (1) responsibility attributions concerning eligibility for *positive* sanctions such as praise or credit; (2) responsibility attributions to the *self;* and (3) responsibility attributions in situations involving judgments of *two or more actors.* Each of these problems will be addressed in some detail later (Section III.), but each also warrants a brief comment here.

It seems reasonable that behaviors or characteristics that are nonnormative in a positive rather than a negative direction, those that "go beyond the call of duty," also elicit personal responsibility attributions (cf. Jones & Davis, 1965; Jones & McGillis, 1976). Thus, it may be departures from norms generally that "excite interest in the ways that entitle us to use the language of responsibility [Feinberg, 1970, pp. 131–132]." Second, there have been few *direct* studies comparing attributions of responsibility to the self and to others (however, see Fincham & Jaspars, 1979). Research on "defensive attribution" (Chaikin & Darley, 1973; Shaver, 1970) refers to but does not directly address this issue, and the evidence on self-attributed responsibility for others' characteristics and conditions is not clear (e.g., Duval, Duval, & Neely, 1979; Ross, Bierbrauer, & Polly, 1974). Would there be systematic differences between responsibility attributions to the self and to others?; by actors and observers? Finally, an observer confronting two or more actors may have two standards for evaluating responsibility: the normative standard referred to earlier, and the standard that the characteristic of each actor provides for the other. This situation touches issues of distributive justice, and the potential differences between individual deserving standards and distributive justice standards, most directly (cf. Cohen, 1979).

Attributions of moral responsibility clearly involve more than assessments of "mere" effective causality, and it is important to distinguish between the two. However, because of their close conceptual linkages, one may reasonably search the vast literature on causal attributions, as well as the more limited literature that focuses specifically on attributions of responsibility, for clues to an understanding of justice (see Fincham & Jaspars, 1980).

Not only are cause and responsibility closely linked conceptually and in the empirical literature; so, too, are responsibility and justice. Both responsibility and justice are moral concepts. Despite lack of clarity in their research, Shaver (1975) concludes from his review that most attribution theorists mean primarily to refer to "evaluations of moral accountability" in their work on responsibility attribution. Such evaluations

can themselves be seen as the allotments, or as precursors to the allotments, that provide the central focus for the concept of justice (cf.
Frankena, 1962). Rescher (1967) describes the basic task of a philosophy
of distributive justice as the provision of "the machinery in terms of
which one can assess the relative merits or demerits of a distribution, the
'assessment' in question being made from the moral or ethical point of
view [p. 9]." Finally, Feinberg says of individual deserving that "if a
person is deserving of some sort of treatment, he must, necessarily, be so
in virtue of some possessed characteristic or prior activity [1970, p. 58;
emphasis in original]." Justice, whether individual or distributive, involves centrally a judgment of the deserving or relative deserving of
recipient units based on their characteristics. The most important dimension of these characteristics is the extent to which they are perceived
to be the responsibility of the recipient units they describe.

Attributions of cause and responsibility have been treated here, as
they are in most of the literature, in terms of judgments about individual
actors. However, there is no reason not to conceptualize recipient units
in collective as well as in individual terms. Attributions of causality and
responsibility may well be relevant to perceptions of social collectivities,
such as racial, sex, and class groupings (e.g., Hamilton, 1979), and these
attributions may then affect perceptions of distributive justice among
them (cf. Schuman, 1968).

C. Implicit Assumptions in Social Psychologies of Justice

None of the major theoretical statements on justice make attributions
a central, and explicit, concern. However, an examination of some of the
most prominent statements suggests that fundamentally important attributional assumptions have been made to develop an understanding of
justice perceptions.

Although not primarily a statement on justice, Thibaut and Kelley's
exchange theory (1959) shares many of the characteristics of two prominent justice statements, those by Homans (1961, 1974) and Adams
(1965). At one point, Thibaut and Kelley define the comparison level for
outcomes (CL) as "a standard by which the person evaluates the rewards
and costs of a given relationship in terms of what he feels he *deserves*
[1959, p. 21; emphasis in original]." Later conceiving of CL as a modal or
average level for all outcomes, each weighted by its salience, they argue
that the outcomes most likely to be salient generally are those for which
the actor is primarily responsible, those over which the actor has some
degree of control. In addition, they argue that the impact of another

individual's outcomes on CL depends on the causal explanation offered for them. A person winning a lottery would have little effect on the CL of the winner's brother. However, if that same person acquired wealth as a consequence of his own efforts, the rewards would be likely to play a role in the brother's evaluation of his own outcomes (1959, p. 88).

Patchen's dissertation (1961) emphasized the importance of perceived responsibility for outcomes on the choice of a comparison standard (cf. Austin, 1977; Goodman, 1974; Greenberg, Chapter 11, this volume). He argued that one important determinant of the choice of a dissonant or consonant comparison was the extent to which the individual accepted personal responsibility for his current position. A person who accepted such responsibility would be ashamed by a dissonant comparison, whereas someone who rejected personal responsibility would choose just such a comparison, and this latter comparison would lead to righteous indignation and justifications for claims to larger outcomes.

Homans (1961, 1974) also refers to the role of attributions. In his discussion of comparison choices, he points to the role of perceived similarity on various dimensions and concludes:

> In effect, if a man is earning less than someone else whose occupation is equal to his own, so that outsiders might judge him to be suffering from injustice, but he says it is his own fault, he is saying that his investments are not really what they seem, not really equal to those of the other, and so the condition of justice is realized. A man is angry when what he gets ranks below what he gives only if he recognizes the apparent injustice to be the result of someone else's actions and not of his own [1974, p. 257].

Potential injustices become "actual" injustices to the person only if and when the discrepancy between actual and deserved outcomes is attributed to something other than the actor's own behavior.

Homans also suggests that an individual is likely to complain about his or her treatment relative to someone else, that is, complain about a condition of potential injustice, "the more successful in redressing the injury his action is likely to be [1974, p. 253]." The injury which is the source of the potential injustice is clearly understood as having been "inflicted" by someone or something else, self-inflicted injury being assumed to be the exception rather than the rule. In addition, Homans seems to suggest that an actor perceives a discrepancy as an actual injustice at one point in time, but that this perception might change if the discrepancy continues. If an individual sees an injury as unlikely to be redressed by his or her own action, the injury either will no longer be seen as an injustice or will cease to elicit complaint. Which is more likely may depend on the individual's causal attributions concerning the probability of successful future action (cf. Fischhoff, 1976; Ross, 1977; Weiner, 1974).

Aside from the evidence provided by implicit assumptions in earlier statements, two recent developments also demonstrate the importance of attributions for justice. In research undertaken in the wake of Lerner's just world hypothesis, individuals show a fairly consistent tendency to derogate a person whom they witness suffering a negative outcome (Lerner & Miller, 1978). In verbal portrayals of such suffering, the tendency to derogate is reduced if the victim can be compensated or if the subject sees the victim as behaviorally responsible for his or her own fate. Apparently, if the victim can be seen as causing his or her own suffering, "there appears to be no need to derogate the victim, presumably because no injustice has occurred [1978, p. 1041]." Implicitly, then, injustice involves a negative outcome for which the actor cannot be held personally responsible. This seems true both for participants *and* for investigators in research on the need to believe in a just world.

Finally, there have been several recent attempts to incorporate research on attributions of the causes of success and failure into research on justice. In a series of papers, Anderson (1974, 1976; Farkas & Anderson, 1979) has described the combinatory rules by which judgments of justice are made from multiple recipient characteristics. Cohen (1978b) has suggested that all of the various recipient characteristics relevant to performances are weighted and signed (positive or negative) according to the personal responsibility for them attributed to the actor. Most recently, research by Kayser and Lamm (1980a,b, in press) has tried to integrate work on responsibility attribution, models of cognitive algebra, and perceptions of justice.

Although more recent work on justice has begun to include reference to the importance of attributions, little explicit acknowledgment has been made in theoretical statements. If social psychologists have to bring their subjects', and their own, attributions of cause and responsibility in the back door to understand perceptions of justice, it seems to be time to suggest that such attributions are crucial.

D. Implicit Assumptions in Recent Philosophies of Justice

Because our purpose is to understand justice, comprehensive philosophical statements should provide fertile ground for our work (see Cohen & Greenberg, Chapter 1, this volume). This is the case not only because testable hypotheses may be gleaned from these statements (e.g.,

Brickman, 1977; Brickman & Bryan, 1976; Curtis, 1979)[2], and not only because these authors try to make the bases of their justice judgments clear. Even a cursory examination of these statements suggests the necessity of systematically including attributions to achieve an understanding of differing perceptions of justice.

Rawls (1971) views as unjust distributive shares any that are "improperly influenced by factors arbitrary from a moral point of view [p. 72]." What are these factors? "Prior distributions of natural assets—that is, natural talents and abilities—as these have been developed or left unrealized, and their use favored or disfavored over time by social circumstances and such chance contingencies as accident and good fortune [p. 72]." He rejects the impact of these factors, and his rejection has centrally to do with the assumptions he makes about the causes of, and the responsibilities for, these characteristics and their consequences:

> It seems to be one of the fixed points of our considered judgments that no one deserves his place in the distribution of native endowments, any more than one deserves one's initial starting place in society. The assertion that a man deserves the superior character that enables him to make the effort to cultivate his abilities is equally problematic; for his character depends in large part upon fortunate family and social circumstances for which he can claim no credit [p. 104].

Thus, Rawls claims that to allow those advantaged by natural endowments or accident, or those further advantaged by the effects of social circumstance, to reap the benefits of those advantages by being given greater shares, is unjust. He appeals to what he claims are our "shared intuitions" and "one of the fixed points of our considered judgments [pp. 72, 104]" in arguing that distributions based on these factors for which recipients are not personally responsible, are unjust.

However widely these intuitions and judgments might be shared otherwise, Nozick (1974) takes strong exception to them. Nozick notes that Rawls makes no mention of how persons have "chosen" to develop their natural assets. "Why is that simply left out? Perhaps because such choices also are viewed as being products of factors *outside the person's control,* and hence as 'arbitrary from the moral point of view' [p. 214; emphasis added]." Nozick further argues that Rawls's strategy here has the effect of

---

[2]It should be noted that Rawls specifically warns against attempts to test his argument empirically in microscopic settings like those employed in much social psychological research. Both Nozick (1974) and Wolff (1977) criticize Rawls for this position. What Rawls, and other philosophers, would say about less microscopic, though still limited, research designs (e.g., Jasso & Rossi, 1977) is not clear.

preventing "the introduction of a person's autonomous choices and actions (and their results) only by attributing *everything* noteworthy about the person completely to certain sorts of 'external' factors [p. 214; emphasis in original]."

Rawls and Nozick disagree in a fundamental way about the extent to which important human characteristics are controllable by human actors.[3] Their attributions of cause and responsibility for these characteristics differ sharply, and it is not surprising to find their preferences for justice differing sharply as a consequence. They agree that characteristics outside actors' control ought not to influence just distributions but disagree as to the status of specific human characteristics and actions. Nozick emphasizes so-called free transfers of holdings from one actor to another. Aside from rectifying past injustices, all holdings, all distributions described by such holdings, are just if they result from "free" exchange and original production. Nozick emphasizes the individual's cultivation of skills necessary to produce holdings of value and to exchange them in transfer.

Rawls, however, emphasizes the limitations imposed by chance and by social circumstances not of the actor's own making. All of these factors are either characteristics of other individuals, random factors, or characteristics of the actor deeply influenced by the action of others (e.g., the socialization behavior of parents). Because of this, the actor's responsibility for them and the outcomes they produce is much diminished. Conscientious effort, a characteristic Rawls believes is very much under the control of the individual actor, is the only individual characteristic he thinks able to justify differences in shares (1971, p. 312).

E. Summary

Perceptions of justice are tied fundamentally to beliefs about the causes of, and responsibility for, important human characteristics. Such links can be seen first in the family resemblance among the concepts of cause, responsibility, and justice. Furthermore, attempts by social psychologists to understand lay perceptions of justice are often forced to invoke implicit assumptions about causal and responsibility beliefs. And, finally, important philosophical disagreements on the nature of justice rest in a fundamental way on differing assessments of the extent to

---

[3]An interesting study by Brickman, Ryan, and Wortman (1975) on causal chains suggests that tendencies to take "long" or "short" views on attributions of cause and responsibility may be related to political belief structure (cf. Schneider, Hastorf, & Ellsworth, 1979).

which persons can be held morally responsible for their characteristics and actions in a given context and social structure.

III. THE ROLE OF ATTRIBUTIONS IN JUSTICE

A. Introduction

In this section, I will discuss the relevance of several key issues that have been addressed by attribution theorists and researchers that are important for an understanding of justice. For each of the issues, I will suggest specific ways in which this understanding would benefit from systematic inclusion of attribution research. No claim is made that this list exhausts all the important ways in which attribution and justice might be related,[4] only that the three issues discussed here belong in prominent places on such a list. In the final section of this chapter, I will offer several additional candidates for inclusion.

B. Divergent Perspectives and Justice

Jones and Nisbett's divergent perspectives hypothesis (1972) suggests the existence of a pervasive tendency for actors to attribute their actions to situational factors, whereas observers tend to attribute those same actions to stable personal dispositions of the actors. Three possible explanations were offered for this difference. Actors and observers were said to differ in visual perspective, in motivation, and in available information. Subsequent research over the past decade generally confirms the hypothesis itself and the importance of each of the three factors offered to explain it (see Kelley & Michela, 1980).

Actors tend to see the causes of their own behavior as environmental, whereas observers locate the causes of the same behavior within the actor (e.g., Arkin & Duval, 1975; Nisbett, Caputo, Legant, & Maracek, 1973; Regan & Totten, 1975; Storms, 1973). In addition, although there is some controversy here, there is also evidence that these different causal perspectives are motivationally based (e.g., Bradley, 1978; Miller & Ross,

---

[4]There have been two systematic attempts at integration. One (Cohen, 1978b) expands Anderson's (1976; Farkas & Anderson, 1979) work on input summation and equity summation to a general model of attributions for, and just allocations to, task performers. The other (Utne & Kidd, 1980) modifies and extends Walster's equity theory (Walster *et al.*, 1978) by including attributional considerations. Recent empirical work on input integration and responsibility attribution has yet to be incorporated into such an attempt (e.g., Kayser & Lamm, 1980a,b, in press).

1975; Miller, 1978; Schuman, 1980; Sicoly & Ross, 1977; Snyder, Stephan, & Rosenfield, 1978; Weary, 1979; Wiley, Crittenden, & Birg, 1979; Zuckerman, 1979). Finally, differences in the information available to actors and observers also seems to contribute to their varying causal perspectives (e.g., Eisen, 1979; Nisbett & Ross, 1980).

There are two closely related, but distinct, interpretations of this general tendency. First, actors and observers disagree as to the causes of the actor's behavior, actors emphasizing environmental and observers emphasizing dispositional forces. This effect is generally referred to as a demonstration of actor/observer differences and involves differences between the attributions of two individuals for the behavior of one of them. Second, an individual tends to emphasize environmental factors as causes of his or her own behavior, while the same individual explains the identical behavior of another person in terms of the other's personal dispositions. This demonstrates a self–other difference and involves differences between two attributions by the same individual, one for his or her own behavior and one for the identical behavior of a distinct other (cf. Zuckerman, 1979).

How might such tendencies affect justice perceptions? Most importantly, actors and observers may disagree about what constitutes a just receipt for the actor. Because of the linguistic and conceptual links between "cause" and "responsibility," observers are not only more likely to attribute the *cause* of behavior to the actor than is the actor him- or herself. Observers are also more likely to attribute *personal responsibility* for the behavior to the actor. Divergent causal perspectives may be associated with, and may give rise to, divergent responsibility perspectives. And interpretations of different causal attributions suggest similar interpretations for the projected differences in responsibility attributions; they may be due to differences in perspective, differences in motivation, or differences in available information. As "responsibility" often involves liability for sanctions, one might expect motivational differences to be most crucial here.

Research on responsibility attributions is consistent with these suggestions, but it comes overwhelmingly from situations in which observers attribute responsibility to a single actor for behavior thought liable for negative sanctions (e.g., Harvey, Harris, & Barnes, 1975). Observers attribute personal responsibility and assign blame to actors whose behavior falls short of normative standards. The research on divergent causal perspectives suggests that the actors themselves would reject that personal responsibility and that blame, as well as any additional negative sanctions that might accompany them. Rejection of personal responsibility may occur because actors' attention is focused on external forces, because such rejection is self-serving and justificatory (on both of which, cf. Duval & Hensley, 1976; Duval & Wicklund, 1972; Wicklund, 1975), or because information available to the actors suggests that such behavior is less characteristic of them than observers take it to be (cf. Ross, Green, & House, 1977). At any rate, behavior that falls short of normative standards will evoke attributions of personal responsibility and blame from observers and may provide justification for administering further, just, punishment. At the same time, actors are likely to reject personal responsibility and blame, and to experience both blame and punishment as unjust.

A straightforward extrapolation to behavior positively discrepant from normative standards suggests that an observer would accord personal responsibility and credit for such behavior, whereas the actor would reject such responsibility and credit. Such a difference appears counterintuitive, even if there are some instances in which actors whose behavior goes beyond the call of duty express modesty and appear to deny or to minimize their personal responsibility for the action, while observers heap praise and other rewards upon them.

Apart from these instances, which may be more true of public than private attributions, the evidence seems to suggest that actors often make self-serving attributions of cause and responsibility (see Section III. D. 3.). There seems to be widespread agreement on the existence of such a tendency amidst serious disagreement about the importance of cognitive and motivational factors in explaining it. Among the most compelling of the cognitive explanations offered is that success and positive discrepancies from normative standards are more likely to be expected and intended than are failure and negative discrepancies, at least for the types of performance situations usually examined (Nisbett & Ross, 1980, pp. 232–234). Whatever their source, these self-serving attributions are consistent with the tendency of actors to attribute their own behavior to external causes when the behavior is liable for negative, but not when it is liable for positive, sanctions. Thus, actor–observer differences in perceptions of the justice of the actor's receipts are more likely to appear for behavior that falls short of normative standards than for behavior that exceeds them.

Those differences that do appear have been interpreted in terms of differing causal attributions for the actor's behavior. However, if attributions of personal responsibility are the result of perceived discrepancies between actual behavior and normative standards, they may also be due to the application of differing normative standards by actors and observers. If, for example, observers set higher normative standards for actors than actors set for themselves, then actual behavior lower than the normative standard set by observers will be seen by those observers as reason for attributing personal responsibility, in the form of blame, to the actor. Here the actor will reject that blame because his or her actual behavior is less negatively discrepant from the lower normative standard he or she sets for the self. Conversely, the actor might see as his or her personal responsibility behavior that is positively discrepant from the lower normative standard set by and for the self, while observers may deny personal responsibility and credit to the actor because the observers' higher normative standards render the behavior "merely" normative. Such a suggestion is consistent with the existence of a false consensus bias (Ross *et al.*, 1977) in which observers regard the behaviors of others as relatively uncommon, and therefore revealing of others' personal dispositions, to the extent that the others' behavior departs from the observers' own, presumably normative, responses in the same situation.

Potential differences between actors and observers are particularly important when the observer is not merely a "passive" perceiver but is in the position of allocating outcomes to the actor. Allocators and recipients may disagree strongly about the justice of a particular outcome (cf. Leventhal, 1976a), and such disagreements may have their roots in differing attributions of responsibility. As more active, involved, observers, allocators may be even more inclined toward personal attributions, of both cause and responsibility, than the relevant actors (cf. Cunningham, Starr, & Kanouse, 1979).

Observers fairly regularly derogate an actor they witness suffering a negative outcome (i.e., experiencing a need) and thereby do not attend to the need by compensating the actor. When actor derogation does *not* occur, the actor is still often not compensated because the victim is perceived to be behaviorally responsible for the need (cf. Lerner & Miller, 1978). Interestingly enough, in situations designed to decrease an observer's attribution of responsibility for the actor's need to the actor, the observer is more likely to offer compensation. This increased helping appears to be mediated by the observer's acceptance of the legitimacy of the need and by his or her acceptance of the responsibility for relieving a need unjustly borne (cf. Barnes, Ickes, & Kidd, 1979; Duval *et al.*, 1979; Schwartz & Fleishman, 1978; Wegner & Schaefer, 1978). "Responsibility" here refers both to responsibility for creating the need and responsibility for alleviating it. Needs for which the person is responsible, either behaviorally or because of some characterological fault, are not seen as unjust. Needs for which the person is not responsible *are* seen as unjust, and responsibility for alleviating them falls, at least in part, to the observer.

Little or no research has examined the question of whether actors would blame themselves (i.e., accept personal responsibility) for their own victim status (Lerner & Miller, 1978). The argument pursued here suggests they would not, preferring instead to attribute the cause of their negative fate to external factors. In what situations self-blame is, or is perceived to be, functional is still a matter of considerable importance and controversy (see Bulman & Wortman, 1977; Buss, 1978; Janoff-Bulman, 1979; Seligman, 1975). I will return to this issue, and its more specific relationship to justice, in the discussion of attributional biases in what follows (Section III. D.).

The self–other interpretation of attributional divergences provides additional possibilities and complexities. It suggests that an individual will cite external causes for his or her own characteristics or behavior, while citing internal causes for identical characteristics in another actor. Three slightly different situations present themselves. In the first, one might examine differences between perceptions of justice for the self as opposed to justice for a single other. One should expect a self-interest effect here, higher outcomes justly administered to the self than to an "identical" other because of differing attributions of responsibility. Again, such an expectation could rely on either a motivational (e.g., Zuckerman, 1979) or a cognitive (Nisbett & Ross, 1980) interpretation of the evidence for "self-serving" attributions. Second, one might examine allocations between the self *and* one or more other recipients. Initially one might also expect a self-interest effect here as well, again because of differing attributions of responsibility. However, because such "differential consideration" smacks so clearly of injustice, almost by definition, these tendencies may be somewhat muted, especially when allocations or justice perceptions are made public.[5]

Third, disagreements between two recipients concerning the justice of a division of outcomes between them can be interpreted in the same way. Each recipient may be inclined to take more personal responsibility for positive and less personal responsibility for negative characteristics than the other would be inclined to accord them. Such differences might again derive either from differences in the availability of information regarding intentions, to plan to approach positive and avoid negative behaviors (e.g., Miller & Ross, 1975; Nisbett & Ross, 1980), or from differences in the impact of self-interested responsibility attributions (e.g., Zuckerman, 1979).

[5]The authors of studies comparing public and private conditions have either not directly assessed perceptions of justice (e.g., Rivera & Tedeschi, 1976) or questioned the plausibility of an attributional interpretation (e.g., Reis & Gruzen, 1976) but the question remains an open one.

A final issue needs to be addressed. Attributions of cause and responsibility are important not only with respect to the characteristics of recipient units, but also with respect to the actual transfer of outcomes involved in making allocations to one or more recipients. The instructions given to allocators in most outcome allocation research include the statement that they are free to allocate any way they wish. One likely consequence of this instruction is that subjects accept personal responsibility for their allocations (cf. Cohen, 1978a; Harvey, 1976). This provides some grounds for countering the allegation that demand characteristics explain many of these data (see, however, the discussion of attributional biases, Section III. D.).

At the same time, the fact that allocators are provided information on specific characteristics of each of the recipients (information as to performance, need, ability, effort, etc.) belies the offer of freedom of choice and the implications it has for acceptance of responsibility. The forces created by these two different portions of the experimental instructions operate in opposite directions, one increasing and the other decreasing the likelihood that the allocator will feel free to make any allocation he or she wishes. Such forces will also affect the degree of personal responsibility allocators accept for their allocations (cf. Harvey, 1976).

Such effects suggest the importance of investigating recipients', as well as allocators', attributions of responsibility for the act of allocation. Several pieces of research indicate that recipients react negatively to, revolt against, allocators who dispense unjust receipts (e.g., Lawler, 1975; Ross, Thibaut, & Evenbeck, 1971). Lawler and Thompson (1978) have demonstrated that this relationship is mediated by recipients' attributions of personal responsibility to allocators. Such an effect also characterizes recipients' reactions to allocators who divide receipts between themselves (the allocator) and the recipient. Allocators described as having control over a receipt division that was unjust in terms of relative performances stimulate greater reciprocal unjust divisions than do allocators who merely administer chance-produced divisions (e.g., Garrett & Libby, 1973; Leventhal, Weiss, & Long, 1969; Libby & Garrett, 1974). Here, it is important to note that reciprocity, as a particular form of justice, is affected by the degree of responsibility attributed to the person engaging in the initial action (see Eckhoff, 1974; Gouldner, 1960; McClintock & Keil, Chapter 10, this volume; Pruitt, 1968).

The work on divergent attributions identifies *potential* conflicts among individuals or among groups as to the cause of and responsibility for certain events. When such conflicts do occur, they are often not "mere" disagreements among "neutral" parties, but heated controversies among "self-interested" individual or collective actors. One way of understanding the "stake" people have in these attributions is to suggest that attributions of cause and responsibility define the context within which the legitimacy of claims to just outcomes is established. Recent work focusing explicitly on attributional conflicts suggests that they are most likely to arise either when a condition or action departs from a normative standard (cf. Horai, 1977), or when there are clear conflicts of interest between actors (cf. Harvey, Wells, & Alvarez, 1978; Orvis, Kelley, & Butler, 1976). Attributional conflicts may thus be most likely to arise in, and are critically important for understanding, the just allocation of blame or credit to an individual actor and just allocations of outcomes among distinct recipient units. Research on the use of verbal and behavioral strategies for pursuing one's interest in such conflicts, strategies such as accounts, excuses, rationalizations, and justifications, may illuminate the underlying structure of debates on justice.

C. Single-Multiple Cases and Justice

Kelley (1973) distinguishes two different cases with which attribution theory can deal in general: (1) the attributor has information from multiple observations; and (2) the attributor has information from only a single observation. Covariation concepts, those that apply to inferences of cause based on observation of covariation of causes and effects, are used to discuss attributions from multiple observations. Configuration concepts, those that apply to causal inferences based on assessments of the contour of the plausible causes of an observed effect, are used to discuss attributions made from a single observation. Distinctions between attributions of cause and responsibility in terms of the number of cases involved may be of critical importance for understanding the impact of the size of the recipient class on perceptions of justice.

The covariation principle suggests that an effect is attributed to that one of its plausible causes with which it varies over time. It operates when the multiplicity refers to observations over time, when the individual possesses "information about the effect at two or more points in time [Kelley, 1973, p. 108]." Kelley also points to self-perception studies in which the attributor "has had a longer series of observations over which to notice the covariation between an effect and possible causes [p. 109]." Examples used later in the article suggest that attributers may be given, or are thought in real life situations to have, multiple information along any one of the three dimensions of the ANOVA cube: times, persons, or entities. Thus, distinctiveness concerns observations on at least two entities, consensus concerns observations on two or more persons, and consistency concerns observations on two or more times.

Kelley points to the idealized nature of his model and suggests that it ought to be regarded merely as the context within which limited samples of observations are made (1973, p. 113). In addition, the attributer often lacks the time and motivation necessary to make multiple observations, in which case "he may make a causal inference on the basis of a *single observation* of the effect [Kelley, 1973, p. 113; emphasis in original]." Even here, however, Kelley suggests that the attributer is likely to have observed similar effects in the past, to have some notions about possibly relevant causes, and to have information about plausible causes of the single observation. Thus, the distinction between single and multiple observations is somewhat ambiguous.

Whatever difficulties there may be in distinguishing clearly the single from the multiple observation cases, the rule operating in multiple observation situations is some form of the covariation principle. For single observation situations, Kelley points to the discounting principle, where the role of a given factor is discounted if other plausible factors are present, and the augmentation principle, where the role of a given factor is increased by the presence of other plausible factors operating in an opposite direction.

Assuming that descriptions of, and distinctions between, these principles are important, what role might they have in contributing to an understanding of justice? When the justice of a single individual's outcome is at issue, one would expect configuration concepts to govern relevant attributions. When the justice of two or more recipients is involved, one would expect covariation concepts to predominate. However, the ambiguity involved in distinguishing the situations to which these two concepts are thought to apply make these expectations less clear than they might be.

With reference to justice for the self, it appears that an individual is dealing with a single case. However, because the individual presumably has confronted situations in the past and thus "has had a long[er] series of observations over which to notice the covariation between an effect and possible causes [Kelley, 1973, p. 109]," the situation actually involves multiple cases where covariation concepts will be employed. Where a perception of justice involves two or more recipients, whether or not the perceiver is also a recipient, multiple observations are clearly involved. These may constitute actual observations of, or information concerning, recipients' performances, needs, and so on. Here, too, one expects covariation principles of attribution to operate.

In fact, one would expect configuration concepts to be operative only in situations involving justice perceptions of a single other recipient. Even here, it might be objected that, as the nature of justice is comparative, there will be some standard involving a specific other recipient (a local comparison) or a reference group (referential comparison; see Berger, Zelditch, Anderson, & Cohen, 1972) in terms of which justice is perceived. This, it may be argued, is what serves the function served by other observations when they are more directly available, and thus covariation concepts will operate here as well. As so little work has been done directly on the role of attributional processes in justice, any decision on the validity of these suggestions will have to await the results of future studies.

Situations involving more than one recipient provide a clear focus for examining the operation of covariation concepts. In allocation situations, an individual is given a total store of outcomes and information about each of the recipients.[6] Frequently, the information concerns performances and factors related to them. For example, if two potential recipients have performed a task with varying degrees of success, the allocator sees a variation in effect and must supply a causal explanation for the variation across persons.

One must note, first, that the focus of the usual attributional task undergoes a shift here. Rather than attributing the cause of, and responsibility for, a single recipient's performance, need, or outcome, an attributer in the situation now under examination must explain two recipients' performances, needs, and so on. If, to take the simplest case, the individual has information on the performances of two recipients, these performances can be equally successful or not. The question the attributer confronts is this: What causes the performances to be similar or different? In effect, the attributer must explain consensus or lack of consensus along the performance dimension.

Whereas consensus information in McArthur's (1972) and in Frieze and Weiner's (1971) work is background to the figure provided by the action under examination, information on consensus here is figural: Two (or more) performances are directly presented. Some previous work has found consensus information to be underutilized, but this may be because it has been presented as background (e.g., McArthur, 1976; Nisbett, Borgida, Crandall, & Reed, 1976; Nisbett & Ross, 1980; Wells & Harvey, 1977). Where performances differ, consensus is by definition low; where performances are identical, consensus is high. According to

[6]Anderson (1974, 1976; Farkas & Anderson, 1979) distinguishes situations in which the allocator has information on two instances of a single dimension, for example, two performances, from situations in which there is a single piece of information for each of two (or more) dimensions, for example, performance and effort. His data suggest the operation of two different combinatory rules, input summation and equity summation, that allocators employ in determining a just distribution of outcomes.

Kelley's attribution cube (1967, 1973), and according to at least some data (e.g., McArthur, 1972), high consensus is a necessary condition for attribution to the stimulus, in this case, to the task. If performances on the same task differ, the task clearly is not the cause of the difference.

Because in most allocation research the entity (the task) is identical for the two potential recipients, differences in performance are likely to be attributed to differences in persons (however, see the discussion of the equal performance conditions in what follows; for an example of a setting in which tasks are described as different, see Leventhal & Michaels, 1969). There is no consistency information given in this research, distinctiveness is low because there are different responses to the same entity, and consensus is low. Where consensus and distinctiveness are low, the likelihood is that attributions for performance will focus on differences between persons. Similarly, attributions for similar performances might be attributed to similarities between the individual performers or, at the very least, differences between persons would be less likely to be cited (cf. Greenberg, 1978).

When attributers are confronted with information concerning two or more recipients, it seems reasonable to suggest that they employ covariation strategies in whatever attributions they make. In most previous attribution research in which multiple observations have been available, they have been multiple observations of a single individual's behavior over time, whether that individual is the attributer or another person. In McArthur's work, for example, subjects are given one current description of behavior (e.g., Paul is enthralled by the painting at the museum), more or less as figure, and consensus, consistency, and distinctiveness information as ground. Thus, information is also provided on how Paul has behaved in similar situations in the past (consistency over time), on how other actors behave toward the entity (consensus over actors), and toward how many other similar entities Paul behaves in the same way (distinctiveness over entities).

In the typical allocation situation, the individual is provided with two current behavior samples, performances of individuals. Often there is little or no information concerning the behavior of other actors; thus little information on consensus apart from the consensus information provided by the two performances themselves. There is often no information on individual's past performances, thus no consistency information. And there is usually no information on the actors' behavior toward similar entities, no distinctiveness information.

In such a situation, consensus information is likely to be that most used because it is the only kind of information directly available. This is interesting because of the evidence of underutilization of such information in attributions concerning the behavior of a single individual. Nisbett and his colleagues suggest that it is the abstractness of consensus information in this research that leads to its underutilization (see Nisbett & Ross, 1980). There is also some evidence that increasing the concreteness of the information increases its use (e.g., Feldman, Higgins, Karlovac, & Ruble, 1976; Hansen & Donoghue, 1977). Finally, some research indicates that consensus information is used when the behavior in question is socially desirable rather than undesirable (Zuckerman, 1978). Attribution researchers would benefit from an examination of allocation research on justice and the ways in which consensus information is used by subjects making these judgments.

Justice researchers would also benefit from attention to the effects of introducing distinctiveness and consistency information on allocation and justice judgment tasks. Information concerning consistency over time and over tasks (distinctiveness) should affect attributions to internal and external factors, and these attributions should affect attributions of personal responsibility and, thus, justice judgments and allocations.

It is also important to note the nature of the information that is *not* presented directly to subjects in research on justice. Performers are almost always described as working on the same type of task. This more or less automatically removes the entity as the focus for attributions of cause regarding differential performances. Also, note that performance on the same task, or at least on tasks of equal difficulty, might be seen as a necessary condition for a widely prevalent norm of justice in this society, equal opportunity for successful performance (cf. Coleman, 1968). Where task difficulties are clearly different, and assuming that actors have not chosen the tasks but have been assigned to them (Cohen, 1974; Leventhal & Michaels, 1969), the "meanings" of performances on these tasks for justice change. Similar predictions could be made for other possible causes of differential performances, particularly differences in abilities and luck. When differences in performance, or need, or outcomes for that matter, are seen as the result of different amounts of luck, or differing task difficulties, the relevance of different performances, needs, and outcomes for justice is altered.

Reviews of both the recipient allocation (Leventhal, 1976a) and achievement evaluation literatures (e.g., Weiner, 1974; Weiner, Frieze, Kukla, Reed, Rest, & Rosenbaum, 1972; Weiner, Russell, & Lerman, 1978) lead to the suggestion that perceptions of just distributions of monetary outcomes and of evaluative feedback depend on the perceivers' attributions of cause and responsibility (Cohen, 1978b). In each case, causal attributions of differential performance to characteristics of the recipients themselves, and particularly to those characteristics for which recipients were likely to be held personally responsible, are *directly* related to perceptions of justice. The relationship between just outcomes and causal factors for which little personal responsibility was attributed, is *inverse*.

These relationships seem particularly clear for the dimension of effort, much less clear for ability, although the relevance of these attributions appears to differ for allocators and recipients (e.g., Kayser & Lamm, 1980b; Lamm & Kayser, 1978; Lamm, Kayser, & Schanz, 1978). This appears to be the case because effort is more likely than ability to be seen as an intentional factor subject to volitional control, *and*, as a consequence, more likely to elicit attributions of personal responsibility related to justice (Cohen, 1978b; Ickes & Kidd, 1976; Kayser & Lamm, 1980a, in press; Lerner, 1971; Weiner *et al.*, 1978; Wittig, Marks, & Jones, 1981).

D. Attributional Biases and Justice

Attribution theorists and researchers have identified several so-called "biases," and Ross's (1977) admittedly incomplete list is, as he suggests, as representative as any other: underestimation of the impact of situational (or external) factors and overestimation of the impact of dispositional factors, what Ross calls the "fundamental attribution error"; increased likelihood of personal attributions when action affects, or is directed at, the attributer (Jones & Davis, 1965), increased attributions of responsibility with increased seriousness of the consequences of behavior (Walster, 1966; however, see the discussion of problems with this research in Section II. B.); and increased attributions of responsibility for acts leading to reward than for acts preventing punishment or loss (Kelley, 1972). Many of these biases, whether their source is cognitive or motivational, involve attributions of cause *and* responsibility, and therefore may be of critical importance to an understanding of justice.

It should be noted first that the concept of "bias" in attributions requires the specification of a valid standard for comparison. Ross (1977), for example, suggests that prediction measures of attribution have a crucial advantage over measurements of causal judgments and inference beyond those of simplicity and seeming objectivity. Predictions can be assessed with regard to their accuracy. Even though this is the case, attribution researchers speak of "biases" when using other tasks because of an assumption about "rational baselines" (Jones & McGillis, 1976) or normative appropriateness based on scientific consensus (Nisbett & Ross, 1980). Whatever the validity of such assumptions, and they can be questioned deeply (e.g., Schneider, Hastorf, & Ellsworth, 1979), most researchers assume the existence of such a standard from which attributional biases clearly can be shown to be departures.

One might instead treat such biases as attributional conflicts (cf. Harvey *et al.*, 1978; Horai, 1977; Orvis *et al.*, 1976); it is this interpretation that, admittedly in another guise, is most familiar to those working on justice. One suspects the presence of "bias" in perceptions of justice when two individuals disagree about an "identical" situation. However, this is less likely to be called "bias" because perceptions of justice are analyzed not by comparing them to some presumably "objective" standard, but according to a standard provided by the viewpoints of other perceivers. To say that "justice is in the eye of the beholder," as social psychologists so often do (cf. Walster, Walster, & Berscheid, 1978), is to suggest that there is no objective standard against which to compare the validity of such perceptions. Justice, it is thought, is a matter of "value," whereas causality is a matter of "fact," at least when the results of rigorous experimental research provide the standard. This "matter of fact" treatment of attributional bias remains a serious question for future work.

1. THE FUNDAMENTAL ATTRIBUTION ERROR

How would the various attributional biases affect the perception of justice? Most generally, if biases affect the relative likelihood of personal as opposed to environmental attributions, they affect the attribution of personal responsibility. Any forces increasing the likelihood of personal attributions will, other things being equal, lead to increased attributions of personal responsibility. The operation of these biases should lead, then, to an increased tendency for individuals to see situations as just and the outcomes of individuals in situations as just. As the relationship among internal factors, responsibility, and just outcomes seems to be based on the perceived intentionality of these factors, there are likely to be important differences between the effects of the biases on the consequences of attributions to effort and ability (cf. Cohen, 1978b; Heider, 1958; Weiner *et al.*, 1978; see also Section III. C. of this chapter).

The hypothesized need to believe in a just world (Lerner, 1975) is, in a sense, one important instance of overestimating the importance of dispositional factors, what Ross (1977) calls the fundamental attribution error. Evidence most often cited for this error involves the tendency for observers to draw "'correspondent' personal inferences about actors who respond[ed] to very obvious situational factors [Ross, 1977, p. 184; for examples, see Bierbrauer, 1973, cited in Nisbett & Ross, 1980; Jones & Harris, 1967]." Lerner's statement of the just world hypothesis is very similar, and the results of research employing that concept suggest that observers frequently derogate or devalue the attributes or personal character of a person who has suffered innocently. The devaluation occurs both in response to reported instances of injustice as well as to injustices that are directly observed (Lerner & Miller, 1978).

As noted previously in this chapter, the first delimiting condition appended to this general conclusion suggests that if the victim can be seen as the behavioral cause of his or her suffering, there appears to be no need to engage in derogation "presumably because no injustice has occurred [Lerner & Miller, 1978, p. 1041]." Attributions of responsibility to a victim alters the individual's perception from one of injustice to justice. As Lerner and Miller point out, even minimal information, such as a random draw of fate, can produce attributions of responsibility to the person, and in some instances observers seem willing to conclude that a victim must have been responsible for his or her own fate in the absence of any supporting evidence whatsoever.

Thus, the fundamental attribution error may not only include the tendency to overestimate the role of personal factors in causal attributions, but may thereby also increase the likelihood of attributions of personal responsibility. This, in turn, may increase the likelihood that justice is perceived to be present. Note here that the emphasis has been on reactions to the situation of a distinct other. Reactions to one's own situation will be discussed later.

Professional attributers have been accused of the same fundamental error. For example, Caplan and Nelson (1973) point out that research on disadvantaged minority groups tends to be directed at discovery of their dispositional characteristics. Such research, if it follows the path outlined here, is likely to lead the consumers of that research (and perhaps to reveal a tendency in the producers of that research) to conclude that members of these groups are personally responsible for their disadvantaged situation, and that their situation is therefore just. Second, Mischel (1974) has demonstrated that the delay of gratification phenomenon, originally interpreted in terms of a dispositional characteristic, is subject to subtle (and perhaps not so subtle) situational influences. Early discussions of this phenomenon (e.g., Lewis, 1966; Mischel, 1958) were employed in the public arena along the path outlined here. The phenomenon was interpreted as revealing dispositional characteristics of the actors, which led often to attributions of personal responsibility for their condition, which in turn led to perceptions of that condition as just (cf. the work by Miller, Reissman, & Seagull, 1972, which is critical of this research and its use for these purposes).

Work on divergent attributional perspectives (Section III. B. of this chapter) can be seen to imply that observers are more prone to the fundamental attribution error than are actors. Aside from the controversy over the relative importance of cognitive or motivational factors here, this suggests a differential application of the consequences of the fundamental attribution error to perceptions of justice for the self as opposed to justice for another. Overemphasis on dispositional characteristics of others should increase the likelihood of personal responsibility attributions to others and should increase the likelihood that the other's situation is seen as just. Underemphasis on dispositional attributions to the self should lead to decreased likelihood of perceiving one's own situation as just. All other things being equal, this suggests a tendency to see an *identical* outcome as less just for the self than for a distinct other, particularly if the individual sees the self as intending to conform to normative standards and as intending success in performance situations (cf. Nisbett & Ross, 1980).

One important condition delimiting the operation of the victim derogation effect is the tendency for the observer to empathize with the victim (Lerner & Miller, 1978). Empathy seems to direct observers' attention to external forces, partially as a consequence of converting observers into "quasi" actors (cf. Cunningham *et al.*, 1979; Storms, 1973; Wegner, Chapter 3, this volume). According to the present argument, such a tendency would decrease the likelihood of internal attributions, decrease the likelihood of personal responsibility attributions, and increase the likelihood that the victim's outcome would be seen as unjust.[7] Those who empathize, and, perhaps more importantly, those "victims" who would induce empathy from onlookers, seem very much aware of these links. Shifting one's perspective may be a necessary condition for a change in perceptions of justice. Appeals for recognition of injustices are often made by attempting to induce this perspectival shift.

Lerner and Miller also point to similarities between victim derogation and self-derogation (1978, p. 1043). One interpretation of this similarity suggests a contradiction, as actors are thought to attribute the cause of their own characteristics and behavior, and responsibility for them, to external forces. However, responses to one's own fate probably appear to be more important to the individual than do responses to another's fate. Thus, as several investigators have suggested, attributions of one's

[7]In some research, an individual attributes causes of another's success or failure in which the attributer has had a clear causal role. In one case, no evidence was found for ego-defensive attributions, but there was evidence for counterdefensive attributions (Ross, Bierbrauer, & Polly, 1974).

own outcomes to one's own characteristics may be functional in leading toward action designed to affect the outcomes or in leading toward understandable explanations of orderliness in the world.[8]

2. EGO-DEFENSIVE BIAS

A focus on the derogation literature points to another important, and frequently investigated bias, the ego-defensive bias. Note first, however, that all the derogation research deals with reactions to individuals who have received negative outcomes. One accepts the designation of "victim" because the outcome is negative and also, perhaps, because the most appealing construction of the experimental setting is that the recipient did nothing that led directly to the outcome. Even if subjects in this research often attribute personal responsibility to the victim, it appears that the authors and professional readers of the research do not.

There seems widespread evidence of self-serving biases in attributions in a wide variety of settings (cf. Bradley, 1978; Snyder et al., 1978; Zuckerman, 1979). Through these biases, attributers are thought to try to maintain or to enhance their general self-esteem or a positive opinion regarding one of their specific dispositions. The clearest cases involve individuals attributing the cause of their own outcomes, where they are inclined to attribute successful outcomes internally and unsuccessful outcomes externally. These results suggest that the fundamental attribution error, which is less likely to be applied to the self, is also less likely to be applied to the self's negative outcomes.

To the extent these biases occur,[9] the fact that they are referred to as "biases" suggests that perceptions of justice are involved. Thus, if actors give themselves more credit for success and less blame for failure than

[8]Several investigators who have commented on the functional nature of self as opposed to external attributions seem to ignore the possible validity and productiveness associated with external attributions. This is the case, at least in part, because external attributions have usually been understood to focus on chance, luck, and so on. In addition, the other major category of external attribution that is discussed, attribution to task difficulty, is seen most often in microlevel terms. The possibility of systematic, structural barriers to performance, similar in their externality and stability to task difficulty, has not often been explored in this work. Only the Gurins and their colleagues (e.g., Gurin, Gurin, & Morrison, 1978) have pointed out the importance of distinguishing attributions to individuals and to structural factors, as well as questioning the productiveness of individualistic attributions of an internal character for members of oppressed groups. Furby (1979) points to a similar "individualistic" bias in closely related work on the concept of locus of control. I will return to this issue in Section III. D. 5. of what follows.

[9]The current state of the evidence convinces most researchers that self-serving biases are widespread, despite some occasional evidence to the contrary (e.g., Ross, Bierbrauer, & Polly, 1974). There *is* still disagreement over the relative importance of cognitive and motivational factors in this bias.

do observers evaluating these same situations, then this constitutes a "bias" not only because a disagreement is noted, but also because the individual seems to be unduly and *unjustly* affected by his or her own self-interest. The individual seems to want more, and to give up less, than others seem to think he or she deserves (cf. Greenberg, 1981). Perceptions of the justice of individuals rest on judgments of their having met appropriate preconditions for obtaining positive or avoiding negative outcomes. If it can be assumed that observers, with little apparent personal stake in the situation other than applications of the standards of deserving, apply these standards "objectively," then this attributional bias suggests that individuals feel their own outcomes are less just than others perceive them to be (cf. Ross & Sicoly, 1979).

The controversy over the relative importance of cognitive and motivational factors in this bias can be of use here. Justice theorists have no qualms about making egoistic assumptions concerning actors' motivations (e.g., Walster *et al.*, 1978, Proposition I), but the attributional concomitants of such assumptions have yet to receive systematic attention. One might interpret the controversy in terms of differential emphasis on the primacy of one factor over the other. Those with cognitive interpretations (e.g., Miller, 1978; Miller & Ross, 1975; Nisbett & Ross, 1980) suggest that more or less rational cognitive processes of the actor, situated as he or she is, yield attributions of cause and responsibility and perceptions of justice that produce positive feelings about the self. Those with motivational interpretations (e.g., Bradley, 1978; Schneider *et al.*, 1979; Snyder *et al.*, 1978; Zuckerman, 1979) seem to suggest that the desire to maintain or to enhance esteem has as its consequences certain kinds of information search and processing. Each views the factor it stresses as primary, the other as derivative.

This suggests an alternative interpretation of self-interest biases that those studying justice claim to find in their subjects. The differential thresholds for the experience of unjust overreward and unjust underreward are usually interpreted in terms of some version of egoism. One might also see these differential thresholds as a consequence of cognitively based attributional processes. For example, if success (at least in test situations) is likely to be anticipated, consistent with past experience, and intentional, whereas failure is more likely to be unanticipated, inconsistent, and unintentional (see Deaux, 1976; Feather & Simon, 1975; Miller, 1978; Miller & Ross, 1975; Nisbett & Ross, 1980), then success may appear to an actor as the result of intention, the "central factor in personal responsibility [Heider, 1958, p. 112]," and thus deserving of a just receipt. Failure would appear to the actor as unintentional, therefore an outcome for which he or she is less personally responsible, and an outcome not justly deserving of blame or punishment. Receiving a specific amount more than deserved (i.e., unjust overreward) may be seen as more just than receiving an identical amount less than deserved, because the former outcome is more easily seen as the result of some intention for which the actor accepts personal responsibility.

Data confirming the existence of a self-serving bias, whatever the source of that bias, provide an important reason for distinguishing between perceptions of justice in which the perceiver's outcomes are directly involved and those in which they are not. Clearly, perceived justice in the former situation is more likely to reflect the impact of the perceiver's desire to attend to his or her own outcomes, whereas this tendency plays less of a role in the latter case.

3. ROLE BIAS

One additional bias may be particularly important to perceptions of justice. Ross (1977) points out that a specific implication of the fundamental attribution error is the tendency for lay attributers to underestimate the effects of roles. Ross's discussion suggests limiting the effects of such an implication to a concern with underestimations of the effects of roles on success in self-presentation, but there appears no good reason to concur in such a restriction. Ross does point to some of the implications of his own research (e.g., Ross, Amabile, & Steinmetz, 1977) for interactions between individuals differing in power:

> Individuals who enjoy positions of power by accident of birth, favorable political treatment, or even their own efforts tend to enjoy advantages in self-presentation. Such individuals, and especially disadvantaged underlings, may greatly underestimate the extent to which the seemingly positive attributes of the powerful simply reflect the advantages of social control. Indeed, this distortion in social judgment threatens to provide a particularly insidious brake upon social mobility, whereby the disadvantaged and powerless overestimate the capabilities of the powerful, who in turn inappropriately deem their own caste well suited to the task of leadership [Ross, 1977, pp. 195–196].

These roles may bias the data available by controlling access to information on which attributional judgments, of cause and responsibility, are made. Control of information on which attributions are based is thus important for understanding the sources of differing perceptions of justice.

Walster and Walster (1975), Homans (1976), and others recently have pointed out that social psychological discussions of justice rarely explore the relationship between justice and power (see also Cohen & Greenberg, Chapter 1, this volume). Wolff (1977) makes a similar critical observation on philosophical discussions of justice. The aspect of power that is crucial in the current context is the ability of an actor or a collectivity to enforce relative attributions of cause and responsibility for (broadly defined) characteristics and outcomes seen as relevant to justice. Ross's suggestion points to the advantages of the powerful in enforcing a particular attributional pattern through control of information. This ability will have clear effects on perceptions of justice. One is reminded again of the relationship between attributions of cause and responsibility, on the one hand, and perceptions of justice, on the other, which distinguish those philosophers, social scientists, and political actors who tend to see current, large-scale institutional arrangements as just (e.g., Friedman, 1962; Nozick, 1974) from those who see these arrangements as unjust (e.g., Bowles & Gintis, 1976; Rawls, 1971; Wolff, 1977).[10]

4. CULTURAL BIAS

Finally, one may point to the existence and impact of a culturally related attributional bias. In their discussion of recent metatheoretical issues in human inferential processes, Nisbett and Ross (1980) point to the widespread belief in a dispositionalist theory deeply imbedded in the texture of our culture:

> According to this view, good or bad luck, accidents of birth, and situational adversities may forestall matters but one's fate will eventually mirror one's character, and one's personal traits and abilities will ultimately prevail over circumstances. . . . It is the set of beliefs which Max Weber (1904) long ago identified as a precondition for the rise of capitalism, and it is consistent with the many philosophical positions that have assigned central roles to the concepts of personal responsibility and free will. [From Richard Nisbett, Lee Ross, *Human Inference: Strategies and Shortcomings of Social Judgement,* © 1980, p. 31. Reprinted by permission of Prentice-Hall, Inc., Englewood Cliffs, N.J.]

The possible prevalence of these beliefs raise several crucial issues for an understanding of perceptions of justice.

First, to the extent that they characterize almost everyone socialized in this culture, these beliefs may have a serious impact on the way justice is perceived *and* discussed. Note the similarity between the beliefs and the charges of cultural bias (cf. Deutsch, 1975; Pepitone, 1976; Sampson, 1969, 1975) that have been directed at the most prominent social psychological statement on justice, equity theory (see also Gergen, Morse, & Gergen, 1980). The usefulness of equity theory (Walster *et al.,*

---

[10]A very similar suggestion has been made by Lenski (1966; also see Section II. D. in this chapter).

1978) rests partially on the assumption that individuals perceive justice as a correspondence between ratios of characteristics and outcomes. It further assumes that individuals feel it is *both* ethically appropriate *and* possible to determine the extent to which each recipient unit is distinguished by a certain level of a relevant characteristic. If it were not *possible* to distinguish recipients in terms of their characteristics, there would be no basis on which to allocate outcomes differentially to them. If it were not ethically appropriate, then what differences there were among recipients would not *justify* differential outcomes. Thus, individuals' beliefs that such differences are both capable of detection and ethically relevant to a conception of justice that distinguishes recipient units are part of the underlying assumptions of equity theory.

Critics of the theory also suggest that it deals solely with recipients' contributions (Leventhal, 1976b), ignoring or misinterpreting the possible importance of recipients' needs and a norm of equality in perceptions of justice. A norm of equality distinct from equity might be based on one of two different beliefs contrary to those described earlier as crucial to equity theory: (1) that different contributions *do not* provide an ethically appropriate justification; or (2) that it is *impossible* to disentangle the contributions of individual recipient units. Those who stress the impact of an equality norm on perceptions of justice usually focus on the first alternative belief. When the second is discussed, it is usually discussed in terms of cognitive limitations of the perceivers (e.g., Leventhal, 1976b), not what might be described as the "objectively" complex task of disentangling individual contributions. Research on allocation is partially misleading here because it usually presents contributions already individualized, as if there were no problem in performing this task. As discussed earlier in this chapter, the impact of needs on justice seems clearly related to the perceivers' beliefs about the recipient's personal responsibility in creating the need.

Whereas most work in attribution has focused on general attributional principles applicable to all perceivers, some investigators have focused on individual differences in the employment of these principles. Most important here is Rotter's distinction between those who tend to employ either internal or external attributions in explaining their own outcomes. One of the most important issues raised by research employing Rotter's I–E scale has been the dimensionality of beliefs about control (e.g., Gurin, Gurin, & Morrison, 1978; MacDonald, 1973).[11]

Perhaps most critical for the present discussion is the distinction

---

[11]I am *not* discussing individual differences in justice perceptions per se here, nor the role of individual differences and situational variables. Such a discussion can be found in Chapter 2 of the current volume by Major and Deaux.

drawn by the Gurins between "personal control," (i.e., individuals' beliefs about the factors controlling events in their own lives), and "control ideology," (i.e., beliefs about the factors controlling the distribution of outcomes in society; Gurin, Gurin, Lao, & Beattie, 1969). The Gurins also have questioned the assumption in much I–E research that an internal orientation is more positive and healthier than an external orientation. At least for some individuals in some situations, an internal orientation might well be extremely counterproductive, and an external orientation, productive.

Both Rotter's original I–E scale (1966) and early research tended to define external control in terms of chance, whereas the Gurins pointed out the importance of external factors not at all related to chance, such as systematic structural discrimination, discrimination that is reasonably predictable and stable. These distinctions may be important for personality measures explicitly linked with the concept of justice (e.g., Greenberg, 1979; Major & Deaux, Chapter 2, this volume; Mirels & Garrett, 1971; Rubin & Peplau, 1975).

However, the distinctions also may be important for pointing to limitations of the distinctions among perceived causes of success and failure that Weiner (1974) has systematized from Heider. Weiner's fourfold taxonomy identifies luck and task difficulty as the primary externally perceived causes of success and failure. Extensions of this taxonomy based on Rosenbaum's introduction of an intentionality dimension (Rosenbaum, 1972) describe external factors in terms of characteristics of other individuals (cf. the use of this expanded classification in Utne & Kidd, 1980, and in Weiner et al., 1978). Such factors are clearly important, but there has been little attention paid to the possibility that the perceived external causes of success and failure include social structural facilitators or constraints.[12]

If it is true that forces accentuating the tendency toward internal causal and personal responsibility attributions reflect a tendency to see the world as just, then one would expect significant correlations between internality and perceived justice. This has been borne out in several investigations (e.g., Mirels & Garrett, 1971; Rubin & Peplau, 1975) despite the fact that these studies did not distinguish personal and ideological internality.[13] This relationship is consistent with earlier suggestions

[12]Although they do call attention to important differences in external attributions, the Gurins do not identify the potential importance of differences in the consequences of two internal attributions: attributions to ability and attributions to motivation. Most of their "internal" items (e.g., Gurin & Gurin, 1976) include references to both. The differential relevance to personal responsibility and perceived justice is thus obscured.

[13]It is important to note that the Just World Scale (Rubin & Peplau, 1975), refers, for the most part, to "justice in general," not justice for a specific individual or justice in the

concerning divergent attributional perspectives (Section III. B.) and the fundamental attribution error (Section III. D. 2.). The link may also be related to differences in philosophical positions on justice. If one believes, as Nozick (1974) does and as Rawls (1971) and Wolff (1977) do not, that political and economic institutions are responsive to the efforts of individuals (individual control ideology), one will tend to see a society supporting those institutions as just. If, however, one believes that there are significant external constraints (external control ideology), one will tend to see the society as unjust.

I have been stressing the role of causal and responsibility attributions in perceptions of justice. One might also look at different attributional patterns as ideological justifications for, or ideological critiques of, different distributions of outcomes. One of the consequences of either lay or scientific causal theories stressing the role of individual effort and responsibility may be the ideological justification of a distribution of outcomes (cf. Furby's [1979] argument concerning a similar characteristic, what she terms an "individualistic bias," in studies of the locus of control concept). One might expect those benefiting from such distributions to be more prone to such theories than to theories emphasizing the structural constraints imposed on individuals. This suggestion points to the importance of work not only on the demographic distribution of justice perceptions, on which substantial progress already can be reported (e.g., Alves & Rossi, 1978; Huber & Form, 1973; Jasso & Rossi, 1977; Rainwater, 1974), but also on the demographic distribution of ideologies of cause and responsibility, on which work has only begun (e.g., Gurin *et al.*, 1978).

IV. CONCLUSION

I have argued in this chapter that an understanding of justice perceptions *demands* an understanding of perceivers' attributions of cause and responsibility. This is no less true for philosophers and social and psychological theorists than it is for the person on the street. Several themes in the attribution literature of the past decade have provided the focus for an examination of the specific role these attributions play.

Work on divergent attributional perspectives points to some of the sources of conflict in justice perceptions across individuals and, perhaps, across groups. It also suggests the dynamics underlying attempts to

---

distribution of outcomes among specified classes of recipients. The distinction between personal control and ideology of control might need to be extended to justice.

change the justice perceptions of particular persons or groups, appeals or demands that they attribute personal responsibility for characteristics thought to be ethically appropriate correlates of deserved outcomes or personal responsibility for the outcomes themselves. Work on the use of covariation principles in causal attribution suggests the crucial dimension of consensus information for perceptions of justice. It also gives reason to believe that those working on attribution and those working on justice have much to learn from each other about the conditions under which individuals employ consensus information. Finally, work on attributional biases points to the importance of distinguishing situations in which the perceiver is also a recipient from those in which he or she is not, to the importance of the perceiver's "stake" in the distribution. This distinction and its importance seem self-evident, but its implications have not been systematically explored, or in some cases even discussed, in much of the work on justice.

There are several other relationships between attributions and justice that might have been explored fruitfully here but were not due to limitations of space. For example, it seems reasonable to suggest that perceptions of justice may, in some instances, be an important factor contributing to attributions of cause and responsibility. Thus, because individuals may see such a close link between attributions of efficient cause and attributions of moral responsibility, they may be reluctant to pursue a "lead" on causal determinants for fear that such a lead, if confirmed, may appear to justify what they consider to be unjust outcomes or distributions.

Second, some evidence has accumulated to suggest that beliefs about the future effects of allocations may affect both the allocations themselves and perceptions of the justice of the current allocation (e.g., Green, 1977; Leventhal, 1976a). Justice may have a retrospective *and* a prospective character. Kelley (1972) has suggested that moral judgments also have a dual character, looking to the past for a judgment of personal responsibility and looking to the future, where "even when they are made of past or imaginary acts, they still serve a dynamic purpose—that of discouraging (or encouraging) similar acts later on [Stevenson, 1967, p. 142, quoted in Kelley, 1972, p. 17]." If it seems reasonable to suggest that perceptions of justice are based not only on judgments of past, but on attempts to influence future, responsibility of relevant actors, an understanding of the psychology of intuitive prediction may become important. The various heuristics involved in such judgments provide a fertile ground for justice researchers (e.g., Fischhoff, 1976; Nisbett & Ross, 1980; Tversky & Kahneman, 1974).

A third additional focus for future work might concern the relationship between perceptions of the justice of differential outcomes of different racial, sexual, and class divisions, and the individual's causal explanations of those differential outcomes. The shift from genetic to environmental explanations for characteristics associated with racial group membership seems to have led a significant portion of the public in the United States to attribute racial differences in occupation, income, and status, not to differences in genetically related abilities, but to personally controllable effort and motivation (e.g., Schuman, 1968). Such attributions would, according to the argument in this chapter, lead to a perception of the justice of racial differences in such outcomes. There is suggestive evidence that similar relationships might obtain for perceptions of the justice of differences between the sexes and between classes, but such possibilities require much additional work (cf. Feldman-Summers & Kiesler, 1974; Huber & Form, 1973; Rainwater, 1974; Taynor & Deaux, 1973; Younger, Arrowood, & Hemsley, 1977).

Finally, throughout this chapter, I have avoided discussing the serious challenges that have been mounted against the internal–external distinction in attribution theory (e.g., Buss, 1978, 1979; Kruglanski, 1975). These critical perspectives suggest the importance of distinguishing "causes" from "reasons" and the possibility that attribution theory has become overly preoccupied with the role of causes in lay understanding and explanation. Buss's critique is particularly relevant here, focusing as he does on a conception of a "reason" as an actor's "justificatory explanation [Buss, 1979, p. 1459]." In the context of his critique of work on divergent attributional perspectives, Buss (1978) suggests that, in most of the situations studied, observers may have been offering causal explanations of the actor's behavior, whereas actors themselves were "all engaged in attempting to *justify* their actions, provide a *rationale* for their actions, make their actions *intelligible* to others, as well as offer a *moral* explanation of their actions—all in the context of their society's rules for 'proper' conduct [Buss, 1978, p. 1315; emphases all in original]."

Buss admits the possibility that actors offer causal explanations, and that observers offer reason explanations, for the actor's behavior. Thus, although causes and reasons may be conceptually distinct, they are also closely related. Their relationship may bear a strong resemblance to the relationship I have been trying to argue for here, between attributions of cause and attributions of responsibility. Understanding a person's perceptions of justice may require an understanding of his or her attributions of cause and responsibility, as well as an understanding of the reasons he or she gives to explain the actions of potential recipients. The nature of these conceptual relationships, and the research they will require, constitutes one final focus for the work to come.

ACKNOWLEDGMENTS

I would like to thank Jerald Greenberg, Philip Brickman, Lita Furby, and Daniel Wegner for their comments on an earlier version of this chapter.

REFERENCES

Adams, J. S. Inequity in social exchange. In L. Berkowitz (Ed.), *Advances in experimental social psychology* (Vol. 2). New York: Academic Press, 1965.

Alves, W. M., & Rossi, P. H. Who should get what? Fairness judgments of the distribution of earnings. *American Journal of Sociology*, 1978, *84*, 541–556.

Anderson, N. H. Cognitive algebra: Integration theory applied to social attribution. In L. Berkowitz (Ed.), *Advances in experimental social psychology* (Vol. 7). New York: Academic Press, 1974.

Anderson, N. H. Equity judgments as information integration. *Journal of Personality and Social Psychology*, 1976, *33*, 192–199.

Arkin, R., & Duval, S. Focus of attention and causal attributions of actors and observers. *Journal of Experimental Social Psychology*, 1975, *11*, 427–438.

Austin, W. Equity theory and social comparison processes. In J. Suls & R. Miller (Eds.), *Social comparison processes: Theoretical and empirical perspectives*. Washington: Hemisphere, 1977.

Barnes, R. D., Ickes, W. J., & Kidd, R. F. Effects of perceived intentionality and stability of another's dependency on helping behavior. *Personality and Social Psychology Bulletin*, 1979, *5*, 367–372.

Berger, J., Zelditch, M., Anderson, B., & Cohen, B. P. Structural aspects of distributive justice: A status-value formulation. In J. Berger, M. Zelditch, & B. Anderson (Eds.), *Sociological theories in progress* (Vol. 2). Boston: Houghton Mifflin, 1972.

Bierbrauer, G. Effects of set, perspective, and temporal factors in attribution. Unpublished doctoral dissertation, Stanford University, 1973. Cited in R. Nisbett & L. Ross, *Human inference: Strategies and shortcomings of social judgment*. Englewood Cliffs, N.J.: Prentice-Hall, 1980.

Bowles, S., & Gintis, H. *Schooling in capitalist America: Educational reform and the contradictions of economic life*. New York: Basic Books, 1976.

Bradley, G. W. Self-serving biases in the attribution process: A reexamination of the fact or fiction question. *Journal of Personality and Social Psychology*, 1978, *36*, 56–71.

Brewer, M. B. An information-processing approach to attribution of responsibility. *Journal of Experimental Social Psychology*, 1977, *13*, 58–69.

Brickman, P. Preference for inequality. *Sociometry*, 1977, *40*, 303–310.

Brickman, P., & Bryan, J. H. Equity versus equality as factors in children's moral judgments of thefts, charity, and third-party transfers. *Journal of Personality and Social Psychology*, 1976, *34*, 757–761.

Brickman, P., Ryan, K., & Wortman, C. B. Causal chains: Attribution of responsibility as a function of immediate or prior causes. *Journal of Personality and Social Psychology*, 1975, *32*, 1060–1067.

Bulman, R. J., & Wortman, C. B. Attributions of blame and coping in the "real world:" Severe accident victims react to their lot. *Journal of Personality and Social Psychology*, 1977, *35*, 351–363.

Buss, A. R. Causes and reasons in attribution theory: A conceptual critique. *Journal of Personality and Social Psychology*, 1978, *36*, 1311–1321.

Buss, A. R. On the relationship between causes and reasons. *Journal of Personality and Social Psychology*, 1979, *37*, 1458–1461.

Caplan, N., & Nelson, S. D. On being useful: The nature and consequences of psychological research on social problems. *American Psychologist*, 1973, *28*, 199–211.

Chaikin, A. L., & Darley, J. M. Victim or perpetrator? Defensive attribution of responsibility and the need for order and justice. *Journal of Personality and Social Psychology*, 1973, *25*, 268–275.

Cohen, R. L. Mastery and justice in laboratory dyads: A revision and extension of equity theory. *Journal of Personality and Social Psychology*, 1974, *29*, 464–474.

Cohen, R. L. *A critique of reward allocation research on distributive justice*. Unpublished manuscript, Bennington College, 1978. (a)

Cohen, R. L. *Toward an integration of equity and attribution perspectives on conceptions of distributive justice*. Unpublished manuscript, Bennington College, 1978. (b)

Cohen, R. L. On the distinction between individual deserving and distributive justice. *Journal for the Theory of Social Behaviour*, 1979, *9*, 167–185.

Coleman, J. The concept of equality of educational opportunity. *Harvard Educational Review*, 1968, *38*, 7–22.

Cunningham, J. D., Starr, P. A., & Kanouse, D. E. Self as actor, active observer, and passive observer: Implications for causal attributions. *Journal of Personality and Social Psychology*, 1979, *37*, 1146–1152.

Curtis, R. C. Effects of knowledge of self-interest and social relationship upon the use of equity, utilitarian, and Rawlsian principles of allocation. *European Journal of Social Psychology*, 1979, *9*, 165–175.

Damon, W. *The social world of the child*. San Francisco: Jossey-Bass, 1977.

Deaux, K. Sex: A perspective on the attribution process. In J. H. Harvey, W. J. Ickes, & R. F. Kidd (Eds.), *New directions in attribution research* (Vol. 1). Hillsdale, N.J.: Erlbaum, 1976.

Deutsch, M. Equity, equality, and need: What determines which value will be used as a basis for distributive justice? *Journal of Social Issues*, 1975, *31*, 137–150.

Duval, S., Duval, V. H., & Neely, R. Self-focus, felt responsibility, and helping behavior. *Journal of Personality and Social Psychology*, 1979, *37*, 1769–1778.

Duval, S., & Hensley, V. Extensions of objective self-awareness theory: The focus of attention-causal attribution hypothesis. In J. H. Harvey, W. J. Ickes, & R. F. Kidd (Eds.), *New directions in attribution research* (Vol. 1). Hillsdale, N.J.: Erlbaum, 1976.

Duval, S., & Wicklund, R. A. *A theory of objective self-awareness*. New York: Academic Press, 1972.

Eckhoff, T. *Justice: Its determinants in social interaction*. Rotterdam: Rotterdam University Press, 1974.

Eisen, S. V. Actor–observer differences in information inference and causal attribution. *Journal of Personality and Social Psychology*, 1979, *37*, 261–272.

Farkas, A. J., & Anderson, N. H. Multidimensional input in equity theory. *Journal of Personality and Social Psychology*, 1979, *37*, 879–896.

Feather, N. T., & Simon, J. G. Reactions to male and female success and failure in sex-linked occupations: Impressions of personality, causal attributions, and perceived likelihood of different consequences. *Journal of Personality and Social Psychology*, 1975, *31*, 20–31.

Feinberg, J. *Doing and deserving: Essays in the theory of responsibility*. Princeton: Princeton University Press, 1970.

Feldman, N. S., Higgins, E. T., Karlovac, M., & Ruble, D. N. Use of consensus information in causal attributions as a function of temporal presentation and availability of direct information. *Journal of Personality and Social Psychology*, 1976, *34*, 694–698.

Feldman-Summers, S., & Kiesler, S. B. Those who are number two try harder: The effect of sex on attributions of causality. *Journal of Personality and Social Psychology*, 1974, *30*, 846–855.

Fincham, F., & Jaspars, J. Attribution of responsibility to the self and other in children and adults. *Journal of Personality and Social Psychology*, 1979, *37*, 1589–1602.

Fincham, F., & Jaspars, J. Attribution of responsibility: From man the scientist to man as lawyer. In L. Berkowitz (Ed.), *Advances in experimental social psychology* (Vol. 13). New York: Academic Press, 1980.

Fishbein, M., & Ajzen, I. Attribution of responsibility: A theoretical note. *Journal of Experimental Social Psychology*, 1973, *9*, 148–153.

Fishhoff, B. Attribution theory and judgment under uncertainty. In J. H. Harvey, W. J. Ickes, & R. F. Kidd (Eds.), *New directions in attribution research* (Vol. 1). Hillsdale, N.J.: Erlbaum, 1976.

Frankena, W. K. The concept of social justice. in R. B. Brandt (Ed.), *Social justice*. Englewood Cliffs, N.J.: Prentice-Hall, 1962.

Friedman, M. *Capitalism and freedom*. Chicago: University of Chicago Press, 1962.

Frieze, I., & Weiner, B. Cue utilization and attributional judgments for success and failure. *Journal of Personality*, 1971, *39*, 591–605.

Furby, L. Individualistic bias in studies of locus of control. In A. R. Buss (Ed.), *Psychology in a social context*. New York: Irvington Press, 1979.

Garrett, J., & Libby, W. L. Role of intentionality in mediating responses to inequity in the dyad. *Journal of Personality and Social Psychology*, 1973, *28*, 21–27.

Gergen, K. J., Morse, S. J., & Gergen, M. M. Behavior exchange in cross-cultural perspective. In H. C. Triandis & R. W. Brislin (Eds.), *Handbook of cross-cultural psychology: Social psychology* (Vol. 5). Boston: Allyn & Bacon, 1980.

Goodman, P. S. An examination of referents used in the evaluation of pay. *Organizational Behavior and Human Performance*, 1974, *12*, 170–195.

Gouldner, A. W. The norm of reciprocity: A preliminary statement. *American Sociological Review*, 1960, *25*, 161–178.

Green, R. M. Intergenerational distributive justice and environmental responsibility. *Bioscience*, 1977, *27*, 260–265.

Greenberg, J. Allocator–recipient similarity and the equitable division of rewards. *Social Psychology*, 1978, *41*, 337–341.

Greenberg, J. Protestant ethic endorsement and the fairness of equity inputs. *Journal of Research in Personality*, 1979, *13*, 81–90

Greenberg, J. The justice of distributing scarce and abundant resources. In M. J. Lerner & S. Lerner (Eds.), *The justice motive in social behavior*. New York: Plenum, 1981.

Gurin, G., & Gurin, P. Personal efficacy and the ideology of personal responsibility. In B. Strumpel (Ed.), *Economic means for human needs*. Ann Arbor: Institute for Social Research, 1976.

Gurin, P., Gurin, G., Lao, R. C., & Beattie, M. Internal–external control in the motivational dynamics of Negro youth. *Journal of Social Issues*, 1969, *25*, 29–53.

Gurin, P., Gurin, G., & Morrison, B. M. Personal and ideological aspects of internal and external control. *Social Psychology*, 1978, *41*, 275–296.

Hamilton, D. L. A cognitive–attributional analysis of stereotyping. In L. Berkowitz (Ed.), *Advances in experimental social psychology* (Vol. 12). New York: Academic Press, 1979.

Hamilton, V. L. Who is responsible? Toward a *social* psychology of responsibility attribution. *Social Psychology*, 1978, *41*, 316–328.

Hansen, R. D., & Donoghue, J. M. The power of consensus: Information derived from one's own and other's behavior. *Journal of Personality and Social Psychology*, 1977, *35*, 294–302.

Harris, B. Developmental differences in the attribution of responsibility. *Developmental Psychology*, 1977, *13*, 257–265.

Harris, R. J. Handling negative inputs: On the plausible equity formulae. *Journal of Experimental Social Psychology*, 1976, *12*, 194–209.

Harvey, J. H. Attribution of freedom. In J. H. Harvey, W. J. Ickes, & R. F. Kidd (Eds.), *New directions in attribution research* (Vol. 1). Hillsdale, N.J.: Erlbaum, 1976.

Harvey, J. H., Harris, B., & Barnes, R. D. Actor–observer differences in the perceptions of responsibility and freedom. *Journal of Personality and Social Psychology*, 1975, *32*, 22–28.

Harvey, J. H., Wells, G. L., & Alvarez, M. D. Attribution in the context of conflict and separation in close relationships. In J. H. Harvey, W. J. Ickes, & R. F. Kidd (Eds.), *New directions in attribution research* (Vol. 2). Hillsdale, N.J.: Erlbaum, 1978.

Heider, F. *The psychology of interpersonal relations*. New York: Wiley, 1958.

Homans, G. C. *Social behavior: Its elementary forms*. New York: Harcourt Brace & World, 1961.

Homans, G. C. *Social behavior: Its elementary forms* (Rev. ed.). New York: Harcourt Brace Jovanovich, 1974.

Homans, G. C. Commentary. In L. Berkowitz & E. Walster (Eds.), *Advances in experimental social psychology* (Vol. 9). New York: Academic Press, 1976.

Horai, J. Attributional conflict. *Journal of Social Issues*, 1977, *33*, 88–100.

Huber, J., & Form, W. *Income and ideology*. New York: Free Press, 1973.

Ickes, W. J., & Kidd, R. F. An attributional analysis of helping behavior. In J. H. Harvey, W. J. Ickes, & R. F. Kidd (Eds.), *New directions in attribution research* (Vol. 1). Hillsdale, N.J.: Erlbaum, 1976.

Janoff-Bulman, R. Characterological versus behavioral self-blame: Inquiries into depression and rape. *Journal of Personality and Social Psychology*, 1979, *37*, 1798–1809.

Jasso, G., & Rossi, P. H. Distributive justice and earned income. *American Sociological Review*, 1977, *42*, 639–651.

Jones, E. E., & Davis, K. E. From acts to dispositions: The attribution process in person perception. In L. Berkowitz (Ed.), *Advances in experimental social psychology* (Vol. 2). New York: Academic Press, 1965.

Jones, E. E., & Harris, V. A. The attribution of attitudes. *Journal of Experimental Social Psychology* 1967, *3*, 1–24.

Jones, E. E., & McGillis, D. Correspondent inferences and the attribution cube: A comparative reappraisal. In J. H. Harvey, W. J. Ickes, & R. F. Kidd (Eds.), *New directions in attribution research* (Vol. 1). Hillsdale, N.J.: Erlbaum, 1976.

Jones, E. E., & Nisbett, R. E. The actor and the observer: Divergent perceptions of the causes of behavior. In E. E. Jones, D. E. Kanouse, H. H. Kelley, R. E. Nisbett, S. Valins, & B. Weiner (Eds.), *Attribution: Perceiving the causes of behavior*. Morristown, N.J.: General Learning Press, 1972.

Kayser, E., & Lamm, H. Input integration and input weighting in decisions on allocations of gains and losses. *European Journal of Social Psychology*, 1980, *10*, 10–15. (a)

Kayser, E., & Lamm, H. *The weight of performance, effort, and ability in the allocation of jointly attained gains and losses*. Unpublished manuscript, University of Mannheim, 1980. (b)

Kayser, E., & Lamm, H. Attribution of responsibility for joint work outcomes in dyads of high and low attraction in a natural setting. *Social Behavior and Personality*, in press.

Kelley, H. H. Attribution theory in social psychology. In D. Levine (Ed.), *Nebraska symposium on motivation*. Lincoln: University of Nebraska Press, 1967.

Kelley, H. H. Moral evaluation. *American Psychologist*, 1971, *26*, 293–300.

Kelley, H. H. Attribution in social interaction. In E. E. Jones, D. E. Kanouse, H. H. Kelley, R. E. Nisbett, S. Valins, & B. Weiner (Eds.), *Attribution: Perceiving the causes of behavior*. Morristown, N.J.: General Learning Press, 1972.

Kelley, H. H. The process of causal attribution. *American Psychologist*, 1973, *28*, 107–128.

Kelley, H. H., & Michela, J. L. Attribution theory and research. *Annual Review of Psychology*, 1980, *31*, 457–501.

Kohlberg, L. Development of moral character and moral ideology. In M. L. Hoffman & L. W. Hoffman (Eds.), *Review of child development research* (Vol. 1). New York: Russell Sage Foundation, 1964.

Kohlberg, L. Moral stages and moralization: The cognitive–developmental approach. In T. Lickona (Ed.), *Moral development and behavior: Theory, research, and social issues.* New York: Holt, Rinehart and Winston, 1976.

Kruglanski, A. The endogenous–exogenous partition in attribution theory. *Psychological Review*, 1975, *82*, 387–406.

Lamm, H., & Kayser, E. The allocation of monetary gain and loss following dyadic performance: The weight given to effort and ability under conditions of low and high intradyadic attraction. *European Journal of Social Psychology*, 1978, *8*, 275–279.

Lamm, H., Kayser, E., & Schanz, V. *Allocation of monetary gain and loss produced by team work: An attributional analysis of the role of differences in members' ability and effort.* Unpublished manuscript, University of Mannheim, 1978.

Lawler, E. J. An experimental study of factors affecting the mobilization of revolutionary coalitions. *Sociometry*, 1975, *38*, 163–179.

Lawler, E. J., & Thompson, M. E. Impact of leader responsibility for inequity on subsequent revolts. *Social Psychology*, 1978, *41*, 264–268.

Lenski, G. *Power and privilege.* New York: McGraw-Hill, 1966.

Lerner, M. J. *Deserving vs. justice: A contemporary dilemma* (Res. Rep. #24). Waterloo, Ontario, Canada: University of Waterloo, Department of Psychology, May 1971.

Lerner, M. J. The justice motive in social behavior: An introduction. *Journal of Social Issues*, 1975, *31*, 1–19.

Lerner, M. J., & Miller, D. T. Just world research and the attribution process: Looking back and ahead. *Psychological Bulletin*, 1978, *85*, 1030–1051.

Leventhal, G. S. The distribution of rewards and resources in groups and organizations. In L. Berkowitz & E. Walster (Eds.), *Advances in experimental social psychology* (Vol. 9). New York: Academic Press, 1976. (a)

Leventhal, G. S. Fairness in social relationships. In J. Thibaut, J. Spence, & R. Carson (Eds.), *Contemporary topics in social psychology.* Morristown, N.J.: General Learning Press, 1976. (b)

Leventhal, G. S., & Michaels, J. Extending the equity model: Perceptions of inputs and allocations of rewards as a function of duration and quantity of performance. *Journal of Personality and Social Psychology*, 1969, *12*, 303–309.

Leventhal, G. S., Weiss, T., & Long, G. Equity, reciprocity, and reallocating rewards in the dyad. *Journal of Personality and Social Psychology*, 1969, *13*, 300–305.

Lewis, O. The culture of poverty. *Scientific American*, 1966, *215*, 19–25.

Libby, W. L., & Garrett, J. Role of intentionality in mediating children's responses to inequity. *Developmental Psychology*, 1974, *10*, 294–297.

MacDonald, A. P. Internal–external locus of control. In J. P. Robinson & P. R. Shaver (Eds.), *Measures of social psychological attitudes* (Rev. ed.). Ann Arbor: Institute for Social Research, 1973.

McArthur, L. Z. The how and what of why: Some determinants and consequences of causal attribution. *Journal of Personality and Social Psychology*, 1972, *22*, 171–193.

McArthur, L. A. The lesser influence of consensus than distinctiveness information on causal attributions: A test of the person–thing hypothesis. *Journal of Personality and Social Psychology*, 1976, *33*, 733–742.

Miller, D. T. What constitutes a self-serving attributional bias? A reply to Bradley. *Journal of Personality and Social Psychology*, 1978, *36*, 1221–1223.

Miller, D. T., & Ross, M. Self-serving biases in the attribution of causality: Fact or fiction? *Psychological Bulletin*, 1975, *82*, 213–225.

Miller, S. M., Riessman, F., & Seagull, A. A. Poverty and self-indulgence: A critique of the nondeferred gratification pattern. In L. A. Ferman, J. L. Kornbluh, & A. Haber (Eds.), *Poverty in America* (Rev. ed.). Ann Arbor: University of Michigan Press, 1972.

Mirels, H. L., & Garrett, J. B. The Protestant ethic as a personality variable. *Journal of Consulting and Clinical Psychology*, 1971, *36*, 40–44.

Mischel, W. Preference for delayed reinforcement: An experimental study of a cultural observation. *Journal of Abnormal and Social Psychology*, 1958, *56*, 57–61.

Mischel, W. Processes in delay of gratification. In L. Berkowitz (Ed.), *Advances in experimental social psychology* (Vol. 7). New York: Academic Press, 1974.

Moschetti, G. J. Calculating equity: Ordinal and ratio criteria. *Social Psychology Quarterly*, 1979, *42*, 172–176.

Nisbett, R. E., Borgida, E., Crandall, R., & Reed, H. Popular induction: Information is not necessarily informative. In J. S. Carroll & J. W. Payne (Eds.), *Cognition and social behavior*. Hillsdale, N.J.: Erlbaum, 1976.

Nisbett, R. E., Caputo, C., Legant, P., & Maracek, J. Behavior as seen by the actor and as seen by the observer. *Journal of Personality and Social Psychology*, 1973, *27*, 154–164.

Nisbett, R. E., & Ross, L. *Human inference: Strategies and shortcomings of social judgment.* Englewood Cliffs, N.J.: Prentice-Hall, 1980.

Nozick, R. *Anarchy, state, and utopia.* New York: Basic Books, 1974.

Orvis, B. R., Kelley, H. H., & Butler, D. Attributional conflict in young couples. In J. H. Harvey, W. J. Ickes, & R. F. Kidd (Eds.), *New directions in attribution research* (Vol. 1). Hillsdale, N.J.: Erlbaum, 1976.

Patchen, M. A conceptual framework and some empirical data regarding comparisons of social rewards. *Sociometry*, 1961, *24*, 136–156.

Pepitone, A. Toward a normative and comparative biocultural social psychology. *Journal of Personality and Social Psychology*, 1976, *34*, 641–653.

Piaget, J. *The moral judgment of the child.* New York: Free Press, 1965.

Pruitt, D. G. Reciprocity and credit building in a laboratory dyad. *Journal of Personality and Social Psychology*, 1968, *8*, 143–147.

Rainwater, L. *What money buys: Inequality and the social meanings of income.* New York: Basic Books, 1974.

Rawls, J. *A theory of justice.* Cambridge: Harvard University Press, 1971.

Regan, D. T., & Totten, J. Empathy and attribution: Turning observers into actors. *Journal of Personality and Social Psychology*, 1975, *32*, 850–856.

Rescher, N. *Distributive justice.* Indianapolis: Bobbs-Merrill, 1967.

Reis, H. T., & Gruzen, J. On mediating equity, equality, and self-interest: The role of self-presentation in social exchange. *Journal of Experimental Social Psychology*, 1976, *12*, 487–503.

Rivera, A. N., & Tedeschi, J. T. Public vs. private reactions to positive inequity. *Journal of Personality and Social Psychology*, 1976, *34*, 895–900.

Rosenbaum, R. M. *A dimensional analysis of the perceived causes of success and failure.* Unpublished doctoral dissertation. University of California, Los Angeles, 1972.

Ross, L. The intuitive psychologist and his shortcomings. In L. Berkowitz (Ed.), *Advances in experimental social psychology* (Vol. 10). New York: Academic Press, 1977.

Ross, L., Amabile, T. M., & Steinmetz, J. L. Social roles, social control, and biases in social perception processes. *Journal of Personality and Social Psychology*, 1977, *35*, 485–494.

Ross, L., Bierbrauer, G., & Polly, S. Attribution of educational outcomes by professional and nonprofessional instructors. *Journal of Personality and Social Psychology,* 1974, *29,* 609–618.

Ross, L., Green, D., & House, P. The false consensus phenomenon: An attributional bias in self-perception and social perception processes. *Journal of Experimental Social Psychology,* 1977, *13,* 279–301.

Ross, M., & DiTecco, D. An attributional analysis of moral judgments. *Journal of Social Issues,* 1975, *31,* 91–109.

Ross, M., & Sicoly, F. Egocentric biases in availability and attribution. *Journal of Personality and Social Psychology,* 1979, *37,* 322–336.

Ross, M., Thibaut, J., & Evenbeck, S. Some determinants of the intensity of social protest. *Journal of Experimental Social Psychology,* 1971, *7,* 401–418.

Rotter, J. B. Generalized expectancies for internal versus external control of reinforcement. *Psychological Monographs,* 1966, *80,* 609.

Rubin, Z., & Peplau, L. Who believes in a just world? *Journal of Social Issues,* 1975, *31,* 65–89.

Sampson, E. E. Studies of status congruence. In L. Berkowitz (Ed.), *Advances in experimental social psychology* (Vol. 4). New York: Academic Press, 1969.

Sampson, E. E. Justice as equality. *Journal of Social Issues,* 1975, *31,* 45–64.

Schneider, D. J., Hastorf, A. H., & Ellsworth, P. C. *Person perception* (2nd ed.). Reading, Mass.: Addison-Wesley, 1979.

Schuman, H. *Free will and determinism in public beliefs about race.* Ann Arbor: Survey Research Center, 1968.

Schuman, H. On the differing perspectives of authors and editors. *Contemporary Sociology,* 1980, *9,* 459.

Schwartz, S. H., & Fleishman, J. A. Personal norms and the mediation of legitimacy effects on helping. *Social Psychology,* 1978, *41,* 306–315.

Sedlak, A. J. Developmental differences in understanding plans and evaluating actors. *Child Development,* 1979, *50,* 536–560.

Seligman, M. E. P. *Helplessness: On depression, development, and death.* San Francisco: Freeman, 1975.

Shaver, K.G. Defensive attribution: Effects of severity and relevance on the responsibility assigned for an accident. *Journal of Personality and Social Psychology,* 1970, *14,* 101–113.

Shaver, K. G. *An introduction to attribution processes.* Cambridge: Winthrop, 1975.

Shaw, M. E., & Sulzer, J. L. An empirical test of Heider's levels in attribution of responsibility. *Journal of Abnormal and Social Psychology,* 1964, *69,* 39–46.

Sicoly, F., & Ross, M. The facilitation of ego-biased attributions by means of self-serving observer feedback. *Journal of Personality and Social Psychology,* 1977, *35,* 734–741.

Snyder, M. L., Stephan, W. G., & Rosenfield, D. Attributional egotism. In J. H. Harvey, W. J. Ickes, & R. F. Kidd (Eds.), *New directions in attribution research* (Vol. 2). Hillsdale, N.J.: Erlbaum 1978.

Stevenson, C. L. *Facts and values: Studies in ethical analysis.* New Haven: Yale University Press, 1967.

Storms, M. D. Videotape and the attribution process: Reversing actors' and observers' points of view. *Journal of Personality and Social Psychology,* 1973, *27,* 165–175.

Taynor, J., & Deaux, K. When women are more deserving than men: Equity, attribution, and perceived sex differences. *Journal of Personality and Social Psychology,* 1973, *28,* 360–367.

Thibaut, J., & Kelley, H. H. *The social psychology of groups.* New York: Wiley, 1959.

Turner, R. H. The self-conception in social interaction. In C. Gordon & K. J. Gergen (Eds.), *The self in social interaction* (Vol. 1). New York: Wiley, 1968.

Turner, R. H. The role and the person. *American Journal of Sociology,* 1978, *84,* 1–23.

Tversky, A., & Kahneman, D. Judgment under uncertainty: Heuristics and biases. *Science,* 1974, *185,* 1124–1131.

Utne, M. K., & Kidd, R. F. Attribution and equity. In G. Mikula (Ed.), *Justice and social interaction.* New York: Springer-Verlag, 1980.

Vidmar, N., & Crinklaw, L. D. Attributing responsibility for an accident: A methodological and conceptual critique. *Canadian Journal of Behavioural Science,* 1974, *6,* 112–130.

Walster, E. Assignment of responsibility for an accident. *Journal of Personality and Social Psychology,* 1966, *3,* 73–79.

Walster, E., & Walster, G. W. Equity and social justice. *Journal of Social Issues,* 1975, *31,* 21–43.

Walster, E., Walster, G. W., & Berscheid, E. *Equity: Theory and research.* Boston: Allyn & Bacon, 1978.

Weary, G. Self-serving attributional biases: Perceptual or response distortions? *Journal of Personality and Social Psychology,* 1979, *37,* 1418–1420.

Weber, M. [*The Protestant Ethic and the spirit of capitalism*]. New York: Scribner, 1930. (Originally published, 1904.)

Wegner, D. M., & Schaefer, D. The concentration of responsibility: An objective self-awareness analysis of group size effects in helping situations. *Journal of Personality and Social Psychology,* 1978, *36,* 147–155.

Weiner, B. *Achievement motivation and attribution theory.* Morristown, N.J.: General Learning Press, 1974.

Weiner, B., Frieze, I., Kukla, A., Reed, L., Rest, S., & Rosenbaum, R. M. Perceiving the causes of success and failure. In E. E. Jones, D. E. Kanouse, H. H. Kelley, R. E. Nisbett, S. Valins, & B. Weiner (Eds.), *Attribution: Perceiving the causes of behavior.* Morristown, N.J.: General Learning Press, 1972.

Weiner, B., & Peter, N. A cognitive–developmental analysis of achievement and moral judgments. *Developmental Psychology,* 1973, *9,* 290–309.

Weiner, B., Russell, D., & Lerman, D. Affective consequences of causal ascriptions. In J. H. Harvey, W. J. Ickes, & R. F. Kidd (Eds.), *New directions in attribution research* (Vol. 2). Hillsdale, N.J.: Erlbaum, 1978.

Wells, G. L., & Harvey, J. H. Do people use consensus information in making causal attributions? *Journal of Personality and Social Psychology,* 1977, *35,* 279–293.

Wicklund, R. A. Objective self-awareness. In L. Berkowitz (Ed.), *Advances in experimental social psychology* (Vol. 8). New York: Academic Press, 1975.

Wiley, M. G., Crittenden, K. S., & Birg, L. D. Why a rejection? Causal attribution of a career achievement event. *Social Psychology Quarterly,* 1979, *42,* 214–222.

Wittig, M. R., Marks, G., & Jones, G. A. The effect of luck versus effort attributions on reward allocation to self and other. *Personality and Social Psychology Bulletin,* 1981, *7,* 71–78.

Wolff, R. P. *Understanding Rawls: A reconstruction and critique of A Theory of Justice.* Princeton: Princeton University Press, 1977.

Wortman, C. B. Causal attributions and personal control. In J. H. Harvey, W. J. Ickes, & R. F. Kidd (Eds.), *New directions in attribution research* (Vol. 1). Hillsdale, N.J.: Erlbaum 1976.

Younger, J. C., Arrowood, A. J., & Hemsley, G. And the lucky shall inherit the earth: Perceiving the causes of financial success and failure. *European Journal of Social Psychology,* 1977, *7,* 509–515.

Zuckerman, M. Use of consensus information in prediction of behavior. *Journal of Experimental Social Psychology,* 1978, *14,* 163–171.

Zuckerman, M. Attribution of success and failure revisited, or: The motivational bias is alive and well in attribution theory. *Journal of Personality,* 1979, *47,* 245–287.

chapter 5

Equity in Attitude Formation and Change

ICEK AJZEN

Social scientists have taken a variety of approaches in their analyses of justice in social exchange (e.g., Adams, 1963; Deutsch, 1975; Homans, 1961; Leventhal, 1976; Stouffer, Suchman, DeVinney, Star, & Williams, 1949; Walster, Berscheid, & Walster, 1973), but most current interest is focused on the role of perceived inequity. Although many investigators have contributed to the formulation of present-day equity theory, its major principles are derived from Festinger's (1957) theory of cognitive dissonance (cf., Adams, 1965). However, in contrast to dissonance theory, which has been a major source of hypotheses for research on attitude formation and change (for reviews, see Fishbein & Ajzen, 1975; Kiesler, Collins, & Miller, 1969; McGuire, 1969), relatively little attention has been paid to the role of equity in this domain; recent developments in equity theory have had no discernable impact on attitude theory and research.

The major objective of the present chapter is to examine the effects of inequity on the formation and change of attitudes in interpersonal relations. Inequity is compared to cognitive dissonance, and the implications of inequity or injustice for attitude formation and change are elaborated. Inequity is usually assumed to be capable of influencing people's attitudes toward their positions in a relationship, toward their partners in the relationship, toward the relationship as a whole, toward the tasks they are to perform, and toward the person or agent responsible for the inequity. The processes whereby inequity is said to affect attitudes of this kind are compared to the predictions made by an information-processing model of attitude formation. These analyses are accom-

161

panied by brief reviews of pertinent empirical literature. The reviews of empirical research are designed to examine the extent to which equity theory permits accurate prediction of attitude formation and change. The chapter concludes with a discussion of the implications of equity theory for influencing behavior in exchange relationships.

I. ATTITUDINAL IMPLICATIONS OF INEQUITY

Generally speaking, inequity is said to exist for a person whenever he or she perceives that the ratio of his or her own outcomes to inputs differs from the outcome-to-input ratio of a comparison other (see Adams, 1965; Walster *et al.*, 1973). To see how such perceived inequity may influence the person's general satisfaction with his or her position as well as the person's more specific attitudes toward aspects of the situation, we must first compare equity theory to the theory of cognitive dissonance from which its major principles were derived.

A. Equity Theory and Cognitive Dissonance

The existence of perceived inequity is assumed to result in distress. When one's own outcomes to inputs fall short of another person's outcomes to inputs (underreward), the predominant emotion should be anger and resentment. In contrast, overreward (an outcome-to-input ratio that favors the individual) is expected to lead to feelings of guilt. The more inequitable the relationship is perceived to be, the greater the distress the individual will feel and, hence, the more he will be motivated to restore equity (cf., Walster, Walster, & Berscheid, 1978).

It can be seen that these propositions are very similar to the principles embodied in Festinger's (1957) theory of cognitive dissonance. As in the case of inequity, dissonance among cognitive elements is assumed to be disturbing and to result in pressures to reduce or to eliminate it. Inequity is often viewed as a special case of cognitive dissonance that involves a perceived discrepancy or inconsistency between one's own inputs and outcomes and those of a reference person or group (Adams, 1963; Wicklund & Brehm, 1976).

A hypothetical example may be instructive. Consider the potential sources of consonance and dissonance in a work situation, the context of most tests of equity theory. Specifically, imagine a lawyer who is working on the staff of a United States senator. The lawyer will hold various beliefs that may be consistent or inconsistent with the knowledge that he

Table 5.1

Hypothetical Example of Absolute Dissonance in a Work Situation

Focal cognitive element "I am working on Senator X's staff."	
Dissonant elements	*Consonant elements*
"I earn less than an insurance salesman without education."	"I am near the center of power."
	"My wife likes life in Washington."
"Nobody cares for my opinions."	
	"I am gaining valuable experience and friends."
"I hardly ever see the senator."	"My work is interesting."

or she is working on the senator's staff. Table 5.1 lists some of the possible consonant and dissonant cognitive elements. Overall dissonance in this situation may be defined by the ratio of dissonant to consonant elements, each weighted by its importance (see Brehm & Cohen, 1962).

Note that in this example cognitive elements are defined as consonant or dissonant without reference to a comparison person. Thus, the element "my work is interesting" is viewed as consonant with being on the senator's staff, irrespective of whether it is more or less interesting than the work of another person. According to equity theory, however, this belief could result in distress if the lawyer viewed his work as interesting but as less (or more) so than the work of a comparison other.

One way of reconciling the two theories is to define cognitive elements in relative terms. For example, the focal element could be redefined as "Other and I have comparable jobs." Some of the relevant consonant and dissonant elements in this case are shown in Table 5.2. It can be seen that the comparison with another person is now built into each cognitive element. Nevertheless, by looking at this hypothetical example, we can

Table 5.2

Hypothetical Example of Relative Dissonance

Focal cognitive element "Other and I have comparable jobs."	
Dissonant elements	*Consonant elements*
"I earn less than Other."	"I work as many hours as Other."
"Other has more clerical assistance."	"Other and I both get company cars."
"My work is more interesting than Other's work."	"Other and I have the same opportunities for promotion."
"My office is bigger than Other's office."	
"I have less experience than Other."	

discern some interesting differences between inequity and cognitive dissonance.

1. UNDERREWARD VERSUS OVERREWARD

First, dissonance theory makes no distinction between cognitive elements that represent inputs (contributions) and those that represent outcomes (rewards). Both kinds of elements can be either consonant or dissonant with the focal cognition. Perhaps of greater importance, there is also no distinction between dissonant elements that describe a state of affairs advantageous to the individual and dissonant elements that describe a disadvantageous state of affairs. Each dissonant element represents an instance of inequity, but the overall magnitude of dissonance present in the situation is defined differently from the overall magnitude of inequity. Holding constant the number of consonant elements, the magnitude of dissonance should be directly proportional to the total number of dissonant elements. In contrast, holding constant the number of equitable (i.e., consonant) elements, inequity should be a function of the imbalance of advantageous and disadvantageous elements; the greater the imbalance, the more the individual's own outcome-to-input ratio differs from that of the comparison other. To illustrate, the element, "I earn less than Other" is both dissonant and inequitable under the assumption of comparable jobs. The additional element, "I have less experience than Other" would, presumably, further increase dissonance (as comparable jobs imply similar experience), but it would lower inequity. Intuitively, the prediction derived from equity theory appears to be more reasonable, pointing to the importance of distinguishing between unfair situations involving underreward and those involving overreward. In fact, as we shall see in what follows, some of the more interesting implications of equity theory relate precisely to this distinction.

The preceding discussion suggests that, although derived largely from dissonance theory, equity theory has introduced some important refinements. First, equity theory makes a distinction between cognitive elements that represent an individual's inputs into an exchange relationship and elements that represent that individual's outcomes. Second, cognitive elements within equity theory involve a comparison of the individual's own inputs and outcomes with those of a reference person or group. Finally, unlike dissonance theory, equity theory distinguishes between inequity that is to the person's advantage and inequity that is to the person's disadvantage. As in dissonance theory, however, both types of inequity are assumed to result in distress and to lead to changes designed to restore equity or, at least, to reduce the magnitude of inequity.

2. RESOLUTION STRATEGIES

The strategies whereby inequity is said to be reduced are again derived from the theory of cognitive dissonance (Brehm & Cohen, 1962; Festinger, 1957). Individuals can increase or reduce their own inputs into the relationship, they can attempt to increase or decrease their outcomes, they can make an effort to influence the comparison other's inputs or outcomes, or they can leave the relationship altogether. Most interesting in the context of the present chapter, however, is the possibility that the individuals will cognitively distort their own or the other person's inputs and outcomes (see Adams, 1965; Wicklund & Brehm, 1976). This possibility suggests some of the ways in which inequity may influence the individual's attitude.

Dissonance and equity theories again appear to diverge with respect to this issue (see Deci, Reis, Johnston, & Smith, 1977; Weick, 1964). Dissonance theorists often view promised or actual reward as "justification" for performing a counterattitudinal or otherwise objectionable behavior. Without sufficient reward, individuals may attempt to justify their behavior by changing their attitudes to become consistent with their behavior. Increasing the amount of reward, however, is said to reduce the magnitude of dissonance created by performing the behavior, and hence, to obviate the need to justify the behavior by means of attitude change. Thus, a person who invests great effort in a task for little reward may attempt to reduce his or her dissonance by developing a more favorable attitude toward the task. The underrewarded effort appears justified if the task is viewed as enjoyable, interesting, important, healthy, and so on. Future task performance is expected to be consistent with the favorable attitude; continued effort reaffirms the task's attractiveness and, hence, serves to further justify past behavior (Weick, 1964).

Different predictions appear to emerge from equity theory. Underreward may increase liking for the task as a result of cognitive distortions designed to increase one's apparent outcomes. Alternatively, or at the same time, inequity may be reduced by lowering one's inputs (i.e., by expending less effort on the task). An increase in effort, as predicted by dissonance theory, could only serve to escalate the inequity.

These conflicting predictions can be reconciled by distinguishing between different modes of dissonance or inequity reduction under different sets of circumstances. A situation common in dissonance research is one in which the participant is induced to perform a task for low reward and no further work on the task is anticipated. Here, the only available strategy for dissonance reduction is attitude change in a favorable direction. If the new attitude persists, it may influence future task performance. A different situation confronts a person who has agreed to, but has not yet performed, the behavior for which he or she has been promised a small reward. People in this situation have at their disposal more than one reasonable mode of dissonance reduction. They can change their attitudes toward the task (to increase their outcomes), they can retain their relatively negative attitude but invest less effort when performing the task (to reduce their inputs), or they can do both simultaneously. In other words, different modes of inequity–dissonance reduction may be invoked prior to, and following, task performance (see also Deci *et al.*, 1977).

Similar considerations may apply in the case of overreward. According to equity theory, overreward will also result in distress, although its magnitude is usually assumed to be smaller than in the case of underreward (Adams, 1965). This distress can be reduced either by lowering one's outcomes or by increasing one's inputs (in addition to the other strategies listed earlier). Using a strategy of cognitive distortion, outcomes can be lowered by developing a more negative attitude toward the task. A relatively boring and unpleasant task may balance any excessive reward. Alternatively, it is possible to reduce inequity resulting from overreward by increasing the amount of effort invested in the task.

It is not clear what predictions dissonance theory would make in the case of excessive reward. Some investigators have argued that any extrinsic reward tends to undermine intrinsic motivation by lowering attitudes toward the task, thus resulting in poorer task performance (see Condry, 1977; Lepper, Greene, & Nisbett, 1973). This should be especially true if the reward is inequitably large.

Both approaches, then, seem to suggest that overreward may lower attitudes toward the task. However, equity theory also predicts increased task performance whereas dissonance theory may be viewed as implying lowered performance in line with the new attitude. It seems again possible to reconcile these discrepant predictions by suggesting that attitude change will be the primary mode of dissonance–inequity reduction following performance of the behavior, and that less effort on the task may be employed whenever inequity is generated by overrewarding a person prior to task performance.

3. SUMMARY

To summarize briefly, although the main principles of equity theory are derived from the theory of cognitive dissonance, there are some important differences between the two theories. Whereas cognitive dissonance is a unitary theoretical construct, equity theory makes a distinction between inequity resulting from underreward and inequity resulting from overreward. Furthermore, although both theories predict that individuals attempt to reduce or eliminate the distress caused by perceived inconsistencies or inequities, their focus is on different modes of stress reduction. Dissonance theory has dealt largely with situations in which behavioral change is ruled out and attitude change is likely to be the primary mode of dissonance reduction. In contrast, equity theory has often been applied to situations in which both attitudinal as well as behavioral changes could serve to reduce perceived inequities.

B. Inequity and Attitudes in Exchange Relationships

According to equity theory, the attainment and maintenance of justice is a positively valued attribute of various aspects of an exchange relationship. Several theorists (e.g., Deutsch, 1975; Leventhal, 1976; Van Avermaet, McClintock, & Moskowitz, 1978), however, have argued that equity may not be the only criterion by which justice or fairness is evaluated. Under certain conditions, equal distribution of rewards regardless of inputs, or distribution of rewards according to needs, may be considered to be more appropriate than an equitable distribution (Sampson, 1975). Defending the generality of equity theory, Walster and Walster (1975) noted that these different rules of justice may be classified as special cases of the equity principle. Equal distribution implies that one's presence is the only input considered relevant in computing outcome-to-input ratios, whereas need-based allocations result when each individual's need is the only relevant input (see Greenberg & Cohen, Chapter 12, this volume). Regardless of the position we adopt on this issue, we are left with the assumption that distributions of reward are guided by considerations of fairness or justice, and that perceived injustice—no matter how it is defined—will affect the attitudes and actions of individuals in the exchange relationship.

1. CONSEQUENCES OF INEQUITY

Our earlier discussion has already referred to some of the ways in which inequity may influence attitudes toward aspects of an exchange relationship. First and foremost, inequity is expected to result in distress, in a belief that the exchange is unfair or unjust, and hence in a general feeling of dissatisfaction with one's position in the exchange (in contrast, see Greenberg, 1979). It has also been suggested that this feeling of dissatisfaction is prompted by anger and resentment in the case of underreward and by guilt in the case of overreward (Walster et al., 1978).

The second potential effect of inequity is related to the individual's attitude toward the task he or she is asked to perform. In an attempt to alleviate the distress produced by inequity, one possibility open to individuals is an adjustment of their attitudes toward the task (see Leventhal, 1964; Weick, 1964). Because the utility, desirability, or intrinsic value of a task affects the individual's outcomes in the relationship, attitudes toward the task should become more favorable when outcomes are perceived to be relatively low (in the case of underreward) and less favorable when outcomes are perceived to be relatively high (in the case of overreward).

Finally, inequity is also expected to influence attitudes toward the person who is viewed as responsible for the inequitable allocation of rewards. This may be the person with whom the individual is in an exchange relationship, or a third person charged with dispensing duties or distributing rewards. Generally speaking, a person held responsible for creating a situation of inequity is expected to be liked less than a person who is perceived to behave in an equitable and fair manner (e.g., Brickman & Bryan, 1975, 1976; Kahn, Lamm, & Nelson, 1977).

It is instructive to compare this analysis of attitudes in exchange relationships with predictions that can be derived from an application of reinforcement or incentive principles (see also Klein, 1973). These principles imply that positive feelings will increase with reward magnitude. The more favorable a person's outcomes in an exchange relationship, the more attracted he or she should be to that relationship (Aronson, 1970) and the more he or she should like the agent responsible for his or her outcomes (Byrne, 1971). Moreover, positive outcomes serve to reinforce task behavior; the greater the reward, the more the person should come to like the task.

Equity theory differs from this analysis in at least two respects. First, according to equity theory, attitudes toward a relationship, a task, or an agent responsible for reward allocation are not a direct function of outcomes received but, rather, of outcomes in relation to a standard of comparison that involves the individual's own inputs and the inputs and outcomes of a reference person or group. Thus, despite a low absolute level of rewards, individuals may be quite satisfied with a relationship or a task if they perceive their inputs to be similarly low, or if they believe that other people's outcome-to-input ratios are about the same as theirs. By the same token, a high absolute reward level does not ensure favorable attitudes. According to equity theory, dissatisfaction will result if the individual views his or her own inputs to warrant even greater rewards, or if he or she believes that a comparison other has a more favorable outcome-to-input ratio.

Of course, a reinforcement or incentive approach could be modified to take into account relative rather than absolute levels of reward (e.g., Thibaut & Kelley, 1959). Such an approach would have greater difficulty, however, in trying to accommodate equity theory's differential predictions concerning the effects of underreward and overreward. One of the most interesting implications of equity theory is the proposition that rewards can be perceived as excessively large and that individuals will be more satisfied in a relationship in which they obtain a smaller but more equitable reward. Even if we defined rewards in relative terms, reinforcement or incentive principles would lead to the opposite prediction. In the case of underreward, the two theoretical approaches are in partial agreement: Both predict that relatively low reward will result in general dissatisfaction with the exchange relationship and in lowered attitudes toward the agent responsible for reward allocation. They again differ, however, with regard to the effects of low rewards on attitudes toward the task. In the case of underreward, equity theory predicts increased liking for the task, whereas the incentive–reinforcement approach implies less liking for a poorly rewarded task.

2. SOME RESEARCH FINDINGS

Over the past 15 years, numerous empirical tests of equity theory have been carried out. Most of these investigations have focused on the effects of inequity on behavior, but a number of studies have examined the influence of inequity on attitudes toward aspects of an exchange relationship. The results of these latter studies are quite disappointing. Although equity manipulations are often reported to influence attitudes, it is difficult to find consistent support for the predictions of equity theory.

a. Attitudes toward the Relationship. Considering first the case of general attitudes toward a relationship, several studies (Austin & Walster, 1974; Finn & Lee, 1972; Pritchard, Dunnette, & Jorgenson, 1972; Walster, Walster & Traupman, 1978; Wicker & Bushweiler, 1970, Study 1) reported the predicted decrease in satisfaction in situations of underreward. Furthermore, two of these studies also found a similar decline of satisfaction in the case of overreward (Austin & Walster, 1974; Walster *et al.*, 1978). To illustrate, Austin and Walster used a 30-item mood adjective check list to assess the reactions of undergraduates who were either equitably paid ($2), underpaid ($1), or overpaid ($3) for their participation in an experiment. The most negative reactions were displayed by underpaid participants and the most positive reactions by equitably paid participants. The attitudes of overpaid participants fell in between the other two groups.

However, a number of studies have reported results that contradict equity theory. They found no reduction or even an increase in satisfaction due to overreward (Moore & Baron, 1973; Pritchard *et al.*, 1972; Wicker & Bushweiler, 1970), and failed to obtain the predicted decrease in satisfaction following underreward (Moore & Baron, 1973; Wicker & Bushweiler, 1970, Study 2). The results of Wicker and Bushweiler (1970) are instructive. The first study described 18 hypothetical situations to college students who were asked to rate the pleasantness of each. The descriptions varied the relative inputs and outcomes of two coworkers, thereby creating underreward, equitable reward, or overreward for the focal person with whom the students were to identify. Respondents rated equitable situations as more pleasant than situations in which they would be at a disadvantage, but they usually preferred overreward to an equitable state of affairs.

The results of Wicker and Bushweiler's (1970) second study were even more damaging for equity theory. Participants worked on a verbal analogies task and were led to believe that they had performed either better than or worse than a confederate. In a manipulation orthogonal to these inputs, participants received either more or less money than the confederate. Ratings of the pleasantness of participating in the experiment revealed no significant effect of inequity. Instead, it was found that attitudes toward the experiment were influenced by the manipulation of inputs: Participants who believed they had performed better than the confederates rated their participation as more pleasant than did participants whose performance fell below that of the confederate. Neither the main effect of outcomes, nor its interaction with inputs, was significant. Furthermore, within-cell correlations between the perceived fairness of outcomes and pleasantness ratings showed no consistent patterns, ranging from $-.14$ to $.61$.

Clearly then, inequity does *not* always result in appreciable distress or dissatisfaction with a relationship. To be sure, generally unfavorable attitudes are often observed when individuals believe they receive less than they deserve. As to attitudes toward an exchange relationship in which the individual is overrewarded, the findings are far from conclusive (see also Pritchard, 1969). Although some studies find a preference for equitable relationships, others report a preference for overreward or no clear difference between the two.

Moreover, an experiment by Rivera and Tedeschi (1976) raises doubts as to the validity of expressed dissatisfaction with overreward. Their findings suggest a strong self-presentation component. In this experiment, two levels of overreward were created, as was an equitable outcome condition. Participants indicated their anger, happiness, guilt, and satisfaction on four-point scales, using either a standard paper-

and-pencil procedure or the bogus pipeline (Jones & Sigall, 1971), a technique designed to elicit more honest responses. Expressed guilt and unhappiness increased significantly with overreward when the paper-and-pencil measure was employed. However, when the bogus pipeline was used, participants expressed feeling *less* guilty and unhappy with increasing overreward. Although it may be possible to find faults with the bogus pipeline technique,[1] these results suggest that we have to exercise caution in our interpretation of expressed dissatisfaction under conditions of overreward (see also Van Avermaet *et al.*, 1978).

 b. Attitudes toward the Reward Allocator.   Results of experimental dealing with liking for an agent who allocates reward equitably or in an inequitable manner are also somewhat inconsistent. Weick (1964) and Brickman and Bryan (1975, 1976) found more favorable attitudes toward a person who allocated rewards equitably; Weick's experiment compared the effects of equitable reward and underreward whereas the studies by Brickman and Bryan involved both underreward and overreward. However, Garrett and Libby (1973), and Libby and Garrett (1974) showed that liking for an allocator of rewards was significantly higher when the allocator overrewarded rather than underrewarded the research participants.[2] Moreover, Kahn *et al.* (1977) found no significant effect of inequity on attitudes toward either an overrewarding or an underrewarding person.

 c. Attitudes toward the Task.   Finally, little support can be found for the predictions of equity theory with respect to attitudes toward the task a person performs under conditions of equity or inequity. Equity theory predicts that, barring inequity reduction by other means, task enhancement should result following underreward, and task derogation should result following overreward. The empirical evidence provides no support for these propositions. Leventhal (1964) and Cook (1969) reported that overreward enhanced rather than lowered attitudes toward a task. They similarly found no significant effect of underreward, a result also reported by Folger, Rosenfield, and Hays (1978) and by Deci *et al.* (1977).

---

[1]For example, because this technique leads respondents to believe that the machine to which they are connected can read their subtle internal reactions, they may attempt to guess what these reactions might be, often—and perhaps erroneously—assuming that these internal reactions are different from their conscious thoughts and feelings.

[2]Because the studies did not include control groups with equitable reward allocation, it is not clear whether liking was reduced by underreward, increased by overreward, or both. In any case, these findings are consistent with research showing a greater tolerance for overreward than for underreward (e.g., Weick & Nesset, 1968; Zadeck & Smith, 1968).

For example, Leventhal (1964) offered college students experimental credits for working on a routine clerical task in a 3-hour experiment. Depending on experimental condition, the number of credits offered exceeded, fell short of, or was about equal to the number of credits students considered appropriate for participation in the experiment. Liking for the task was assessed on a 101-point graphic scale. Contrary to equity theory predictions, overrewarded subjects—rather than depressing task attitudes—actually responded by giving significantly more favorable evaluations of the task than did either equitably rewarded subjects or underrewarded subjects. The attitudes of the subjects in the latter two conditions did not differ significantly from each other. Exactly the same pattern of results was reported by Cook (1969).

Some investigators have suggested that the effect of inequity on liking for a task depends on the presence or absence of other factors, such as freedom of choice (Folger *et al.*, 1978) or ambiguity of inequity (Deci *et al.*, 1977). The search for variables that moderate the effects of inequity on attitudes toward a task is reminiscent of much dissonance research that attempted to identify the conditions that must be met to observe the predicted consequences of behavior under insufficient justification (e.g., Calder, Ross, & Insko, 1973; Collins, Ashmore, & Hornbeck, 1970). This research led to an ever increasing set of requirements, including commitment to the behavior, awareness of and personal responsibility for its consequences, freedom of choice, and violation of an expectancy related to the self concept (for a review, see Fishbein & Ajzen, 1975, Chapter 10). These requirements, if accepted in their entirety, would impose such severe limitations on the predicted phenomenon as to rob it of any practical significance. Although equity research has a long way to go, pursuit of this road is likely to result in a deadlock much like the one encountered by dissonance research.

C. Equity and Information-Processing Theories of Attitude

In attempting to account for the inconsistent effects of inequity on attitudes in an exchange relationship it will be helpful to consider the role of inequity in the context of more general theories of attitude formation and change. Although a variety of attitude theories have been proposed, information-processing approaches appear to have gained the most widespread acceptance in recent years (see Ajzen, 1977; Anderson, 1971; Fishbein & Ajzen, 1975; Schneider, 1976). From an information-processing perspective, an individual's evaluation of or attitude toward any object is determined by his or her information about the object. If the information is generally favorable, the individual will form a positive attitude toward the object; if the information is unfavorable, the individual's evaluation of the object will be negative. Note, however, that the attitude depends not so much on the information that is (objectively) available as on the beliefs about the object formed on the basis of that information (see Ajzen, 1977; Fishbein & Ajzen, 1972, 1975). A person's belief about an object may be defined as his or her subjective probability that the object has a given attribute. The terms *object* and *attribute* are used in the generic sense and they refer to any discriminable aspect of the individual's world. In the context of equity research, the object of interest may be the exchange relationship, the task, or the agent who allocates rewards. For example, an individual might indicate an 80% chance that his job pays less than comparable jobs held by other people. The belief object *my job* is linked to the attribute "pays less than comparable jobs" with a subjective probability of .8.

According to Fishbein's (1963, 1967) theory of attitude, a person's evaluation of an object is a function of his or her salient beliefs about that object. Each belief links the object with a valued attribute. The attitude is determined by the person's evaluation of the attributes associated with the object and by the strength of these associations. Specifically, the evaluation of each salient attribute contributes to the attitude in proportion to the person's subjective probability that the object has the attribute in question. Theories of a similar nature, although narrower in scope, have been proposed by Edwards (1954), Rosenberg (1956), and others (e.g., see Feather, 1959; Fishbein & Ajzen, 1975). This information-processing theory of attitude is presented symbolically in Eq. (5.1), where A stands for attitude, b_i is the belief (subjective probability) that the attitude object has attribute i, e_i is the evaluation of attribute i, and the sum is over the n salient beliefs. Thus:

$$A = \sum_{i=1}^{n} b_i e_i. \tag{5.1}$$

1. INEQUITY AND PERCEIVED FAIRNESS

In terms of the preceding discussion, perceived justice or fairness can best be defined as a *belief* about an exchange relationship. Equity theory can then be viewed as an attempt to specify the determinants of the belief that a relationship is fair or unfair. As we saw earlier, these determinants involve people's beliefs concerning their inputs and outcomes relative to the inputs and outcomes of a comparison individual or group. Specifically, equity theory states that both relative overcompensation as well as relative undercompensation will be regarded as less fair than equitable outcome-to-input ratios.

Empirical research provides clear support for this aspect of equity theory. In an early study, Homans (1953) showed that workers in higher status positions thought they should be paid more than lower status workers. More direct support for the idea that perceived inequities are judged to be unfair can be found in studies that report checks on their equity manipulations (e.g., Brickman & Bryan, 1975, 1976; Kahn, 1972; Wicker & Bushweiler, 1970). For example, Wicker and Bushweiler found that equitable outcome-to-input ratios received significantly higher fairness ratings than did inequitable ratios. This difference was observed for judgments in hypothetical as well as actual exchange relationships. More important, inequitable exchanges were rated as unfair not only when the individual was underrewarded but also when she was overrewarded. Confirmation of the latter effect can be found in Rivera and Tedeschi (1976). In this study a supervisor either distributed rewards equitably or created one of two levels of inequity by overrewarding the participants. The fairness and equitableness of the supervisor, rated on 7-point scales, was found to decline as the amount of overreward increased.

2. INEQUITY AND SALIENT BELIEFS IN AN EXCHANGE RELATIONSHIP

Clearly, then, degree of inequity influences the judged fairness of a relationship, and of the person responsible for the inequity, in the predicted manner. We saw previously, however, that the effects of perceived fairness on attitudes toward the relationship and its major elements are often found to contradict equity theory predictions. From the perspective of an information-processing model of attitude formation, the inconsistent research findings are not unexpected. According to the theory outlined above, people's attitudes are a function of the *total set* of their salient beliefs about the object of the attitude [see Eq. (5.1)]. It follows that varying the degree of inequity in an exchange will influence a given attitude only if it affects this cognitive foundation of the attitude in question.

a. Effects of Inequity on Beliefs and Attribute Evaluations. Examination of Eq. (5.1) suggests that there are two ways in which inequity could have an impact on a person's attitude. First, inequity may influence some of the person's salient beliefs about the attitude object. To illustrate, we saw above that inequitable relationships are regarded as being unfair. Because, at least within Western culture, fairness is valued positively (see Leventhal, 1976), this belief taken in isolation would tend to lower people's attitudes toward an inequitable relationship in comparison to a relationship that is perceived to be equitable.

However, the degree to which a relationship is perceived to be fair or unfair is only one of many beliefs people usually hold about their relationships. For example, research has shown that attitudes toward work relationships (i.e., job satisfaction) are determined by a variety of beliefs about the work itself, about supervision, coworkers, pay, and promotion (see Greenberg, Chapter 11, this volume; Smith, Kendall, & Hulin, 1969). Although the belief concerning justice or fairness may often be important, the individual's attitude toward his or her job will be determined by the totality of the individual's salient beliefs about this relationship. Only by considering the effects of inequity on all salient beliefs can we gain an understanding of its impact on attitudes toward the relationship.

A second way in which inequity may influence attitudes is related to the effects it may have on attribute evaluations [see Eq. (5.1)]. To return to the work situation, imagine a worker who, among other things, believes that there are few opportunities for promotion on the job. His or her own evaluation of this job attribute (few opportunities for promotion) is likely to depend at least in part on perceived equity. If the worker believes that relevant comparison others have more opportunities for promotion, his or her evaluation of the attribute in question will probably be negative. If, however, the worker believes that others have about the same opportunities for promotion, the evaluation of his or her own opportunities is likely to be less negative. Equity with respect to promotional opportunities may thus result in a more favorable attitude toward one's job than any inequitable promotional opportunities. Or, to turn to work-related beliefs, people who perceive their work to be boring may develop a negative attitude toward the work. Again, however, their evaluation of this attribute—and hence their attitudes toward their work—are likely to be more favorable when the work of relevant others is viewed as equally boring than when it is viewed as more interesting.

The same arguments can be made regarding evaluations of attributes associated with pay, supervision, coworkers, or any other aspect of the work relationship. Equity or inequity may be viewed as influencing the value individuals place on the attributes they believe to be associated with the relationship in question. Note again, however, that considerations of equity may not be the only factor influencing attribute evaluations. A person may have a negative evaluation of low pay even if he or she realizes that others in comparable positions are paid about the same. Perhaps more obvious, inequity to a person's advantage may seldom result in negative attribute evaluations. Thus, people who believe they are being paid much more than others in the same position may realize that this state of affairs is inequitable. At the same time, however, they are also likely to believe that their high pay enables them to buy various products, to travel, to gain status in the community, and so on. Because all of these beliefs, and not only their concern about equity, will influence people's evaluations of being paid more than others, their attitude toward that pay is likely to be favorable despite the inequity it involves. In fact, they could be more favorable than their attitudes toward lower but equitable pay.

Similar considerations apply to the effects of inequity on attitudes toward the person responsible for reward allocation and on attitudes toward the task a person is asked to perform. One salient belief about a person who allocates rewards inequitably is likely to be the belief that the person in question is unfair, unjust, or even dishonest. As most people's evaluations of these attributes are quite negative, an inequitable allocator of rewards may often be liked less than one who allocates rewards equitably. Here too, however, the attitude toward another person is usually based on many beliefs about the person, in addition to the belief that he is fair or equitable. To be sure, resentment produced by underreward may be strong enough to result in an overall negative attitude toward the person held responsible for it. It is more difficult to see why an overrewarding agent should be disliked. Although such an agent may be viewed as unfair, he may at the same time be perceived as generous, friendly, and as having the individual's interests at heart. Overall, such an agent may be liked more than one who distributes rewards in a scrupulously equitable manner.

b. Empirical Support.   Some support for this analysis can be found in existing empirical research. In a laboratory experiment involving a concept-identification task, Weick (1964) assessed attitudes as well as a set of beliefs with respect to the experimenter who was responsible for equitable or inequitable reward allocation. The college students who participated in the study expected to receive one experimental credit for their participation. In the equity condition, they were in fact offered the expected credit, but in the underreward condition they were told that they could not be given any credit for participating in the experiment. Although inequity had no effect on the extent to which the experimenter was perceived to be interested, courteous, friendly, impersonal, or professional, in comparison to equitably treated students, underrewarded students rated the experimenter as more dishonest, pushy, unenthusiastic, and discouraging. Consistent with these effects on beliefs, the inequitable experimenter was also liked less than the experimenter who offered the expected reward.

The important mediating role of beliefs can also be seen in a study by

Kahn *et al.* (1977) even though these investigators did not obtain direct measures of beliefs. College students read a description of a three-person group that had earned $3.30 for its work on an experimental task, and in which one of the group members was asked to distribute the reward. Each group member had made a different contribution to the group's performance. Depending on the condition, the allocator's own inputs were either low, moderate, or high, and he or she distributed the money either in an equitable manner or equally to each of the three group members. By distributing the reward equitably, allocators in this situation assured themselves an amount of money that, depending on condition, was either more than, the same as, or less than the $1.10 they could obtain by distributing the reward equally. Each respondent's attitude toward the allocator was assessed by means of several evaluative semantic differential scales and the two liking items on Byrne's (1961) interpersonal judgment scale.

Contrary to the predictions of equity theory, respondents did not prefer the equitable allocator to a group member who distributed the reward equally. (In fact, a nonsignificant trend in the opposite direction was obtained.) The analysis of variance instead revealed increased liking for an allocator who, by the choice of an allocation norm, took less money for himself or for herself than could have been secured by choosing the alternative norm. It thus appears that liking for allocators in this situation was influenced not so much by whether they were equitable, but rather, by whether respondents could infer from the allocators' behavior that they were generous or unselfish.[3]

A similar conclusion emerges from a sequence of studies by Brickman and Bryan (1975, 1976). Elementary school children watched a movie in which a girl redistributed her own outcomes and the outcomes of several fictitious others. Depending on experimental condition, this redistribution reduced, increased, or left unchanged the girl's own outcomes; increased or reduced the equality of the outcomes; and increased or reduced the equity of the outcomes (Brickman & Bryan, 1976). Attitudes toward the girl were affected by each of the three manipulations: Students liked the girl more when she increased rather than reduced equity, when she raised rather than lowered equality, and when she gave up some of her own reward rather than when she transferred the outcomes of others to herself. This latter finding again suggests that when reward allocation affects the allocator's own outcomes, liking may be influenced

[3]Unfortunately, these results were not replicated in a study using a German subject population.

by the extent to which her behavior can be interpreted as generous or altruistic.[4]

Examination of the likely effects of inequity on salient beliefs can also help to explain the negative findings concerning the relation between inequity and task attitudes. Unlike the case of attitudes toward a relationship in general or toward the allocator of rewards, inequitable pay for task performance need not result in the belief that the task is unfair. Instead of searching for consistent relations between underreward and overreward, on the one hand, and liking for the task, on the other, the information-processing theory of attitude formation suggests that we examine the effects of inequitable rewards on the person's salient beliefs about the task. Existing salient beliefs may change, and new salient beliefs may be formed, depending on the exact circumstances surrounding task performance and perhaps also upon individual difference variables. Some of these changes may increase, whereas others may reduce, liking for the task; but by considering the total set of a person's salient beliefs, we should be able to predict his or her attitude toward the task following equitable or inequitable rewards.

A study by Lawler and O'Gara (1967) provides limited support for this analysis. Students at Yale University spent two hours interviewing other students about their college-related experiences. They were paid either 25¢ per interview, a rate considered equitable, or only 10¢ per interview. At the conclusion, they were asked to rate the interviewing task on four 7-point scales whose endpoints were boring–interesting, important–unimportant, simple–complex, and challenging–unchallenging. Each of these items may be considered a belief about the task. Data analyses showed that inequity had no significant effects on beliefs concerning the task's importance or its complexity. Underrewarded students, however, rated the task as significantly more interesting, but also as significantly less challenging. Although it is not clear what other beliefs about the task may have been influenced by the equity manipulation, had a general measure of attitude toward the task been obtained, it might have reflected these contradictory effects. That is, since inequity changed one belief in a favorable direction but the other belief in an unfavorable direction, the overall effect of underreward might be to leave attitudes toward the task unaffected. Nonsignificant effects of inequity on

---

[4]Note that the studies just discussed used observers of, rather than participants in, inequitable relationships. It is not clear whether equity theory would predict that observers will experience the same kind of distress due to inequity as will actual participants. Walster *et al.* (1978) argued that observers will react in the same way as do participants, although the reactions of observers are expected to be less passionate.

task attitudes were, in fact, reported by Leventhal (1964) and by Cook (1969).

In short, we cannot expect strong or even consistent effects of inequity on attitudes in an exchange relationship. Depending on other beliefs individuals hold, they may be more, equally, or less satisfied with a relationship that is inequitable than with one that is equitable. To be sure, everything else being equal, most people would prefer an equitable to an inequitable relationship. Unfortunately, other things are seldom equal. Our beliefs about equitable relationships differ in many important ways from our beliefs about inequitable relationships, quite apart from our beliefs concerning their fairness. The extent to which a relationship is fair or unfair may often not be a particularly salient attribute of that relationship, in which case it will have relatively little effect on the individual's attitudes.

II. BEHAVIORAL IMPLICATIONS OF INEQUITY

In the context of equity theory, attitude change serves to reduce or to eliminate perceived inequities. Alternatively, people can affect their inputs or outcomes, and hence establish a more equitable situation, by changing their behavior. Thus, people who are underrewarded may reduce their effort and quality of performance on a task, whereas overrewarded individuals may increase their effort and performance (see Lawler, 1968). Given the compensatory nature of attitude and behavior change as alternative modes of inequity reduction, it is tempting to propose that the inconsistent effects of inequity on attitudes may be explained by its effects on behavior. If, in some cases, individuals cope with inequity by changing their behaviors, whereas in others, they cope by adjusting their attitudes, apparently inconsistent results would appear to be inevitable.

Unfortunately, relatively few studies have assessed the effects of inequity on attitudes as well as on behavior. Most of these investigations have varied the inequity of a reward given for performance on a task and have examined the effects of this manipulation on the participants' attitudes toward the task and on the quantity or quality of their task behavior. We saw earlier that the effects of inequity on attitudes toward the task participants are asked to perform are found to be inconsistent and are largely nonsignificant. Results concerning behavioral change in these studies are equally disappointing, irrespective of the effects of inequity on attitudes. Some studies (e.g., Cook, 1969; Folger *et al.*, 1978; Pritchard *et al.*, 1972) reported largely nonsignificant effects of inequity on task behavior; some (e.g., Lawler & O'Gara, 1967; Moore & Baron, 1973) found greater quality of performance in situations of equitable reward than in situations of underreward, whereas others (e.g., Weick, 1964) found the reverse to be true. With respect to quantity of output, Weick (1964) and Lawler and O'Gara (1967) found underreward to be superior to equitable reward, whereas Deci *et al.* (1977) found that participants produced more when they were paid equitably than when they received less than they expected.

A. Attitudes and Behavior in Exchange Relationships

Clearly, equity theory cannot account for these inconsistent effects of inequity even if changes in attitudes and behavior are considered simultaneously.[5] In the more general context of attitude theory and research, however, inconsistent effects due to inequity may again not be altogether unexpected. According to equity theory, changes in attitudes and behavior follow directly from perceived inequity; as means of inequity reduction, they are functionally equivalent. By way of contrast, an attitudinal perspective suggests a two-stage process according to which the effect of perceived inequity on behavior depends on (1) its effects on attitudes, and (2) the relation between these attitudes and the behavior in question.

We have already seen that perceived inequity is only one of many beliefs that may influence attitudes toward an exchange relationship and that, therefore, no simple, consistent effect of inequity on attitudes can be expected. The potential impact of inequity on behavior must be regarded as even more tenuous because of the additional uncertainties concerning the relation of attitude to behavior. Recent work on the attitude–behavior relationship (for reviews, see Ajzen, 1979; Ajzen & Fishbein, 1977) has shown that its magnitude depends largely on the degree of *correspondence* between the measure of attitude and the measure of behavior. The two measures can be said to correspond when they involve at least the same action and target elements (see Ajzen & Fishbein, 1977). For example, the behavior "coming to work on time" corresponds directly to the worker's attitude toward "coming to work on

---

[5]Many other studies have, of course, tested equity theory in relation to behavior change. Most of these studies, however, have not obtained measures of attitude and their findings are thus beyond the scope of this chapter.

time," but not to his attitude toward his job or toward his employer. Similarly, the global attitude toward an exchange relationship corresponds to a general index of different behaviors vis-à-vis the relationship, but not to any given action, such as exerting effort on task performance.

It can be seen that, even when inequity is found to influence attitudes, this effect will not be reflected in behavior unless the attitude that has changed corresponds to the behavior under consideration. Although it is difficult to arrive at clear generalizations, especially concerning the effects of overreward, we saw that underreward often depresses attitudes toward the exchange relationship in general and toward the agent responsible for it. As to attitudes toward the task individuals are asked to perform, neither overreward nor underreward is found to have a consistent effect on attitudes. Given this pattern of results it is hardly surprising that inequity has no reliable impact on task performance. Attitudes toward the relationship and toward the reward allocator fail to correspond to this behavior in both action and target elements; neither attitude refers to the action of working on a task, and their targets (the relationship and the rewarding agent) differ from the target of the behavior (the task). Attitude toward the task corresponds to the behavior in the target element (the task) but it too fails to specify an action (e.g., exerting effort). Moreover, as inequity usually has little effect on task attitudes, this partial correspondence between task attitudes and performance can be of only little value.

B. Inequity and Social Influence

Before concluding this chapter, a few words concerning the role of inequity in the social influence process may be in order. We saw that equity theory has close links to the theory of cognitive dissonance, which deals at least in part with the process of social influence and persuasion (see Fishbein & Ajzen, 1975). The theory of cognitive dissonance predicts that we can influence people's attitudes (and their subsequent behavior) by inducing them to act in contradiction to their attitudes under dissonance-arousing conditions. Although it is now generally agreed that this prediction is limited to a very unique set of circumstances (see Wicklund & Brehm, 1976), it may be tempting to argue that the motive to avoid inequity could similarly be used as an influence strategy. That is, we could conceivably administer rewards in such a fashion as to obtain a particular pattern of attitudes and behavior. Underreward could be used to raise attitudes toward a task or to increase quantity of performance, and equitable pay could be used to generate liking for a supervisor.

The dangers involved in such strategies should by now be apparent. Research findings concerning the effects of inequity on attitudes and behavior give us little reason to expect that we can, in our present state of knowledge, exert social influence by manipulating inequities. Any such manipulation can easily "boomerang" and produce the opposite of the desired effect. Until more is learned about the conditions under which a given state of inequity will result in a particular kind of attitude or behavior, we would be well advised to exercise great caution in using equity theory as a basis for devising social influence strategies (see also Greenberg, Chapter 11; Greenberg & Cohen, Chapter 12, this volume).

III. SUMMARY AND CONCLUSIONS

This chapter has dealt with the role of equity in attitude formation and change. According to equity theory, the distress resulting from perceived inequities in an exchange relationship has predictable effects on the individual's attitudes toward various aspects of that relationship. Apart from producing general dissatisfaction and unhappiness, inequity is assumed to affect attitudes toward the task as well as toward the agent held responsible for it. Although underreward is expected to generate greater distress than is overreward, both types of inequity are said to result in distress, and hence, to influence attitude formation and change.

This analysis was compared to an information-processing approach to the formation of attitudes. From the perspective of an information-processing approach, perceived inequity is only one of many beliefs that may influence attitudes toward various aspects of an exchange relationship. Because beliefs about equitable and inequitable relationships will often differ in various ways other than perceived fairness, we cannot expect that inequity will have a consistent impact on an individual's attitudes.

Few, if any, studies have provided clear comparisons of equity and information-processing approaches to attitude formation,[6] but the empirical research reviewed in this chapter tends to support the information-processing analysis. Variations in degree of inequity are often found to have no impact on attitudes, and when they do influence attitudes, the findings often conflict with the predictions of equity theory. In contrast, a few studies have reported results suggesting that

---

[6]Comparisons of equity and "expectancy" theories have usually assessed only one or two beliefs (e.g., Klein, 1973), and have typically dealt with task performance rather than with attitudes (for a review, see Lawler, 1968).

attitudes in exchange relationships can be predicted and understood by considering the beliefs on which they are based.

A brief consideration of attitude–behavior relationships revealed that perceived inequity can also not be expected to have a consistent effect on behavior. From this perspective, for equity to affect behavior, it must not only influence attitudes but there must, in addition, be a strong relation between these attitudes and the behavior in question. The attitudes and behaviors considered in most equity research, however, fail to correspond to each other in their essential elements. As might therefore be expected, the few studies that have observed behavior in addition to assessing attitudes have, in fact, found no consistent impact of inequity on behavior.

It must be emphasized that the failure to find consistent support for equity theory's predictions concerning attitudes in exchange relationships does not imply that the theory is equally ineffective in other contexts. Several chapters in this book illustrate the generality and utility of the theory in a variety of different applications. Nevertheless, it appears that some claims for the theory's great power and generality (e.g., Walster *et al.*, 1978) must be regarded as overly optimistic and perhaps a bit too ambitious. Although perceived inequity in social relations may sometimes be a powerful motivating force, it must be realized that it is only one of many factors that influence attitudes and behavior. The analysis in the present chapter suggests that use of an information-processing approach can help accommodate both beliefs concerning equity and fairness as well as other types of beliefs that influence the formation of attitudes in an exchange relationship.

ACKNOWLEDGMENTS

I am grateful to George Levinger and the editors for their helpful comments on an earlier draft of this chapter.

REFERENCES

Adams, J. S. Toward an understanding of inequity. *Journal of Abnormal and Social Psychology*, 1963, *67*, 422–436.

Adams, J. S. Inequity in social exchange. In L. Berkowitz (Ed.), *Advances in experimental social psychology* (Vol. 2). New York: Academic Press, 1965.

Ajzen, I. Information-processing approaches to interpersonal attraction. In S. W. Duck (Ed.), *Theory and practice in interpersonal attraction*. London: Academic Press, 1977.

Ajzen, I. *On behaving in accordance with one's attitudes*. Paper presented at the Second Ontario Symposium, Waterloo, 1979.

Ajzen, I., & Fishbein, M. Attitude–behavior relations: A theoretical analysis and review of empirical research. *Psychological Bulletin*, 1977, *84*, 888–918.

Anderson, N. H. Integration theory and attitude change. *Psychological Review*, 1971, *78*, 171–206.

Aronson, E. Some antecedents of interpersonal attraction. In W. J. Arnold & D. Levine (Eds.), *Nebraska symposium on motivation*. Lincoln: University of Nebraska Press, 1970.

Austin, W., & Walster, E. Reactions to confirmation and disconfirmation of expectancies of equity and inequity. *Journal of Personality and Social Psychology*, 1974, *30*, 208–216.

Brehm, J. W., & Cohen, A. R. *Explorations in cognitive dissonance*. New York: Wiley, 1962.

Brickman, P., & Bryan, J. H. Moral judgment of theft, charity, and third-party transfers that increase or decrease equality. *Journal of Personality and Social Psychology*, 1975, *31*, 156–161.

Brickman, P., & Bryan, J. H. Equity versus equality as factors in children's moral judgments of theft, charity, and third-party transfers. *Journal of Personality and Social Psychology*, 1976, *34*, 757–761.

Byrne, D. Interpersonal attraction and attitude similarity. *Journal of Abnormal and Social Psychology*, 1961, *62*, 713–715.

Byrne, D. *The attraction paradigm*. New York: Academic Press, 1971.

Calder, B. J., Ross, M., & Insko, C. A. Attitude change and attitude attribution: Effects of incentive, choice, and consequences. *Journal of Personality and Social Psychology*, 1973, *25*, 84–99.

Collins, B. E., Ashmore, R. D., Hornbeck, F. W., & Whitney, R. E. Studies in forced compliance: XIII, XV. In search of a dissonance-produced forced compliance paradigm. *Representative Research in Social Psychology*, 1970, *1*, 11–23.

Condry, J. Enemies of exploration: Self-initiated versus other-initiated learning. *Journal of Personality and Social Psychology*, 1977, *35*, 459–477.

Cook, T. D. Temporal mechanisms mediating attitude change after underpayment and overpayment. *Journal of Personality*, 1969, *37*, 618–635.

Deci, E. L., Reis, H. T., Johnston, E. J., & Smith, R. Toward reconciling equity theory and insufficient justification. *Personality and Social Psychology Bulletin*, 1977, *3*, 224–227.

Deutsch, M. Equity, equality, and need: What determines which value will be used as the basis of distributive justice? *Journal of Social Issues*, 1975, *31*, 137–149.

Edwards, W. The theory of decision making. *Psychological Bulletin*, 1954, *51*, 380–417.

Feather, N. T. Subjective probability and decision under uncertainty. *Psychological Review*, 1959, *66*, 150–164.

Festinger, L. *A theory of cognitive dissonance*. Evanston, Ill.: Row, Peterson, 1957.

Finn, R. H., & Lee, S. M. Salary equity: Its determination, analysis, and correlates. *Journal of Applied Psychology*, 1972, *56*, 283–292.

Fishbein, M. An investigation of the relationship between beliefs about an object and the attitude toward the object. *Human Relations*, 1963, *16*, 233–240.

Fishbein, M. A behavior theory approach to the relations between beliefs about an object and the attitude toward that object. In M. Fishbein (Ed.), *Readings in attitude theory and measurement*. New York: Wiley, 1967.

Fishbein, M., & Ajzen, I. Attitudes and opinions. *Annual Review of Psychology*, 1972, *23*, 287–544.

Fishbein, M., & Ajzen, I. *Belief, attitude, intention, and behavior: An introduction to theory and research*. Reading, Mass.: Addison-Wesley, 1975.

Folger, R., Rosenfield, D., & Hays, R. P. Equity and intrinsic motivation: The role of choice. *Journal of Personality and Social Psychology*, 1978, *36*, 557–564.

Garrett, J., & Libby, W. L. Jr. Role of intentionality in mediating responses to inequity in the dyad. *Journal of Personality and Social Psychology*, 1973, *28*, 21–27.

Greenberg, J. Justice perceived versus justice enacted. In J. Greenberg (Chair), *Recent developments in interpersonal justice theory and research*. Symposium presented at the meeting of the American Psychological Association, New York, September 1979.

Homans, G. C. Status among clerical workers. *Human Organization*, 1953, *12*, 5–10.

Homans, G. C. *Social behavior: Its elementary forms*. New York: Harcourt Brace & World, 1961.

Jones, E. E., & Sigall, H. The bogus pipeline: A new paradigm for measuring affect and attitude. *Psychological Bulletin*, 1971, *76*, 349–364.

Kahn, A. Reactions to generosity or stinginess from an intelligent or stupid work partner: A test of equity theory in a direct exchange relationship. *Journal of Personality and Social Psychology*, 1972, *21*, 116–123.

Kahn, A., Lamm, H., & Nelson, R. E. Preferences for an equal or equitable allocator. *Journal of Personality and Social Psychology*, 1977, *35*, 837–844.

Kiesler, C. A., Collins, B. E., & Miller, N. *Attitude change*. New York: Wiley, 1969.

Klein, S. M. Pay factors as predictors to satisfaction: A comparison of reinforcement, equity, and expectancy. *Academy of Management Journal*, 1973, *16*, 598–610.

Lawler, E. E., III., & O'Gara, P. W. Effects of inequity produced by underpayment on work output, work quality, and attitudes toward the work. *Journal of Applied Psychology*, 1967, *51*, 403–410.

Lawler, E. E., III. Equity theory as a predictor of productivity and work quality. *Psychological Bulletin*, 1968, *70*, 596–610.

Lepper, M. R., Green, D., & Nisbett, R. E. Undermining children's intrinsic interest with extrinsic reward: A test of the "over-justification" hypothesis. *Journal of Personality and Social Psychology*, 1973, *28*, 129–137.

Leventhal, G. S. Reward magnitude, task attractiveness, and liking for instrumental activity. *Journal of Abnormal and Social Psychology*, 1964, *68*, 460–463.

Leventhal, G. S. *Fairness in social relationships*. Morristown, N.J.: General Learning Press, 1976.

Libby, W. L. Jr., & Garrett, J. Role of intentionality in mediating children's responses to inequity. *Developmental Psychology*, 1974, *10*, 294–297.

McGuire, W. J. The nature of attitudes and attitude change. In G. Lindzey & E. Aronson (Eds.), *The handbook of social psychology* (2nd ed., Vol. 3). Reading, Mass.: Addison-Wesley, 1969.

Moore, L. M., & Baron, R. M. Effects of wage inequities on work attitudes and performance. *Journal of Experimental Social Psychology*, 1973, *9*, 1–16.

Pritchard, R. D. Equity theory: A review and critique. *Organizational Behavior and Human Performance*, 1969, *4*, 176–211.

Pritchard, R. D., Dunnette, M. D., & Jorgenson, D. O. Effects of perceptions of equity and inequity on worker performance and satisfaction. *Journal of Applied Psychology*, 1972, *56*, 75–94.

Rivera, A. N., & Tedeschi, J. T. Public versus private reactions to positive inequity. *Journal of Personality and Social Psychology*, 1976, *34*, 895–900.

Rosenberg, M. J. Cognitive structure and attitudinal affect. *Journal of Abnormal and Social Psychology*, 1956, *23*, 367–372.

Sampson, E. E. On justice as equality. *Journal of Social Issues*, 1975, *31*, 45–64.

Schneider, D. J. *Social psychology*. Reading, Mass.: Addison-Wesley, 1976.

Smith, P. C., Kendall, L. M., & Hulin, C. L. *The measurement of satisfaction in work and retirement: A strategy for the study of attitudes*. Chicago: Rand McNally, 1969.

Stouffer, S. A., Suchman, D. E., DeVinney, L. C., Star, S. A., & Williams, R. M., Jr. *The American soldier: Adjustment during army life*. Princeton, N.J.: Princeton University Press, 1949.

Thibaut, J. W., & Kelley, H. H. *The social psychology of groups.* New York: Wiley, 1959.

Van Avermaet, E., McClintock, C. G., & Moskowitz, J. Alternative approaches to equity: Dissonance reduction, pro-social motivation, and strategic accommodation. *European Journal of Social Psychology,* 1978, *8,* 419–437.

Walster, E., Berscheid, E., & Walster, G. W. New directions in equity research. *Journal of Personality and Social Psychology,* 1973, *25,* 151–176.

Walster, E., & Walster, G. W. Equity and social justice. *Journal of Social Issues,* 1975, *31,* 21–43.

Walster, E., Walster, G. W., & Berscheid, E. *Equity: Theory and research.* Boston: Allyn & Bacon, 1978.

Walster, E., Walster, G. W., & Traupman, J. Equity and premarital sex. *Journal of Personality and Social Psychology,* 1978, *36,* 82–92.

Weick, K. E. Reduction of cognitive dissonance through task enhancement and effort expenditure. *Journal of Abnormal and Social Psychology,* 1964, *68,* 533–539.

Weick, K. E., & Nesset, B. Preferences among forms of equity. *Organizational Behavior and Human Performance,* 1968, *3,* 400–416.

Wicker, A. W., & Bushweiler, G. Perceived fairness and pleasantness of social exchange situations: Two factorial studies of inequity. *Journal of Personality and Social Psychology,* 1970, *15,* 63–75.

Wicklund, R. A., & Brehm, J. W. *Perspectives on cognitive dissonance.* Hillsdale, N.J.: Erlbaum, 1976.

Zadeck, S., & Smith, P. C. A psychophysical determination of equitable payment: A methodological study. *Journal of Applied Psychology,* 1968, *52,* 343–347.

chapter 6

Effects of Conformity Pressure on Justice Behavior[1]

VERNON L. ALLEN

I. INTRODUCTION

Concepts such as justice and injustice lend themselves only too easily to a discussion at the abstract theoretical and philosophical level without appearing to require recourse to the world of mundane data. Yet, these concepts certainly should not remain isolated from relevant areas of empirical inquiry in psychology. The purpose of this chapter is to explore some of the points of contact between concepts of justice and existing theory and data concerning conformity to group norms, one of the traditional areas of research in social psychology. At first glance it might seem that there is little relationship between the areas of conformity and justice. If this initial impression is sustained as we examine the topics more closely, this chapter will indeed be a succinct one. It would be very surprising, however, were points of intersection between these two areas not discovered in view of the complex interdependency of all aspects of human behavior.

The various concepts of justice have been defined thoroughly by the editors, so it is unnecessary to repeat that discussion here. Many authors have noted that cultural norms have evolved concerning the equitable distribution of outcomes as a justice norm; that is, people believe that there should be a positive relation between effort and reward, between input and outcome, among the members of a group or society (Adams,

---

[1]This chapter was written while the author was a fellow at the Institute for Advanced Study in the Humanities and Social Sciences, The Netherlands.

EQUITY AND JUSTICE
IN SOCIAL BEHAVIOR

1965; Lerner, 1975; Walster, Berscheid, & Walster, 1976). It has also been noted that social pressure exists within a group to induce individuals to accept and to conform to the norms that specify the apportioning of outcomes. Broad and sweeping assertions of this kind tend to have an ipse dixit quality, of course, but there is no doubt that some relevant evidence can be marshaled in support of these generalizations. Other norms of justice exist, however, and may in some cases be stronger than the equity norm. Thus, the conception of justice is based on equality or need in some groups and societies (Deutsch, 1975). Further differentation is offered by Lerner (1975), who suggests six different forms of justice: needs, entitlement, parity, equity, law (or Darwinian justice) and justified self-interest. In everyday life, it is possible for some combination of different norms of justice to be involved in a particular situation.

It is worth noting an explicit distinction between equity and justice that has been suggested by some authors (Wilkins, 1976), even though the terms frequently are used interchangeably. The concept of *justice* is often used to denote a fixed ideal or an absolute reference point, whereas *equity* is used in the sense of making comparisons with other persons. To state the distinction another way, for its reference justice "looks up" and equity "looks around." According to this distinction, then, justice includes the concept of equity, but equity does not include the concept of justice. To draw the distinction another way, equity refers to only one of the rules for allocating outcomes among recipients—namely, according to their contributions. But the concept of justice is a broad one that can be understood as subsuming all the particular rules for allocating outcomes. Unless specifically noted, the more general term will be employed in the present chapter, except when specifically restricting the scope of the discussion to equity theory (Adams, 1965; Walster *et al.*, 1976).

A chapter on the relationship between the areas of conformity and justice runs the risk of rambling far afield into abstract speculations about related areas such as ethics or law. In an attempt to avoid the dangers of undisciplined meandering, the chapter will focus on suggestions from the area of conformity that might provide a better understanding of behavior associated with equity and justice.[2] After a few brief comments about conformity and norms in the first section, the second

[2]It is possible to look at the other side of the relationship, namely, the contribution of equity theory to the understanding of conformity and nonconformity. Attempts have been made to use social exchange theory as an integrative model in the area of conformity (Nord, 1969), and to explain the relation between status and deviation from group norms (Hollander, 1958). Nevertheless, to maintain a focus on justice as the central behavioral phenomenon under discussion, I shall not venture in this direction.

section discusses the influence that conformity pressure can exert upon the elements involved in any judgment about justice. The third section offers observations concerning the role of conformity pressure in promoting or impeding justice outcomes in concrete situations. A few concluding remarks are offered in the final section.

II. NORMS, CONFORMITY, AND JUSTICE

A. Group Influence

Before discussing aspects of justice behavior, a few comments about social influence and conformity are in order. Conformity is a term that has been used in a rather imprecise way to refer to several varieties of social influence exerted by the group toward the individual. Terms such as conformity, compliance, anticonformity, and independence have been used to describe the nature of a person's response to group pressure: When subjected to social pressure, an individual's response may take the form of moving closer toward the group's norm, moving farther away, or not changing at all (Stricker, Messick, & Jackson, 1970; Willis, 1965). The term *conformity* will be used here in a broad sense to refer to any influence on the individual's behavior due to the presence of a norm or group consensus.

In its most common usage in psychology conformity is considered to be almost synonymous with public compliance without an accompanying private change—that is, going along with the group without really agreeing. In Asch's (1956) experiments, the subjects' agreement with the erroneous group did seem to represent public compliance without a corresponding private agreement in most cases. But evidence is available to indicate that the change process produced by group norms does often result in true private change instead of mere public compliance with the group (Allen, 1965). It should also be pointed out that behavior that is initially public compliance may change over time to private acceptance (Raven, 1959). Moreover, many issues that require a response in everyday social life are less objective and clear-cut than the perceptual judgments (length of lines) used in Asch's research. When the situation is ambiguous or the individual has not formulated a strong position on a topic, conformity pressure does not involve a direct and obvious conflict between the individual and the group norm. Social influence takes a more subtle form in the absence of a clearly noticeable conflict between the individual and the group's position, and the individual may be unaware that his or her response is the consequence of influence by the group norm. In particular, changes that occur gradually over time are quite imperceptible and thus difficult to identify as being due to social influence. Furthermore, a group norm may produce influence on the less obvious dimensions of perception, belief, and affect, as well as on overt behavior (Allen, 1965).

It should be pointed out that an individual conforms to the perceived rather than to the objective norm; and one's perception of a norm will not always be veridical. A person must "receive" the norm being "sent" by the group (Rommetveit, 1955) before it can be used as a guide for taking any action whatsoever, whether conformity, independence, or anticonformity. Lack of congruence between the sent norm (as it exists in actuality) and the received norm (as the individual sees it) sometimes will occur. Objective evidence concerning expectations about a norm can be obtained easily from direct experience, observation, or the reactions of other persons toward deviates. Yet, in many instances, relevant cues are not readily available or the existing information is ambiguous or misperceived; pluralistic ignorance does exist concerning some aspects of behavior (Korte, 1972). In such cases the perceived norm will be at variance with reality. It is important to emphasize again that it is the received or presumed norm that influences a person's behavior rather than the objective norm (Gordon, 1952; McKeachie, 1954). As the form of justice will vary according to the nature of the situation, type of group, and desired goal or outcome, an individual is faced with the necessity of trying to garner relevant information about the nature of the justice norm being used by the group; often, available information will be limited. Hence, we should not assume that information about a justice norm is readily accessible, a priori, for the individual. Our analysis should begin prior to the stage of an individual's response to the norm. There may be instances in which behavior that apparently indicates non-conformity to a justice norm might, instead, be the result of an erroneous perception about the group norm.

B. Norms and Fairness

A few general comments should now be devoted to the issue of the importance of social norms as the foundation upon which conceptualizations of justice are ultimately based. The idea of fairness can be attributed to social norms, as most theorists concede (Blau, 1967). When conformity to such a norm exists, justice or fairness will be an important determinant of behavior. A distinction can be made between two normative aspects of justice: a norm that stipulates that one ought to behave justly (whatever it may be), and a norm specifying the principles of justice that one ought to conform to. The former is a metanorm concerning the intensity of evaluative expectations with regard to a certain realm of behavior relative to others, and the latter is a specification of the particular content of the behavior in question.

It is obvious that the relative importance of justice differs strongly across societies and across time within a given society. At certain times (e.g., national emergency) justice will clearly take a subsidiary position relative to other considerations. Wide differences also exist among subcultures concerning the type of behavior that is accepted as constituting fairness. For instance, criminals often tend to accept norms that define behavior under a certain set of circumstances as being "fair" rather than exploitative (Roebuck, 1964; Yochelson & Samenow, 1976). Even when a strong norm exists concerning justice, its importance relative to other determinants of behavior will depend upon the degree of conformity to the norm. Strong feelings about the desirability of justice will have little impact if most people fail to conform to the norm.

Democratic–egalitarian societies place a great deal of stress on the distributive justice norm; but this norm is less strong and ubiquitous in many other societies. In the United States, for instance, strong conformity pressures are directed toward attaining equitable outcomes, so distributive justice is a salient factor among the determinants of behavior. Social pressure promotes conformity to the norm of equity even when a person might have been satisfied with an inequitable situation. Concern with equity can reach such a level of intensity as to become almost a preoccupation, with everyone comparing the fairness of his own outcomes to those of other persons, other groups, or other sections of the country. It would be expected that, in highly materialistic societies, the concern with equity would be very pervasive because allocation of material goods is easily calculated by objective means. By contrast, other types of goods (such as purity of heart or kindness) are less easily quantified. Perhaps it is not accidental that early empirical work in equity was conducted in industry where outcomes such as work and money are easily noticeable.

The precise nature and the content of justice and injustice demonstrate a great variability among human societies, as even a cursory excursion into history and anthropology will document. What is considered to be just or unjust depends on time and place. The reasons for the particular form, shape, and content of justice and injustice must be sought in historical, religious, or economic forces, or even in fortuitous factors. The tremendous degree of variation across cultures and through history in the beliefs about social justice is a vivid testimony to the power of social norms in creating social reality. Aristotle, in his *Nichomachean Ethics*

(Ross, 1925), commented on the problem of variability long ago: "For all men agree that what is just in distribution must be according to merit in some sense, though they do not all specify the same sort of merit, but democrats identify it with the status of freeman, supporters of oligarchy with wealth (or noble birth), and supporters of aristocracy with excellence [p. 1131]." The ancient Greeks accepted slavery without any sense of its constituting an unjust practice. Punishments that would cause extreme revulsion among individuals currently living in western societies—if applied to any crime—were considered just and reasonable for even minor infractions of laws only a few centuries ago (for instance, hanging and quartering for stealing a small amount of money or food).

Conformity plays a central role in the acceptance and the perpetuation of a particular set of norms and rules that constitutes a system of justice. Once a system of rules and norms exists in a society, (voluntary) conformity by individuals implies that the existing system is seen as being just and reasonable. (If adherence to norms is perceived as due to coercion, then conformity would convey a different implication about the justice of the system.) Through the processes of socialization, the cultural norms are transmitted across generations, although some degree of distortion often occurs. During childhood, one is taught to conform to the cultural norms and rules that define just and unjust behavior. Widespread conformity to a social norm results in uniformity of behavior that will facilitate the perception and learning of the "normative expectations of what constitute 'fair' correlations between inputs and outcomes [Adams, 1965, p. 279]."

For most people, primitive (i.e., unreflective) conformity to existing norms and rules is the terminal point of their cognitive processes about justice and injustice (Kohlberg, 1964). To attempt to engage in the complex, subtle, and abstract processes required for making an independent judgment about the degree of justice or injustice in every given instance of behavior would not only be unacceptably time-consuming but would be a stressful experience as well. As in all areas of life, conformity to norms and rules helps simplify our behavior by providing preestablished guidelines and acceptable definitions of that part of social reality dealing with justice. Specific occurrences that depart significantly from accepted norms and rules are seen as instances of injustice.

What is considered to be just, then, depends to a very great extent upon what other persons around us agree is just. An experiment by Berkowitz and Walker (1967) compared the impact of peer consensus and criminal laws on individuals' judgments about the morality of an action. Results showed that knowledge about an existing law and knowledge about the consensus of peers both exerted a significant influence on students' judgments about the moral propriety of an action; more interestingly, from the point of view of the present discussion, the consensus of opinion among peers exerted a stronger effect on judgment than knowledge of the relevant laws.

In a stable society where the norms are clear and where strong pressure exists for conformity, there will be little overt disagreement about what constitutes fairness and unfairness. By contrast, there will be less agreement in times of flux or social change about the relevant criteria and the weight they should receive (e.g., affirmative action programs). One looks to the norms of one's own reference group in such times for guidance—to see what others think—as opposed to making an absolute evaluation. In these ambiguous circumstances it is as if a person were saying: "What do other people believe to be fair? I will agree with them." In summary, in most societies, a set of norms and rules defines justice and injustice, and a person's judgment about concrete cases reflects his or her conformity to the cultural norms (Zimring & Hawkins, 1977). In most instances, the person is probably not even aware that the perception of justice is so largely dependent upon conformity to the cultural norms. Thus, a rough and ready sense of the just and unjust is predetermined for most people by their adherence to the cultural norms (the content of which is extremely flexible).

III. ELASTICITY OF THE DISTRIBUTIVE JUSTICE CALCULUS

One of the important conclusions reached in the area of social psychology is that group norms exert a profound impact on an individual's cognitions, emotions, and behavior. Conformity to social norms can also play a major role in judgments made about fairness; for illustrative purposes, consider the several phases that are implicated in the eventual judgments concerning distributive justice.[3] The following discussion will be restricted to judgments about the fairness of outcomes for only two persons. Although usually not bothering to discuss or elaborate the point, theorists who deal with distributive justice have asserted that the determinants of a person's judgment are the perceived elements—rather than the objective state of affairs (Adams, 1965; Walster *et al.*, 1976).

---

[3]We are not concerned here with attempting to offer a theoretical model of judgments about justice, but with emphasizing the potential influence of conformity pressure at any of the stages into which one may decompose the total sequence of or processes that contribute to the final judgment. For systematic expositions of justice-judgment models, see the articles by Farkas and Anderson (1979) and Leventhal (1976).

Behavior connected with justice is susceptible to influence from conformity at each of the points leading to the eventual judgment about fairness: inputs and outcomes (costs–rewards), choice of comparison other, type of comparison other, and the decision itself.

A. Social Pressure Points

1. DETECTION

Before discussing the psychological processes that terminate in a judgment of justice or injustice, we should acknowledge a prior cognitive stage that is critical, although usually not discussed explicitly. Formulations about distributive justice assume that the relevant inputs and outcomes are noticed by the individual (Adams, 1965). The objective existence of these elements is not sufficient; it is necessary that they exist in a psychological sense for the individual as well. To take notice of another person's inputs or outcomes is the first necessary step before the evaluation process can begin.

The salience of an event is determined by its distinctiveness in relation to its surroundings. Thus, homogeneity of inputs or outputs provides a stable background against which variation is likely to be detected. The existence of a high degree of conformity to a norm creates uniformity of behavior that renders deviation distinctive and hence easily noticeable— the perceptual ground on which any difference in behavior is a highly salient figure. One could predict that whether or not a given input–outcome is noticed (and hence the type of comparison with self that eventually takes place) will be determined by the degree of uniformity (conformity) of behavior in a given domain. Another person who has inputs or outcomes different from one's own would be more likely to be noticed under conditions of group homogeneity on certain characteristics (e.g., one female in a group of males; Taylor & Fiske, 1978).

2. INFORMATION INTEGRATION

After relevant events in the environment have been detected by the individual, they are weighted, summed, and evaluated (Anderson, 1976). At these phases, the effect of normative pressure can be quite pronounced. Most of the stimuli involved in justice judgments are subjective or ambiguous; under such conditions of low physical reality one must rely on other people to establish social reality (Festinger, 1954). The nature of the perception of social reality by an individual will be strongly influenced by the consensus of other people's behavior. Ample research is available indicating that consensus is capable of producing rather remarkable changes in the meaning and interpretation given to a standard stimulus (Allen & Wilder, 1980).

A high degree of consensus among other persons creates change in both cognitions and behaviors. In fact, research conducted by Allen and Wilder (1980) suggests that cognitive change may, in part, mediate behavioral change. It was hypothesized that a person reinterprets the meaning of the stimulus object when facing unpopular responses from a unanimous group, and that this change in meaning leads to a shift in the behavioral response toward the group's position. In the first experiment, several opinion items were presented. Subjects observed either unpopular responses supposedly made earlier by a unanimous group or by a group having one dissenter (social support), or no responses at all (control). Subjects merely gave their interpretation of the meaning of a key word or phrase in each opinion statement—they did not give their own opinions. Results showed that subjects gave more uncommon meanings to the stimuli in the unanimous conditions than in the social support and control conditions. In another experiment subjects observed scores that corresponded to the interpretation (meaning) produced by the unanimous and control conditions in the first experiment. After observing the consensually produced meanings of these items, the subjects shifted their own opinions toward the position held by the unanimous group in Experiment 1. It was concluded, therefore, that group consensus affects the perceived meaning of a stimulus, and that change in meaning is, in turn, responsible for the shift in opinion.

3. COMPARISON OTHER

A crucial determinant of judgments about distributive justice is, of course, the characteristics of the person with whom one compares rewards and costs. One of the difficulties with equity theory (Walster *et al.*, 1976) is its vague specification of the "other" which is used in making evaluations of fairness by an individual (Austin, 1977). What sort of others are used in making comparisons? It is generally agreed that the comparison other must be similar on certain relevant dimensions (what these dimensions consist of is not always apparent). Research in the field (Austin, 1977) indicates that the comparison other usually consists of either: (*a*) a reference group (i.e., others in a similar position, role, or status); or (*b*) another person with whom an individual is linked by a relationship or through interaction. Thus, the source for making justice comparisons may be a reference group or a reference person. At a more abstract level, Austin (1977) suggests that the referents used for equity comparisons can vary along the dimensions of proximity, similarity, and instrumentality. However thoroughly theorists conceptualize categories of referents, the task of determining, a priori, the choice that an individual will use for a comparison group or comparison other remains an obstinate problem; it is a problem that we will not attempt to deal with here. The importance of the choice of the particular referent for making a comparison is clearly a critical determinant of one's ultimate evaluation about the degree of justice or injustice in any specific case.

Depending upon the characteristics of the persons used for comparison, the behavioral outcome may vary sharply. In an experiment by Israel (1964), subjects reported that they had successfully resisted social pressure by imagining how certain salient referent persons such as "best friend" or "parents" would answer in the situation. Even an imaginary or fictitious comparison person can be effective in influencing one's behavior. In his book, *Profiles in Courage,* John F. Kennedy (1964) described several instances in which United States senators faced severe social pressure from their contemporaries. In one case a senator resisted social pressure by viewing his present behavior in the light of an evaluation as it might be made by a future historian. Thus, the person who seemed to be "out of step" not only was hearing a "different drummer" but, in this case, hearing one who had not yet been born. In summary, other persons who are not physically present can be used as guides for evaluating one's own behavior in important situations.

Great importance should be attached to factors determining the choice of the comparison person. Merton (1957), among others, has mentioned several factors that seem to influence the choice of reference group. Almost all the discussions on this problem emphasize the importance of similarity between persons along some central social dimension; in addition, shared fate also seems to be an important factor. Findings from our own experiments on behavior under group pressure indicate that the similarity of the situation in general is also important in contributing to the effectiveness of a reference person who is not physically present (Allen & Wilder, 1979). The choice of comparison other may also represent conformity to the ingroup's observed (or presumed) behavior in this area. In other words, the choice of reference group (or person) by an individual may be due to conforming to the choice that other members of one's group make under similar circumstances. Moreover, one's group can even specify that it is not acceptable to compare one's outcomes with those of other persons at all, and thus can strongly discourage using a comparison person in evaluating one's outcomes.

4. JUDGMENT

The actual process of judgment is susceptible to conformity pressures, quite independent of any prior effects that conformity may have had on the detection, selection, and interpretation of stimuli, or on the choice of comparison other. In a very direct and explicit fashion, social pressure can determine a person's judgment and behavior concerning the fairness of an act. For example, in Morse, Gruzen, and Reis's (1976) research, the behavior of subjects who were responsible for allocating rewards was influenced to some extent by the perceived expectations of the experimenter. Whether conformity to a norm under such circumstances represents mere public compliance (without private acceptance) is not known. For the allocator who faces the problem of distributing rewards, conformity to an external norm has distinct advantages. Ascribing the distribution of rewards to the demands of an external norm tends to deflect any dissatisfaction felt by the recipients away from the allocator and toward the external (and impersonal) norm. Allocators often try to convince recipients that the uneven distribution of rewards has a normative basis, whether or not the claim is entirely true.

Empirical research indicates that social factors are important determinants of public responses to injustice (Kidder, Bellettirie, & Cohn, 1977; Mikula & Schwinger, 1978). The general interpersonal norm of politeness, modesty, and responsibility seems to be an important factor influencing type of allocation in face-to-face situations. An interesting pattern of behavior has been observed in a two-person work situation that is appropriate for an equitable (distributive) allocation of outcomes (Mikula & Schwinger, 1978). Subjects in these experiments tended to choose the mode of allocation that gave a greater reward to their partners than to themselves. Thus, the person who contributed more than the partner chose the equality principle (giving more to the low-contributing partner than would have occurred with the equity principle); similarly, the person who contributed less than the partner chose the equity principle (thereby giving more to the high-performing partner than would occur with the equality principle). Each person in the group seemed to be guided by what Mikula calls the "politeness ritual," a kind of "Alphonse-Gaston" courtesy norm. The pattern of results described by the politeness ritual occurred when the affective relationship between partners was negative or neutral, as well as positive; in all cases the politeness norm seemed to prevail.

Some available evidence suggests that an individual's apparent support for the equity norm is due in part to self-preservation tactics—that is, compliance to norms concerning behavior that is thought to elicit social approval. For example, it was found in one study that adherence to the equity norm was greater when the subject's behavior was known to the experimenter than when the response was made in private (Morse et al., 1976). Public and private responses to positive inequity (overpayment) were investigated in one experiment by use of the bogus pipeline technique (Rivera & Tedeschi, 1976). When subjects received more than their fair shares, they expressed guilt publicly, but they were actually happier according to data from the bogus pipeline, which provides a more valid measure of one's private response. Because acting in a just manner is highly valued in our society, it is to be expected that publicly conforming to justice norms could be used as a means of gaining social approval from others. A study by Tjosvold (1977) indicates that persons did conform to the justice norm when it had been invoked by a fellow group member; and, according to the author, they did so because conformity is seen as leading to social esteem from group members.

Nevertheless, it would be unwarranted and premature to conclude that any public response given in the presence of a group is always inauthentic or discrepant from one's true belief. Agreement with a group's position may indicate that a real, underlying change has occurred. In a study by Prator and Greenberg (1982), subjects either responded anonymously or expected to discuss their answers later with other group members. Results failed to show any significant overall effect for public–private conditions of responding. There was an interaction with sex of subject, however. In the underpayment condition (in which subjects were led to believe that their fellow group members underpaid a target person), female subjects conformed more to the group in the public condition than in the private condition; the males did not show this type of difference. As the underpayment condition represented the most extreme group norm, it was suggested that the greater public conformity by females might be due to their greater concern about preserving interpersonal relationships and group harmony.

The general lack of difference between the public and private conditions in the Prator and Greenberg (1982) study had very interesting implications. Group pressure directed toward issues of justice may indeed sometimes produce true or private change rather than simply public compliance or overt agreement with the group. The consensual responses of a group can supply information that helps to define social reality for the individual; that is, they can provide a frame of reference for determining the meaning of a stimulus and the correctness of a response in a particular situation.

5. RESPONSES TO INJUSTICE

Finally, conformity to social norms can determine the nature of one's response to injustice, including the appropriateness of potential ways of reducing it. Reactions to injustice carry the serious potential danger of disrupting the social system (or creating additional acts perceived as unjust as well) if left entirely to the individual's discretion—or to collective action unchecked by societal norms. Thus, social norms govern such behavior in most cases. Most contemporary societies have established normative prohibitions against seeking personal retribution for injustice committed against one's self or relatives. Yet in some North American Indian tribes, it was one's duty to revenge a wrong to one's self or family (Hoebel, 1954); social disapproval would be expressed if retribution were not forthcoming. In many cases, even the method of taking retribution is socially prescribed. (In the old west, shooting one's enemy in the back was frowned upon.)

Even when the objective evidence in an unjust situation normally would lead to a sense of distress,[4] one's group can provide social norms that will attenuate or prevent such a reaction by invoking other elements or by shifting the perspective to other levels. Thus, present injustice loses its potential for creating distress if it is perceived as being necessary to conform to another norm, such as contributing to societal progress. In this way, current unjust distributions may be legitimized because of the positive long-term consequences (e.g., greater general economic growth that will ultimately benefit even those persons currently receiving unfair outcomes).[5] The ideology of upward mobility may function in the same way. And, of course, religion offers many good examples. Outcomes in the present time will not be considered to be unfair if future outcomes in another realm of existence are seen as even more important: "It is not unfair that my outcomes are unsatisfactory now, because I'll obtain greater rewards than other people in another world: So I'm not dissatisfied." [As counterpart to Austin and Walster's (1975) concept of "equity with the world," we can coin the term "equity with the universe" to describe this situation.] It is difficult to maintain beliefs about the importance of outcomes in an unknowable future relative to the insistent reality of present circumstances except by the bolstering of social reality that can be provided by social norms. Strong conformity pressures can encourage an individual to take into consideration this level of "irreality" (Lewin, 1951) when responding to present injustice.

6. SUMMARY

In summary, an attempt has been made to specify the possible influence exerted by conformity at each of the several phases that contribute

[4]To an unknown degree, the distress and anger felt in certain inequitable situations (i.e., when the individual feels his or her outcomes are less than desirable) may be due not to the violation of the fairness norm, per se, but to the emotion of envy, which seems to be a powerful panhuman phenomenon (Foster, 1972).

[5]A temporal dimension is explicitly invoked in the distinction between equity as a goal of social interaction or as an interpersonal strategy that may be instrumental in the pursuit of various long-term motives (Van Avermaet, McClintock, & Moskowitz, 1978).

to an evaluation of justice or injustice by the individual. It is clear that normative influences operate at every point, affecting to an unknown degree the resultant assessment made about fairness. An important task for further research is to specify the conditions under which conformity to social norms influences behavior (and to what degree) at the specific phases involved in the processes leading to decisions about justice.

B. Group Level Factors

The role of group membership in justice behavior deserves a brief discussion at this point. The categorization of people into in-group and out-group is a ubiquitous cognitive process; and the perceptual and behavioral consequences of in-group or out-group membership have been demonstrated in many studies (Allen & Wilder, 1975; Tajfel, 1970, 1978). It has been shown that a person will favor in-group members at the expense of out-group members even when group membership is based on the mere categorization of individuals on some trivial response. When an in-group member has a choice of awarding points between an in-group and an out-group member, results show that he or she favors the in-group member. Tajfel (1970) explains these findings as being due to the social norm that stipulates that one is expected (ought) to discriminate in favor of one's own group members. Whatever the correct explanation may be, in-group favoritism has direct relevance to the outcomes of comparisons between in-group and out-group members.

At the same time, the results of recent studies disclose that a person does not favor the in-group member at the expense of the out-group member as strongly as it is possible to do (Billig & Tajfel, 1973; Commins & Lockwood, 1979). To be completely fair would require one to give an equal number of points to the out-group member as to the in-group member. In this situation, then, a conflict exists between the norm of in-group loyalty and the norm of fairness (which is very important in our culture). The data from these experiments indicate that subjects compromise in their behavior by favoring the in-group members somewhat (by awarding them a greater number of points than the out-group member); but the behavior is still not as biased as it is possible to be. Such favoritism toward the in-group member cannot be accounted for by the possibility of face-to-face social pressure from other in-group members, as the task of awarding points in these studies is usually private and the recipients are anonymous members of the in-group or out-group. Also, it is important to emphasize that in this experimental paradigm the subject never allocates rewards to the self, so self-interest (or, at any rate, direct self-interest) cannot be invoked as an explanation for the findings.

In summary, the norm of fairness in these experiments is in conflict with the norm of ingroup bias. As noted previously, subjects are not completely fair under such conditions; they compromise between fairness and complete favoritism to ingroup members.

Several implications can be drawn from results of the series of in-group–out-group categorization experiments. First, predictions made on the basis of the assumed operation of the fairness norm are not supported: Here is a situation in which the subjects do not behave fairly between in-group and out-group members. Other research supports this conclusion more directly. Commins and Lockwood (1979) examined the behavior of persons toward in-group and out-group members under conditions of equity and inequity (which was disadvantageous either to the in-group or to the out-group). Results did not support the predictions made from equity theory: In-group bias occurred in all conditions. It appears that the opportunity to restore equity will be ignored in preference to behavior that contributes to a positive social identity for one's own in-group. And, of course, a very effective way of achieving positive distinctiveness for one's own group is by discriminating against out-groups. A second point is that subjects in these studies faced a situation that is only too common in everyday life: a conflict between two opposing norms. In many cases of behavior that involves justice, the situation is of this sort—which is a great deal more complicated than assumed by theories of equity or justice. Thus, one must be cognizant of the counter-vailing forces toward conformity to social norms that are in conflict with the direction of the behavior predicted by justice considerations alone. The relative weight of each norm in such a norm-conflict situation is an empirical question, so the outcome will vary across specific instances; but, more importantly, it is also a general theoretical problem that needs to be dealt with. The relative strength of the opposing norms of discrimination and fairness is affected by many situational factors. A recent study demonstrated that the norm for fairness is stronger in less cohesive groups and in groups having superior status (Branthwaite, Doyle, & Lightbown, 1979). On the basis of available experimental research (Billig & Tajfel, 1973; Branthwaite *et al.*, 1979), it can be suggested that variables that increase the strength of the discrimination norm relative to the fairness norm (i.e., similarity of members, cohesiveness, low status, explicit reference to the group), all tend to increase the salience of group identity. A third implication from the in-group–out-group studies is that group membership can be identified as one of the important factors that modulates the impact of justice processes on behavior. Group membership clearly alters the results that would be predicted from considering theories of equity or justice taken in isolation.

A number of other interesting questions arise from considerations of in-group–out-group categorization. Because justice situations do often involve an out-group member, some discrepancy from expected results should obtain when questions of justice involve in-group versus out-group members. Likewise, behavioral results are likely to differ when justice considerations involve making a comparison between in-group members as opposed to making a comparison between out-group members. Conformity to norms stipulating favoritism toward in-group members makes it unlikely that one will exhibit the identical reactions when an in-group member and an out-group member have received unjust treatment. Techniques that would tend to enhance a person's empathy or identification with an unjustly treated out-group member should increase the probability of one's undertaking behavior designed to mitigate the plight of the mistreated out-group member (Lerner, Miller, & Holmes, 1976). Group membership also becomes an important factor in justice behavior at another point—the choice of reference group. Very different consequences will occur depending on whether an ingroup or an out-group is taken as a referent for comparison purposes. Also, a person has the choice of selecting an individual or a group as a basis for the comparison of own rewards and costs. A group should be a much more stable source for purposes of comparison than a single person.

To belong to a group means, among other things, expressing agreement with other members regarding certain important matters of belief, values, and the like. The "we" feeling of a group is an acknowledgment of acceptance and conformity regarding the many norms that are shared among group members. In most social groups (although not in all) conformity is a desired and valued behavior, as indicated by the negative reactions that nonconformity elicits from other group members. As a case in point, consider the group pressure manifested against "rate busting [Homans, 1961]" and other disapproved actions in industrial settings; intense social pressure can be brought to bear on nonconformers. When conformity is a positively valued commodity, it will be taken into account as an input when judgments are made about the allocation of outcomes among group members.

The role of group membership is particularly important because the opportunity for surveillance of behavior and for applying sanctions within a group will increase the pressure to conform to the norms. When one's own group is threatened or group membership is salient, for any reason, these commonalities will be especially emphasized. Furthermore, socioemotional relationships among group members and norms about solidarity are better served by making an appeal for justice for one's group relative to other groups, even if it means neglecting issues of distributive justice at the level of the individual group members. Thus, salience of group membership can shift the center of gravity in justice considerations from the self to the group as a whole (Eckhoff, 1974). We do not know the answer to the important question of the extent to which a person is able to obtain personal satisfaction from one's own group having received justice relative to other group, even though it entails a personal loss. There are many fascinating problems for further research in this area. Similar issues have been raised by Runciman (1966) in his distinction between egoistic and fraternal relative deprivation.

In addition to the in-group–out-group distinction, individuals may be categorized at two different units of analysis, as intimated earlier: level of the person or level of the group. Thus, four persons who are in close physical proximity may be categorized as either: (*a*) at the individual level (as a four-person aggregate); or (*b*) at the group level (as being members of the same group). Research has shown that categorizing behavior at the individual or at the group level results in a standard sequence of behavior being perceived and interpreted differently by an observer (Wilder, 1978). Thus, in contrast to an aggregate, when persons are perceived as a group there tends to be (*a*) a perception of the existence of greater similarity of belief among the members; and (*b*) the attribution of greater external causality for a member's behavior that is constant across members but of greater internal causality when the behavior of one member differs from that of the majority.

In summary, an individual's perceptions and responses are influenced by the way the other person's behavior has been categorized (in-group versus out-group, or individual versus group level). In many instances, these factors will significantly modify the predictions made solely on the basis of theories of justice. The role of the group in justice behavior is a neglected area that could yield important results in future research. One important type of small, face-to-face group would seem to provide a particularly appropriate and instructive setting for numerous problems pertinent to justice—the family. One could observe in this type of small group the interplay between ideas of justice (need, equality, distributive, or other) and the conformity to norms that exist within and outside the group. Moreover, there are naturally existing status differences among family members that are modified as the children grow; hence, it is possible to observe changes in the nature of the tactics used by family members to attain compliance to norms of equity and justice. It is, additionally, a setting in which ideas of justice and fairness are often in conflict with the concrete realities of the demands for group members to conform to certain behaviors that are justified by appeal to motives other than justice. Finally, the contribution to children's learning about justice from their observation of the conformity (with and without private acceptance) of other family members could be readily subjected to investigation in this type of small group.

IV. FACILITATING AND IMPEDING JUSTICE

Up to this point we have discussed conformity pressure primarily in terms of its impact on cognitive processes—that is, the perception of the discrete elements involved in judgments about justice. There was no intention of suggesting that a discrepancy existed between private beliefs and public behavior under many conditions of social pressure. As we said earlier, social influence that produces conformity will often also result in a true change in cognition, perception, or affect (belief, opinion, attitude). But conformity pressure does, of course, produce overt behaviors that are discrepant with one's private beliefs or values—the situation usually denoted by the term *compliance*.

A. Contemporaneous Social Pressure

Regardless of the nature and outcome of a judgment about justice, the overt action taken by the person as a result of conformity pressures can produce varying degrees of fairness–unfairness or justice–injustice that may be discrepant with one's own private preference. An individual may also support the norm endorsed by the group without perceiving any conflict between it and his or her own private position. That is, an individual may not have any opinion at all or have no preference for one alternative over another.

The most interesting situations are those in which an individual has a clear and strong private preference for a course of action which is either supported or opposed by social pressure from the group. Four categories can be created by combining two levels of the following dimensions: An individual has a private preference for behaving in a way that leads to just or to unjust outcomes; and group pressure is advocating behavior that leads to just or to unjust outcomes. Four categories result from these two dimensions. In two categories the direction of the group pressure is consistent with the individual's own preferred type of behavior; and, in two other categories, there is a conflict between the preferred behavior of the individual and the direction advocated by the group.

1. GROUP UNJUST–INDIVIDUAL JUST

Let us consider first the category in which group pressure produces injustice in conflict with the individual's preference. The norm of the group may be in conflict with one's own beliefs (or internal norm) about what constitutes justice behavior in a given situation. Subjected to social pressure from an external source, we would expect that a person's own behavior might be influenced—that a person would move toward a group's position although it conflicts with his or her personal beliefs. Extensive research in the area of conformity indicates that social pressure can significantly influence an individual's public behavior across a wide range of tasks and content; there is no reason to think that justice behavior should be an exception.

Life is so full of examples of this sort that it hardly seems necessary to enumerate them; unfair behavior or the miscarriage of justice seems to be readily produced by group pressure. It is very easy for a person to succumb to social pressure and participate in unjust behavior that is in conflict with one's own private disposition at the time, as indicated by instances of summary justice perpetrated by lynch mobs and by other cases of crowd phenomena. A very poignant example of the strength of social pressure over the judgment of individuals is depicted in an account of the hanging of an innocent person in the early American West in the novel, *The Oxbow Incident* (Clark, 1943). We should recognize that group pressure is effective not only in the case of stable and long-lasting norms, but also with norms that develop rapidly within a transient behavioral situation—"emergent norms" to use Turner's (1964) term. According to Turner (1964), during a crowd situation the behavior of an individual is strongly influenced by the norms that evolve during the interaction and that serve to guide and control ongoing behavior.

Relevant social psychological research is also available. In one variation of Milgram's (1965) well-known studies of obedience, a group unanimously chose to assign very dangerous levels of electric shock to a victim. The consensus of the group was very effective in producing compliance in the single naive subject. A survey study by Pettigrew (1958) disclosed that pressure to conform to social norms concerning racial segregation seemed to be one of the strongest factors affecting the behavior of whites toward blacks in the south. And it is well known that expedient compliance often becomes transformed over time into true change or internalization (Allen, 1965).

A study conducted by Prator and Greenberg (1982) attempted to create a clear conflict between an individual's belief about justice and the responses given by a group of peers. Using the allocation of payment as

the task, the experimenter created several different types of group pressure that deviated from the equitable allocation of payment. After being
informed of the production of two hypothetical workers, the subjects
were asked to allocate the percentage of pay that each should receive.
Data from the control condition indicated that when subjects responded
in the absence of information about the group members' answers they
tended to adhere quite closely to the equity norm in allocating pay between the two workers. It does appear, as others have noted (Lane &
Messé, 1971; Walster et al., 1976) that equity tends to be the prevailing
justice norm in the absence of cues to the contrary. Social pressure
consisted of subjects' observing the responses allegedly given by five
peers; the group's responses departed from an equitable distribution for
the two workers by either overpayment, underpayment, or equality of
payment.

Results revealed that, overall, the social pressure from the group did
influence the subjects' allocation; that is, there was a movement toward
the allocation of pay that was advocated by the peer group responding
before the subject's turn. (Only in the equality norm condition did the
results fail to differ significantly from the control condition.) It is most
important to note, however, that the group pressure exerted only a
limited degree of influence on the subjects' responses. Thus, although
responses shifted in the direction of the group's allocation of payment,
the degree of movement was far short of the group's position. For
example, in the overpayment condition, the group allocated 90% of the
pay to the better worker; the mean response for subjects was 71%, which
is significantly greater than in the control and equity conditions (61%)
but still short of the amount given by the group (90%). A similar result
occurred in the underpayment condition. Interestingly, the subjects
moved toward the group approximately one-third of the available distance. This percentage of movement toward the group has often been
reported in the conformity literature (Allen, 1965), so findings for justice behavior are in accord with results obtained with other types of
content used in group pressure studies.

Prator and Greenberg take pains to emphasize that the results of their
study attest to the strength and stability of the internal justice norm of
equity. Stress is placed on the fact that the responses of subjects never
completely converged with those given by the inequitable group (i.e.,
there was a significant difference between the group's position and the
subjects' responses). The authors' conclusion is correct, of course, but, at
the same time, it must be acknowledged that the group's position did
cause a significant shift toward the inequitable position relative to responses given in the control condition. To the extent that justice or

injustice is a matter of degree (as it almost always is in reality), it must be concluded that pressure from the group is clearly capable of moving an individual's response away from his or her internal norm (e.g., equity)—away from the response that would be given in the absence of the group norm.

2. INDIVIDUAL UNJUST–GROUP JUST

The second type of individual–group conflict is the situation in which the individual has a disposition to behave in a way that leads to unjust outcomes but group pressure leads to a just outcome. Social pressure that is directed toward a fair distribution when an individual might prefer an unequal share for the self is an example of this type of benign outcome of conformity pressure. Another example of social pressure producing a just outcome is group pressure that promotes nondiscriminative behavior toward members of minority groups despite one's private preferences to the contrary.

3. INDIVIDUAL–GROUP CONSISTENCY

In the categories of consistency between the individual and the group (and when the individual has no preference), there is an absence of conflict. Willingness to conform to the group norm may produce either a just or an unjust outcome because the individual does not have a private preference. Social pressure in the process of eye-witness identification of suspects is an example (Buckhout, 1974). Group pressure that produces just and unjust behavior in these types of situations helps to establish social reality for the individual. What Le Bon said long ago about the role of the social group still seems to be applicable today: "The action of a group consists mainly in fortifying hesitant beliefs. An individual conviction that is weak is reinforced when it becomes collective [Le Bon, 1912, p. 102]." We may tend to overlook the importance of conformity to group norms as a means of strengthening behavior—whether just or unjust—in instances where there is consistency between an individual's disposition and group pressure.

B. Nonconformity and Social Change

It is clear that social pressure is effective in producing overt behavior that is discrepant with one's private position. The most socially relevant form of such behavior is the case of conforming to unjust behavior despite one's private belief to the contrary. Numerous cases have been discussed in which extensive conformity to conditions (or at least lack of active protest) has existed in the face of egregious injustice. Moreover, the group often brings social pressure to prohibit an individual from actively engaging in behavior that opposes existing injustices. Such situations have often existed in prisons and concentration camps (Moore, 1978). Strong social pressures are marshaled by inmate groups in these situations to discourage persons from resisting the injustices because of the dangers that such action would bring for the safety and survival of the entire group of captives. Injustice is often maintained, then, by social pressures to conform to unjust situations and by complementary social pressure to inhibit behavior that could be directed toward resisting the status quo. In this way, questions such as "Why do people not revolt under conditions of injustice?" can be answered in part.

There are two other subtle forms of social pressure that are important in considering justice and injustice. First, there is the subtle yet effective social pressure brought to bear on an individual to remain silent rather than to speak out about injustices. In his discussion of the notion of "groupthink," Janis (1972) argues that groups that are characterized by high cohesiveness and high morale are especially susceptible to this form of social pressure. Injustices are perpetuated when members of the oppressing group conform to social pressure against speaking out or taking action on an issue; history is replete with examples such as the McCarthy period in the United States and the Nazi era in Germany. This type of group pressure is particularly insidious, as Crutchfield notes, because the person "eventually comes not only to yield on particular opinions but to yield even his right to *express* an opinion [Kretch, Crutchfield, & Ballachy, 1962. p. 506; italics in original]." A somewhat different form of subtle social pressure may also contribute to the continuation of injustice: social pressure in the form of discouraging a person from maintaining a neutral position. Oppressing groups will sometimes demand of a person an explicit declaration of his or her position: "You are either with us or against us." More often, the social pressure is less direct yet no less insistent. An experiment was designed, using the Asch-type situation, which allowed the subject the opportunity on each trial of abstaining by not responding at all (Allen, 1975). Results showed that the subjects did not utilize the available option of not responding. Even though escape from the group pressure was possible, the subjects still responded—and conformed to the group's answers. It appears that conformity involves both pressure from the group to answer instead of remaining silent and, in addition, directional pressure to agree with the group's position. On important issues, then, a person will find that social pressure to commit one's self makes it difficult to remain neutral in the face of undesirable conformity forces.

In view of the pervasiveness and strength of conformity pressure, it is not surprising that injustices often persist. Yet we know that people do not always conform to injustice, that injustice is sometimes resisted, and that social change does occur. It is not possible in the space available here to discuss all the conditions that contribute to the combating of injustice. Certainly, there are economic, political, ideological, religious, and personality factors, among others, that may play a role in any particular instance. For the present we will only mention briefly some important situational factors that are derived from research in the area of conformity.

For persons attempting to resist pressures to conform, the crucial role of a partner who provides social support cannot be overemphasized. One of the well-known findings in research in the Asch-type situation is that when another person disagrees with the group (agreeing with the subject) conformity is almost completely eradicated (Allen, 1975). It seems that having social support enables a person to resist conformity pressure quite effectively. The applicability of these findings to important issues of injustice is indicated by results of a social support condition in the Milgram (1965) obedience situation. A unanimous group was very effective in inducing the subject to agree to assign severe shocks to the victim. But it was found that, in the presence of a single person who opposed the group, the subject was willing to resist the authority. A considerable amount of research has demonstrated the generality of social support as a technique for reducing conformity, and has specified some of the processes contributing to its effectiveness (Allen, 1975).

Social support is a sufficient psychological condition for producing nonconformity, but nonconformity does not (in the short run) bring about a change in the social norm that is responsible for maintaining the group-supported behavior. The group majority may simply denigrate or reject the nonconforming minority and render ineffective its attempts to alter the existing group norm. Even so, producing nonconformity by social support is at least a first step. Recent research suggests that it is possible for the nonconforming minority to influence members of the majority and to bring about a change in social norms. Moscovici (1976) and colleagues have demonstrated that the behavioral style of the minority—and, in particular, the consistency of its behavior—is one means by which it can effectively influence the majority over time. Consistency of behavior by the minority creates a cognitive conflict in the majority, which may lead to a restructuring of beliefs and opinions. In this manner it is possible for the powerless minority to influence a powerful majority in the long run. It is interesting to note that justice and injustice are capable of evoking very intense cognitive and affective responses in some persons (Cahn, 1949); because of their strong commitment, a few persons may be willing to persist for a very long time even in the face of an unsympathetic majority in the pursuit of their goal of changing the norm. Moscovici (1976) cites numerous examples of individuals who spent most of their lives working to change conditions in society that provoked in them a sense of outrage at the existing injustices. Although initially the accepted beliefs and practices may have been opposed by only a few nonconforming persons, it is indeed possible ultimately to produce a change in prevailing norms.

Questions concerning equity and justice often tend to be posed in a static way, as if these conceptions were fixed and unchanging. It is clear that changes do, indeed, occur; and conceptions of fairness and justice do evolve over time. Yet little is known about the determinants of such changes. The possibility of a consistent minority producing a change in norms has been mentioned; but deviant behavior is a complicated situation that may either produce social change or serve to strengthen the existing norms. The punishment of deviants can reinforce the perception of the legitimacy of norms concerning justice (especially on those occasions when one might find it expedient to violate the norm). The presence of a deviant can reinforce conformity not only by providing justification for one's own behavior, but also by helping to clarify the limits or boundaries of acceptable behavior. In short, the important role played by nonconformity or deviance should not be underestimated. Research is needed to clarify the conditions under which deviation from a norm results in changing the norm or in merely strengthening it. Further information on this problem should increase our understanding of the nature of the changes that occur over time in connection with norms that are integral to justice.

C. Procedural Justice

Any discussion of fairness and justice would be incomplete without giving some attention to procedural justice, that is, the methods or procedures used to resolve conflicts or to determine the allocation of outcomes (Folger, 1977; Thibaut & Walker, 1975). It is possible for individuals to view a procedure as being just or unjust independently of the judgment they may have about the justice or injustice of the outcome. Procedural justice is concerned with the rules rather than with the consequences of the rules.

At several steps during the process of procedural justice, there are ample opportunities available for conformity pressures to operate. In the course of deliberation among members of a jury, social influence and conformity pressures are likely to arise, just as in an interaction among members of any small, face-to-face, group (Brooks & Doob, 1975). It would not be fair to prejudge the effect of conformity pressure on the nature of eventual outcomes on the justice–injustice continuum. Happily, most instances of social pressure do not have unfortunate consequences of the sort described in a recent cartoon in the *New Yorker*. A burly "criminal type" is shown in the witness stand in a courtroom, responding to a question from an attorney standing in front of him: "I hit big Angie eight times with the fire ax and then threw him into the East River because of peer pressure." It is at least as likely, theoretically, for conformity pressure to enhance the quality of justice as it is to diminish it. Merely because the paradigm used in most of the contemporary research equates conformity with inaccuracy does not mean that this is always the case. In fact, research on groups that uses other paradigms indicates that the decision-making and problem-solving ability of a group is often superior to that of an individual (Steiner, 1972).

V. EPILOGUE

We must remember that judgments about justice and the behavior connected with injustice are made by persons who at the same time are subjected to all the influences that stem from having contact with other people and from being part of a broader social system of roles and groups. It is important to understand the motivational bases for a person's judgment and behavior concerning justice if accurate predictions are to be made. For example, when a person behaves in accordance with the distributive justice norm specifying that one ought not to receive more than comparable others or ought not to work less than comparable others, it is important to know whether such behavior is the result of conformity pressure alone (public compliance) or of internal beliefs and values that are consistent with the group's expectations. The motivational basis of the response could be ascertained by determining any difference in the behavior when privacy is assured as compared to a condition of public surveillance by other persons (Kidder *et al.*, 1977; Morse *et al.*, 1976).

It appears that there may be a tendency to perceive justice norms as operative in many situations even when such is not the case. According to the "just world" hypothesis (Lerner *et al.*, 1976), people are motivated to believe that others get what they deserve—that justice exists—and perceptions and evaluations of other people and events will be distorted in such a way as to increase the correspondence between what others deserve and what they get. If individuals want to believe in a just world, there may be a tendency to perceive erroneously the existence of a justice norm in many situations where it is not actually present. The upshot of this line of thinking is that one's behavior may frequently be influenced by a fictitious justice norm.

Justice theorists acknowledge that inputs–outcomes judgments and reactions to unjust outcomes will vary greatly from individual to individual, and will be dependent upon the person's perceptions rather than the objective characteristics of the elements in question (Adams, 1965; Eckhoff, 1974; Walster *et al.* 1976). It has frequently been remarked in passing that an implicit social "contract" (norm) plays an important role in specifying the relative weight of certain types of inputs and outcomes and the types of outcome seen as being "fair." Yet, research in the justice area has largely neglected the investigation of normative factors. It is important for both practical and theoretical reasons to pay more attention to an analysis of normative factors and their influence on judgments and reactions about justice. Research along these lines might be able to bring a greater degree of specification to the highly abstract (and content-free) conceptualizations of equity and justice theory, and might also help to clarify the functions of these elements in relation to the broader social structure in which the individual is enmeshed (role, group, organization, subculture, culture).

ACKNOWLEDGMENTS

For helpful comments, thanks are extended to P. Allen, W. Bowerman, P. Defares, R. van der Vlist, and J. Whyte.

REFERENCES

Adams, J. S. Inequity in social exchange. In L. Berkowitz, *Advances in experimental social psychology* (Vol. 2). New York: Academic Press, 1965.

Allen, V. L. Situational factors in conformity. In L. Berkowitz (Ed.), *Advances in experimental social psychology* (Vol. 2). New York: Academic Press, 1965.

Allen, V. L. Social support for nonconformity. In L. Berkowitz (Ed.), *Advances in experimental social psychology* (Vol. 8). New York: Academic Press, 1975.

Allen, V. L., & Wilder, D. A. Categorization, belief similarity, and intergroup discrimination. *Journal of Personality and Social Psychology*, 1975, *32*, 971–977.

Allen, V. L., & Wilder, D. A. Social support in absentia: The effect of an absentee partner on conformity. *Human Relations*, 1979, *32*, 103–111.

Allen, V. L., & Wilder, D. A. Impact of group consensus and social support on stimulus meaning: Mediation of conformity by cognitive restructuring. *Journal of Personality and Social Psychology*, 1980, *39*, 1116–1124.

Anderson, N. H. Equity judgment as information integration. *Journal of Personality and Social Psychology*, 1976, *33*, 291–299.

Asch, S. E. Studies of independence and conformity: I. A minority of one against a unanimous majority. *Psychological Monographs*, 1956, *70*, No. 9 (Whole No. 416).

Austin, W. Equity theory and social comparison processes. In J. M. Suls & R. L. Miller (Eds.), *Social comparison processes.* New York: Wiley, 1977.

Austin, W., & Walster, E. "Equity with the world": The trans-relational effects of equity and inequity. *Sociometry*, 1975, *38*, 474–496.

Berkowitz, L., & Walker, N. Laws and moral judgments. *Sociometry*, 1967, *30*, 410–422.

Billig, M. G., & Tajfel, H. Social categorization and similarity in intergroup behavior. *European Journal of Social Psychology*, 1973, *3*, 27–52.

Blau, P. M. *Exchange and power in social life.* New York: Wiley, 1967.

Branthwaite, A., Doyle, S., & Lightbown, N. The balance between fairness and discrimination. *European Journal of Social Psychology*, 1979, *9*, 149–163.

Brooks, W. W., & Doob, A. N. Justice and the jury. *Journal of Social Issues*, 1975, *31*, 171–182.

Buckhout, R. Eyewitness testimony. *Scientific American*, 1974, *321*, 23–31.

Cahn, E. *The sense of injustice.* New York: New York University Press, 1949.

Clark, W. V. T. *The ox-bow incident.* New York: Signet, 1943.

Commins, B., & Lockwood, J. The effects of status differences, favored treatment, and equity on intergroup comparisons. *European Journal of Social Psychology*, 1979, *9*, 281–289.

Deutsch, M. Equity, equality, and need: What determines which value will be used as the basis of distributive justice? *Journal of Social Issues*, 1975, *31*, 137–150.

Eckhoff, T. *Justice: Its determinants in social interaction.* Rotterdam, Holland: Rotterdam University Press, 1974.

Farkas, A. J., & Anderson, N. H. Multidimensional input in equity theory. *Journal of Personality and Social Psychology*, 1979, *37*, 879–896.

Festinger, L. A theory of social comparison processes. *Human Relations*, 1954, *7*, 117–140.

Folger, R. Distributive and procedural justice: Combined impact of "voice" and improvement on experienced inequity. *Journal of Personality and Social Psychology*, 1977, *35*, 108–119.

Foster, G. M. The anatomy of envy: A study in symbolic behavior. *Current Anthropology*, 1972, *13*, 165–186.

Gordon, R. L. Interaction between attitude and the definition of the situation in the expression of opinion. *American Sociological Review*, 1952, *17*, 50–58.

Hoebel, E. A. *The law of primitive man.* Cambridge: Harvard University Press, 1954.

Hollander, E. P. Conformity, status, and idiosyncrasy credit. *Psychological Review*, 1958, *65*, 117–127.

Homans, G. *Social behavior: Its elementary forms.* New York: Harcourt Brace & World, 1961.

Israel, J. Experimental change of attitude using the Asch-effect. *Acta Sociologica*, 1964, *7*, 95–104.

Janis, I. L. *Victims of groupthink.* Boston: Houghton Mifflin, 1972.

Kennedy, J. F. *Profiles in courage.* New York: Harper & Row, 1964.

Kidder, L. H., Bellettirie, G., & Cohn, E. S. Secret ambitions and public performances: The effects of anonymity on reward allocations made by men and women. *Journal of Experimental Social Psychology*, 1977, *13*, 70–80.

Kohlberg, L. Development of moral character and moral ideology. In M. Hoffman & L. Hoffman (Eds.), *Review of child development research* (Vol. 1). New York: Russell Sage Foundation, 1964.

Korte, C. Pluralistic ignorance about student radicalism. *Sociometry*, 1972, *35*, 576–587.

Krech, D., Crutchfield, R. S., & Ballachey, E. L. *Individual in society*. New York: McGraw-Hill, 1962.

Lane, I. M. & Messé, L. A. Equity and the distribution of rewards. *Journal of Personality and Social Psychology*, 1971, *20*, 1–17.

Le Bon, G. [*The psychology of revolutions*]. London: Allen & Unwin, 1912. (Originally published as *La revolution française et la psychologie des revolutions*.)

Lerner, M. J. The justice motive in social behavior: An introduction. *Journal of Social Issues*, 1975, *31*, 1–19.

Lerner, M. J., Miller, D. T., & Holmes, J. G. Deserving and the emergence of forms of justice. In L. Berkowitz & E. Walster (Eds.), *Advances in experimental social psychology* (Vol. 9). Academic Press, 1976.

Leventhal, G. S. The distribution of rewards and resources in groups and organizations. In L. Berkowitz & E. Walster (Eds.), *Advances in experimental social psychology* (Vol. 9). New York: Academic Press, 1976.

Lewin, K. *Field theory in social science*. New York: Harper, 1951.

McKeachie, W. J. Individual conformity to attitudes of classroom groups. *Journal of Abnormal and Social Psychology*, 1954, *49*, 282–289.

Merton, R. K. *Social theory and social structure*. Glencoe, Ill.: The Free Press, 1957.

Mikula, G., & Schwinger, T. Intermember relations and reward allocation: Theoretical considerations of affects. In H. Brandstatter, J. H. Davis, & H. Schuler (Eds.), *Dynamics of group decisions*. Beverly Hills, Calif.: Sage, 1978.

Milgram, S. Liberating effects of group pressure. *Journal of Personality and Social Psychology*, 1965, *1*, 127–134.

Moore, B., Jr. *Injustice: The social bases of obedience and revolt*. White Plains, N.Y.: M. E. Sharpe, 1978.

Morse, S. J., Gruzen, J., & Reis, H. T. The nature of equity-restoration: Some approval-seeking considerations. *Journal of Experimental Social Psychology*, 1976, *12*, 1–8.

Moscovici, S. *Social influence and social change*. New York: Academic Press, 1976.

Nord, W. R. Social exchange theory: An integrative approach to social conformity. *Psychological Bulletin*, 1969, *71*, 174–208.

Pettigrew, T. F. Personality and sociocultural factors in intergroup attitudes: A cross-national comparison. *Journal of Conflict Resolution*, 1958, *2*, 27–42.

Prator, S. C. & Greenberg, J. *Sex differences in conformity to social justice norms*. Manuscript submitted for publication, 1982.

Raven, B. H. Social influence on opinions and the communication of related content. *Journal of Abnormal and Social Psychology*, 1959, *58*, 119–128.

Rivera, A. N. & Tedeschi, J. T. Public versus private reactions to positive inequity. *Journal of Personality and Social Psychology*, 1976, *34*, 895–900.

Roebuck, J. The short con man. *Crime and Delinquency*, 1964, *10*, 240–246.

Rommetveit, R. *Social norms and roles*. Minneapolis, Minn.: University of Minnesota Press, 1955.

Ross, W. D. (Ed.). *The Oxford translation of Aristotle, Vol. IX: The Nichomachean Ethics*. London: Oxford University Press, 1925.

Runciman, W. G. *Relative deprivation and social justice*. Berkeley: University of California Press, 1966.

Steiner, I. D. *Group process and productivity*. New York: Academic Press, 1972.

Stricker, L. J., Messick, S., & Jackson, D. N. Conformity, anticonformity, and indepen-dence: Their dimensionality and generality. *Journal of Personality and Social Psychology,* 1970, *16,* 494–507.

Tajfel, H. Experiments in intergroup discrimination. *Scientific American,* 1970, *223,* 96–102.

Tajfel, H. (Ed.), *Differentiation between social groups: Studies in the social psychology of intergroup relations.* London: Academic Press, 1978.

Taylor, S. E., & Fiske, S. T. Salience, attention, and attribution: Top of the head phenomena. In L. Berkowitz (Ed.), *Advances in experimental social psychology* (Vol. 11). New York: Academic Press, 1978.

Thibaut, J. & Walker, L. *Procedural justice: A psychological analysis.* Hillsdale, N.J.: Erlbaum, 1975.

Tjosvold, D. Commitment to justice in conflict between unequal status persons. *Journal of Applied Social Psychology,* 1977, *7,* 149–162.

Turner, R. H. Collective behavior. In R. E. L. Faris (Ed.), *Handbook of modern sociology.* Chicago: Rand McNally, 1964.

Van Avermaet, E., McClintock, C., & Moskowitz, J. Alternative approaches to equity: Disso-nance reduction, pro-social motivation and strategic accommodation. *European Journal of Social Psychology,* 1978, *8,* 419–437.

Walster, E., Berscheid, E., & Walster, G. W. New directions in equity research. In L. Berkowitz & E. Walster (Eds.), *Advances in experimental social psychology* (Vol. 9). New York: Academic Press, 1976.

Wilder, D. A. Perceiving persons as a group: Effects on attributions of causality and beliefs. *Social Psychology,* 1978, *41,* 13–23.

Wilkins, L. T. Equity and republican justice. *The Annals of the American Academy of Political and Social Science,* 1976, *423,* 152–161.

Willis, R. H. Conformity, independence, and anticonformity. *Human Relations,* 1965, *18,* 373–388.

Yochelson, S., & Samenow, S. E. *The criminal personality* (Vol. 1). New York: Aronson, 1976.

Zimring, F., & Hawkins, G. The legal threat as an instrument of social change. In J. L. Tapp & F. J. Levine (Eds.), *Law, justice, and the individual in society.* New York: Holt, Rinehart & Winston, 1977.

chapter 7

Moral Evaluation in Intimate Relationships

WILLIAM AUSTIN
JOYCE TOBIASEN

I. INTRODUCTION

Our purpose in this chapter is to address the important issues in a consideration of "friendship and fairness." In raising questions about this topic, we have discovered that few empirical studies have directly investigated the role of moral evaluations in close relationships. In fact, some theorists have maintained that considerations of fairness are irrelevant in such relationships. However, the critics seem to be in the minority. In tackling this general topic, we will use the pioneering and provocative ideas of Elaine Hatfield and her colleagues on "equity theory and intimate relationships" (see Walster, Walster & Berscheid, 1978). Her approach applies equity and exchange theories to love relationships. Of course, opposing positions on love, such as the views of Erich Fromm, will need to be entertained. We will review the sparse research that does exist in this area, and close by suggesting an integrated approach that draws upon ideas from clinical psychology and recent studies on attribution processes in close relationships.

Austin (undated) has often used an hypothetical case as a pedagogical tool for introducing undergraduate college students to the topic of fairness. This case, which is labeled "I love you, but ... ," concerns the romantic and mundane day-to-day concerns of John and Mary—newlyweds:

> John and Mary had been undergraduates at the same school, and lived together for two years before getting married after graduation. Following graduation, John entered law school and Mary continued to work for an accountant. Mary was so competent at her job that the

217

EQUITY AND JUSTICE
IN SOCIAL BEHAVIOR

firm had offered her an executive position with the possibility of
becoming a partner after she completed her graduate degree. Mary
wanted very much to attend graduate business school. However,
John proposed that in order for them to avoid financial chaos that
Mary should continue working for her firm and support them while
John went to law school. John did not want them to borrow money.
After law school, John would be making a healthy salary and would
put Mary through graduate school. They also decided that since
Mary would be working and John busy with school, it would be
absolutely necessary for them to equally share in domestic chores.

The relationship and marriage went well at first. There was a
honeymoon period. Both partners were very benevolent and loving
toward one another. Mary enjoyed her work though it was demanding; John was excited about law school. Each partner found time for
the other and they shared in household duties. But gradually, Mary
began to assume more and more responsibility around the house.
She found herself doing almost all of the cooking and cleaning,
buying the groceries, and keeping things organized financially.

Things steadily got rougher for John and Mary. John spent more
and more time at the library, leaving less time for Mary. The initial
bargain had clearly broken down. When Mary mentioned this to
John, he admitted his neglect and apologized... ("I love you so
much. I know it's hard for you. You work all day and come home to
dinner and house stuff.") Subsequently, John was more attentive.
But only for a short while. John continued to overwork at school and
underwork at home.

Tension began to mount. Mary, feeling the pressure at work,
domestic chores, and lack of attention and stimulation from her
husband, again confronted John about what she saw as his unfair
treatment of her. John said she was turning into a nag. The next
night, John called Mary at work to tell her that he was bringing a
friend for dinner and would be there at 6:30, the time they usually
ate dinner. Mary exploded ... not only was it a last minute notice,
but it was *his* turn to fix dinner. He again apologized for his lack of
help in domestic things, but said he must work very hard at school
for *them*. This incident caused a major quarrel. Mary told John that
he should pick something up on his way home for John and his
friend to eat because Mary had to work late. John protested, "we
can't afford to eat out." Mary told John that not only was he insensi-
tive to her needs, but that he was "cheap" as well. That night John
tried to "make up" to Mary and promised to be a better partner.
Mary, still mad, turned off his sexual advances. John told Mary she
must be frigid.

The saga of John and Mary may read a bit like a soap opera. Nonetheless, most of us are familiar with existing intimate relationships in which

the same issues are involved. We also know that people respond in quite different ways to the pressures of this type of situation. Some would feel that love is unconditional and that one must accept the "bad with the good." Some couples would insist on talking about the issues to try to work out a compromise that suits them both. Some would insist on a "fair" relationship—period.

During class discussions of this case, students concur that, although a number of lingering questions remain on how intimacy colors perceptions of fairness, it is clear that intimate relationships are indeed scrutinized in moral terms: fair or unfair, just or unjust treatment, respectful or disrespectful, and so on. We agree with this assumption and will attempt to identify the role that moral evaluation processes seem to play in close relationships.

In this chapter, we will try to provide some tentative answers to questions that arise when one begins to confront "moral" evaluations in intimate relations. We will draw on two research literatures in social psychology. The first, on how individuals judge relationships to be fair or unfair and what they do in response to their judgments, is well developed. Excellent theorizing and empirical studies exist in this area. Unfortunately, there is very little evidence on how different types of relationships influence judgments and behavior. Most of the research on fairness consists of laboratory studies with virtually no studies on fairness in long-term relationships. The second—on the dynamics of intimate relationships—is less systematic, consisting of theoretical and philosophical statements from a variety of sources, and with little reliable research. We will not attempt to undertake an exhaustive review of these literatures. A number of excellent reviews on fairness in social relations exist (see Berkowitz & Walster, 1976; Walster, Walster, & Berscheid, 1978). In addition, although social psychologists have thoroughly researched the topic of interpersonal attraction (see Berscheid & Walster, 1978; Burgess & Huston, 1979), they have barely touched on intimacy; here the empirical research is sparse (see Hatfield, Utne, & Traupmann, 1979; Rubin, 1970; Walster & Walster, 1978). Given that the scientific study of intimacy has been generally taboo, it is not surprising that little research exists on how intimates evaluate the fairness of their relationships.

This may be changing. The rising divorce rate has convinced many scientists that the study of issues of intimacy, especially of factors that shape marital satisfaction, are critically important. In this chapter, we will review a few studies that argue these issues and offer some practical advice for dealing with dilemmas of marital fairness and unfairness.

This chapter is organized into four sections, each dealing with a different aspect of fairness and intimacy. In Section II, we define intimacy–nonintimacy, and consider whether intimates are equally concerned with issues of fairness.

In Section III, we discuss the nature of fairness in social relations. We will discuss social comparison processes, the use of justifications for harmful acts, and the importance of situational factors for moral evaluations.

In Section IV, we will attempt to tie together the separate theory and research on the topics of intimacy and fairness. One particular theory— equity theory—shows promise in this respect. As the topic of fairness in intimate relationships is a relatively new research topic, we will be forced to engage in a good bit of speculation. At times, the best we will be able to do is to draw on clinicians' anecdoctal observations of the processes engaged in by couples caught up in marital conflict. In addition, we will review several laboratory studies showing how the type of relationship enjoyed by two people affects the way they distribute rewards between themselves. Because the generality of these studies may be limited by the somewhat unusual laboratory environment in which they were conducted, we will next review a series of field studies that provide insights into the structure of moral evaluations among intimates.

The final section examines fairness in the context of the family system, with particular emphasis on the parent–child relationship. Is the question of "what is fair?" relevant to the parent? To the child? A review of the changing history of the parent–child relationships from eighteenth-century child-rearing practices through the contemporary childrens' rights movement suggests that the question is germane to our topic. Writings of developmental psychologists and pediatric specialists support this view.

II. THE NATURE OF INTIMACY

Two distinguishing features of intimate relationships are clear to most observers. First, intimacy is subjective; it is truly in the "eye of the beholder." Second, there are different degrees of intimacy, and different types of intimate relationships.

A. Definitions of Intimacy

Webster's New Collegiate Dictionary (1959, p. 441) provides four definitions of intimacy:

1. Intrinsic; innermost; inmost; hence; very personal; private.
2. Characterized by or arising from close union, contact, association, acquaintance, investigation, or the like; as, *intimate* friends or knowledge.
3. Having illicit sexual relations (with).
4. Closely personal;—of garments.

These formal definitions are too general to be of much use in a scientific analysis. Although, not surprisingly, scientists have also had trouble defining intimacy, their definitions are a little more useful.

Hatfield *et al.* (1979) considered intimacy to be a *static* state—something that a couple had either achieved or had not achieved: *Intimacy:* A relationship between loving persons whose lives are deeply entwined (p. 106). Perlmutter and Hatfield (1980) considered intimacy to be a process—a way of relating "a process in which a dyad—via sharing of ideas, (via verbal and nonverbal communication), affect, and behavior emotions, and behavior—attempts to move toward more complete communication, on all levels of the communicational transaction. [p. 18]."

B. Role Expectations in Intimate Relationships

There are different types of intimate relationships. The labels of the varied roles we play—mother, brother, lover—describe them.

1. Romantic relationships
   a. Married
   b. Dating
2. Parent–child relationships
3. Other family relationships
   a. Siblings
   b. Extended family
4. Same sex versus different sex "best friends"

Many sociologists argue that the concept of role is critically important in understanding the dynamics of intimate relationships. They argue that roles—which prescribe certain behaviors and proscribe others—structure virtually all of our relationships (Goffman, 1971). Intimate relations are no exception.

There may be a tendency for intimates to see an intimate's primary role as isomorphic with his or her identity. He is the breadwinner. She is the mother. John is the son. Turner (1978) observes:

The greater the extent to which members of a social circle are bounded to role incumbents by ties of identification, the greater the tendency for them to conceive the person as revealed by the role.... The more intimate the role relationship among actors and social circle, the greater the tendency for members of the social circle to conceive the person as revealed by the role [p. 7].... A relationship of intimacy requires that customary defenses be dropped—that usual boundaries of self-disclosure be abandoned. The person whose role involves intimate revelations, such as the counselee, reveals aspects of behavior, attitude, and sentiment that could be quite damaging if the counselor were to betray the trust and pass on the revelations. Accordingly it is nearly impossible to remain in such a relationship unless the counselee assumes that the counselor displayed in the role corresponds to the person [p. 8]. [Reprinted by permission from R. H. Turner, "The Role and the Person," *American Journal of Sociology*, 1978, *84*, 1–23. Copyright © 1978 by the University of Chicago Press.]

Expectations of how to act out certain roles in intimate relationships are learned (although not necessarily endorsed) in a broad cultural milieu (e.g., "cultural learning"). In particular, how we act out romantic and parent–child roles are subject to explicit and powerful norms that are vested with pressures from deep historical traditions. The fact that they are perhaps the most basic intimate roles we are exposed to in our lives amplifies pressures to conform to the expectations.

If a culture is a stable one, roles come to be so taken for granted, so much in the actor's "bones," that "what is" comes to be seen as "what is right." How society says people have to behave, is generally accepted as how it is "fair" to expect people to behave.

However, social institutions sometimes change. Revolutions, although never rendering a complete change, take place. Recently, role expectations between men and women and between parents and children have been undergoing rapid change. We have witnessed the feminist and childrens' rights movements. Inconsistencies between old and new cultural learning creates stress in ongoing family systems. This is most apparent in romantic relationships, which in turn, affect parent–child relationships. Examples of how past and contemporary man and woman prescriptions come into conflict is implied by the late Erich Fromm (1956): "The polarity of the sexes is disappearing, and with it erotic love, which is based on this polarity [p. 15]." Perhaps even more striking evidence of the role conflict experienced by the modern Western woman are the pronouncements of Pope Paul VI, who communicated that "the women's liberation movement could make women too masculine and threaten their spiritual and moral integrity [UPI, Feb. 1, 1976]." In light of the pressures for intimate relationships to maintain themselves as we have already discussed, it is easy to see how both women and men can feel pushed and pulled by their perceived role demands. They want to be the contemporary woman or man as well as the ideal mother or father. People often do not know which way to turn. We will discuss in the following sections how successful negotiation of conflicting role demands among intimates is essential to their perceptions of fairness, happiness, and likelihood of staying together.

Roles have a second function: They tell us how one ought to behave to symbolize feelings of intimacy. There are familiar rituals: goodnight kisses from children, romantic dinners between lovers, and displays of unconditional sharing by friends. (We will review some of the *specific* characteristics that distinguish intimate relationships from casual encounters in the next section.)

The notion that role requirements tell intimates how they *ought* to behave is somewhat paradoxical in view of the fact that many theorists conceive of intimate relations as the only relationship in which people are not bound by role constraints—the only role in which people can freely express all facets of themselves (see Perlmutter & Hatfield, 1980; Zaretsky, 1978).

C. Characteristics of Intimate Relationships

Sociologists observe that intimate relationships have very different role requirements than casual relationships. But exactly how do they differ? Social psychologists have itemized a number of the differences.

Hatfield *et al.* (1979) argue that when we reflect upon relationships between friends, lovers, spouses, and parents and children, it appears that they are generally marked by a number of characteristics:

1. Intensity of feelings
2. Communication: Depth and breadth of information exchange
3. Commitment
4. Value of resources exchanged
5. Variety of resources exchanged
6. Interchangeability of resources
7. The unit of analysis from "you" and "me" to "we"

We will discuss each of these in turn.

1. INTENSITY OF FEELINGS

Love relationships are emotionally complex. Intimates' love and hate for one another intertwine in a complicated web. Both joy and guilt are present. There are ups and downs. But whatever it is they feel, intimates feel intensely. Fromm (1956) describes the intensity of passionate love:

> If two people who have been strangers . . . suddenly let the wall between them
> break down, and feel close, feel one, this moment of oneness is one of the
> most exhilarating, most exciting experiences in life. . . . This miracle of sud-
> den intimacy is often facilitated if it is combined with, or intimated by, sexual
> attraction and consummation. . . . However, this type of love is by its very
> nature not lasting. The two persons become well acquainted, their intimacy
> loses more and more its miraculous character, until their antagonism, their
> disappointments, their mutual boredom kill whatever is left of the initial
> excitement [p. 4].

The role of passion in the *development* of marital love is well understood
(Berscheid & Walster, 1974; Walster & Walster, 1978).

The feelings in parent–child relations are just as conspicuous; they
often persist for a lifetime (Friday, 1977), but they have not been so
extensively studied (see Section V of this chapter).

Casual acquaintances' feelings for one another are usually more tepid.

2. COMMUNICATION: DEPTH AND BREADTH OF INFORMATION EXCHANGE

Casual relationships tend to be superficial. The participants do not
really know one another. Intimates generally have access to information
about one another's histories, values, hopes and fears, strengths and
weaknesses, and so on.

Altman and Taylor (1973), Derlega and Chaikin (1975), Jourard
(1971), and Perlmutter and Hatfield (1980) maintain that the process of
mutual sharing—from reporting on one's mundane day-to-day activities,
to inner secrets—is what turns casual relationships into intimate ones. At
first, people are wary. They reveal something about themselves making
themselves vulnerable, and await a response; they wait to see what the
other will do. If he or she responds with a reassuring comment or an
equally revealing statement, the process continues. This process of building trust has been well documented by researchers in a variety of settings
(e.g., Huesman & Levinger, 1976; Kurth, 1970; Worthy, Gary, & Kahn,
1969). Apparently, the more intimate we are with others, the more willing we are to reveal ourselves to them, and the more we expect them to
reveal to us. Reciprocity is the rule.

3. COMMITMENT

One way to view the role of self-disclosure in the development of
intimacy is as an ingredient in building commitment to the relationship.
The process of reciprocal self-disclosure thus acts as an emotional adhe-
sive that binds two people together. Similarly, just as self-disclosure must
be reciprocal for a relationship to develop, so too does commitment
need to be balanced:

In brief, it seems that commitments must keep abreast for a love relationship to develop into a lasting mutual attachment. If one lover is considerably more involved than the other, his greater commitment invites exploitation or provokes feelings of entrapment, both of which obliterate love. Whereas rewards experienced in the relationship may lead to its continuation for a while, the weak interest of the less commited or the frustrations of the more commited probably will sooner or later prompt one or the other to terminate it. Only when two lovers' affection for and commitment to one another expand at roughly the same pace do they tend mutually to reinforce their love [Blau, 1964, pp. 84–85]. [This quotation and following quotations cited to Blau (1964) are from *Exchange and Power in Social Life* by P. M. Blau. Copyright © John Wiley & Sons, Inc. Reprinted by permission of John Wiley & Sons, Inc.]

Commitment is revealed in terms of its relative permanency. Intimate affairs are expected to endure, and generally do endure, for a long time. "Til death do us part" is still our cultural ideal for marriage. This is another way of saying that commitment is a necessary part of intimate relationships.

4. VALUE OF RESOURCES EXCHANGED

Casual acquaintances can please or discomfort us. Intimates can make us ecstatically happy or plunge us into deep despair. The characteristics of intimacy—such as intensity of feeling and commitment—"cause" the behaviors of intimate partners to be valued more highly. The stakes are higher.

Many theorists have observed that intimates' rewards are especially potent. Levinger *et al.* (1970) pointed out that the same reward, for example, "You're a fine man," may be far more touching when it comes from an intimate than from a casual acquaintance. In addition, because intimates know one another, they know exactly what the other cares about. In addition, intimates possess a bigger storehouse of rewards than do casuals. Generally, people are more willing to invest their resources—time, effort, intimate information, money, and so on—in intimate affairs than in casual encounters.

Another reason why intimate relationships are often so rewarding is that we use a different scale in judging intimates than in judging strangers. We often accentuate the positive and eliminate the negative qualitites of those close to us. This attributional bias is perhaps most conspicuous when negative activities of a loved one threaten the existence of the relationship, or worse, the stability of an entire family unit. A good example of this process is reported by Yarrow, Schwartz, Murphy, and Deasy (1955) in their study of wives' reactions to their husbands' mental illnesses. In this empirical study, Yarrow *et al.*, discovered a typical response pattern in which the wife persevered in her search for plausible explanations for ostensibly abnormal behavior. It is a process of periodic discounting of what appears to be, until a point is reached where she *must* acknowledge the deviance and the threat to the family unit. This process seems to be characterized by intermittent shifting of perceptions from the deviant to the normal and back again. The wife is confused and wants to rationalize away the threat.

Intimates' rewards may be unusually potent but so are the punishments they can inflict on each other. As Aronson (1970) succinctly put it: "Familiarity may breed reward, but it also breeds the capacity to hurt."

The most potent punishment, of course, is the ability to end an intimate relationship. Break-ups are generally traumatic for intimates. Reactions to divorce by spouses (Hunt, 1974) and children (Levitin, 1980) document this process.

5. VARIETY OF RESOURCES EXCHANGED

Casuals exchange only a few things. Intimates usually provide one another with a great variety of rewards and punishments. Foa and his colleagues (Donnenwerth & Foa, 1974; Turner, Foa, & Foa, 1971) argue that people exchange six classes of resources: (1) love; (2) status, (3) information; (4) money; (5) goods; and (6) services.

Hatfield (in press a) speculates that casuals generally exchange only a *few* types of resources. Because casual relationships are such short-term relationships, casuals probably are satisfied if they can exchange a few things. They are simply not "in business" long enough to work out very complicated exchanges. In intimate exchanges, however, partners generally exchange resources from all six classes. They can afford to go to the trouble to negotiate more complicated exchanges. They are in business for a long time.

6. INTERCHANGEABILITY OF RESOURCES

We would speculate that, within a particular exchange, acquaintances tend to be limited to exchanging a narrow band of resources. If I mow my neighbor's lawn while he is away on vacation, then I would expect him to reciprocate when I am away. I would not expect an invitation to dinner as payment for the favor because this would be a sign that our relationship is progressing to a deeper level. I might not feel comfortable with such an idea; my neighbor might appear presumptuous.

In contrast, intimate relationships exist in a variety of contexts. Intimates feel freer to exchange resources from entirely different classes. The wife who appreciates her husband's kindness to her mother, may tell him so, bake him a pie, or vow to be understanding when he comes home tired and uncommunicative. This "open market" atmosphere in intimate relationships means that intimates spend much of their time negotiating the "terms" of their relationship. Some support for this contention comes from Scanzoni (1972), Turner *et al.* (1971), and Donnenwerth and Foa (1974).

7. THE UNIT OF ANALYSIS: FROM "YOU" AND "ME" TO "WE"

Another characteristic of intimate relationships is that intimates maintain their own identity and yet, through identification with and empathy for their partners, come to define themselves as "one."

What are the key elements in this so-called identification process? According to Blau (1964), part of the answer lies in the intrinsic motivation developed through repeated reinforcement of sharing, selfless-like behavior:

> Human beings evidently derive pleasure from doing things for those they love and sometimes make great sacrifices for them. This tendency results partly from the identification with the other produced by love, from the desire to give symbolic expression to one's devotion, from the function providing rewards has for strengthening a loved one's attachment to oneself, and perhaps partly from the process previously termed reverse secondary reinforcement. The repeated experience of being rewarded by the increased attachment of a loved one after having done a variety of things to please him may have the effect that giving pleasure to loved ones becomes intrinsically gratifying [p. 77].

It does not follow from this process of developing a sense of "weness"—of altering one's identity—that one loses his or her sense of personal identity. Rather, we are describing the natural consequences of becoming dependent on another. In the case of intimacy, there is mutual dependency of the kind that is qualitatively different from the kind of dependency experienced by casuals simply by the fact of their interaction (e.g., if we go to dinner at a fine restaurant, our satisfaction is *dependent* on the fine cuisine and good service of the chef and waiter; their satisfaction is *dependent* on our compliments, tips, and payment of the bill). Blau (1964), again, provides an insightful description of dependency in romantic relationships. In the courting phase of romance, partners frequently are not totally honest with one another regarding the extent of their dependency and feeling for the other. This becomes apparent in flirting behavior:

> Flirting involves largely the expression of attraction in a semiserious or stereotyped fashion that is designed to elicit some commitment from the other in advance of making a serious commitment oneself. The joking and

ambiguous commitments implied by flirting can be laughed off if they fail to
evoke a responsive cord or made firm if they do. But as long as both continue
to conceal the strength of their affection for the other while both become
increasingly dependent on the other's affection, they frustrate one another
[Blau, 1964, p. 77].

Dependency is sometimes communicated in romantic relationships by
displays of possessiveness or jealousy. Such feelings may reflect a
number of individual factors such as insecurity or lack of trust, but they
also indicate that certain types of intimate relationships produce the
sense of uniqueness—or an "I *must* have" sensation. One spouse "truly
needs" the other; the parent "wouldn't know what to do without" the
child, and vice versa. These are the manifestations of how dependency
fosters a sense of we-ness, and in turn, how this perception creates further dependency.

A plausible scenario, then, in describing the development of intimate
relationships, and how they survive, goes something like this:

1. Intimates become acquainted
2. They get to "know" one another through reciprocal self-
disclosure; there is natural attraction
3. Initial dependencies are created
4. A mutual commitment is made
5. A belief that the relationship is "unique" emerges (The spouse
truly "needs" the other. No one else will do. The parent "would not
know what to do" without the child and vice versa.)
6. A sense of liking–loving steadily grows in intensity throughout this
process
7. A sense of we-ness or unit formation develops.

Intensity of feeling, knowing (e.g., self-disclosure), dependency,
commitment, and perception of uniqueness combine to create a belief
that the intimates' identity is defined in terms of the relationship and
that the relationship fulfills an indispensable number of needs for the
person. The net result of this general process, is to exclude the possibility
of alternative relationships. It is difficult, although not impossible, to
have more than a few "best friends," and more than one lover, more
than one set of parents or children.

Intimate relationships very often are "for better or for worse" because
it is difficult to terminate them. Thibaut and Kelly's (1959) exchange
theory concepts of comparison level (CL) and comparison level for alternatives (CL_{alt}) are useful in describing this consequence of intimacy.
People enmeshed with others will be satisfied to the extent that the other

is meeting their expectations and treating them as they feel they deserve; these are expectations formed from past relationships and the dependencies of the immediate relationship. These expectations constitute a person's CL. The CL_{alt} is another standard we use to evaluate ongoing relationships. It refers to the options available to us, or what kind of treatment we can potentially receive from other, alternative relationships. If there is a large discrepancy between our current satisfaction (as it is influenced by our CL) and our imagined satisfaction in a different relationship, we are more likely to think of a change. The practical difficulties associated with extricating oneself from an unsatisfying intimate relationship ("divorce is a messy business," etc.), results in individuals setting their CL_{alt} extraordinarily high. The potential gains of breaking away must be weighed against the likely costs. The result of this type of pressure is that people in unhappy intimate relationships have feelings of being "trapped." They want to leave, but they feel they cannot. To hear comments such as "I hate the S.O.B., but I must stay with him" strikes observers as inherently irrational. However, considering how personal identities are intertwined and the dependencies that develop in love relationships, it is not surprising that the partners tenaciously hold on to the bonds of their relationships—even though they are being unfairly treated. For to end a deeply involving, long-term relationship, be it with a spouse, a parent, or a best friend, is like killing part of oneself.

III. FAIRNESS IN INTERPERSONAL RELATIONS

A. Nature of Fairness

Clinical psychologists have stressed the importance of moral evaluations—reflected in self-blame, depression, or excessive anger—in interpersonal problems (Beck & Shaw, 1977; Ellis, 1977). A major point in these clinical writings is that a client's extreme emotional reaction to the perception of treating another unfairly or being treated unfairly by another person is an important element in the symptomatology of a variety of clinical disturbances.

Although little direct scientific evidence exists on the role of moral evaluations in complex relationships, social psychologists have extensively studied reactions to perceptions of unfairness in less involved relationships. If we can accept the assumption that perceived *fairness* represents the experiential core of moral evaluation, this research tradition can serve as the basis for describing the key elements of moral evaluations, which may apply to intimate relationships.

Fairness, or its more formal label of justice, was long thought to lie in the exclusive domain of moral philosophers and legal scholars. During the last two decades, however, social psychologists have published a number of theoretical papers and empirical studies that collectively describe the general processes underlying perceptions of fairness (see Berkowitz & Walster, 1976; Lerner, 1975; Walster *et al.*, 1978).

Austin (1979) attempted to describe the major characteristics of fairness. He points out that fairness is a very general concept. In any specific situation, there are a multitude of rules for determining what is fair or unfair. (The case of "John and Mary" conveys the complexity of deciding what is fair in ongoing relationships.) According to Austin, the most central components of perceived fairness are (1) subjectivity; (2) comparativeness, and (3) involvement of a balancing operation.

1. FAIRNESS AS SUBJECTIVE

The perception of fairness, like beauty, is in the eye of the beholder. People may see the same events, but form opposing moral evaluations. What Mary sees as "being taken advantage of," John may view as "necessary under the circumstances." This aspect of fairness forces researchers to take into account individual past histories and differences in values before making predictions about reactions to unfairness.

2. FAIRNESS IS COMPARATIVE

Most theorists agree that individuals must make a comparison with some type of standard before they can determine whether a relationship is a fair one. Most justice evaluations are made on the basis of social comparisons, usually with a person in *similar* circumstances. However, perceived fairness may be based on other types of comparisons, such as absolute standards, or even with oneself in terms of how the person is accustomed to being treated by others (see Austin, McGinn, & Susmilch, 1980). The comparisons that are drawn act as points of reference providing an individual with a perceptual background for making contextual judgments on what is fair in a particular situation.

3. FAIRNESS AS A BALANCE

The successful negotiation of what is fair in a relationship requires that parties reach a balance between different claims that are asserted and in the rewards received. Each must acknowledge merit in the other's point of view. Compromise is necessary when conflict arises. Aristotle (1966) referred to this sense of justice in a relationship as the "mean" and "intermediate." Thus, Mary must see that circumstances have changed since John entered law school; John must try to relieve Mary of some of the home responsibilities. Otherwise, the marital tensions will continue.

B. Theories of Fairness

Research on perceptions of fairness evolved from a popular viewpoint in social psychology known as exchange theory (Blau, 1964; Homans, 1974; Thibaut & Kelley, 1959), which represents the most general theoretical framework for studying interpersonal attraction.

The exchange theories characterize every human interaction as an exchange of activities—verbal and nonverbal messages, psychological rewards (e.g., love, status, praise) and punishments (e.g., insults, withholding of love, etc.), and material goods (e.g., money, jobs).

Exchange theorists have invoked numerous concepts to explain how individuals seek satisfaction from their interpersonal dealings. They have always stressed rewards, punishment, and reinforcement (Homans, 1974). However, they have also found it necessary to employ other general concepts for describing the dynamics of exchange relationships. These concepts include interpersonal power (Homans, 1974; Scanzoni, 1972); norms, expectations, and values (Blau, 1964; Homans, 1974); communication patterns (Secord & Backman, 1974); and role demands (Blau, 1964; Homans, 1974). These concepts help to dictate research questions that are important in predicting satisfaction with various interpersonal encounters, intimate and nonintimate alike:

1. What activities are seen as rewarding and punishing, and to what degree?
2. Who has control over which important activities? Who is the dominant person? The leader? Are there coalitions among group members?
3. What expectations and values are brought to the relationship and are they being confirmed?
4. How have the participants structured the relationship with norms and roles? Are they conscious of the roles? Were the role expectations agreed upon in advance?
5. How effectively are the individuals communicating? Are misunderstandings interfering with the ability to play preferred roles and obtain goals?
6. What alternative behaviors and relationships are available to the participants? What are the costs involved in changing the relationship?

Exchange theory thus easily generates a wide-ranging analysis associated with the multiple dimensions of real-life relationships.

Theorists of interpersonal justice, such as Adams (1965); Homans (1961, 1974), and Walster, Berscheid, and Walster, (1973) have utilized an exchange theory framework to discuss issues of fairness. All of these theories *start* with the notion that there is a norm of fairness. This norm is reflected in rules that specify how rewards should be allocated in relationships.

The most encompassing rule is Aristotle's rule of *distributive justice* (Homans, 1961), which stipulates that rewards be distributed in terms of personal deserving, or in proportion to what one puts into a relationship. Furthermore, to be seen as fair, this proportion of rewards to contributions must be perceived by the person as equal to the proportional rewards being received by some comparison person (e.g., Mary looks to John, or to other spouses of law students). Other rules of distributive justice are *equality,* where contributions are ignored (Sampson, 1975) and *need,* where rewards are based on needs of participants in a relationship (e.g., small infants).

The exchange theories of fairness share other common features. They predict that, when it is clear to a person that a given rule of distributive justice should govern an exchange but that it is not being applied correctly, the person will react emotionally. People who feel they are getting more than they deserve feel guilty. Those who feel they are getting too little feel angry.

Theorists have documented that an assortment of situational factors may hasten or mitigate the perception of unfairness. Examples include the intention to do harm (Glass, 1964), previous reward level of the victimized (Austin & Walster, 1975), and the relevance of goals other than fairness, such as productivity (Leventhal, Michaels, & Sanford, 1972).

These theories have proved to be quite successful in predicting reactions to perceived unfairness in casual relationships.

C. Role Expectations and Fairness

John and Mary, like other intimate partners, organize their relationship in terms of the roles they play: husband–wife; money earner–student, and so on. Roles carry with them specific expectations of behavior. Some couples agree that they will share roles and responsibility for certain behaviors—housekeeping, child rearing, and money earning. It is generally accepted that roles and their accompanying expectations are necessary to lend predictability to casual and to intimate relationships (Sarbin & Allen, 1968). Sometimes, people are aware of their expectations. Generally, they are not. Couples only become more aware of their "contracts" when their partners fail to live up to their unspoken expectations (Sager, 1976).

Researchers have consistently demonstrated that disconfirmed role expectations generate dissatisfaction with a relationship (Sarbin & Allen, 1968). Because role expectations are articulated as "oughts" or "shoulds," one would expect perceptions of unfairness to mediate role-related dissatisfaction. Recent theoretical papers by Hamilton (1978) and Turner (1978) propose that a close relationship exists between behavior that deviates from role prescriptions and moral evaluations. (Thus, Mary assigns moral blame to John for not sharing the domestic role responsibilities that he agreed to.) However, researchers have yet to verify this appealing idea. This empirical gap may be due to the tendency of social psychologists to shy away from studying long-term relationships (where the importance of role expectations is stressed). In addition, social psychologists who have studied fairness have focused on effects of different distributions of rewards to the exclusion of other sources of perceived unfairness in relationships—such as violations of role behaviors.

If we think of roles as day-to-day *procedures* for organizing activities in relationships, then recent research on *procedural justice* in social psychology provides a conceptual basis for the proposition that role violations should create perceptions of unfairness. This new literature demonstrates that judgments of fairness are affected by the structure of procedure and their proper implementation (see Austin & Tobiasen, in press; Karuza & Leventhal, 1976; Lerner & Whitehead, 1980; Thibaut & Walker, 1975). However, these studies have been limited to individuals' ratings of formal procedures used for dispute resolution rather than reactions to role violations.

One situation in which we would expect role-related behavior to influence judgments of fairness is one of external events creating pressures to change the allocation of role responsibilitites. When a chain of events requires that the initial "contract," explicit or implicit, be renegotiated, then there is an increased opportunity for perceptions of unfairness to arise. Such perceptions may threaten the existence of the relationship. There is some support for this notion. Komarovsky (1940), in a survey study conducted during the Depression, discovered after the husband lost his job that many marriage partners changed the structure of their marriage from a traditional patriarchal one toward one with a more equal distribution of authority. Sometimes the status of husbands and wives in the family were even reversed. These changes were necessary for the marriage to be seen as "fair," and to survive.

IV. FAIRNESS IN INTIMATE RELATIONSHIPS

In this section we will attempt to integrate our separate analyses of intimacy and fairness. First, we will reconsider the exchange theories, and review what insights they may give us as to the issues of fairness that are likely to arise in any relationship. Then, we will focus on one specific exchange theory—equity theory.

A. Exchange Theories and Intimate Relations

It is clear from the diversity of questions we deduced from the exchange theories that this approach is intended to apply to all types of relationships. It is our view that concepts such as reinforcement, dominance, norm, and role are applicable to all types of relationships. Blau (1964), for example, remarks:

> Exchange processes occur in love relations as well as in social associations of only extrinsic significance. Their dynamics, however, are different, because the specific rewards exchanged are merely means to produce the ultimate reward of intrinsic attention in love relations, while the exchange of specific rewards is the very objective of the association in purely instrumental social relations. In intrinsic love attachments, as noted earlier, each individual furnishes rewards to the other not to receive proportionate extrinsic benefits in return but to express and confirm his own commitment and to promote the other's growing commitment to the association. An analysis of love reveals the element of exchange entailed even in intrinsically significant associations as well as their distinctive nature [p. 76].

Although Blau feels that love relationships have qualitatively distinct defining characteristics (such those described in Section II), he nonetheless describes them in exchange terms.

It is not surprising, then, that the research most relevant to fairness in intimate relationships has been carried out within an exchange orientation. However, the data are sparse. Levinger's field research on marital couples is one promising example (e.g., Huesman & Levinger, 1976; Levinger, 1976; Levinger & Snoek, 1972;). In one of these studies (Levinger, 1966), 600 couples were interviewed after they had filed for divorce. Their interview responses were coded into 12 categories of conflict, or complaints, about their partners. Some of these categories included verbal abuse, physical abuse, lack of love, and so on. One would expect that these are the types of complaints that lead to perceptions of unfairness. According to Levinger, these complaints, or "marital costs," are evaluated relative to one's comparison level, or what we call the expected level of deservingness—much as a dissatisfied employee would evaluate his job. Levinger reasoned that a partner will consider divorce when marital costs pull net rewards below his or her CL, and an attractive alternative is open (e.g., another relationship, or perhaps freedom from involvement). Whereas Levinger's study provides data relevant to the role of perceived unfairness in marital break-ups, the data were interpreted in terms of marital dissatisfaction rather than the mediating role of unfairness.

B. Equity Theory and Intimate Relationships

Probably the theory that has sparked the most research on fairness is equity theory (Adams, 1965; Walster et al., 1973). This theory assumes that judgments of fairness are made in approximately ratio form: "Am I receiving rewards in proportion to my contribution?" Social comparison processes are also stressed: "Is my proportion of contributions to outcomes (e.g., rewards received–costs incurred) equal to the proportion received by other individuals in similar circumstances?" (The propositions of equity theory are described elsewhere in this book; see Chapter 10 by Donnerstein and Hatfield.)

According to equity theory, when partners are confronted with the fact that there is a gross imbalance in their relationship, they should be inclined to try to "set things right." They have three options. They can:

1. Try to make their relationship actually more equitable
2. Try to convince themselves (and their partners) that things are fairer than they seem to be
3. Withdraw from their relationship

Recently, Hatfield and her colleagues have attempted to apply equity theory's propositions to intimate relationships (see Walster et al., 1978; Hatfield et al., 1979; Hatfield, in press-b).

Hatfield (in press, b) admits that intimate and casual relations differ in some ways:

1. Many people feel they are not "supposed" to care about "what's in it for me." "Am I giving as good as I get"—but they do.
2. Most people hope for different things from their love relations than from their casual ones. Intimates usually care more about *love* than anything else. Casuals may be more concerned about material benefits.
3. Participants in casual versus intimate relationships should differ in how easy it is to tolerate temporary imbalances. Casuals may be

fully aware that unless existing imbalances are redressed *immediately,* they will probably never be redressed at all. Intimates, committed to a lifetime together, should barely notice momentary imbalances. They take it for granted that, because they care for their partners, and their partners care for them, in the normal course of events, things will balance out.

It is only when things get grossly out of hand, that couples become uneasy. "How did this happen? Doesn't my partner care about me any more? Is it just an accident?" It is only then that they feel pressure to set things right.

The following five hypotheses are examples of the impact that equity considerations should have on intimate relationships:

> *Hypothesis 1:* Men and women should be most likely to continue to date, to live together and to marry, if they feel their relationship is an equitable one (Hatfield *et al.,* 1979, pp. 162–175).
>
> *Hypothesis 2:* Men and women in equitable relationships should be fairly content. Men and women who feel they've received either far more, or far less, than they deserve, should be uncomfortable. The more inequitable their relationships, the more distressed they should be (Hatfield *et al.,* 1979, p. 113).
>
> *Hypothesis 3:* Since inequitites are disturbing, couples may be expected to keep chipping away at them over the course of their marriages. Underbenefitted men and women, who feel that they are contributing far more than their fair share to the relationship, should be motivated to demand more from their partners. Their guilty partners may well agree to provide such rewards. Thus, all things being equal, relationships should become more and more equitable over time (Hatfield *et al.,* 1979, p. 114).
>
> *Hypothesis 4:* Expectations need to be periodically reviewed and renegotiated. In all marriages there are crisis periods; for example, when the dating couple marries, moves in together, and begins to discover what marriage is really like; when the first child arrives; when the children leave home; when someone loses his or her job . . . or retires. At such times of precipitous change, a couple may find that their once equitable relationship is now woefully unbalanced. Equity theorists would predict that if we contacted couples just before such crises, in the midst of such crises, and then again, after couples had a chance to deal with the crisis, we would find that the couples would have found the crisis period very unsettling, and had worked hard to reestablish the equitableness of their relationships . . . or that their relationship would be floundering (Walster *et al.,* 1978, pp. 176–182).
>
> *Hypothesis 5:* Equitable relationships will be especially stable relationships (Walster, *et al.,* 1978, pp. 176–182).

1. THE THEORETICAL DEBATE

Marriage and family researchers are in sharp debate as to whether or not considerations of fairness are relevant to intimate relationships.

Some critics indignantly insist that intimate relations are special relations—untainted by crass considerations of social exchange. For example, Morris (1971) states:

> In a partnership one merely exchanges favours; the partner does not give for the sake of giving. But between a pair of adult human lovers there develops a relationship like that between mother and child. A total trust develops and, with it, a total bodily intimacy. There is no "give and take" in true loving, only giving. The fact that it is "two-way giving" obscures this, but the "two-way receiving" that inevitably results from it is not a condition of the giving, as it is in a partnership, it is simply a pleasing adjunct to it [p. 72].

Many other eminent theorists share this view that love relationships are above the self-interested concerns of other exchange relationships (see Fromm, 1956; Meeker, 1971; Mills & Clark, in press; Murstein, in press; Rubin, 1973).

Another group of prominent theorists would seem to agree with Walster *et al.* (1978) and Hatfield (in press, b). For example, Patterson (1971) proposes that the perception of fair exchanges as central to stable marriages: "There is an odd kind of equity which holds when people interact with each other. In effect, we get what we give, both in amount and in kind. Each of us seems to have his own bookkeeping system for love, and for pain. Over time, the books are balanced [p. 26]."

Other theorists agree that, in love relationships—as in all other relationships—considerations of exchange and fairness are salient. See, for example, Bernard (1964), Blau (1964), McCall (1966), Scanzoni (1972), Storer (1966), and Lederer and Jackson (1968).

2. THE EVIDENCE

Theorists have debated the relevance of fairness considerations for intimates in absolute terms (e.g., fairness is either relevant, or it is not). Researchers, however, have asked *how* the type of relationship influences moral evaluations. The data on this issue come from several sources: (1) experimental studies of reward allocation; (2) field studies of perceived fairness in ongoing relationships; and (3) reports by clinical psychologists, mainly family therapists. The data clearly indicate that intimates are sensitive to fairness in their relationship, and readily judge their partners in these terms. However, at this time, little is known about the dynamics of fairness processes in complex relationships; or how partners, best friends, families and so on negotiate "fair expectations" to make the relationship a fair and satisfying one. Let us review the research evidence, which points to this conclusion.

3. EXPERIMENTAL STUDIES OF REWARD ALLOCATION

Experimental studies of how people allocate rewards in relationships of different degrees of closeness suggest that the positions of both equity theorists and its critics may be partly correct. These studies indicate that friendship often operates openly as exchange behavior, but that the type of relationship influences the rule chosen for distributing rewards. Instead of choosing a proportional contributions rule, so that rewards reflect differences in the quality and quantity of inputs to a relationship, these studies suggest that friends choose equality in reward allocations.

Austin (1980) offers a clear demonstration of this tendency. In this study, college roommates and pairs of strangers allocated monetary rewards between themselves and their partner on the basis of their score on a word puzzle task. Half of the subject pairs thought that they had scored higher; the other half much lower on the task. As Table 7.1 shows, roommates generally opted for an equality rule that downplayed differences in performance. Strangers, however, generally chose either merit or equality rules in a manner that maximized their material interest, yet could be justified as fair. Fairness thus seemed to be defined by friends so as to reflect a commitment to the relationship.

Other researchers have reported similar findings. Curtis (1978) found that when a positive relationship was created between two subjects

Table 7.1
Effect of Type of Relationship and Task Performance on Individuals' Allocation Behavior[a]

Task performance	Type of Relationship		Average for performance
	Roommates	Strangers	
Low inputs	7–17–1[b]	2–12–11	10–29–12
	2.45[c]	2.52	2.49
	49.0[d]	50.4	49.7
High inputs	3–21–1	15–3–7	18–24–8
	2.57	2.87	2.72
	51.4%	57.4%	54.4%
	11–38–2	17–15–18	
	2.51	2.70	
	50.2%	53.9%	

[a] Reconstructed from Austin, 1980.
[b] The sequence represents the number of subjects choosing proportional merit, equality, or a compromise between merit and equality respectively.
[c] Average money allocated to self, where $2.50 = equal split and $3 = allocation based strictly on merit.
[d] Percentage of money allocated to self.

in a laboratory setting, high and low scorers took significantly less money for themselves. Indirect support for this finding comes from several other experimental studies. First, Greenberg (1978) found that perceived *similarity* between strangers resulted in equal divisions of reward even though the subjects had performed relatively better on a task. Second, closeness of relation reveals itself in *bargaining studies.* Schoeninger and Wood (1969) found that married couples emphasize common interests whereas ad hoc pairs focus on conflicts of interest; Morehous (1966) reports that cooperation is positively related to length of a bargaining game. These findings support Lerner, Miller, and Holmes's (1976) prediction that partners in close or "unit" relationships should choose less self-interested rules of fairness. Thus, it seems that, although friends feel quite comfortable interacting in a explicit exchange manner, their behaviors are different from casuals, reflecting their commitment and concern for the other.

4. FIELD STUDIES ON INTIMACY AND FAIRNESS

Some support for equity theory Hypotheses 1–5 comes from the work of Hatfield and her colleagues (in press, a). Let us review a sampling of this research:

Hypothesis 1: Men and women should be most likely to continue to date, to live together, and to marry if they feel their relationship is an equitable one.

Walster, Walster, and Traupmann (1978) interviewed 537 college men and women who were casual or steady daters. The authors measured fairness via the Walster Global Measures Scale (see Walster *et al.,* 1978): "Considering what you put into your dating relationship, compared to what you get out of it ... and what your partner put in compared to what s(he) gets out of it, how does your dating relationship "stack up"? [p. 178]." From students' estimates, it was possible to classify men and women who felt overbenefited, ("I am getting a much better ... somewhat better ... or slightly better ... deal than my partner"), fairly treated ("We are both getting an equally good ... or bad ... deal"), or underbenefited ("My partner is getting a slightly better ... somewhat better ... much better deal than I am") in their love affairs.

The authors chose to measure a relationship's potential in several ways. First, they asked couples how sexual their relationships were. They found that couples in fair relationships had experimented with a higher degree of sex. Generally, couples in fair relationships were having sexual intercourse. Both the greatly underbenefited and the greatly overbenefited tended to stop before engaging in intercourse.

The authors then asked respondents who *had* had intercourse, why they had done so. The participants in relatively fair relations were most likely to say that they had intercourse because they *both* wanted to (i.e., to say that "Mutual curiousity", the fact that "We are/were in love", "We like each other," or "Mutual physical desire, enjoyment" were their reasons for having intercourse. Those who felt extremely overbenefited or extremely underbenefited were less likely to say that sex was a mutual decision.

Why are men and women in fair relationships so willing to experiment sexually?—Perhaps because they are confident that their relationship would last. As predicted, the authors found that men and women in relationships perceived as fairly balanced were generally in stable relationships, and that they expect them to remain that way. They are confident that they would still be together 1 year and 5 years into the future. Their confidence may well be warranted. In a follow-up study, three and one half months later, couples in fair relationships were more likely to be still dating than were other couples. Both the overbenefited (who have every reason to wish their relationships would last) and the underbenefited (who have every reason to hope that something better would come along) were pessimistic about the future. If their relationships were not already in disarray, they expected that they soon would be.

Hypothesis 2: Men and women in fair relationships should be fairly content. Men and women who feel they have received either far more or far less than they deserve should be uncomfortable. The more unfair their relationships are, the more distressed they should be.

Utne *et al.* (1978) interviewed 118 newlywed couples. Couples varied in age from 16 to 45. (The average groom was 26+ and the average bride was 24+.) Most couples had dated seriously for over 2 years before marrying. For 80% of the couples, this was their first marriage. The couples had a variety of occupations—including housewives, accountants, teachers, farmers, and construction workers. A few were students.

The interview covered a variety of topics, including the history of the relationship, perceived fairness of the relationships, and Austin's (1972) measure of contentment–distress with the fairness of the marriage.

The authors found that fairness considerations did have an important impact on how contented–distressed the couples felt about their relationships. Couples in fair relations were the most contented and happy. Newlyweds who felt they were getting more than they deserved from the relationship (as did John), felt slightly ill at ease—they felt guilty about the status quo. As one might expect, the underbenefited were even more distressed (as was Mary). They felt angry about the status quo.

Hypothesis 3: Because inequities are disturbing, couples may be expected to keep chipping away at them over the course of their marriages. Thus, all things being equal, relationships should become more and more fair over time. As yet, there is no evidence as to whether or not this is so. Careful longitudinal studies remain to be conducted.

Hypothesis 4: In all marriages, there are certain crisis periods that demand that expectations be renegotiated. Couples contacted just before, in the midst of, and after such crises would have found the crisis period very unsettling, and would have worked hard to reestablish fairness in their relationships, otherwise, their relationship would be floundering.

Unfortunately, most of the evidence in support of the contention that mismatched couples try to "fine tune" their relationship, is anecdotal. There are some data suggesting that when a person's physical appearance changes drastically (through accident, plastic surgery, or dieting) his expectations may change too.

For example, Jones (1974), in "Marriage and the Formerly Fat: The Effect Weight Loss Has on Your Life Together," warned *Weight Watchers* magazine readers that: "Marriage, like all relationships, is a balance. When one partner is overweight, the fact has been considered, perhaps unconsciously, in setting up the balance. Obviously, when you remove the obesity, you upset the balance. The relationship shifts and takes on a different complexion." In the same article, Jones (1974) adds: "Gone are ... the attempts to buy love through acquiescence and the overweight's traditional don't-make-waves-they-may-throw-you-out-policy. In their place comes a new pride, an awareness of rights and a tendency to speak up for those rights [pp. 23–50]."

Obviously, changes in physical appearance may affect partners' satisfaction with their marriage in subtle, yet powerful ways. Whether such changes would affect perceived fairness is difficult to determine. However, empirical studies showing that people "match-up" with partners of comparable physical attractiveness suggest that this factor is related to perceived fairness (see Berscheid & Walster, 1978; Huston, 1973; Murstein, 1972).

Significant changes in a marriage that require renegotiating expectations, are more likely to come from events external to a marriage. A limited amount of survey data supports the contention that external events send reverberations throughout an entire family system. Expectations that regulate day-to-day activities then need to be renegotiated to maintain fairness and satisfaction (Fogarty, Rapoport, & Rapoport, 1971; Komarovsky, 1971).

Hypothesis 5: Equitable relationships will be especially stable relationships. Utne, *et al.,* (1978), interviewed newlyweds about their marriages.

The authors measured newlyweds' perceptions of how overbenefited, fairly treated, or underbenefited they were in their marriages as well as how stable they believed their marriages to be. The authors proposed that spouses who feel fairly treated will perceive their marriages to be more stable than will spouses who feel underbenefited *or* overbenefited. The authors measured perceived stability in marriage by asking their respondents (1) How certain they were that the two of them would be together in four years; (2) How often they had considered moving out; (3) How often they had considered divorce; and (4) How stable they felt this marriage was. As predicted, the more unfair the relationship, the more newlyweds thought about the possibility of abandoning it. Men and women who felt fairly treated in their relationships were more secure about their marriages than were either the overbenefited or the underbenefited.

C. Clinical Perspectives and Fairness

The experimental studies and Hatfield *et al.'s* research demonstrate that fairness is relevant to both casual and intimate relationships. The experimental studies show that friends downplay differences in input in favor of bolstering the relationship by allocating rewards equally. Hatfield's interview studies show that intimates readily assess the fairness of their relationships in terms of relative inputs. Also, intimates at quite different stages of involvement (e.g., dating; newlyweds; married for a long time) respond to fairness questions with equal ease.

Unfortunately, these types of data only constitute very preliminary steps in understanding fairness processes that characterize the day-to-day dynamics of close relationships. Systematically conducted longitudinal studies are needed to provide descriptive information and to test our theories of fairness and intimacy. In lieu of these ideal data, however, we can look to the theories and case studies of clinical psychologists. This literature enables us to speculate on pertinent day-to-day processes that, hopefully, social psychologists will soon incorporate into their research efforts.

1. EXCHANGE AND THE "MARRIAGE CONTRACT"

Many marriage counselors and family therapists think that fairness considerations are so critical in a relationship that they train their clients to think in exchange and fairness terms. They argue that by making the processes of exchange salient, conflict can be managed more effectively. For example, Lederer and Jackson (1968) proposed:

> Marriage is an interlocking, self-contained system. The behavior and the attitudes of one partner *always* stimulate some sort of reaction from the other.... We call this system of behavioral responses the *quid pro quo* (or "something for something").... The *quid pro quo* process is an unconscious effort of both partners to assure themselves that they are equals, that they are peers. It is a technique enabling each to preserve his dignity and self-esteem. Their equality may not be apparent to the world at large; it may be based upon values meaningless to anyone else, yet serve to maintain the relationship because the people involved perceive their behavioral balance as fair and mutually satisfying [pp. 177–79].

Watzlawick, Weakland, and Fisch (1974) suggest how this view of marriage translates into helping solve marital conflict:

> In general, the problems encountered in marriage therapy more often than not have to do with the almost insurmountable difficulty of changing the *quid pro quo* on which the relationship was originally based. Of course, this *quid pro quo* is never the outcome of overt negotiation, but is rather in the nature of a tacit contract whose conditions the partners may be quite unable to verbalize, even though they are extremely sensitive to any violations of these unwritten clauses. If conflict arises, the partners typically attempt to solve it within the framework of the contract [p. 73].

Thus, some marital therapists explicitly focus on the exchange of behaviors and the perception of fairness as a means of reducing conflict in intimate relationships.

2. PROCEDURAL ASPECTS: RULES AND ROLES

An extension of this exchange approach to marriage is to view marriage as a system of rules and role allocations. Marriage is thus seen as a system of rules that define the nature of the relationship.

For example, Haley (1963/1972) describes these rules as (1) explicit understandings of specific acts that one spouse can do; (2) implicit understandings that are acted out, and that the spouses would acknowledge if they were pointed out; and (3) hidden rules that observers would surmise govern behavior in the marriage, but the spouses would deny their existence.

Haley (1963/1972) suggests how this typology of rules in marriage translates into types of marital conflict: "Marital conflict centers in (*a*) disagreements about the rules for living together, (*b*) disagreements about who is to set those rules, and (*c*) attempts to enforce rules which are incompatible with each other [p. 188]."

The marital rules are based on the way role expectations are defined. Thus, conflict over rules often means perceived unfairness is due to disconfirmed role expectations. For example, the hypothetical account of John and Mary portrays a relationship where conflict stemmed directly from disconfirmed role expectations, which led to the perception that things were unfair. When John violated the negotiated arrangement of shared role demands, it was procedurally unfair. Mary incurred unfair costs. She was incensed. (For an example of how roles are related to fairness in parent–child relationships see the clinical case history in Section V.)

3. COMMUNICATION AND NEGOTIATION

Sager (1976) notes that people possess many more or less unconscious ideas as to what they have a right to expect in their relationships. Some of these expectations are eminently reasonable; some are wildly unrealistic.

Ellis (undated), calling marriage the "hotbed of neurosis," itemizes a number of the unrealistic expectations in marriage:

1. Marriage will overcome deficiencies in one's self.
2. A person will never feel unloved or alone after marriage.
3. One's frustrations (including sexual) will be overcome by marriage.
4. Marriage will make a person perfect.
5. Children will be perfect and will appreciate all that we do for them.

When expectations such as these are not met, people perceive that the relationship is unfair. Frustration and disappointment follow.

When we realize that role demands keep changing (e.g., the wife begins to work, or the husband loses his job, or there is a dramatic change in the identity and values of one spouse), and that many of people's expectations are impossible to articulate, it is no wonder marriage is the "hotbed of neurosis."

Because marital partners often enter marriages with unrealistic expectations and because they change in assorted ways during the course of the marriage, a therapist may be needed to help partners renegotiate the terms of the marriage contract. Watzlawick *et al.* (1974) maintain: "Tacit interpersonal contracts . . . are bound to become obsolete, if only as the result of the passage of time, and the necessary change then has to be a change of the contract itself . . . and not merely a change in the bounds of the contract [p. 73]." Marriage counselors thus teach couples how to negotiate effectively. Sometimes couples are even encouraged to draw up explicit marriage contracts. (Azrin, Naster, & Jones, 1973; Rappaport and Harrell, 1972; Scanzoni, 1972; and Sussman, 1975, provide an overview of such therapeutic marriage contracts).

At the heart of effective negotiation, and marital satisfaction generally, is good communication among intimates (Sager, 1976). Unrealistic expectations can be examined; motivations can be better understood. Researchers confirm that married couples experiencing serious conflict exchange fewer positive messages and are less receptive to problem-solving acts (Billings, 1979). Bach and Wyden (1968) teach us the important point that what is seen as unfair among intimates has as much to do with *how* a message is said as it does with *what* a partner says or does. These therapists see the rising divorce rate as a search for intimacy in modern society rather than as a fleeing from it [p. 35]. They believe that by training people to "fight fairly" (since people need to vent their inevitable frustrations), better communication and stronger relationships will result. One tip they offer is: "One of the first bits of advice we gave them is that wise marital combatants always try to measure their weapons against the seriousness of a particular fight issue. Nuclear bombs shouldn't be triggered against pea-shooter causes; or, as we sometimes warn trainees: 'Don't drop the bomb on Luxembourg [p. 23].'"

How intimates are able to deal with changing expectations and their ability to communicate about other issues combine to affect perceptions of fairness. Consider, for example, Komarovsky's (1940/1967) study of role changes in the Depression family. Without the ability to communicate effectively, couples would not be able to fairly implement changes in role expectations so that the marriage could survive.

D. Attributional Studies of Intimates and Conflict: Toward an Integrated Approach

Scientific understanding of phenomena often progresses through the efforts of researchers attempting to integrate parallel theories and research. The complexity of intimate relationships demands an integrated approach. In attempting to understand how moral evaluation functions in an intimate context, it would seem wise for researchers in the future to combine the strengths of social psychological studies, experimental and surveys, with clinical writings. An integrated approach could combine the rigorous empirical methodology and theory construction techniques found in social psychology with clinicians' accounts of individual variation and their creative problem solving to apply to real life fairness dilemmas among intimates.

Recent exploratory studies that have applied attribution theory to intimate relationships offer clues as to how the social and clinical psychology literatures can be drawn closer together (Harvey, Wells, & Alvarez, 1978; Orvis, Kelley, & Butler, 1976). Attribution theory (see Harvey, Ickes, & Kidd, 1976; 1978 for review) is emerging as a dominant perspective in social psychology. Viewing humans as rational information processors, attribution theorists have proposed various rules of inference that we may use in attempting to understand the causes of our own and others' behaviors. In making causal attributions, individuals appear to apply these rules to the contextual information (e.g., personal and situational factors) to gain control over their environments.

Regan (1978), after reviewing research relevant to interpersonal attraction and attribution, proposes that attribution processes may operate quite differently in the case of intimates:

> There is the suggestion in some studies that as a person becomes involved with another whose actions are hedonically and personalistically relevant for the perceiver, sensitivity to "contextual" factors . . . may be reduced. It may be the case that the highly rational processing of contextual information that forms such a central aspect of attributional theories is not likely to dominate evaluative reactions to another when the perceiver is significantly involved in the interaction [p. 229].

This viewpoint is strikingly similar to that of clinicians who have described the irrationality of cognitions and the lack of communication among intimates. For example, Albert Ellis's rational emotive therapy (Ellis & Harper, 1975) describes the role of irrationality in psychopathology; R. D. Laing (Laing, Phillipson, & Lee, 1966) refers to the role of miscommunication in family dysfunction as, "A vicious circle of mismatched interpretations, expectancies, experiences, attributions and counter-attributions [p. 28]."

The similarity of Regan's (1978) view, as a social psychologist, and those of Ellis and Laing *et al.* strike us as encouraging with respect to the possibility of working towards an integrated approach. Empirical support for this possibility (albeit in preliminary form) is offered by Orvis *et al.* (1976) and Harvey *et al.* (1978). These studies present descriptive data on the attributions that married and dating couples use in trying to explain their partner's behavior.

Orvis *et al.* (1976) asked 41 dating and married college couples to list examples of their own and their partner's behaviors. Next, a sample of these behaviors was selected for subjects to write about in detail. These responses were then categorized in terms of the kinds of attributions subjects made about their partner's behavior.

Orvis *et al.* found typical attribution themes: internal versus external; stable versus unstable, and so on. However, the data seemed to confirm

Regan's (1978) idea that intimates do indeed use attributions differently than nonintimates. Orvis *et al.* suggest that attributions are not used by intimates to achieve mastery of their environment. Rather, there were indications that attributions serve a communication function when conflict arises. Thus, Orvis *et al.* describe "attributional communication," which is seen as part of a more general evaluative process. These researchers found that college intimates listed many more negative behaviors than positive, and that their attributions took the form of justifications or "accounts" of these unsavory acts. We believe that the Orvis *et al.* analysis sets the stage for future studies on what might be called "moral negotiation" among intimates. That is, how do intimates implicitly communicate what is fair or unfair about their partner's behaviors?

Although Orvis *et al.* admit that their data are quite preliminary, they suggest, "that the dynamics of [intimacy] require intra-couple communication of discrepant interpretations of behavior." Harvey *et al.* (1978) reinforce this position. These researchers began with the assumption that a key to a stable relationship is an understanding of the partner's view of oneself. This view is similar to Laing *et al.*'s (1966) analysis of metaperspective taking in human interaction. Good communication, then, may require an actor not only to be cognizant of another's opinion of him or her, but the other's view of how the actor is viewing the relationship as well.

Harvey *et al.* (1978) conducted an interview study of unmarried couples and a case history study of married couples who were recently separated. Their interview data showed that subjects both under- and overestimated the ability of their partner to predict their attributions. Using the categories of conflict developed by Levinger (1966), they found that: "even in these relatively long-term close relationships, individuals tend to be inaccurate in their perceptions of how their partners see the world in terms of areas of conflict [p. 247]." Moreover, the couples did not know they differed in their attributions. Thus, these subjects were not particularly adept at metaperspective taking (i.e., Laing *et al.*, 1966) and were unaware of that fact. Thus, it is not surprising that marriages can become a "vicious cycle" of misattribution, as Laing *et al.* propose.

Not surprisingly, Harvey *et al.*'s case history data show that separated married couples employ a heavy dose of negative evaluations of their partners, with a high degree of blame assigned to the partner for the failure of the relationship. This study points to the need for longitudinal data on the development of "blaming" among intimates. Like the Orvis *et al.* study, these data fall short of analyzing the dynamics of moral evaluation among intimates. However, these studies suggest how researchers can move in this direction. In addition, we believe these data pave a path for researchers who would attempt to integrate the fairness, clinical, and attributional perspectives.

V. FAIRNESS IN
   ## PARENT-CHILD RELATIONSHIPS

Social psychologists have not yet applied their theories to judgments of fairness between parents and children. No empirical studies have been conducted. Yet, if we purport to understand the rudiments of moral evaluation in intimate relationships, we must at least speculate about the dynamics of parent-child intimacy.

Critics of the role of moral evaluation among intimates might be even more inclined to resist this analysis in the case of children. For parent-child intimacy, even more so than that of lovers and best friends, is characterized by dependencies and commitment to the relationship. Fromm (1956) makes this point:

> The relationship of mother and child is by its very nature one of inequality, where one needs all the help, and the other gives it. It is for this altruistic, unselfish character that motherly love has been considered the highest kind of love, and the most sacred of all emotional bonds. . . . This is so in spite of the fact that they do not "get" anthing in return from the child, except a smile or the expression of satisfaction on his face [p. 58].

We are reluctant to disagree with this eloquent statement. Yet, consider the parent of the adolescent son or daughter who remarks in the midst of a petty disagreement, "I hate you! You don't understand me!" The parent feels he or she has sacrificed a thousand times for the child. Or, consider the case of child who has been physically abused or emotionally neglected. In these cases how else does the parent or child initially define the relationship other than to say it is not fair? The child is seen as ungrateful; the abusing parent as cruel. No doubt, researchers will begin to study this topic in the future.

The parent-child relationship, like other intimate relationships, is multifaceted. There are times when both parties act selflessly, giving unconditionally to the other. Elements of deserving creep in, though. The child deserves a new set of clothes; the parents deserves "respect" from their offspring. Few parents would disagree.

A. A Clinical Case Study

The perception of unfair treatment in parent–child relationships often stems from the opinion that behavior departs from role expectations. Perhaps no other intimate relationship is more closely tied to role definitions than that between parent and child. These roles help define the personal identities of the participants.

Questions of fairness are usually the result of parents asserting control and/or children reaching for autonomy. Fairness issues with children are prevalent during adolescence, but serious problems of fair treatment arise in the 6–12-year-old range as well.

Issues of fairness between parent and child possess a rule-centered focus. Children voice their dislike for the creation and imposition of rules—for example, those concerning chores, bedtime hour, homework, dating, and so on. Direct challenges to the legitimacy of parental authority itself are not uncommon. Thus, fairness takes on a particularly procedural character in the parenting context due to issues surrounding control and authority. In addition, the fact that the family is a small group means that it must develop a coherent body of rules and roles, and a set of procedures to carry out the rules and role expectations to function effectively. A recent family therapy case seen by Austin illustrates how issues of fairness concerning the definition of parent–child roles arise, and how they are expressed in terms of a challenge to the legitimacy of parental authority.

During the first session, the father of a 9-year-old boy and a 12-year-old daughter described their problem as "too much anger; we can't even talk anymore." The mother initially said that she "just wanted to treat her children fairly." After these opening comments by the parents, the children volunteered that the father was bossy. The therapist encouraged this dialogue with the joint goal of further defining the problem and opening up communication among family members. The Father remarked that the son was "too big for his britches." Next, the son, pulling his knees up under his chin and glaring at his father, defiantly stated: "You're too big for your britches! You just think you have to be in charge. Who said you're in charge? Why do you have to be the one? Why you?" With this statement, the son challenged the legitmacy of the authority normally vested in the parental role—it was not fair for the father to try to control the son's behavior.

The therapist diagnosed the family as one where the parents were reluctant to exercise the power endemic to their role as parents. Children and parents were confused about the boundaries between parent and child, and the obligations that accompany each role. The father wanted to exercise control, but was afraid to do so in a consistent manner; the mother voiced her fear of the destructive use of parental authority—she did not want to "destroy their spontaneity." The result of this trepidation with which the parents enacted their roles was a high degree of stress when control was attempted and the perception of pervasive unfairness. The son challenged the basis of his parents' authority; the daughter felt her brother received preferential treatment; and the father felt isolated and suffered from the lack of responsiveness from the children. Of gravest concern, however, was the fear by all family members that the son would lose control. In fact, this was a "family secret." Although he was a model student at school, where limits on his behavior were imposed, the son was a "tyrant" at home. All other family members dreaded the rage he held toward his parents. The son had effectively used "tantrums" and "explosions" to get his own way at home.

This family found itself in a quandary because the roles had not been clearly defined; expectations concerning rule making and enforcement were ambiguous. The expression of unfairness was the vehicle through which fear was expressed—the fear of parents exercizing their authority and children afraid of the power they found in their own hands.

B. Distinctive Features of Parent–Child Relationships

1. CULTURAL LEARNING

There are several factors that influence how fairness affects parent–child intimacy. The most important factor is the pervasive influence of cultural learning on parental behavior. We *learn* how to act out all of our intimate roles from the surrounding culture, but this learning is more explicit in the case of parent–child relationships.

The image of the passive, receiving child and the powerful, active, giving parent has guided research in developmental psychology for the past 40 years (Martin, 1975). Although, on the whole, many investigators have indicated a dissatisfaction with this general approach (Bell, 1968; Kessen, 1979; Martin, 1975) there is some evidence that the orientation, if not the findings, have had a powerful effect on mother–child relationships through the mass availability of child care manuals (Weiss, 1978) that stress child-centeredness and caretaker sacrifice.

Manuals published in the early 1900s could be classified as "mother survival kits," while at the same time providing tips for good child care.

For example, Weiss (1978) states: "Early toilet training relieved women of laundry burdens and also built good habits for the child. Early supper and bedtime were healthy for a child and also gave a frayed mother time to devote time to other activities. Strict scheduling spared mothers from being on call all day and developed habits of regularity in the baby [p. 39]."

However, the concern with mutuality began to fade after World War II. According to Weiss, the manuals became more child-centered and the mother became more trapped by her powers over the child. Quoting from the *United States Children's Bureau Manuals*, Weiss (1973), illustrates the change in emphasis toward child rights and mother's responsibilities. For example, if a child broke a treasured vase, the mother, not the child, is chastized because: "The mother should not have left it where the baby could get hold of it [p. 16]." On giving advice to mothers on how to make a baby most happy, the manual explained;

> In fact, [the child's] needs cannot be satisfactorily met unless the mother's are too. If she does not plan so that she will not be overburdened, she will be in no condition to be sunny and pleasant. Fitting her day around the child's routines in such a way that she does not become completely exhausted by night will help her to be a good companion to her husband too [p. 48].

It is difficult to estimate the effects that these manuals have had on generations of mothers and fathers [*Baby and Child Care* (Spock, 1976) alone sold 24,000,000 copies!].

2. "SPECIALNESS" OF THE CHILD

The emphasis in child care books has changed. They now share a common point: For parent *and* child to be satisfied, there must be a balance in meeting the needs of the other. Fairness in this context is mutual need satisfaction. However, the scales remain tipped in favor of the child. For example, Ainsworth (1973) warns mothers who are considering a vacation that the "respite may be bought too dearly if adequate substitute care is not arranged. The postseparation disturbances of the child may outweigh any vacation relief experienced by the parents [p. 79]." Thus, fairness to the committed parent may mean that intermittent symbolic gestures of appreciation will have to suffice as one's return on investment.

We believe this hypothesis is plausible because of the cultural and historical context of child development. The child is seen as deserving of "special" treatment. Children used to be treated as property and part of a man's estate (Aries, 1962), and recent highly publicized egregious cases of child abuse are proof that children are sometimes exploited. However, the childrens' rights movement has helped to securely establish for children a special status in society. We have seen the "International Year of the Child," White House Conferences, Public Law 94-142 guaranteeing special education rights for all children, and guarantees of new legal rights in the courtroom for minors.

This special status, backed by cultural norms, places pressures on parents to justify behavior by children that would be held as morally reprehensible in adults. Parents establish "psychological equity" with children by securing promises from the child to behave better in the future, or by simply feeling their son or daughter is "just being a child; he'll grow up soon."

3. CHILD REARING—MAKING ROOM FOR RECIPROCITY

Children do grow up and must assume more responsibility as a result. Parents and peers do demand "fair treatment." Realistically, the scales are still unbalanced in favor of the older child—but less so.

Even in the case of younger children, however, researchers are beginning to uncover more reciprocity in parent–child exchanges than was previously thought. Bell (1979) has summarized this recent research on reciprocal exchanges.

Interview studies of child-rearing practices by Baumrind (1967; 1971) provide some insights into fairness in parent–child interactions by focusing on reciprocity of exchange. Baumrind found that parental patterns of behavior that introduced a standard of fairness to the parent–child relationship resulted in the most satisfying relationship. These patterns were found among a group of parents who exerted more control over the child's behavior, but did so in manner that was pleasant and positive for the child and parent. Children in this group were expected to behave in an age-appropriate manner; maturity demands were made by soliciting the child's opinion and through an open verbal exchange. Both parents and children in this group were openly affectionate toward one another. Parents used less punishment and a greater percentage of child-initiated response sequences resulted in satisfaction for the child. Thus, the parents' exercise of control and demands for maturity occurred in a context in which the parents encouraged verbal give-and-take, listened to the child's point of view, occasionally retracted a demand on the basis of the child's expression, and provided a generous measure of affection and approval that was, to some extent, contingent on the child's performance. Thus, fairness in child rearing appears to reflect participation by the children, but also requires firm control by parents, behavior that requires clear role definitions.

C. Fairness in Unusual Parent–Child Relationships

We have argued that fairness is relevant in all intimate relationships, but that there are cultural constraints that limit the degree of reciprocity in parent–child relations. The great majority of parents adjust to this reality. But what of those parents who have responsibility for rearing handicapped children?

Fawcett (1978), in a cross-cultural study, reports commonly listed rewards of child rearing reported by parents in six countries: companionship, observing children grow in maturity and responsibility; pride in children's accomplishments; completeness of family life; and continuity of family name and tradition. Parents who give birth to a child who is either deformed or handicapped will most likely be frustrated in realizing some of these positive returns. Families of disabled children tend to experience not only marital and person distress (Gath, 1974; Klaus & Kennel, 1976), but mutually distressing mother–child relationships. The young blind child, for example, is more likely to encounter emotional indifference by the parents because of the child's reduced facial expressiveness and the absence of contingent smiling (Fraiberg, 1974). The young cerebral palsy child is more likely to experience a diminishing amount of maternal warmth during his or her second or third years—especially if the child is not yet walking (Kogan & Tyler, 1973).

Certainly, these findings are only empirical generalizations. Many parents are able to adapt to the greater responsibility of raising a handicapped child. Awareness of handicapped children as real people with rights has increased through new federal legislation. However, the deleterious effects of a child's disability on mothers (Cummings, Bayley, & Rie, 1966) and fathers (Cummings, 1976) are well documented. Mothers of mentally retarded children differed in the following areas: (a) increased occurrence of depressed feelings; (b) increased preoccupation with the involved child; (c) increased difficulty in handling anger at the child; (d) decreased enjoyment of the child; and (e) feelings of rejection toward the child. The fathers showed greater depression, decreased enjoyment of the child, and decreased interpersonal satisfaction with wife and other children.

The handicapped child in some cases is not able to provide the many positive pleasures of a normal child, while at the same time imposing unusual demands on his or her caretakers. The handicapped child's reduced sensory and/or response capacity often makes the child appear to be unresponsive to parents' care (Korn, Chess, & Fernandez, 1978). It is not surprising, therefore, that parents may feel some anger and resentment toward the child. The relationship is judged as unfair by the parent. *The justifications for the culturally mandated imbalance in favor of the child are gone; the symbolic gestures of appreciation by the child may be missing.*

Finally, investigators have recently identified what they call "difficult" infants. Despite attention from parents, these infants cry extensively and inconsolably; their moods are negative and unpredictable (Thomas, Chess, Birch, Hertzig, & Korn, 1963; Thomas, Chess, & Birch, 1968). According to Lamb (1978), premature infants are at greater risk of abuse by their parents. In one sense, they possess short-term physical handicaps. These infants neither look nor sound like full-term babies. They have a high pitched aversive cry, are physically less attractive than full term babies, and are unable to smile as long as full-term babies. Lamb (1978) argues that the difficult baby syndrome, combined with real world stress on the family and the personalities of the parents, may be the major contributing cause of child abuse. The argument is persuasive when it is coupled with findings on the role of the infant in its own abuse. Parents who abused their child saw the child as the cause (Gelles, 1970), mentioning annoying persistent crying or abrasive behaviors not present in other siblings. Furthermore, battered children continue to be harmed in foster homes (Bell & Harper, 1977). These data suggest that child abuse is partly determined by the unsatisfactory nature of the parent relationship with an infant who provides few rewards and demands large sacrifices. We would like to suggest, as do Kempe and Kempe (1978), that irrational judgments of unfairness by parents mediates child abuse.

IV. CONCLUDING COMMENT

In this chapter, we have attempted to provide a general overview of the role of moral evaluation in intimate relationships. We have drawn upon several distinct areas of theory and research: interpersonal attraction, fairness, marital and family therapy, and attribution theory. Our goal was to indicate what psychologists know at this point about intimacy *and* fairness, and then to suggest how these two topics can be integrated. Each of these areas of research appear to share common features. We have attempted to show how these common links serve as the basis for an integrated approach to both theoretical analysis and practical problem solving of fairness dilemmas among intimates.

ACKNOWLEDGMENTS

The authors gratefully acknowledge the many helpful comments and editorial assistance of Elaine Hatfield in the preparation of this chapter.

REFERENCES

Adams, J. S. Inequity in social exchange. In L. Berkowitz (Ed.), *Advances in experimental social psychology* (Vol. 2). New York: Academic Press, 1965.

Ainsworth, M. D. S. The development of infant–mother attachment. In B. M. Caldwell & H. M. Ricciuti (Eds.), *Review of child development research* (Vol. 3). Chicago: University of Chicago Press, 1973.

Altman, I., & Taylor, D. A. *Social penetration: The development of interpersonal relationships.* New York: Holt, Rinehart & Winston, 1973.

Aries, P. *Centuries of childhood* (R. Baldick, trans.). New York: Knopf, 1962.

Aronson, E. Some antecedents of interpersonal attraction. In W. J. Arnold & D. Levine (Eds.), *Nebraska Symposium on Motivation.* Lincoln: University of Nebraska Press, 1970.

Austin, W. *Theoretical and experimental explorations in expectancy theory.* Unpublished master's thesis, University of Wisconsin, Madison, 1972.

Austin, W. Equity theory and social comparison processes. In J. Suls & R. Miller (Eds.), *Social comparison theory: Theoretical and empirical perspectives.* Washington, D. C.: Hemisphere, 1977.

Austin, W. Justice, freedom, and self-interest in intergroup relations. In W. G. Austin & S. Worchel (Eds.), *The social psychology of intergroup relations.* Belmont, Calif.: Brooks/Cole, 1979.

Austin, W. Friendship and fairness: Effects of type of relationship and task performance on choice of distribution rules. *Personality and Social Psychology Bulletin,* 1980, *6,* 401–408.

Austin, W., McGinn, N. C., & Susmilch, C. Internal standards revisited: Effects of social comparisons and expectancies on judgments of fairness and satisfaction. *Journal of Experimental Social Psychology,* 1980, *16,* 426–441.

Austin, W., & Tobiasen, J. Legal justice and the psychology of conflict resolution. In R. Folger (Ed.), *Justice: Emerging psychological perspectives.* New York: Plenum, in press.

Austin, W., & Walster, E. Equity with the world: The transrelational effects of equity and inequity. *Sociometry,* 1975, *38,* 474–496.

Azrin, N. H., Naster, B. J., & Jones, R. Reciprocity counseling: A rapid learning-based procedure for marital counseling. *Behavior Reserch, and Therapy,* 1973, *11,* 365–382.

Bach, G. R., & Wyden, P. *The intimate enemy: How to fight fair in love and marriage.* New York: Avon, 1968.

Baumrind, D. Child care practices anteceding three patterns of preschool behavior. *Genetic Psychology Monographs,* 1967, *75,* 43–83.

Baumrind, D. Current patterns of parental authority. *Developmental Psychology Monographs,* 1971, *4*(1).

Beck, A. T., & Shaw, B. F. Cognitive approaches to depression. In A. Ellis & R. Greiger, (Eds.), *Handbook of Rational Emotive Therapy.* New York: Springer, 1977.

Bell, R. Q. A reinterpretation of the direction of effects in studies of socialization. *Psychological Review,* 1968, *75,* 81–95.

Bell, R. Q. Parent, child, and reciprocal influences. *American Psychologist.* 1979, *34,* 821–826.

Bell, R. Q., & Harper, L. V. *The effects of children on parents.* Hillsdale, N.J.: Erlbaum, 1977.

Berkowitz, L., & Walster, E. (Eds.). *Advances in experimental social psychology* (Vol. 9). New York: Academic Press, 1976.

Bernard, J. The adjustments of married mates. In H. T. Christensen (Ed.), *Handbook of marriage and the family.* Chicago: Rand McNally, 1964.

Berscheid, E., & Walster, E. *Interpersonal attraction* (2nd ed.). Reading, Mass.: Addison-Wesley, 1978.

Berscheid, E., & Walster, E. A little bit about love. In T. L. Huston (Ed.), *Foundations of interpersonal attraction*. New York: Academic Press, 1974.

Billings, A. Conflict resolution in distressed and nondistressed married couples. *Journal of Consulting and Clinical Psychology*, 1979, *47*, 368–376.

Blau, P. M. *Exchange and power in social life*. New York: Wiley, 1964.

Burgess, R. L., & Huston, T. L. (Eds.). *Social exchange in developing relationships*. New York: Academic Press, 1979.

Cummings, S. The impact of the child's deficiency on the father. A study of fathers of mentally retarded and chronically ill children. *American Journal of Orthopsychiatry*, 1976, *46*, 246–255.

Cummings, S., Bayley, S., & Rie, H. Effects of the child's deficiency on the mother. A study of mothers of mentally retarded, chronically ill, and neurotic children. *American Journal of Orthopsychiatry*, 1966, *36*, 595–608.

Curtis, R. C. Effects of knowledge of self-interest and social relationships upon the use of equity, utilitarian, and Rawlsian principles of allocation. *European Journal of Social Psychology*, 1979, *9*, 165–175.

Derlega, V. J., & Chaikin, A. L. *Sharing intimacy: What we say to others and why*. Englewood Cliffs, N.J.: Prentice-Hall, 1975.

Donnenwerth, G. V., & Foa, U. G. Effect of resource class on retaliation to injustice in interpersonal exchange. *Journal of Personality and Social Psychology*, 1974, *29*, 785–793.

Ellis, A. *Marriage: The hotbed of neurosis*. New York: Institute for Rational Living, undated audio casette.

Ellis, A. Theoretical and conceptual foundations of rational-emotive therapy. In A. Ellis & R. Greiger (Eds.), *Handbook of rational emotive therapy*. New York: Springer, 1977.

Ellis, A., & Harper, R. A. *A new guide to rational living*. Englewood Cliffs, N.J.: Prentice-Hall, 1975.

Fawcett, J. The value and cost of the first child. In W. Miller & L. Newman (Eds.), *The first child and family formation*. Chapel Hill, N.C.: University of North Carolina Press, 1978.

Fogarty, M. P., Rapoport, R., & Rapoport, R. N. *Sex, career and family*. Beverly Hills, Calif.: Sage, 1971.

Fraiberg, S. Blind infants and their mothers: An examination of the sign system. In M. Lewis & L. A. Rosenblum (Eds.), *The effect of the infant on its care-giver*. New York: Wiley, 1974.

Friday, N. *My mother/myself*. New York: Dell, 1977.

Fromm, E. *The art of loving*. New York: Harper & Row, 1956.

Gath, A. Sibling reactions to mental handicap: A comparison of the brothers and sisters of mongol children. *Journal of Child Psychology and Psychiatry*, 1974, *15*, 187–198.

Gelles, R. J. Violence toward children in the United States. *American Journal of Orthopsychiatry*, 1970, *48*, 580–592.

Glass, D. C. Changes in liking as a means of reducing cognitive discrepancies between self-esteem and aggression. *Journal of Personality*, 1964, *32*, 531–549.

Goffman, E. *Relations in public*. New York: Basic Books, 1971.

Greenberg, J. Allocator–recipient similarity and the equitable division of rewards, *Social Psychology*, 1978, *41*, 337–341.

Haley, J. Marital therapy. In G. D. Erickson & T. P. Hogan (Eds.), *Family therapy: An introduction to therapy and techique*. Monterey, Cal.: Brooks/Cole, 1972. (Originally published in *Archives of General Psychiatry*, 1963, *8*, 213–234.)

Hamilton, V. L. Who is responsible? Toward a *social* psychology of responsibility attribution. *Social Psychology*, 1978, *41*, 316–328.

Harvey, J., Ickes, W., & Kidd, R. F. *New directions in attribution research* (Vol. 1). Hillsdale, N.J.: Erlbaum, 1976.

Harvey, J., Ickes, W., & Kidd, R. F. *New directions in attribution research* (Vol. 2). Hillsdale, N.J.: Erlbaum, 1978.

Harvey, J. H., Wells, G. L., & Alvarez, M. D. Attribution in the context of conflict and separation in close relationships. In J. Harvey, W. Ickes, & R. F. Kidd (Eds.), *New directions in attributions research* (Vol. 2). Hillsdale, N.J.: Erlbaum, 1978.

Hatfield, E. Passionate love. In B. Wolman (Ed.), *Handbook of developmental psychology*. Englewood Cliffs, N.J.: Prentice-Hall, in press. (a)

Hatfield, E. *Love, sex, and the marketplace*. New York: Academic Press, in press. (b)

Hatfield, E., Utne, M. K., & Traupmann, J. Equity theory and intimate relationships. In R. Burgess & T. L. Huston (Eds.), *Social exchange in developing relationships*. New York: Academic Press, 1979.

Homans, G. *Social behavior: Its elementary forms*. New York: Harcourt Brace & World, 1961.

Homans, G. *Social behavior: Its elementary forms* (2nd ed.). New York: Harcourt Brace Jovanovich, 1974.

Huesmann, L. R., & Levinger, G. Incremental exchange theory: A formal model for progression in dyadic social interaction. In L. Berkowitz & E. Walster (Eds.), *Advances in experimental social psychology* (Vol. 9). New York: Academic Press, 1976.

Hunt, M. *Sexual behavior in the 1970s*. New York: Dell, 1974.

Huston, T. L. Ambiguity of acceptance, social desirability, and dating choice. *Journal of Experimental Social Psychology*, 1973, *9*, 32–42.

Jones, A. In M. Palmer, "Marriage and the formerly fat: The effect weight loss has on your life together." *Weight Watchers*, March, 1974, *7*(2).

Jourard, S. M. *Self-disclosure*. New York: Wiley, 1971.

Karuza, J., & Leventhal, G. S. *Justice judgments: Role demands and perception of fairness*. Paper presented at the meeting of the American Psychological Association, Washington, D.C., September 1976.

Kempe, R. S., & Kempe, C. H. *Child abuse*. Cambridge, Mass.: Harvard University Press, 1978.

Kessen, W. The American child and other cultural inventions. *American Psychologist*, 1979, *34*, 815–820.

Klaus, M., & Kennell, J. *Maternal infant bonding*. St. Louis, Mo.: C. V. Mosby, 1976.

Kogan, K., & Tyler, N. Mother–child interaction in young physically handicapped children. *American Journal of Mental Deficiency*, 1973, *77*, 492–497.

Komarovsky, M. *Blue-collar marriage*. New York: Vintage, 1967. (Originally published, 1940.)

Komarovsky, M. *The unemployed man and his family*. New York: Octagon, 1971.

Korn, S., Chess, S., & Fernandez, P. The impact of children's physical handicaps on marital quality and family interaction. In R. Lerner & G. Spanier (Eds.), *Child differences on marital and family interaction*. New York: Academic Press, 1978.

Kurth, S. B. Friendship and friendly relations. In G. J. McCall, M. K. Denzin, G. D. Suttles, & S. B. Kurth (Eds.), *Social relationships*. Chicago: Aldine, 1970.

Laing, R. D., Phillipson, H., & Lee, A. R. *Interpersonal perception*. New York: Harper & Row, 1966.

Lamb, M. Influence of the child, marital quality, and family interaction during the prenatal and infancy periods. In R. Lerner & G. Spanier (Eds.), *Child influences on marital and family interaction*. New York: Academic Press, 1978.

Lederer, W. J., & Jackson, D. D. *The mirages of marriage*. New York: Norton, 1968.

Lerner, M. J. (Ed.). The justice motive in social behavior. *Journal of Social Issues*, 1975, *31*, (whole issue).

Lerner, M. J., Miller, D. T., & Holmes, J. G. Deserving and the emergence of forms of justice. In L. Berkowitz & E. Walster (Eds.), *Advances in experimental social psychology* (Vol. 9). New York: Academic Press, 1976.

Lerner, M. J., & Whitehead, L. A. Procedural justice viewed in the context of justice motive theory. In G. Mikula (Ed.), *Justice and social interaction*. New York: Springer-Verlag, 1980.

Leventhal, G. S., Michaels, J. W., & Sanford, C. Inequity and interpersonal conflict: Reward allocation and secrecy about reward as methods of preventing conflict. *Journal of Personality and Social Psychology*, 1972, *23*, 88–102.

Levinger, G. Sources of marital dissatisfaction among applicants for divorce. *American Journal for Orthopsychiatry*, 1966, *36*, 803–807.

Levinger, G. A social psychological perspective on marital dissolution. *Journal of Social Issues*, 1976, *32*, 21–47.

Levinger, G., Senn, D. J., and Jorgensen, B. W. Progress toward permanence in courtship: A test of the Kerckhoff-Davis hypothesis. *Sociometry*, 1970, *33*, 427–443.

Levinger, G., & Snoek, J. D. *Attraction in relationship: A new look at interpersonal attraction.* Morristown, N.J.: General Learning Press, 1972.

Levitin, T. Children of divorce. *Journal of Social Issues, 1980*, *35*, 1–25.

Martin, B. Parent–child relations. In F. D. Horowitz (Ed.), *Review of child development research* (Vol. 4). Chicago: University of Chicago Press, 1975.

McCall, M. M. Courtship as social exchange: Some historical comparisons. In Bernard Farber (Ed.), *Kinship and family organization*. New York: Wiley, 1966.

Meeker, B. F. Decisions and exchange. *American Sociological Review*, 1971, *36*, 485–495.

Mills, J., & Clark, M. S. Exchange in communal relationships. In E. Hatfield (Ed.), *Love, sex, and the marketplace*, New York: Academic Press, in press.

Morehous, L. G. One-play, two-play, five-play, ten-play runs of prisoner dilemma. *Journal of Conflict Resolution*, 1966, *10*, 354–362.

Morris, D. *Intimate behaviour*. New York: Random House, Bantam Books, 1971.

Murstein, B. I. The limit of exchange in equity theories. In E. Hatfield (Ed.), *Love, sex, and the marketplace*. New York: Academic Press, in press.

Murstein, B. I. Physical attractiveness and marital choice. *Journal of Personality and Social Psychology*, 1972, *22*, 8–12.

Orvis, B. R., Kelley, H. H., & Butler, D. Attributional conflict in young couples. In J. Harvey, W. Ickes, & R. F. Kidd (Eds.), *New directions in attribution theory* (Vol. 1). Hillsdale, N.J.: Erlbaum, 1976.

Patterson, G. R. *Families: Applications of social learning to family life*. Champaign, Ill.: Research Press, 1971.

Perlmutter, M., & Hatfield, E. Intimacy, intentional metacommunication, and second-order change. *American Journal of Family Therapy*, 1980, *8*, 17–23.

Rappaport, A. F., & Harrel, J. A behavioral exchange for marital counseling. *Family Coordinator*, 1972, *21*, 203–213.

Regan, D. T. Attribution aspects of interpersonal attraction. In J. Harvey, W. Ickes, & R. F. Kidd (Eds.), *New directions in attribution research* (Vol. 2). Hillsdale, N.J.: Erlbaum, 1978.

Rubin, Z. The measurement of romantic love. *Journal of Personality and Social Psychology*, 1970, *16*, 265–273.

Rubin, Z. *Liking and loving. An invitation to social psychology.* New York: Holt, Rinehart & Winston, 1973.

Sager, C. *Marriage contracts and couple therapy*. New York: Brunner/Mazel, 1976.

Sampson, E. E. On justice as equality. *Journal of Social Issues*, 1975, *31*, 45–64.

Sarbin, T. R., & Allen, V. L. Role theory. In G. Lindzey & E. Aronson (Eds.), *The handbook of social psychology* (Vol. 1). Reading, Mass.: Addison-Wesley, 1968.

Scanzoni, J. *Sexual bargaining: Power politics in the american marriage.* Englewood Cliffs, N.J.: Prentice-Hall, 1972.

Schoeninger, D. W., & Wood, W. D. Comparison of married and ad hoc mixed-sex dyads. *Journal of Experimental Social Psychology,* 1969, *5,* 483–499.

Secord, P. F., & Backman, C. W. *Social psychology* (2nd ed.). New York: McGraw-Hill, 1974.

Spock, B. *Baby and child care.* New York: Pocket Books, 1976.

Storer, N. W. *The social system of science.* New York: Holt, Rinehart & Winston, 1966.

Sussman, M. Ties that bind. *Time.* September, 1975, p. 62.

Thibaut, J., & Kelley, H. H. *The social psychology of groups.* New York: Wiley, 1959.

Thibaut, J., & Walker, L. *Procedural justice. A psychological analysis.* Hillsdale, N.J.: Erlbaum, 1975.

Thomas, A., Chess, S., & Birch, H. G. *Temperament and behavior disorders in children.* New York: New York University Press, 1968.

Thomas, A., Chess, L., Birch, H. G., Hertzig, M. E., & Korn, S. *Behavioral individuality in early childhood.* New York: New York University Press, 1963.

Turner, J. L., Foa, E. B., & Foa, U. G. Interpersonal reinforcers: Classification in a relationship and some differential properties. *Journal of Personality and Social Psychology,* 1971, *19,* 168–180.

Turner, R. H. The role and the person. *American Journal of Sociology,* 1978, *84,* 1–23.

United States Children's Bureau. *Infant care.* Washington, D.C.: U.S. Government Printing Office, 1973.

Utne, M. K., Hatfield, E., Traupmann, J., & Greenberger, D. *Equity, marital satisfaction, and stability.* Unpublished manuscript, University of Wisconsin, Madison, 1978.

Walster, E., Berscheid, E., & Walster, G. W. New directions in equity research. *Journal of Personality and Social Psychology,* 1973, *25,* 151–176.

Walster, E., & Walster, G. W. *A new look at love.* Reading, Mass.: Addison-Wesley, 1978.

Walster, E., Walster, G. W., & Berscheid, E. *Equity: Theory and research.* Boston: Allyn & Bacon, 1978.

Walster, E., Walster, G. W., & Traupmann, J. Equity and premarital sex. *Journal of Personality and Social Psychology,* 1978, *36,* 82–92.

Watzlawick, P., Weakland, J., & Fisch, R. *Change: Principles of problem formation and problem resolution.* New York: Norton, 1974.

Webster's New Collegiate Dictionary. Cambridge, Mass.: G & C Merriam, 1959.

Weiss, N. The mother–child dyad revisited: perceptions of mothers and children in twentieth century child-rearing manuals. *Journal of Social Issues,* 1978, *34,* 29–45.

Worthy, M., Gary, A. L., & Kahn, G. M. Self-disclosure as an exchange process. *Journal of Personality and Social Psychology,* 1969, *13,* 63–69.

Yarrow, M. R., Schwartz, C. G., Murphy, H. S., & Deasy, L. C. The psychological meaning of mental illness in the family. *Journal of Social Issues,* 1955, *11,* 12–24.

Zaretsky, E. *Capitalism, the family, and personal life.* New York: Harper Colophon Books, 1976.

chapter 8

Prosocial Behavior, Equity, and Justice

DENNIS KREBS

During the last decade, the study of what has come to be called prosocial, or positive social behavior has achieved prominence in social and developmental psychology. At least seven books on the subject have been published recently (Bar-Tal, 1976; Mussen & Eisenberg-Berg, 1977; Rushton, 1980; Staub, 1978; Wispe, 1978; Eisenberg-Berg, 1982; and Rushton and Sorrentino, 1981). However, at present, research on prosocial behavior is, by and large, a partially woven tapestry of loosely connected threads.

As with much of social psychology, the lack of theoretical integration in the area of prosocial behavior is not unusual. In the words of Walster, Walster, and Berscheid (1978), "there is one thing . . . that conscientious social scientists can agree on—psychology desperately needs a general theory of social behavior [p. 1]." Walster *et al.* (1978) offer equity theory as a promising candidate for such a theory. The central purpose of this chapter is to examine the extent to which theories of equity and justice can help investigators of prosocial behavior weave their findings into more highly integrated patterns. And, in a project such as this, it would only be proper to search for ways in which research on prosocial behavior can reciprocate.

The term *prosocial behavior* refers to acts that benefit others. Included within this domain are behaviors such as donating to charity, sharing, helping others with small tasks, and intervening in emergencies. Although the ostensible effect of these behaviors is similar—they supply some benefit to another—it may be misleading to subsume them under the same rubric. The label *prosocial* is a rough description of a group of

261

EQUITY AND JUSTICE
IN SOCIAL BEHAVIOR

externally similar behaviors that may stem from qualitatively different motives. Of particular significance, the common assumption that because a behavior is prosocial it is altruistic is entirely gratuitious: people often help others in order to help themselves (see Krebs, 1978a; Krebs & Russell, 1981).

Three areas in the study of prosocial behavior seem particularly relevant to considerations of equity and justice—sharing and distributing resources, compensatory helping, and reciprocity. The first section of this chapter will be devoted to an examination of the structure of resource allocation; the second to research on compensatory helping; and the third to prosocial reciprocity. Consideration of these issues will raise questions about the capacity of theories and research on equity and justice to help elucidate the relationship between prosocial behavior and a number of determinants that hitherto have been examined in relative isolation from one another. In particular, the discussion will consider the effects of social norms, parameters of situations, cognitive development, moral reasoning, guilt, shame, general negative affect, the need to believe in a just world, and interpersonal attraction.

I. SHARING AND RESOURCE ALLOCATION: DISTRIBUTIVE JUSTICE

A. Definitional Problems

Deciding how to divide resources is one of the central problems of social existence. Inevitably, some people possess things that other people want. In most cases, the person who allocates the resources has some claim to the goods. In other cases, the allocator may be a disinterested third party charged with distributing resources among others. When examining the behavior of people with some claim to resources, two central questions arise (1) to what extent will they behave selfishly or generously; and (2) to what extent will their allocation behavior conform to one of several relevant principles of justice. In the case of impartial third-party allocators, only the second consideration arises.

1. GENEROSITY AND SELFISHNESS

What do investigators mean when they use the terms *generous* and *selfish?* As a type of prosocial behavior, generosity is plagued with the definitional ambiguity endemic to the more general construct. Typically, investigators define generosity (and selfishness) operationally in terms of the proportion of resources allocators give to themselves, relative to others (or relative to their inputs), without any attempt to discover its motivational underpinning. But giving someone else the lion's share need not necessarily be a generous act. It could be an act of expiation, cowardice, conformity, or ingratiation. Nor need keeping the lion's share be selfish. Behavior is ambiguous. The results of a recent study by Greenberg (1978) exemplify this point well.

Greenberg found that subjects behaved "generously" (i.e., gave more resources to others than the others deserved from their contributions) in two situations: (1) when the subjects possessed valuable resources and the recipients had little power; and (2) when the subjects possessed valuable resources and the recipients had a great deal of power. According to Greenberg, in the first situation "the social responsibility norm was apparently activated . . . by allocators' increased feelings of personal responsibility for their co-workers' fate"; but in the second situation the "allocators appeared to have been attempting to obligate their more powerful co-recipients to reciprocate their apparent generosity by giving them a large share of a more valuable reward [p. 376]." Clearly, if Greenberg's interpretation is correct, the two externally similar behaviors have qualitatively different underpinnings.

Another source of ambiguity surrounding the constructs of generosity and selfishness concerns their status as principles of justice. Generosity (and prosocial behavior in general) may or may not serve as a principle of justice, depending on the conditions under which it is displayed. People may behave generously even though they believe it is wrong; and they may behave selfishly because they believe it is right. Generosity may be unjust, and selfishness may be just. Whether either type of behavior qualifies as a principle of justice depends on whether it follows from the belief that it is the right thing to do.

2. PRINCIPLES OF JUSTICE

Among the many possible principles of justice an allocator could evoke, three have received special attention—humanitarianism, equality, and equity. Principles of justice supply a basis for giving people what they deserve, for balancing the competing claims of interested parties. However, they may well not be equally adequate. Some may meet the ideal of justice, fairness, and deserving more effectively than others. This, of course, is the overriding philosophical question of normative ethics. Psychologists do not always agree on the conclusion. For example, Walster et al. (1978) view equity as the most adequate principle of justice. Deutsch (1975) disagrees, suggesting that the basis for self-respect and mutual respect is undermined by the norm of equity because it signifies that various participants in the relationship do not have equal value.

Deutsch suggests further that the principle of equality meets the ideal of justice more adequately, because it provides support for the basis of mutual respect.

To conduct research on principles of justice, investigators must define and operationalize them. Defining equality as a type of distributive justice is relatively easy: It involves giving everyone involved the same proportion of the resources, regardless of their contributions. Humanitarianism is somewhat more difficult to define (see Mikula, 1980). Humanitarianism involves rewarding people in accordance with their need. But how should need be determined: In the context of the situation in question; in the context of the relationships involved; or in the context of a person's overall life? And how should we decide what needs are relevant? The behavioral result of humanitarian allocation may be an equal distribution of resources (when everyone's need is equal) or it may be unequal (when everyone's need is not). In some cases, humanitarian behavior, like generosity, may be construed as a principle of justice; and in others it may be construed as a violation of a principle of justice. For example, one allocator might give a recipient additional resources because the allocator believes that people deserve to have their needs met; whereas another might behave in exactly the same way with the intention of giving the recipient more than he or she deserves.

Of the three most salient principles of justice, the principle of equity is the most unwieldly and difficult to define. In a general sort of way, equity involves rewarding people in proportion to their costs and contributions. If one gives more, he or she gets more. However, it is often unclear what counts as costs and contributions, and how they should be weighed. Following Homans (1961) and Adams (1965), Walster *et al.* (1978) define equity broadly, arguing that, as the overriding principle of distributive justice, all other principles are subsumed in it. In this formulation, for example, need and equality are viewed as inputs in interactions. In contrast, other investigators (Deutsch, 1975; Leventhal, 1976; Sampson, 1975) construe equity more narrowly, as the principle of justice prescribing that people's contributions should be the primary determinants of what they deserve. I will adopt the latter, more narrow definition in this chapter.

a. Standards of Comparison in Equity. Even in cases where equity is defined narrowly and where inputs can be quantified reliably, there may still be considerable ambiguity about the appropriate standard of comparison for equity. At least five different factors could be balanced to achieve equity: (1) the ratio of one person's inputs and outcomes with that of a partner; (2) the ratio of a person's inputs and outcomes with that of a reference group; (3) one's inputs with one's outcomes; (4) a partner's inputs with his or her outcomes; and (5) the net input–outcome ratio in all of one's relationships. Austin (1977) distinguishes between the first and second types, calling them *person-other* and *reference group* comparisons. In the first case, for example, a worker might compare his or her productivity and wages to those of another worker. In the second the worker would use all other workers in the company as a standard of comparison.

The difference between the first, third, and fourth standards of comparison can be seen by considering the following example. Imagine that your partner works 2 hours and builds four toy airplanes, and you work 1 hour and build two. You are given $6 to divide between you. The obvious way to achieve equity is by giving your partner $4 and keeping $2 for yourself. However, note that there are at least three different standards of equity in this exchange: (1) that associated with the relationship between your inputs and outcomes, irrespective of the inputs and outcomes of your partner, (2) that associated with your partner's inputs and outcomes, irrespective of yours, and (3) that associated with the relationship between your inputs and outcomes and those of your partner.

In the theory set forth by Adams (1965) and Walster *et al.* (1978) the object of equity is the *relationship* between two or more people. Equity obtains when each person's outcomes relative to his or her inputs (assets or liabilities) are equal. As such, the theory is a social comparison theory. However, in many of the experimental situations constructed by equity theorists (and assumed to supply tests of Adams's and Walster *et al.*'s equity theories), the resources that are made available lend themselves to a division that satisfies all three forms of equity. What, we might ask, would happen if the amount a person were given to share did not lend itself to the simultaneous satisfaction of them all? This question was investigated by Lane and Messé (1972). These investigators found, as we would expect, that subjects divided payment for a job equally when they and their partners had performed an equal amount of work, and had been paid sufficiently. However, when (with input equal) subjects were either overpaid or underpaid, they did not share the resources equitably. When they were underpaid, they gave themselves what *they* deserved, and left the (insufficient) remainder for the other. When they were overpaid, they gave the other what he deserved, and kept the rest for themselves.

Findings such as these raise the question: "Equity with whom?" They suggest that people do not necessarily calculate equity in terms of comparisons with other people. Although many studies have established that people often compare the ratio of their inputs and outcomes to those of others, there is, in the words of Lane and Messé (1972), also evidence "which indicates that (a) persons evaluate both their own and the other's ratios in terms of some internal standard that varies as a function of inputs, and (b) concerns with own equity are stronger than concerns with other equity [p. 233]."

Finally, focusing on the fifth type of equity balance, people may disregard their contributions to a relationship and the contributions of others, and seek to maintain "equity with the world," which, as defined by Austin and Walster (1975), is "the degree of equity present in the totality of a person's relationships during a given period of time [p. 478; see also Austin & Walster, 1974]." In Austin's (1977) terms, equity with the world differs from person–other equity because it is "transrelational." The question is, under what circumstances will people attempt to maintain equity with the world instead of equity with specific others? According to Austin (1977) "common observation suggests that person-specific equity is the primary mode of inter-personal justice [p. 299]," but that people will sacrifice person-specific equity when they are not able to maintain it (because, for example, the appropriate other is not available), when the cost of maintaining it is high, and when they are not accountable (i.e., when they will never see the other again).

3. SUMMARY

To summarize, whether or not people are guided by principles of distributive justice, and if so, what principles they employ, may depend on whether or not they are a potential recipient of the resources they are charged with allocating. To determine whether a behavior is selfish or generous (i.e., prosocial) an investigator must discover its motivational underpinnings and specify the standard from which it veers. Generosity may or may not qualify as a principle of justice. Although the definition of equality is relatively clear, there is considerable ambiguity surrounding the operationalization of principles of humanitarianism and equity. In particular, it is unclear whether allocators strive to maintain "own equity," "other equity," "equity in relationships," or "equity with the world." With these considerations in mind, let us turn now to the empirical research on resource allocation, first among adults, then among children.

B. The Structure of Resource Allocation among Adults

One of the behaviors commonly considered prosocial is sharing. When we think of sharing, the incidents that come most readily to mind are those that are spontaneous—a child shares some candy with a friend; a worker shares his lunch with a colleague; we let a neighbor use our lawnmower. In situations such as these, there is no direct connection between the costs people have incurred in obtaining resources and the resources they share; and there is no ambiguity about who possesses, owns, or has the preemptive right to the resources. There has been virtually no research on spontaneous sharing in adults, and only a few studies on sharing in children.

Most research on the division of resources has investigated what is commonly called resource allocation. In research of this sort, subjects who may or may not have participated in a project are given the responsibility to allocate resources to people who make varying contributions to the task. The subjects do not really own the resources or have a preemptive right to them; rather, they are cast in the role of purveyors, allocators, or transfer agents. In this sense, the task they face is qualitatively different from the task faced by a person in a position to share. However, in cases where allocators are potential recipients of resources, they may infer that, because they have been given the resources to allocate, they own them; and, therefore, they may define their task in terms of sharing. The critical difference between sharing and resource allocation lies in whether the person who possesses the resources believes that they are his or hers. The conclusions that people draw about their rights to the resources they are asked to allocate (and, therefore, whether they define their task as sharing or resource allocation) may well reflect a great deal about the form of their justice reasoning.

A large number of studies have investigated allocation behavior among adults. The central question behind such research is: What principle characterizes the distribution of the resources: How do people decide what they and others deserve? Do they divide resources equally, equitably, or in proportion to each recipient's need? As jaded social psychologists have come to expect, the best answer to questions such as these is usually "all of the above." A large number of studies have found that when subjects are asked to allocate resources, they allocate them equitably. To quote Coon, Lane, and Lichtman (1974), "The results of the adult reward distribution research have, for the most part, supported equity theory [p. 302]." However, as indicated by Leventhal (1976), studies have also found that allocators sometimes do not reward recipients according to their inputs, but rather, according to their needs, or even equally. And, to make matters even more complicated, there is evidence to indicate that, whereas subjects tend to divide resources equitably when they have contributed less than their partners, they tend to divide resources equally when they have contributed more—a phenomenon termed "the politeness ritual" by Mikula and Schwinger (1978).

What, then, causes the variation? The most popular answer to this question is different norms. As stated by Staub (1978), "in the course of socialization, growth, and development, most people accept some social values and norms as their own. . . . Subsequently these values and norms guide their behavior [p. 43]." The four norms most frequently evoked to explain prosocial behavior are the norms of social responsibility or humanitarianism (Berkowitz & Daniels, 1963; Schwartz, 1975), equality (Sampson, 1969), equity (Leventhal, 1976), and reciprocity (Gouldner, 1960). In addition, other investigators have evoked norms such as that of giving (Leeds, 1963) and the norm of deservingness, (Staub, 1972).

1. NORMATIVE EXPLANATIONS OF PROSOCIAL BEHAVIOR

Krebs (1970) considered the general capacity of norms to explain prosocial behavior and reached the following conclusion:

> The notion that people act in accordance with normative standards of conduct seems quite sound as far as it goes. It would seem, though, that it does not go far enough . . . a particular response can be predicted on the basis of a norm. If it occurs, the norm is said to have had an effect. If it does not occur, the situation is said to fall outside the range of the norm. . . . The danger with normative analysis is that norms can be invented post hoc to explain almost anything [pp. 294–295].

This general problem applies to norms of allocation. According to Leventhal (1976): "Allocation norms are important determinants of an allocator's decisions. . . . However, several norms are often salient at one time and each may favor a different distribution of reward, thus an allocator must decide which allocation norm or combination of norms to follow [p. 129]." The question is, how do people decide which norms to follow?

A number of investigators have considered this question, and concluded that people abide by the norms that are (a) the most salient to them; (b) the most functional; and/or (c) the most appropriate to the situations they are in. For example, Staub (1978) considers ways in which the "contradictory forces" of the norm of sharing and the norm of deserving combine, and suggests that the norm of deserving is "probably intensified after children enter school, since within most schools, the notion of earning is stressed and has substantial influence for some time [p. 284]." Leventhal (1976) suggests that people often follow "those norms which are approved and accepted by others [p. 129]" and those that produce the pattern of benefits that are appropriate to the situations to which they pertain. In particular, "an allocator may follow the equity norm to maximize productivity; follow the equality norm to reduce dissatisfaction and conflict; and follow the norm of adherence to commitments to foster harmony and reduce cognitive strain [p. 123]." Closely related to Leventhal's model is the notion that the goal of resource allocation is a significant determinant of the principles that govern it. Mikula (1980, pp. 158–160) reviews research documenting this point.

Deutsch (1975) also has offered an analysis that is similar to Leventhal's, suggesting that particular situations call out particular norms and values. In particular, he holds that equity is the dominant principle in situations involving economic productivity; equality is the dominant principle in situations involving enjoyable social relations; and need is the dominant principle in situations involving personal development and personal welfare.

Deutsch recognizes that many situations call out two or more of these norms, which then come into conflict. He suggests that the conflict is resolved in terms of the following principle: "*the typical consequences of a given type of social relation tend to elicit that relation* [p. 147]." Thus, for example, "if a social situation were characterized by impersonality, competition, maximization, an emphasis on comparability rather than uniqueness, largeness in size or scope, etc., then an economic orientation and the principle of equity are likely to be dominant in the group or social system [p. 148]."

Lerner *et al.* (1976) also consider the difficult question of how people select brands of fairness or justice. They base their answer on the nature of the perceived relationship between a person and the object of his or her concern; the type of perceived relationship is thought to elicit the specific form of justice applied. Lerner *et al.* (1976) suggest that in antagonistic ("nonunit") relationships, people go for all they can get. Competitive games and many business and legal exchanges are cases in point. In situations where people view themselves as similar to or interdependent with others ("unit relationships"), they tend to share fairly. In particular, they tend to share equally when they view themselves as part of the same "team" (see Schwinger, 1975); and they tend to share equitably when they perceive themselves to be in a similar role. Finally, when people identify with others, they tend to behave altruistically. In particular, they are prone to give others as much help as they need, regardless of what the others contributed, when they empathize with them; and they attempt to do what is best for others in the long run when they take their role (see Krebs, 1978a). Relations between parents and children, lovers, and in some cases even spouses are cases in point.

Although normative models such as those of Staub (1978), Leventhal (1976), Deutsch (1975), and Lerner *et al.* (1976) may help to specify the conditions under which particular norms obtain, they are limited in at least two ways: (1) they do not account for more microscopic parameters of situations that affect the form of resource allocation; and (2) they do not account for individual differences. Mikula (1980, pp. 153–160) supplies an excellent review of the impact of specific situational variables on the structure of resource allocation. In it he cites studies reporting effects for the following aspects of situations: anticipation of future interaction, affective quality of relationships involved, the size of contributions, openness of the allocation decision, the value of the reward, and guidelines and goals set by experimenters. A study by Greenberg (1978) supplies a representative example of the impact of two microscopic aspects of allocation situations. Greenberg (1978) manipulated the value of resources and the opportunity to engage in future interaction with the recipient, and found that subjects (a) behaved selfishly when the value of the resources they possessed was high and when they did not expect to engage in any future exchanges with their co-workers; (b) allocated equally when the rewards were worth little, whatever the possibility of future exchange; and (c) allocated equitably when they expected the recipient to have an opportunity to reciprocate, across all values of reward.

The second way in which normative analyses are limited is in their neglect of individual differences. If situations exert predominant control over the norms that are evoked to guide allocation behavior, most people would behave the same way in the same situations. But this, as Major and Deaux indicate in Chapter 2 of this volume, is often not the case. Of particular significance, there is persuasive evidence that children of different ages tend to allocate resources in terms of different principles (in the same situations). Let us review research on how children allocate resources, then explore its implications for a more comprehensive explanation of distributive justice.

C. The Structure of Resource Allocation among Children

Like research on adults, most research on resource distribution among children has investigated allocation rather than sharing. What evidence on sharing there is suggests that children begin to share early in life, and that the incidence of sharing increases with age. Rheingold, Hay, and West (1976) observed 15–24-month-old children, and noted that they engaged in a considerable amount of sharing. Most of it involved giving things to parents and other children and permitting or encouraging playmates to play mutually with their toys. The incidence of such sharing increased over the 15–24-month span. In another study, Murphy (1937) observed a substantial amount of naturalistic sharing in nursery school children. Other studies (see Krebs, 1970; and Staub, 1978 for reviews) have found that, in general, generosity increases with age.

Turning to the preponderance of research—on the allocation of resources among children—a study by Leventhal and Anderson (1970) serves as a representative prototype. In this study, kindergarten children were asked to do some work (pasting stickers on a sheet of paper), and led to believe that a partner also was working at the same task. After the children had pasted up either 5 or 15 stickers, they were stopped, informed that their partner had pasted up either 5 or 15 stickers, and given 20 attractive stickers to divide as a reward. Leventhal and Anderson found that, by and large, the children divided the rewards equally. The only deviation from an approximately 50/50 split was among boys who did more than their share. These boys kept an average of 2.5 more stickers for themselves, tending toward an equitable distribution. In a close replication of this study, Lerner (1974, Experiment 1) obtained almost identical results.

Lane and Coon (1972) divided kindergarten-aged children into a group of 4-year-olds and a group of 5-year-olds. Like the previous investigators, Lane and Coon failed to find any differences in the proportion of rewards given to recipients as a function of their relative inputs. However, Lane & Coon did find an age difference. The 4-year-olds tended to behave selfishly—keeping an average of from 2.5 to 4.5 more stickers for themselves. In contrast, the 5-year-olds, like the kindergarten subjects in other studies, tended to divide the rewards 50/50.

In another study, Lerner (1974) adapted the Leventhal and Anderson procedure to make it appropriate for fifth graders. He found that children of this age divided resources equitably, but, like the adults in the Lane and Messé (1972) study, their equitable behavior was tinged with self-interest. When given five ball-point pens to share, they almost always gave three to the person who had done the most work. However, when given six pens to share, some of the fifth-grade children kept half, even though they had done less than half of the work.

In the Leventhal and Anderson (1970), Lerner (1974), and Lane and Coon (1972) studies, children were required to divide the resources between themselves and others. If they divided them in terms of a principle of fairness or justice, we would expect them to behave in much the same way in situations where they were not one of the recipients. Several studies have assessed the behavior of children in the role of supervisor, charged with dividing up resources between two workers. In one study, Peterson, Peterson, and McDonald (1975) found that kindergarten children divided 10 pieces of candy approximately evenly between two imaginary workers, despite the fact that they contributed unequally. (However, 42% of the children behaved inconsistently across three situations). Lerner (1974) found that there was little difference between the behavior of self-interested and supervisory kindergarten allocators, with both tending to divide resources between workers evenly regardless of their input. There was a slight tendency for supervisors to give workers who had contributed only one-fourth to the outcome less than the workers gave themselves. Fifth grade children also behaved similarly in supervisory and self-interested roles. However, at this age, they tended to allocate resources equitably (with a tendency to give a little less to the worker who did more, and a little more to the worker who did less).

In a recent article, Hook and Cook (1979) reviewed the literature on allocation in children. The results of the studies surveyed in their more exhaustive review support the trends indicated by the ones considered here. Young 3- and 4-year-old children tend to behave in a self-interested manner. Slightly older 4- and 5-year-olds tend to divide resources equally. Then, from ages 6–12, what Hook and Cook (1979) called *ordinal equity* becomes the preferred mode of resource allocation. In ordinal equity, those who contribute more are given more, but not necessarily an amount equivalent to their contributions. Hook and Cook contrast ordinal with *proportional equity,* (where rewards are equivalent to contributions), and suggest that proportional equity occurs only among adolescents and adults. Hook and Cook also document the absence of systematic differences between the behavior of allocators who are potential recipients and the behavior of allocators who serve in third-party roles (except of course, that third-party allocators cannot behave in a self-interested manner).

In the studies on resource allocation among children that we have been considering, the children were given resources that lent themselves to divisions that simultaneously satisfied own, other, and relationship equity. A study on children patterned after that of Lane and Messé (1972) compared the allocation behavior of children who were given "sufficient," "insufficient," and "over-sufficient" resources to allocate. Coon et al. (1974) found that the children in their study allocated sufficient resources equitably. However, when the resources were either insufficient or oversufficient, most children gave the recipient who had done less more than his share. Only fourth- and sixth-grade children who were given insufficient resources to allocate departed from this trend, allocating more equitably. Because the allocators were not potential recipients (as they were in the Lane & Messé, 1972, study), self-interest was controlled. The results of this study remind us that the age trends observed in other studies pertain to a limited array of situations.

1. DESERVING

Overpaying and underpaying children for work they have done is assumed by most investigators to entail giving them more or less than they deserve. In an interesting intersection between research on equity and research on prosocial behavior, investigators have found that children who have been given gratuitious rewards (Staub, 1973) or have been overpaid (Long & Lerner, 1974) share more and donate more to charity than those who have been paid what they deserve. In a study patterned after that of Leventhal and Anderson (1970), Olejnik (1976) tested and confirmed the assumption that children believe that they should be paid in proportion to the work they do, then paid two groups of children the same amount for doing unequal amounts of work. Olejnik found that kindergarten children who were overpaid gave more to a needy refugee than children who were paid what they deserved (but there was a consistent tendency for this effect to diminish from first to third grade).

In the most elaborate study to date on deserving in children, Miller and Smith (1977) overpaid, underpaid, and properly paid children for participating in a task, then gave them an opportunity to donate some of their money to another child. Consistent with the principle of equity, these investigators found that the overpaid children gave more to the other child than the properly paid children; and, as we might expect, the underpaid children gave less. Miller and Smith (1977) also manipulated the circumstances surrounding the recipients' need. In one group, the recipients ostensibly had been properly paid, but had lost their money carelessly. In the other group, the responsibility for their predicament was not attributed to them. These investigators found that children in two of their three groups (those who had been properly paid and those who had been underpaid) gave more money to the recipients who were not responsible for their misfortune (i.e., who did not deserve to suffer) than to recipients who were responsible.

Studies showing developmental changes in the structure of allocation behavior in similar situations demonstrate that there is more to variations in "norms" or principles of resource allocation than variations in situations. Conversely, studies on deserving demonstrate that there is more to variations in resource allocation than variations in age. To understand the ways in which person-specific and situational forces exert their effects, we must discover how children of different ages process the information they are given—what goes on in their heads before they make a decision about how to divide resources. The external analysis of norms and situations must be supplemented by an internal analysis of cognition. A number of approaches have been adopted.

2. COGNITIVE DETERMINANTS OF RESOURCE ALLOCATION

a. Decision-Making Models. One way to investigate the cognitive inputs in resource allocation is to examine the decision-making process. Focusing on humanitarian norms, Schwartz (1975) has offered an eight-step model of what goes on in people's minds when they make decisions about helping those in need. In this analysis, Schwartz makes what I believe to be an important distinction—between *social* norms, defined as "expectations held by a group that persons ought to behave (act, think, believe) in particular ways" and *personal* or internalized norms, defined as those for which sanctions are "tied to the self-concept," and can relate to specific acts in specific situations as a sort of "subtype of attitude [pp. 122–123]." Although I would not call the latter cognitions norms, I believe, with Schwartz, that we must understand how people interpret their obligations toward others in particular situations to account for the ways in which they allocate resources.

The main method that Schwartz employs to discover what personal norms people have internalized is to ask them how obliged they would feel to help particular people in particular situations. For example, one of his questions reads "If a stranger to you needed a bone-marrow transplant and you were a suitable donor, would you feel a moral obligation to donate bone marrow?" As concerns the relationship among such feelings of moral obligation (i.e., personal norms), Schwartz (1977) writes:

> Values and norms are organized in vertical structures connecting values to general norms which foster their attainment and to more specific norms which articulate them in concrete situations. . . . Norms and values are also linked horizontally at given levels of abstraction. . . . The strength of horizontal structuring refers to the extent to which an action relevant to a given norm or value is perceived as having inescapable implications for others at the same level, so that they jointly influence the evaluation of the anticipated action [p. 232].

Schwartz (1975) considers the question of why people behave equitably in one situation and generously in others, and, like other investigators, roots his answer in situational constraints. He suggests that norms of exchange are intended to influence further exchanges, but humanitarian norms are not. However, as research on equity demonstrates, people appear to employ norms of exchange in one-shot encounters with strangers. Schwartz also suggests that humanitarian norms are activated by the perception of need in others; but, as Schwartz indicates, social psychologists have not yet supplied a satisfactory explanation of what happens when humanitarian norms conflict with other norms after they are aroused. More importantly in the present context, this model does not account for developmental changes. The natural place to look for such a theory is in the cognitive–developmental camp.

b. Extrapolations from Cognitive Development. Hook and Cook (1979) account for the systematic developmental changes in allocation behavior in terms of systematic changes in cognitive development. Citing research on Piaget's theory, they supply compelling evidence for a close association between age-related changes in "logico-mathematical" reasoning and age-related changes in the structure of allocation behavior: "allocation behaviors seem to follow a sequence of stages similar to those of thought in general and are roughly correspondent to Piaget's sequential stages of intellectual development [pp. 441–442]."

It is important to note that, in contrast to Schwartz's model, which concerns the content of thought (i.e., values, attitudes, and "personal norms"), cognitive–developmental theory focuses on the organization or structure of thought. Cognitive–developmental theorists are less concerned with *what* people feel morally obliged to do than with *how* they make moral decisions. One of their central concerns is with deciphering the principles underlying the vertical and horizontal organization of attitudes.

The thrust of Hook and Cook's analysis is that the ability to calculate first ordinal, then proportional equity is a necessary condition for employing these principles as a basis for allocation. Thus, an appropriately sophisticated degree of cognitive development is a necessary prerequisite for the ability to use sophisticated principles of distributive justice. These investigators outline the structure of logic associated with equality, ordinal equity, and proportional equity calculations, showing how each successive type is more complex than its predecessor.

Hook and Cook implicitly assume that when children think about justice, they employ the same cognitive structures that they do when they think about nonsocial relationships. This assumption is controversial. Piaget (1965) appears to endorse it, but later cognitive–developmental theorists such as Kohlberg (1976) and Turiel (1977) do not, arguing that, although cognitive development may be a necessary condition for moral development, structures of justice develop independently from other cognitive structures (see Krebs & Gillmore, in press). Whatever their exact position on this issue, a number of cognitive-developmental theorists have investigated the structure of justice reasoning in children.

c. Direct Investigations of the Structure of Justice Reasoning. Part of Piaget's (1965) analysis of moral development in children concerned distributive justice. Piaget's central conclusion was that children's conceptions of distributive justice go through three stages of development. In the first, "the germs of equalitarianism" do not produce any "genuine manifestations." In the second, "equalitarianism grows in strength and comes to outweigh any other consideration." And in the third, "mere equalitarianism makes way for a more subtle conception of justice which we may call 'equity,' [which involves] never defining equality without taking account of the way in which each individual is situated [pp. 284–285]."

Over the years, Piaget's early studies have been replicated and refined many times. Although his basic findings have proven to be relatively resilient, more precise research has found, as social psychologists would predict, that minor variations in the structures of the situations contained in his stories frequently produce significant differences in the responses they elicit (see Krebs, 1978b).

Since the time Piaget published his early analysis of the development of conceptions of justice, a number of psychologists have undertaken additional, more precise investigations. Kohlberg's work (1969, 1976) is notable in this respect; but the most thorough analysis of the development of conceptions of distributive justice has been offered by William Damon. It is worth considering Damon's research in some detail.

The basic method employed by Damon (1977) is to obtain children's reactions to stories similar to those employed by Piaget, but more elaborate. Consider the following story and questions from Damon (1977):

> Here are four little children just about your age. Well, actually, George here is a couple of years younger than the other three. Let's pretend that they were at school one day when their teacher, Miss Townsend, asked them to go outside with a couple of men. The men told the four kids that they really like bracelets made by little children, and they asked the kids if they would make some bracelets for them. The kids spent about fifteen or twenty minutes making lots of bracelets for the men. Michele, here, made a whole lot of bracelets, more than anyone else, and her's were the prettiest ones too. John and Ellen made some nice bracelets too; and, as you can see, John is the biggest boy there. George, the younger kid didn't do so well. He only made half of a bracelet, and it was not very pretty.
>
> Well, one of the men thanked them all for making bracelets, and put before them ten candy bars, which he said was their reward for making the bracelets. But he said that the kids would have to decide what the best way

was to split up the candy bars between themselves. Let's pretend that these are the ten candy bars [represent with poker chips]. How do you think the kids should split them up between themselves?

1. Should Michele get some extra for making the most and the prettiest? Is that fair? Why?
2. Should John get some extra for being the biggest boy? Is that fair? Why? What about Ellen?
3. Should George, the younger kid, get less than the other kids because he didn't do so well? Is that fair? Why?
4. Should the boys get more than the girls? Or should the girls get more than the boys? Why?
5. What's the best way to divide the candy bars? Why is that a good way?
6. What if you were . . . [the kid who made the most, the biggest boy, girl; ask about each in turn]? Would you think that this was the best way to split them up? Why [pp. 64–65]?

Damon's research and structural analysis produced the conceptions of justice outlined in Table 8.1. Note that according to Damon (1977), young children believe that resources should be shared *equally;* that

Table 8.1
Brief Descriptions of Early Positive Justice Levels[a]

Level 0-A:	Positive justice choices derive from S's wish that an act occur. Reasons simply assert the choices rather than attempting to justify them (that is, I should get it because I want to have it).
Level 0-B:	Choices still reflect S's desires but are now justified on the basis of external, observable realities such as size, sex, or other physical characteristics of persons (that is, We should get the most because we're girls). Such justifications, however, are invoked in a fluctuating, *a posteriori* manner, and are self-serving in the end.
Level 1-A:	Positive justice choices derive from notions of strict equality in actions (that is, that everyone should get the same). Justifications are consistent with this principle but are unilateral and inflexible.
Level 1-B:	Positive justice choices derive from a notion of reciprocity in actions: that persons should be paid back in kind for doing good or bad things. Notions of merit and deserving emerge. Justifications are unilateral and inflexible.
Level 2-A:	A moral relativity develops out of the understanding that different persons can have different, yet equally valid, justifications for their claims to justice. The claims of persons with special needs (that is, the poor) are weighed heavily. Choices attempt quantitative compromises between competing claims (e.g., He should get the most, but she should get some too).
Level 2-B:	S coordinates considerations of equality and reciprocity, so that S's positive justice choices take into account the claims of various persons and the demands of the specific situation. Choices are firm and clearcut, yet justifications reflect the recognition that all persons should be given their due (though, in many situations, this does not mean equal treatment).

[a] From Damon (1977) p. 75.

concerns with reciprocity and *equity* ("merit and deserving") emerge later; and that concerns with *need* emerge later still.

Cognitive–developmental research on distributive justice focuses on the way children think. Social psychological research on distributive justice focuses on the way children behave. There is a remarkable convergence between the two types of research. As children get older, they both *say* that people should allocate resources in terms of principles of justice (first equality, then equity), and they *behave* in accordance with these principles when they allocate. However, the observed association is very general. It reflects only rough age trends across different studies, and says little about the nature of the relationship underlying the association. Do children who possess the cognitive capacity to understand equity actually employ this type of reasoning when they allocate resources in their everyday lives; and if so, does it have any systematic effect on their behavior?

d. Hypothetical Reasoning, Practical Reasoning, and Behavior. Damon (1977) tested the relationship between hypothetical and real-life reasoning. He gave one group of children the hypothetical dilemma about sharing described earlier, then, 2 months later, placed them in an equivalent situation. In addition, he placed a second group of children in the situation, then, 2 months later, gave them the hypothetical dilemma. The results of the study revealed a high correlation ($r = .78$) between the level of justice reasoning of children in real and hypothetical situations. However, only about 50% of the children obtained the same score, with about a third obtaining more advanced scores on hypothetical than real-life reasoning.

Damon also assessed the children's behavior. If children behaved in a manner that paralleled their justice reasoning, the children at the lowest level should have behaved in a self-interested manner; the children at Level 1A (Table 8.1) should have distributed the candies equally; the children at Level 1B should have given more to the meritorious child; and the children of Level 2 should have given more to the younger, less competent child. Only the first two predictions were supported. There was a pervasive tendency for all children to distribute the candy equally; and none of the children at any of the justice levels distributed it equitably. However, children at justice levels 1B and above gave themselves significantly more candy bars when they had made the "prettiest and most" bracelets than they did in other conditions, suggesting that "although self-interest does not disappear with development, its nature changes. The claim of merit . . . was more accessible to children at 1B and above than to younger children and therefore was used disproportionately at the highest levels in constructing self-serving distributions [p. 116]." Overall, Damon was forced to conclude that "predicting a child's social conduct from his or her reasoning remains a complex and risky task," and that "predictions concerning children's conduct must also consider the different ways in which self-interest may influence different modes of reasoning in different contexts [p. 116]."

It is interesting to compare the results of Damon's study with the results of a study by Gunzburger et al. (1977). Gunzburger et al. assessed the level of moral development of a group of adolescents from the ninth to the twelfth grades, then determined how they allocated $5.60 among people who had made unequal contributions to a project. The results of this study indicated that (1) virtually none of the subjects at any age allocated in a self-interested manner; (2) about 20–25% of the subjects at all stages allocated resources equally; (3) the majority of subjects at Kohlberg's Stage 3 moral development (but at no other stage) allocated equitably; (4) the majority of subjects at Kohlberg's Stages 4, 5, and 6 allocated in accordance with a humanitarian principle (i.e., they gave a worker who worked less than his share of the time through no fault of his own as much as workers who had done their share); and (5) a minority (25%) of Stage 6 subjects compensated the worker who had blamelessly failed to contribute his share, out of their own earnings.

The first notable feature of these findings is that it is stage of development, not age, that is of primary concern in the cognitive–developmental analysis of resource allocation—there were no significant effects for age in the Gunzburger et al. study. Second, the findings suggest that equity is not the ultimate principle of allocation. Rather, in the type of situation typically investigated, it may peak at Stage 3 (which children typically approach in early adolescence). People at mature stages of moral development appear to behave in more humanitarian ways. Finally, although selfish behavior seems minimal (in experimental situations) in all but very immature children, people at all stages of moral development may employ principles of equality.

D. Sharing and Resource Allocation: General Conclusions

Justice involves the optimal balance of the rights and duties among interdependent people. In the words of Deutsch (1975), "the 'natural values of justice' are thus the values which foster effective social cooperation to promote individual well-being [p. 140]." Unmitigated self-interest is fine, until others follow the same course. Children quickly learn the limits of selfishness. In the view of Lerner et al. (1976), a child comes to realize the long-term benefits of relinquishing the power he or she has to gratify impulses immediately, and "makes a 'personal contract' with himself to orient himself to the world on the basis of what he earns or deserves via his prior investment rather than on the basis of what he can get at any given moment [p. 135]." Having made this contract, children develop an investment in the idea that it will pay off (i.e., that their world is a just one in which people get what they deserve). In this way, they derive a need to promote justice, and enter into a "social contract" with others. Whether the development of a sense of social justice occurs in this manner, more directly through indoctrination, or through the more general perception that things work better when people behave fairly, the evidence suggests that, when it comes to dividing resources at least, it begins to influence the social behavior of children at a very early age.

Research on resource allocation gives rise to five central conclusions: (1) from about age 4 or 5 on, resource allocation is patterned after principles of justice, although even among adults, these principles are often bent in the direction of self-interest; (2) the situations that people are in exert a strong influence on the principles they employ; (3) general intellectual ability and justice reasoning affect the ways in which people reach decisions about resource allocation; (4) structures of reasoning change with development, and (5) there is an association between thought and behavior, but it is complex.

Social psychological research indicates that the structure of resource allocation is determined by the structure of situations. Cognitive–developmental research indicates that the structure of resource allocation is determined by the structure of thought. Together this research indicates that the way in which people allocate resources is determined by the interaction between the structure of reasoning and the structure of situations. The circumstances surrounding situations affect the way goods are distributed, but different individuals may behave differently in the "same" situation because they view it from different perspectives.

Looked at only in terms of developmental changes in justice reasoning in equity-conducive situations, the evidence suggests that humanitarian principles are superior to the principle of proportional equity, which in turn is superior to the principle of ordinal equity, which is superior to the principle of equality, and so on. Interpreted superficially, this reserch would appear to support the value judgments of those who believe that humanitarianism and equity are the most adequate principles of justice. However, this conclusion ignores the input from situations. Although it may well be the case that humanitarianism and proportional equity are most just in the situations constructed by experimenters, other principles may be more adequate in other situations.

Indeed, only certain principles may be relevant to many incidents that involve the distribution of resources. For example, in most cases where individuals are asked to donate to charity, nothing is known about the inputs of the recipients, and, therefore, considerations of equity may be irrelevant.

Developmental research indicates that the cognitive ability to comprehend proportional equity takes time to develop, and, therefore, it is not available to young children as a principle of justice. Developmental research also indicates that the principle of proportional equity takes more factors into consideration, is based on finer distinctions, and so on, than, for example, the principle of equality—in situations that are structured in appropriate ways. In the Gunzburger *et al.* (1977) study, the ability to understand equity was a logical prerequisite to making the humanitarian adjustment. However, there is nothing in the developmental analysis that precludes the possibility that other principles, for example, more sophisticated principles of equality, will not ultimately subsume principles of humanitarianism and equity. The value of the developmental perspective lies in its ability to identify sequences of cognitive acquisitions. The challenge of the perspective lies in the difficult task of deciphering the logic that underlies the growth of ideas—which may supply a basis for evaluating them. I suspect that ultimately the principles that lie at the top of the hierarchy will not be principles such as equality, equity, and humanitarianism. Rather, they will be higher-order principles that prescribe the circumstances under which these principles should prevail.

II. REDRESSING INEQUITY: COMPENSATORY HELPING

However benign and benevolent we may be, even the best of us cannot help occasionally hurting other people. Hurting others and getting hurt is a fact of life. But there is one redeeming aspect of this unfortunate state of affairs: even though harm doing is an intrinsically antisocial type of behavior, it sometimes produces prosocial results. In particular, research on prosocial behaviors has shown that under some circumstances harming another induces "compensatory helping." At present, however, it is unclear why this effect occurs. Different investigators interpret it in different ways. For example, Freedman, Wallington, and Bless (1967) attribute it to *guilt;* McMillen (1971) to *shame;* Cialdini, Darby, and Vincent (1973) to a *general negative affective state*; and Berscheid and Walster (1967) to *equity*.

A. Guilt

In one of the earliest studies on compensatory helping, Darlington and Macker (1966) placed subjects in a situation in which the amount of money partners earned depended on their performance. The partner (a confederate of the experimenters) indicated that he or she was badly in need of money. Darlington and Macker found that subjects who "failed" to help the "needy other" were subsequently more prone to volunteer to donate blood than other subjects. In a later study, Carlsmith and Gross (1969) found that subjects who believed that they had given another subject painful electric shocks were more willing than other subjects to volunteer to assist on a socially useful project (making phone calls to save redwood trees in California). In a third study, Freedman *et al.* (1967) found that subjects who were induced to knock over a pile of index cards were more willing to volunteer for an experiment than subjects who were not. Freedman *et al.* (1967) also arranged for a confederate to divulge information to subjects about a test they were waiting to take, then asked the subjects whether they had received any prior information. Most subjects lied. Subsequently, these subjects evidenced a much greater willingness than other subjects to volunteer for another experiment, without pay. The authors of these four studies and others concluded that feelings of guilt, whether induced by harming another or transgressing, induce people to behave prosocially.

Guilt is a negative state, and as such, presses for relief. Theorists have long recognized that people employ three main tactics to allay guilt— reparation, expiation, and confession. Reparation is intrinsically prosocial: Making amends inevitably involves doing something for others. In contrast, the primary motive in expiation is to punish oneself. Confession falls somewhere in between. In some cases, for example when people agree to suffer on someone else's behalf, it is unclear whether the motivation underlying compensatory helping is to make expiation, reparation, or both. For example, in one study, Wallace and Sadalla (1966) found that subjects who were led to believe that they had broken an experimenter's machine were more willing than other subjects to sign up for an experiment in which they would receive electric shocks. In another study, Rawlings (1968) found that subjects whose errors caused their partners to suffer subsequently divided the duration of electric shocks between themselves and a third person in a way that was unfavorable to themselves. However, in other cases, a separation can be made.

Among the studies on compensatory helping, only one has supplied clear evidence for expiation (without reparation) following transgression. Wallington (1973) found that subjects who had been induced to transgress inflicted more painful shocks on themselves than did control subjects, even though their sacrifice conferred no benefits on anyone else. Subjects in this study were not given a chance to make reparation. Other studies have shown that when subjects are given a choice, they prefer reparation to expiation. For example, Freedman *et al.* (1967) found that subjects who had been induced to transgress did not choose to redress their transgression by volunteering for the more unpleasant of two experiments; and Berscheid and Walster (1967) found that harm doers were more likely to compensate their victims when they could make amends exactly than when they could only pay more.

How good an explanation for helping following harm doing does the construct of guilt offer? Although intuitively appealing, I believe that it is theoretically limited. Guilt is a hypothetical construct about which countless investigators have theorized, but for which none has as yet produced a valid measure. Before this construct can assume a more secure position among explanatory principles, the theory that specifies its parameters must be more explicit. In addition, there are at least two findings that suggest that there is more involved in compensatory helping than allaying guilt. It is generally assumed that guilt is a private, internal, self-judgmental reaction that people impose upon themselves. If this assumption is valid, private acts of harm doing should evoke as much guilt and compensatory helping as those that are witnessed by others. However, at least two studies have found that subjects who believed that their harm doing went undiscovered were less prone to engage in subsequent helping than those who did not (Silverman, 1967; Wallace & Sadalla, 1966). Second, several studies have found that witnessing others being hurt results in as much or more "compensatory helping" than hurting them (Cialdini *et al.*, 1973, Rawlings, 1968; Regan, 1971). The first set of findings suggests that the force that mediates the harm doing effect may be better construed as *shame* than as guilt. The second suggests that it may be a much more diffuse unpleasant state than either. Let us consider each of these possibilities in greater detail.

B. Shame

Shame implies looking bad in the eyes of others—even if the audience is only imaginary. In most of the studies on compensatory helping, the harm doing is public. Therefore, the motivation underlying the helping may be more to restore a tarnished self-image than to allay guilt. When you give another person painful shocks, you present yourself in a rather unfavorable way. When you knock over a pile of index cards, you seem like a "klutz." One good way to make yourself look good again is to engage in an impressive display of charitable behavior.

Robert Baer and I conducted a study (Krebs, 1970, see p. 266) on the effects of success and failure on helping. There were four conditions in the study: success that aids another, success that aids only oneself, failure that harms another, and failure that harms only oneself. We found that subjects who failed at a task and thereby publicly harmed another donated significantly more of their earnings to charity than subjects in other groups. Subjects who succeeded and thereby helped another donated significantly less. We interpreted these findings in terms of the motivation to maintain an optimally positive self-image, and attributed the compensatory helping of the subjects who harmed another to shame. However, the results also were consistent with the idea that the subjects were attempting to maintain equity.

McMillen (1971) supplied more persuasive evidence that feelings of shame may motivate compensatory helping. This study and another by McMillen and Austin (1971) found that subjects who took an experimentally created opportunity to cheat were, as we would expect, more inclined to help than those who did not. However, the disposition to help was reduced significantly in subjects when a confederate raised their self-esteem during the period intervening between the cheating and the opportunity to help. Apparently, looking good in front of another allayed the shame induced by the transgression.

Although the construct of shame may well supply a more adequate characterization of the distress evoked by harming another than the construct of guilt in many situations, it does not explain why blameless witnesses are disposed to help people they see harmed. What, then, would cause those who witness one person harming another to take measures to compensate the victim?

C. Feeling Bad

Troubled by the inability of constructs like guilt and shame to account for the harm-doing effect, Cialdini et al., (1973) suggested that "the sight of another's suffering . . . produce[s] a general, negative affective state [p. 505]," and that one way to relieve this state is to engage in prosocial behavior. In Cialdini's view people learn, through socialization, to feel good when they behave altruistically. Altruism serves "to alleviate a negative state because it is a personally gratifying and thus, mood-enhancing experience [Cialdini & Kenrick, 1976, p. 908]." In a study designed to test this model, Cialdini et al. (1973) arranged to have subjects knock over a set of index cards. As expected, these subjects were more disposed to help (by making telephone calls) than were control subjects. In addition, Cialdini *et al.* gave some of their subjects an unexpected reward of social approval during the time between the harm-doing incident and the opportunity to behave prosocially. As we would expect from McMillen's findings on the effect of shame, subjects whose self-esteem was elevated did not volunteer to help any more than did control subjects. However, Cialdini *et al.* also assessed the helping behavior of a group of subjects who merely witnessed the harm doing. They found that these subjects behaved very similarly to the harm doers in comparable conditions, suggesting that the motivation underlying the "compensatory helping" was not to relieve guilt or shame, but, rather, to allay a more general negative state induced by witnessing an unpleasant event.

The interpretations of compensatory helping that we have been considering are based on two general explanatory constructs—the idea that harming another or transgressing creates an imbalance that must be righted, and the idea that perpetrating or witnessing harm doing makes people feel bad. Equity theory, as outlined by Walster *et al.* (1978), is based on the assumption that imbalances in the relative outcomes of interpersonal relationships produce distress that motivates equity-redressing behavior. To what extent can it subsume the other explanations of compensatory helping?

D. Inequity Distress

Inasmuch as harm doing involves one person committing an act that "causes his partner's relative outcomes to fall short of his own [Walster *et al.,* 1978, p. 154]," it perpetrates an imbalance that, according to equity theory, should produce distress. To equity theorists, the precise form assumed by the distress is relatively unimportant. In the words of Walster *et al.* (1978), "compelling evidence exists to support the contention that an individual does feel intense distress after exploiting others.... Some theorists label it 'guilt'; others call it 'fear of retaliation'; still others label it 'dissonance,' 'empathy,' or 'conditioned anxiety' [p. 22]." What matters is that this distress gives rise to inequity-reducing behavior. And, of course, the most straightforward way to reestablish equity is by compensating the victim.

Equity theory improves on other positions by supplying a clear indication of the form that compensatory behavior should assume. Corollary 1, Proposition IV of Walster's theory states that "other things being equal, the more adequate an exploiter perceives an available equity-restoring technique to be, the more likely he is to use this technique to restore equity [p. 36]." It seems plausible that people would not be motivated to overcompensate victims, but equity theory also assumes that they should not be motivated to undercompensate them. A number of studies support this assumption. For example, Berscheid and Walster (1967) arranged to have women from a church auxiliary prevent their partners from winning two books of trading stamps during a game. These investigators found that the willingness of the subjects to help the victim in a second game depended on the extent to which they could compensate her equitably. Subjects who could help the victim win two books of stamps (and thus establish equity) helped her significantly more than subjects who had the opportunity to help her win either more or less. These findings were replicated by Berscheid, Walster, and Barclay (1969). In addition, there is evidence that impartial observers are motivated to redress inequities. Baker (1974) arranged for subjects to observe players receive an inequitable share of the winnings from a game. Later, when the subjects were given an opportunity to allocate resources, they tended to permit the inequitably treated players to catch up.

On the surface, equity theory would appear to offer an adequate account of the results of studies that have been interpreted in terms of guilt. The concepts of expiation and reparation can be quite readily translated into equity theory. Expiation involves restoring equity by reducing the resources of the overpaid; and reparation involves restoring equity by increasing the resources of the underpaid. The evidence suggests that reparation is preferred to expiation. According to Walster et al. (1978), "Other things being equal, the less costly an exploiter perceives an available equity-restoring technique to be, the more likely he is to use this technique to restore equity [p. 36]." Helping a person you have harmed is generally less costly than evening then score by harming yourself.

The equity account also is consistent with the results of studies that have evoked the construct of shame. According to Walster et al. (1978), the distress following harm doing "is presumed to arise from two sources: fear of retaliation and threatened self-esteem [p. 22]." There is a close connection between self-esteem, esteem from others, and shame (Turner, 1968). In cases where inequities are public, people generally have more to lose by failing to redress them than when they are private. Thus, at this level, equity theory also appears able to account for the results of research that has attributed compensatory harm doing to shame.

Finally, the idea of equity is consistent with some of the findings from research on the effects of negative states. Walster *et al.* (1978) assume that all inequities produce "distress." However, whereas Cialdini assumes that the positive lift people get from helping others is a result of early conditioning, equity theory attributes it to the relief from distress associated with righting a wrong or restoring equilibrium. A central difference between the equity and negative state explanations is that, according to the latter, people should be able to give themselves a lift by helping others when they feel down for any reason, whereas equity theory focuses only on the relief from distress obtained by redressing inequity.

It should not be surprising that the construct of equity supplies a satisfying explanation for the main results of research on compensatory helping. After all, the concept of compensation implies restoring some form of balance or equity. As indicated by Walster *et al.* (1978), there has been more research by equity theorists on exploiter–victim relations than on any other issue. However, there are at least three problems with the idea that the motivation underlying compensatory helping is to redress inequity. First, in most of the studies on compensatory helping, the harm doers do not actually compensate their victims; rather, they help *third persons*. Second, it is not immediately obvious how the prosocial behavior of people who *witness* harm doing serves to redress equity. And finally, some studies have found that *witnesses* to harm doing become disposed to help *third persons*. Let us consider each of these problems in turn.

E. Problems with the Equity Explanation of Compensatory Helping

1. GENERALIZED COMPENSATION

Looked at in terms of the concrete relationships involved, there is nothing equity restoring about harming one person, then helping someone else—it leaves the original victim exploited, and it creates an inequity in the helper's relationship with the third party. The results of studies showing that people are more prone to, for example, donate to charity, after they have perpetrated a misdeed raise, once again, the question "equity with whom?"

Walster *et al.* (1978) have considered this question as it pertains to exploiter–victim relationships. In their words, "Conventional Equity researchers would argue that the injustices one inflicts on a partner (or suffers at his hands) should motivate one to right things with his partner—and only his partner [p. 205]." However, they suggest, people may compensate third parties to maintain "equity with the world." In a study designed to investigate this possibility, Austin (see Walster *et al.*, 1978) hypothesized (1) that when a person cannot restore equity with a victim, the person "may settle for paying back (or victimizing) a totally different partner in a totally different situation, and at least maintaining equity with the world [p. 206];" and, (2) that when a person "is secure that he will never see his second partner again, he may be quite willing to abandon the equitableness of his relationship with a specific partner in order to maintain equity with the world [p. 206]." Austin tested these hypotheses by arranging for women to be either equitably paid, over-paid, or underpaid by a partner on one task, then giving them an oppor-tunity to share some of the money they made with a different partner, on a second task. Austin found that when the women expected to see their partners again, they split the money equally. However, when they did not, the women who previously had been underpaid took more for themselves; and the women who previously had been overpaid took (slightly) less.

These findings extend those of Lane and Messé (1972). They suggest that when people balance inputs and outputs on the scales of justice they retain considerable flexibility in whom they put on the "others" side of the scale. Austin showed that people may perpetuate inequity in one relationship to promote equity in another one. Given the vast range of conceivable standards of comparison, almost any outcome could be jus-tified as equitable. It is easy to imagine some people believing that, because their lot in life has been particularly unfortunate, the "world" or "fate" owes them compensation, and, therefore, that it is equitable for them to grab everything they can get. Equity theorists have not pro-duced a clear statement of the principles that define people's choice of comparison others. In the words of Walster *et al.* (1978): "about all they can say is that many individuals compare themselves with a surprising variety of groups [p. 208]."

Although there is little evidence on people's preference for compari-son others in the prosocial literature, there is a suggestion that, given a choice, people prefer to compensate third parties rather than their victims, especially if compensating their victims entails facing them (Freedman, 1970; Rawlings, 1970). In almost all the studies on compen-satory helping, harm doers are not required to face their victims after they harm them. They are not in an ongoing relationship with them. In this circumstance, the evidence suggests that people are motivated to counterbalance their misdeed with a good deed, and to reestablish a more internal equilibrium. The central factors that people would appear to balance in these situations are either (*a*) their conceptions of them-selves as good people and the goodness of their behavior in their own eyes (guilt) and in the eyes of others (shame); or (*b*) what they get from the world in general, and what they give ("equity with the world").

2. THE PROSOCIAL WITNESS

The evidence that proved most problematic to the guilt and shame explanations of harm doing—the prosocial effect of witnessing harmdoing—also is problematic to equity theory. Because witnesses are not involved in the perpetration or receipt of inequity (i.e., because they are not part of an inequitable relationship) there ought not be any reason for them to engage in compensatory helping. The prosocial behavior of witnesses could, of course, be dismissed as irrelevant to concerns of equity and justice. It might, for example, be attributed to empathy or some other affective response (see Bateson & Coke, 1981). However, witnessing harm doing could violate observers' sense of equity and justice; and the resulting behavior could be aimed at redressing the perceived injustice. If this were the case, it would require an even greater elaboration of existing theories than we have hitherto considered.

The idea that people are motivated to insure that others are treated justly is consistent with Lerner's notion that people have a personal investment in preserving the assumption that the world is just—that people get what they deserve. Lerner and others have established quite convincingly that when people are able to compensate innocent victims, they tend to do so; but when they cannot, they derogate them (Lerner, 1975; 1977; Lerner & Simmons, 1966). In Lerner's view, the need to believe that the world is just is derived from the personal need to believe that one's efforts will be rewarded. It also could be more directly acquired as an aspect of moral reasoning (see Piaget, 1965). Whatever its origin, it seems safe to conclude that people are not only motivated to foster equity in their relations with others and to insure that, in general, they personally get what they deserve, they also sometimes are motivated to insure that others are treated justly, even when it involves taking action that is costly and inequitable to themselves.

3. GENERALIZED COMPENSATORY HELPING: THE PROSOCIAL WITNESS

It is unclear whether present formulations of equity theory are flexible enough to account for generalized compensatory helping and the helping behavior of prosocial witnesses. Even if they were, research on prosocial behavior contains one last double-barreled challenge. When witnesses are unable to compensate victims (and perhaps even when they are), they may behave prosocially toward third parties. It is difficult to imagine how the existing versions of equity theory could be stretched to

account for this phenomenon. Although the witness's charitable behavior may enhance the recipient's equity with the world, the connections between this behavior and the observation of harm doing to someone else is unclear. Perhaps the observation of injustice instills within
people the desire to redress it, which, when it cannot be satisfied directly,
becomes generalized to other situations. Perhaps witnesses behave prosocially to establish to themselves that they are different from the harm
doers they have observed. At present, the internal cognitive dynamics of
the people who engage in generalized compensatory prosocial behavior
remain largely unexplored.

F. Compensatory Helping: General Conclusions

Research on compensatory helping may be interpreted as leading to
two quite different conclusions. First, it indicates that if the behavior of
those who help after perpetrating or witnessing harm is motivated by a
sense of injustice, this sense is a large and flexible one. People are concerned not only with maintaining equity between themselves and those
with whom they are in a relationship, but also with internal standards
and with the world in general. When they harm others, they are
motivated to behave prosocially toward people who were not party to the
original injustice. When they witness harm, they not only compensate
the victims, they also often help people who were in no way involved.

This conclusion assumes that all the findings we have considered can
be accounted for by a single theory or explanatory principle—in this case
the motive to preserve equity or justice. Alternatively, there may be
qualitatively different dynamics involved in different cases. For example, witnessing a person getting hurt may evoke an empathic response
that may motivate prosocial behavior completely independently from
whether the victim deserved to get hurt or not (and, in general, regardless of whether or not the observer feels that there has been an injustice;
see Krebs, 1975). If this alternative conclusion were valid, it would
support the current tendency for social psychologists to interpret findings on compensatory helping in terms of the particular constructs that
appear to supply the most plausible explanation for their particular
findings.

III. REDRESSING INEQUITY:
PROSOCIAL RECIPROCITY

Disrupting the harmony of interpersonal relations has a negative
ring. This ring resonates appropriately around behaviors that harm

others. However, the delicate balance of interpersonal exchange can be disrupted in other, more benign ways—for example, by helping others. A spate of research on prosocial behavior suggests that people are motivated to correct the imbalance created when they receive gratuitous help, and that the most common way of doing it is to reciprocate the assistance (see, for example, Blau, 1963; Pruitt, 1968; Regan, 1971; Schopler, 1970; Staub & Sherk, 1970; and Wilke & Lanzetta, 1970). In contrast to research on compensatory helping, which focuses on the reactions of the *perpetrator* of *harm*, research on prosocial reciprocity focuses on the reactions of the *recipient* of *help*.

Gouldner (1960) has argued that reciprocity is a universal norm. Subsequent evidence has shown that if not universal, reciprocity is certainly pervasive. It has been observed in young children (Durkin, 1961), in other cultures (Gergen, Ellsworth, Maslach, & Seipel, 1975; Mauss, 1954), and even in other species (Trivers, 1971). But reciprocity is not unconditional, in humans at least. Gouldner (1960) has specified four factors that regulate it: (1) the recipient's need; (2) "the resources of the donor"; (3) the "motives imputed to the donor"; and (4) the voluntariness of the act of giving (p. 171). Subsequent studies have supplied support for all four conditions. (See, for example, Garrett & Libby, 1973; Goranson & Berkowitz, 1966; Greenberg, 1968; Greenberg & Frisch, 1972; Gross & Latané, 1974; Leventhal, Weiss, & Long, 1969; Muir & Weinstein, 1962; Nadler, Fisher, & Streufert, 1974; Nemeth, 1970; and Thibaut & Reicken, 1955.)

A. Why Do People Reciprocate Assistance?

There is little doubt that the form of many helping exchanges is reciprocal; but why are people disposed to reciprocate assistance? Researchers have considered four main reasons: (1) people become attracted to those who help them; (2) people desire to abide by the norm of reciprocity; (3) people feel "indebted"; and (4) people seek to redress inequity.

1. INTERPERSONAL ATTRACTION

It makes sense to suspect that receiving help from someone would cause one to like the person, and, therefore, to become increasingly prone to help the person in return. However, research has not supplied much support for this plausible idea. Several studies have failed to find a positive relationship between attraction and reciprocity. For example, Stapleton, Nacci, and Tedeschi (1973) found that subjects reciprocated the rewards they received from "partners" equivalently, regardless of their attractiveness; and Regan (1971) found that the willingness of confederates to reciprocate a favor was not affected by their subsequent liking for the person who proferred it. Studies by Greenberg, Block, and Silverman (1971) and Nemeth (1970) have supported these findings. In addition, a number of studies have found that receiving favors that cannot be reciprocated evokes resentment toward the donor.

2. NORMS

In his early influential paper, Gouldner (1960) argued that reciprocity is a universal norm that prescribes "(1) people should help those who have helped them; and (2) people should not injure those who have helped them [p. 171]." Some of the first psychological studies on prosocial behavior (for example, Berkowitz & Daniels, 1964) also viewed reciprocity as a norm. I discussed some of the problems with normative explanations of prosocial behavior earlier. They also apply to the norm of reciprocity.

3. INDEBTEDNESS

According to Greenberg (1968), receiving favors may produce an unpleasant psychological state akin to cognitive dissonance that he calls "indebtedness" (see also Greenberg, 1980; Greenberg & Shapiro, 1971). Reformulating and extending the conditions of reciprocity laid down by Gouldner (1960), Greenberg suggests that the sense of indebtedness is affected by (1) the relative difference between the recipient's and donor's rewards and costs; (2) the extent to which helping behavior is evoked by the recipient, the donor, and external factors; (3) (with Gouldner) the donor's motives; and (4) the reactions of third parties. Studies by Saxe and Greenberg (1974) and Tessor, Gatewood, and Driver (1968) have supported these points.

4. EQUITY

Equity is a rarified and mercurial state. It is disrupted when people harm others; and it is sent awry when people render assistance. All else equal, helping another induces a state of inequity. Thus, according to equity theory, helpers and recipients of help should feel distress. In the words of Hatfield *et al.* (1978):

> Undeserved gifts produce inequity in a relationship. If the participants know the recipient can and will reciprocate, the inequity is viewed as temporary, and thus it will produce little distress. If the participants know the recipient cannot or will not reciprocate, however, a real inequity is produced; the participants will experience distress [p. 133].

Walster *et al.* (1978) have espoused the hope that their equity theory would supply a "general theory of social behavior." Earlier I examined its ability to subsume the various explanations of compensatory helping. Here I will examine its ability to subsume the other explanations of reciprocity.

As far as the central constructs go, Walster's equity theory would seem easily able to encompass both the normative explanation of reciprocity and Greenberg's theory of indebtedness; and it would seem able to explain the lack of support for the explanation based on interpersonal attraction. Quite simply, the norm of reciprocity could be interpreted as a general statement about one of the forms that equity can assume; the construct of indebtedness could be construed as one type of inequity distress; and the lack of attraction for donors felt by recipients could be attributed to their resentment for the distress the donors have evoked. In addition, Walster's equity theory would appear to take the analysis of reciprocity further. The norm of reciprocity dictates that people should repay assistance, but it does not specify the form that the repayment should assume. People could repay the assistance equally; they could return more help than they received; they could reciprocate a token amount, or they could reciprocate an amount equivalent to the donor's losses relative to his or her gains. Equity theory, of course, prescribes that the preferred form of reciprocity should maximize the balance between the gains of each participant in the relationship, relative to his or her costs.

A number of studies have supported the assumption that, when people reciprocate favors, they tend to do so equitably. The research cited earlier supporting Gouldner's contention that reciprocity is affected by the recipient's need and the donor's resources, and research supporting Greenberg's contention that indebtedness is affected by the relative difference between the recipient's and donor's rewards and costs support the equity formulation. In another study, (Tesser et al., 1968) subjects indicated that they would feel more gratitude if they received a picture from a poor aunt (i.e., one whose inputs were low) than from one who was well off. And Pruitt (1968) found that subjects playing a mixed motive game reciprocated more when they received a high proportion of their partner's resources than when they received a larger absolute amount. Thus, in the same way that the findings of several studies indicate that the preferred form of compensatory helping is equitable, the findings of several studies indicate that people prefer to reciprocate assistance equitably. However, of course, positive findings such as these do not negate the possibility that other forms of reciprocity sometimes prevail.

Although research on reciprocal helping contains considerable support for the central assumptions of Walster et al.'s equity theory, it, like research on compensatory helping, also contains a number of findings that are problematic. In particular, equity theory would appear to have difficulty acounting for (1) the influence of the motives imputed to the donor; (2) the phenomenon of generalized reciprocity; and (3) evidence that receiving unearned benefits evokes distress. Let us consider each of these issues in turn.

5. PROBLEMS WITH THE EQUITY EXPLANATION OF PROSOCIAL RECIPROCITY

a. The Motives of the Giver   Considering the conditions of reciprocity and indebtedness laid down by Gouldner and Greenberg, we might ask, why, from the perspective of equity theory, should voluntarily given assistance evoke more reciprocity than compulsorily given assistance. It seems reasonable to assume that the costs of giving would be higher for donors who were disinclined to give than for those who were more positively motivated, and, therefore, that it would be equitable for them to receive more rather than less in return. And why, in general, should people's motives be so important? Motives need not necessarily affect the balance of inputs and outcomes.

Walster *et al.* (1978) consider these questions: "Why, in equity terms, should a recipient have such different reactions to the altruistic giver than to the giver who was forced to give or who had "ulterior motives? [p. 99]." They give two answers: (1) "goodness, unselfishness, and moral character [may be perceived as] positive inputs to a relationship, in and of themselves"; and (2) because the recipient may want to "cement his relations" with well versus poorly motivated helpers. I must say that I do not find these explanations very satisfying. First, people sometimes exploit altruistic donors of good character rather than treating them equitably (see Nemeth, 1970). And, second, most of the exchanges that have been investigated experimentally are one-shot affairs in which subjects do not expect to see their partners again. In most psychological theories, the construct of equity refers primarily to relatively tangible inputs and outcomes. It is, of course, possible to argue that anything that affects the form of an exchange is an input. However, accounting for the influence of motives in this manner seems inadequate. Our sense of indebtedness to people is strongly influenced by our perception of their intentions. In many cases we do not feel obliged to repay people who were forced to help us; and we feel strongly beholden to those who wanted to help, but could not (see Piaget, 1965). The motives underlying helping seem to be more a precondition for the desire to reciprocate than merely an aspect of the inputs to an exchange. If motives are to be construed as inputs, they are a very special kind—one, clearly, that warrants more attention in equity theory than it has received.

b. Generalized Reciprocity.   Reciprocity makes sense. If someone helps you and you help back, you are "even," and the relationship between the two of you is left in a balanced state. Observing incidents of reciprocity leads us to believe that the people involved are motivated to maintain balanced relations with others. However, as we have seen, behavior that balances the input–outcome ratios *between* two people may also serve to balance the ratio of costs and gains *within* each individual, or between an individual and the world. In the same way that studies on compensatory helping have found that people who have harmed another are disposed to behave prosocially to those they have not harmed, studies on reciprocity have found that people who receive favors also are prone to help third parties (Goranson & Berkowitz, 1966; Greenglass, 1969). This phenomenon has been called *generalized reciprocity*, although, as I argued in an earlier paper (Krebs, 1970, p. 296), it is unclear whether such generalized helping actually involves reciprocity. The phenomenon of "generalized reciprocity" leads to a significant enlargement of the context of social exchange. It suggests that receiving help from one person engenders the motivation to help any number of other people. Thus, inasmuch as prosocial behavior is governed by a desire to maintain a balance between what we give and what we get, the means of maintaining it are magnified infinitely.

The problems raised for equity theory by "generalized" or "displaced" reciprocity are similar to the problems raised by third person helping following harm doing. If we confine the equity analysis to the particular relationships in question, receiving the initial help creates an inequitable relationship between the two people involved, and giving help to a third person creates an inequitable relationship between the original recipient and the third person. However, viewed from another angle, "generalized reciprocity" balances the inputs and outcomes of the person who first receives, then gives; and it may serve to maintain "equity with the world." As with research on generalized compensatory helping, research on generalized reciprocity suggests that the principles of justice that guide prosocial behavior are larger and more flexible than those that pertain to the concrete exchanges between specific people.

c. How Do You Feel When You Receive Assistance?   Proposition III of Walster *et al.*'s formulation of equity theory contends that inequity evokes a negative affective state that they call "distress." Although, as pointed out by Adams and Freedman (1976), there has been little phenomenological research on the nature of affective reactions to inequity, this proposition seems eminently plausible in situations (*a*) where we are victims and get less than we deserve; and (*b*) where we perpetrate inequities by harming others. But equity theory also contends that we feel bad when we receive gratuitous help—when we get more than we deserve. Thus, it implies that people should resist favors and assistance unless they feel that they deserve them or can pay them back. A number of studies have supported this somewhat counterintuitive proposition. Studies by Berkowitz (1968), Berkowitz and Friedman (1967), Greenberg (1968), and Morris and Rosen (1973), have shown that subjects in psychological experiments are more willing to accept gifts when they can reciprocate them than when they cannot. In a naturalistic study, Krebs and Baldwin (see Krebs & Whitten, 1972) found that students could not even give away dollar bills to people leaving a subway in Boston Commons (although there are a number of alternative explanations for this finding). Gergen and Gergen (1971) found that countries preferred aid from the United States that could be reciprocated over aid that could not. And, in a somewhat more elaborate study, Gergen et al. (1975) found that the subjects like donors who requested exact repayment for "gifts" they had given more than either generous or mercenary donors. Findings such as these support the assumption that receiving assistance can induce distress, and that this distress can be relieved by reciprocating the assistance. However, if that were all there was to the matter, more people would punish their enemies by doing them favors. Other research has shown that receiving favors does not necessarily produce distress.

Isen and her colleagues designed a series of studies in which subjects received gratuitious favors, then were given an opportunity to behave prosocially. In one study, Isen and Levin (1972) gave students who were studying in the library a cookie, then, later, arranged for a confederate to ask them to participate in an experiment on creativity. In another, Isen and Levin (1972) arranged for people to find dimes in telephone booths, then watched to see whether they would help a confederate pick up a manila folder full of papers. In a third, people who found dimes were given an opportunity to mail a lost letter (Levin & Isen, 1975). In a fourth study, Isen, Clark, and Schwartz (1976) gave people a free packet of stationary, then tested their willingness to make a phone call for a person in distress who ostensibly had used his or her last dime and called them by mistake. In all of these studies, the subjects who received unexpected favors behaved more helpfully than those who did not.

From an equity perspective, we would expect the subjects in Isen's studies to have experienced distress because they received an unreciprocated favor, and to have engaged in "generalized reciprocity" to reduce the distress. However, Isen interpreted her findings in a quite different way. She argued that her subjects experienced a "warm glow of goodwill" from receiving a favor, not distress, and that the warm glow gave rise to the prosocial behavior. Later studies supported this formulation (Isen & Levin, 1972; Isen *et al.*, 1976). In one study, Isen *et al.* (1978) showed that positive experiences such as receiving an unexpected gift and winning a game caused subjects to rate a car and television set more positively and to recall more positive words than other subjects. Isen concluded that positive experiences produce a positive outlook that increases people's benevolence.

Evidence on the affective mediators of reciprocity creates a quandry. Some studies suggest that receiving a favor makes people feel bad, and that these people behave prosocially to relieve distress; but others suggest that receiving favors makes people feel good, and that they behave prosocially because they are in a benevolent mood. We could turn to studies that have focused more directly on the nature of the affective mediators of helping in search of a resolution, but these studies also have produced contradictory results. Some research has found that positive affective states mediate helping, but others have found that helping is mediated by negative affective states. In support of the first relationship, Aderman (1972) found that reading happy statements resulted in an increase in prosocial behavior; Moore, Underwood, and Rosenhan (1973) found that reminiscing about happy experiences fostered helping, (whereas reading and reminiscing about sad events did not); and Underwood *et al.* (1977) found a linear decrease in the number of pennies children donated as the moods the children experienced varied from happy to neutral to sad. However, in support of the second relationship, Cialdini and Kenrick (1976) found that inducing elementary and high school students to reminisce about *sad* experiences resulted in an increase in donations; Cialdini *et al.* (1973) found that elevating people's moods by giving them a reward or social approval resulted in a *reduction* in prosocial behavior; and Cialdini and Kenrick (1976) found that, whereas children are more likely to behave prosocially when they feel good than when they feel bad, adults behave in exactly the opposite way.

The conclusion I draw from these seemingly contradictory studies is that receiving a favor may make people feel either good or bad, depending on the meaning and function associated with it. There are at least two important differences between, for example, the Gergen studies, where recipients appeared to resent the favor, and Isen studies, where recipients appeared to appreciate the favor: (1) subjects in Gergen's studies received assistance from identifiable others with whom they tended to be in a relationship, whereas subjects in Isen's studies received benefits accidentally or from fleeting donors; and (2) subjects in

Gergen's studies were required to indicate how they felt about their benefactors, whereas subjects in Isen's studies were not. It appears more likely that the subjects in Gergen's studies would have made social comparisons that served to increase the salience of the donor's status. The reason why these subjects resented the favors they received may have related to the loss in status accompanying them. In the words of Homans (1961) "Anyone who accepts from another a service he cannot repay in kind incurs inferiority as a cost of receiving the service. The esteem he gives the other he foregoes himself [p. 320]." Typically, those with high status give, and those with low status receive. One way to establish your status is to give to others who cannot repay. There is a great deal of anthropological evidence on gift giving that demonstrates the validity of this principle. The potlatch or gift-giving battle engaged in by West Coast Indians, where the amount one can give is a direct measure of his prestige, is a particularly clear case in point (see Walster *et al.*, 1978). In exchanges of this sort, those who receive a disproportionate share of the tangible goods pay for it with interest in their loss of esteem.

Another circumstance under which the receipt of favors may produce distress is when the favors are given tactically, to create obligation. Brehm and Cole (1966), and Schopler and Thompson (1968) have found that, when people feel manipulated, they may experience a distressful state called *reactance*. However, in these studies, subjects who experienced distress were *less* likely to reciprocate a favor than those who did not.

In contrast, people may feel good after receiving favors when their need for assistance is great, when the cost of helping is low, and when the people who give the assistance do not achieve gains in relative status. We do not usually feel bad toward a person who calls an ambulance and comforts us after an accident. And, as the Isen studies indicate, people appear to feel good when they are given gratuitious help from strangers even though their need is low.

Although there is little evidence on the issue, I suspect that most affective states that mediate prosocial behavior will prove to be epiphenomenal or at least of secondary significance to the cognitive states associated with them. It is less whether people feel good or bad that determines whether they will help, than why they feel good or bad, and how the helping behavior relates to the meaning attached to the events that caused their affective state (i.e., the function it serves). Staub (1978) has outlined a model that focuses on the significance of the comparison between (a) people's current affective states and their customary affective states; and (b) people's affective states and the affective states of others. In Staub's model, people behave prosocially when they feel better than usual relative to how much better than usual others feel. The assumption that the significance of affective experiences is assessed vis a vis some standard or comparison level is consistent with the findings of studies indicating that people attempt to maintain "own equity" and "equity with the world." However, I suspect that ultimately people's behavior will prove to be determined more by what they *think* about how they feel vis a vis various standards, and, in particular, how they think they *deserve* to feel, than by relative affective comparisons. When people feel better than they believe they deserve to feel, they will sacrifice resources, help others, and even punish themselves to even the score. If people feel worse than they believe they should, they will take measures to elevate their affective state—in some cases by behaving selfishly (buying themselves a present) and in some cases by behaving generously (and, for example, reaping enhanced esteem).

In conclusion, whether receiving gratuitous favors produces distress or not depends on the meaning attached to them and the context in which they occur. When they are perceived as godsends, they may make their recipients feel good. When they signal status differences or create obligation, they make recipients feel bad. People behave prosocially when they feel both good and bad. It is less people's affective states that determine how they behave than their interpretation of their affective state in the context of how they usually feel, how others feel, and how they deserve to feel. Inasmuch as a sense of inequity entails a sense of injustice, it should be accompanied by distress (whether there can be just inequities depends, of course, on how one defines inequity). However, receiving gratuitous favors may not violate a recipient's sense of justice; and people may, as Isen and her colleagues have suggested, behave prosocially simply because they feel good.

B. Prosocial Reciprocity: General Conclusions

There can be little question that people possess a wide-ranging disposition to reciprocate assistance, that receiving undeserved favors often evokes distress and that, in some situations, the form the assistance takes is equitable. However, the equity account of prosocial reciprocity fails to supply satisfying explanations for why the motives attributed to benefactors affect the reactions of recipients, why people engage in generalized reciprocity, and why recipients sometimes feel good when they receive undeserved favors. Equity theory appears to apply only to a subset of situations. Ultimately, people's reactions to favors are determined by their attributions of motives, their interpretation of the meaning of the gift, their overriding sense of justice, and their anticipation of the consequences of their behavior.

IV. PROSOCIAL BEHAVIOR, EQUITY, AND JUSTICE: GENERAL CONCLUSIONS

A substantial amount of research indicates that people may behave prosocially to maintain equity and justice in interpersonal relations. It is also the case, of course, that people may behave prosocially for other reasons, and that people may employ other forms of behavior to foster equity and justice. The relationship between prosocial behavior, equity, and justice is far from perfect. Prosocial behavior may produce inequities; and inequities may be redressed through antisocial behavior and psychological devices.

An examination of the relationship between prosocial behavior and justice leads quite naturally to a focus on the reactions of perpetrators of harm and recipients of help. It is important to note that compensatory helping and prosocial reciprocity occur in response to inequities—after the balance of a relationship has been disrupted. The association between prosocial behavior and equity is far less firm in balanced relationships. Indeed, in these cases, prosocial behavior is intrinsically *inconsistent* with equity. To quote Walster *et al.* (1978) "The benefactor who gives and gives and gets little in return is a participant in an inequitable and unprofitable relationship. His recipient is a participant in an inequitable albeit profitable relationship [p. 102]."

Even in situations where inequities have occurred, people may redress them through antisocial or "psychological" means. Recipients of harm may retaliate. Benefactors may demand compensation. And perpetrators of harm may restore "psychological equity" by derogating their victims, convincing themselves that their victims are not really suffering, or denying responsibility.

Whether people will attempt to restore actual equity or psychological equity, and why, is at present poorly understood. Walster *et al.* (1978) suggest that people will employ the most effective and least costly technique. For example, Hatfield, Walster, and Piliavin (1978) interpret the behavior of bystanders in emergencies in these terms, citing studies that have found that people tend not to help when the cost is high (because, for example, the victim had blood trickling from his mouth (Piliavin & Piliavin, 1972) or a port wine stain birthmark (Piliavin, Piliavin, & Rodin, 1975). However, these interpretations tend to be post hoc and incomplete. Indeed, it is unclear whether the subjects in these studies even experience a sense of inequity. I do not intend to explore the issue of psychological versus actual equity at great length here; however, I would like to express some reservation about the dichotomy. Inasmuch as equitable behavior is determined by the cognitive processes that mediate it, "psychological" devices are not orthogonal to "actual" behavior. The way in which people process information may or may not give rise to equitable behavior. It may or may not distort reality or be defensive. It makes sense to assume that "psychological" analyses may be affected by the costs and availability of various behavioral options. However, people sometimes engage in equitable behavior at great cost, in situations where few options exist. Certainly some of the subjects in the Piliavin studies helped in the "high cost" condition. A full analysis of the conditions under which people employ "psychological" versus "actual" equity-restoring techniques must attend to the interaction between aspects of people such as their level of cognitive and moral development (the cognitive forces that mediate psychological analyses) and aspects of situations such as cost and availability. Decision-making models such as that of Schwartz (1977) supply one way of attacking this problem. Models of moral reasoning such as that of Damon (1977) supply another.

There is no invariant relationship between any principle of justice and any prosocial or altruistic behavior. One of the primary functions of principles of justice is to resolve conflicts between self and others. In some cases, a just solution is in a person's immediate self-interest. In other cases, it is in the interest of others. For example, whether a humanitarian norm prescribes "selfish" or "altruistic" behavior depends on whether you or someone else has the greater need. This is not to say that different principles of justice do not tend to prescribe differentially "altruistic" behavior. During the first decade or so of a child's life, principles of fairness would appear to conflict quite consistently with self-interest. Thus, behaving "fairly" often entails behaving "altruistically" (i.e., understanding that others may have a conflicting point of view [role-taking], and learning to accommodate to their rights). The tendency for children to behave increasingly generously through the elementary and high school years may reflect the growing power of increasingly sophisticated principles of fairness. However, as I have argued elsewhere (Krebs, 1978a), although the principles of justice that evolve during the first three stages of moral development become increasingly conducive to "altruistic behavior," this conduciveness may well peak at Kohlberg's Stage 3. The principles that evolve after that prescribe an increasing attentiveness to the larger social context, sometimes in a way that is inconsistent with generosity toward individuals. For example, at Stage 3 people might give money to a beggar because they feel sorry for him, but at later stages they may refuse to give because they believe that such "generosity" is ultimately destructive to the social system that they (and the beggar) have an obligation to preserve.

The central purpose of the present chapter was to examine the capacity of equity theory and other theories of justice to supply an overriding framework for three subsets of research on prosocial behavior, and to explore the implications of research in these areas for existing theories of equity and justice. It seems safe to conclude that, whatever the ultimate potential of theories of justice to explain resource allocation, compensatory helping, and prosocial reciprocity, existing theories are not yet mature enough to account for all of the findings in these areas. At present, existing formulations have not succeeded in supplying a "general theory of [pro]social behavior [Walster *et al.*, 1978]."

The central product of this brief encounter between the two domains was the clarification of critical questions of relevance to both. Research reviewed here indicated that from age 4 or 5 years on, people are guided by principles of justice. However, it also revealed that a great deal remains to be learned about how people decide which principles to employ: Different principles of justice appear to prevail in different circumstances, and different people appear to favor certain principles over others. In general terms, justice decisions appear to be determined by the interaction between the structure of thought and the structure of situations, each affecting the other reciprocally.

The most plausible way of accounting for the interaction between the way people think about justice and the demands of situations is to assume that as children acquire an understanding of increasingly complex principles of justice, they become increasingly able to apply those that are most appropriate to particular situations. Mature people do not necessarily analyse all situations in terms of high order humanitarian principles because these principles are not always relevant. Thus, humanitarian principles are not always the "best." Rather, the distinguishing feature of moral maturity may well be the ability to analyse situations and apply the principles that are most appropriate (i.e., foster the greatest justice). This is another way of saying that one of the defining qualities of maturity is flexibility. There may well be several principles that are more adequate than humanitarianism. Indeed, both psychological research (Kohlberg, 1976) and philosophical theory (Rawls, 1971) indicate that there are. Implicit in this analysis is a characterization of the relationship between equity and justice—equity is treated as one of several principles of justice.

A great deal remains to be learned about the nature of principles of justice, the relationship among different principles, the ways in which different principles are selected, and the processes through which they affect behavior. Particularly problematic is the question of who (or what) individuals employ as standards of comparison in decisions about equity and justice. Research on prosocial behavior demonstrates that people are sensitive to more than the ratio of their inputs and outcomes relative to that of a particular other. Indeed, research on third-person generalized compensation and reciprocity indicated that if principles of justice help to mediate these behaviors, the standards of comparison they contain are exceptionally abstract and independent from the relationships in question.

What guidance, then, do these observations offer to future researchers? In my view, they point most clearly to the value of more direct investigations of the cognitive and affective processes that mediate decisions about how resources should be divided and whether or not people should behave prosocially. Cognitive processes seem to be most central in decisions about resource allocation, and affective processes appear to play a powerful role in compensatory helping and reciprocity. Undoubtedly, affective reactions are structured by cognitions, and cognitions are energized by affect; but the nature of these relationships and the ways in which they affect prosocial behavior are, at present, quite unclear. It is possible that the most parsimonious explanation of phenomena such as third-person generalized compensation and reciprocity relates to the relief of unpleasant affective states relatively independent from justice decisions.

The original purpose of considering the relationship between justice theory and prosocial behavior was to explore the possibility of an adoption—to determine whether, and to what extent, justice theory could incorporate the findings from resource allocation, compensatory helping, and reciprocity. The evidence indicates that justice theory is not, as yet, sufficiently mature to provide an adequate home for prosocial behavior. But the meeting between the two domains was far from unproductive. It has made it clear that each contains the capacity to help the other grow. Hopefully, the two will meet, to their mutual benefit, many times again.

REFERENCES

Adams, J. S. Inequity in social exchange. In L. Berkowitz (Ed.), *Advances in experimental social psychology* (Vol. 2). New York: Academic Press, 1965.

Adams, J. S., & Freedman, S. Equity theory revisited: Comments and annotated bibliography. In L. Berkowitz & E. Walster (Eds.), *Advances in experimental social psychology* (Vol. 9). New York: Academic Press, 1976.

Aderman, D. Elation, depression, and helping behavior. *Journal of Personality and Social Psychology*, 1972, *24*, 91–101.

Austin, W. Equity theory and social comparison processes. In J. M. Suls & R. L. Miller (Eds.), *Social comparison processes*. Washington, D.C.: Hemisphere, 1977.

Austin, W., & Walster, E. Participants' reactions to equity with the world. *Journal of Experimental Social Psychology*, 1974, *10*, 528–548.

Austin, W., & Walster, E. "Equity with the World": The trans-relational effects of equity and inequity. *Sociometry*, 1975, *38*, 474–496.

Baker, K. Experimental analysis of third-party justice behavior. *Journal of Personality and Social Psycholgoy*, 1974, *30*, 307–316.

Bar-Tal, D. *Prosocial behavior: Theory and research*. Washington, D.C.: Hemisphere, 1976.

Bateson, D., & Coke, J. Empathic motivation for helping: Egoistic or altruistic? In J. P. Rushton & R. M. Sorrentino (Eds.), *Altruism and helping behavior*. Hillsdale, N.J.: Erlbaum, 1981.

Berkowitz, L. Responsibility, reciprocity, and social distance in help giving: An experimental investigation of English social class differences. *Journal of Experimental Social Psychology*, 1968, *4*, 46–63.

Berkowitz, L., & Daniels, L. R. Responsibility and dependency. *Journal of Abnormal and Social Psychology*, 1963, *66*, 429–436.

Berkowitz, L., & Daniels, L. R. Affecting the salience of the social responsibility norm. *Journal of Abnormal and Social Psychology*, 1964, *68*, 302–306.

Berkowitz, L., & Friedman, P. Some social class differences in helping behavior. *Journal of Personality and Social Psychology*, 1967, *5*, 217–225.

Berscheid, E., & Walster, E. When does a harm-doer compensate a victim? *Journal of Personality and Social Psychology*, 1967, *6*, 435–441.

Berscheid, E., Walster, E., & Barclay, A. Effect of time on tendency to compensate a victim. *Psychological Reports*, 1969, *25*, 431–436.

Blau, P. M. *The dynamics of bureaucracy: A study of interpersonal relations in two government agencies* (Rev. ed.). Chicago: University of Chicago Press, 1963.

Brehm, J. W., & Cole, A. H. Effect of a favor which reduces freedom. *Journal of Personality and Social Psychology*, 1966, *3*, 420–426.

Carlsmith, J. M., & Gross, A. E. Some effects of guilt on compliance. *Journal of Personality and Social Psychology*, 1969, *11*, 232–239.

Cialdini, R. B., Darby, B. L., & Vincent, J. E. Transgression and altruism: A case for hedonism. *Journal of Experimental Social Psychology*, 1973, *9*, 502–516.

Cialdini, R. B., & Kenrick, D. T. Altruism as hedonism: A social development perspective on the relationship of negative mood state and helping. *Journal of Personality and Social Psychology*, 1976, *34*, 907–914.

Coon, R., Lane, I., & Lichtman, R. J. Sufficiency of reward and allocation behavior. *Human Development*, 1974, *17*, 301–313.

Damon, W. *The social world of the child*. San Francisco: Jossey-Bass, 1977.

Darlington, R. B., & Macker, C. E. Displacement of guilt-produced altruistic behavior. *Journal of Personality and Social Psychology*, 1966, *4*, 442–443.

Deutsch, M. Equity, equality, and need: What determines which value will be used as the basis of distributive justice? *Journal of Social Issues*, 1975, *31*, 137–150.

Durkin, D. The specificity of children's moral judgments. *Journal of Genetic Psychology*, 1961, *98*, 3–13.

Eisenberg-Berg, N. (Ed.). *Development of prosocial behavior*. New York: Academic Press, 1982.

Freedman, J. L. Transgression, compliance, and guilt. In J. Macaulay & L. Berkowitz (Eds.), *Altruism and helping behavior*. New York: Academic Press, 1970.

Freedman, J. L., Wallington, S. A., & Bless, E. Compliance without pressure: The effect of guilt. *Journal of Personality and Social Psychology,* 1967, *7,* 117–124.

Garrett, J. B., & Libby, W. L., Jr. Role of intentionality in mediating responses to inequity in the dyad. *Journal of Personality and Social Psychology,* 1973, *28,* 21–27.

Gergen, K. J., & Gergen, M. K. International assistance from a psychological perspective. In *The yearbook of international affairs* (Vol. 25). London: London Institute of World Affairs, 1971.

Gergen, K., Ellsworth, P., Maslach, C., & Seipel, M. Obligation, donor resources, and reactions to aid in 3 cultures. *Journal of Personality and Social Psychology,* 1975, *31,* 390–400.

Goranson, R. E., & Berkowitz, L. Reciprocity and responsibility reactions to prior help. *Journal of Personality and Social Psychology,* 1966, *3,* 227–232.

Gouldner, A. W. The norm of reciprocity: A preliminary statement. *American Sociological Review,* 1960, *25,* 161–179.

Greenberg, J. Effects of reward value and retaliative power on allocation decisions: Justice, generosity, or greed? *Journal of Personality and Social Psychology,* 1978, *36,* 367–379.

Greenberg, M. S. A preliminary statement on a theory of indebtedness. In M. S. Greenberg (Chair), *Justice in social exchange.* Symposium presented at the meeting of the Western Psychological Association, San Diego, September 1968.

Greenberg, M. S. A theory of indebtedness. In K. Gergen, M. S. Greenberg, & R. H. Willis (Eds.), *Social exchange: Advances in theory and research.* New York: Plenum, 1980.

Greenberg, M. S., Block, M. W., & Silverman, M. A. Determinants of helping behavior: Person's rewards versus other's costs. *Journal of Personality,* 1971, *39,* 79–93.

Greenberg, M. S., & Frisch, D. M. Effect of intentionality on willingness to reciprocate a favor. *Journal of Experimental Social Psychology,* 1972, *8,* 99–111.

Greenberg, M. S., & Shapiro, S. P. Indebtedness: An adverse aspect of asking for and receiving help. *Sociometry,* 1971, *34,* 290–301.

Greenglass, E. R. Effects of prior help and hindrance on willingness to help another: Reciprocity or social responsibility. *Journal of Personality and Social Psychology,* 1969, *11,* 224–231.

Gross, A. E., & Latané, J. G. Receiving help, reciprocation, and interpersonal attraction. *Journal of Applied Social Psychology,* 1974, *4,* 210–223.

Gunzburger, D., Wegner, D. M., & Anooshian, L. Moral judgment and distributive justice. *Human Development,* 1977, *20,* 160–170.

Hatfield, E., Walster, G. W., & Piliavin, J. A. Equity theory and helping relationships. In L. Wispé (Ed.), *Altruism, sympathy, and helping.* New York: Academic Press, 1978.

Homans, G. C. *Social behavior: Its elementary forms.* New York: Harcourt Brace & World, 1961.

Hook, J. G., & Cook, T. D. Equity theory and the cognitive ability of children. *Psychological Bulletin,* 1979, *86,* 429–445.

Isen, A., Clark, M., & Schwartz, M. Duration of the effect of good mood on helping: "Footprints in the sands of time." *Journal of Personality and Social Psychology,* 1976, *34,* 385–393.

Isen, A. M., & Levin, P. F. Effect of feeling good on helping: Cookies and kindness. *Journal of Personality and Social Psychology,* 1972, *21,* 384–388.

Isen, A. M., Shalker, T. E., Clark, M., & Karp, L. Affect, accessibility of material in memory, and behavior: A cognitive loop? *Journal of Personality and Social Psychology,* 1978, *36,* 1–13.

Kohlberg, L. Stage and sequence: The cognitive–developmental approach to socialization. In D. Goslin (Ed.), *Handbook of socialization theory and research.* Chicago: Rand McNally, 1969.

Kohlberg, L. Moral stages and moralization: The cognitive–developmental approach. In T. Lickona (Ed.), *Moral development and behavior*. New York: Holt, 1976.

Krebs, D. Altruism—an examination of the concept and a review of the literature. *Psychological Bulletin*, 1970, *73*, 258–302.

Krebs, D. L. Empathy and altruism. *Journal of Personality and Social Psychology*, 1975, *32*, 1134–1146.

Krebs, D. A cognitive–developmental approach to altruism. In L. Wispé (Ed.), *Altruism, sympathy, and helping*. New York: Academic Press, 1978. (a)

Krebs, D. The moral judgment of the child: Reconsidered. *Human Nature*, January, 1978. (b)

Krebs, D., & Gillmore, J. The relationship among the first stages of cognitive development, role-taking, and moral development. *Child Development*, in press.

Krebs, D., & Russell, C. Role-taking and altruism. In J. P. Rushton & R. M. Sorrentino (Eds.), *Altruism and helping behavior*. Hillsdale, N.J.: Erlbaum, in press.

Krebs, D., & Whitten, P. Guilt-edged giving. *Psychology Today*, 1972, January, 50–52, 76–77.

Lane, I., & Coon, R. Reward allocation in preschool children. *Child Development*, 1972, *43*, 1382–1389.

Lane, I. M., & Messé, L. A. Distribution of insufficient, sufficient, and oversufficient rewards: A clarification of equity theory. *Journal of Personality and Social Psychology*, 1972, *21*, 228–233.

Leeds, R. Altruism and the norm of giving. *Merrill-Palmer Quarterly*, 1963, *9*, 229–240.

Lerner, M. The justice motive: "Equity" and "parity" among children. *Journal of Personality and Social Psychology*, 1974, *29*, 539–550.

Lerner, M. J. The justice motive in social behavior: Introduction. *Journal of Social Issues*, 1975, *31*, 1–20.

Lerner, M. J. The justice motive: Some hypotheses as to its origins and forms. *Journal of Personality*, 1977, *45*, 1–53.

Lerner, M. J., Miller, D. T., & Holmes, J. G. Deserving and the emergence of forms of justice. In L. Berkowitz & E. Walster (Eds.), *Advances in experimental social psychology* (Vol. 9). New York: Academic Press, 1976.

Lerner, M. J., & Simmons, C. H. Observer's reaction to the "innocent victim": Compassion or rejection? *Journal of Personality and Social Psychology*, 1966, *4*, 203–210.

Leventhal, G. S. The distribution of rewards and resources in groups and organizations. In L. Berkowitz & E. Walster (Eds.), *Advances in experimental social psychology* (Vol. 9). New York: Academic Press, 1976.

Leventhal, G. S., & Anderson, D. Self-interest and the maintenance of equity. *Journal of Personality and Social Psychology*, 1970, *15*, 57–62.

Leventhal, G. S., Weiss, T., & Long, G. Equity, reciprocity, and reallocating the rewards in the dyad. *Journal of Personality and Social Psychology*, 1969, *13*, 300–305.

Levin, P. F., & Isen, A. M. Further studies on the effect of feeling good on helping. *Sociometry*, 1975, *38*, 141–147.

Long, G. T., & Lerner, M. J. Deserving, the "personal contract," and altruistic behavior by children. *Journal of Personality and Social Psychology*, 1974, *29*, 551–556.

Mauss, M. *The gift: Forms and functions of exchange in archaic societies*. Glencoe, Ill.: Free Press, 1954.

McMillen, D. L. Transgression, self-image, and compliant behavior. *Journal of Personality and Social Psychology*, 1971, *20*, 176–179.

McMillen, D. L., & Austin, J. B. Effect of positive feedback on compliances following transgression. *Psychonomic Science*, 1971, *24*, 59–61.

Mikula, G. On the role of justice in allocation decisions. In G. Mikula (Ed.), *Justice and social interaction.* New York: Springer-Verlag, 1980.

Mikula, G., & Schwinger, T. Intermember relations and reward allocation. In H. Brandstätter, J. H. Davis, & H. Schuler (Eds.), *Dynamics of group decision.* Beverly Hills, Calif.: Sage, 1978.

Miller, D. T., & Smith, J. The effect of own deservingness and deservingness of others on children's helping behavior. *Child Development,* 1977, *48,* 617–620.

Moore, B., Underwood, B., & Rosenham, D. C. Affect and altruism. *Developmental Psychology,* 1973, *8,* 99–104.

Morris, S., & Rosen, S. Effects of felt adequacy and opportunity to reciprocate on help seeking. *Journal of Experimental Social Psychology,* 1973, *9,* 265–276.

Muir, D. E., & Weinstein, E. A. The social debt: An investigation of lower-class and middle-class norms of social obligation. *American Sociological Review,* 1962, *27,* 532–539.

Murphy, L. B. *Social behavior and child personality: An exploratory study of some roots of sympathy.* New York: Columbia University Press, 1937.

Mussen, P., & Eisenberg-Berg, N. *Roots of caring, sharing, and helping.* San Francisco: Freeman, 1977.

Nadler, A., Fisher, J. D., & Streufert, S. The donor's dilemma: Recipient's reactions to aid from friend or foe. *Journal of Applied Social Psychology,* 1974, *4,* 275–285.

Nemeth, C. Bargaining and reciprocity. *Psychological Bulletin,* 1970, *74,* 297–308.

Olejnik, A. B. The effects of reward-deservedness on children's sharing. *Child Development,* 1976, *47,* 380–385.

Peterson, C., Peterson, J., & McDonald, N. Factors affecting reward allocations by preschool children. *Child Development,* 1975, *46,* 942–947.

Piaget, J. [The moral judgment of the child]. New York: Free Press, 1965. (Originally published, 1932.)

Piliavin, I. M., Piliavin, J. A., & Rodin, J. Costs, diffusion, and the stigmatized victim. *Journal of Personality and Social Psychology,* 1975, *32,* 429–438.

Piliavin, J. A., & Piliavin, I. M. The effect of blood on reactions to a victim. *Journal of Personality and Social Psychology,* 1972, *23,* 253–261.

Pruitt, D. G. Reciprocity and credit building in a laboratory dyad. *Journal of Personality and Social Psychology,* 1968, *8,* 143–147.

Rawlings, E. I. Witnessing harm to other: A reassessment of the role of guilt in altruistic behavior. *Journal of Personality and Social Psychology,* 1968, *10,* 377–380.

Rawlings, E. I. Reactive guilt and anticipatory guilt in altruistic behavior. In J. Macaulay & L. Berkowitz (Eds.), *Altruism and helping behavior.* New York: Academic Press, 1970.

Rawls, J. *A theory of justice.* Cambridge, Mass.: Harvard University Press, 1971.

Regan, D. T. Effects of a favor and liking on compliance. *Journal of Experimental Social Psychology,* 1971, *7,* 627–639.

Rheingold, H. L., Hay, D. F., & West, M. J. Sharing in the second year of life. *Child Development,* 1976, *47,* 1148–1158.

Rushton, J. P. *Altruism, socialization, society.* Englewood Cliffs, N.J.: Prentice-Hall, 1980.

Rushton, J. P., & Sorrentino, R. M. (Eds.). *Altruism and helping behavior.* Hillsdale, N.J.: Erlbaum, in press.

Sampson, E. E. Studies of status congruence. In L. Berkowitz (Ed.), *Advances in experimental social psychology* (Vol. 4). New York: Academic Press, 1969.

Sampson, E. E. On justice as equality. *Journal of Social Issues,* 1975, *31,* 21–43.

Saxe, L., & Greenberg, M. *Reaction to a help request: Importance of locus of help initiation and negative outcome.* Paper presented at the meeting of the Eastern Psychological Association, Philadelphia, 1974.

Schopler, J. An attribution analysis of some determinants of reciprocating a benefit. In J. Macaulay & L. Berkowitz (Eds.), *Altruism and helping behavior.* New York: Academic Press, 1970.

Schopler, J., & Thompson, V. Role of attribution processes in mediating amount of reciprocity for a favor. *Journal of Personality and Social Psychology,* 1968, *10,* 243–250.

Schwartz, S. The justice of need and the activation of humanitarian norms. *Journal of Social Issues,* 1975, *31,* 111–136.

Schwartz, S. H. Normative influences on altruism. In L. Berkowitz (Ed.), *Advances in experimental social psychology* (Vol. 10). New York: Academic Press, 1977.

Schwinger, T. Zur Entstehung gruppen-spezifischer Normen der Gewinnaufteilung. Phil. Diss. Graz, 1975.

Silverman, I. W. Incidence of guilt reactions in children. *Journal of Personality and Social Psychology,* 1967, *7,* 338–340.

Stapleton, R. E., Nacci, P., & Tedeschi, J. T. Interpersonal attraction and the reciprocity of benefits. *Journal of Personality and Social Psychology,* 1973, *28,* 199–205.

Staub, E. Instigation to goodness: The role of social norms and interpersonal influence. *Journal of Social Issues,* 1972, *28,* 131–151.

Staub, E. *Children's sharing behavior: Success and failure, the "norm of deserving," and reciprocity in sharing.* In S. Crockenberg (Chair), *Helping and sharing: Concepts of altruism and cooperation.* Symposium presented at the meeting of the Society of Research in Child Development, Philadelphia, March 1973.

Staub, E. *Positive social behavior and morality* (Vol. 1). New York: Academic Press, 1978.

Staub, E., & Sherk, L. Need approval, children's sharing behavior, and reciprocity in sharing. *Child Development,* 1970, *41,* 243–253.

Tesser, A., Gatewood, R., & Driver, M. Some determinants of gratitude. *Journal of Personality and Social Psychology,* 1968, *9,* 233–236.

Thibaut, J. W., & Riecken, H. W. Some determinants and consequences of the perception of social causality. *Journal of Personality,* 1955, *24,* 113–133.

Trivers, R. L. The evolution of reciprocal altruism. *Quarterly Review of Biology,* 1971, *46,* 35–57.

Turiel, E. Distinct conceptual and developmental domains: Social–conventional and morality. In C. E. Keasey (Ed.), *Nebraska symposium on motivation,* 1977. Lincoln: University of Nebraska Press, 1977.

Turner, R. H. The self-conception in social interaction. In C. Gordon & K. Gergen (Eds.), *The self in social interaction* (Vol. 1). Wiley, 1968.

Underwood, B., Froming, W. J., & Moore, B. S. Mood, attention, and altruism: A search for mediating variables. *Developmental Psychology,* 1977, *13,* 541–542.

Wallace, L., & Sadalla, E. Behavioral consequences of transgression, I: The effects of social recognition. *Journal of Experimental Research in Personality,* 1966, *1,* 187–194.

Wallington, S. A. Consequences of transgression: Self-punishment and depression. *Journal of Personality and Social Psychology,* 1973, *28,* 1–7.

Walster, E., Walster, G. W., & Berscheid, E. *Equity: Theory and research.* Boston: Allyn & Bacon, 1978.

Wilke, H., & Lanzetta, J. T. The obligation to help: The effects of amount of prior help on subsequent helping behavior. *Journal of Experimental Social Psychology,* 1970, *6,* 483–493.

Wispé, L. (Ed.). *Altruism, sympathy, and helping.* New York: Academic Press, 1978.

chapter 9

Aggression and Inequity[1]

EDWARD DONNERSTEIN
ELAINE HATFIELD

I. INTRODUCTION

Equity theory claims to be a general theory—providing insights into all social encounters (Berkowitz & Walster, 1976). In this chapter, we will attempt to assess the theory's relevance, or irrelevance, for explaining what goes on in aggressive encounters. In Section II, we will briefly review equity theory. (Those who already know more about this theory than they wish to know, can proceed directly to Section III.) In reviewing the vast aggression literature, we found that equity considerations do seem to be critically important in determining how people respond in potentially aggressive settings. We will review these findings in Section III. But not everything fits. In Section IV, we will discuss the cases in which Equity theory and the data do not seem to mesh very well.

II. A BRIEF OVERVIEW OF EQUITY THEORY

Equity theory consists of four propositions (see Hatfield, 1980).

Proposition I: Individuals will try to maximize their outcomes (where outcomes equals rewards minus punishments).

[1] Preparation of this chapter was supported in part by NIMH grant 1F32 MH07788-01 to Donnerstein, and in part by a National Institute of Health Grant for Biomedical Research to Hatfield.

309

Proposition II A: Groups (or, rather, the individuals comprising these groups) can maximize collective outcomes by evolving accepted systems for equitably apportioning rewards and punishments among members. Thus, groups will evolve such systems of equity and will attempt to induce members to accept and adhere to these systems.

Proposition II B: Groups will generally reward members who treat others equitably and generally punish members who treat others inequitably.

Proposition III: When individuals find themselves participating in inequitable relationships, they will become distressed. The more inequitable the relationship, the more distress they will feel.

Proposition IV: Individuals who discover they are in inequitable relationships will attempt to eliminate their distress by restoring equity. The greater the inequity that exists, the more distress they will feel, and the harder they will try to restore equity.

A. Who Decides Whether a Relationship Is Equitable

According to equity theory, equity is in the eye of the beholder. People's perceptions of how equitable a relationship is will depend on their assessment of what is "fair." Thus, in any aggressive encounter, people may well disagree about such basic things as "Who's the victim? . . . Who was victimized?", much less such subtle things as "Were the perpetrators justified in aggressing?" "Was their aggression too little, too late?" "Was it fair or excessive?" "Are the victims entitled to retaliate?" "How should outside observers respond?" "Should they try to set things right or do nothing?"

B. The Psychological Consequences of Inequity

According to equity theory (Proposition III), when people treat others unfairly, or are unfairly treated themselves, it is upsetting. When people take advantage of others, they tend to feel "guilt," "dissonance," "empathy," "fear of retaliation," or "conditioned anxiety" (Austin & Walster, 1974). When they are taken advantage of, they feel "shame," "dissonance," or "anger." Essentially, however, both aggressor and victim's feelings are similar—they both experience subjective distress accompanied by physiological arousal (see Austin & Walster, 1974; Walster, Walster, & Berscheid, 1978).

C. Techniques by Which Aggressors-Victims May Reduce Their Distress

Proposition IV proposes that individuals who are distressed by inequity will try to eliminate their distress by restoring either actual equity or psychological equity to their relationships.

1. ACTUAL EQUITY

People can try to "set things right" in a variety of ways. The child who has said cruel things to a friend, can recognize what he has done, repent, and try to set things right. The man who is jilted by a woman can spread mean rumors behind her back.

2. PSYCHOLOGICAL EQUITY

People can restore equity to a relationship in a second way—by changing their definition of the situation. The battered child can convince himself that, really, he "asked for it"—or that's how his father expresses his love ("He was doing it for my own good—It hurt him more than it hurts me.") or that God will get his father in the end.

3. ACTUAL VERSUS PSYCHOLOGICAL EQUITY RESTORATION

At this point, equity theorists confront a crucial question: When will an aggressor–victim try to restore actual equity to a relationship?—When will he or she settle for restoring psychological equity? According to equity theory (Propositions I and IV), cost–benefit considerations should determine how men and women respond to injustice. Whether people respond by attempting to restore actual equity, by distorting reality, or by doing a little of both, has been found to depend on the costs and benefits associated with each strategy (see, e.g., Berscheid & Walster, 1967; Berscheid, Walster, & Barclay, 1969; Weick & Nesset, 1968).

D. Summary

Equity theorists concur that people try to maximize their outcomes (Proposition I). Group members can maximize their collective outcomes by devising an equitable system for sharing resources. Thus, all groups try to hammer out acceptable systems for allocating outcomes and trying to induce members to adhere to these standards; that is, they try to ensure that all participants receive equal relative outcomes. Groups can do this in only one way: by making it profitable to be fair. They must reward members who behave equitably and punish those who do not

(Proposition II). When socialized individuals find themselves enmeshed in inequitable relationships, they experience distress (Proposition III). They can reduce their distress by restoring either actual equity or psychological equity to their relationships (Proposition IV).

III. THE APPLICATION OF EQUITY THEORY TO AGGRESSOR-VICTIM RELATIONSHIPS

When we review the aggression literature, we see that considerations of fairness and justice seem to be extremely important in determining: (1) whether or not people aggress against one another; and (2) how they feel about their aggressive versus passive reactions.

A. Definition of Terms

Baron (1977) defines *aggression* as "any form of behavior directed toward the goal of harming or injuring another living being who is motivated to avoid such treatment [p. 7]." We should keep in mind that in this definition we are referring to intentional aggression. That is, we do not mean acts of harm that might occur by accident.

In many situations, who is defined as an "aggressor," who the "victim," depends on how one punctuates a chain of events. Consider a typical aggression paradigm:

A college student, enthusiastic about contributing to science, or at least earning some money, reports to the lab. The experimenter greets her and introduces another student (actually, an experimental confederate). Suddenly, in the experimental condition, without warning, the confederate attacks the student. He tells her she is stupid, subjects her to intense electric shock for no apparent reason. Then, the tables are turned. The student must now teach her "fellow student" the task. If she wishes, she can combine her teaching with a little aggressive punishment (all for the other's "own good," of course). In the control conditions, the student is not angered.

Traditionally, aggression researchers have labeled this interaction in the following way:

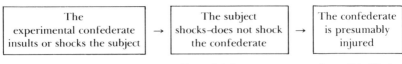

| The experimental confederate insults or shocks the subject | → | The subject shocks–does not shock the confederate | → | The confederate is presumably injured |

Potential Aggressor ⟶ Ostensible Victim

For purposes of an equity analysis (and in line with conventional wisdom) we would label this interaction in quite another way:

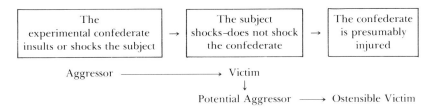

Initially, it is the *experimental confederate* who is the aggressor; the student, the victim. Then the tables are turned. The student is given an opportunity either to aggress or to refuse to do so. The confederate is put in the role of a potential victim.

B. Applying the Theory

It is obvious that equity theory *ought* to have a great deal to say about people's reactions in aggression encounters. We plan to organize our analysis and discussion as shown in Figure 9.1. We will examine the sequence of events from the viewpoint of the subject by looking at five different issues. First, is there any justification for the subject to act aggressively. Second, what are the feelings of those who are provoked or treated in a neutral manner. Third, how does the subject react? Does he or she aggress back, or is a nonaggressive response elicited from the subject. If the subject does aggress, how much aggression, in comparison to what was received, is administered? Fourth, how does the subject feel after acting aggressively or nonaggressively. And finally, what does the individual do at this time?

1. IS THE SUBJECT GIVEN ANY JUSTIFICATION FOR AGGRESSING?

Considerations of fairness seem to be critically important in determining how people respond to one another. Generally, aggression researchers must provide compelling reasons for subjects to behave aggressively before subjects will even *consider* doing so. Researchers have found a variety of techniques to be effective in enticing people to aggress.

Sometimes, for no apparent reason, subjects are physically attacked via electric shock (see Borden, Bowen, & Taylor, 1971; Dengerink & Bertilson, 1974; Dengerink & Myers, 1977; Taylor, 1967). Sometimes, subjects are gratuitously insulted—they are told they are stupid, un-

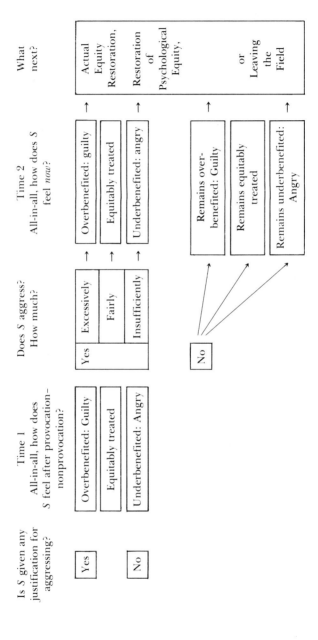

Figure 9.1. A flowchart of the aggression–equity sequence.

motivated, or have unappealing personalities (e.g., Baron & Bell, 1975; Geen, 1968). Baron (1977) points out that these insults hurt as much as, and perhaps even more, than would a physical attack. Greenwell and Dengerink (1973) note: "While attack is an important instigator of aggressive behavior, it appears that the physical discomfort experienced by a person may be subordinate to the symbolic elements that are incorporated in that attack [p. 70]." Sometimes, students are arbitrarily cheated out of rewards they have earned (Worchel, 1974). Essentially, all these procedures are designed to provide the subject with ample justification for aggressing in return. As equity theory would predict, such justifications are critically important in sparking distress and aggressive counterattack. Baron (1977) observes that unless researchers provide adequate justification, subjects will often fail to become upset or fail to retaliate: "Indeed, there is some indication in this research that fully justified and expected frustrations often fail to induce either physiological arousal (Zillman & Cantor, 1976) or subsequent attack against the source of the thwarting [p. 90]." When researchers provide adequate justifications, subjects do both (see Baron & Bell, 1976; Donnerstein, Donnerstein, & Evans, 1975; Geen, 1968).

2. TIME 1: ALL-IN-ALL, HOW DOES THE SUBJECT FEEL AFTER PROVOCATION–NONPROVOCATION?

In real-life confrontations people often have a history. They may feel that in *previous* encounters with their partners they were treated far better than they had a right to expect (they were overbenefited), they got just what they had coming (they were equitably treated), or less (they were underbenefited). Such past history should have a profound effect on how any *specific* provocation affects a person. The older brother who has been teasing his sister unmercifully for days, may well feel he "has it coming," when she turns the tables. The couple who have shared a lifetime of equitable exchange, will probably see a single provocation as merely a momentary imbalance in the marital give-and-take. The battered wife may respond in quite a volatile way to yet another provocation; for her, it may be "the last straw." In real life, it is often impossible to disentangle who did what, to whom, and when. That information is lost in the mists of time. It is difficult to know *how* to rate a relationship's fairness.

In a laboratory setting, however, people start afresh. Participants enter the laboratory with no past history in that situation and with those specific people. It is relatively easy to classify things. In the typical aggression experiment in the last section, experimental subjects are assaulted mentally or physically without warning. As a consequence, they are likely to feel underbenefited—and angry. The control subjects have every reason to feel equitably treated.

3. HOW DOES THE SUBJECT RESPOND TO PROVOCATION? DOES HE OR SHE AGGRESS? HOW MUCH?

> Anybody can become angry—that is easy; but to be angry with the right person, and to the right degree, and at the right time, and for the right purpose, and in the right way—that is not within everybody's power and is not easy.
>
> —Aristotle; in Paynton & Blackey, 1971, p. 11

According to equity theory, the provoked feel most comfortable when they retaliate *appropriately*. If they go overboard—destroying a fly with a sledgehammer—when they cool off, and think back on what they have done, they feel ashamed. If they respond to provocation with too little, too late, when they think back on their ineffectual reaction, they feel equally ashamed.

Theoretically, then, it is critically important to know how the provoked, who choose to aggress or avoid aggression, later come to view their actions. In existing studies, however, it is very difficult for us to classify subjects' responses as excessive, appropriate, or inadequate. The researchers shock the hapless subjects. Their action is insulting *and* painful. How do you weigh that? How much electric shock does it take in retaliation to balance things out?

Luckily a few researchers have investigated this issue and find that people do try to retaliate, both in kind and amount. For example, O'Leary and Dengerink (1973) attempted to determine whether aggressors and victim–aggressors generally behave in a highly reciprocal manner. To investigate this question, they paired subjects with opponents who adopted one of four strategies during the session. In the *low attack group,* the aggressors gave the subjects very mild shocks, time after time. In the *decreasing attack group,* the aggressors *started* by giving the subjects very painful shocks, but over time, they began to set gentler and gentler shock levels. In the *increasing attack group,* the aggressors followed the opposite strategy; they started out administering mild shocks, but trial by trial, their shocks became increasingly painful. Finally, in the *high attack group,* the aggressors gave the subjects intensely painful shocks every time they got a chance.

The authors found that subjects did behave in a highly reciprocal fashion. They "gave as good as they got." Subjects in the *low attack group* gave mild shocks, those in the *increasing* and *decreasing attack groups* matched their partner's level of ferocity, and those in the *high attack group* gave consistently painful shocks of their own.

The notion that things should be "set right" via *exact* punishment is a deeply engrained one. *The Code of Hammurabi* (about 2250 B.C.) was based on just that philosophy. "If one break a man's bone, they shall break his bone [Harper, 1904, p. 73]." Today, philosophers are more sophisticated. After thinking about the question for 4000 years, they now have absolutely no one idea why society punishes wrongdoers. Does society punish people to restore equity? To protect society by isolating wrongdoers? To set a harsh example for other potential harm doers? To rehabilitate them? Philosophers cannot agree. Despite philosophers' disagreements, however, almost everyone else feels that, at least in part, wrongdoers should expiate their crimes by suffering, and that the punishment should fit the crime (Fry, 1956; Rose & Prell, 1955; Sharp & Otto, 1910).

4. TIME 2: ALL-IN-ALL, HOW DOES THE SUBJECT FEEL NOW? WHAT NEXT?

In the studies we have focused on thus far, the experimenters either provoked or did not provoke the subjects, and then they observed whether these victims–potential aggressors did or did not retaliate. Most aggression studies end at this point. But our curiosity does not. What happens next? What happens when potential aggressors get angry and go too far? Do they try to make amends? Justify their behavior? Escape? What about subjects who refuse to retaliate, or are afraid to? Theorists generally assume that it is good for people to control their aggressive responses. But is it? What happens to the provoked when they decide not to retaliate? Do they end up trying to get back at others in a multitude of *little* ways? Do they end up justifying the provoker's cruel behavior?—convincing themselves that they had it coming? Do they displace their aggression?

Considerable evidence—collected in very different contexts—suggests that aggressors–nonaggressors, may do exactly these things. Before considering this evidence, a caution is in order. From Figure 9.1, it is obvious that, at this point, we could offer a laborious enumeration of myriad possibilities. Subjects who are provoked or not provoked could feel overbenefited, equitably treated, or underbenefited. Afterwards they may do nothing, or retaliate—excessively, adequately, inadequately, and as a consequence, feel guilty, just fine, or angry. To avoid having to run through all the possibilities to make our point, let us make a simplifying assumption: For this equity analysis, we need not worry about "who hit who first and what happened next." For our purposes, we need only calculate whether or not, by Time 2, the subject feels overbenefited, equitably treated, or underbenefited. We will label as *aggressors* those who, at Time 2, have hurt the other more than the other has hurt them. (This includes experimenters and confederates who provoke subjects, subjects who get angry and go overboard in paying them back.) Let us label as *victims*, those who have been hurt more than they have hurt others. (This includes subjects who have been victimized but have had no chance to retaliate—or who do not dare to retaliate—or who retaliate too little too late.) Our discussion, in equity theory terms, of how the aggressor and victims might be expected to set out, at Time 2, to remedy the *status quo* can now proceed from here.

According to equity theory (Proposition III), people who feel they have treated others unfairly and those who have been treated unfairly themselves, should feel acutely uncomfortable. Walster *et al.* (1978) review the considerable evidence that they do.

Both aggressors and their victims can attempt to set things right in two very different ways: They can attempt to restore actual equity or psychological equity to their relationships. Or if all else fails, they can leave the field.

a. Restoring Actual Equity. Aggressors often voluntarily compensate their victims or acquiesce when they retaliate. Evidence in support of this contention comes from Berscheid and Walster (1967), Walster and Prestholdt (1966), and Walster, Aronson, Abrahams, and Rottman (1966).

Not surprisingly, it is often the victims who insist that things be set right. Victims are quick to seek restitution (see Leventhal & Bergman, 1969; Marwell, Schmitt, & Shotola, 1971). If that is not possible, victims are not hesitant to "get even" by retaliation. Much of the evidence in support of this contention was reported earlier in this chapter (see also Brown, 1968; Thibaut, 1950; Ross, Thibaut, & Evenbeck, 1971).

Often, then, both aggressor and victim follow Aristotle's dictum. They try to make sure justice is done to the right person, at the right time, in the right amount.

But what happens when it is not? What about angry people who go too far? Or do not go far enough? The existing evidence suggests that when aggressor–victims think back on things, they will feel uneasy and will try to make themselves feel better by rationalizing the status quo.

b. Restoring Psychological Equity. As we noted earlier, both aggressors, victims, and outside observers can restore psychological equity to a relationship by distorting reality. Aggressors convince themselves that their victims deserved to be hurt (see Berkowitz, 1962; Davidson, 1964; Davis & Jones, 1960; Glass, 1964; Katz, Glass, & Cohen, 1973; Sykes &

Matza, 1957; Walster & Prestholdt, 1966), that they did not *really* suffer or at least did not suffer very much (Brock & Buss, 1962; Sykes & Matza, 1957), or that *they* are not responsible for their suffering ("It's not me folks, I was only following orders") (Brock & Buss, 1962, 1964; Sykes & Matza, 1957).

That we often justify our cruelties to others was apparent even to the ancients. Let us consider a typical experiment. Davis and Jones (1960) reasoned that, because most of us think of ourselves as kind and fair persons, anytime we hurt another deeply, we feel uncomfortable. Ironically, it is the kindest and fairest of us who feel worst when we hurt others, and thus are most likely to try to make ourselves feel a little better, by deciding that our hapless victims deserved what they got. Davis and Jones also argued that the more responsible we feel for our decisions to hurt others, the more uncomfortable we will feel, and thus the more eager we will be to denigrate our victim.

Finally, these investigators were also interested in the fact that, in some situations we can withdraw, or take back cruel behavior. When we have hurt others by insulting them, we can say "I didn't mean it," or "I was playing a joke," and thereby partially eliminate the harm we have done. Davis and Jones hypothesized that when such "taking back" is possible, we will not denigrate the victim, but will choose to make amends.

To test these hypotheses, Davis and Jones (1960) cajoled half of their subjects (those in the choice condition) into *volunteering* to read an extremely harsh evaluation to a fellow student. He essentially *forced* the remaining students (those in the no-choice condition) to read it. (He simply told them they *must* read the negative evaluation.) In addition, some of the subjects were led to believe they would be able to meet the other person later (and thus they could explain they had not really meant their harsh criticism). The experimenter led the remaining students to believe that a subsequent meeting was impossible (and thus there was no way the injury could be undone). After the subjects read the negative evaluation to the other, the experimenter asked them to rate the other's likability, warmth, conceit, intelligence, and adjustment.

How did students feel about the other *after* insulting him or her? Davis and Jones (1960) found that men and women were most likely to derogate the victim when they: (1) believed that they had some freedom not to behave in the harmful manner; and (2) realized that they could not easily take back their behavior in a subsequent meeting. Davis and Jones, then, confirmed the notion that people who insult others may end up by convincing themselves that their hapless targets deserved to suffer.

In a particularly interesting study, Sykes and Matza (1957) found that juvenile delinquents often defend their victimization of others by arguing that their victims are homosexuals, or bums, or possess other traits that make them deserving of punishment. In tormenting others, then, the delinquents can claim to be restorers of justice rather than harm doers. A number of subsequent researchers have confirmed the fact that aggressors do often denigrate their victims (see Berkowitz, 1962; Davidson, 1964; Davis & Jones, 1960; Glass, 1964; Katz, Glass, & Cohen, 1973; Walster & Prestholdt, 1966).

Of course, their victims can restore psychological equity in exactly the same ways. Often victimized individuals find it less upsetting to distort reality and justify their victimization, than to acknowledge that the world is unjust and that they are too impotent to elicit fair treatment (see Lerner & Matthews, 1967). Victimized individuals have been found to restore equity in several ways. Sometimes they console themselves by imagining that they were not really victimized (see Jecker & Landy, 1969; Walster & Prestholdt, 1966) or that their victimization will bring compensary benefits (Solomon, 1957; Thibaut & Kelley, 1959). Sometimes victims console themselves by concluding that, in the long run, their tormentors will be punished as they deserve.

c. Escape.   Of course, if all else fails, the guilty aggressor or the humiliated victim can reduce the discomfort by fleeing. Baron and Bell (1975, 1976) found that many subjects find aggressive settings so threatening that all they think about is escape. As one subject observed, "The only thing I thought about was getting the hell out of here!"

d. What Determines whether Participants Respond to Injustice by Restoring Actual or Psychological Equity?   Thus far, we have reviewed evidence that demonstrates that aggressors and their victims sometimes restore actual equity, sometimes psychological equity, to their relationships. But this is not enough. What determines which of these two techniques aggressors or victims will use? According to equity theory, people's responses are shaped by cost–benefit considerations. According to Walster *et al.* (1978):

> Proposition IV: Corollary 1: Other things being equal, the more adequate an exploiter perceives an available equity-restoring technique to be, the more likely he is to use this technique to restore equity.
>
> Proposition I: Corollary 2: Other things being equal, the less costly an exploiter perceives an available equity-restoring technique to be, the more likely he is to use this technique to restore equity [p. 36].

There is some evidence that cost–benefit considerations *are* vitally important in determining how both the aggressive and *potentially* aggressive person (and his or her actual or *potential* victim) will respond.[2] According to equity theory, when people contemplate unjustly hurting others or actually *do* hurt others, they feel distressed. Basically, this distress is presumed to arise from two sources: threatened self-esteem and fear of retaliation.

According to equity theory, anything that (a) makes potential aggressors aware that they will experience self-concept-distress if they injure others; or (b) makes them aware that the victim, the victim's sympathizers, or God may retaliate—should cause them to think twice before aggressing. The evidence suggests that it does.

1. Self-Concept and Aggression–Nonaggression

Researchers have collected considerable evidence that people are likely to hesitate before aggressing, if they know that they will suffer pangs of conscience if they act out. Some examples:

a. Researchers have found that people who *anticipate* pangs of remorse or stings of self-censure for engaging in assaults against others, are especially likely to refrain from such actions (see Donnerstein & Donnerstein, 1973, 1976; Gambaro & Rabin, 1969; Knot, Lasater, & Shuman, 1974; Meyer, 1967).

b. People who are eager for social approval, or who are unusually anxious, are less aggressive (Conn & Crowne, 1964; Dengerink, 1971; Dorsky & Taylor, 1972; Fishman, 1965; Taylor, 1970). (Of course, with enough provocation, even the meekest, most mild-mannered individuals might—like the proverbial worm—turn on their tormentors.)

c. When people realize they are responsible for their own actions, they are most likely to think through what they are doing. Tilker (1970) found that when potential aggressors had been told that the responsibility for the victim's health and welfare rested entirely with them, they were less willing to injure other subjects.

d. Finally, researchers have found that, once aggressors begin to assault others, whether or not they *continue* seems to be influenced by cost–benefit considerations. Whether or not they continue to behave aggressively is influenced by the victims' reactions.

Sometimes aggressors are so angry at a victim, and so uninhibited about aggressing that, when they observe an enemy's suffering, they are encouraged. When individuals are "highly" angry, signs of victims' pain

---

[2]Here, *because of its relevance*, we are primarily interested in the factors that elicit or dampen a potential *aggressor's* aggressive response. Readers interested in the parallel data concerning factors that influence the reaction of a potential *victim* of aggression should consult Walster *et al.* (1978).

will increase aggression. For example, Baron (1974a, 1977), Feshbach, Stiles, and Bitter (1967), Hartmann (1969), and Swart and Berkowitz (1976) found that, if people were strongly provoked, the victim's pain and suffering served as a form of reinforcement.

However, some aggressors' anger is so tempered, or they are so opposed to aggression, that when they observe their victim in pain, they are horrified. They immediately cease their aggressive activity (see Baron, 1971b, 1974a; Geen, 1970; Rule & Leger, 1976). Under conditions of no anger or mild anger, victim pain generally tends to reduce aggression.

2. Fear of Retaliation and Aggression–Nonaggression

Similarly, according to equity theory's cost–benefit analysis, anything that makes potential aggressors aware that the victim, the victim's sympathizers, or God, may retaliate against them, should make them think twice before aggressing. Again, there is some evidence that this is so.

a. In their now classic monograph, Dollard, Doob, Miller, Mowrer, & Sears (1939) observed that "It is evident, of course, that all frustrating situations do not produce overt aggression. Few arrested motorists jeer at policemen; guests at formal dinners do not complain when the meat is tough; German Jews do not strike Nazi stormtroopers [p. 32]." Their conclusion? "The strength of inhibition of any act of aggression varies positively with the amount of punishment anticipated to be a consequence of that act [p. 33.]" A quarter of a century later Berkowitz (1962) noted that "the strength of an individual's aggressive tendencies is directly associated with the extent that he anticipates punishment or disapproval for aggression [p. 93]."

b. Borden (1975) found that an audience can facilitate or inhibit aggression—depending on its assumed values. A variety of authors have found that people are far less likely to aggress if they anticipate social disapproval for doing so (Brown & Elliot, 1965; Brown & Tyler, 1968; Deur & Parke, 1970; Donnerstein & Donnerstein, 1978; Hollenberg & Sperry, 1951; Tyler & Brown, 1967).

c. Donnerstein et al. (1972), Donnerstein and Donnerstein (1975, 1976), and Wilson and Rogers (1975) found that people are less likely to aggress when they know their potential victims have the power to retaliate than when they know they do not. For example, in a series of investigations (see Donnerstein et al., 1972) in which college men had to teach "fellow students" a task, half of the time the fellow student was white; half of the time he or she was black. As is usual, the student was required to deliver electric shock to the fellow student every time he or she made a mistake. Half of the time, in the *anonymous condition*, the students were led to believe that the victims would never know their (the aggressor's) identity. The remainder of the time, in the *nonanonymous condition*, they were informed that they could both see and identify the aggressors over closed circuit TV. Furthermore, within each of *these* groups, half of the students—those in the *prior role-switching instructions condition*—were informed before the shock trials even began that their victims would have the opportunity to retaliate when they finished. The remaining students—those in the *subsequent role-switching instructions condition*—were not told about this supposed reversal of roles until after they had finished shocking the victim. As might be expected, students' aggression was strongly affected by cost–benefit considerations. They were more aggressive when they felt anonymous than when they did not, and more aggressive when the victims could not retaliate than when they could.

Interestingly enough, Donnerstein *et al.* (1972) found that the victim's race interacted strongly with both of the preceding factors influencing subjects behavior. White men were actually more aggressive toward a black than a white when they believed they could attack with total impunity. They were less aggressive toward a black than a white target when they believed that retaliation was probable.

d. Cohen (1955), and Graham, Charwat, Honig, and Weltz (1951) found that provoked people are more willing to aggress against low status and low social power people than their more powerful peers. Of course, a potential victim's threats must be more than "empty" threats if they are to be effective. As one might expect, such threats are most likely to be effective when they are creditable and potent (see Baron, 1971c, 1973, 1974b).

In summarizing the data on the link between anticipation of retaliation and aggression, Baron (1977) observes: "the threat of punishment from the victim seemed to produce a shift from direct, easily recognized forms of aggression to less direct, readily concealable forms [p. 253]."

It is evident, then, that equity theory notions *do* seem to have some validity. Cost–benefit considerations do seem to have a critical impact on whether provoked people respond with aggression or with passive withdrawal.

5. WHAT NEXT: WHERE DOES IT ALL END?

Of course, real life is an endless stream. In real life, the sequence would not end there. Aggression breeds anger and retaliation or inhibition of aggression. Retaliation–nonretaliation then stirs up new feelings. Did the retaliatory–nonretaliatory act set things right? If so fine. But what if—on thinking it through—the subjects realize that they have acted too hastily or too excessively, or did not go far enough? When that is the case, they may be left with guilt and anger. And those feelings will, in turn, spur new activity designed to "set things right."

IV. BEYOND EQUITY THEORY

In Section III, we attempted to demonstrate that the equity paradigm is a useful framework for organizing much of the aggression data. In fact, from what we have written so far, it sounds as if equity theory can account for every step in an aggressive encounter. It cannot. Under some conditions, equity considerations seem surprisingly unimportant in determining how people behave. On occasion, people aggress against the wrong people, at the wrong time, for the wrong reasons, and out of all proportion to the provocation. Let us discuss some of these exceptions.

A. Who Do We Aggress Against?

Currently, aggression theorists are engaged in a debate as to whether or not people are equally *satisfied* when they can aggress directly against their tormentors, as opposed to being forced to displace their aggression onto someone else. For example, Berkowitz (1965) argues that equity considerations are critically important in determining whether or not people's "aggressive drive" is reduced by direct–indirect aggression.

Others, such as Feshbach (1964, 1970), and Zillmann (1979), reject the notion that the aggressive drive can be reduced only through injury to the source of frustration. For example, they point out that when prejudiced people are provoked, they often choose to attack those they dislike—whether or not those people deserve it (Buss, 1961; Donnerstein *et al.*, 1972; Kaufmann, 1970).

Regardless of their assumptions about how the provoked *feel* after directly aggressing or displacing their aggression, researchers are in agreement about what people *do*. Sometimes the provoked injure those who "have it coming." But if they are unwilling to attack those who have injured them, they may well displace their aggression onto a totally innocent victim (Berkowitz, 1969; Dollard *et al.*, 1939; Fenigstein & Buss, 1974; Ferson, 1959; Miller, 1948; Murray & Berkun, 1955; Thibaut & Coules, 1952). An interesting example of this process is provided in a study by Konecni and Doob (1972). In this study subjects were angered or not angered by a confederate of the experimenter. Some subjects were given an opportunity to retaliate against this same person. A second group of subjects were given an opportunity to attack another individual. When subjects were given a final opportunity to aggress, it was found that those subjects who had an opportunity to attack the confederate the first time, did in fact show a reduction in aggressive behavior compared to those subjects who were not given any such cathartic experience. In addition, those who were given an opportunity to attack another individual also showed a reduction in subsequent aggressive behavior.

Although these types of results would not seem to fit well with equity theory, one could look at the situation quite differently. For instance, the subject has incurred the cost of being shocked (angered) while another individual in the experiment has not (the displaced target). It is possible that the subject could restore equity to the entire situation by acting aggressively toward this "other" individual (see Tedeschi & Lindskold, 1976).

B. Why Do People Aggress?

Researchers have found that they can stimulate aggression *via* a variety of techniques. And, some of the things that seem to facilitate or inhibit aggression have nothing to do with "fairness."

They have catalogued a potpourri of factors—none of which has anything to do with fairness—that (a) determine whether or not people are *ready* for aggression in the first place; which (b) intensify or moderate their *emotional response;* and which (c) determine whether or not they will *express* their aggression overtly.

1. FRUSTRATION: A FACTOR THAT DETERMINES WHETHER OR NOT PEOPLE ARE PREDISPOSED TO AGGRESS

Currently, theorists are engaged in a heated debate as to whether or not frustration, in and of itself, breeds aggression. Traditional theorists (e.g., Miller *et al.,* 1941) assumed that frustration was a necessary and sufficient cause of aggression. Recently, however, researchers have begun to argue that, generally, simple frustration is *not* enough to stimulate aggression (see Gentry, 1970; Kuhn, Madsen, & Becker, 1967; Rule & Hewitt, 1971; Taylor & Pisano, 1971). Buss (1966) concludes, "It is clear that . . . pure frustration is a relatively unimportant antecedent of physical aggression [p. 161]." Baron (1977) argues that only *high levels* of frustration provoke aggression. "With few exceptions, investigations that yielded negative results regarding the aggression enhancing influence of frustration have employed relatively mild levels of thwarting, while those which have reported positive findings have involved stronger levels of this factor [p. 88; see also, Harris, 1974]."

In fact, once an individual has been frustrated, it seems unlikely that aggression can be "halted" even if information that might restore equity to the situation is provided. A good example is the research of Zillmann (e.g., Zillmann & Cantor, 1976; Zillmann, Bryant, Cantor, & Day, 1975), which has shown that when a frustrating source gives reasons for behaving in a certain manner (e.g., emotionally upset), the frustrated individual will still aggress against the source even if this information is provided after the frustration. It would seem that, once anger is aroused, the question of what is "fair" is not as important as the act of aggression itself.

Therefore, at least in some cases, people may be predisposed to aggress against others simply because they have been severely frustrated, not because it is fair that they do so.

2. FACTORS HAVING NOTHING TO DO WITH FAIRNESS
   THAT INTENSIFY OR MODERATE PEOPLE'S
   EMOTIONAL RESPONSES

According to Bandura (1973), if people are already feeling angry, anything that intensifies their angry feelings should increase the likelihood that they will aggress—and aggress harshly. Experiments have shown that provoked people can be "pushed over the brink" by a startling array of arousing events such as: *crowding* (Freedman, 1975), *noise* (Donnerstein & Wilson, 1976; Geen & O'Neal, 1969; Konecni, 1975b), *heat* (Baron, 1972a; Baron & Bell, 1975; Baron & Lawton, 1972; Griffitt, 1970; Griffitt & Veitch, 1971), *vigorous exercise* (Zillmann, 1979), *competitive activities* (Christy, Gelfand, & Hartmann, 1971), *general emotional arousal* (Zillmann, 1979), and *sexual arousal* (Baron & Bell, 1977; Donnerstein & Barrett, 1978; Donnerstein *et al.*, 1975; Donnerstein & Hallam, 1978; Jaffee, Malmuth, Feingold, & Feshbach, 1975; Meyer, 1972; Zillmann, 1971).

In reviewing all the evidence, it seems clear that if people are provoked, their anger can be intensified by a variety of arousing experiences, and these intensified feelings can easily "spill over" into aggression (Donnerstein & Wilson, 1976; Konecni, 1975b; Zillmann & Bryant, 1975; Zillmann, Johnson, & Day, 1974).

3. FACTORS HAVING NOTHING TO DO WITH FAIRNESS
   THAT DETERMINE WHETHER OR NOT PEOPLE
   BEHAVE AGGRESSIVELY

   a. Instrumental Conditioning.   According to learning theory, a person can *learn* to behave aggressively or nonaggressively. One learns to do what is necessary to attain reward and to avoid punishment (Bandura, 1973; Zillmann, 1979).

There seem to be a variety of offers one "can't refuse." Children and adults have been found to act aggressively or nonaggressively to secure any number of rewards. Among these are (1) self-reinforcement: (sometimes, people "pat themselves on the back" for aggressing or turning the other check; see Bandura, 1973; Feshbach, 1970; Toch, 1959): (2) various material incentives such as money, desired objects, toys, and candy (Buss, 1971; Gaebelein, 1973; Walters & Brown, 1963); (3) social approval (Geen & Stonner, 1971; Gentry, 1970); or (4) the alleviation of aversive treatments (Patterson, Littman, & Bricker, 1967).

b. Modeling. In addition, people often acquire new forms of behavior—including patterns of aggression or passivity—simply by observing the actions of others (see Bandura, 1973; Goranson, 1970).

The powerful impact of aggressive models has been illustrated in studies of media violence (Bandura, 1965; Bandura, Ross, & Ross, 1963a, 1963b), in laboratory studies (Baron, 1971c; Baron & Bell, 1975; Baron & Kepner, 1970; Berkowitz & Alioto, 1973; Buvinic & Berkowitz, 1976; Donnerstein & Donnerstein 1976; Geen & Stonner, 1972; Grusec, 1972; Hanratty, O'Neal & Sulzer, 1972; Liebert & Baron, 1972; Rice & Grusec, 1975; Wheeler & Caggiula, 1966), and in long-term field studies (Leyens, Camino, Parke, & Berkowitz, 1975; Parke, Berkowitz, Leyens, & Sebastian, 1975).

There are comparable data showing that nonaggressive models, who refuse to be provoked, powerfully *inhibit* aggressive behavior (Baron, 1971c, 1972b; Baron & Kepner, 1970; Donnerstein & Donnerstein, 1977).

c. Conformity. People will aggress if they are ordered to (see Borden & Taylor, 1973; Milgram, 1963, 1965a, 1965b, 1974).

d. Aggressive Cues. According to Berkowitz (1965a, 1969, 1971, 1973), anger induces the *readiness* for overt aggression. But it is the presence or absence of aggressive cues—stimuli associated with the previous or present anger instigation or with aggression generally—that determines whether or not an aggressive *response* will occur. For example, Berkowitz and his colleagues (see Berkowitz, 1965b, 1974; Berkowitz & Geen, 1966; Berkowitz & LePage, 1967; Geen & Berkowitz, 1966) found that people were more likely to aggress against others if they found themselves in a room that had guns, rather than sports equipment, strewn about. Berkowitz (1968) concludes: "Guns not only permit violence, they can stimulate it as well. The finger pulls the trigger, but the trigger may also be pulling the finger [p. 22]."

In the same view, Baron (1977) has argued that the presence or absence of cues associated with responses that are *incompatible* with aggression—empathy, laughter, or lust—may *inhibit* aggression. There is some evidence that Baron may be correct: When people find themselves in pleasant settings—where they are surrounded by good-natured humor, pleasant sexual arousal—they find it very hard to get angry, much less to express their anger (see Baron, 1976; Baron & Bell, 1974; Baron & Byrne, 1977; Landy & Mettee, 1969; Leak, 1974; Mueller & Donnerstein, 1977; Zillmann & Sapolsky, 1977).

e. Drugs: Alcohol and Marijuana.   From the existing evidence, it appears that alochol tends to release aggression; marijuana tends to inhibit it (Taylor & Gammon, 1975; Taylor, Vardaris, Rawitch, Gammon, Cranston, & Lubetkin, 1976).

f. Conclusion.   There are a variety of factors having nothing to do with fairness that can influence people to behave aggressively or nonaggressively.

By now, then, we have come full circle. We see that Aristotle was right: Ideally, we would always be angry with the right person, to the right degree, at the right time, for the right purpose, and in the right way—but that is *not* within everyone's power and is *not* easy. As we have seen in Section III, we sometimes get angry, not at the people who most deserve our anger, but at people we hate, people too weak, too downtrodden to fight back. We are sometimes at such a good place in our lives, so amused, sexually aroused, high that we do not fight back when we should. We sometimes are in such pain, so angry, that we respond when we should not, and out of all proportion.

V. A CONCLUDING NOTE

In looking over the preceding chapter, a consistent pattern seems to emerge. This pattern can be summarized in two observations.

First, at every point in the aggressive sequence, the attributions people make in explaining what is happening to them, why they are responding as they are, and so on, seem to be critically important.

Sometimes people know perfectly well what is happening to them and why (a fellow student attacks them, because he does not like Presbyterians, etc.). Then it is easy to decide what is fair and what is not. But often, in experiments, it is hard for people to know what has hit them. Who would ever even consider the possibility that perhaps they assaulted another because it was a little too hot or a little too cool in the room? Who could admit that they hurt another, because they were afraid to attack the real source of their frustration and were displacing their aggression? In such cases, the attributions people make, "I am bad," "He is irritating," may be critically important.

Second, people seem to behave most in accord with Aristotle's ideal—and most equitably—when they are calm, cool, and collected. When people are intensely angry, or intensely aroused, considerations of equity seem to go by the wayside. There is evidence in support of this contention: Several authors have found that anything that makes people self-conscious about their behavior, increases the chance that they will behave fairly. For example, researchers have found that anything that increases people's "objective self-awareness," looking in a mirror, and so on, causes them to behave more in accord with their values and standards (Carver, 1974, 1975; Scheier, Fenigstein, & Buss, 1974; Wicklund, 1975). For example, under conditions of objective self-awareness, traditional men are less likely to aggress against women than under other conditions (Carver, 1974; Scheier et al., 1974); those who disapprove of physical punishment are especially likely to act in accord with their beliefs (Carver, 1975).

Berscheid et al. (1969) found that, when people had time to think, they were more likely to treat others fairly than when their decisions had to be hurried. Conversely, when people are angry, considerations of logic go out the window (Baron, 1973). Of course, as Ovid observed: "Like fragile ice, anger in time passes away (Ut fragilis glacies, interit ira mora) [Ovid, Ars Amatoria, Bk. 1, 1. 374]." And when people cool down, they may well realize that they have behaved badly and feel the need to "set things right." At this cooling down point, considerations of justice may well sweep back into a position of prominence.

REFERENCES

Aristotle. In C. T. Paynton & R. Blackey (Eds.), Why revolution? Theories and analyses. Cambridge, Mass.: Schenkman, 1971.

Austin, W., & Walster, E. Reactions to confirmations and disconformations of expectancies of equity and inequity. Journal of Personality and Social Psychology, 1974, 30, 208–216.

Bandura, A. Influence of models' reinforcement contingencies on the acquisition of imitative responses. Journal of Personality and Social Psychology, 1965, 1, 589–595.

Bandura, A. Aggression: A social learning analysis. Englewood Cliffs, N.J.: Prentice-Hall, 1973.

Bandura, A., Ross, D., & Ross, S. A. Imitation of film-mediated aggressive models. Journal of Abnormal and Social Psychology, 1963, 66, 3–11. (a)

Bandura, A., Ross, D., & Ross, S. A. Vicarious reinforcement and imitative learning. Journal of Abnormal and Social Psychology, 1963, 67, 601–607. (b)

Baron, R. A. Aggression as a function of magnitude of victim's pain cues, level of prior anger arousal, and aggressor–victim similarity. *Journal of Personality and Social Psychology*, 1971, *18*, 48–54. (a)

Baron, R. A. Exposure to an aggressive model and apparent probability of retaliation as determinants of adult aggressive behavior. *Journal of Experimental Social Psychology*, 1971, 7, 343–355. (b)

Baron, R. A. Reducing the influence of an aggressive model: The restraining effects of discrepant modeling cues. *Journal of Personality and Social Psychology*, 1971, *20*, 240–245. (c)

Baron, R. A. Aggression as a function of ambient temperature and prior anger arousal. *Journal of Personality and Social Psychology*, 1972, *21*, 183–189. (a)

Baron, R. A. Reducing the influence of an aggressive model: The restraining effects of peer censure. *Journal of Experimental Social Psychology*, 1972, *8*, 266–275. (b)

Baron, R. A. Threatened retaliation from the victim as an inhibitor of physical aggression. *Journal of Research in Personality*, 1973, 7, 103–115.

Baron, R. A. Aggression as a function of victim's pain cues, level of prior anger arousal, and exposure to an aggressive model. *Journal of Personality and Social Psychology*, 1974, *29*, 117–124. (a)

Baron, R. A. Threatened retaliation as an inhibitor of human aggression: Mediating effects of the instrumental value of aggression. *Bulletin of the Psychonomic Society*, 1974, *29*, 217–219. (b)

Baron, R. A. The reduction of human aggression: A field study of the influence of incompatible reactions. *Journal of Applied Social Psychology*, 1976, *6*, 260–274.

Baron, R. A. *Human aggression*. New York: Plenum, 1977.

Baron, R. A., & Bell, P. A. Aggression and heat: Mediating effects of prior provocation and exposure to an aggressive model. *Journal of Personality and Social Psychology*, 1975, *31*, 825–832.

Baron, R. A., & Bell, P. A. Aggression and heat: The influence of ambient temperature, negative affect, and a cooling drink on physical aggression. *Journal of Personality and Social Psychology*, 1976, *33*, 245–255.

Baron, R. A., & Bell, P. A. Sexual arousal and aggression by males: Effects of type of erotic stimuli and prior provocation. *Journal of Personality and Social Psychology*, 1977, *35*, 79–87.

Baron, R. A., & Byrne, D. *Social psychology: Understanding human interaction* (2nd ed.) Boston: Allyn & Bacon, 1977.

Baron, R. A., & Kepner, C. R. Model's behavior and attraction toward the model as determinants of adult aggressive behavior. *Journal of Personality and Social Psychology*, 1970, *14*, 335–344.

Baron, R. A., & Lawton, S. F. Environmental influences on aggression: The facilitation of modeling effects by high ambient temperatures. *Psychonomic Science*, 1972, *26*, 80–83.

Baron, R. A., & Ball, R. L. The aggression-inhibiting influence of nonhostile humor. *Journal of Experimental Social Psychology*, 1974, *10*, 23–33.

Berkowitz, L. *Aggression: A social psychological analysis*. New York: McGraw-Hill, 1962.

Berkowitz, L. The concept of aggressive drive: Some additional considerations. In L. Berkowitz (Ed.), *Advances in experimental social psychology* (Vol. 2). New York: Academic Press, 1965. (a)

Berkowitz, L. Some aspects of observed aggression. *Journal of Personality and Social Psychology*, 1965, *2*, 359–369. (b)

Berkowitz, L. Impulse, aggression, and the gun. *Psychology Today*, 1968, *2*(4), 18–22.

Berkowitz, L. The frustration–aggression hypothesis revisited. In L. Berkowitz (Ed.), *Roots of aggression*. New York: Atherton, 1969.

Berkowitz, L. The contagion of violence: In W. J. Arnold & M. M. Page (Eds.), *Nebraska symposium on motivation*. Lincoln: University of Nebraska Press, 1971. Pp. 95–135.

Berkowitz, L. Control of aggression. In B. M. Caldwell & H. M Ricciutti (Eds.), *Review of child development research* (Vol. 3). Chicago: Chicago University Press, 1973.

Berkowitz, L. Some determinants of impulsive aggression: The role of mediated associations with reinforcements for aggression. *Psychological Review*, 1974, *81*, 165–176.

Berkowitz, L., & Alioto, J. T. The meaning of an observed event as a determinant of its aggressive consequences. *Journal of Personality and Social Psychology*, 1973, *28*, 206–217.

Berkowitz, L., & Geen, R. G. Film violence and the cue properties of available targets. *Journal of Personality and Social Psychology*, 1966, *3*, 525–530.

Berkowitz, L., & LePage, A. Weapons as aggression-eliciting stimuli. *Journal of Personality and Social Psychology*, 1967, *7*, 202–207.

Berkowitz, L., & Walster, E. (Eds.). *Advances in experimental social psychology* (Vol. 9). New York: Academic Press, 1976.

Berscheid, E., & Walster, E. When does a harm doer compensate a victim? *Journal of Personality and Social Psychology*, 1967, *6*, 435–441.

Berscheid, E., Walster, E., & Barclay, A. Effect of time on tendency to compensate a victim. *Psychological Reports*, 1969, *25*, 431–436.

Borden, R. J. Witnessed aggression: Influence of an observer's sex and values on aggressive responding. *Journal of Personality and Social Psychology*, 1975, *31*, 567–573.

Borden, R. J., Bowen, R., & Taylor, S. P. Shock-setting behavior as a function of physical attack and extrinsic reward. *Perceptual and Motor Skills*, 1971, *33*, 563–568.

Borden, R. J., & Taylor, S. P. The social instigation and control of physical aggression. *Journal of Applied Social Psychology*, 1973, *3*, 354–361.

Brock, T. C., & Buss, A. H. Dissonance, aggression, and evaluation of pain. *Journal of Abnormal and Social Psychology*, 1962, *65*, 197–202.

Brock, T. C., & Buss, A. H. Effects of justification for aggression in communication with the victim on postaggression dissonance. *Journal of Abnormal and Social Psychology*, 1964, *68*, 403–412.

Brown, B. R. The effects of need to maintain face on interpersonal bargaining. *Journal of Experimental Social Psychology*, 1968, *4*, 107–122.

Brown, D. G., & Tyler, V. O., Jr. Time out from reinforcement: A technique for dethroning the "duke" of an institutionalized group. *Journal of Child Psychology and Psychiatry and Allied Disciplines*, 1968, *9*, 203–211.

Brown, P., & Elliott, R. Control of aggression in a nursery school class. *Journal of Experimental Child Psychology*, 1965, *2*, 103–107.

Buvinic, M. L., & Berkowitz, L. Delayed effects of practiced versus unpracticed responses after observation of movie violence. *Journal of Experimental Social Psychology*, 1976, *12*, 283–298.

Buss, A. H. *The psychology of aggression*. New York: Wiley, 1961.

Buss, A. H. The effect of harm on subsequent aggression. *Journal of Experimental Research in Personality*, 1966, *1*, 249–255.

Buss, A. H. Aggression pays. In J. L. Singer (Ed.), *The control of aggression and violence*. New York: Academic Press, 1971.

Carver, C. S. Facilitation of physical aggression through objective self-awareness. *Journal of Experimental Social Psychology*, 1974, *10*, 365–370.

Carver, C. S. The facilitation of aggression as a function of objective self-awareness and attitudes toward punishment. *Journal of Experimental Social Psychology*, 1975, *11*, 510–519.

Christy, P. R., Gelfand, C. M., & Hartmann, D. P. Effects of competition-induced frustration on two classes of modeled behavior. *Developmental Psychology*, 1971, *5*, 104–111.

Cohen, A. R. Social norms, arbitrariness of frustration, and status of the agent of frustration in the frustration–aggression hypothesis. *Journal of Abnormal and Social Psychology*, 1955, *51*, 222–226.

Conn, L. K., & Crowne, D. P. Instigation to aggression, emotional arousal, and defensive emulation. *Journal of Personality*, 1964, *32*, 163–179.

Davidson, J. Cognitive familiarity and dissonance reduction. In L. Festinger (Ed.), *Conflict, decision, and dissonance*. Stanford, Calif.: Stanford University Press, 1964.

Davis, K. E., & Jones, E. E. Changes in interpersonal perception as a means of reducing cognitive dissonance. *Journal of Abnormal and Social Psychology*, 1960, *61*, 402–410.

Dengerink, H. A. Aggression, anxiety, and physiological arousal. *Journal of Experimental Research in Personality*, 1971, *5*, 223–232.

Dengerink, H. A., & Bertilson, H. A. The reduction of attack instigated aggression. *Journal of Research in Personality*, 1974, *8*, 254–262.

Dengerink, H. A., & Myers, J. D. The effects of failure and depression on subsequent aggression. *Journal of Personality and Social Psychology*, 1977, *35*, 88–96.

Deur, J. D., & Parke, R. D. Effects of inconsistent punishment on aggression in children. *Developmental Psychology*, 1970, *2*, 401–411.

Dollard, J., Doob, L., Miller, N., Mowrer, O. H., & Sears, R. R. *Frustration and aggression*. New Haven, Conn.: Yale University Press, 1939.

Donnerstein, E., Donnerstein, M., & Evans, R. Erotic stimuli and aggression: Facilitation or inhibition. *Journal of Personality and Social Psychology*, 1975, *32*, 237–244.

Donnerstein, E., Donnerstein, M., Simon, S., & Ditrichs, R. Variables in interracial aggression: Anonymity, expected retaliation, and a riot. *Journal of Personality and Social Psychology*, 1972, *22*, 236–245.

Donnerstein, E., & Wilson, D. W. The effects of noise and perceived control upon ongoing and subsequent aggressive behavior. *Journal of Personality and Social Psychology*, 1976, *34*, 774–781.

Donnerstein, M., & Donnerstein, E. Modeling in the control of interracial aggression: The problem of generality. *Journal of Personality*, 1977, *45*, 100–116.

Donnerstein, E., & Donnerstein, M. Variables in interracial aggression: Potential ingroup censure. *Journal of Personality and Social Psychology*, 1973, *27*, 143–150.

Donnerstein, E., & Donnerstein, M. The effect of attitudinal similarity on interracial aggression. *Journal of Personality*, 1975, *43*, 485–502.

Donnerstein, E., & Donnerstein, M. Research in the control of interracial aggression. In R. G. Geen & E. C. O'Neal (Eds.), *Perspectives on aggression*. New York: Academic Press, 1976.

Donnerstein, E., & Barrett, G. The effects of erotic stimuli on male aggression towards females. *Journal of Personality and Social Psychology*, 1978, *36*, 180–188.

Donnerstein, E., & Hallam, J. The facilitating effects of erotica on aggression toward females. *Journal of Personality and Social Psychology*, 1978, *36*, 1270–1277.

Dorsky, F. S., & Taylor, S. P. Physical aggression as a function of manifest anxiety. *Psychonomic Science*, 1972, *27*, 103–104.

Fenigstein, A., & Buss, A. H. Association and affect as determinants of displaced aggression. *Journal of Research in Personality*, 1974, *7*, 306–313.

Ferson, J. E. The displacement of hostility. *Dissertation Abstracts*, 1959, *19*, 2386–2387.

Feshbach, S. The function of aggression and the regulation of aggressive drive. *Psychological Review*, 1964, *71*, 257–272.

Feshbach, S. Aggression. In P. H. Mussen (Ed.), *Carmichael's manual of child psychology*. New York: Wiley, 1970.

Feshbach, S., Stiles, W. B., & Bitter, E. The reinforcing effect of witnessing aggression. *Journal of Experimental Research in Personality*, 1967, *2*, 133–139.

Fishman, C. G. Need for approval and the expression of aggression under varying conditions of frustration. *Journal of Personality and Social Psychology*, 1965, *2*, 809–816.

Freedman, J. L. *Crowding and behavior*. San Francisco: Freeman, 1975.

Fry, M. Justice for Victims. *Journal of Public Law*, 1956, *8*, 155–253.

Gaebelein, J. W. Third-party instigation of aggression: An experimental approach. *Journal of Personality and Social Psychology*, 1973, *27*, 389–395.

Gambaro, S., & Rabin, A. K. Diastolic blood pressure responses following direct and displaced aggression after anger arousal in high- and low-guild subjects. *Journal of Personality and Social Psychology*, 1969, *12*, 87–94.

Geen, R. G. Effects of frustration, attack, and prior training in aggressiveness upon aggressive behavior. *Journal of Personality and Social Psychology*, 1968, *9*, 316–321.

Geen, R. G. Perceived suffering of the victim as an inhibitor of attack-induced aggression. *Journal of Social Psychology*, 1970, *81*, 209–215.

Geen, R. G., & Berkowitz, L. Name-mediated aggressive cue properties. *Journal of Personality*, 1966, *34*, 456–465.

Geen, R. G., & O'Neal, E. C. Activation of cue-elicited aggression by general arousal. *Journal of Personality and Social Psychology*. 1969, *11*, 289–292.

Geen, R. G., & Stonner, D. Effects of aggressiveness habit strength on behavior in the presence of aggression-related stimuli. *Journal of Personality and Social Psychology*, 1971, *17*, 149–153.

Geen, R. G., & Stonner, D. Context effects in observed violence. *Journal of Personality and Social Psychology*, 1972, *25*, 145–150.

Gentry, W. D. Effects of frustration, attack, and prior aggressive training on overt aggression and vascular processes. *Journal of Personality and Social Psychology*, 1970, *16*, 718–725.

Glass, D. C. Changes in liking as a means of reducing cognitive discrepancies between self-esteem and aggression. *Journal of Personality*, 1964, *32*, 520–549.

Goranson, R. E. Media violence and aggressive behavior: A review of experimental research. In L. Berkowitz (Ed.), *Advances in experimental social psychology* (Vol. 5). New York: Academic Press, 1970.

Graham, F. K., Charwat, W. A., Honig, A. S., & Weltz, P. C. Aggression as a function of the attack and the attacker. *Journal of Abnormal and Social Psychology*, 1951, *46*, 512–520.

Greenwell, J., & Dengerink, H. A. The role of perceived versus actual attack in human physical aggression. *Journal of Personality and Social Psychology*, 1973, *26*, 66–71.

Griffitt, W. Environmental effects on interpersonal affective behavior: Ambient effective temperature and attraction. *Journal of Personality and Social Psychology*, 1970, *15*, 240–244.

Griffitt, W., & Veitch, R. Hot and crowded: Influence of population density and temperature on interpersonal affective behavior. *Journal of Personality and Social Psychology*, 1971, *17*, 92–98.

Grusec, J. E. Demand characteristics of the modeling experiment: Altruism as a function of age and aggression. *Journal of Personality and Social Psychology*, 1972, *22*, 139–148.

Hanratty, M. A., O'Neal, E., & Sulzer, J. L. Effect of frustration upon imitation and aggression. *Journal of Personality and Social Psychology*, 1972, *21*, 30–34.

Harper, R. F. *The code of Hammurabi: King of Babylon about 2250 B.C.* Chicago: The University of Chicago Press, 1904.

Harris, M. B. Mediators between frustration and aggression in a field experiment. *Journal of Experimental Social Psychology*, 1974, *10*, 561–571.

Hartmann, D. P. Influence of symbolically modeled instrumental aggression and pain cues on aggressive behavior. *Journal of Personality and Social Psychology*, 1969, *11*, 280–288.

Hatfield, E. *Love, sex, and the marketplace*. Unpublished manuscript, 1981.

Hollenberg, E., & Sperry, M. Some antecedents of aggression and effects of frustration in doll play. *Personality*, 1951, *1*, 34–43.

Jaffe, Y., Malamuth, N., Feingold, J., & Feshbach, S. Sexual arousal and behavioral aggression. *Journal of Personality and Social Psychology*, 1974, *30*, 759–764.

Jecker, J., & Landy, D. Liking a person as a function of doing him a favor. *Human Relations*, 1969, *22*, 371–378.

Katz, I., Glass, D. D., & Cohen, S. Ambivalence, guilt, and the scapegoating of minority group victims. *Journal of Experimental Social Psychology*, 1973, *9*, 423–436.

Kaufmann, H. *Aggression and altruism*. New York: Holt, 1970.

Knott, P. D., Lasater, L., & Shuman, R. Aggression–guilt and conditionability for aggressiveness. *Journal of Personality*, 1974, *42*, 332–344.

Konecni, V. J. Annoyance, type and duration of postannoyance activity, and aggression: The "cathartic effect." *Journal of Experimental Psychology: General*, 1975, *104*, 76–102. (b)

Konecni, V. J., & Doob, A. N. Catharsis through displacement of aggression. *Journal of Personality and Social Psychology*, 1972, *23*, 379–387.

Kuhn, D. Z., Madsen, C. H., & Becker, W. C. Effects of exposure to an aggressive model and "frustration" on children's aggressive behavior. *Child Development*, 1967, *38*, 739–745.

Landy, D., & Mettee, D. Evaluation of an aggressor as a function of exposure to cartoon humor. *Journal of Personality and Social Psychology*, 1969, *12*, 66–71.

Leak, G. K. Effects of hostility arousal and aggressive humor on catharsis and humor preference. *Journal of Personality and Social Psychology*, 1974, *30*, 736–740.

Lerner, M. J., & Matthews, G. Reactions to the suffering of others under conditions of indirect responsibility. *Journal of Personality and Social Psychology*, 1967, *5*, 319–325.

Leventhal, G. S., & Bergman, J. T. Self-depriving behavior as a response to unprofitable inequity. *Journal of Experimental Social Psychology*, 1969, *5*, 153–171.

Leyens, J. P., Camino, L., Parke, R. D., & Berkowitz, L. Effects of movie violence on aggression in a field setting as a function of group dominance and cohesion. *Journal of Personality and Social Psychology*, 1975, *32*, 346–360.

Liebert, R. M., & Baron, R. A. Some immediate effects of televised violence on children's behavior. *Developmental Psychology*, 1972, *6*, 469–475.

Marwell, G., Schmitt, D. R., & Shotola, R. Cooperation and interpersonal risk. *Journal of Personality and Social Psychology*, 1971, *18*, 9–32.

Meyer, R. G. The relationship of blood pressure levels to the chronic inhibition of aggression. *Dissertation Abstracts*, 1967, *28*, 2099.

Meyer, T. P. The effects of sexually arousing and violent films on aggressive behavior. *Journal of Sex Research*, 1972, *8*, 324–333.

Milgram, S. Behavioral study of obedience. *Journal of Abnormal and Social Psychology*, 1963, *67*, 371–378.

Milgram, S. Liberating effects of group pressure. *Journal of Personality and Social Psychology*, 1965, *1*, 127–134. (a)

Milgram, S. Some conditions of obedience and disobedience to authority. *Human Relations*, 1965, *18*, 57–76. (b)

Milgram, S. *Obedience to authority*. New York: Harper & Row, 1974.

Miller, N. E. The frustration–aggression hypothesis. *Psychological Review*, 1941, *48*, 337–342.

Miller, N. E. Theory and experiment relating psychoanalytic displacement to stimulus–response generalization. *Journal of Abnormal and Social Psychology*, 1948, *43*, 155–178.

Mueller, C., & Donnerstein, E. The effects of humor-induced arousal upon aggressive behavior. *Journal of Research in Personality*, 1977, *11*, 73–82.

Murray, E. J., & Berkun, M. M. Displacement as a function of conflict. *Journal of Abnormal and Social Psychology*, 1955, *51*, 47–56.

O'Leary, M. R., & Dengerink, H. A. *Journal of Experimental Research in Personality*, 1973, *7*, 61–70.

Parke, R. D., Berkowitz, L., Leyens, J. P., & Sebastian, R. The effects of repeated exposure to movie violence on aggressive behavior in juvenile delinquent boys: Field experimental studies. In L. Berkowitz (Ed.), *Advances in experimental social psychology* (Vol. 8). New York: Academic Press, 1975.

Patterson, G. R., Littman, R. A., & Bricker, W. Assertive behavior in children: A step toward a theory of aggression. *Monographs of the Society for Research in Child Development*, 1967, *32*, No. 5 (Serial No. 113).

Rice, M. E., & Grusec, J. E. Saying and doing: Effects on observer performance. *Journal of Personality and Social Psychology*, 1975, *32*, 584–593.

Rose, A. M., & Prell, A. F. Does the punishment fit the crime? *The American Journal of Sociology*, 1955, *61*, 247–259.

Ross, M., Thibaut, J., & Evenbeck, S. Some determinants of the intensity of social protest. *Journal of Experimental Social Psychology*, 1971, *7*, 401–418.

Rule, G. B., & Hewitt, L. S. Effects of thwarting on cardiac response and physical aggression. *Journal of Personality and Social Psychology*, 1971, *19*, 181–187.

Rule, B. G., & Leger, G. J. Pain cues and differing functions of aggression. *Canadian Journal of Behavioral Science*, 1976, *8*, 213–222.

Scheier, M. F., Fenigstein, A., & Buss, A. H. Self-awareness and physical aggression. *Journal of Experimental Social Psychology*, 1974, *10*, 264–273.

Sharp, F. C., & Otto, M. C. Retribution and detterence in the moral judgments of common sense. *International Journal of Ethics*, 1910, *20*, 428–458.

Solomon, L. *The influence of some types of power relationships and motivational treatments upon the development of interpersonal trust.* New York: Research Center for Human Relations, New York University, 1957.

Swart, C., & Berkowitz, L. Effects of a stimulus associated with a victim's pain on later aggression. *Journal of Personality and Social Psychology*, 1976, *33*, 623–631.

Sykes, G. M., & Matza, D. Techniques of neutralization: A theory of delinquency. *American Sociological Review*, 1957, *22*, 664–670.

Taylor, S. P. Aggressive behavior and physiological arousal as a function of provocation and the tendency to inhibit aggression. *Journal of Personality*, 1967, *35*, 297–310.

Taylor, S. P. Aggressive behavior as a function of approval motivation and physical attack. *Psychonomic Science*, 1970, *18*, 195–196.

Taylor, S. P., & Gammon, C. B. Effects of type and dose of alcohol on human physical aggression. *Journal of Personality and Social Psychology*, 1975, *32*, 169–175.

Taylor, S. P., & Pisano, R. Physical aggression as a function of frustration and physical attack. *Journal of Social Psychology*, 1971, *84*, 261–267.

Taylor, S. P., Vardaris, R. M., Rawitch, A. B., Gammon, C. B., Cranston, J. W., & Lubetkin, A. I. The effects of alcohol and delta-9-tetrahydrocannabinol on human physical aggression. *Aggressive Behavior*, 1976, *2*, 153–161.

Tedeschi, J. T., & Lindskold, S. *Social psychology.* New York: Wiley, 1976.

Thibaut, J. W. An experimental study of the cohesiveness of underprivileged groups. *Human Relations*, 1950, *3*, 251–278.

Thibaut, J. W., & Coules, J. The role of communication in the reduction of interpersonal hostility. *Journal of Abnormal and Social Psychology*, 1952, *47*, 770–777.

Thibaut, J. W., & Kelley, H. H. *The social psychology of groups.* New York: Wiley, 1959.

Tilker, H. A. Socially responsible behavior as a function of observer responsibility and victim feedback. *Journal of Personality and Social Psychology*, 1970, *14*, 95–100.

Toch, H. *Violent men.* Chicago: Aldine, 1969.

Tyler, V. O., Jr., & Brown, G. D. The use of swift, brief isolation as a group control device for institutionalized delinquents. *Behavior Research and Therapy,* 1967, *5,* 1–9.

Walster, E., & Prestholdt, P. The effect of misjudging another: Overcompensation or dissonance reduction? *Journal of Experimental Social Psychology,* 1966, *2,* 85–97.

Walster, E., Walster, G. W., & Berscheid, E. *Equity: Theory and research.* Boston: Allyn & Bacon, 1978.

Walster, E., Aronson, V., Abrahams, D., & Rottman, L. Importance of physical attractiveness in dating behavior. *Journal of Personality and Social Psychology,* 1966, *4,* 508–516.

Walters, R. H., & Brown, M. Studies of reinforcement of aggression III: Transfer of responses to an interpersonal situation. *Child Development,* 1963, *34,* 536–571.

Weick, K. E., & Nesset, B. Preferences among forms of equity. *Organizational Behavior and Human Performance,* 1968, *3,* 400–416.

Wheeler, L., & Caggiula, A. R. The contagion of aggression. *Journal of Experimental Social Psychology,* 1966, *2,* 1–10.

Wicklund, R. A. Objective self-awareness. In L. Berkowitz (Ed.), *Advances in experimental social psychology* (Vol. 8). New York: Academic Press, 1975.

Wilson, L., & Rogers, R. W. The fire this time: Effects of race of target, insult, and potential retaliation on black aggression. *Journal of Personality and Social Psychology,* 1975, *32,* 857–864.

Worchel, S. The effect of three types of arbitrary thwarting on the instigation to aggression. *Journal of Personality,* 1974, *42,* 301–318.

Zillmann, D. Excitation transfer in communication-mediated aggressive behavior. *Journal of Experimental Social Psychology,* 1971, *7,* 419–434.

Zillmann, D. *Hostility and aggression.* Hillsdale, N.J.: Erlbaum, 1979.

Zillmann, D., Bryant, J., Cantor, J. R., & Day, K. D. Irrelevance of mitigating circumstances in retaliatory behavior at high levels of excitation. *Journal of Research in Personality,* 1975, *9,* 282–293.

Zillmann, D., & Cantor, J. R. Effect of timing of information about mitigating circumstances on emotional responses to provocation and retaliatory behavior. *Journal of Experimental Social Psychology,* 1976, *12,* 38–55.

Zillmann, D., Johnson, R. C., & Day, K. D. Attribution of apparent arousal and proficiency of recovery from sympathetic activation affecting activation transfer to aggressive behavior. *Journal of Experimental Social Psychology,* 1974, *10,* 503–515.

Zillmann, D., & Sapolsky, B. S. What mediates the effect of mild erotica on hostile behavior by males? *Journal of Personality and Social Psychology,* 1977, *35,* 587–596.

chapter 10

Equity and Social Exchange[1]

CHARLES G. McCLINTOCK
LINDA J. KEIL

In this chapter we will be concerned with describing equity in historical terms and indicating two major classes of distributional behaviors to which the term has been applied. In doing so, we will arbitrarily constrain most of our subsequent discussion of equity and exchange to one of these two classes of transfer behavior. Next, we will define and describe several alternative theoretical paradigms that have been elaborated to explain the functional bases of the exchange of resources between human actors. Here, too, we will limit our discussion to a consideration of a subset of the possible conceptual approaches to social exchange. Such restrictiveness will help make the final task of examining the relationship between equity and social exchange more manageable. It should not be taken to imply that those classes of equitable behaviors or theories of social exchange included in the final analysis are more representative or important than those excluded.

Before proceeding, a few comments on definition are in order. First, there are a large number of terms in English that have been employed as synonyms for equity in its most *generic* sense: just, rightful, fair, impartial, equal, lawful, legitimate, dispassionate, appropriate, considered, and so forth. Some of these apply primarily to the outcomes of human transactions; others principally to the procedures that produce such out-

[1]The senior author would like to thank the London School of Economics for providing an appropriate intellectual environment for the initial phase of this effort, and NSF (NSF Grant 77-03862) and the University Faculty Research Committee for financial assistance during the preparation of this chapter.

337

comes. Second, equity has been afforded a number of more specific meanings, two of which are of particular relevance here.

In *sociology* the construct of equity has been used to justify the legitimization of authority in bureaucracies. Thus, beginning with Weber (1947), various organizational theorists including Simon (1957) and Presthus (1960) have viewed equity as providing a moral basis for the premise that those in authority have the *right* to demand obedience; those subject to authority, the *obligation* to obey. These and other theorists then proceed to define various criteria that societies employ to distribute authority. Similar types of assumptions are made in political theories concerned with social contracts and the doctrine of political obligation. Although legitimization, as Katz and Kahn (1978) observe, has not been used as an explanatory construct in social psychology, Milgram's (1974) findings on obedience are certainly consistent with Weber's theoretical assumptions.

In *social psychology* a somewhat different and more specific definition of equity dominates most contemporary research and theory. Beginning with Homans's notion of distributive justice (1961), and including its formalization by Adams (1965), equity has been defined as one of several specific rules that may be employed to determine what is a fair distribution of outcomes. Namely, the rule of equity asserts that one's outcome should be proportional to one's input or contribution. To avoid the definitional confusion that often attends discussions of equity, we will attempt to indicate which usage of the term is being employed in the various discussions that follow.

I. EQUITY

Equity, in its most generic sense, refers to those decision rules that humans employ to define how and when a just and fair distribution of valued resources obtains between actors. The rules themselves may be more or less codified, and may be quite general or specific to a particular relationship. The value of the resources distributed may be positive or negative, that is, they may be rewarding or punishing to the participants. The resources themselves may represent activities, physical commodities, affective states, or any other valued condition. Thus, for example, one may afford another a positive resource by verbally expressing love, presenting a gift, or changing a tire.

Defining what is fair or equitable has been and continues to be a principal activity of human actors who are dependent upon one another, that is, interdependent, in terms of achieving valued outcomes. As such, the study of equity is of central importance to understanding the various types of human relationships and organizations whether these be legal, political, economic, religious, social, or cultural in form. And to the extent that considerations of equity are central in relationships of interdependence, then describing how decision rules regarding fairness are formed and operate is essential to developing valid functional explanations of behavior at all levels of social analysis proceeding from the most basic unit of human social interaction, the dyad, to the most complex of societies.

One dominant characteristic of equity is that what is considered equitable and fair not only changes continuously through time, but it often appears ambiguous at any given time. Newman (1973), in introducing a recent comparative study of equity as it relates to legal systems throughout the world, notes that there has been a continuing search for the meaning of justice since the time of the Academy of Athens. He comments on the indeterminacy of equity in the legal system by pointing to the strange role it plays in the structure of law, a role that is both distinct from and yet tied to legal norms: "Much of the uncertainty that surrounds the meaning of equity is due to the fact that the law must balance the interests of the individual against the interests of society, and each set of interests is differently affected by moral codes [p. 15]." Obviously, the weights assigned to the importance of the individual relative to the society may vary not only between societies but within societies as a function of the nature of decision agencies involved, and of fluctuations in community norms.

Lord Kames (1760), a noted Scottish jurist, described both the reasons why equity is requisite to human affairs, as well as why it can be reached in legal decisions only in certain instances. Equity, he asserted, is required because humans are endowed with a limited capacity for displaying benevolence. Kames argued, though we are constrained by duty not to cause injury to others, we are not compelled to be universally good. We are compelled by nature to show benevolence only toward those with whom we are more or less strongly connected, namely, toward family and friends, and at times toward those with whom we share a more or less common fate, for instance, someone with whom we are shipwrecked on a desert island. Rules of equity become necessary as a means to ensure fairness in our relationships with persons with whom we are loosely connected.

In tracing the history of equity in the legal system of Scotland, Kames observed that initially questions of equity in human action, because of their intrinsic interpersonal complexity, were not handled as matters of common law, but were appropriated to the King and his Council. In time, of course, this system of appeal became too cumbersome, and in

Scotland, a separate court to consider questions of "just, equal and salutary" outcomes was constituted, the Court of Sessions. And, the subsequent history of Western law is in part the history of the slow extension of legal norms and decision making to areas of fairness beyond those relating strictly to the distribution of physical goods and property. Thus, the twentieth century has seen equity depart from the "positivism of law, which would protect the rights of personality only if some property right . . . was present in the case. Only equity . . . has been able to solve the many problems of contemporary society caused by the emergence of new forms of property, and by changing economic and social conditions [Brown, 1973, pp. 221-222]."

A. Equity in Reciprocation and in Allocation

Eckhoff (1974), in his brilliant treatise on justice, notes that problems of justice or equity occur in situations where there is "transfer" of resources, namely, where one party takes some action in relation to another party to which the latter attaches positive or negative value. Parties can be individuals, groups or societies. Eckhoff distinguishes two major classes of transfer, given instances where two or more transfers are interconnected, namely those of *reciprocation* and of *allocation*. Reciprocation exists where there is "give and take" between two parties, and where "one transfer is conditioned by another." This may occur when there is an *exchange* of positive resources such as parents exchanging kisses with their children at bedtime. Or the reciprocation may involve parties inflicting negative outcomes upon each other. (Eckhoff limits his use of the specific term, exchange, to instances of positive reciprocation.)

The second major class of transfers Eckhoff defines as the *allocation* of resources. Such allocations involve the division by an allocator between recipients of one set of objects, or of differing sets which are comparable. In terms of fairness, one can then talk about whether a parent has fairly allocated presents to his or her children at Christmas time, or whether the criminal justice system has allocated fair punishments to two offenders, one of whose crimes is more serious than the other's.

A somewhat similar distinction has been made by Gulliver (1969) who examined the ways conflicts of interest are settled in differing cultures. After reviewing a number of societies in differing social and ecological states, he concludes that all possess negotiation procedures for the reciprocal transfer of resources between parties, but only some have methods for arbitration. Arbitration in this instance implies that some individual or group external to the conflict of interest acts as an arbitrator, or in

Eckhoff's terms, as an allocator of resources. Hence, negotiations represent universal first party *reciprocated* procedures for conflict resolution in which compulsion is exercised by the opposing party and not by an overriding external authority. Arbitration, however, implies resource *allocation decisions* being made by a third party such as might obtain in a binding labor arbitration.

The Eckhoff distinction is of considerable importance for the present chapter insofar as we plan by and large to restrict our primary analysis of equity and social exchange to the structural relationship of reciprocation or negotiation. In so doing, we will consider equity as it relates to the behaviors of actors who are in a first party relationship, and who may directly exercise control over one another's outcomes. This in no way implies that equity is not equally important when looking at relationships of allocation. In fact, as is apparent in the present volume, there seems to have been considerably more speculative, theoretical, and empirical effort in the social sciences devoted to examining equity in relationships where first- or third-party allocations of resources are made to some dependent other. This obtains for the evaluation of equity in its most generic sense: What constitutes fair rules of process and outcome, the study of the legitimization of authority in bureaucratic systems and political life, and the use of the more specific rule that asserts actors' outcomes should be directly proportional to their inputs.

There are undoubtedly numerous reasons for this difference in theoretical and empirical effort. One of the more important ones relates to another assertion made by Lord Kames (1760), that those processes defining human behavior in "personal circumstances" of reciprocity are extremely complex, and not subject to the same form of legal and normative analysis as behaviors that obtain between "loosely connected" individuals. Furthermore, in its bureaucratic and political usage, equity helps to rationalize the division of authority, a division that helps to determine which actors will exercise the right to make resource allocations. And finally, most social psychological theories of human behavior are too weakly formulated to conceptualize even simple forms of interpersonal relationships (for an exception, see Kelley & Thibaut, 1978). Conversely, the allocation model of equity is quite isomorphic with the stimulus–response model that underlies most social psychological explanations of human social behaviors.

B. Equity and the Theory of Social Value

One fundamental characteristic of actors who are in a relationship of reciprocation is that they are interdependent in terms of achieving outcomes. That is, the behavior pursued by one actor often affects both the actor's own and others' outcome. And the obverse is true as well: Others' behaviors affect both their own and actor's outcomes. This relationship of interdependence has profound implications for the formation and expression of human values. It implies that, as a social agent developing criteria for action, an individual must often consider the implications that his or her choices have for both own *and* others' outcomes. Such a consideration is requisite to the extent that humans have been evolutionarily programmed and/or socialized to place value on others' outcomes. And the functional necessity of this weighting process is obvious: Given reciprocation, actors' rewards and punishments and, in fact, survival, are determined by others' behavior as well as their own and vice versa. Hence, in interdependent settings, one's choice of behaviors is conditioned to a significant degree by the outcomes one has obtained previously as a result of others' behavior. And, of course, the obverse obtains as well.

C. Social Values

McClintock has, with the help of a number of colleagues and students, attempted to develop a general conceptual paradigm that defines an actor's social values in terms of the outcome interdependence that exists between that actor and others (McClintock, 1972, 1977). In this paradigm, it is first noted that "in situations of social interdependence one's access to one's own valued outcomes ... is dependent upon the value assigned by other to their possible outcomes [and vice versa]," a condition central to the theory of games (see Luce & Raiffa, 1957). Furthermore, in a step that takes us beyond game theory, it is asserted that "the attractiveness of a particular alternative for one actor may be influenced not only by the outcomes she (or he) receives but also by the outcomes she (or he) judges other will receive [McClintock, 1977, p. 54]."

These two assertions combine to produce a social being who is both interdependent with others and who seeks to distribute physical, psychological, and social resources between self and others in particular ways. The nature of this interdependence and the outcome preferences of participating actors play a major part in determining the structure and the functional nature of relationships of exchange (see Wyer, 1969, 1971).

Given the previous reasoning, one can go on to assume that consistent preferences for particular patterns of outcomes for self and other(s) reflect particular social values. One way to represent such preferences is as a set of vectors in a two-dimensional space in which the magnitude or quality of an actor's outcomes is defined on one axis, and those of other on the other axis. Griesinger and Livingston (1973) describe such a spatial model of values in which various combinations of own and other's outcomes can be designated as points in the two-dimensional space formed by the two axes. Figure 10.1 illustrates vectors that define a subset of social values that are frequently expressed in settings where there are two or more interdependent actors, including those that maximize other's outcomes, joint outcomes, own outcomes, relative advantage of own over other's outcomes, and one that minimizes other's outcomes. Although there are an infinite number of possible preference rules, those social values common to "naive" as well as to scientific descriptions of human social behavior seem to fall on vectors that correspond with the principal own and other outcome axes, or that are 45 degrees removed from them.

One additional characteristic of social values that McClintock (1977) has stated previously in propositional form is also important to note. In any choice situation where actors are interdependent in terms of the attainment of outcomes, a preference may reflect either (1) an actor's most valued outcome (a social goal or motive); and/or (2) a strategic response designed to affect other's subsequent choices so as to increase the likelihood that an actor can subsequently achieve a highly valued outcome.

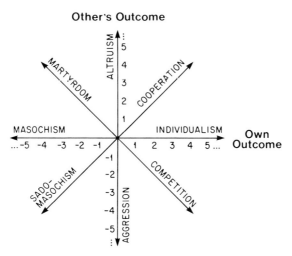

Figure 10.1. Vectors that define a subset of social values. (Given a particular value orientation, an actor should select that combination of available own and other's outcomes that has the greatest projection on the correspondent vector.)

In effect, this proposition asserts that making a choice that is consistent with a particular value may reflect one of two intentions on the part of an actor. It may be a response that is consistent with the actor's preferred goal or end state, for example, a preference for a cooperative or competitive outcome. Or, it may reflect an attempt to modify other's subsequent choices in such a way that an actor may be able to achieve some preferred outcome that is partially under the control of other; that is, actor's choice may represent an instrumental or strategic action such as ingratiation. This distinction is important because confusion between goals and strategies can impede the social scientist's attempts to understand an actor's behavior, and can be an obstacle to the development of trust between actors within a relationship.

Finally, it should be noted that an actor's dominant value may shift within a given setting or as the actor moves from one interdependence setting to another. Thus, although there may be individual differences in value (see, for example, Kuhlman & Marshello, 1975; Messick & McClintock, 1968; Radzicki, 1976), it is obvious that situations can also strongly affect the dominance of social values.

D. Values of Fairness

Van Avermaet, McClintock, and Moskowitz (1978) attempt to examine whether several rules for the fair distribution of outcomes can also be appropriately characterized as social values. And, indeed, two of the more specific rules of fairness, proportional equity and equality, can be represented in a two dimensional own–other outcome space. Given its proportional representation, equity does not take a linear form. Rather, as depicted in the example in Figure 10.2, an individual intent upon maximizing the equity of his own and other's outcomes would follow a decision rule in which the ratio of self to other's outcomes would be proportional to the ratio of their respective inputs. Given equal inputs, as in Figure 10.2, actors would prefer choices on a line with a slope value of 1, and would prefer those points in the outcome space for which the ratio between own and other's outcomes most closely approximates 1.

The dashed lines in Figure 10.2 deserve brief comment. They represent indifference lines or curves, a concept developed by decision theorists to describe various combinations of two commodities between which a buyer has no preference. As depicted in Figure 10.2, actors choosing equitably would prefer the own–other outcome point falling on the indifference line closest to the Slope 1 line. However, they would be indifferent between the points defining a given indifference line because the ratio of own and other's outcomes to inputs falling on this line are

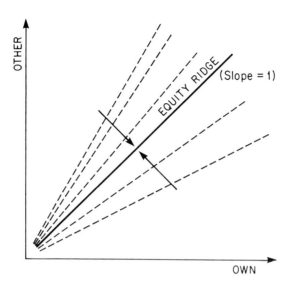

Figure 10.2. Equity given equal inputs by self and other. (The most equitable distribution of own and other's outcomes would fall on the equity ridge. Dashed lines represent indifference curves defined by their proximity to the ridge and where the ratio of self to other's outcomes are proportional to the ratio of their respective inputs.)

proportionally equal. Indifference proves to be a very useful concept in defining and assessing an actor's decision rules.

Figure 10.2 depicts an instance of equity given equal inputs; Figure 10.3 illustrates an equity preference structure for a hypothetical own–other input ratio with a slope of 2. This implies that other has contributed twice as much input as self, and hence deserves twice as much of the available payoffs. In fact, for any given own–other input ratio, the corresponding equity preference structure can be mapped onto a two dimensional payoff space. And, of course, if an actor were motivated to behave equitably, then he or she should consistently select that distribution of outcomes which most closely approximated the slope defined by the existing ratio of inputs.

It should be strongly emphasized that equity and equality are two of a number of patterns of outcomes between actor and other(s) that may and indeed have been labeled as fair or just. Any systematic preference structure of an individual for outcome distributions between self and other(s) can be depicted in such an outcome space. And a sizable number of these structures or rules have been employed to define specific rules of fairness by differing actors within and between various social settings at various times in history. For example, winner-take-all, every man for himself, Pareto optimality, the distribution of outcomes by need, and

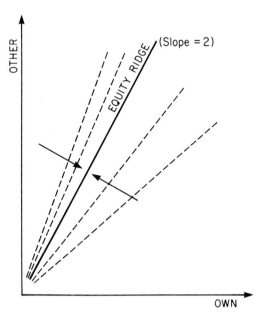

Figure 10.3. Equity given other's inputs are twice own inputs. (The most equitable distribution falls on the equity ridge. Dashed lines represent indifference curves defined as in Figure 10.2.)

noblesse oblige have all have been described as fair or just rules for resource distribution.

E. Attributions and Misattributions of Social Values

One of the principal activities of actors who are in relationships of reciprocity is the exchange of various types of activities, resources, and affect. Theories that describe these exchange processes will be described in the next section. Here, we want to point out why it is difficult at times for both a "naive" actor or observer, as well as a more sophisticated observing social scientist, to decode accurately which social values are being expressed by an actor toward an interdependent other. The resulting inaccuracies in the decoding process may become a significant problem to both actor and other because they often raise the costs of maintaining the relationship, and thereby jeopardize its viability. For the social scientist, of course, misunderstanding an intention behind an act may reduce the validity and reliability of descriptions or explanations of the choice behavior of actors in settings of reciprocity.

For example, when an actor selects one of several ways to distribute outcomes between self and other, the behavior is subject to a variety of interpretations. One possible source of attributional confusion may be obtained in interpreting an act as a goal rather than as a strategy. Mary's attributing John's act of giving her something as being an end in itself instead of an instance of ingratiation can markedly affect not only her view of him, but also what kinds of outcomes she will mediate for him in the future. And even if attributions are restricted to goal oriented behaviors, there is still room for major errors. For example, suppose John had the opportunity to afford Mary $500 and himself $500, or to afford Mary $300 and himself $600, and he chose the second alternative. Mary could reasonably make the attribution that John was not behaving in a prosocial manner toward her. He did not choose to maximize her outcome or their joint outcomes. Furthermore, he rejected the fairness norm of equality. However, Mary still does not have sufficient information to judge how antisocial John's behavior was intended to be. For his choice maximized his own outcome, his competitive advantage over her, and minimized Mary's outcome. Obviously, she does not have the information on the basis of John's choice to decide whether he was individualistic, competitive, or aggressive in motivation. Of course, which of these three orientations Mary chooses to attribute to John will affect her future behavior toward him, including the types of outcomes she would mediate for him. This, in turn, will influence John's subsequent behavior toward Mary, and so on.

II. SOCIAL EXCHANGE THEORY

In the previous sections, we have defined equity in a limited sense as one of several social values that an actor may pursue in settings where there is outcome interdependence between self and other(s). In the present one, we will examine theories that attempt to describe the reasons, rules, and processes that underlie behaviors in interdependent relationships where two or more actors seek to trade or exchange valued resources with one another. In a subsequent section, we will consider the possible roles of fairness in this exchange process.

One of the first investigations of social exchange was conducted by Mauss (1967), who examined the significance of the exchange of gifts in a number of "simple" societies. He observed that, although gifts appeared to be proffered in a voluntary manner within and between various societies, they were in fact given and repaid under obligation. He further noted that, with regard to the nature of exchange, the following obtained: "what they exchange is not exclusively goods and wealth, real and personal property, and things of economic value. They exchange rather courtesies, entertainments, ritual, military assistance, women, children, dances, and feasts; and fairs in which the market is but one element and the circulation of wealth but one part of a wide and enduring contract [p. 3]."

Lévi-Strauss (1969), like Mauss, also examined the interparty exchange of goods within a variety of societies. He concluded that the exchange of goods is not only pervasive but has meaning far beyond the realization of simple economic values permitting a participant "to gain security and fortify oneself against risks incurred through alliances and rivalry [p. 76]."

Blau (1964a), in setting forth his theory of exchange, substantially widened the conception of exchange resources. He asserted that "social exchange can be observed everywhere once we are sensitized by this conception of it, not only in market relations but also in friendship and love." Blau includes within his definition of resources all "actions that are contingent on rewarding reactions from other, and cease when these expected reactions are not forthcoming [p. 6]." Thus, the expression of affection, conforming to normative demands, ignoring insults, or making love can be represented as resources that can be exchanged in settings of reciprocity and outcome interdependence. Such a broad definition of social exchange is also implied by Homans's work (1961, p. 1) where social interaction is defined as the "exchange of activity, tangible or intangible, and more or less rewarding or costly between at least two persons." Thibaut and Kelley (1959; see also Kelley & Thibaut, 1978) would concur with both Homans and Blau in extending the definition of exchange resources to include objects, events, or affective states that actors find rewarding.

In one of the few attempts after Mauss (1967) to define what is typically exchanged in human relationships, Foa (1971) has postulated six classes of resources: (1) status; (2) love; (3) service; (4) information; (5) material goods; and (6) money. These he orders along two dimensions, *particularism* and *concreteness*. Particularism is a dimension that defines the degree to which the specific individual with whom the resource is to be exchanged constitutes a condition for the exchange to occur. Hence, one would expect that love would be the most particularistic resource and money, the least. The second dimension is one of symbolism with status and information falling on the more symbolic end of the continuum, and services and goods on the other. Foa uses this classification scheme in an inventive way to help to define similarity between resources and to predict which classes of resources are likely to be exchanged for one another.

Thus, social exchange theories are concerned with the structural and functional nature of relationships that obtain between two or more actors who are outcome interdependent, and who reciprocally determine the delivery of various classes and amounts of resources to one another.

A. Social Psychological Exchange Theory: The Economic and Anthropological Antecedents

Prior to describing the major *social psychological* theories of exchange in more individual terms, we will attempt to depict two other major exchange traditions that preceded them, namely, the *economic* model of exchange as applied to transactions in the marketplace, and the *social anthropological* model that considers the exchange of social as well as physical commodities in the service of social and economic ends at the societal level. We will examine the economic model first, and in more detail, because there is greater comparability between it and contemporary social psychological models of exchange. Before discussing exchange theories in greater detail, we should acknowledge our indebtedness to Heath (1976) for his major analytic work in the area. We have encountered no single source that is more valuable to one interested in a critical, and often profound, analysis of the role that exchange theories have and should play in explanations of human social behavior.

1. THE ECONOMIC MODEL OF EXCHANGE

Robbins (1932), in an often-quoted definition, asserts that economics is "a science which studies human behaviour as a relationship between ends and scarce means with alternative uses [p. 15]." In effect, Robbins argues that economics is concerned with how humans should and do make decisions or choices regarding the employment of scarce resources (e.g., money) in the pursuit of preferred outcomes. Exchange processes become important because many economic decisions involve two or more interdependent actors. In the process of developing an economic exchange model, a general paradigm of human decision making has emerged that is applicable to human behavior in noneconomic as well as economic contexts. This decision-making paradigm of rational choice, in fact, parallels that which provides the conceptual basis for the previously described theory of social values. Hence, it provides a common meeting ground between the models of economic and social exchange to be described subsequently.

The theory of rational choice asserts that an individual actor should and often does make choices in a purposive manner so as to obtain preferred outcomes in an effective way, that is, to maximize the value of his or her outcomes. If an actor has complete control over achieving the outcomes available, he or she merely makes the choice that will access the most preferred goal. If, as is often the case, the likelihood that a particular outcome can be obtained is not certain, one is compelled to take into consideration both the probability of obtaining the outcome as well as its utility, in maximizing the expected value of one's outcomes. In economics, the dominant value that is assumed to dictate human economic behavior is the maximization of *own* economic utilities or outcomes.

Given a theory of rational choice for maximizing the expected value of outcomes, economists next asked the question of whether one can define a preference space that would describe an actor's attempts to maximize outcomes in regard to preferred combinations of two or more commodities. To handle this problem, the economists developed what we described in our earlier discussion of social values as indifference curves. These curves, which can also be mapped into a two dimensional geometrical outcome space, depict a series of points defined by a particular combination of two or more commodities between which an actor is indifferent.

Generally, economists (see MacCrimmon & Toda, 1969) assume in drawing sets of indifference curves that a consumer would prefer to have more of both commodities than less; that the consumer's choices are transitive, that is, the consumer has consistent preferences and hence indifference curves will not intersect; and finally, they assume some notion of diminishing marginal utility applies, namely, the more a consumer has of a particular commodity, the less valuable will be the next additional unit of that commodity. In terms of the theory of social values defined earlier, the two commodities are own and other's outcomes.

The most interesting part of economic theory as it relates to exchange theory concerns instances where one has two buyers and/or sellers who each want something that the other has. In effect, much of economic theory and all of exchange theory is concerned with the dynamics of actors' behaviors in settings where the outcomes can be improved more within a relationship than outside of it. In some instances, actors directly mediate rewards and/or costs for one another. In other instances, external constraints may make the rewards within a relationship, no matter how low, higher than the costs of leaving the relationship. The latter defines what is sometimes called an involuntary relationship.

Most major theories of economic exchange consider the case of bilateral monopoly where two actors have something to trade or exchange, and where each attempts to maximize own profits. The economists again use the notion of indifference curves to represent this instance, but this time map actors' preference structures for the distribution of the two commodities to be traded in a geometric space, what is in economics termed an *Edgeworth Box*. Blau (1964a), for example, uses such a box diagram to extend economic theory to an analysis of an exchange between two actors who possess two social commodities, one who has expert "problem-solving ability" and the other "resources of willing compliance," that is, the ability to confer status or esteem.

A simple depiction of Blau's example is given in the "box diagram" in Figure 10.4. In effect, the box illustrates relations between Persons A and B who can trade their two social commodities in varying amounts. If one assumes that each person has some amount of each commodity prior to an exchange, then one can represent their initial position in the box, say at point X in Figure 10.4. Also represented in the box are two indifference curves, one for Person A: a_1 a_3, and one for B: b_1 b_3. These two curves intersect, and define the sets of outcomes between which both are indifferent. The space within the two sets of indifference curves defines a region in which both actors would prefer to be in terms of their relative distribution of Blau's two commodities, "problem-solving ability" and "willing compliance."

Once we have identified such a region, the next question becomes,

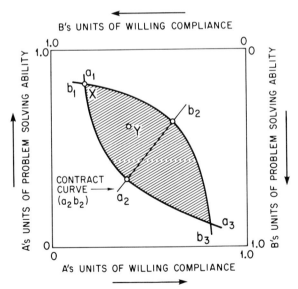

Figure 10.4. An Edgeworth box depicting a possible exchange relationship between Actor A and Actor B for the commodities of problem-solving ability and units of willing compliance. (a_1, a_3 is an indifference curve for A; b_1, b_3 for B. Together they define a common region [shaded] of jointly preferred outcomes. Y represents an outcome preferred by A and B to X. a_2 is A's most preferred outcome; b_2 is B's. The line a_2, b_2 defines a contract curve, that is, the region of maximum joint benefit.)

what actual trades should or will be made? Consider the point Y in the space. Both persons are better off here than at their present location, X. However, note that there remain numerous points at which both would be even better off in terms of their preference structure. It can be seen, for example, that the optimal point for Person A is at a_2 and for B at b_2. And in fact, a line connecting the two points defines the parties' maximum joint benefit. Economic theory argues that exchanges will tend to occur along this a_2 b_2 line, called the contract line, but that the particular point on the line is indeterminant *a priori*. In effect, this line represents a region where bargaining is required, as movement along either indifference curve away from the contract line will worsen one person's position at no added advantage to the other.

This bilateral monopoly model, as Cook and Emerson (1978) note, leaves the *specific* outcome of two-person exchange indeterminate along the contract line. Because economic theory is based on a model of individual decision making in an asocial market in which actors, although more or less interdependent, tend to be numerous and unacquainted, there are no normative allocation rules once a contract line is reached. Social theories of exchange, in fact, address this indeterminancy. Namely, they consider how concepts such as social value, equity, power, social comparison, distributive justice, profit, and so on help to define the processes that influence the formation and maintenance of relations, as well as help to predict the specific outcomes that actors will obtain in exchange relationships.

Finally, one other aspect of economic theory that has been important in the development of social exchange models is the theory of price. Both Blau and Homans in their theories of social exchange use the economic assumption that the actual or equilibrium price of a commodity is given by the intersection of demand and supply curves. For this to obtain, in economics, a number of assumptions must be made, such as that the commodities are homogeneous; that there are large numbers of buyers and sellers; and that buyers and sellers have knowledge of the prices at which others are willing to buy and sell. Both Blau and Homans relax these assumptions. Blau, for instance, utilizes the concept of price to help define the relative stability of relationships formed for the exchange of two resources, problem-solving ability and willing compliance (conformity). Homans uses the theory of price in yet another way, namely to help explain why some members of a group are afforded more status than others. He argues, for example, that expert advice is characteristically in scarcer supply than conformity, and hence engenders greater approval and status from the group. Again the pricing of advice or conformity may not be strictly determinant, and the setting of prices for these social commodities is subject to negotiation and the operation of various social decision rules.

These two theories then, bilateral monopoly and price, are central in both theories of economic and social exchange. A third economic paradigm, game theory, a model that considers decision making in social settings where actors are outcome interdependent, will be outlined and discussed subsequently when we consider Thibaut and Kelley's conceptualization of social exchange.

2. THE ANTHROPOLOGICAL MODEL OF EXCHANGE

The works of Mauss and Lévi-Strauss, cited earlier, stand in sharp contrast to the preceding economic model of exchange, and in fact, to the social psychological exchange theories as well. They fall within a collectivist tradition in anthropology and sociology that generally eschews as principles for explaining social behavior both the rational decision assumptions of economics, and the individualistic reward and cost formulations of behavioral psychology. Whereas most social psychological theories of exchange ask how individual actors behave and interact given the constraints of norms, roles, and other institutional arrangements, the more collectivistic theories are concerned with understanding the origins and functioning of these institutional variables themselves. And whereas the former see individual self-interest, needs, and social values as the motivating forces propelling human action and interaction, the collectivist tradition postulates that understanding social phenomena, including the behavior of "individuals," is dependent upon identifying and assessing those social processes that contribute more or less to the successful functioning of societies and subgroups within them. And the laws that govern such societal processes are assumed to be irreducible to the level of the individual, that is, to have emergent properties.

Durkheim (1947), of course, is often cited as the sociologist who has most convincingly argued that utilitarian economic assumptions and psychological variables are irrelevant to both sociological and anthropological explanations. Others, such as Parsons (1968) and Blau (1964a), have argued that a synthesis between individualistic and collectivistic explanations is possible. And Ekeh (1974), who has written a very thorough, although not always objective, review of exchange theory from both explanatory traditions, maintains that, although a synthesis between them is not possible, their polemic opposition is functional in stimulating theoretical and methodological advances within both.

To provide one instance of the collectivist orientation to social exchange, let us briefly consider the work of Lévi-Strauss. As Ekeh (1974, p. 43) points out, Lévi-Strauss, who is concerned in particular with exchange as it relates to the structure of kinship, takes a strong position against the economic theory of kinship exchange proposed by Frazer (1919). The latter, in one of the earliest exchange explanations of social behavior, viewed the exchange of sisters, for example, as illustrating a simple instance of barter pursued as a means to obtain a wife. Lévi-Strauss strongly attacks this utilitarian form of explanation as simple and naive on several grounds. First, he takes strong exception to deductive forms of theorizing where social exchange laws are deduced from economic principles that in turn are viewed to derive from more inclusive "natural" laws. Second, he sees no need to distinguish economic from social laws of exchange. And finally, he asserts, even if one could distinguish them, Frazer provides no means for formulating autonomous laws of social exchange. In fact, Lévi-Strauss argues that the nature of the goods exchanged is irrelevant to understanding the process of exchange. He observes: "The exchange relationship comes before the things exchanged, and is independent of them. If the goods considered in isolation are identical, they cease to be so when assigned their proper place in the structure of reciprocity [1969, p. 139]."

B. Social Psychological Models of Exchange

There are three major social psychological theories of exchange: those propounded by Homans in *Social Behavior: Its Elementary Forms* (1961, 1974), by Blau in *Exchange and Power In Social Life* (1964a) and by Thibaut and Kelley in the *Social Psychology of Groups* (1959) and by Kelley and Thibaut in *Interpersonal Relations: A Theory of Interdependence* (1978). Before briefly indicating some of the major points of emphasis within each of the models, we would like to specify some of the major assumptions that they hold in common:

1. Human actors are outcome interdependent, insofar as each human actor mediates rewards for others who in turn mediate rewards for the actor.
2. Human beings tend to form and continue in those relationships that afford them rewards, and that are profitable in the sense that the rewards obtained outweigh the costs of maintaining the relationships. Continuance is based on both parties finding the relationship mutually profitable.
3. Actors within a relationship are compelled to reciprocate rewards to assure the continuity of exchange. In effect, an actor must take into consideration the welfare of other to assure his or her own.
4. Exchange is not restricted to economic activities—social exchange,

as Blau has observed, is ubiquitous, and any resources actors value may be exchanged.

5. The *a priori* or continuing distribution of valued resources between actors within an exchange relationship may or may not be symmetrical. Generally, the actor who has more of a valued resource or resources is assumed to have the capability to exercise more influence or power within the relationship.

6. Finally, although the social psychological models to be described differ in the degree to which they emphasize the centrality of various economic and psychological principles, they universally assume that the understanding of institutional arrangements is not sufficient for describing the processes of social exchange. Rather, they would see such arrangements as setting limits within which human interaction and exchange occur.

1. THE EXCHANGE THEORY OF HOMANS

Homans's theory is strongly psychological in orientation. The major propositions that he sets forth as the fundamental determinants of exchange are based on the principles of behavior set forth by Skinnerian behavioral psychologists, principles that were formulated and tested in studies of animal behavior. Homans assumes that the propositions can be employed to describe the nature of human interdependence and exchange: "Nothing emerges that cannot be explained by propositions of individuals as individuals, together with the given conditions [within which] they tend to be interacting [1974, p. 12]." More complex institutional arrangements are viewed as ultimately reducible to these same propositions: "The characteristics of social groups and societies are resultants, no doubt complicated, but still resultants, of the interactions between individuals over time—and they are not more than that [1974, p. 12]."

The psychological propositions that Homans believes govern all human action are paraphrased in what follows, and are to be found either in his initial formulation (1961) or the later revision (1974) of his book on social behavior:

Success Proposition: The more often a given act is rewarded, the more likely an actor is to perform it. (Subject to the constraints stated in the Deprivation–Satiation Proposition)

Stimulus Proposition: If in the past a particular event has resulted in actor's behavior being rewarded, then the more similar the present event to the past one, the more likely it is that actor will again perform the same or a similar act.

Value Proposition: The more valuable to a person is the result of his action, the more likely he is to perform the action. Positive values may imply rewards or the avoidance or escape from punishment; negative ones, punishment, withholding rewards, or reward forgone as a result of choice.

Deprivation–Satiation Proposition: The more recently a reward has been received, the less valuable any further unit of the reward.

Aggression–Approval Proposition: If a person does not receive a reward he expected his action to produce or receives less than he expected, he will become angry and will be more likely to act aggressively as the results of such behavior become more valuable to him. Conversely, if a person receives an expected reward, and especially if he receives more than expected, he will be more likely to perform and value approving behavior.

Rationality Proposition: In choosing between alternative actions, a person will choose that one for which, as perceived by him at the time, the value, V, of the results, multiplied by the probability, p, of getting the results, is greatest.

The final proposition summarizes Homans's first three propositions, and is a restatement of the expected value hypothesis that underlies most economic models of human decision making. Homans believes that this proposition provides a link between his behavioral propositions, and an economic model of human action and exchange.

In fact, the economists' expected value hypothesis depicts human decision makers behaving in a purposive and rational manner taking the future into account. Homans, whose propositions are based primarily upon the observations of pigeons, would not describe action as either purposive or future oriented, as probability and value are strictly matters of accumulated past experience. The economist, however, assumes that a rational human decision maker employs past, present, and future expectancies to both define utilities and to estimate probabilities. As Heath (1976) cogently points out in regard to estimating probabilities: "If an unbiased coin has come up heads on one trial, Homans's pigeon is apt to believe that it will come up heads on the subsequent trial too. But the rational man who has been told about probability theory does not make this mistake. He knows that there is a fifty–fifty chance of heads on each and every trial. His expectations are thus different from the pigeon's, and so will be his behavior [p. 14]." In fact, of course, humans also use history inappropriately in estimating probabilities of equally likely events, but not to the degree that Homans's pigeons would.

Although not stated in formal theoretical terms, Homans makes a

number of assertions concerning the nature of social exchange that derive more or less directly from his fundamental psychological propositions. He observes that exchange occurs in interaction when the action
of one actor rewards another and vice versa, and that an actor will
approach that other person who is likely to offer the highest rewards in
relation to the costs of approach. He notes further that an *impersonal*
relation exists when an actor enters into a single exchange with another
for a single reward that is readily available elsewhere, because it is the
nature of the reward and not the identity of the particular person that is
important. The relationship is a *personal* one where actors enter into
multiple exchanges of reward that are specific to the particular actors
involved. He defines psychic profit as reward minus cost where cost is
defined as the reward forgone in not performing some alternative ac-
tion(s). No exchange continues unless both parties are making a profit.
And conflict and anger can be engendered if one actor perceives that
another has achieved an unfair advantage. Finally, Homans sets forth his
well-known principle of distributive justice: An actor in an exchange
relationship with another will expect the rewards of each to be proportional to the costs . . . and the net rewards or profits of each man to be
proportional to his investment such that the greater the investment, the
greater the profit.

Homans proceeds to illustrate these propositions and assertions by
examining the procedures and findings of a number of laboratory and
field studies that consider such fundamental social processes as group
cohesiveness, social approval and liking, the exercise of power, worker
satisfaction and morale, and social justice and fairness. It is apparent that
Homans's view of man conforms to the Skinnerian model of an individual organism that solves the problems of achieving rewards and
avoiding punishments in a social context by taking into account past
experience. Further, Homans's model, unlike the economic one, depicts
man as a potentially emotional creature who experiences affect when
discrepancies occur between expected and obtained rewards and
punishments.

2. BLAU'S MODEL OF EXCHANGE

The principles of exchange as set forth by Blau differ from those of
Homans in a number of ways. First, rather than employing the principles of behavioral psychology as the building blocks of a theory, Blau is
much more eclectic in his approach, relying on a combination of economic and decision theoretic principles, on social rather than behavioral
assertions at the psychological level, while simultaneously employing the
more sociological and anthropological arguments set forth by Mauss and

others. Rather than taking the strongly reductionistic position of Homans, Blau asserts that understanding the behavior of individuals is essential, but not sufficient for understanding social exchange, and that the same relationship obtains between understanding the processes of exchange and more complex institutional arrangements. "Emergent properties are essentially relationships between elements in a structure. The relationships are not contained in the elements, though they could not exist without them, and they define the structure [Blau, 1964a, p. 3]."

Although Blau does not, like Homans, enumerate a set of limited propositions from which to further derive theorems and hypotheses concerning social exchange and more complex institutional arrangements, he does make a number of basic assertions that provide a theoretical basis for much of his subsequent analysis. For example, he observes that actors are attracted to rewarding associations. Rewards, according to Blau, may be *spontaneous* (ends in themselves) or *calculated* (means to other ends). Blau further enumerates three types of costs that may affect the value of rewards: *investment* costs such as those associated with the acquisition of skills; *direct* costs such as occur when an actor complies to other's demands in an exchange setting; and *opportunity* costs that include the alternative forgone in pursuing a given act.

An actor is assumed to choose between alternative potential relationships or courses of action by first evaluating both prior and expected rewards and costs associated with each, and then selecting the best. Blau notes that a fundamental characteristic of social exchange is that an actor who supplies a rewarding service to another obligates the other to furnish a benefit in return. Social exchange differs from economic transactions insofar as the nature of the required return benefit is diffuse, often unstructured in regard to time, and both dependent upon trust as well as a condition for its continuation. Exchange processes are also seen to give rise to the differentiation of power. An actor who services others' needs, and who is independent of any services at others' command, attains power over others by making the satisfaction of others' needs contingent on others' compliance to the actor. And finally, Blau provides a dynamic for the exchange process: Actors are interested in maintaining a balance between inputs and outputs and staying out of debt in social transactions; hence, producing a strain toward reciprocity. At the same time, actors aspire to achieve an exchange balance in their own favor, by which they would accumulate credit, making their status superior to that of others; hence, producing a strain toward imbalance.

Blau provides us with a much richer social portrayal than Homans of human actors who form relationships because of mutual attraction, an attraction based on fulfillment of the needs and values of both. Blau does not provide a social psychological description of the needs and values of individual actors, but, assuming them as given, goes on to define and evaluate dyadic and group processes that guide social exchange. In doing so, he examines such phenomena as impression formation and maintenance, the formation of groups, the differentiation of power and status, the emergence and functioning of group norms, the development of interpersonal trust, as well as a number of other more collective phenomena.

3. THIBAUT AND KELLEY'S MODEL OF INTERDEPENDENCE

The work of Thibaut and Kelley (1959) is the most social psychological of the three models of exchange considered here. They are fundamentally concerned with the structural nature of social interdependence, and its impact on patterns of social interaction. And in their analysis, they employ a form of game theory based on earlier economic models of multiperson decision making. In doing so, they argue that an interaction between an actor and another can be depicted as a game-type matrix for which one axis represents items in actor's behavioral repertoire, and the other axis those in other's repertoire. Entered in each cell of the matrix are outcomes that represent a composite of the rewards and costs experienced by actor and by other for a particular combination of their behaviors. The specific value of each outcome is a function of variables exogenous to the relationship, such as the needs of the actor and the resources of other, and endogenous variables, such as the prior history of dyadic interaction or existing incompatibilities between actor's various response alternatives.

An interaction between actor and other will be initiated or will continue based on the value of the outcomes experienced by both parties relative to two general criteria. *Comparison level* (*CL*) is the standard one uses to evaluate the attractiveness of a relationship in terms of beliefs about whether one "deserves" the outcome provided. If the outcomes fall above the comparison level, then the relationship is "relatively" satisfying; below, unsatisfying. The level is set on the basis of one's prior history, real or symbolic, of outcomes experienced. *Comparison level for alternatives* (CL_{alt}) is the lowest level of outcome that one will accept in a relationship given available alternative relationships. When outcomes fall below the comparison level for alternatives, an actor will leave the relationship. The more above one's CL_{alt} one's outcomes are in a given relationship, the more one is dependent on that relationship. An actor may be in an unsatisfying relationship where the level of rewards is below actor's CL. However, the actor may be constrained to the relation-ship because these outcomes are above actor's CL_{alt}.

An actor has power over other to the extent that variations in his or her behavior can affect the quality of other's outcome. Two basic kinds of power are defined. Actors have *fate control* if they can affect other's outcome regardless of what other does. Actors have *behavior control* over another if they can affect the probability that other will act in a particular way to maximize other's outcomes.

Thibaut and Kelley (1959) use these constructs to examine a number of increasingly complex social phenomena. *First,* they ask how the pro-cesses just described relate to the following questions concerning dyadic relations: (*a*) What variables influence participants' rewards and costs to make the continuation of a relationship more viable; (*b*) how does re-sponse interference raise the costs of a relationship; (*c*) what factors influence how rewards and costs are sampled during the formation of a relationship; and (*d*) how do various patterns of mutual and unilateral fate and behavior control affect the development and maintenance of relationships? *Second,* they examine how these preceding dyadic pro-cesses: (*a*) affect the functioning of groups in terms of the development of norms and roles; (*b*) interact with the characteristics of a task to affect group performance and morale; and (*c*) influence actors' adaptability to new situations given that they are involuntarily subject to the dictates of a group. *Third,* they look at interdependence within large groups, examin-ing the types of influence that are exerted upon members by groups of various size and complexity, and the manner in which roles are defined and interrelated to promote the functioning of larger groups.

Kelley and Thibaut's (1978) theoretical work extends their analysis of outcome matrices as a way of depicting the structure of social inter-dependence. Such matrices were initially defined and formally explored by mathematicians and economists as a method for developing prescrip-tive models of rational choice given varying structures of outcome inter-dependence and exchange. Subsequently, these matrix games have been used both theoretically and methodologically by social psychologists to explore patterns of cooperation, competition, and bargaining in rela-tionships where two or more actors were outcome interdependent and where the behaviors of each mediated rewards and punishments for themselves and others.

Thibaut and Kelley's conception of the exchange process thus focuses on outcome interdependence. Individual rewards and costs, two major forms of evaluation of outcomes, and the capability to exercise control over own and other's outcomes and behaviors are initially defined at an individualistic level, albeit at the level of a very social individual who maximizes socially defined outcomes such as status and prestige, and who compares own with other's outcomes. However, for Thibaut and Kelley, a more fundamental understanding of social exchange and interdependence necessarily occurs at the level of an interacting dyad or group. Thus, in one sense, Thibaut and Kelley come closer to building a model of social exchange that falls at a level of analysis intermediate between psychology and sociology than does either Homans or Blau.

C. The Status of Exchange Theory

The primary purpose of the present chaper is *not* to provide an indepth analysis of exchange theories of human action. Rather we want to examine the role equity plays within relationships of reciprocity or exchange. To do this, it is first necessary to characterize the current status of theories of exchange. It is perhaps a commentary on the current conceptual and methodological weaknesses in the social sciences to observe that none of the prior theoretical models of exchange, whether economic, political, anthropological, sociological or social psychological in emphasis, has been strongly operationalized and empirically tested. That is, there has been relatively little in the way of those kinds of efforts that are required to build and validate theories of ongoing social process—namely, the sequence of operationalization, testing, reformulating, reoperationalizing, retesting, reformulating, and so on. This does not mean, however, that the preceding conceptual efforts have not had an impact within the various disciplines in the social sciences.

What one does observe is that a particular construct or process outlined in one or more of the preceding exchange theories is incorporated within a more limited behavioral paradigm. For example, the reward–cost notions concerning the formation and maintenance of relationships, as initially set forth by Homans, Blau, Thibaut and Kelley, are represented in almost all current conceptualizations of social attraction. Furthermore, one finds repeated references to Thibaut and Kelley's ideas concerning comparison level and comparison level for alternatives in various paradigms that attempt to define the bases for satisfaction within human relations. And, of course, Homans's principle of distributive justice dominates current social psychological research on equity and fairness. In addition, there are individual propositions borrowed from exchange theory that can be found in contemporary paradigms relating to game and bargaining behavior, and to the process of coalition formation. And recently, there have been attempts to extend theories of exchange to include processes that are perhaps essential for their successful operationalization and validation. For example, Kelley (1979) has recently begun to define more specifically the structural relationships that may obtain within exchange, the way in which actors assign values to their own and other's outcomes, the kinds of controls or influence that actors can and do exert over one another, and the forms of attributions they make during the interactive process regarding their own and other's past and future intentions and behaviors—all of which represent or influence processes fundamental to the determination of human behavior in settings of reciprocity.

III. EQUITY AND SOCIAL EXCHANGE

In this third section we will examine how various theorists have viewed the relationship between the processes of social exchange and the use of various rules of fairness including equity. Examples of empirical research that have examined this relationship will be included in a fourth section.

A. Reciprocity and Allocation Revisited

As noted earlier, Eckhoff (1974) in his analysis of justice makes a strong distinction between two types of transfers that occur in human affairs, reciprocity and allocation. Reciprocal transfers are, of course, identical to what are commonly described as exchange relationships insofar as actors interact and mediate outcomes for one another. Transfer by allocation does not necessarily assume reciprocity or interdependence, and hence is not necessarily isomorphic with theories that consider resource exchange. And in fact, as we will discuss subsequently, allocation studies of justice in social psychology are primarily concerned with "reactive" processes, namely with what criteria actors use to evaluate the fairness or unfairness of a given resource distribution, and how they subsequently adapt cognitively or behaviorally to this evaluation. An exchange approach to fairness in contrast would necessarily focus on why, when, and how interdependent actors behave in ways that produce reciprocal outcomes that are consistent with one or more definitions of equity.

B. The Relationship between Equity and Reciprocity

There have been a number of ways in which fairness and justice have been defined and described in terms of their relationship to the processes of reciprocity and social exchange. The definitions have been both prescriptive and descriptive in character. An example of a prescriptive definition of equity is provided by Mauss (1967) in his study of the reciprocation of gift giving: "A wise precept has run right through human evolution, and we would be wise to adopt it as a principle of action. We should come out of ourselves and regard the duty of giving as a liberty, for in it there lies no risk. A fine Maori proverb runs: . . . 'Give as much as you receive and all is for the best' [p. 67]."

Eckhoff also defines a prescriptive set of principles of justice that have been observed in a number of situations of reciprocity, and which are illustrated by the following phrases: (a) "good shall be repaid by good"; (b) "hurt can be repaid by hurt"; (c) "a wrong shall be righted" (restitution); and (d) "after receiving an advantage one may expect a disadvantage [p. 30]." Eckhoff defines the preceding principles as instances of *retributive justice* differentiating them from the principle of justice that is central to allocation settings, namely, the familiar notion of *distributive justice*.

Malinowski (1922, p. 39) provides a more functional description of the relationship between fairness and social exchange. A fair relationship is characterized as "occurring within a standing partnership, or associated with definite social ties or coupled with mutuality in noneconomic matters" and as entailing "mutual dependence . . . [being] realized in the equivalent arrangement of reciprocal services [p. 55]." It is the "equivalent arrangement of reciprocal services" that defines for Malinowski how fair outcomes are achieved given various divisions of labor between interdependent actors.

Gouldner (1960) takes a somewhat similar functional stance to Malinowski, and goes on to assume the existence of a universal norm of reciprocity that in effect defines the requirements for fairness in human action: "(1) people should help those who have helped them, and (2) people should not injure those who have helped them [p. 88]." Gouldner then describes four conditions or standards that help to define the imputed value of the resource the potential reciprocator has received from a donor: (a) the intensity of the recipient's need; (b) the resources available to the donor; (c) the motives imputed to the donor; and (d) the nature of the constraints existing when the resource was donated. Given Gouldner's model, the utility of the resource initially transferred would be perceived to be greater if the recipient were in strong need, the donor had little in the way of that resource to give (but gave), and if the donor gave without external pressures being applied and without thought of own gain. In terms of social value theory outlined earlier, each of these conditions adds weight to the perception that the actor giving resources was concerned with increasing or maximizing other's outcomes as an end in itself. The norm of reciprocity then sets an expectation for some form of repayment as a requirement for fair exchange.

Homans (1961, 1974) defines fairness in exchange relationships in terms of the previously cited principle of distributive justice. In applying the principle of distributive justice descriptively, Homans uses both situations of reciprocity and of allocation. In describing justice in the Norton Street Gang, originally described in W. F. Whyte's *Street Corner Society* (1943), Homans employs the principle of reciprocity: "The value of what a member receives by way of a reward from the members of the group in one field of activity should be proportional to the value to them of the activities he contributes to another field [p. 234]." However, most of Homans's analysis of justice is based on descriptions of fairness in the Western Electric Company (Roethlisberger and Dickson, 1939), and in the Eastern Utilities Company (Homans, 1954). Justice in these industrial contexts is generally framed in terms of relationships of allocation or of complementarity (Gouldner, 1960) rather than of exchange and reciprocity. That is, Homans is not principally concerned in his analysis of fairness with the exchange of resources between worker and management per se. Rather, he examines how a given worker or a group of similar workers define and evaluate the fairness of the outcomes they are allocated by a corporation for their work investment relative to the outcomes others receive for their investment.

Thus, Homans assumes that equity is based on a learned expectancy that outcomes to self and others will conform to the rule of distributive justice. Violations of this distributive principle give rise to perceptions of unfairness, and to possible anger and guilt. It is a short conceptual step from Homans's assumption concerning expectancy violation, particularly as set forth in his 1974 book, to Festinger's (1957) assumptions regarding dissonance and dissonance reduction. And it is the marriage of distributive justice and dissonance that has produced the dominant contemporary theories of fairness in social psychology, namely, those advanced by Adams (1965) and by Walster, Berscheid, and Walster (1973).

Blau, in his 1964 book, accepts Homans's definition of distributive justice but also asserts that, rather than being derivable from the principles of operant conditioning, it is normatively given. He argues that equity represents "a social norm that prescribes just treatment as a moral principle [1964a, p. 157]," a norm that is reinforced initially by socializing third parties, and may be subsequently internalized by an actor, thereby producing feelings of guilt if violated. In effect, Blau argues that equity is initially a social fact that may become an individual social value.

In a subsequent paper, Blau (1964b) criticizes Homans for deliber-ately limiting his evaluation of equity to the exchange of rewards and punishments between two persons, and for not considering the more important normative aspects of justice. Blau is quite incorrect in his first assertion, as Homans does little to analyze equity in terms of the interac-tive processes within two-party exchanges. But he is correct in asserting that Homans does not perform a normative analysis of equity, although Homans does use the construct of norms in other contexts. Blau then extends Homans's notion of distributive justice by examining how value becomes assigned to its principal components: the returns received for services, and the investment costs incurred for providing them. He ar-gues, using principles derived from the economic laws of supply and demand, that it is society that assigns values to the rewards and costs experienced and hence that defines the values attached to fairness in a relationship of direct exchange. And then, in characteristic fashion, Blau argues that an understanding of these more elementary processes can be used to help define more complex and higher level processes such as those that affect allocation decisions made by groups in settings of indi-rect exchange. In effect, Blau uses evidence gained from examining the processes of direct exchange between two actors as a beginning point from which to develop more complex theories of indirect exchange such as those, for example, that would define social welfare.

Thibaut and Kelley (1959), in their initial statement on social inter-dependence, do not include fairness or justice in their analysis of the processes or rules that help to define the nature of interdependence relationships. They do note, however, in this initial statement, that an individual's CL for outcomes provides a standard that may be used to evaluate both the goodness and fairness of outcomes obtained within a relationship. In their more recent theoretical statement, Kelley and Thibaut (1978) do relate two of the major constructs of fairness, equity and equality, to the interpersonal processes of negotiation and ex-change. In their analysis of the structural properties of social inter-dependence, they imply a two-stage process. They argue that an actor *first* uses a transformational calculus to translate objective own–other outcome matrices into *effective* or operational matrices. The calculus they suggest an actor employs is quite similar to that which was elaborated in our discussion of social values except that equity and equality are subject to bilateral negotiation, and introduced as possible outcome rules during the second stage.

Kelley and Thibaut argue that if, after the transformation process, actors' preferences are not perfectly correspondent, a second stage is entered during which actors may pursue individually or collectively three possible courses of action: (1) they can act on their own to obtain the best available outcome for themselves, perhaps taking into account the other's likely behaviors; (2) they can behave in an agreed upon coordinated way in the interest of providing both with better outcomes through time, given their respective effective matrices, than they could obtain by behaving independently; and (3) they may behave in a coordinated way under the coercion produced when one or both actors threaten or lower other's outcomes below what could be obtained through coordination.

Equity and equality become possible decision rules to be invoked by actors to define outcome distributions acceptable to both parties during the second stage. In discussing how equity and equality may be used in negotiation, Kelley and Thibaut claim that actor and other probably use both the value of the outcomes they are likely to obtain in taking independent action, as well as the strength of the strategic threats they can deploy against other, as multiple baselines for evaluating the goodness of various possible distributions of outcomes between self and other. The range of own and other outcome combinations that become negotiable are those that are bilaterally acceptable given these baselines, and in terms of the theory of bargaining or negotiation, these combinations define the *frontier* of a plot of all pairs of possible negotiated outcomes. This frontier is analogous to the contract curve depicted in Figure 10.4. In situations where actors have made differential inputs, Kelley and Thibaut claim one would expect that an advantaged actor would seek the equitable frontier point, whereas the nonadvantaged actor would maintain that the equal outcome frontier point would indeed represent a fairer distribution of resources. In regard to the resulting impasse, the same that Cook and Emerson (1978) address in their analysis of the indeterminancy of bilateral monopoly models of economic exchange, Kelley and Thibaut observe: "At this point our model has made its predictions about the progress [of negotiation], and must leave some uncertainty about the outcome. In general, we might expect the final agreement to be some compromise between those indicated by the two arguments [p. 293]."

It should be acknowledged that Kelley and Thibaut's description of the role that equality and equity may play in negotiations between interdependent actors is quite similar to that proposed by Komorita and Chertkoff (1973) in their theoretical paper on bargaining. In fact, one of their ten major theoretical assumptions states: "Assumption 3: A person strong in resources is more likely to expect and advocate the parity norm as a basis for reward division, while a person weak in resources is more likely to expect and advocate the equality norm [p. 152]." Partial support, for both the Kelley and Thibaut and the Komorita and Chertkoff assumptions, is reported in the earlier cited article by Van Avermaet *et al.* (1978). In an allocation study, it was observed that, when allocators were not in a position of reciprocity with others, and were assured anonymity in their distribution of outcomes, they used an equity or parity rule when they had contributed more input than other, and used an equality rule when they had contributed less input than other. However, it should also be reported that when the distribution was made in a public setting, allocators who had contributed less input shifted from an equity to a parity rule, taking less of the monetary outcome for self than they afforded others.

Cook and Emerson (1978) also examine fairness within relationships of direct exchange. They observe first that the proportional formulations of equity set forth by such theorists as Homans (1961, 1974), Adams (1965), and Walster *et al.* (1973) are more applicable to settings where some "central allocator or third party" distributes rewards between contributors than to settings where there is a direct two-party exchange of resources. In effect, as we would argue, these researchers view the preceding equity statements as more applicable to instances of allocation than to those where there is reciprocity and outcome interdependence. Cook and Emerson then use the economic paradigm of bilateral monopoly to formulate one of the few definitions of equity that is appropriate to direct two-party exchange relationships. Within the bilateral monopoly paradigm, it is assumed that two persons (A and B) each have a monopoly on a single resource (x and y respectively). In such a situation, the input of one person to an exchange becomes the other person's outcome. The equity of the exchange can be determined by comparing the relative values of the resources given and received by each party using what Cook and Emerson term the *rule of equitable exchange*. The rule, according to Cook and Emerson, can be specified in terms of the following equation:

$$\alpha\, yY - \alpha\, xX = \beta\, xX - \beta\, yY \qquad (10.1)$$

where $\alpha\, x$ and $\alpha\, y$ are the unit values of the resources x and y to person A. And $\beta\, x$ and $\beta\, y$ are the unit values of the resources x and y to person B. X and Y refer to the number of units *exchanged* between the two actors, and the equality expression defines an equilibrium state of equal profits.

Cook and Emerson, following some earlier work by Emerson (1972), further postulate that equity as a solution will obtain in a situation of bilateral monopoly when two conditions are met: (1) both participants know how much each profits from the transaction relative to the other, which is likely to occur if both share a common culture and a history of prior interaction; and (2) the rule of equitable exchange is activated and honored. This becomes more likely if future interaction is anticipated, and if the utilities of x and y are high. These preconditions are not sufficient to meet what appears to be a requirement for the interpersonal comparison of utilities by participants to an exchange, a comparison process that has proven a nemesis for a number of theories of social and collective decision making.

Gamson (1961) proposed a somewhat similar process in his early formulation regarding coalition formation:

> Our general hypothesis stated that participants will expect others to demand from a coalition a share of the payoffs which is proportional to the amount of the resources which they are contributing to it. Each participant will estimate the value of any coalition strategy as the total payoff to a coalition multiplied by his share [p. 382].

Finally, there have been several, very tentative attempts to look at how exchange relationships develop through time and, in a few instances, the relation between fairness and reciprocity is also considered. Such analyses have been made primarily for male–female interactions of progressive intimacy and interdependence. For example, Huesmann and Levinger (1976) have recently developed a computer simulation model of incremental exchange through time. Its assumptions reflect both expected value theory and some of the previously described assertions in Thibaut and Kelley's (1959) interdependence formulation. The model provides a more systematic way to describe the development of varying patterns of male–female exchange and mutual involvement through time than does Blau's (1964a) earlier described effort.

Huston and Burgess (1979) have observed that a number of social psychologists argue that intimate relationships are not adequately characterized by exchange models: "Even those who believe exchange principles can be usefully applied to a wide variety of situations and relationships sometimes shy away from applying them to close relationships (e.g., Deutsch, 1975; Lerner, 1975; Rubin, 1973; Sampson, 1975) [p. 10]." The preceding critics generally assume that the underlying motive assumed in exchange is material self-interest, whereas intimate relationships involve more prosocial forms of motivation and interdependence. This concern, in part, reflects the failure of contemporary theorists of social value, interdependence, and exchange to convincingly assert that the early anthropologists were correct when they claimed that exchange principles encompass all forms of human relationships whether they occur in the marketplace or in the bedroom, whether they obtain between buyer and seller or between husband and wife, and whether the goals pursued in exchange are money, sexual satisfaction, or altruism.

A second reason why critics such as Rubin, Deutsch, and Sampson question the appropriateness of an exchange model for describing intimate relationships is that the field of social psychology has generally and quite inappropriately described the equity paradigms of Adams (1965) and of Walster *et al.* (1973) as concerned with exchange processes. In fact, of course, both models have focused upon the determinants and consequences of allocation behaviors. Finally, these critics argue that Adams's equity model in emphasizing equity rather than equality tends to assume or create differences in status that are inimical to the cooperation required for sustaining intimate forms of relationship. Unfortunately, regardless of whether they stress the fairness rules of equity or equality, most current social psychological theories do *not* treat fairness as sets of alternative procedural and distributional rules for resource distribution that apply to *sequences* of interaction between interdependent actors, rules that may remain relatively constant or vary between settings and through time.

A possible exception to this is Caldwell's (1979) suggestion regarding how fairness operates within stable two-party exchange relationships that include both sexual and affective reciprocity. Borrowing the notion of bookkeeping from the field of accounting, she suggests that partners to a relationship literally keep "books" regarding the "inputs" and "outcomes" of their interactions through time. That is, interdependent actors are assumed to "maintain" ledgers in which they enter the services they render other, and the services received from other, a record of exchanges. Obviously, what is entered as service rendered by one actor becomes an entry under services received by the other. To understand what is occurring in an exchange relationship at any time, particularly with regard to the question of credits and debits, Caldwell maintains then that an observer must have the history of prior transactions as they are perceived by both participants. Or, at least, an observer needs to know in an ahistorical sense what the running totals are at the moment of observation. Obviously, the participants' ledgers will not be mirror images of one another, as perceptions of services rendered and those received will vary between actors. Such inconsistencies are assumed to give rise to discussion, to negotiation, to conflict, to open warfare, and, at times, to the dissolution of a relationship.

IV. THE SOCIAL PSYCHOLOGY OF EQUITY

In this final major section we will attempt a somewhat finer grained analysis of the differing approaches, including exchange, that have been or can be taken in investigating the social psychology of fairness or equity. In doing so, we will impose several organizational rules. First, we will describe separately the conceptual approaches that have been or can be included within the two models of equity that have been repeatedly distinguished in the present chapter: namely, those of allocation and those of reciprocity or exchange. Second, because there is a very large empirical literature, much of which is examined in the present volume, that assumes an allocation model of fairness, we will not attempt to cite particular studies as examples of the more specific approaches to allocation. However, because of their highly limited numbers, and because of the focus of the present chapter, we will cite examples of studies that illustrate various approaches to the study of fairness within relationships of exchange.

A. Fairness and Allocation Models of Human Judgment and Behavior

Most social psychological theory and research that has examined fairness and equity has addressed one of the following issues:

1. How do two or more persons who are in an allocation relationship with a third party evaluate or judge the comparative fairness of the outcomes they receive?
2. What kinds of cognitive and behavioral adjustments do such individuals make if they judge that their own or other's outcomes are unfair?
3. What allocations do actors actually make to self and other and how do they rationalize these when they are charged with the responsibility of distributing a fixed set of resources given variations in own and other's task inputs?
4. What factors influence the fairness judgments third parties make when they observe the resource allocations of others?

As noted previously, these questions derive primarily from a psychological model that depicts humans as reactive creatures who make judgments concerning fairness given some prior set of events, and who then adjust their cognitions or behaviors to reduce any resulting discomfort or dissonance (see, for example, analyses by Leventhal, 1980; Mikula, 1977). Implicit in this formulation is the assumption that actors learn from others in their environment fairness rules that produce discomfort when violated (Walster, *et al.*, 1973).

Lerner (1970) argues that another form of inconsistency contributes to discomfort and the search for fair behavior. Namely, he believes that actors feel uncomfortable if they believe that others are not obtaining those outcomes that they deserve. Given a fair or just world, actors can then safely defer immediate gratification, and work for more satisfying remote goals. Such a deferral is seen as functional in increasing the ultimate rewards available to the individual and to the society. And, Lerner concludes, people try to protect their view of a just world by attempting cognitively and behaviorally to redress injustice.

The preceding approach to fairness has tended to focus on a restricted or limited set of events. Namely, actors are viewed as making single judgments concerning justice or injustice, and then displaying or not displaying some cognitive or behavioral response. Neither the judgmental process nor the reactions to injustice are examined as part of the ongoing interactive processes that characterize most of human social behavior. Rather, the more traditional, unidirectional stimulus–cognitive processing–response paradigm of individual psychology is employed. Although this approach certainly does not provide an adequate model for understanding the more complex and dynamic character of human behavior in interdependent exchange relationships, findings concerning the judgments individuals make in allocation settings, as well as their reactions to unfairness, permit one to understand judgments and behaviors in simple social settings, and can serve as important inputs in understanding more complex forms of exchange behavior. For this reason, we will very briefly examine how each of the preceding four issues has been addressed using an allocation model of fairness.

1. EVALUATING THE FAIRNESS OF ALLOCATIONS

Leventhal (1976) provides a very comprehensive analysis of the allocation paradigm of justice from a judgmental standpoint. In it, he enumerates a number of criteria that seem to play a major role in affecting an observer's evaluations as to whether fair allocations have been achieved. This represents, of course, an extension of the more simplistic models of equity set forth by Homans (1961), Adams (1965), and Walster *et al.* (1973) suggesting that contributions represent the single input variable for determining distributive justice. Leventhal asserts that a single criterion approach is not representative of the information humans employ in making justice judgments (Cook & Parcel, 1977, advance a similar argument). Leventhal suggests that the following summary formula for deserved outcomes more adequately characterizes observers' views of the world of fairness:

$$\text{Deserved outcomes} = w_c D \text{ by contributions} + w_n D \text{ by need} + w_e D \text{ by equality} + w_o D \text{ by other rules}$$

In the equation, D implies deservingness for a particular criterion, and w refers to the weight that observers assign to each criterion.

After specifying those criteria that define deserved outcomes, Leventhal proceeds to examine a variety of factors that help determine the weights that may be assigned to the various deservingness criteria. For example, one factor he assumes to be of central importance to the weighting process is social comparison (Austin, 1977; Festinger, 1954).

2. REACTION TO UNFAIR ALLOCATIONS

Once a person perceives that deservingness D has been violated, there are a number of activities that may be engaged in to achieve consistency. Among the "adaptive" responses to inequity that have been considered conceptually or empirically are the following:

1. The person may distort his or her perception concerning the outcomes that other actually obtained.
2. The person, as has been observed in a number of studies, may derogate others who have been treated unfairly to a level where deservingness and outcomes are consistent, which has been found to obtain particularly in those instances where the derogator is also responsible for initially providing other with inappropriate outcomes.
3. The person may merely avoid interacting with an unfairly treated other (i.e., 'out of sight-out of mind').
4. The person may change the level of other's outcomes to bring them in line with what the person perceives other fairly deserves.
5. If other is in fact receiving more resources than he deserves, the person may take some action to change other's behaviors such that his or her contributions fairly match his or her outcomes (Lerner & Miller, 1978).

3. ACTOR'S SELF-OTHER ALLOCATION BEHAVIOR

Actors not only evaluate and react to others' allocations, they make allocations themselves. The most frequently employed paradigm to study this behavior requires two persons, a subject and another (real or simulated), to perform a common task for a third party, often the experimenter. The experimenter then manipulates the relative contribution feedback provided to the subject. That is, the other person is said to have accomplished more, the same, or less than the subject. Some rationale is then provided as to why the subject should distribute the available outcome resources between self and other.

Using this technique, a number of interesting results have been found. For example, children's outcome distributions or allocations between self and other have been shown to vary as a function of age. Very young children do not attend strongly to cues concerning relative own-other contributions, and tend to afford themselves a generous proportion of the outcomes. With increasing age and socialization, children begin to distribute the outcome resources equally, at least when adults observe their behaviors. With further increases in age, children begin to take into account the relative contributions made to the task by self and other, and to employ the rule of distributive justice. Hook (1978) and Hook and Cook (1979) have recently observed that this sequence of development in fairness rules is under the control of changes in both moral and cognitive development.

4. FAIRNESS JUDGMENTS BY THIRD PARTIES

Two of the more interesting empirical investigations of settings in which outsiders, whose own self-interests are not directly involved, make judgments concerning the appropriateness of others' allocation behaviors, were conducted by Brickman and Bryan (1975, 1976). These investigators observed that when children served as third-party observers, both the nature of the outcome distribution rule followed (whether equity or equality), and the nature of the means by which an allocation was made (charity or theft), affected children's judgments of fairness. Based on these findings, the investigators argue that third-party justice judgments are affected both by the ends others seek, and the means they follow to achieve them. In terms of the theory of social values described earlier, judgments of justice are affected both by others' perceptions of actor's goals and the strategies actor pursues to achieve those goals.

5. A PERFORMANCE EXPECTATION MODEL OF FAIRNESS OF ALLOCATIONS

At the beginning of this chapter, we noted that fairness could, from a sociological perspective, be related to Weber's notions concerning the legitimization of power within bureaucracies. Such an approach to fairness is strongly represented in the work of Berger, Zelditch, Anderson, and Cohen (1972a) and Berger, Cohen, and Zelditch (1972b), who maintain that the most important fairness issue concerns the distribution and legitimization of power, prestige and status within task oriented groups. This consideration was central to Weber's analysis as well. Berger *et al.* (1972a,b) claim that status is neglected in both Homans's and Adams's approaches to distributive justice. Homans (1976) has recently made a similar accusation regarding other social psychological equity paradigms claiming that they "do not much try to ... relate equity to other kindred social phenomena about which a good deal is already known ... I do not hear much about either power or status, though they have close if somewhat ambiguous relations with equity [p. 241]." Berger *et al.* (1972a,b) also argue, as we have in the present chapter, that Homans's, Adams's and other models of distributive justice are reactive insofar as they stress primarily the consequences of perceived inequity. They then proceed to emphasize the importance of an activation model of distributive justice that predicts the differentiation and allocation of power between actors on the basis of task-related abilities.

There is an additional difference between the Berger *et al.* (1972a,b) approach to justice and the more traditional one. First, the former distinguish individual from collective criteria of fairness or justice. In situations of individual justice, an actor compares his or her outcomes with an immediate comparison other, and makes a local judgment of fairness. Berger *et al.* (1972a,b) assert, however, that this is only one source of judgment; a more important evaluation obtains when an actor concludes that both he or she and a comparison other have been collectively mistreated relative to some other general referential standard of fairness. And they assume that it is the latter comparison that provides normative expectations regarding appropriate allocations of power and prestige.

Parcel and Cook (1977) have suggested that one can with some ease achieve an integration between three theoretical paradigms: (1) the Berger *et al.* performance model; (2) the status differentiation theory of Kimberly (1966, 1972); and (3) the more traditional notions of distributive justice advocated by Homans, Adams, and others. One can assume that an assignment of power and prestige based on performance produces status differentiation within groups. This in turn results in the differential allocation of economic rewards, particularly when status and performance are seen to be correlated. The assumptions of distributive justice are met if status and performance are viewed as the relevant inputs for the fair allocation of economic outcomes. Parcel and Cook go on to evaluate this integration both conceptually and empirically.

Like the prior questions addressed in this section, performance expectation work represents but a more sociological analysis of the justice of allocation. It does not provide much in the way of a conceptual or methodological means to examine the roles that fairness plays within ongoing exchange relationships, regardless of whether the standards of fairness in interaction are local or referential.

B. Fairness and Exchange Models of Human Actions

As observed earlier, if by an exchange model of human action, one implies an explanatory system that considers how two or more actors attempt to obtain resources in settings of mutual outcome control, then one must unfortunately conclude that there have been relatively few conceptual attempts to specify how rules of equity and fairness regulate the formation and maintenance of such relationships. And there have been even fewer attempts to examine fairness in such relationships empirically. Still, there have been bits and pieces of effort that are relevant to the development of the area.

To provide a framework for organizing these bits and pieces, we will attempt to order examples of work on fairness and exchange on a continuum of interdependence. (A somewhat simpler effort to accomplish such an ordering can be found in Mikula & Schwinger, 1978.) The continuum ranges from the simplest possible interdependence setting to the most complex along a bipolar dimension with allocation behavior at one end and reciprocation at the other. Each point represents one possible conceptual and empirical approach to questions of the use of fairness rules within an exchange relationship. Thus, although the first two points describe allocation behaviors, the underlying model does not pertain to either the judgmental or reactive bases of fairness as described in the previous section, but rather considers the degree of interdependence between actors pursuing outcomes in a purposive manner. At one end of the continuum, the *first* point, one actor unilaterally and anonymously controls the distribution of available resources to self and other(s). Interdependence is generally operationalized as the actors' contributions to a common task. The unilateral control of resources by the allocator represents a form of fate control that serves to minimize both the normative demands and the strategic considerations of interpersonal influence. Another contributing factor to the minimization of these factors is that the allocation occurs at only one time point. Van Avermaet (1975) has observed that adults having such outcome control are likely to select fairness rules isomorphic with self-interest. At a judgmental level, Severts (1976) found that, in a private condition, children favorably evaluated unjust favorable allocations made to them by a third party, but expressed disfavor of such allocations when they were made public. Reis and Gruzen (1976), in a behavioral study, report: "Allocators enhanced their own rewards beyond normative values only when their choices were completely private [p. 487]." And Lane and Messé (1971) obtained similar results. These research examples suggest that anonymity and unilateral control enhance self-interested behaviors.

A *second* point on the continuum is represented by research settings in which an allocator unilaterally controls the outcome distribution on a one-time basis, but knows that the experimenter and/or the other task contributor will be aware of both the task input and the distribution of outcomes. Such a situation adds normative demands to the minimal

setting just described. Most prior behavioral research on fairness falls at
this point at the allocation end of the continuum. The various chapters
of this book provide numerous examples of such research. Most of it
attempts to answer the previously posed questions regarding what allocations actors make when charged with the responsibility of distributing
a fixed set of resources between self and other under varying conditions
of relative task input. Attention is focused on the normative demands of
the situation and the fact of interdependence is neglected. For example,
the question of future interaction between participants is generally left
ambiguous. Hence, the contribution of subject's concern about other's
possible future response to subject's allocation is not known. Theoretically, however, if such interpersonal considerations are controlled by
removing strategic considerations, findings at this second continuum
point should be useful in providing a description of distribution behavior that includes normative demands.

A *third* point involves instances where an actor has fate control over
the outcome distribution at a given time and does expect to interact with
other in the future. Von Grumbkow, Deen, Steensma, and Wilke (1976)
have found that possible future interactions between allocator and other
affect the former's allocation behavior. Advantaged actors expecting future interaction distributed outcomes in a manner approximating
equality; those expecting no future interaction approximated an equity
rule. Future interaction is also implied in the manipulation and measurement of the effects of friendship (Benton, 1971; Morgan & Sawyer,
1967; Wright, 1942). Under conditions of friendship, one might expect
that the anticipation of a continuing interaction would affect allocation
behavior. Benton, for example, has found a sex by friendship interaction
such that boys made equity choices both with friends and nonfriends
whereas girls made equality choices with friends but equity choices with
nonfriends. At this third point on the proposed continuum, reciprocity
or exchange begins to become a factor insofar as actors anticipate that
others will react to their resource distribution in some way. Conceptually, the situation is even more complex, as actor is not only likely to
perceive that other will react, but also that other may affect actor's own
future outcomes. Thus, the setting for actor becomes one of perceived
interdependence, and actor's behavior toward other is likely to be defined both by considerations of interpersonal strategy and by normative
demands.

The *fourth* point on the continuum is reached when an allocator actually expects to exchange roles or to take turns with the recipient in the
future in the same or a similar task. At this point, the time frame is
expanded and the eventual control of resources is seen as bilateral rather
than unilateral. Thus, we might expect to observe task-specific strategies

on the part of the subjects that are designed to influence other to make more favorable future allocations to the subjects. In one of our own current research programs (McClintock & Keil, 1980), half of the children expect the recipient of their reward distribution will have an opportunity to reciprocate in the future; half are informed there will be no future interaction. Preliminary findings indicate that less self-interested distributions of resources are made in the expected reciprocity condition. Greenberg (1978) recently examined the effects of anticipated reciprocity upon the distributional behaviors of adults and reports that justice standards were adhered to by allocators expecting exchanges with equally powerful co-workers. Self-interested responses were made when recipients had no retaliative power, particularly when the reward was lucrative.

Shapiro (1975) used the presence or absence of expectations of future interaction to explain differences between the findings reported by Leventhal and Anderson (1970), Leventhal and Lane (1970), and Leventhal and Michaels (1969) indicating that equity is the principal distributional response to unequal inputs, and those reported by others (Gamson, 1961; Morgan & Sawyer, 1967; Wiggins, 1966), implying that equality was the principal rule. In his own research, Shapiro found that allocators with higher inputs, when future interaction was expected, divided the reward equally; when future interaction was not expected, rewards were divided according to equity. At this fourth continuum point the exchange characteristics of the setting are still implicit, although the expanded time frame and the shift to bilateral control of resources adds a complexity that more closely approximates full exchange relationships.

The *fifth* point on the continuum is one in which the exchange relationship is explicit, where there is a strong form of outcome interdependence that is restricted to the immediate setting. Thus, although a reciprocal relationship exists within the time period of the exchange, there is little concern with future interaction, hence with long-term considerations of interpersonal strategy. Laboratory studies of bargaining and negotiation as well as of coalition formation are the best examples of research at this continuum point. In a broader context, Homans (1961, 1974) defines this form of relationship as an impersonal one that is characterized by a single exchange of a single reward that is readily available elsewhere. It is the nature of the reward and not the identity of the particular other person that is important to this form of exchange. Homans defines a relationship as personal when it involves multiple exchanges of reward that are specific to the particular actors involved. Similar distinctions have been made by Boulding (1978) and by Kelley and Thibaut (1978).

Most of the theoretical and empirical work concerned with a decision theoretic and empirical understanding of bargaining and coalition formation that fall at this point on the continuum have assumed that actors are fundamentally self-interested in orientation, and have attempted to define what strategies they employ to optimize their own outcomes. Pruìtt (1977), in discussing various integrative approaches to conflict resolution, has observed that bargaining, whereby parties attempt to coerce or persuade their adversaries into making great concessions while conceding as little as possible, is but one of several general approaches to conflict resolution. Another involves the application of rules or norms including those that define various kinds of fairness. However, as Kelley and Thibaut (1978) have observed, the availability of multiple rules of fairness enables actors to select those most consistent with self-interest. For example, a bargainer with fewer inputs and/or less power may recommend equality as a fair distribution rule whereas one with more inputs or greater power will recommend equity as a fair distribution rule.

Komorita and Kravitz (1979) have also looked at the role various fairness rules may play in the distribution of outcomes given various alternative outcomes that each actor will realize if a bargain is not reached. For example, they consider an instance where Person A would receive 40 points and Person B would receive 20 points if an agreement were not reached; and both could split 100 points if a bargain were reached. They suggest that three fairness rules might provide a bargained outcome: equality, whereby each party takes 50 units; equity, whereby Person A would take two-thirds, Person B, one-third; and finally, the rule of equal excess which states that each player would take points directly comparable to the points they would receive without an agreement, and the remainder would then be equally split between actors. The latter, given that the outcomes for nonagreement are specified, is comparable to the well-known bargaining solutions of Nash (1950, 1953) and Shapeley (1953). Komorita and Kravitz found empirically that on differing occasions all three of these rules are used. Although we do not yet know under what conditions one or the other will dominate, this research provides an example of how various fairness rules may affect outcomes in a bargaining task.

With regard to research in coalition formation, Komorita and Brinberg (1977) conclude on the basis of a review of the literature and their own research findings that the motives associated with self-interest and with fairness are present in most coalition tasks:

> Equal strategic power (players can form an equal number of alternative winning coalitions) but unequal outcomes (players with larger resources received a larger share)—suggest that there are two opposing motivational forces op-

> erating in a coalition situation: the motive to maximize one's own share of the prize, based upon strategic bargaining power, and a norm of equity (distributive justice) which prescribes that an individual with larger resources should receive larger outcomes [p. 359].

In general, self-interest has been found to be a stronger determinant of outcomes in coalition studies than has fairness. This probably obtains because, as Stryker (1972) has noted, the differential allocation of resources to subjects is accomplished in a nonmeaningful way (i.e., randomly or without reason). Furthermore, to the extent that the relations in coalition studies are impersonal, fairness should be weaker than when they are personal in nature.

Just as our fifth point represents a narrow and relatively impersonal type of relationship, the *sixth* and final point on our continuum implies a personal, long-term relationship. The sixth point is thus defined by a social exchange relationship where there is reciprocity in fate and behavior control, and the expectation of continuing interpersonal interaction. The complexity inherent in such a relationship where the choices of interdependent actors are conditioned by their past exchanges, their expectations regarding the effects of their present behavior upon their own and other's future behaviors, as well as the goals that each may ultimately seek, undoubtedly account for the dearth of work at this continuum point. Most conceptual approaches necessarily restrict their attention to a specific aspect of interdependence or exchange within a more or less narrowly defined time interval.

For example, Walster, Walster, and Traupmann (1978) classified dating relationships as equitable or inequitable on the basis of partners' self-reports of their contributions to the relationship and their feelings about the benefits they received from it. Within inequitable relationships, partners who felt they were receiving less than they deserved were termed *underbenefited;* those who felt they were gaining a disproportionate share of benefits were termed *overbenefited.* Drawing on their dissonance model of equity, the researchers suggested that inequitable dating relationships should be characterized by feelings of distress. Furthermore, they proposed that attempts to attain a more balanced, equitable relationship could take one of two forms: restoration of psychological equity or restoration of actual equity. Restoration of psychological equity occurs primarily as a denial by the partner that an imbalance exists. The restoration of actual equity can occur in a variety of ways. For example, Walster *et al.* suggest the underbenefited partner, who is receiving far less than he or she deserves in the relationship, may feel entitled to have a greater voice in decisions about what activities the couple will engage in. Specifically, Walster *et al.* proposed that the underbenefited partner would feel entitled to dictate the intimacy level of the couple's sexual relationship. Although support was found for the expectation that partners in inequitable relationships feel uneasy about their relationships, no support was found for their more behavioral hypotheses concerning sexual intimacy and exchange.

Hatfield, Utne, and Traupmann (1979) have expanded the previous arguments into a more general statement concerning the centrality of equity considerations within intimate relationships. They conclude, citing research by Walster, Traupmann, and Walster (1978) on marital relationships, that equitable relationships will be stable relationships or exchanges and inequitable relationships will be fragile ones.

A very important requirement for description of fairness relationships at the sixth continuum point is the development of models that focus on exchange through time. Huesmann and Levinger's (1976) previously cited model, as well as Caldwell's (1979) work on negotiation, suggest the importance of this variable. Caldwell, for example, suggests that in more intimate, longer-term relationships, participants may operate as bookkeepers maintaining cognitive records of contributions or services rendered to and received from others through time. This running record is then employed as a means to evaluate the fairness of a relationship on a continuing basis. But to date, social psychologists, perhaps having no previously elaborated economic model to fall back on, have done rather poorly in elaborating conceptual paradigms that examine how the multiple criteria of fairness influence and help maintain interdependent relationships of exchange between individuals in dyads and small groups through time.

One recent attempt to conceptualize the development of relationships over time is provided by Scanzoni (1979) who suggests a three-stage model of "progressive interdependence." The theoretical roots of this model derive from Gouldner's (1960) notion that reciprocity is the dynamic that maintains ongoing social relationships. The major questions one needs to ask about continuing relationships, according to Scanzoni, are how they are maintained, and how they progress to greater interdependence levels. Both questions can be answered in terms of two forms of reciprocity: as a response to rewards or benefits provided by another; and as a moral obligation.

Progress to greater interdependence levels is conceptualized by Scanzoni as a three-stage process. The stages, labeled *exploration, expansion,* and *commitment,* are linked by "purposive-action processes" such as communication, bargaining, power, and distributive justice, all of which serve to expand mutual reciprocity in both its moral obligation and reward response senses. This model, although more conceptual than empirical, provides some insight into what kind of empirical work is needed for the assessment of reciprocity and fairness within close relationships.

Burnstein and Katz (1972) have observed that equitable distributions of outcomes, which may be deleterious to the performance of a group on a given task, are more likely to be made when there are strong ties of interdependence between the members of a group. The researchers view this use of a fairness rule as serving several strategic functions for a group, although it may lower the immediate level of performance of the group on some tasks. For example, by reducing invidious comparison, equitable distributions of resources both decrease intragroup antagonism and the likelihood that group members will not work together. The researchers further report that if decision making is centralized, more efficient distribution of status may be made that may in turn improve group performance, but decrease group equity and integration. Such distributions are particularly likely to obtain when decisions involve a single individual as an allocator, and when they are in the allocator's own self-interest.

The most integrated conceptual approach to long-term exchange relationships can be found in Kelley's (1979) work on close heterosexual dyadic relationships. Kelley has developed a model that describes three levels of interdependence that exist in a hierarchical ordering within close personal relationships. Couples may be more or less interdependent in terms of (a) the specific behaviors of each; (b) the norms and role expectations each brings to the relationship; and (c) the personality traits and attitudes each possesses. A major assumption here is that persons incur rewards and costs from all three of these sources or levels of interdependence. The implications of the preceding levels of analysis for fairness in exchange relationships is set forth by Braiker and Kelley (1979) in their "central assumption": "The higher levels (of interdependence) serve to govern events at the lower levels. Each person's normative preferences determine his decisions at the level of specific behaviors—how he weighs his own and his partner's interests, the value he attaches to equity, turn-taking, equal sharing in decisions, etc. [p. 141]." Thus, according to this approach, evaluation of the fairness of outcomes for each partner depends upon the interaction of personality traits, attitudes and beliefs at the personal level, the expectations at the normative level, and the joint behaviors emitted by actors who share outcome interdependence.

Finally, exchange relationships can exist in instances where actors are defined as firms or nation-states. Winham (1977, pp. 354–355) provides several examples of such relationships of reciprocity between such actors in his analysis of complex international economic and political affairs. He observes, for example, that reciprocity as a construct plays an important role in structuring participants' definitions of what information is relevant to the negotiation process. This structuring is important because there is usually a large and complex set of circumstances underlying such negotiations. He observes further that at this level of negotiation, "No negotiator will accept an agreement unless he can defend it as 'reciprocal' . . . [although] there is no definition of reciprocity beyond the idea of 'fair exchange,' nor are there exact procedures of measuring reciprocity [p. 354]." At the same time, although the constructs of reciprocity and fairness may indeed perform the function of simplifying the required informational structure in complex negotiations between economic and political actors, it would not be surprising to find that various criteria of fairness, in interaction with the structural characteristics of the interdependence relationship, may play a significant role in defining what outcomes are achieved by international as well as by individual actors.

V. CONCLUSION

It is fair to say that as yet there exist neither sophisticated nor powerful theories of social interaction and exchange. We have not come very far from the early theoretical speculations of Mauss (1967) and others on reciprocity in gift giving and other human activities. Those theoretical advances that have occurred can be traced primarily to economics and the concern for the exchange of economic commodities, the principal one being money. But even here the assumptions concerning the motives of human actors as well as the structure of their interdependence have been very narrow, if not naive. And the range of exchange situations, as well as resources, to which economic theories are applicable are limited, to say the least. Still the economists can hardly be faulted for making greater advances in modeling human exchange and interdependence than other social scientists. An exception to the foregoing is to be found in the very strong conceptualization of social interdependence recently stated by the social psychologists Kelley and Thibaut (1978) and Kelley (1979).

Given the limitations in current theorizing on interdependence and exchange, as well as the current fixation of social psychologist's energies upon processes of social cognition, it is perhaps not surprising that most social psychological theories of equity are not primarily concerned with interpersonal processes per se, but with how experienced inequities are defined and rationalized by the favored, the disfavored, or some external observer. Such an emphasis is consistent with those individualistic models of human behavior that have dominated the social sciences and social psychology in particular over the past several decades. Such an orientation is strongly reflected in a number of the chapters of the present volume. Explanations of the processes underlying perceived injustice, as well as various attempts to determine what factors may influence an individual's predisposition toward such judgments of justice or injustice, as well as the equitable or inequitable allocations, are undoubtedly essential to understanding the role that fairness plays in human behavior. But the greatest advances in understanding rules of fairness in relation to human behavior will occur when we begin to understand how they help to define and to determine the structure and the ongoing processes of human interdependence and exchange. Such an understanding will have profound implications for theoretical advances in all of the social sciences. To date, the uneven progress toward this kind of understanding has been facilitated by efforts in a number of disciplines. One would hope that more rapid progress will occur in the future with social psychology playing a more dominant role than it has thus far.

ACKNOWLEDGMENTS

The authors are grateful to the editors of this volume for providing them an opportunity and excuse for carefully reading and evaluating materials that they should have otherwise read. In particular, we are indebted to Ron Cohen, whose advice on issues and authors played a major role in defining the boundaries of the present project. Because we were in part new to the terrain enclosed within these boundaries, we actively sought criticisms of an initial draft of the present chapter from friends, relatives, students, former students, colleagues and an occasional scholar. We have met to varying degrees the universally helpful suggestions of Valerie Dull, Dan Katz, Sam Komorita, George Levinger, Evie McClintock, James McClintock, Dave Messick, Gary Namie, Thijs Poppe, Glenn Reeder, Frank Stech, John Thibaut, Bob Wyer, as well as of our editors.

REFERENCES

Adams, J. S. Inequity in social exchange. In L. Berkowitz (Ed.), *Advances in experimental social psychology* (Vol. 2). New York: Academic Press, 1965.

Austin, W. Equity theory and social comparison processes. In J. Suls & R. Miller (Eds.), *Social comparison processes*. Washington: Hemisphere, 1977.

Benton, A. Productivity, distributive justice, and bargaining among children. *Journal of Personality and Social Psychology*, 1971, *18*, 68–78.

Berger, J., Zelditch, M., Anderson, B., & Cohen, B. Structural aspects of distributive justice: A status-value formulation. In J. Berger, M. Zelditch, & B. Anderson (Eds.), *Sociological theories in progress* (Vol. 2). Boston: Houghton Mifflin, 1972. (a)

Berger, J., Cohen, B., & Zelditch, M. Status characteristics and social interaction. *American Sociological Review*, 1972, *37*, 241–255. (b)

Blau, P. *Exchange and power in social life*. New York: Wiley, 1964. (a).

Blau, P. Justice in social exchange. *Sociological Inquiry*, 1964, *34*, 193–206. (b)

Boulding, K. *Ecodynamics*. Beverly Hills: Sage, 1978.

Braiker, H., & Kelley, H. H. Conflict in the development of close relationships. In R. L. Burgess & T. L. Huston (Eds.), *Social exchange in developing relationships*. New York: Academic Press, 1979.

Brickman, P., & Bryan, J. H. Moral judgment of theft, charity, and third-party transfers that increase or decrease equality. *Journal of Personality and Social Psychology*, 1975, *31*, 156–161.

Brickman, P., & Bryan, J. H. Equity versus equality in children's moral judgment of thefts, charity, and third-party transfers. *Journal of Personality and Social Psychology*, 1976, *34*, 757–761.

Brown, B. F. Equity in the law of the United States. In R. A. Newman (Ed.), *Equity in the world's legal systems*. Brussels: Establishments Emile Bruylant, 1973.

Burnstein, E., & Katz, S. Decisions involving equitable and optimal distributions of status. In C. G. McClintock (Ed.), *Experimental social psychology*. New York: Holt, Rinehart & Winston, 1972.

Caldwell, M. *Negotiation in sexual encounters*. Unpublished doctoral dissertation. University of California, Santa Barbara, 1979.

Cook, K., & Emerson, R. Power, equity, and commitment in exchange networks. *American Sociological Review*, 1978, *43*, 721–739.

Cook, K., & Parcel, T. Equity theory: Directions for future research. *Sociological Inquiry*, 1977, *47*, 75–88.

Deutsch, M. Equity, equality, and need: What determines which value will be used as the basis for distributive justice? *Journal of Social Issues*, 1975, *31*, 137–149.

Durkheim, E. *Division of labor in society*. New York: Free Press, 1947.

Eckhoff, T. *Justice: Its determinants in social interaction*. Rotterdam: Rotterdam University Press, 1974.

Ekeh, P. *Social exchange theory: The two traditions*. London: Heinemann, 1974.

Emerson, R. Exchange theory. Part 1: A psychological basis for social exchange. In J. Berger, M. Zelditch, & B. Anderson (Eds.), *Sociological theories in progress* (Vol. 2). Boston: Houghton Mifflin, 1972.

Festinger, L. A theory of social comparison processes. *Human Relations*, 1954, *7*, 117–140.

Festinger, L. *A theory of cognitive dissonance*. Evanston, Ill.: Row, Peterson, 1957.

Foa, U. G. Interpersonal and economic resources. *Science*, 1971, *171*, 345–351.

Frazer, J. G. *Folklore in the Old Testament* II. London: Macmillan, 1919.

Gamson, W. A. A theory of coalition formation. *American Sociological Review*, 1961, *26*, 372–382.

Gouldner, A. The norm of reciprocity: A preliminary statement. *American Sociological Review*, 1960, *25*, 161–179.

Greenberg, J. Effects of reward value and retaliative power on allocation decisions: Justice, generosity, or greed? *Journal of Personality and Social Psychology*, 1978, *36*, 367–379.

Griesinger, D., & Livingston, J., Jr. Toward a model of interpersonal motivation in experimental games. *Behavioral Science*, 1973, *18*, 173–188.

Gulliver, P. H. Dispute settlements without courts: The Ndendevil of Southern Tanzania. In L. Nader (Ed.), *Law in culture and society*. Chicago: Aldine, 1969.

Hatfield, E., Utne, M. K., & Traupmann, J. Equity theory and intimate relationships. In R. L. Burgess & T. L. Huston (Eds.), *Social exchange in developing relationships*. New York: Academic Press, 1979.

Heath, A. *Rational choice and social exchange: A critique of exchange theory.* Cambridge: Cambridge University Press, 1976.

Homans, G. C. The cash posters. *American Sociological Review,* 1954, *19,* 724–733.

Homans, G. C. *Social behavior: Its elementary forms.* New York: Harcourt Brace & World, 1961.

Homans, G. C. *Social behavior: Its elementary forms* (Rev. ed.). New York: Harcourt Brace Jovanovich, 1974.

Homans, G. C. Commentary. In L. Berkowitz & E. Walster (Eds.), *Advances in experimental social psychology* (Vol. 9). New York: Academic Press, 1976.

Hook, J. The development of equity and logico-mathematical thinking. *Child Development,* 1978, *49,* 1035–1044.

Hook, J., & Cook, T. D. Equity theory and the cognitive ability of children. *Psychological Bulletin,* 1979, *86,* 429–445.

Huesmann, L. P., & Levinger, G. Incremental exchange theory: A formal model for progression in dyadic social interaction. In L. Berkowitz & E. Walster (Eds.), *Advances in experimental social psychology* (Vol. 9). New York: Academic Press, 1976.

Huston, T. L., & Burgess, R. L. Social exchange in developing relationships: An overview. In R. L. Burgess & T. L. Huston (Eds.), *Social exchange in developing relationships.* New York: Academic Press, 1979.

Kames, Lord. *The principles of equity.* Edinburg, 1760.

Katz, D., & Kahn, R. *The social psychology of organizations* (2nd ed.). New York: Wiley, 1978.

Kelley, H. H. *Personal relationships: Their structures and processes.* Hillsdale, N.J.: Erlbaum, 1979.

Kelley, H. H., & Thibaut, J. *Interpersonal relations: A theory of interdependence.* New York: Wiley, 1978.

Kimberly, J. A theory of status equilibration. In J. Berger, M. Zelditch, & B. Anderson (Eds.), *Sociological theories in progress* (Vol. 1). Boston: Houghton Mifflin, 1966.

Kimberly, J. Relations among status, power, and economic rewards in simple and complex social systems. In J. Berger, M. Zelditch, & B. Anderson (Eds.), *Sociological theories in progress* (Vol. 2). Boston: Houghton Mifflin, 1972.

Komorita, S. S., & Brinberg, D. The effects of equity norms in coalition formation. *Sociometry,* 1977, *40,* 351–361.

Komorita, S. S., & Chertkoff, J. A bargaining theory of coalition formation. *Psychological Review,* 1973, *80,* 149–162.

Komorita, S. S., & Kravitz, D. The effects of alternatives in bargaining. *Journal of Experimental Social Psychology,* 1979, *15,* 147–157.

Kuhlman, D., & Marshello, A. Individual differences in game motivation as moderators of preprogrammed strategy effects in Prisoner's Dilemma. *Journal of Personality and Social Psychology,* 1975, *32,* 922–931.

Lane, I. M., & Messé, L. A. Equity and the distribution of rewards. *Journal of Personality and Social Psychology,* 1971, *20,* 1–17.

Lerner, M. J. The desire for justice and reactions to victims. In J. Macaulay & L. Berkowitz (Eds.), *Altruism and helping behavior.* New York: Academic Press, 1970.

Lerner, M. J. The justice motive in social behavior: An introduction. *Journal of Social Issues,* 1975, *31,* 1–19.

Lerner, M. J., & Miller, D. T. Just world research and the attribution process: Looking back and ahead. *Psychological Bulletin,* 1978, *85,* 1030–1051.

Leventhal, G. S. Fairness in social relationships. In J. Thibaut, J. Spence, & R. Carson (Eds.), *Contemporary topics in social psychology.* Morristown, N.J.: General Learning Press, 1976.

Leventhal, G. S. What should be done with equity theory? New approaches to the study of fairness in social relationships. In K. Gergen, M. Greenberg, & R. Willis (Eds.), *Social exchange theory.* New York: Plenum, 1980.

Leventhal, G. S., & Anderson, D. Self-interest and the maintenance of equity. *Journal of Personality and Social Psychology,* 1970, *15,* 57–62.

Leventhal, G. S., & Lane, D. W. Sex, age, and equity behavior. *Journal of Personality and Social Psychology,* 1970, *15,* 312–316.

Leventhal, G. S., & Michaels, J. W. Extending the equity model: Perception of inputs and allocation of reward as a function of duration and quantity of performance. *Journal of Personality and Social Psychology,* 1969, *12,* 303–309.

Lévi-Strauss, C. *The elementary structures of kinship.* Boston: Beacon, 1969.

Luce, D., & Raiffa, H. *Games and decisions: Introduction and critical survey.* New York: Wiley, 1957.

MacCrimmon, K., & Toda, M. The experimental determination of indifference curves. *Review of Economic Studies,* 1969, *36,* 433–452.

Malinowski, B. *Argonauts of the Western Pacific.* London: Routledge and Kegan Paul, 1922.

Mauss, M. *The gift.* New York: Norton, 1967. (Originally published, 1925. Published by Norton by arrangement with Routledge & Kegan Paul Ltd.)

McClintock, C. G. Social motivation—A set of propositions. *Behavioral Science,* 1972, *17,* 438–454.

McClintock, C. G. Social motivations in settings of outcome interdependence. In D. Druckman (Ed.), *Negotiation behavior.* Beverly Hills, Calif.: Sage, 1977.

McClintock, C. G., & Keil, L. *The effects of cognition, reward, and social interdependence upon children's fairness behaviors.* NSF Proposal #80-63, 1980.

Messick, D., & McClintock, C. G. Motivational bases of choice in experimental games. *Journal of Experimental Social Psychology,* 1968, *4,* 1–25.

Mikula, G. *Considerations of justice in an allocation situation.* Paper presented at the meeting of the European Association of Experimental Social Psychologists, September 1977.

Mikula, G., & Schwinger, T. Intermember relations and reward allocation: Theoretical considerations of effects. In H. Brandstatter, J. H. Davis, & H. Schuler (Eds.), *Dynamics of group decisions.* Beverly Hills, Calif.: Sage, 1978.

Milgram, S. *Obedience to authority.* New York: Harper & Row, 1974.

Morgan, W., & Sawyer, J. Bargaining, expectations, and the preference for equality over equity. *Journal of Personality and Social Psychology,* 1967, *6,* 139–149.

Nash, J. F. The bargaining problem. *Econometrica,* 1950, *18,* 155–162.

Nash, J. F. Two-person cooperative games. *Econometrica,* 1953, *21,* 128–140.

Newman, R. A. (Ed.). *Equity in the world's legal systems.* Brussels: Establishments Emile Bruylant, 1973.

Parcel, T. L., & Cook, K. Status characteristics, reward allocation and equity. *Sociometry,* 1977, *40,* 311–324.

Parsons, T. Utilitarianism II: Sociological thought. In D. Sills (Ed.), *International encyclopedia of the social sciences* (Vol. 16). New York: Macmillan, 1968.

Presthus, R. Authority in organizations. *Public Administration Review,* 1960, *20,* 88–91.

Pruitt, D. Twenty years of experimental gaming: Critique, synthesis and suggestions for the future. *Annual Review of Psychology,* 1977, *28,* 363–392.

Radzicki, J. Technique of conjoint measurement of subjective value of own and others' gain. *Polish Psychological Bulletin,* 1976, *7,* 179–186.

Reis, H. T., & Gruzen, J. On mediating equity, equality, and self-interest: The role of self-presentation in social exchange. *Journal of Experimental Social Psychology,* 1976, *12,* 487–503.

Robbins, L. *An essay on the nature and significance of economic science*. London: Macmillan, 1932.

Roethlisberger, F., & Dickson, W. *Management and the worker*. Cambridge: Harvard University Press, 1939.

Rubin, Z. *Liking and loving*. New York: Holt, Rinehart & Winston, 1973.

Sampson, E. E. On justice as equality. *Journal of Social Issues*, 1975, *31*, 45–64.

Scanzoni, J. Social exchange and behavioral interdependence. In R. L. Burgess & T. L. Huston (Eds.), *Social exchange in developing relationships*. New York: Academic Press, 1979.

Severts, A. *Billykheid en gelijkheid en het verdeelgedrag van 6-jarige kinderen*. Unpublished manuscript, K. U. Leuven, 1976.

Shapeley, L. S. A value for n-person games. In H. W. Kuhn & A. W. Tucker (Eds.), *Contributions to the theory of games, II*. Princeton: Princeton University Press, 1953.

Shapiro, E. G. Effects of expectations of future interaction on reward allocations in dyads: Equity or equality. *Journal of Personality and Social Psychology*, 1975, *31*, 873–880.

Simon, H. Authority. In C. M. Arensberg (Ed.), *Research in industrial human relations*. New York: Harper, 1957.

Stryker, S. Coalition behavior. In C. G. McClintock (Ed.), *Experimental social psychology*. New York: Holt, Rinehart & Winston, 1972.

Thibaut, J., & Kelley, H. H. *The social psychology of groups*. New York: Wiley, 1959.

Van Avermaet, E. *Equity: A theoretical and experimental analysis*. Unpublished doctoral dissertation, University of California, Santa Barbara, 1975.

Van Avermaet, E., McClintock, C. G., & Moskowitz, J. Alternative approaches to equity: Dissonance reduction, pro-social motivation, and strategic accommodation. *European Journal of Social Psychology*, 1978, *8*, 419–437.

Von Grumbkow, J., Deen, E., Steensma, H., & Wilke, H. The effect of future interaction on the distribution of rewards. *European Journal of Social Psychology*, 1976, *6*, 119–123.

Walster, E., Berscheid, E., & Walster, G. W. New directions in equity research. *Journal of Personality and Social Psychology*, 1973, *25*, 151–176.

Walster, E., Traupmann, J., & Walster, G. W. Equity and extramarital sex. *Archives of Sexual Behavior*, 1978, *7*, 121–141.

Walster, E., Walster, G. W., & Traupmann, J. Equity and premarital sex. *Journal of Personality and Social Psychology*, 1978, *36*, 82–92.

Weber, M. *The theory of social and economic organization* (Edited by T. Parsons and translated by A. M. Henderson & T. Parsons). New York: Oxford University Press, 1947.

Whyte, W. F. *Street corner society*. Chicago: University of Chicago Press, 1943.

Wiggins, J. A. Status differentiation, external consequences, and alternative reward distributions. *Sociometry*, 1966, *29*, 89–103.

Winham, G. Complexity in international negotiation. In D. Druckman (Ed.), *Negotiations: Social psychological perspectives*. Beverley Hills, Calif.: Sage, 1977.

Wright, B. Altruism in children and the perceived conduct of others. *Journal of Abnormal and Social Psychology*, 1942, *37*, 218–233.

Wyer, R. Prediction of behavior in two-person games. *Journal of Personality and Social Psychology*, 1969, *13*, 222–228.

Wyer, R. The effects of outcome matrix and partner's behavior in two-person games. *Journal of Experimental Social Psychology*, 1971, *7*, 190–210.

chapter 11

Approaching Equity
and Avoiding Inequity
in Groups and Organizations

JERALD GREENBERG

I. PROLOGUE

A. The Pervasiveness of Justice in Groups and Organizations

That considerations of equity and justice are basic to the functioning of groups and organizations cannot be denied.[1] Perhaps more so than any other topic covered in this volume, it is in the area of group and organizational dynamics that the themes of equity and justice are most pervasive.

Because the pioneering work on equity theory by Adams (1963, 1965) was derived from analyses of behavior in employer–employee relationships, it is not surprising that it is in this context that most equity research has been conducted. Most of the preceding theoretical accounts of justice were also analyzed within the context of groups and organizations (e.g., Homans, 1961; Jacques, 1961; Patchen, 1961). The emphasis on studying justice in work settings derived from these theoretical state-

---

[1]In this chapter, the term *equity* will be used to refer to a specific norm of social or interpersonal justice, or to specific theories using this term in their names. Cohen and Greenberg discuss the distinction between equity and justice in Chapter 1 of this volume.

EQUITY AND JUSTICE
IN SOCIAL BEHAVIOR

ments is indicated by a formidable body of empirical research (see review by Adams & Freedman, 1976).

However, it is not merely due to historical precedent that much of our knowledge of equity behavior is housed in the context of business settings. It has been noted that the nature of equity theory, with its emphasis on social comparison processes, as well as explicit specification of rewards (outcomes) and contributions (inputs), makes it particularly well suited to studying workers' reactions to payment (Walster, Walster, & Berscheid, 1978). Hence, the context of the business world has provided a viable backdrop for use in studying equity and justice. Moreover, studies of groups and organizations have benefited from the use of justice concepts. Reflecting on this, Weick (1966) was moved to conclude that, "Equity theory appears to be among the more useful middle-range theories of organizational behavior [p. 439]."

B. The Motivational Properties of Equity and Inequity

It is, perhaps, the most rudimentary requirement of any discussion relating justice notions to the dynamics of behavior in groups and organizations to consider the motivational properties of equity and inequity. This assessment is supported by a variety of evidence, not the least important of which is the detailed discussion of equity theory appearing in Campbell and Pritchard's (1976) chapter on industrial motivation in the *Handbook of Industrial and Organizational Psychology*. Moreover, both the original position (Adams, 1963, 1965) as well as more recent theoretical statements (e.g., Walster, Berscheid, & Walster, 1973) emphasize that behavior is motivated by considerations of equity and inequity. Yet, there is considerable disagreement surrounding the exact nature of the motivational processes involved. The present chapter will critically review some of the positions and controversies germane to this topic.

My presentation will be organized around the distinction between viewing equity as a reactive concept or a proactive concept (see Van Avermaet, McClintock, & Moskowitz, 1978). In other words, I will consider whether behavior, particularly in group and organizational milieus, is motivated by attempts to escape from, or avoid, inequitable conditions (a reactive approach), or by attempts to actively secure, or approach, equitable conditions (a proactive approach). As we will see, some interesting theoretical and practical implications arise from this distinction.

II. REACTIVE AVOIDANCE OF INEQUITY

A. Description

Both traditional equity theory (Adams, 1965) and subsequent reformulations (e.g., Walster *et al.*, 1973) have postulated that inequity produces stress, and that persons strive toward equity to escape the aversive internal state of perceived inequity. Hence, equity theory holds that responses to inequity are *reactive*.

Equity theory, as described in detail elsewhere (Adams, 1965; Goodman & Friedman, 1971; Pritchard, 1969; Walster *et al.*, 1973; see also Chapter 1, this volume) asserts that the presence of an inequitable state of affairs motivates behavior aimed at returning exchange participants to their formerly equitable conditions. Specifically, the theory postulates that a perceived inequity creates tension in the perceiver that is proportional to the magnitude of the inequity, and that the perceiver is motivated by this tension to reduce the inequity. The strength of this motivation is proportional to the magnitude of the perceived inequity (Adams, 1965).

From this perspective, equity theory is essentially a drive reduction theory. Changes in behavior or cognition in response to inequity are conceived as reactions motivated by attempts to reduce stress. Accordingly, we are led to the general assertion of the reactive position that *inequity motivates behavior*.

B. Reactions to Inequity

With this in mind, the literature germane to the reactive viewpoint will be reviewed. A series of studies designed to test predictions derived from Adams's (1963, 1965) theory of inequity were performed in the period immediately following the appearance of his initial theoretical statement. Because this research has already been reviewed extensively elsewhere (e.g., Adams & Freedman, 1976; Goodman & Friedman, 1971; Lawler, 1968a; Mowday, 1979; Pritchard, 1969), only the highlights of this work will be presented here. Particular attention will be paid to recent studies, and to the identification and assessment of theoretical and empirical problems.

The focus of this section will be on actual performance differences, although it should be understood that cognitive, psychological, reactions to inequity are also likely to occur (Greenberg, 1979a). These alternative modes of response to inequity have received scant research attention, particularly in work settings, but the little available evidence suggests that nonperformance responses to payment on the job (e.g., social responses, such as subgroup formation) are indeed consistent with an equity orientation (Hinton, 1972). However, the bias toward performance measures is in keeping with the emphasis on motivating performance that stimulated a good deal of equity research in work organizations (Campbell & Pritchard, 1976). To enhance comparability with previous reviews, I will follow the practice of distinguishing between cases of overpayment inequity and underpayment inequity.

1. UNDERPAYMENT

Equity theory hypothesizes that *underpaid hourly* workers will be less productive than equitably paid workers. By reducing their inputs, workers could effectively raise the ratio of their outcomes to inputs such that it would potentially match the higher ratio of a comparison other, thereby reducing inequity. In an analogous manner, *underpaid piece-rate* workers are expected to produce a larger amount of low quality units than are equitably paid workers. This strategy serves to reduce inequity by bringing about an increase in outcomes without demanding greater inputs.

Overall, research in which subjects have been underpaid has confirmed these expectations (e.g., Andrews, 1967; Lawler & O'Gara, 1967; Pritchard, Dunnette, & Jorgenson, 1972). An interesting archival study by Lord and Hohenfeld (1979) provides some additional support for the predicted underpayment effect. These researchers compared the performance of 23 major league baseball players who, because of contractual reasons, were paid lower salaries in the 1976 season than in 1975. Support was obtained for the hypothesis that these players would perceive themselves as undercompensated relative to self-referents from the previous year. These perceptions were associated with lowered performance as assessed by significant reductions in batting averages, home runs, and runs-batted-in (however, see Duchon & Jago, 1981).

The above research suggests that decreases in performance quantity or quality appear to be a likely behavioral reaction to underpayment inequity. Hence, underpayment inequity motivates performance decrements.

2. OVERPAYMENT

Analogous theorizing has also been applied to predicting the reactions of overpaid workers. The theory predicts that *overpaid hourly* workers will raise their performance level in response to overpayment and will be more productive than equitably paid workers. By bringing their inputs into line with their disproportionately high outcomes, workers overpaid on an hourly basis can reduce the extent of their overpayment equity. It is expected that *overpaid piece-rate* workers will be less productive, but perform higher quality work than equitably paid workers. This prediction follows from the reasoning that simply producing more would just exaggerate the inequity because the contingent pay system would bring still higher pay to more productive workers. Instead, increasing work quality allows overpaid workers to raise their performance inputs without raising their outcomes, thereby lowering their outcome–input ratios and escaping inequity.

In general, the majority of the studies on the effects of overpayment on task performance have supported equity theory predictions (e.g., Adams & Jacobsen, 1964; Adams & Rosenbaum, 1962; Andrews, 1967; Friedman & Goodman, 1967; Goodman & Friedman, 1968, 1969; Lawler, 1968b, Lawler, Koplin, Young, & Fadem, 1968; Weiner, 1970; Wood & Lawler, 1970). Yet, as several critics have noted, this support is not entirely unequivocal. Insightful critiques of this evidence have been broached by several observers, including Goodman & Friedman (1971), Lawler, (1968a), and Pritchard (1969), who have pointed out some weaknesses of these studies and have offered a number of alternative interpretations of the findings.

Perhaps the most compelling criticism levied against the research demonstrating overpayment effects is the assertion that the usual overpayment induction procedure may have had the effect of threatening subjects' self-esteem (Lawler, 1968a; Pritchard, 1969). In the Adams and Rosenbaum (1962) study, and in many of the subsequent experiments (e.g., Goodman & Friedman, 1968, 1969; Lawler *et al.*, 1968; Wood & Lawler, 1970), the manner of leading subjects to believe they were overpaid involved telling them that they were unqualified for the task, but would none the less be paid at the advertised rate (which, of course, was inappropriately high for such an unqualified person). As a result, it has been argued, it is possible that the workers' self-esteem may have been unintentionally threatened as a by-product of manipulating overpayment in this manner. Accordingly, the alternative explanation cannot be ruled out that the impressive performance of overpaid workers was due to these workers' attempts to convince themselves and their employers that they were actually quite capable after all.

Evidence in support of this possibility is derived from a role-playing study by Andrews and Valenzi (1970). Subjects were asked to imagine how they would feel if they were the employee in a situation like that in the Adams and Rosenberg paradigm, in which their job qualifications were challenged. Interestingly, about 44% of the subjects expressed awareness that their self-esteem would be threatened, whereas virtually no subjects expressed any awareness of a wage inequity. Further evidence of the contaminating effects of threatened qualifications is provided in several more direct tests (e.g., Evans & Molinari, 1970; Lawler, 1968b; Weiner, 1970). The study by Lawler (1968b) makes a particularly cogent case. It was found that the tendency for overpaid subjects to be more productive than equitably paid ones was manifest when the Adams and Rosenberg procedure of inducing overpayment by challenging job qualifications was replicated, but *not* when subjects were led to believe that they were overpaid as a result of external circumstances. Overpayment effects also failed to occur in a study by Hinton (1972) in which payment was based on external circumstances. On this basis, it would appear that the overpayment effect *may* be an artifact created by the process of threatening self-esteem while attempting to induce overpayment inequity.

In commenting on these findings, however, Adams (1968) has noted the possibility that Lawler's (1968b) "overpaid by circumstance" subjects may not have felt that they were inequitably paid at all, just highly paid. This possibility is quite likely, considering that subjects were told they were paid more than workers on past projects, but the same as other workers on the same project. Thus, it is possible that Lawler's overpayment induction procedure might not have created feelings of inequitable payment, just high payment, thereby accounting for the failure to find the overpayment effect predicted by equity theory.

In direct support of the theory are several studies that find the predicted overpayment effects in the absence of a manipulation threatening self-esteem. For example, Andrews (1967) overpaid subjects by circumstance on a laboratory task and still found evidence supporting equity theory predictions. Likewise, in a work-simulation study, Pritchard *et al.* (1972) manipulated overpayment by telling subjects that an error in advertising had occurred, and found that overpaid subjects were more productive than equitably paid ones. Using an extremely ingenious induction procedure, Garland (1973) led subjects to believe that they were overpaid by having their coworkers casually announce their own lower rate of pay. Even though this procedure did not challenge workers' self-esteem, equity theory predictions were supported (i.e., overpaid subjects tended to produce less work of higher equality than did equitably paid subjects). On the basis of this evidence, and Adams's (1968) arguments rebutting Lawler's (1968b) nonsupportive evidence, it seems reasonable to conclude that the overpayment effect is *not* limited to settings in which the overpayment induction is confounded with threats to self-esteem. Rather, it appears that overpayment effects are relatively reliable across a variety of induction procedures.

A related criticism levied against studies supporting equity theory's interpretation of responses to overpayment is that overpaid subjects felt in jeopardy of being fired (Pritchard, 1969). Because they were paid more than their qualifications merited, Adams and Rosenbaum's (1962) overpaid subjects might have worked as hard as they did to protect their job security. However, this explanation assumes that the possibility of termination or of future employment existed. However, analogous results were found even when job security was assured and when future employment was impossible (Arrowood, 1961; Lawler et al., 1968). Accordingly, the threatened job security explanation is lacking in empirical support.

Another potential problem noted by several critics (e.g., Anderson & Shelly, 1971; Opshal & Dunnette, 1966; Pritchard et al., 1972) is that the instructions to the overpaid subjects placed greater emphasis on the importance of good work quality than did the instructions to the equitably paid subjects. However, in view of the consistency of findings using procedures devoid of this potentially biasing procedure (e.g., Garland, 1973; Pritchard et al., 1972), the viability of this criticism must be questioned (Walster et al., 1978).

3. THE PROBLEM OF INPUT–OUTCOME AMBIGUITY

The success of equity theory in being able to predict behavioral reactions to inequity is based on the assumption that persons hold clear perceptions of what factors constitute inputs and outcomes. The pay and the work studied in highly controlled equity investigations comprise just a small segment of a wide array of inputs and outcomes existing in actual organizations (Belcher, 1974). Other factors, such as vacations and insurance plans, represent other possible outcomes; a person's age and seniority represent other possible inputs. However, theorists have noted that some job elements are difficult to classify as either an input or an outcome (Goodman & Friedman, 1971; Pritchard, 1969). Consider responsibility as an example. If an employee is given an increase in responsibility, it is uncertain whether this constitutes an increase in outcomes (added prestige and respect), or inputs (more challenging duties to perform). This problem has some important implications for work behavior and attitudes.

An interesting approach to this problem was taken by Tornow (1971), whose central thesis was that if there were differences in what job factors are seen as being inputs and outcomes, then these differences would either facilitate or attenuate the effects of inequitable payment. Specifically, persons may perceive ambiguous job elements (such as having to make decisions, doing complex work, making use of abilities) either as indicating a contribution they must make (i.e., as inputs), or as something about the job that is valuable and intrinsically interesting (i.e., as outcomes). Conceiving this as an individual difference, Tornow (1971) developed a test designed to identify those who perceive ambiguous job elements as inputs and those who perceive them as outcomes.

It was hypothesized that in an underpayment inequity work situation, greater inequity would be experienced by subjects who tend to perceive ambiguous job elements as inputs; putting these ambiguous elements on the input side of the equity ratio would exaggerate the degree of inequity. Conversely, workers who tend to view ambiguous job elements as outcomes were expected to see potentially inequitable work situations as less inequitable because additional perceived rewards would raise the outcome–input ratio. For cases of overpayment inequity, of course, the predictions were reversed.

Tornow (1971) reanalyzed the data from the large-scale simulation study by Pritchard et al. (1972) after recontacting the subjects who participated in that study and distinguishing them on the basis of their responses to his input–outcome checklist. In this manner, Tornow found good, although not unequivocal, support for his hypotheses in terms of both reported feelings of inequity and actual work performance. Accordingly, reactions to inequity were either augmented or attenuated by individual beliefs regarding what constituted job rewards and responsibilites.

I agree with Campbell and Pritchard's (1976) assessment that Tornow's (1971) work is worth emulating, and would like to share some ideas for theoretical and applied research inspired by it. First, it would be interesting to do a predictive study or a concurrent study, rather than a postdictive one. Because turnover is related to feelings of underpayment inequity (Finn & Lee, 1972; Telly, French, & Scott, 1971), it may be expected that employees resigning because they feel inadequately paid (as determined via an exit interview; e.g., Hinrichs, 1971) are more likely to be classified among those perceiving ambiguous job elements as inputs than as outcomes.

Another researchable idea, and one with possible practical import, involves revising employees' perspectives so they shift their views of various job responsibilities from inputs to outcomes.[2] The need for such a shift may be especially pronounced when a laborer initially enters the ranks of management. A union laborer may be expected to perceive many job responsibilities as inputs that a manager may perceive as outcomes. Because attitudinal shifts have been documented as occurring upon entry into management (Lieberman, 1956), it is an interesting possibility

---

[2]This assumes, of course, that workers are more likely to feel underpaid than overpaid (Weick & Nesset, 1966; Zedeck & Smith, 1968).

that perceptions of ambiguous job factors as inputs or outcomes may make a like shift. Inculcating these attitudes should be an integral part of management training, as failure to be adequately socialized in this manner may breed heightened feelings of inequity, possibly leading to dissatisfaction (Finn & Lee, 1972), and excessive turnover (Telly *et al.*, 1971). Such intervention programs should be researched, both to determine their effectiveness, and to test theoretical hypotheses about how reactions to inequity are influenced by such cognitive restructuring and resocialization.

C. Using Inequity as a Motivator

Given that inequitably high pay appears to lead to enhanced performance, it follows that pay administrators (or allocators in general) interested in inducing high performance would succeed by purposely creating overpayment inequities. The strategic use of overreward would seem to be an effective inducement to productivity to the extent that workers will attempt to raise their performance in attempting to alleviate the aversiveness of overpayment inequity (see also Chapter 5 by Ajzen in this volume).

Appealing as this proposition may be, there are two critical questions that must be addressed. First, will allocators actually follow such a policy? And, if so, what factors will limit its use? Each of these questions will now be considered.

1. IS IT DONE?

There is evidence from several studies to suggest that allocators interested in raising performance levels *will* administer inequitably high levels of reward. For example, in a series of experiments, Lanzetta and his colleagues (Bankart & Lanzetta, 1970; Lanzetta & Hannah, 1969) examined the sanctioning behavior of persons attempting to train others through the administration of rewards and punishments. These studies found that incompetent performers tended to be treated *less punitively* than were competent performers. Similarly, a pair of experiments by Rothbart (1968) revealed that subjects attempting to elicit better performance from workers tended to administer generous rewards following trials with poor performance.

Still more direct evidence of this effect is provided by some of the author's own research (Greenberg, 1978a; Greenberg & Leventhal, 1976). For example, Greenberg and Leventhal (1976, Study 1) directly compared the allocation practices of subjects instructed to allocate reward equitably with those instructed to allocate reward so as to motivate recipients' performance. It was found that low-level performers, particularly those in failing groups, were given higher levels of reward by subjects attempting to motivate high performance than by those attempting to maintain equity. Corroborating evidence was found in a follow-up study (Greenberg & Leventhal, 1976, Study 2) in which poor performers were also given higher rewards by subjects attempting to motivate than by subjects attempting to maintain equity. Questionnaire responses from this study revealed that subjects implicitly believed in the efficacy of overreward relative to underreward as a motivational tactic. A similar tendency for allocators to violate the equity norm to elicit high performance was also reported in another study by Greenberg (1978a).

Further support for the contention that conventional wisdom embraces the instrumental virtues of the overreward strategy is revealed in a recent account appearing on the sports pages (Associated Press, 1979). On September 14, 1979, in a football game between the Baltimore Colts and the Cleveland Browns, Baltimore kicker Toni Linhart missed three easy field goals, costing his team a 13–10 defeat. Instead of being chastised, Linhart found himself the recipient of a $10,000 raise provided by this team's president and treasurer, Robert Irsay. Irsay was quoted as saying, "He'll be the best kicker from now on. . . . Maybe a little more money will get some people interested in playing a little harder." To this, he added, "You always reward people when they do something good; well, I figured I'd give him the reward ahead of time." This incident provides interesting anecdotal support for the tendency of allocators to overreward poor performers in the hopes of motivating them.

There appear to be several possible reasons for the popular use of the overreward strategy as a motivator. For example, Greenberg and Leventhal (1976) have suggested that subjects' past experiences may have made them aware of the tendency for overpaid workers to be more productive than equitably paid workers (e.g., Adams & Jacobsen, 1964; Adams & Rosenbaum, 1962). For this reason they may purposely overreward workers to motivate them to perform at higher levels.

It has also been suggested (Leventhal, 1976) that the use of the overreward tactic is related to subjects' attempts to create obligations on the part of performers to reciprocate allocators' generosity by improving their subsequent performance. The possibility that the norm of reciprocity (Gouldner, 1960) may enhance obligations to repay previous generous acts has been considered one of the most basic principles underlying the use of managerial compensation as a motivational tool (Nash & Carroll, 1975). In fact, statements embracing the reciprocity norm are often included in the managerial compensation policies of many companies (Nash & Carroll, 1975). This would appear to be the reasoning behind Colts' president and treasurer Irsay's generosity toward Linhart.

Despite all of this laboratory research and anecdotal support for the use of overreward as a motivational tactic, there appears to be no strong evidence to suggest that allocators actually follow an overreward strategy in organizations. The few field studies that could potentially have documented supervisors' attempts to elevate subordinates' poor performance by offering them generous rewards have failed to find that they actually do so (e.g., Kipnis & Lane, 1962; Kipnis & Cosentino, 1969). In commenting on this, Kipnis (1976) has observed:

> Indeed it would be difficult to locate many managers who attempt to correct incompetence with pay raises. Organizations do not encourage the use of rewards as a means of changing the performance of noncompliant workers. Such a use of power might be viewed as a "bribe" and, hence, as being illicit. Furthermore, having to honor a promise to reward a worker who has previously annoyed a supervisor by his poor work may in fact be personally distasteful, and would certainly anger satisfactory workers. [Reprinted by permission from D. Kipnis, *The Powerholders* (Chicago: University of Chicago Press, 1976), p. 69. Copyright © 1976 by the University of Chicago Press.]

This observation raises some interesting questions about the conditions under which allocators may actually use or refrain from using the overreward strategy for instrumental purposes.

2. LIMITATIONS

Under what conditions will an overreward strategy be used? What are the implications of its use on organizational functioning?

Clearly, a key mediating factor appears to be the allocator's temporal frame of reference. Subjects in the studies by Robert (1968) and Bankart and Lanzetta (1970) had little time to stimulate improvement; similarly, subjects in Greenberg and Leventhal's (1976) studies were in an "emergency situation." I agree with Leventhal's (1976) position that the one-time only, short-term, or emergency measures taken in these studies might not have been taken if it were possible for subjects to consider a long-term perspective. Similarly, Van Avermaet *et al.* (1978) have also noted that inequitable behavior may be an effective way of reaching short-term goals, but not long-term goals. If inequity is indeed aversive, the decision to purposely create it may be unfavorably received and eventually lead to rebellion—a potentially counterproductive result.[3]

Leventhal's (1976) conclusion that the tactic of using overpayment as a motivator may only be temporary fits in well with the evidence suggesting that heightened performance in response to overpayment may itself only be temporary. The majority of studies examining the effects of

---

[3]Disillusionment with scientific management (Taylor, 1911) is likewise based on the belief that workers respond better to supervision devoid of aversive external control (McGregor, 1960).

overpayment have typically employed brief periods of observation in a single experimental session (see Goodman & Friedman, 1969). However, the effect of overpayment has been found to diminish in at least one study monitoring performance over several sessions (Lawler *et al.*, 1968). Thus, it appears that overpayment inequity may have only temporary motivating effects, and that overpayment may only be employed as a motivational strategy in short-term situations.

Another possible factor mediating the use of overreward as a motivational strategy has to do with workers' initial levels of performance. Greenberg and Leventhal (1976), for example, noted that subjects only gave inequitably high pay to poor performers, but avoided paying already good performers an inequitable wage. It was suggested that subjects were afraid of disrupting good performers with an inequitable wage. Thus, as the saying goes, "the squeaky wheel" may indeed "get the grease." Kipnis (1976) too agrees that managers often refrain from disrupting particularly good performers with extreme levels of payment, but cautions that managers may sometimes have to revert to using extreme payment when they suspect that high levels of performance can no longer be taken for granted and may soon deteriorate.

By similar reasoning, it follows that allocators may refrain from over-rewarding one worker if they fear repercussions from others. This is especially likely in interdependent groups, where rewarding one member more than he or she deserves may lead other members who compare themselves to this person to feel that they have been unfairly treated. It would not have been surprising, for example, if Toni Linhart's team members felt that Linhart's being rewarded for poor performance was unfair to them. Under these circumstances, of course, these team members may begin to feel underrewarded, and lower their performance. Accordingly, the use of overreward would appear to be an inappropriate motivational strategy when a high degree of group member interdependence enhances the possibility of unfavorable wage comparisons on a group level. Baltimore Colts' ownership appears to have eventually accepted this, and subsequently fired Linhart, and then Irsay.

D. Self-Justification

In addition to equity theory, the tradition of research on insufficient and oversufficient justification (e.g., Deci, 1975; Lepper & Greene, 1978) can also be viewed as taking a reactive approach to motivation.

The "overjustification effect" refers to the tendency for persons who are paid to perform a task to subsequently show a decrement in intrinsic interest in performing that task. The assumption is that the pay provides excessive cognitive justification for performing the task; hence, the belief that it was the pay and not the inherently interesting task that motivated performance. Similarly, persons who are not paid for performing a task are forced to create some justification for their performance, and can do so by reporting greater interest in the task, and by being more productive. This is known as the "inadequate justification" effect. (The reader is referred to Lepper and Greene, 1978, for a more sophisticated description of these effects.)

The idea that inadequate payment leads to high performance (inadequate justification) and that adequate payment leads to low performance (overjustification) assumes a reactive mechanism. That is, the reason for the different performance comes about as a result of an attempt to cognitively justify an existing state of affairs. Individuals, therefore, are reacting to the degree of justification they believe they have for performing a task. It is this justification that motivates performance.

It is not surprising that, like equity theory, these self-justification theories are reactive in nature, as they share a common ancestry in cognitive dissonance theory (Festinger, 1957), which, itself, is a reactive theory. Unlike equity theory, however, there *appear* to be very different predictions made regarding the effects of payment on performance by self-justification theories.

As discussed earlier, equity theory predicts that, relative to equitably paid persons, persons who are overpaid will raise their performance, and that persons who are underpaid will lower their performance. This action is taken as a behavioral attempt to adjust performance so as to bring the ratio of one's rewards to performance into line with the ratios of others. However, an *ostensibly* contradictory finding has been obtained by researchers studying the phenomena of insufficient and oversufficient justification. Specifically, research in this tradition has reported that persons paid for performing intrinsically interesting tasks tend to perform these tasks less frequently in free-choice situations than do subjects who are not paid for performing (Deci, 1971; Lepper, Greene, & Nisbett, 1973). These results have been explained by suggesting that subjects enhanced their performance to create adequate justification for performing a task when existing justification seemed inadequate. Conceptually similar explanations have been offered by research on task-enhancement (Weick, 1964) and cognitive evaluation theory (Deci, 1975).[4]

---

[4]An interesting alternative explanation rooted in classical learning theory has been recently offered by Garland and Staff (1979).

Yet, equity theory can also account for these findings. Specifically, equity theory allows that persons may cognitively distort their liking for a task to justify performing it under conditions in which alternative justification is lacking. Weick (1964) has found that when this occurs, persons are highly motivated to perform well, thereby maintaining consistency between their positive attitudes and productive behavior. Subsequent research has corroborated this finding (for a review, see Weick, 1967), and has also established that overreward can lead to disliking for a task and lowered productivity (see Lepper & Greene, 1978). Thus, responses to inequity can come in the form of either increased or decreased liking and productivity.

This raises the question of *when* each type of response to inequity will occur. In an attempt to reconcile these conflicting responses, Deci (1975) proposes explanations based on several mediational variables. Since the time of Deci's analysis, additional research bearing on these and other possible explanations has been conducted. The discussion that follows will focus on these various mediational factors.

1. AMBIGUITY OF INEQUITY

One factor proposed as mediating the type of inequity reaction that will occur is the degree of ambiguity surrounding the inequity. To explain how ambiguity of inequity accounts for the mode of inequity resolution, Deci (1975) cites a basic proposition of equity theory asserting that the less cognitive distortion is required to restore an inequity, the more likely will an individual be to employ such a distortion (Adams, 1965; Walster, Berscheid, & Walster, 1970). When the existence of an inequity is ambiguous, less distortion will be required to redress it than when the inequity is unambiguous, making cognitive distortion more likely under conditions of ambiguous inequity.

Evidence directly supporting this reasoning has been reported by Deci, Reis, Johnson, and Smith (1977) in a study in which the degree of inequity ambiguity was explicitly manipulated. Their underpaid subjects were more productive when inequity was ambiguous than when inequity was unambiguous. The degree of ambiguity argument is also used to explain the tendency for performance decrements to be found in studies of underpayment inequity (where the experimental situations and instructions make the inequity clear), and for performance increases to be found in inadequate justification studies (where the existence of an inequity is often uncertain; Deci, 1975).

Deci's analysis is complemented and extended by the findings of Curtis, Kessler, Pendleton, and Sagotsky (1978). These investigators reported that subjects who were sufficiently paid for performing a dull task referred to as a "job" reduced the time spent performing the task after the session was allegedly over, whereas unpaid subjects did not show any change. Hence, the overjustification effect occurred. Interestingly, no such pattern of results obtained when the task performed was referred to as "play." By labeling the task as "a job," subjects were likely to attribute their behavior to being motivated by the extrinsic rewards associated with performance, hence, heightening the tendency to reduce performance in response to the termination of payment. However, by labeling the task as "play," the tendency for subjects to reduce their performance in response to pay withdrawal would be diminished because an intrinsically based explanation for their behavior was likely (cf. Pittman, Cooper, & Smith, 1977).

It is interesting, although this experimental situation was depicted as a work setting, that an overjustification effect was still found. This is not particularly surprising, however, as subjects worked alone, and, except when overpaid, were not given an external basis of comparison. Such conditions made the possibility of inequity quite ambiguous, thereby inviting overjustification. Similarly, when subjects were overpaid at the job, the inequity was made exceedingly explicit, and the usual overpayment effects occurred (i.e., sufficiently paid subjects were less productive than overpaid ones). Interestingly, when the task was referred to as play, no significant overpayment effects were observed. Apparently, the inappropriateness of pay for play invalidated the pay sufficiency information.

Despite Deci *et al.*'s (1977) finding that performance was high when inequity was ambiguous, it would appear to be unwise to propose that industrial managers should ambiguously underpay their workers to increase their intrinsic interest, and thereby, their performance. Organizational research suggests that ambiguity of payment equity may actually be aversive. The equity or inequity of a person's pay may certainly be considered to be ambiguous when clear information is lacking regarding the outcomes of significant reference persons, as in secret pay policies. Research by Lawler (e.g., 1965, 1967) has shown that secret pay policies in organizations often leave managers to perceive that their own pay levels are comparatively worse than they really are. For example, managers tended to overestimate the pay of others at their same level and below, and expressed dissatisfaction with their pay. As a result, Lawler asserts that workers will feel their job performance is unimportant in determining pay, thereby undermining motivation, as subsequent research has verified (Dansereau, Cashman, & Graen, 1973). Lawler (1965, 1967) argues that such adverse effects of the "hidden costs of secrecy" may be avoided by providing employees with unambiguous information about salary.[5] In fact, it is a basic aspect of the Filipino system of *Pakikisama* to maintain openness about salaries so that employees can monitor the fairness of pay systems (Gellerman, 1967).

The suggestion that openness about pay serves to avoid the adverse impact of inequity appears to contradict Deci's research and theorizing (1975; Deci *et al.*, 1977) suggesting that underpayment leads to improved performance when the inequity is ambiguous. This contradiction is readily explained by the fact that Deci *et al.*'s (1977) subjects were participants in a short-term laboratory experiment and may have been willing to cognitively justify the apparent inequity, whereas actual employees whose livelihoods were threatened by inadequate payment would not be expected to so willingly adapt in this way to an inequity. A similar warning against extrapolating from laboratory research on intrinsic motivation to organizational phenomena has been previously expressed (Notz, 1975).

2. FREEDOM OF CHOICE

Deci (1975) has also postulated that the type of response to inequity that will be observed depends upon individuals' beliefs about the extent to which they have a choice over, and responsibility for, their behavior. Citing the results of forced-compliance research (e.g., Collins & Hoyt, 1972; Linder, Cooper, & Jones, 1967), Deci argues that individuals have a greater need to justify their behavior if they feel personally responsible for having engaged in it. A high degree of choice regarding whether or not to engage in an activity typically exists in insufficient justification studies (e.g., Weick, 1964; Linder *et al.*, 1967), thereby leading subjects to enhance their task performance and attitudes to justify their freely made decision to perform without payment. However, subjects in the usual underpayment inequity study arrive committed to perform a task without knowing their pay, making the inequity a *fait accompli*, a situation in which justification is unlikely (Cooper & Brehm, 1971), and lowered performance may result. Hence, Deci reconciles the apparently contradictory findings of inadequate justification studies and inequity studies by pointing to the differential levels of freedom of choice experienced by subjects in these investigations.

This post hoc explanation is substantiated by a pair of studies by Folger and his associates (Folger, Rosenfield, & Hays, 1978; Folger, Rosenfield, Hays, & Grove, 1978). Subjects in these studies were either

---

[5]To the extent that knowledge of others' rewards may breed interpersonal conflict, allocators may actually prefer to maintain secrecy about allocation policies (for a review of relevant evidence, see Leventhal, 1976, pp. 110–112).

underpaid or overpaid for performing a task on which they worked after being given a choice or no choice as to whether or not to work. Consistent with Deci's (1975) theorizing, underpaid subjects were highly productive when given a choice to perform (the usual inadequate justification effect), but were less productive when performing without a choice (the usual underpayment inequity effect). Hence, it appears that reactions to inequity in any situation may be mediated by the availability of choice in that situation.

There are some interesting implications of the finding that persons may be motivated to work for low wages only when they have some choice in the matter. It may be the case that persons freely accepting inadequately paying jobs represent a unique segment of the population whose needs for money are low. Indeed, in Hinton's (1972) research, subjects knew in advance that they would be inequitably paid, and not surprisingly, failed to perform as expected by the theory. Apparently, those who showed up for the study after being informed in advance that they would be paid an inequitable wage (and these were fewer in the underpayment conditions) appear to represent a biased, self-selected group.[6]

Because of a variety of external constraints, such as a lack of alternative jobs, workers are often forced to accept underpayment as a *fait accompli*. Employees who feel they have little choice but to continue working for inadequate pay attempt to redress inequity not by leaving, but by performing poorly. Thus, extrapolating from Folger's research, it appears that when external constraints reduce workers' perceived freedom of choice, the probability of quitting is increased as an alternative response to inequity. Evidence in support of this supposition is provided by data showing that turnover is positively associated with level of business activity and perceived alternative opportunities (Armknecht & Early, 1972). Although it may seem immediately profitable and tempting for businesses to hire workers at a very low level of pay in a tight labor market, it appears wise to reiterate Folger, Rosenfield, and Hays's (1978) caveat that such a practice may ultimately be costly in terms of lowered performance.[7]

[6]The interesting possibility should be noted here that an allocator's belief that a recipient's need for money is low may sometimes be a convenient post hoc justification for underpaying certain persons. As Cohen (1979) has recently noted, giving lower salaries to women is often justified in this manner.

[7]The fear of getting fired because of inadequate performance may conflict with the tendency to perform poorly under conditions of limited job possibilities, thereby dissuading extremely poor performance and virtually enslaving workers. However, the high cost of selecting and training new personnel may inhibit management from taking advantage of employees, thereby balancing the situation.

3. COST OF INEQUITY

Evidence for an additional mediating variable is provided in a recent study by the present author (Greenberg, 1980a) suggesting that the choice of an inequity resolution strategy depends upon the personal cost of the inequity experienced. It was reasoned that persons experiencing unprofitable inequity who had no viable behavioral means of reducing the inequity would express their feelings of inequity attitudinally, but that the nature of these attitudes would depend on the personal cost of the inequity. Specifically, it was hypothesized that unprofitable inequity would lead to lowered satisfaction when the personal cost of the inequity was low, but that raised satisfaction would result from experiencing a costly inequity. This reasoning was based on the idea that a minor inequity would be less likely to stimulate the use of cognitive distortion as a means of reducing inequity (Walster *et al.*, 1970).

A telephone survey was taken to assess satisfaction with the United States postal system before and after an increase in the rate of first class postage. The postal rate increase was viewed as a potentially inequitable situation as customers were forced to pay higher prices for the same services. The sample was dichotomized with respect to whether they were relatively high-use or low-use customers. As expected, high users of stamps responded to the rate increase by expressing temporarily greater satisfaction with the postal service, thereby justifying the costly inequity to themselves (i.e., being more satisfied with the service justified the price increase). In contrast, low users, those expected to find the inequity not too costly, admitted a temporary dissatisfaction with the postal service. Hence, responses to inequity came in the form of increased liking when the personal cost of the inequity was high, and decreased liking when the personal cost was low.

It is noteworthy in this study that very few subjects reported an actual or anticipated behavioral response to the inequity (i.e., buying fewer stamps). It was reasoned that the attitudinal responses observed may have been different if subjects were willing to alter their behavior (use fewer stamps), but such a response may have proven too costly and inconvenient. Certainly, it is easier to express changes in satisfaction than to limit one's use of postage stamps.

Extrapolating from this study, it may be a good idea for workers to be given formalized means of expressing their job satisfaction or dissatisfaction. Such mechanisms may give workers a viable method of "letting off steam," while preserving the level of their performance. Several mechanisms already exist that may serve this purpose, such as formal grievance procedures (Pettefer, 1970), and the suggestion box (Whitwell, 1963). Both of these mechanisms could potentially provide an effective channel for expressing inequity without threatening more destructive and costly modes of expression, such as pilferage or lowered performance.

4. REVIEW AND CONCLUSIONS

The literature reviewed here has revealed three variables that mediate the nature of responses to inequity. Specifically, responses predicted by equity theory (i.e., high performance in response to overpayment, and low performance in response to underpayment) were found to be more likely than responses predicted by self-justification theories (i.e., low performance and little intrinsic interest in response to paid work, and high performance and great intrinsic interest in response to unpaid work) when: (a) the inequity is ambiguous; (b) the choice of whether or not to perform is low; and (c) the personal cost of the inequity is low.

However, as both equity theory and self-justification theories are derived from cognitive dissonance theory, the conflict between these two traditions appears to be based more on a divergence in theoretical perspectives than on a fundamental contradiction. Hence, the operative question becomes: "Which mode of response to inequity will occur?" and not whether equity or self-justification theory is correct. Both approaches are reactive in the sense that they posit that behavior is motivated by attempts to avoid unpleasant states, whether they be called underpayment inequity, or inadequate justification. Research derived from these traditions appears to have some practical import, although the limited external validity of much of the laboratory research leaves certain practical questions unanswered.

E. Status Inconsistency

An approach similar to equity theory, but more general, is based on the idea that people react negatively when either their own or others' rankings across various status dimensions are dissimilar. Such a condition is commonly referred to as inconsistency or status incongruency (also known as status disequilibration, and status crystallization), and is based on the pioneering sociological theorizing of Benoit-Smullyan (1944), Goffman (1957), and Lenski (1954). Theorists have proposed that status inconsistency is an aversive condition as it creates conflicting expectations about others' behavior (Berger, Conner, & Fisek, 1974), or states of social incertitude (Homans, 1961; Zaleznik, Christenson, & Roethlisberger, 1958). Behavioral expectations are likely to be in conflict when others' statuses are inconsistent, causing anxiety and dissatisfying social relations. These conditions are described as being stressful, and individuals are hypothesized to behaviorally or cognitively realign inconsistent ranks (Runciman & Bagley, 1969).

Such a point of view is doubtlessly reactive, as it proposes that behavior is motivated by attempts to avoid status inconsistency. This approach is quite similar to equity theory, but asserts that an aversive state results from inconsistency between reward and performance ranks (as would be expected for *any* ranks that are socially expected to be aligned), and *not* because the result is an "injustice" per se.

1. COMPARISON TO EQUITY

The most comprehensive comparison of the equity and status inconsistency viewpoints has been undertaken by Sampson (1969). It is Sampson's thesis that *both* the notions of justice and certitude (or mastery, the need to eliminate conflicting expectations) are needed as explanatory concepts. He proposes that the congruence of reward and cost ranks may be considered fair only when prevailing standards of justice so suggest. Even inconsistent rankings may be considered fair or just when they confirm prevailing expectations. However, when no prevailing standards for the division of reward and cost statuses exists, justice demands that these be distributed equally, even if the result is an inconsistency. Thus, when the norm of equity prevails, status congruence *and* justice are simultaneously accomplished; when the norm of equality prevails, maintaining consistency between statuses is in itself a miscarriage of justice.

Cast in general terms, Sampson's (1969) argument is that whether or not one is interested in mere congruence between statuses or justice is situational—it depends on the nature of the status dimensions available to a person for evaluation (e.g., see Brandon, 1965). If these are dimensions suggesting equity, then alignment of status dimensions is just; but, if these are dimensions suggesting equality, then alignment of statuses is unjust. In addition to Sampson (1969, 1975), several other theorists have argued that either equity or equality may be appropriate justice norms in certain situations (Deutsch, 1975; Leventhal, 1976).

People often fail to maintain congruency between reward status and investment status when investments fail to be reflected in outcomes (Parcel & Cook, 1977; Suchner & Jackson, 1976). As Blau (1964) has said: "Earning superior status in a group requires not merely impressing others with outstanding abilities but actually using these abilities to make contributions to the achievement of the collective goals of the group and the individual goals of its members [pp. 126–127]." Contributions must also be perceived as under internal control for congruence to be maintained with rewards. Rewards for externally mediated contributions tend to be distributed equally (e.g., Cohen, 1974; Greenberg, 1980b; Wittig, Marks, & Jones, 1981). In summary, evidence supports Sampson's (1969) assertion that justice does not always require status congruence.

2. RESEARCH ON THE EFFECTS OF STATUS INCONSISTENCY

The notion of status inconsistency has been applied to understanding a wealth of social phenomena such as attitudes toward immigrants (Runciman & Bagley, 1969), suicide (Gibbs & Martin, 1958), political liberalism, preference for social change, and other matters (Geschwender, 1967; Sampson, 1969). Much of this research has been reviewed by Stryker and Macke (1978), and will not be discussed here. Instead, I will focus on the effects of status consistency and inconsistency on group and organizational behavior.

Attempts to examine the effects of status inconsistency in groups and organizations have a formidable history, dating back over half a century to the Hawthorne studies (Roethlisberger & Dickson, 1939). Accounts of this pioneering research reveal that employees with lower status occupations were often relegated menial tasks while in social cliques that included higher status persons (see also Homans, 1961, pp. 235–236). Hence, workers attempted to keep the various statuses of their fellows consistent, an action in keeping with the Claudian saying, "Nothing is more annoying than a low man raised to a high position."

Subsequent accounts of status inconsistency have been more systematic and have focused on its effects on job performance and attitudes. The earliest research in this area dates back almost three decades to when Homans (1953) reported the results of a field study in which higher status employees, ledger clerks, reported greater dissatisfaction over being paid identical wages with lower status employees, cash posters. In that same year, Stuart Adams (1953) also reported that dissatisfaction was associated with status incongruence in a study involving Air Force flight crews. An index of status congruence calculated on the basis of age, rank, flight experience, and other status factors was found to be positively related to satisfaction. Moreover, within a specified range, technical performance also covaried with status congruence.

Research in the late 1950s provided corroborating evidence of the beneficial effects of status consistency. For example, Clark's dissertation in 1958 (cited in Homans, 1961, pp. 255–262) examined how the degree of status congruence between members of work teams at supermarket checkout counters (ringers and bundlers) influenced labor efficiency. It was found that work teams enjoying the greatest amount of congruence on social statuses tended to be the most efficient. Low degrees of status congruence within work teams reduced "social ease," and was associated with lower efficiency and higher turnover. Analogous results were reported in an early laboratory study by Exline and Ziller (1959) in which groups whose members had congruent statuses were more congenial and efficient that groups whose members had incongruent statuses.

In the 1960s, research on status inconsistency became popular among psychologists interested in industrial work groups. For example, research by Lawler (1965) has shown that workers tend to overestimate the salaries of their subordinates, and that this is associated with job dissatisfaction. Viewed in terms of status inconsistency, employees did not feel that their reward status matched their position status within the company. Similarly, Hunt (1968, 1969) noted that increased conflict potential and anxiety, as well as decreased satisfaction and productivity may result from status inconsistency on the job. Accordingly, it has been argued that the negative effects of inconsistent organizational statuses can be avoided by accompanying good performance appraisals with adequate compensation (Hunt, 1968, 1969).

Another popular line of research has dealt with the factors influencing a group's tendency to alter congruent or incongruent status ranks. For example, Burnstein and Zajonc (1965) noted that group members worked to reduce status incongruence, especially when it was large. Subsequent studies from this program of research have shown that persons may even purposely make their statuses incongruent (i.e., give one person more importance than another) to maximize joint rewards, but only when unjustly treated individuals have alternative opportunities to be compensated (Burnstein & Katz, 1972, Experiment IV; Burnstein & Wolosin, 1968).

The allocation of statuses has also been studied by Susman (1970) in an industrial setting. His subjects, oil refinery workers, were required to rate their coworkers with respect to their perceived competence in performing various tasks and the amount of skill believed necessary to perform them. Field observations and informal interviews also identified the extent to which various tasks were assigned to workers. Consistent with status consistency hypotheses, workers judged more competent by their coworkers tended to be assigned to tasks judged as requiring more skill.

More recent studies have examined the relationship between group status and bias. Research by Dion (1973, 1979) has shown that groups composed of equal status members tended to be highly cohesive and biased toward their own group—a state known as "status equity." When group members have different statuses, "status inequity" exists, and there is less ingroup favoritism. A group's self-bias can also be enhanced by increasing its overall status relative to that of other groups (Commins & Lockwood, 1979). These studies suggest that status consistency can be rewarding, and bind groups together.

III. PROACTIVE APPROACHING OF EQUITY

A. Description

The view that equity is proactive asserts that behavior is motivated by a positive concern for fairness. Equity, then, may be conceived as a valued goal in itself, as opposed to the reactive position that equity is a state achieved by escaping from inequity. Hence, the proactive view contends that *equity motivates behavior.*

The proactive approach to equity has been popularized in several recent theoretical statements. The following sections will review these various theoretical accounts, and consider their practical implications for understanding group and organizational behavior.

B. Theoretical Perspectives

1. JUSTICE MOTIVE THEORY

Lerner's (1975, 1977a, 1977b; Lerner & Whitehead, 1980) conceptualization of justice motive theory easily qualifies as a proactive approach. The theory "assumes a preeminent guiding perinciple or motive in the commitment to deserving which serves to organize most goal-seeking behavior [Lerner, 1977a, p. 23]." Similarly, Lerner (1977b) has asserted that, "rather than playing a dependent, derivative role in human affairs the concern with justice seems to provide a central and guiding theme in our lives [p. 4]." These statements highlight the proactive nature of justice motive theory.

Structurally, the theory proposes that various forms of justice emerge from persons' perceptions of the kinds of relations they have with others, and where they and others stand in relation to the desired resources (for a more formalized, and extended account, see Lerner, 1977b; Lerner & Whitehead, 1980). The central tenet of the theory is that a commitment to deserving, what is called the "personal contract," develops in the course of maturation. The personal contract represents a person's resolution to "orient himself to the world on the basis of what he earns or deserves via his prior investments [Lerner, Miller, & Holmes, 1976, p. 135]."

One interesting aspect of the theory is the idea that highly formalized contractual agreements between individuals may alter the perceived relationships between them, and therefore, the form of justice they follow. Lerner and Whitehead (1980) propose that the imposition of formal contracts may be a necessary part of a complex society, but that they may also impose their costs by suggesting to people that their formerly friendly relationships may have become antagonistic. Hence, it is an interesting possibility that institutionalized contracts may threaten the integrity of personal contracts.

There are a number of organizational phenomena that may be viewed as resulting from the imposition of formalized, institutionalized regulations about deserving (also see Section III. D.). The growing problem of distrust may be seen as one by-product of the imposition of formalized rules of deserving in organizations. The suggestion is that systems that preclude the possibility of showing trustworthiness tend to suppress the personal contract of deserving. Individuals become oriented to the systematized structures for determining desert, as opposed to personalized ones. For example, in a study of problem-solving groups, Zand (1972) observed that one person's trusting behavior tended to evoke trusting behavior from others. Subjects who were instructed to trust their fellow group members tended to develop closer personal relationships with them, and to more freely exchange relevant ideas than did untrusting groups. In a study by Kruglanski (1970), subjects playing a supervisory role expressed a concern for attaining distributive justice as a reason for trusting subordinates. Taken together, this evidence supports Lerner and Whitehead's (1980) supposition that the imposition of formalized structures of exchange may affect persons' trust for others, which will affect their social relationships and their method of exchanging resources.

Another extrapolation from justice motive theory can be made. Given that different justice norms may emerge from persons in different types of social relationships, it would be potentially problematic for individuals at different organizational levels to maintain peer relationships outside the organization. Just as role demands in organizations may be conflicting (see Katz & Kahn, 1966), it may be expected that justice motive demands might come into conflict when persons share different types of personal relationships inside and outside an organization (Lerner & Whitehead, 1980). If one considers the potential for organizational and personal strain arising from such justice motive conflicts, it is not surprising that organizational policies sometimes frown upon fraternization between personnel. The segregation of recreational facilities for personnel at different levels in the military, and in many private organizations, may be seen as attempts at avoiding such problems.

2. LEVENTHAL ON "THE INSTRUMENTAL VALUE OF EQUITABLE ALLOCATIONS"

Leventhal (1976) has also contended that people proactively strive to maintain equity. He assumes that the motivation to distribute reward equitably is derived from the belief that equitable allocations are the most profitable in the long run. Leventhal hypothesizes several possible reasons for this, all of which are supported by studies of group and organizational behavior.

First, Leventhal (1976) notes that equitable pay policies may be perceived as being profitable because they bring essential resources to those who could use them most effectively. Allocators are particularly likely to distribute limited resources in a manner favoring recipients whose past history makes them appear to be most likely to use them beneficially (Pondy & Birnberg, 1969) and least likely to waste them (Leventhal, Weiss, & Buttrick, 1973).

Second, it is argued that equitable allocations reinforce good performance and punish poor performance, thereby helping to attract good new personnel and weed out poor performers. Support for this contention is derived from a field study by Finn and Lee (1972) in which inequitably paid employees were found to be more likely than equitably paid employees to voluntarily terminate their employment. Corroborating evidence is provided by another industrial study in which it was reported that effective leaders were likely to resign under conditions in which the link between reward and performance was so low that equitable payment could not be obtained (Dansereau et al., 1973). In addition, laboratory evidence (e.g., Schmitt & Marwell, 1972; Valenzi & Andrews, 1971) further supports the contention that equitable payment helps to maintain effective group membership.

Finally, Leventhal (1976) argues that equitable allocations result in productive behavior, as such a practice clearly links performance and rewards. Evidence for this position is provided by a sizable body of empirical and theoretical accounts (e.g., Collins & Guetzkow, 1964; Julian & Perry, 1967). A study by Weinstein and Holzbach (1973), for example, found that subjects who were differentially rewarded for their performance were more productive than those who received equal payment. Industrial research has clearly shown that workers are more productive when their pay is linked to their performance than when no such contingency is perceived (Lawler, 1971; Porter & Lawler, 1968). Research of this type helps explain the success of wage incentive plans (see Section III. D.).

3. SOCIAL MOTIVATION MODEL

McClintock's (1972) model of social motivation presupposes that behavior is motivated by attempts to attain the most highly valued distribution of outcomes. The social motivation model is clearly proactive; it "emphasizes the predecisional attractiveness of equity, whereas the dissonance model accentuates the postdecisional aversiveness of inequity [Van Avermaet *et al.*, 1978, p. 435]."

Extending this theorizing, Van Avermaet *et al.* (1978) have conceived of equity as both a valued goal, and as a strategy designed to attain other goals. In viewing equity as a goal, they note that "people are assumed to behave equitably because of the intrinsic reward value of the corresponding distributions of outcomes to self and others [p. 431]." They also note that equity can be viewed as a strategy (i.e., as a means of attaining a goal). This possibility assumes that people "behave equitably because of the extrinsic, instrumental value of such behavior"; hence, as an "indirect manifestation of a concern with maximizing one's own absolute or relative long-term gains [Van Avermaet *et al.*, 1978, p. 431]."

The question of whether equity is a goal or a strategy designed to achieve other goals has led Van Avermaet *et al.* to reason that if equity is a goal in itself, then it should always be followed; but, that if it is a strategy, then it will be followed only when the environmental cues suggest that following it may help achieve a desired goal. This hypothesis is supported by several studies showing that social pressure may, in fact, lead individuals toward or away from equitable behavior.

A clear example of this is provided in a study by Rivera and Tedeschi (1976) in which subjects expressed responses to overpayment inequity using either a paper-and-pencil measure, or a bogus pipeline device. Responses made in the paper-and-pencil condition were subject to faking (i.e., these subjects could report feelings to the experimenter that presented themselves in the most favorable light), but responses made using the bogus pipeline were not subject to faking because individuals were led to believe that the machine would detect lies. It was found that subjects publicly reported feeling unhappy about the overpayment, but privately reported feeling quite pleased about it. These results suggest that responses to inequity only follow the hypothesized pattern when they are publicly observable, and that privately made responses may be opposite. Thus, publicly feigning displeasure with inequitably high reward may help to attain the goal of fostering favorable self-presentation.

If subjects were motivated to avoid the inequity itself, they would have been expected to display similar displeasure privately. Thus, in this study, equity appears to be taken as a path toward another goal, rather than as a goal in itself.

The tendency for equitable behavior to be enhanced by exposing one's behavior to an experimenter has also been reported elsewhere (e.g., Morse, Gruzen, & Reis, 1976; Reis & Gruzen, 1976). Similarly, other research has demonstrated that allocators may refrain from taking an inequitably high share of reward when others can retaliate, either socially (Althoff, Hoyenga, & Garrett, 1974; Austin & McGinn, 1977; Shapiro, 1975; Von Grumbkow, Deen, Steensma, & Wilke, 1976), or economically (Greenberg, 1978b). Moreover, the belief that one may or may not be held publicly accountable for one's own actions is known to influence the tendency to allocate rewards and punishments in a manner consistent with sex-role expectations (Greenberg, 1979b; Kidder, Bellettirie, & Cohn, 1977). Hence, it appears that equitable behavior may be enacted when situational demands lead to the belief that displaying equitable behavior can (a) enhance the experimenter's impression of oneself; (b) avoid social or financial retaliation; or (c) maintain sex-role demands. In each of these ways, equitable behavior may be seen as a strategy used for maintaining another goal.

Van Avermaet et al. (1978) argue that if equity were a socially valued goal in itself, then it would always be followed regardless of these various mediating variables. However, this need not be so if one views equity as just one of several possible goals orienting behavior at any time. It is questionable to assume that equity is not a goal because it is sometimes supplanted by other goals. Any goal may be subverted by the opportunity to attain a more valued goal. In the cases just noted, other concerns appear to have subordinated interest in attaining equity. The assumption that equity is followed because it maximizes long-term profits may be true, but so also may other goals, at least as much. The subversion of equity, then, cannot in itself be taken as *prima facie* evidence of its status as a motive instead of a goal.

It is my contention that maintaining equity may be a valued goal, but it is not prepotent. Other coexisting goals may conflict with the goal of achieving equity. Hence, individuals may be faced with the situation of determining which of several mutually exclusive goals to attain at any one time. The experimental manipulations that stress the potential for pressures from peers or experimenters merely enhance the salience of the goal of favorable impression management over the goal of obtaining equity. Although equity may, in the long run, be profitable, so might showing deference to others, and recognizing other social norms. Simply put, the fact that equitable behavior may be suppressed, disguised, or even violated does not mean that equity is not a goal. It may only mean that equity is not a preeminent goal, and not the only goal that an individual may be seeking at any moment.

4. EXPECTANCY × VALENCE THEORIES

Expectancy × valence theories may be considered proactive as they characterize behavior as purposive, and oriented toward achieving positively valued states. Cast in the simplest terms, this position asserts that the force to behave in a particular manner is a function of individuals' beliefs that effort will result in attaining various outcomes (i.e., expectancy), multiplied by the value attached to these outcomes (i.e., valence). The conceptual roots of this approach go back to Tolman (1932), who postulated the existence of such cognitive processes in accounting for learning in rats. More recently, the approach has been the basis of several influential theories of industrial motivation, such as those proposed by Vroom (1964), Porter and Lawler(1968), Graen (1969), and Campbell and Pritchard (1976). An encyclopedic review of this work has appeared in Campbell and Pritchard (1976), and will not be undertaken here.

It is perhaps clearest in the case of expectancy × valence theories of motivation how proactive approaches differ from reactive ones, such as original equity theory (Adams, 1965). One aspect of this difference that has generated a good deal of theoretical and empirical interest, mostly in the late 1960s and early 1970s, concerns the differing predictions that the two theoretical approaches make about the effects of payment inequities on work performance.

As stated by Adams (1965), equity theory contends that persons strive to balance their inputs against their outcomes to form a ratio matching that of another person with whom they are comparing themselves. Accordingly, it is possible to create conditions (such as overreward) in which people restrict their opportunities to maximize their profits, for the sake of maintaining equity with another. In contrast, the expectancy × valence approach contends that individuals will attempt to maximize their profits. So, for example, when an individual values money, and believes that money is contingent upon performance (as in a piece-rate system), he or she would be expected to work hard, even if so doing exaggerates an inequity. This difference may be summarized by quoting Lawler: "Expectancy theory can be said to emphasize persons trying to maximize their positive outcomes, while equity theory emphasizes persons trying to balance their inputs against their outcomes [1968a, p. 598]."

In attempting to reconcile these different positions, Lawler (1968a) has argued that methodological flaws in the early equity theory studies have rendered them imperfect tests of the theory, and suggests that the results might actually be accounted for by an expectancy × valence approach. (Many of these problems have been identified in Section II. B. 2 of this chapter.) For example, he raises the possibility that subjects in Adams's early research (e.g., 1963; Adams & Jacobsen, 1964) may have been made to feel insecure about their future on the job by virtue of the fact that the overpayment inequity was created in a manner that challenged their qualifications. The result, a decrease in performance quantity and an increase in quality was interpreted by Lawler as attempts on the part of subjects to secure future employment by showing the experimenter that they can indeed perform high quality work despite their inadequate qualifications. The key point is that this behavior can be interpreted as an attempt to maximize long-term profit, and is consistent with an expectancy × valence orientation. In a similar manner Lawler has reinterpreted many other equity theory results as predictable from expectancy × valence theory (see summary by Campbell & Pritchard, 1976, p. 109).

In concluding his post hoc reevaluation of the two approaches, Lawler recommends that equity be incorporated within a general expectancy × valence framework by including feelings of equity as one of many positively valent outcomes. He argues that such a combined approach would have better predictive power than would either approach alone, and has incorporated an equity component in his version of expectancy × valence theory (Porter & Lawler, 1968). A less formal approach incorporating expectancy × valence considerations into an equity framework has been proposed by Klein (1973).

In response to Lawler's (1968b) critique, Adams (1968) has rebutted that what really needs to be done is to identify the conditions under which each position is most predictive, and not just which position is correct. The study by Dansereau *et al.* (1976) reflects this concern. In this longitudinal study, comparisons were made between the turnover rates of workers whose jobs were such that the leadership structure imposed differing expectations about the degree to which pay was contingent upon performance. An expectancy × valence approach would predict that conditions clearly linking pay to performance would not benefit poor performers, leading them to resign. An equity approach would predict that low pay–performance contingencies would not benefit good performers, leading them to resign. Both hypotheses were confirmed, suggesting that both theoretical approaches may be useful, but under different conditions. In this regard, recent research has also shown that behavior consistent with equity theory or expectancy theory predictions may be moderated by individual differences, such as stage of moral development (Vecchio, 1981).

It is not surprising that empirical results reflect the predictive value of both approaches, and that theoretical models have incorporated each of these models with the other (e.g., Klein, 1973; Porter & Lawler, 1968). As Campbell and Pritchard (1976) have concluded, "The two models are not really in conflict [p. 109]." This statement reflects a more general idea—namely, that reactive and proactive approaches to equity are not in conflict; they merely focus on different aspects of equity behavior.

All of the proactive approaches reviewed here have stressed that long-term maximization of outcomes may accrue by following the equity norm. Yet, it is not inconsistent for approaches asserting that individuals attempt to escape from inequity to also assume the existence of a desire to maximize profits. In fact, the Walster *et al.* (1973) version of equity theory does just this by proposing that individuals learn that society rewards equitable behavior. With this in mind, it is not surprising that integrations and complementary findings have derived from attempts to compare expectancy × valence theories and equity theory.

C. Challenges and Limitations

It should be noted that there is a good deal of empirical research and theoretical thought that calls into question the prevalence and the universality of proactive approaches to equity. I am not speaking here of the complementary reactive approaches described earlier, but rather, of the possibility that equity might not be sought at all.

1. THE EGALITARIAN CHALLENGE

Several complementary arguments have been advanced suggesting that—under some circumstances, at least—the preferred manner of distributing rewards follows from the equality norm (e.g., Deutsch, 1975; Leventhal, 1976; Sampson, 1975). In contrast to justice as equity, which differentially rewards individuals on the basis of various investments, justice as equality "is based on a principle that divides resources equally, arguing that differential investments do not provide a legitimate basis for making claims to differential outcomes [Sampson, 1975, p. 49]."

There is mounting evidence suggesting that equally distributed rewards may promote positive interpersonal relations, which, in turn, facilitate the attainment of other valued goals. I will now identify and describe a few of the conditions under which equal rewards are used for instrumental purposes.

a. Long-term Relationships. A great deal of evidence suggests that the norm of equality prevails in long-term relationships. It would appear as if strictly following the equity norm in each exchange episode would connote that the relationship would be equitable if it were ended at any time. However, in long-term relationships, one may expect "the score" to even out in the long run; over repeated exchanges, each party will get what he or she deserves from the other. Under such conditions, imposition of an equity standard may be interpreted as a threat to the integrity of the friendship, an attempt to "cash in one's chips," in a manner of speaking. As Deutsch (1975) has said of the equity principle, it may disrupt social relations because "it undermines the bases for mutual respect and self-respect necessary for enjoyment of such relations [p. 146]." Hence, Deutsch proposes that the equality principle will prevail when the fostering or maintenance of enjoyable relationships is emphasized.

One reason why the equity norm may predominate in so many laboratory studies of reward allocation (see Leventhal, 1976) is that subjects are in a very short-term and highly anonymous situation. However, some studies have explicitly led subjects to believe that they would be having an extended interaction with or get to meet the recipients of the reward they disbursed (e.g., Althoff *et al.*, 1974; Austin & McGinn, 1977; Shapiro, 1975; Von Grumbkow *et al.*, 1976). Under these conditions, subjects typically followed the equality norm, presumably in an attempt to avoid the interpersonal conflict associated with distributing rewards unequally (Bales, 1955; Leventhal, 1976).

Better examples of the equality performance in long-term relationships come from laboratory studies examining allocations between real-life partners. For example, Schoeninger and Wood (1969) compared the negotiation behavior of married couples and ad hoc mixed-sex dyads. Not surprisingly, it was found that married couples demonstrated more cooperative behavior; they were more likely to accept equal distributions of earnings, and more quickly arrived at an agreement than did ad hoc dyads.

A number of recent studies have shown that equality norm is the preferred allocation practice among friends. For example, Austin (1980) compared the way female college students who were roommates and those who were strangers divided a monetary reward between themselves following unequal task performance. Not surprisingly, adherence to the equality norm was far more prevalent among roommates (75%) than among strangers (30%). Moreover, strangers tended to follow whichever norm was more profitable to them—equality when their inputs were low, and equity when their inputs were high. However, friends followed the equality norm regardless of immediate monetary profitability. Similarly, in studying elementary school girls, Benton (1971) found that equal reward divisions were preferred to more profitable distributions among friends, but that the reverse occurred among nonfriends. These findings are further complemented by the work of Morgan and Sawyer (1967, 1979) suggesting that equality has different connotations among friends and nonfriends. Together, these studies support Blau's (1964) observation that the greater formality between nonfriends than among friends makes unjust outcomes less tolerable.

One factor that appears to underlie the preference for equality among friends is perceived similarity. This is evidenced in a study by Greenberg (1978c) in which subjects believing they had superior inputs refrained from keeping more than half the available reward when their corecipient was described as similar, but kept significantly more than half when their corecipient was described as dissimilar. Analogous preferences for equal allocations among similar persons have also been demonstrated in other studies using a variety of different procedures (e.g., Banks, 1976; Carles & Carver, 1979; Curtis, 1979).

This evidence is consistent with other theoretical positions. For example, Lerner's justice motive theory (see Section III. B. 1.) predicts that the "parity" norm (equivalent to equality) would prevail under conditions in which personal similarity is stressed. From another perspective, others who are seen as similar may be viewed as having a common "situated identity" (Mead, 1934), and should be treated as equals. Applying this concept to equality behavior, Sampson (1975) has noted that, "Equality oriented behavior communicates the situated identity of cooperation among status equals with common interests [p. 54]."

On the basis of the foregoing theory and evidence, it appears that equality is preferred to equity in long-term relationships such as marriage and friendship. Moreover, there is good reason to believe that this is based on the notion that similar others deserve to be treated equally.

b. Interdependent Groups. Another line of research has emphasized the popularity of the equality norm under conditions in which the fates of group members are interdependent. (This is in contrast to the predominance of the equity norm in situations in which persons are independent; see Sections II. C. 2 and III. B. 2.). For example, Valentine (cited in Leventhal, 1976) found that experimental instructions encouraging interdependence prompted superior performers to lower their shares of reward toward equality. Mikula (1974) reported a similar effect among individuals drawn together by sharing the common condition of being aliens residing in a foreign country. Analogous results have been reported by Kahn (1972), and by Pepitone (1971).

Another line of research has demonstrated that equal rewards foster higher productivity within groups whose members are interdependent. Over 30 years ago, in fact, Deutsch (1949) reported that cooperating group members (those whose fates were interdependent) were more productive and more favorably disposed toward the group and its work than those who were in competing groups (those whose fates were independent). Similarly, Miller and Hamblin (1963) have reported that differential rewarding (such as that required by the equity norm) disrupts performance under conditions of high task interdependence.

As Zander (1977) has explained, conditions of interdependence may result in products that can only be credited to the group as a whole, and not to any particular member. If task interdependence is high, individual group members may become "more concerned about the quality of the group's performance than about quality of their own personal performance and develop a desire for group success [p. 47]." The consequences of crediting individual performance under these conditions should be quite clear. Doing so is definitely inequitable, and could create serious socioemotional problems that may undermine group effectivenss (Lawler, 1971; Leventhal, 1976).

Organizational research has demonstrated that conflict often does result from unequal distributions of reward between interdependent units. It has been shown, for example, that conflict is likely to emerge when separate performance rather than overall combined performance is emphasized (Walton & Dutton, 1969). Conflict also results when one industrial group which is dependent upon another benefits at the other's expense (e.g., Dalton, 1959; Strauss, 1964). In summary, it appears that equality tends to reduce conflict, in turn, facilitating productivity in interdependent groups.

An interesting application of the equality norm exists within sports teams. Although team members' degree of interdependence varies from one sport to another, team sports provide a good example of interdependent groups (Jones, 1974). As a result, it is not surprising to find that members of sports teams tend to receive equal shares of rewards, such as prize money. Thus, although winning teams receive more than losing teams, members *within* each team typically share rewards equally.

This practice appears to be wise in view of evidence suggesting that the use of equality within groups fosters greater respect, admiration, positive identity, and less conflict than does the use of equity (Branthwaite, Doyle, & Lightbown, 1979). Complementing this evidence is Leventhal, Michaels, & Sanford's (1972) finding that persons explicitly attempting to avoid conflict will tend toward making equal allocations. Because players often attribute team slumps to problems of envy and conflict within their teams (the New York Yankees notwithstanding), it appears to be a sound practice to follow the justice norm of equality when dividing team rewards (for an extended discussion of justice in sports, see Greenberg, 1979c).[8]

2. NATIONALITY: IS EQUITY MOTIVATION UNIQUELY AMERICAN?

Now that several cross-national studies of equity have been conducted, one may question the international universality of the equity norm. In fact, commenting on national differences in attitudes toward compensation, Barrett and Bass (1976) have remarked that, "What managers value becomes translated into what they feel is an equitable system of pay [p. 1654]." Research conducted in several nations suggests that societal differences may influence the prevalance of the equity norm, and mediate its use as a motivator.[9]

a. Great Britain. A good deal of this work has directly compared the relative use of the equity standard in the United States and England. For example, Lawler (1971) has reported that British managers are less willing to base pay raise decisions on performance than are their American counterparts. Instead, they place greater emphasis on nonperformance factors, such as security and need. These findings are consistent with the findings of Robinson and Bell (1978) suggesting that Americans more greatly value monetary success, whereas the British value a "just society," more broadly conceived. However, accounts of the British system of wages and incentives reveal that the practice of relating individuals' wages to their performance is indeed quite prevalent (Dore, 1973). Thus, it would be incorrect to say that the British do not employ equitable pay systems (i.e., those in which individual pay is contingent upon performance); rather, the British practice of assessing performance

---

[8]It should be cautioned that the equality norm does not appear to be employed with respect to salaries. Traditionally, base pay is determined by individual efforts. It is only when special group efforts have led to special group rewards that these are allocated equally.

[9]Only some of the research germane to this topic will be reviewed here (see also Yuchtman's, 1972, analysis of pay in Israeli kibbtzim). Readers interested in the more general issue of cross-cultural differences in equity behavior are referred to Chapter 2 by Major and Deaux in the present volume, and to the recent review by Gergen, Morse, and Gergen (1980). For a review of national differences in organizational behavior, see Barrett and Bass (1976).

takes into account a wider array of nonperformance factors than does the American system.

b. Japan. In sharp contrast to either the British or American methods of using wage incentives, a drastically different approach is employed in Japan. For example, in his account of workers at the Hitachi factory in Japan, Dore (1973) notes that individual incentives are less prevalent than group incentives (which tend to blur the connection between individual performance and wages). At Hitachi, the wage system is dominated by the belief that the firm is buying a lifetime's work; the company seeks to maintain wages to promote cooperation between workers and to tend to their needs, such as their familial responsibilities. This appears to be true in Japan in general, where compensation is seen as a means by which employers can fulfill their obligation to promote their employees' welfare. It is not surprising, therefore, that the concept of performance appraisal is so widely rejected in the Orient as a whole (Gellerman, 1967). In summary, then, the prevailing social values of Japan preclude the use of equitable wages as a motivator.

c. The Soviet Union. In the Soviet Union, however, wages are very closely tied to performance. The operative principle of "to each according to his work" is uncharacteristic of socialist ideals, but is widespread at even the highest organizational levels.[10] This lies in contrast to the United States, where wage incentive plans are usually reserved for lower-level, piece-rate employees. Another difference between American and Soviet incentive plans is that a very large share of Russian managers' salaries are composed of bonuses, whereas a much smaller proportion of salary is based on bonuses in the United States (Granick, 1960). So variable, in fact, is the Soviet incentive system, that incentives and reverse incentives ranging from 30% above base salary to 25% below base salary are generally permitted ("Russia Sets Programs of Wage Incentives," 1970).

d. The Netherlands. Another nation in which unique national values have affected the equity norm is the Netherlands. The Calvinistic heritage of the Dutch has been described as making them passionately independent, interested in working hard, and concerned about money only to the extent that their basic needs are fulfilled (Weick, Bougon, & Maruyama, 1976). It is therefore not surprising that the Dutch express a greater preference for high inputs regardless of their outcomes than do

[10]This practice is even employed at high scientific levels to overcome areas of technical deficiency (Granick, 1960).

Americans (Weick *et al.*, 1976), and tend to perform at a consistent level regardless of payment equity or inequity (Wilke & Steur, 1972).

e. Conclusion. The research we have reviewed here brings together work based on laboratory studies, cultural observations, and industrial surveys to suggest that the motivational properties of equity appear to be strictly culture bound. Although we cannot conclude that the motivational effects of equitable pay would only occur in the United States, it does appear that the cultural norms of various nations appear to make the equity norm more or less prevalent and/or potent as an incentive.

D. Practical Application: Wage Incentives

The theory and research on proactive approaches to equity suggest several interesting practical applications for the administration of pay plans in organizations. In writing on this topic, Lawler (1971) has indicated that the most basic issue concerning the use of pay as a motivator of work performance is to "create a belief among employees that good performance will lead to high pay [p. 157]." Pay that is proportional to performance can be considered equitable. One popular method of making the pay–performance contingency explicit in organizations is by implementing "incentive plans."

Wage incentive plans are pay policies by which employees' pay is directly linked to their job performance, as measured in some precise manner. Such plans take many forms, ranging from individual piece-rate systems to group incentive plans. The goals of such plans are, blatantly, "to promote or increase the productivity of an employee [Zollitsch, 1975, p. 61]." To accomplish this, incentive plans "must provide a sound basis for a just monetary reward for job performance, as measured by job standards [Zollitsch, 1975, p. 64]." An incentive plan, it has been said, "comes the closest of any method of paying the employee a fair day's pay for a fair day's work [Zollitsch, 1975, p. 63]." [These quotations and following quotations from Zollitsch (1975) are used by permission from "Productivity, Time Study, and Incentive-Pay Plans," by H. G. Zollitsch, Chapter 6.3 of *ASPA Handbook of Personnel and Industrial Relations,* copyright 1979 by The Bureau of National Affairs, Inc., Washington, D.C.]

Industry surveys suggest that such plans are in widespread use. Figures range from almost universal use in top management (Belcher, 1974) and about 80% in sales work (Dauner, 1972), down to around 25% in manufacturing work (Davis, 1972), and negligible use in office work (Cox, 1971).

The great popularity of these plans would appear to be an indication of their efficiency. Particularly dramatic evidence comes from a survey of 29 industrial groups (Dale, 1958), which showed an average production increase of 63.5%. More conservative reviews have reported productivity increases at a still impressive 10% to 20% (Lawler, 1971).

Despite these impressive figures, there is good evidence that in many organizations pay may be unrelated, or even negatively related, to performance (see review by Lawler, 1971, especially p. 158). This state of affairs appears to be attributable, in great measure, to employees' lack of acceptance of such plans (Lawler, 1971). This reluctance appears to stem from a lack of trust in management, and a fear that, once workers start earning too much, standards will be changed (Davis, 1972).[11] This is consistent with Lerner and Whitehead's (1980) assertion that institutionalized contracts may breed interpersonal distrust (see Section III.B.1.). Awareness of this possibility has led one management specialist to offer the following warning: "An incentive plan can work well in a firm only when employees and their management have confidence and trust in the fairness of each other and both are interested in having an incentive plan [Zollitsch, 1975, p. 64]." On this basis, it is not particularly surprising that one survey found that 21% of industrial grievances were related to wage incentives ("The Truth About Wage Incentives," 1959), and that wage incentive plans tend to be more effective when management and labor share a common acceptance of them (Corina, 1970).

The discussion in Section III.D.1.*b.* emphasized the potentially disruptive effects of equitable allocations within interdependent groups. This possibility, coupled with the effectiveness of individual incentive plans, has led to a compromise in many organizations—the development of "group incentive plans." Group plans are newer and less frequently implemented than individual wage incentive plans, but are rapidly growing in popularity (Zollitsch, 1975). One popular group incentive plan is profit sharing (Metzger, 1966), a plan in which employees are paid a monetary supplement based on their company's profits. Other group incentive plans include the Scanlon plan (Lesieur, 1958), and the Lincoln Electric Company plan (Wecksler, 1966).

Such plans do *not* promote a link between individual effort and reward, but distribute all gains between employer and employee. Group incentive plans are particularly well suited for jobs in which workers are highly interdependent upon each other, and individual contributions to

[11]Such beliefs are not unfounded, as standards often do change once workers start earning what management deems to be too much (e.g., see Braverman, 1974).

the group product cannot be determined (Lawler, 1971, especially p. 170). They tend to promote the spirit of teamwork, harmony, and joint cooperation within the group, and feelings of partnership with management (Best, 1961), which in some cases facilitates greater profits (Metzger, 1966). As we have discussed earlier (see Section III. C. 1. *b*), sports teams provide a good example of interdependent groups whose members share bonus profits equally.[12]

IV. EPILOGUE

The research, theory, and applications reviewed here have compared the positions contending that performance is motivated by either equitable pay or inequitable pay. The focus has been on pay because its ready quantifiability has made it the variable of choice in most studies of equity and inequity. Some theorists (e.g., Herzberg, Mausner, & Snyderman, 1959), though, have called into question the fundamental issue of whether pay, equitable or inequitable, is a motivator at all. Because prevailing justice models are cast in general terms, such as inputs and outcomes, they are not forced to take a stand on this issue. Their assumption is that it is the equity or inequity of rewards, pay or any other, and not the rewards themselves that motivates behavior. The community of justice researchers need to begin assessing this assumption by studying rewards other than pay in future equity research. Indeed, some recent research has demonstrated that rewards other than pay, such as status (Greenberg, 1980c) and workspace (Burt & Sundstrom, 1979), also operate within an equity framework. Research of this type is encouraging to the possibility of wider application of the equity concept in groups and organizations, and promises to uncover a wealth of currently unappreciated ideas.

REFERENCES

Adams, J. S. Toward an understanding of inequity. *Journal of Abnormal and Social Psychology*, 1963, *67*, 422–436.

---

[12]However, unlike the equal allocation of prize monies among sports team members, industrial workers in most group incentive plans do not receive an absolutely equal share of the profit. Instead, they typically receive an equal proportion of the profits relative to their base salary. This procedure represents a compromise between absolutely equal sharing of profits, and sharing of profits based on individual contributions.

Adams, J. S. Inequity in social exchange. In L. Berkowitz (Ed.), *Advances in experimental social psychology* (Vol. 2). New York: Academic Press, 1965.

Adams, J. S. Effects of overpayment: Two comments on Lawler's paper. *Journal of Personality and Social Psychology*, 1968, *10*, 315–316.

Adams, J. S., & Freedman, S. Equity theory revisited: Comments and annotated bibliography. In L. Berkowitz & E. Walster (Eds.), *Advances in experimental social psychology* (Vol. 9). New York: Academic Press, 1976.

Adams, J. S., & Jacobsen, P. R. Effects of wage inequities on work quality. *Journal of Abnormal and Social Psychology*, 1964, *69*, 19–25.

Adams, J. S., & Rosenbaum, W. B. The relationship of worker productivity to cognitive dissonance about wage inequities. *Journal of Applied Psychology*, 1962, *46*, 161–164.

Adams, S. Status congruency as a variable in small group performance. *Social Forces*, 1953, *32*, 16–22.

Althoff, L., Hoyenga, K. I., & Garrett, J. B. *Interactive effects of sex and anticipated partner interaction upon equity behavior.* Paper presented at the meeting of the Midwestern Psychological Association, Chicago, May 1974.

Anderson, B., & Shelly, R. K. Reactions to inequity, III: Inequity and social influence. *Acta Sociologica*, 1971, *14*, 236–244.

Andrews, I. R. Wage inequity and job performance: An experimental study. *Journal of Applied Psychology*, 1967, *51*, 39–45.

Andrews, I. R., & Valenzi, E. R. Overpay inequity or self-image as a worker: A critical examination of an experimental induction procedure. *Organizational Behavior and Human Performance*, 1970, *5*, 266–276.

Armknecht, P. A., & Early, J. F. Quits in manufacturing: A study of their causes. *Monthly Labor Review*, 1972, *95*(11), 31–37.

Arrowood, A. J. *Some effects on productivity of justified and unjustified levels of reward under public and private conditions.* Unpublished doctoral dissertation, University of Minnesota, 1961.

Associated Press. Linhart misses once, twice, three times—for $10,000. *New Orleans States-Item*, September 18, 1979, Section C, pp. 1, 4.

Austin, W. Friendship and fairness: Effects of type of relationship and task performance on choice of distribution rules. *Personality and Social Psychology Bulletin*, 1980, *6*, 402–407.

Austin, W., & McGinn, N. C. Sex differences in choice of distribution rules. *Journal of Personality*, 1977, *45*, 379–394.

Bales, R. F. Adaptive and integrative changes as a source of strain in social systems. In Hare, A. P., Borgatta, E. F., & Bales, R. F. (Eds.), *Small groups: Studies in social interaction.* New York: Knopf, 1955.

Bankart, C. P., & Lanzetta, J. T. Performance and motivation as variables affecting the administration of rewards and punishments. *Representative Research in Social Psychology*, 1970, *1*, 1–10.

Banks, W. C. The effects of perceived similarity upon the use of reward and punishment. *Journal of Experimental Social Psychology*, 1976, *12*, 131–138.

Barrett, G. V., & Bass, B. M. Cross-cultural issues in industrial and organizational psychology. In M. D. Dunnette (Ed.), *Handbook of industrial and organizational psychology.* Chicago: Rand McNally, 1976.

Belcher, D. W. *Compensation administration.* Englewood Cliffs, N.J.: Prentice-Hall, 1974.

Benoit-Smullyan, E. Status, status types and status interaction. *American Sociological Review*, 1944, *9*, 151–161.

Benton, A. A. Productivity, distributive justice, and bargaining among children. *Journal of Personality and Social Psychology*, 1971, *18*, 68–78.

Berger, J., Conner, T. L., & Fisek, M. H. *Expectation states theory.* Cambridge, Mass.: Winthrop, 1974.

Best, R. D. Profit sharing and motivation for productivity. In *A symposium of profit sharing and productivity.* Madison, Wis.: Center for Productivity Motivation, 1961.

Blau, P. *Exchange and power in social life.* New York: Wiley, 1964.

Brandon, A. C. Status congruency and expectations. *Sociometry*, 1965, *28*, 272–288.

Branthwaite, A., Doyle, I., & Lightbown, N. The balance between fairness and discrimination. *European Journal of Social Psychology*, 1979, *9*, 149–163.

Braverman, H. *Labor and monopoly capital.* New York: Monthly Review Press, 1974.

Burnstein, E., & Katz, S. Group decisions involving equitable and optimal distribution of status. In C. G. McClintock (Ed.), *Experimental social psychology.* New York: Holt, Rinehart & Winston, 1972.

Burnstein, E., & Wolosin, R. J. The development of status distinctions under conditions of inequity. *Journal of Experimental Social Psychology*, 1968, *4*, 415–430.

Burnstein, E., & Zajonc, R. B. The effect of group success on the reduction of status incongruence in task-oriented groups. *Sociometry*, 1965, *28*, 349–362.

Burt, R. E., & Sundstrom, E. *Work space and job satisfaction: Extending equity theory to the physical environment.* Paper presented at the meeting of the American Psychological Association, New York, September 1979.

Campbell, J. P., & Pritchard, R. A. Motivation theory in industrial and organizational psychology. Chicago: Rand McNally, 1976.

Carles, E. M., & Carver, C. S. Effects of person salience versus role salience on reward allocation in a dyad. *Journal of Personality and Social Psychology*, 1979, *37*, 2071–2080.

Cohen, R. L. Mastery and justice in laboratory dyads: A revision and extension of equity theory. *Journal of Personality and Social Psychology*, 1974, *29*, 464–474.

Cohen, R. L. *Attribution, justice, and sex discrimination at work.* Unpublished manuscript, Bennington College, 1979.

Collins, B. E., & Guetzkow, H. *A social psychology of group processes for decision making.* New York: Wiley, 1964.

Collins, B. E., & Hoyt, M. F. Personal responsibility for consequences: An integration of the "forced compliance" literature. *Journal of Experimental Social Psychology*, 1972, *8*, 558–593.

Commins, B., Y Lockwood, J. The effects of status differences, favoured treatment and equity on intergroup comparisons. *European Journal of Social Psychology*, 1979, *9*, 281–289.

Cooper, J., & Brehm, J. W. Prechoice awareness of relative deprivation as a determinant of cognitive dissonance. *Journal of Experimental Social Psychology*, 1971, *7*, 571–581.

Corina, J. *Forms of wage and salary payment for high productivity.* Paris: Organization for Economic Cooperation and Development, 1970.

Cox, J. H. Time and incentive pay practices in urban areas. *Monthly Labour Review*, 1971, *74*, 53–56.

Curtis, R. C. Effects of knowledge of self-interest and social relationship upon the use of equity, utilitarian, and Rawlsian principles of allocation. *European Journal of Social Psychology*, 1979, *9*, 165–175.

Curtis, R. C., Kessler, S., Pendleton, S., & Sagotsky, E. *Payment, overpayment, equity, and overjustification.* Paper presented at the meeting of the American Psychological Association, Toronto, Canada, September 1978.

Dalton, M. *Men who manage.* New York: Wiley, 1959.

Dansereau, F., Cashman, J., & Graen, G. Instrumentality theory and equity theory as complementary approaches in predicting the relationship of leadership and turnover among managers. *Organizational Behavior and Human Performance*, 1973, *10*, 184–200.

Dale, J. D. *Wage incentives and productivity*. New York: The George Elliott Company, 1958.

Dauner, J. R. Salesmen's compensation: Have we kept pace? *Akron Business and Economic Review*, 1972, *3*, 33–37.

Davis, K. *Human behavior at work* (4th ed.). New York: McGraw-Hill, 1972.

Deci, E. L. Effects of externally mediated rewards on intrinsic motivation. *Journal of Personality and Social Psychology*, 1971, *18*, 105–115.

Deci, E. L. *Intrinsic motivation*. New York: Plenum, 1975.

Deci, E. L., Reis, H. T., Johnston, E. J., & Smith, R. Toward reconciling equity theory and insufficient justification. *Personality and Social Psychology Bulletin*, 1977, *3*, 224–227.

Deutsch, M. An experimental study of the effects of cooperation and competition upon group processes. *Human Relations*, 1949, *2*, 199–231.

Deutsch, M. Equity, equality, and need: What determines which value will be used as the basis of distributive justice? *Journal of Social Issues*, 1975, *31*, 137–149.

Dion, K. L. Cohesiveness as a determinant of ingroup–outgroup bias. *Journal of Personality and Social Psychology*, 1973, *28*, 163–171.

Dion, K. L. Status equity, sex composition of group, and intergroup bias. *Personality and Social Psychology Bulletin*, 1979, *5*, 240–244.

Dore, R. *British factory—Japanese factory*. Berkeley, Calif.: University of California Press, 1973.

Duchon, D., & Jago, A. G. Equity and the performance of major league baseball players: An extension of Lord and Hohenfeld. *Journal of Applied Psychology*, 1981, *66*, 728–732.

Evans, M. G., & Molinari, L. Equity, piece rate overpayment, and job security: Some effects on performance. *Journal of Applied Psychology*, 1970, *54*, 105–114.

Exline, R. V., & Ziller, R. C. Status congruency and interpersonal conflict in decision-making groups. *Human Relations*, 1959, *12*, 147–162.

Festinger, L. *A theory of cognitive dissonance*. Evanston, Ill.: Row, Peterson, 1957.

Finn, R. H., & Lee, S. M. Salary equity: Its determination, analysis and correlates. *Journal of Applied Psychology*, 1972, *56*, 283–292.

Folger, R., Rosenfield, D., & Hays, R. P. Equity and intrinsic motivation: The role of choice. *Journal of Personality and Social Psychology*, 1978, *36*, 557–564.

Folger, R., Rosenfield, D., Hays, R., & Grove, R. Justice versus justification effects on productivity: Reconciling equity and dissonance findings. *Organizational Behavior and Human Performance*, 1978, *22*, 465–473.

Friedman, A., & Goodman, P. Wage inequity, self-qualifications, and productivity. *Organizational Behavior and Human Performance*, 1967, *2*, 406–417.

Garland, H. The effects of piece-rate underpayment and overpayment on job performance: A test of equity theory with a new induction procedure. *Journal of Applied Social Psychology*, 1973, *3*, 325–334.

Garland, H., & Staff, P. E. The overjustification effect: Reward contrast or reattribution in rats? *Motivation and Emotion*, 1979, *3*, 35–49.

Gellerman, S. W. Passivity, paranoia, and "pakikisana." *Columbia Journal of World Business*, September–October, 1967, 59–66.

Gergen, K. J., Morse, S. J., & Gergen, M. M. Behavior exchange in cross-cultural perspective. In H. C. Triandis & R. W. Brislin (Eds.), *Handbook of cross-cultural psychology: Social psychology* (Vol. 5). Boston: Allyn & Bacon, 1980.

Geschwender, J. A. Continuities in theories of status consistency and cognitive dissonance. *Social Forces*, 1967, *46*, 160–171.

Gibbs, J. P., & Martin, W. T. Status integration and suicide. *American Sociological Review*, 1958, *23*, 140–147.

Goffman, I. W. Status consistency and preference for change in power distribution. *American Sociological Review*, 1957, *22*, 275–281.

Goodman, P. S., & Friedman, A. An examination of the effect of wage inequity in the hourly condition. *Organizational Behavior and Human Performance*, 1968, *3*, 340–352.

Goodman, P. S., & Friedman, A. An examination of quantity and quality of performance under conditions of overpayment in piece rate. *Organizational Behavior and Human Performance*, 1969, *4*, 365–374.

Goodman, P. S., & Friedman, A. An examination of Adams' theory of inequity. *Administrative Science Quarterly*, 1971, *16*, 271–288.

Gouldner, A. W. The norm of reciprocity: A preliminary statement. *American Sociological Review*, 1960, *25*, 161–178.

Graen, G. Instrumentality theory of work motivation: Some experimental results and suggested modifications. *Journal of Applied Psychology*, 1969, *53*, 1–25. (Monograph)

Granick, D. *The red executive*. Garden City, N.Y.: Doubleday, 1960.

Greenberg, J. Equity, motivation, and effects of past reward on allocation decisions. *Personality and Social Psychology Bulletin*, 1978, *4*, 131–134. (a)

Greenberg, J. Effects of reward value and retaliative power on allocations decisions: Justice, generosity, or greed? *Journal of Personality and Social Psychology*, 1978, *36*, 367–379. (b)

Greenberg, J. Allocator–recipient similarity and the equitable division of rewards. *Social Psychology*, 1978, *41*, 337–341. (c)

Greenberg, J. Justice perceived versus justice enacted. In J. Greenberg (Chair), *Recent developments in interpersonal justice theory and research*. Symposium presented at the meeting of the American Psychological Association, New York, September 1979. (a)

Greenberg, J. *Sex differences in redressing injustice and punishing harmdoers*. Paper presented at the meeting of the Midwestern Psychological Association. Chicago, May 1979. (b)

Greenberg, J. Equity and justice in sports and games. In J. Levy (Chair), *Play behavior*. Research Symposium on Leisure Research sponsored by the Society of Park and Recreation Educators, New Orleans, October 1979. (c)

Greenberg, J. Reactions to a postal rate increase: Justification or inequity distress? *Journal of Applied Social Psychology*, 1980, *10*, 184–190. (a)

Greenberg, J. Attentional focus and locus of outcome causality as determinants of equity behavior. *Journal of Personality and Social Psychology*, 1980, *38*, 579–585. (b)

Greenberg, J. *Status-induced inequity as a cheap but temporary motivator*. Unpublished manuscript, Tulane University, 1980. (c)

Greenberg, J., & Leventhal, G. S. Equity and the use of overreward to motivate performance. *Journal of Personality and Social Psychology*, 1976, *34*, 179–190.

Herzberg, F., Mausner, B., & Snyderman, B. *The motivation to work* (2nd ed.). New York: Wiley, 1959.

Hinrichs, J. R. Employees coming and going: The exit interview. *Personnel*, 1971, *48*, 30–35.

Hinton, B. L. The experimental extension of equity theory to interpersonal and group interaction situations. *Organizational Behavior and Human Performance*, 1972, *8*, 434–499.

Homans, G. C. Status among clerical workers. *Human Organization*, 1953, *12*, 5–10.

Homans, G. C. *Social behavior: Its elementary forms*. New York: Harcourt Brace & World, 1961.

Hunt, J. G. Status congruence in organizations: Effects and suggested research. *Academy of Management Proceedings*, 1968, pp. 178–184.

Hunt, J. G. Status congruence: An important organization function. *Personnel Administration*, 1969, *32*, 19–24.

Jacques, E. *Equitable payment*. New York: Wiley, 1961.

Jones, M. B. Regressing group on individual effectiveness. *Organizational Behavior and Human Performance*, 1974, *11*, 426–451.

Julian, J. W., & Perry, F. A. Cooperation contrasted with intra-group and inter-group competition. *Sociometry*, 1967, *30*, 79–90.

Kahn, A. Reactions to generosity or stinginess from an intelligent or stupid work partner: A test of equity theory in a direct exchange relationship. *Journal of Personality and Social Psychology*, 1972, *21*, 116–123.

Katz, D., & Kahn, R. L. *The social psychology of organizations*. New York: Wiley, 1966.

Kidder, L. H., Bellettirie, G., & Cohn, E. S. Secret ambitions and public performances. The effects of anonymity on reward allocations made by man and women. *Journal of Experimental Social Psychology*, 1977, *13*, 70–80.

Kipnis, D. *The powerholders*. Chicago: University of Chicago Press, 1976.

Kipnis, D., & Cosentino, J. Use of leadership powers in industry. *Journal of Applied Psychology*, 1969, *53*, 460–466.

Kipnis, D., & Lane, W. P. Self-confidence and leadership. *Journal of Applied Psychology*, 1962, *46*, 291–295.

Klein, S. M. Pay factors as predictors to satisfaction: A comparison of reinforcement, equity, and expectancy. *Academy of Management Journal*, 1973, *16*, 598–610.

Kruglanski, A. J. Attributing trustworthiness in supervisor–worker relations. *Journal of Experimental Social Psychology*, 1970, *6*, 214–232.

Lanzetta, J. T., & Hannah, T. E. Reinforcing behavior of "naive" trainers. *Journal of Personality and Social Psychology*, 1969, *11*, 245–252.

Lawler, E. E. Managers' perceptions of their subordinates' pay and of their superiors' pay. *Personnel Psychology*, 1965, *18*, 413–422.

Lawler, E. E. Secrecy about management compensation: Are there hidden costs? *Organizational Behavior and Human Performance*, 1967, *2*, 182–189.

Lawler, E. E., III. Equity theory as a predictor of productivity and work quality. *Psychological Bulletin*, 1968, *70*, 596–610. (a)

Lawler, E. E., III. Effects of hourly overpayment on productivity and work quality. *Journal of Personality and Social Psychology*, 1968, *10*, 306–313. (b)

Lawler, E. E. *Pay and organizational effectiveness: A psychological view*. New York: McGraw-Hill, 1971.

Lawler, E. E., III, Koplin, C. A., Young, T. F., & Fadem, J. A. Inequity reduction over time in an induced overpayment situation. *Organizational Behavior and Human Performance*, 1968, *3*, 253–268.

Lawler, E. E., III, & O'Gara, P. W. Effects of inequity produced by underpayment on work output, work quality, and attitudes toward the work. *Journal of Applied Psychology*, 1967, *51*, 403–410.

Lenski, G. E. Status crystallization: A nonvertical dimension of social status. *American Sociological Review*, 1954, *19*, 405–413.

Lepper, M. R., & Greene, D. (Eds.). *The hidden costs of reward*. Hillsdale, N.J.: Erlbaum, 1978.

Lepper, M. R., Greene, D., & Nisbett, R. E. Undermining children's intrinsic interest with extrinsic rewards: A test of the "overjustification" hypothesis. *Journal of Personality and Social Psychology*, 1973, *28*, 129–137.

Lerner, M. J. The justice motive in social behavior: An introduction. *Journal of Social Issues*, 1975, *31*, 1–20.

Lerner, M. J. The justice motive: Some hypotheses as to its origins and forms. *Journal of Personality*, 1977, *45*, 1–52. (a)

Lerner, M. J. *The justice motive in social behavior: Hypotheses as to its origins and forms, II.* Research grant proposal to the Canada Council, October 1977. (b)

Lerner, M. J., & Whitehead, L. A. Procedural justice viewed in the context of justice motive theory. In G. Mikula (Ed.), *Justice and social interaction.* New York: Springer-Verlag, 1980.

Lerner, M. J., Miller, D. T., & Holmes, J. G. Deserving and the emergence of forms of justice. In L. Berkowitz & E. Walster (Eds.), *Advances in experimental social psychology* (Vol. 9). New York: Academic Press, 1976.

Leventhal, G. S. The distribution of rewards and resources in groups and organizations. In L. Berkowitz & E. Walster (Eds.), *Advances in experimental social psychology* (Vol. 9). New York: Academic Press, 1976.

Leventhal, G. S., Michaels, J. W., & Sanford, C. Inequity and interpersonal conflict: Reward allocation and secrecy about reward as methods of preventing conflict. *Journal of Personality and Social Psychology*, 1972, *23*, 88–102.

Leventhal, G. S., Weiss, T., & Buttrick, R. Attribution of value, equity, and the prevention of waste in reward allocation. *Journal of Personality and Social Psychology*, 1973, *27*, 276–286.

Lesieur, F. G. (Ed.), *The Scanlon plan.* New York: Wiley, 1958.

Lieberman, S. The effects of changes in roles on the attitudes of role occupants. *Human Relations*, 1956, *9*, 385–402.

Linder, D. E., Cooper, J., & Jones, E. E. Decision freedom as a determinant of the role of incentive magnitude in attitude change. *Journal of Personality and Social Psychology*, 1967, *6*, 245–254.

Lord, R. G., & Hohenfeld, J. A. Longitudinal field assessment of equity effects on the performance of major league baseball players. *Journal of Applied Psychology*, 1979, *64*, 19–26.

McClintock, C. G. Social motivation—a set of propositions. *Behavioral Science*, 1972, *17*, 438–454.

McGregor, D. *The human side of enterprise.* New York: McGraw-Hill, 1960.

Mead, G. H. *Mind, self, and society.* Chicago: University of Chicago Press, 1934.

Metzger, B. L. *Profit sharing in perspective* (2nd ed.). Evanston, Ill.: Profit Sharing Research Foundation, 1966.

Mikula, G. Nationality, performance, and sex as determinants of reward allocation. *Journal of Personality and Social Psychology*, 1974, *29*, 435–440.

Miller, L. K., & Hamblin, R. L. Interdependence, differential rewarding, and productivity. *American Sociological Review*, 1963, *28*, 768–778.

Morgan, W. R., & Sawyer, J. Bargaining, expectations, and the preferences for equality over equity. *Journal of Personality and Social Psychology*, 1967, *6*, 139–149.

Morgan, W. R., & Sawyer, J. Equality, equity, and procedural justice in social exchange. *Social Psychology Quarterly*, 1979, *42*, 71–75.

Morse, S. J., Gruzen, J., & Reis, H. T. The nature of equity restoration: Some approval-seeking considerations. *Journal of Personality and Social Psychology*, 1976, *12*, 1–8.

Mowday, R. T. Equity theory predictions of behavior in organizations. In R. M. Steers &

L. W. Porter (Eds.), *Motivation and work behavior* (2nd ed.). New York: McGraw-Hill, 1979.

Nash, A. N., & Carroll, S. J., Jr. *The management of compensation.* Monterey, Calif.: Brooks/ Cole, 1975.

Notz, W. W. Work motivation and the negative effects of extrinsic rewards: A review with implications for theory and practice. *American Psychologist,* 1975, *30,* 884–891.

Opshal, R. L., & Dunnette, M. D. The role of financial compensation in industrial motivation. *Psychological Bulletin,* 1966, *66,* 94–118.

Parcel, T. L., & Cook, K. S. Status characteristics, reward allocation, and equity. *Sociometry,* 1977, *40,* 311–324.

Patchen, M. *The choice of wage comparisons.* Englewood Cliffs, N.J.: Prentice-Hall, 1961.

Pepitone, A. The role of justice in interdependent decision making. *Journal of Experimental Social Psychology,* 1971, *7,* 144–156.

Pettefer, J. C. Effective grievance administration. *California Management Review,* 1970, *13*(2), 12–18.

Pittman, T. S., Cooper, E. E., & Smith, T. W. Attribution of causality and the overjustification effect. *Personality and Social Psychology Bulletin,* 1977, *3,* 280–283.

Pondy, L. R., & Birnberg, J. G. An experimental study of the allocation of financial resources within small hierarchical task groups. *Administrative Science Quarterly,* 1969, *14,* 192–201.

Porter, L. W., & Lawler, E. E. *Managerial attitudes and performance.* Homewood, Ill.: Richard D. Irwin, 1968.

Pritchard, R. A. Equity theory: A review and critique. *Organizational Behavior and Human Performance,* 1969, *4,* 176–211.

Pritchard, R. A., Dunnette, M. D., & Jorgenson, D. O. Effects of perceptions of equity and inequity on worker performance and satisfaction. *Journal of Applied Psychology,* 1972, *56,* 75–94.

Reis, H. T., & Gruzen, J. On mediating equity, equality, and self-interest: The role of self-presentation in social exchange. *Journal of Experimental Psychology,* 1976, *12,* 487–503.

Rivera, A. N., & Tedeschi, J. T. Public versus private reactions to positive inequity. *Journal of Personality and Social Psychology,* 1976, *34,* 895–900.

Robinson, R. V., & Bell, W. Equality, success, and social justice in England and the United States. *American Sociological Review,* 1978, *43,* 125–143.

Roethlisberger, F. J., & Dickson, W. J. *Management and the worker.* Cambridge, Mass.: Harvard University Press, 1939.

Rothbart, M. Effects of motivation, equity, and compliance on the use of reward and punishment. *Journal of Personality and Social Psychology,* 1968, *9,* 353–362.

Runciman, W. G., & Bagley, C. R. Status consistency, relative deprivation, and attitudes toward immigrants. *Sociology,* 1969, *3,* 359–375.

Russia sets programs of wage incentives in scientific work. *The Wall Street Journal,* June 1, 1970, p. 12.

Sampson, E. E. Studies of status congruence. In L. Berkowitz (Ed.), *Advances in experimental social psychology* (Vol. 4). New York: Academic Press, 1969.

Sampson, E. E. On justice as equality. *Journal of Social Issues,* 1975, *31,* 45–64.

Schmitt, D. R., & Marwell, G. Withdrawal and reward allocation as responses to inequity. *Journal of Experimental Social Psychology,* 1972, *8,* 207–221.

Schoeninger, D. W., & Wood, D. W. Comparison of married and ad hoc mixed-sex dyads negotiating the division of a reward. *Journal of Experimental Social Psychology,* 1969, *5,* 483–499.

Shapiro, E. G. Effect of expectation of future interaction on reward allocation in dyads: Equity or equality. *Journal of Personality and Social Psychology*, 1975, *31*, 873–880.

Strauss, G. Work-flow frictions, interfunctional rivalry, and professionalism: A case study of purchasing agents. *Human Organization*, 1964, *23*, 137–149.

Stryker, S., & Macke, A. S. Status inconsistency and role conflict. In R. H. Turner, J. Coleman, & R. C. Fox (Eds.), *Annual review of sociology*, (Vol. 4). Palo Alto, Calif.: Annual Reviews, 1978.

Suchner, R. W., & Jackson, D. Responsibility and status: A causal or only a spurious relationship. *Sociometry*, 1976, *39*, 243–256.

Susman, G. I. The concept of status congruence as a basis to predict task allocations in autonomous work groups. *Administrative Science Quarterly*, 1970, *15*, 164–175.

Taylor, F. W. *Principles of scientific management*. New York: Harper, 1911.

Telly, C. S., French, W. L., & Scott, W. G. The relationship of inequity to turnover among hourly workers. *Administrative Science Quarterly*, 1971, *16*, 164–172.

Tolman, E. C. *Purposive behavior in animals and men*. New York: Appleton-Century-Crofts, 1932.

Tornow, W. W. The development and application of an input–outcome moderator test on the perception and reduction of inequity. *Organizational Behavior and Human Performance*, 1971, *6*, 614–638.

The truth about wage incentives and work measurement today. *Factory Management and Maintenance*, April, 1959, p. 82.

Valenzi, E. R., & Andrews, I. R. Effect of hourly overpay and underpay inequity when tested with a new induction procedure. *Journal of Applied Psychology*, 1971, *55*, 22–27.

Van Avermaet, E., McClintock, C., & Moskowitz, J. Alternative approaches to equity: Dissonance reduction, pro-social motivation and strategic accommodation. *European Journal of Social Psychology*, 1978, *8*, 419–437.

Vecchio, R. P. An individual-differences interpretation of the conflicting predictions generated by equity theory and expectancy theory. *Journal of Applied Psychology*, 1981, *66*, 470–481.

Von Grumbkow, J., Deen, E., Steensma, H., & Wilke, H. The effect of future interaction on the distribution of rewards. *European Journal of Social Psychology*, 1976, *6*, 119–123.

Vroom, V. H. *Work and motivation*. New York: Wiley, 1964.

Walster, E., Berscheid, E., & Walster, G. W. The exploited: Justice or justification? In J. McCauley & L. Berkowitz (Eds.), *Altruism and helping behavior*. New York: Academic Press, 1970.

Walster, E., Berscheid, E., & Walster, G. W. New directions in equity research. *Journal of Personality and Social Psychology*, 1973, *25*, 151–176.

Walster, E., Walster, G. W., & Berscheid, E. *Equity: Theory and research*. Boston: Allyn & Bacon, 1978.

Walton, R. E., & Dutton, J. M. The management of interdepartmental conflict: A model and review. *Administrative Science Quarterly*, 1969, *14*, 73–84.

Wecksler, A. N. *The Lincoln Electric Company's approach to cutting costs and reducing selling prices*. Cleveland: Lincoln Electric Company, 1966.

Weick, K. E. Reduction of cognitive dissonance through task enhancement and effort expenditure. *Journal of Abnormal and Social Psychology*, 1964, *68*, 533–539.

Weick, K. E. The concept of equity in the perception of pay. *Administrative Science Quarterly*, 1966, *11*, 414–439.

Weick, K. E. Dissonance and task enhancement: A problem for compensation theory? *Organizational Behavior and Human Performance*, 1967, *2*, 189–207.

Weick, K. E., Bougon, M. G., & Maruyama, G. The equity context. *Organizational Behavior and Human Performance*, 1976, *15*, 32–65.

Weick, K. E., & Nesset, B. Preferences among forms of equity. *Organizational Behavior and Human Performance*, 1968, *3*, 400–416.

Weinstein, A. G., & Holzbach, R. L. Impact of individual differences, reward distribution, and task structure on productivity in a simulated work environment. *Journal of Applied Psychology*, 1973, *58*, 296–301.

Whitwell, W. C. *Suggestion systems are profitable.* Englewood Cliffs, N.J.: Prentice-Hall, 1963.

Wiener, Y. The effects of "task-" and "ego-oriented" performance on 2 kinds of of over-compensation inequity. *Organizational Behavior and Human Performance*, 1970, *5*, 191–208.

Wilke, H., & Steur, T. Overpayment: Perceived qualifications and financial compensation. *European Journal of Social Psychology*, 1972, *2*, 273–284.

Wittig, M. A., Marks, G., & Jones, G. A. The effect of luck versus effort attributions on reward allocation to self and other. *Personality and Social Psychology Bulletin*, 1981, *7*, 71–78.

Wood, I., & Lawler, E. E. Effects of piece rate overpayment on productivity. *Journal of Applied Psychology*, 1970, *54*, 234–238.

Yuchtman, E. Reward distribution and work-role attractiveness in the kibbutz—reflections on equity theory. *American Sociological Review*, 1972, *37*, 581–595.

Zaleznik, A., Christenson, C. R., & Roethlisberger, F. J. *The motivation, productivity, and satisfaction of workers.* Cambridge, Mass.: Harvard University Press, 1958.

Zand, D. E. Trust and managerial problem solving. *Administrative Science Quarterly*, 1972, *17*, 229–239.

Zander, A. *Groups at work.* San Francisco: Jossey-Bass, 1977.

Zedeck, S., & Smith, P. C. A psychophysical determination of equitable payment. *Journal of Applied Psychology*, 1968, *52*, 343–347.

Zollitsch, H. G. Productivity, time study, and incentive-pay plans. In D. Yoder & H. G. Heneman, Jr. (Eds.), *Motivation and commitment.* Washington, D.C.: Bureau of National Affairs, 1975.

chapter 12

Why Justice? Normative and Instrumental Interpretations[1]

JERALD GREENBERG
RONALD L. COHEN

I. INTRODUCTION

In our opinion, the chapters in this volume have shown that matters of justice are no less the unique domain of any one subgroup of social psychologists than they are concerns relevant to the discipline as a whole. We have seen how theories, concepts, and research findings generated from an interest in justice have been applied to a wide range of social phenomena and, in addition, how advances in various fields of social psychology have contributed to our knowledge of justice.

The contributions to this volume have presented many different ideas regarding people's concerns about justice in social behavior. From among these, we see two analytically distinct approaches emerging. The normative approach suggests that behaviors coincident with various justice norms are enacted because they are dictated by prevailing social practices. The instrumental approach suggests that when people behave justly, they do so because they believe that ostensible displays of just behavior can facilitate the attainment of other goals. We admit at the outset that the "normative" and "instrumental" interpretations of justice are neither completely independent of one another, nor are they the only motives behind justice behavior (see Section IV).

[1]This chapter was prepared while the senior author was in residence as a Fulbright research scholar at the Université Catholique de Louvain, Louvain-la-Neuve, Belgium. We acknowledge the support of that institution and the Commission for Educational Exchange between the United States of America, Belgium, and Luxemburg.

437

Our descriptions of justice as generated by normative or instrumental considerations are not offered as opposing views. As such, we do not mean to imply that there are proponents of each viewpoint arguing from either side of a theoretical fence. To the contrary, as our discussion will reveal, many of the major theorists have been involved in both perspectives. Accordingly, the distinction we make here is not presented as a historical account of a clearly formulated debate. Instead, it is offered as a heuristic device for extracting some of the emerging themes of this volume and for organizing some of the important research questions that have captured the attention of social psychologists studying justice.

To this end, our plan of attack calls for discussing the normative and instrumental perspectives of justice in terms of the body of theory and research germane to each. Our analyses will focus on the various research questions generated by each perspective and in the ways in which the contributions to this volume may be integrated within these lines of investigation. Finally, we will conclude by analyzing the interrelationships between the justice motives related to each of these perspectives, and the prospects offered by interpreting justice as a philosophical and moral ideal.

II. JUSTICE AS NORMATIVE

One reason people behave justly is that it is normative to do so. Prevailing social practices and social structures encourage individuals to respond to injustices in various ways and to distribute rewards in ways that are defined as just according to the situation in which they find themselves. This is not to suggest that such behaviors may not facilitate other goals or be rewarding in themselves, but rather, that the motive to "be just" is in part governed by normative dictates providing the impetus for just behavior and defining the form which that behavior takes. For example, Leventhal (1976a) defines an "allocation norm" as, "a social rule which specifies criteria that define certain distributions of rewards and resources as fair and just [p. 94]." He also notes that these normative bases of just behavior are dictated by the prevailing social system: "Prevailing rules and practices may encourage the allocator to follow certain norms and ignore others [Leventhal, 1976a, p. 95]."

In Section IV. C. of Chapter 1 we identified the issue of competing norms of justice as one of the focal issues of contemporary justice researchers, an assessment shared by others (e.g., Reis, 1979). Although there are many facets of this issue, two that seem most basic involve (1) identifying and describing the various competing norms; and (2) determining the conditions under which they are each applied. The first two subsections will describe the current state of affairs with respect to each of these related lines of inquiry. Relating this background material to the contributions of this volume, the final two sections will offer an integration of the normative view of justice, and discuss some of the limitations of the normative view.

A. How Many Justice Norms? What Are They?

How do individuals divide resources between themselves in a just manner? Theorists appear to disagree over what normative standards are employed in addressing this question. Some theorists have argued that there is but one norm—proportionate equity (e.g., Walster & Walster, 1975), whereas others have conceptualized equity as merely one of several distinct normative standards of justice ranging in number from two (e.g., Sampson, 1969, 1975) or three (e.g., Deutsch, 1975; Leventhal, 1976a), to six (e.g., Lerner, 1975, 1977) or more (e.g., Reis, 1979). Let us examine this more closely.

The most parsimonious view espouses that justice is best conceptualized as adherence to a single norm of proportionate equity. Specifically, Walster and Walster (1975) have argued that what appear to be different forms of justice may actually be accounted for by recourse to a single norm of proportionate equity. The underlying assumption of this position is that the equity principle can explain a wide variety of different distributive practices by virtue of the elasticity of the concept of "inputs." Accordingly, if one assumes that various inputs are seen as relevant in different situations, then different amounts of reward may be deemed fair. If people feel that an equal distribution of reward is fair, this may be taken as an indication of their belief that the relevant inputs are equal. Thus, equality is seen as a special case of more general principle of proportionate equity. The most popular version of this view is represented by equity theory (Walster, Berscheid, & Walster, 1973): "Regardless of which inputs a society believes are relevant in a given situation, the same theoretical framework—equity theory—predicts when men will feel equitably or inequitably treated and how they will respond to their treatment [Walster & Walster, 1975, p. 29]."

Critics of this view have contended that such a position unreasonably stretches the equitable calculus beyond any practical utility, and is a "move towards unwise parsimony [Sampson, 1969, p. 264]." Sampson (1969) notes that the equity view gives too much attention to the internal psychological processes of dissonance reduction at the expense of normative social processes. As he suggests, "equity is not as much a psychological law about human nature as it is a psychological outcome of a culture's economic socialization practices [Sampson, 1975, p. 58]." Thus, equity is presented as a norm of justice, but not the only one. Instead, he has argued that there exists a second distinct norm of justice—equality—that is needed to explain distributive behavior, and that it is incorrect to conceive of equality as a special case of equity. Equality is offered as a separate justice norm that dictates that outcomes be distributed equally regardless of contributions. The basis of this argument is that, "By nature, man is not an equity theorist [1975, p. 49]." He proposes that two contrasting solutions have been offered to the distributive problem—an equity solution and an equality solution—and that these are "founded upon differing assumptions about the fundamental nature of persons and their collective accommodation [Sampson, 1975, p. 48]."

Other theorists seem to have accepted Sampson's view that equality is a fundamentally different form of justice distinct from equity. For example, Deutsch (1975) and Leventhal (1976a, 1976b, 1980) have included both equity and equality in their own conceptualizations of justice, but have added a third justice norm—need. As Leventhal (1976b) has stated, "Three justice rules—the contributions [i.e., equity], needs and equality rules—are the most important determinants of Person's conception of distributive fairness [p. 212]." In general terms, the needs norm of justice dictates that outcomes should be distributed so as to satisfy recipients' legitimate desires, and to prevent their suffering.[2]

As theorists continued to proliferate their listings of justice norms, fortunately, they imposed some orderly structure to better understand them. An example of a conceptually derived model is that of Lerner (1975, 1977), who extended the list of three justice norms to six by imposing a 3×2 conceptual scheme. Briefly stated, Lerner suggests that the form justice takes will depend on the type of relationship we perceive we have with another, and whether we perceive the other as a person or as an occupant of a position. Type of relationship is characterized in terms of the degree of psychological separation between parties, and ranges from the most distant, "nonunit" relationships, to closer, "unit" relationships, to the closest, "identity" relationships. Not only are equity, equality (what he calls "parity"), and need located in this system, but so are other norms such as entitlement–social obligations, law–Darwinian justice, and justified self-interest. The reader is referred to Lerner's

---

[2]We should note that both Leventhal (1976b, 1980) and Deutsch (1975) also identify other norms, but base their conceptualizations primarily on equity, equality, and need.

(1975, 1977) original statement for a more detailed description, which is beyond the scope of this chapter (see also Chapter 1, this volume).

More recently, Reis (in press) has attempted to uncover the basic dimensions of perceived fairness by using a multidimensional scaling technique. In contrast to Lerner (1975, 1977), who conceptually derived various forms of justice from two underlying dimensions, Reis (in press) empirically determined what dimensions subjects perceived as underlying various norms of justice. Specifically, he began by generating a list of justice norms suggested by the psychological literature, as well as those noted in historical, philosophical, and legal analyses. This resulted in a list of 17 justice rules, which he then had subjects rate in terms of their relative similarity. Multidimensional scaling of these similarity judgments yielded three dimensions that accounted for 78% of the variance.

Although Reis (in press) cautions that his results are preliminary, it seems worthwhile to share his conceptualizations of the resulting underlying dimensions. The first dimension distinguishes between norms favoring an immediate gratification of needs with those allowing long-term need gratification. A second dimension seems to run from materially oriented justice norms (e.g., proportional equity) to interpersonally oriented norms (e.g., equality). Finally, he describes a third dimension which appears to distinguish between norms for benefitting oneself from norms for benefitting others. Despite the fact that this work is preliminary and subject to different interpretations, it does suggest that persons intuitively recognize the existence of several different norms of justice.

B. Which Norm When?

From the foregoing discussion, it seems clear that it is a more popular viewpoint among justice theorists to conceive of justice as a number of distinct normative standards, each of which plays a part in determining what is fair in various situations, than to conceive of justice only as equity. We agree with the assessment that the multiple norms position has greater utility in being able to understand behavior in various situations (cf. Goode, 1978; Reis, 1979; Schwinger, 1980). Indeed, most of the theorists identifying different justice norms have done so in an attempt to determine how these norms influence behavior.

The predominant research emphasis has been on determining the conditions under which various justice norms are activated. The assumption underlying this line of investigation is that different normative standards are socially appropriate under different situations, and that behaviors in line with these standards predominate when these conditions are manifest. Although, as we have noted, there appear to be other norms of justice, the most popularly studied ones are clearly equity, equality, and need. As a result, we know the most about when each of these justice norms will predominate.

1. EQUITY

Looking first at the equity norm, theorists have agreed that it is primarily activated in economically oriented situations. In this regard, Deutsch (1975) has proposed that: "In cooperative relations in which economic productivity is a primary goal, equity rather than equality or need will be the dominant principle of distributive justice [p. 143]." In his justice-judgment model, Leventhal (1976b) has made a similar assumption regarding activation of what he calls "the contributions rule" (i.e., allocating resources in accordance with one's contributions—or, in accordance with the equity norm). Like Deutsch (1975), Leventhal (1976b) has noted that such a rule may be expected to predominate under conditions in which "receivers' primary responsibility is to perform effectively [p. 216]." Analogously, Lerner's justice motive theory asserts that equity is likely to be the predominant justice norm when individuals in a "unit" relationship with one another (i.e., they share similar fates) perceive each other as occupants of a social role, rather than as unique individuals.

In summary, then, it has been suggested that the equity norm is likely to prevail in economically oriented situations, such as business relationships, where individuals are likely to see each other as role occupants whose behavior directly affects economic productivity. Research evidence reviewed in this volume (e.g., Greenberg, Chapter 11) and elsewhere (e.g., Leventhal, 1976a) substantiates these claims, and will not be reiterated here.

2. EQUALITY

In contrast, theorists have noted that the equality norm tends to predominate under conditions of cooperation and social harmony. Specifically, Deutsch (1975) has remarked that equality will prevail in situations in which "fostering or maintenance of enjoyable social relations [p. 146]" is emphasized. Likewise, Leventhal (1976b) proposes that equality will predominate whenever "maintenance of harmony and solidarity among receivers is important [p. 218]." Similarly, Lerner (1975, 1977) has noted that seeing another as an individual rather than as an incumbent of a social position is an important precondition for activation of the equality norm. As in the case of the equity norm, evidence in support of these claims is widely available (e.g., Greenberg, Chapter 11; Leventhal, 1976a).

3. NEED

Another justice norm that has received attention is need. As a norm of distributive justice, the need principle implies that resources should be distributed to recipients in accord with their legitimate need for them, regardless of their relative contributions. As such, when a group of recipients' relative needs for rewards differ, but not in a manner paralleling their relative contributions, the need norm conflicts with the norms of equity and equality.

Under what condition is the need norm salient? Deutsch (1975) has proposed that the need principle will predominate in situations in which persons are interested in fostering personal welfare and development. Several theorists have noted that this is likely to occur when persons have a very close, friendly relationship (e.g., Lerner, 1977; Leventhal, 1976b; Mikula & Schwinger, 1978). Although there has been much less research generated by the need norm than by either equity or equality, the few relevant studies that have been reported tend to support these theoretical statements (see reviews by Lamm, Kayser, & Schwinger, 1981; Leventhal, 1976a).

C. Justice Norms in Social Relationships: An Integration

The point has been made that adherence to justice norms is moderated by considerations of the nature of the social relationship between individuals. It is not too difficult to apply Deutsch's (1975) and Leventhal's (1976b) theorizing about the situations dictating equity, equality and need to various types of social relationships in which these conditions may exist. Indeed, Lerner's (1975, 1977) theoretical conceptualization is based, in part, on the nature of the relationship between individuals.

1. OVERVIEW OF INTEGRATIVE ANALYSIS

What justice norms are associated with various types of social relations? Attempts to consider this question have been most seriously undertaken in this volume by Austin and Tobiasen (Chapter 7), and by McClintock and Keil (Chapter 10), although the matter is also addressed by Wegner (Chapter 3) and by Greenberg (Chapter 11). Austin and Tobiasen propose that the nature of the social relationship between two persons—specifically, the level of intimacy between them—is a key determinant. Another factor, the degree of outcome interdependence between individuals, forms the basis of McClintock and Keil's analyses. Our analysis combines both these factors.

Our use of the terms interdependence and intimacy is not intended to be distinct from the ways they have been used in this volume, or the literature in general. Nevertheless, clarity demands that we define these terms as they will be used in our analysis. We define *interdependence* as the degree to which participants in a social exchange have control over each other's resources. By dichotomizing relationships along this dimension, we can identify those relationships characterized by persons having relatively little control over each other's resources (low interdependence), or by a relatively high degree of control over each other's resources (high interdependence). We define *intimacy* as the closeness of the social bond between individuals (for a more extensive discussion of this dimension, see Austin & Tobiasen, Chapter 7). Dichotomizing this variable enables us to distinguish between relationships characterized by relatively weak social bonds (low intimacy), or relatively strong social bonds (high intimacy).

In an attempt to integrate these factors, we propose that interdependence and intimacy can be conceptualized as independent dimensions, and that various types of social relationships can be located at the points of intersection. The model we will employ is depicted in Figure 12.1. To

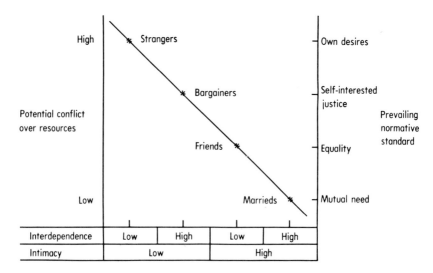

Figure 12.1. Prevailing normative standards in social relations characterized by levels of interdependence and intimacy.

simplify our analysis, we will dichotomize interdependence and intimacy as previously noted. By combining high or low levels of each, we get a fourfold categorization. In this resulting taxonomy, we may identify: *strangers* as being low in intimacy and low in interdependence, *bargainers* as low in intimacy and high in interdependence, *friends* as high in intimacy and low in interdependence, and *marrieds* as high in intimacy and high in interdependence. These are, of course, merely representative examples of relationships that may be characterized by combinations of these factors.

One may also note the existence of a single unifying dimension that underlies these conceptual categories. We propose that a dimension of *potential conflict over resources* accounts for ordering these four types of relationships along a single dimension. By conflict over resources, we mean a concern for self-interest in distribution relative to other-interest. If we assume that persons are always interested in their own well-being, we can differentiate persons' relationships with others in terms of the degree to which their interest in other's well-being approximates their own. In cases in which a person's interests and others' interests are most divergent, we may expect the greatest conflict over resources—"every man for himself." This may be expected to be the case among strangers. In cases in which persons' own interests and those of another are coincident, then conflict over resources may be very low, or nonexistent, since what gratifies one person also gratifies the other. Ideally, this describes the relationship between married persons.

Of course, there are also middle points along the continuum at which a person's interests and another's interests are shared to intermediate degrees. For example, bargainers may well be expected to have a relatively high degree of conflict over resources, as their basic positions are antagonistic to each other, each wanting to increase his or her own share relative to the other. However, because their bargaining relationship may be expected to create a relatively high degree of interdependence, bargainers may be expected to be less selfish than strangers. In the case of friends, greater intimacy may be expected to create concern over the other's well-being, resulting in less conflict over resources. Because friends are less interdependent on each other than marrieds, they may be expected to manifest a relatively higher level of selfish behavior than marrieds.

2. LINKING NORMS TO RELATIONS

A specific normative standard seems to be logically suggested by each of these continuum points. Moreover, there is empirical evidence to suggest that each of these norms does indeed prevail for each of the different types of relations along the continuum, thereby providing convergent validity for our model.

a. Strangers.   Among strangers, the practice of acting selfishly—in accord with one's own desires—appears to be normative. Indeed, imagine the scene that would be created by emptying a bag of $100 bills in the middle of a busy street. Passersby could probably be imagined frantically scurrying about attempting to scoop up as much loot as possible before the others depleted the supply. This sort of situation hardly prompts people to consider each other's needs, and to leave some money for them. Instead, it would be normative to be selfish. Unfortunately, we are aware of no field study that has employed this scenario.

However, some laboratory research has simulated such selfishness. For example, Greenberg (1978) has reported that allocators took disproportionately large shares of reward when they had unilateral control over resources that were highly valuable. It seems reasonable to imply that unilateral control over resources makes individuals relatively low on interdependence, as only one individual is dependent on the other for resources. The level of intimacy between individuals in this study was low as subjects had no knowledge of the other, nor were they led to believe that they would have any further interaction with each other. A similar tendency for unilateral control over resources to promote selfishness has also been observed by Lane and Messé (1971), who noted that this tendency was particularly potent when subjects were able to maintain their anonymity, thereby keeping the level of intimacy relatively low.

b. Bargainers.   In the typical study on bargaining and negotiation, the level of intimacy between participants is usually quite low, although the degree of interdependence between them is high. Bargainers can typically control each others' access to resources, and attempt to maximize their own at the other's expense. However, because bargainers are more interdependent than strangers, we can also expect them to temper their distributive behavior with less selfishness. The successful continuity of the bargaining relationship requires some adherence to normative standards that allow for simultaneous concern over self-interest and ostensible displays of concern for the other's welfare (e.g., a "politeness ritual"; see Schwinger, 1980). Recourse to principles of justice appear to be the solution as they discourage unreasonable and counterproductive acts.

However, a question arises as to what norm to follow. Different norms result in different distributions. Because bargainers are in an essentially antagonistic relationship, we submit that they would each advocate adherence to a justice norm that benefits themselves. Such a decision is simultaneously justifiable by recourse to existing normative precedents, and advances one's own interest relative to that of the other.

Indeed, there exists research evidence in support of this proposition. For example, Komorita and Kravitz (1979) have noted that persons playing a bargaining game tended to prefer the equality norm to the norm of equal excess, when doing so would be beneficial to them. Similarly, studies have shown that it is the partner with the greater inputs who is more likely to prefer the equity norm to the equality norm (e.g., Leventhal & Anderson, 1970). Lerner (1971; Lerner & Lichtman, 1968) has shown that people in competitive relationships take actions to benefit themselves when they believe that it is normatively justifiable—what he refers to as the norm of "justified self-interest." Bargaining relationships may be seen as "him or me" situations, making it "entirely legitimate to do what one can *within the rules* to get the desired outcome [Lerner, Miller, & Holmes, 1976, p. 158; emphasis added]."

c. Friends.   In more intimate relationships, such as friendships, persons may be expected to maintain greater concern over each other's interests. With concern over other's interests approaching those of oneself, it would be expected that an equality norm would predominate. Indeed, several studies have shown that equal distributions of reward predominate among friends (e.g., Austin, 1980; Benton, 1971; Morgan & Sawyer, 1967, 1979).

Support for this contention is also derived from Lerner's (1975, 1977) suggestion that persons in "unit" relationships—those who perceive themselves as similar to others and belonging with them, such as friends—may be expected to follow the "parity," or equality, norm. Deutsch (1975) also suggests that the mutual interest of friends to promote enjoyable relationships is best achieved by distributing resources equally. This avoids the potential conflict created by making allocations that promote self-interest, and that encourage discrimination between friends, thereby threatening the "sameness" on which the friendship may be based (cf. Bales, 1955; Greenberg, Chapter 11, this volume; Leventhal, 1976a).

d. Marrieds.   The situation is somewhat different, however, among married persons because their dependence on each other for resources may be expected to be far greater than it would among friends.[3] Al-

---

[3]We do not mean to imply that exchanges of resources between friends are *in*dependent, merely that relationships between friends typically involve less *inter*dependence than relationships between marrieds. (For one reason at least, marrieds can be expected to have

though the research reviewed in this volume by Greenberg (Chapter 11, Section III. C. 1. *b*.) suggests that the equality norm tends to be followed in interdependent groups, that research has, for the most part, failed to focus on groups whose members are as intimately related, or as highly interdependent on each other, as marrieds. We cannot say that equality is not as important among marrieds as it is among friends, but we can say that among marrieds the concern for mutual needs is predominant. Ideally, in marriage, what benefits one spouse also benefits the other such that there should be little or no conflict over resources; allocations result in mutual gratification of needs. (We *did* say "ideally," and recognize that failures do occur.)

As noted by several contributors to this volume, (e.g., Allen, Chapter 6; Austin & Tobiasen, Chapter 7) and others (e.g., Blau, 1964), the sense of "we feelings" and shared identity is likely to emerge in relationships characterized by extremely high levels of intimacy and interdependence. Married relationships are typically so characterized, thereby making individuals sensitive to satisfying the mutual needs of their family members. Lerner (1975, 1977) suggests the same thing in characterizing an "identity relation" between individuals as one in which there is "a minimal psychological separation between them. What happens to one 'happens empathically to the other [Lerner *et al.*, 1976, p. 154]." He notes that, in such relationships, individuals tend to be responsive to the other's needs. This is not surprising as other's needs and own needs may be identical, and mutually satisfied.

The assertion that adherence to a principle of allocation in accord with mutual needs is expected in married relationships is consistent with Clark and Mills' (1979) work suggesting that benefits are administered with others' needs in mind in "communal relationships"—those in which members feel responsible for each other's welfare. It also receives support from Wegner's analysis of tacit–focal awareness in this volume (Chapter 3). Specifically, he contends that tacit awareness of another can be expected to foster an orientation toward that person's needs. Because tacit awareness involves perceiving another through oneself—empathically—it is not surprising that married persons may share an awareness of each other on this level.

---

longer-lived and more complicated networks of resource exchanges.) The same caveat also applies to the distinction between strangers and bargainers as regards interdependence. Strangers may not always be completely independent of one another (e.g., the scenario in which the money is dropped creates a zero-sum situation, thereby connoting some interdependence), although they may be less interdependent than bargainers.

3. SUMMARY

We have proposed that two factors—intimacy and interdependence—can be combined to reflect one dimension of potential conflict over resources. Various social relationships can be located along this dimension, and specific normative standards appear to be associated with each. When intimacy is low and interdependence is low; conflict over resources may be highest. Strangers fall into this category, and can be expected to follow the practice of selfishly satisfying their own desires. Conflict is lower when intimacy is low and interdependence is high, as is the case among bargainers. Persons in this type of relationship tend to prefer whatever justice norm is most advantageous to them. Among friends intimacy is high and interdependence is relatively low. The degree of conflict over resources is lower, and the equality norm prevails. Finally, when intimacy and interdependence are both high, conflict is lowest. Ideally, such is the case among married persons who, therefore, adhere to the norm of satisfying their mutual needs.

D. Some Limitations of the Normative View

Krebs (1970; Chapter 8, this volume) has called attention to the limitations of "merely" normative analyses of altruism and of justice. Although the type of social relation among individuals may be an important factor in defining the appropriate justice norm, there are doubtlessly many factors that may limit or qualify the impact of norms on behavior. Two distinct types of factors have been highlighted in this volume and will concern us in the first two subsections: (1) the focal person's perspective as an actor or observer; and (2) his or her individual characteristics. A third factor, the structure of power among individuals in the situation, has received less explicit attention (see, however, Austin & Hatfield, 1980; Cohen & Greenberg, Chapter 1, this volume), but seems crucial for an understanding of how normative constraints are expressed in overt action. We address this factor in the third following subsection.

1. ACTORS' VERSUS OBSERVERS' PERSPECTIVES

Various studies of justice have focused on different roles of the focal person: either as an allocator of reward, as a recipient, or as an outside party (see also Major & Deaux, Chapter 2, Section I). Because parties outside an exchange relationship may be unaffected by it, we can expect that the justice or injustice of that relationship may only be viewed abstractly, without practical relevance. However, persons in an exchange relationship with each other are very much affected by the justice or injustice of the exchange, although their perspectives on what constitutes just behavior may differ.

In Chapter 4, Cohen suggests that parties involved in social exchange will hold different views of justice as a function of their position as actors or observers. For purposes of an example, we may consider an allocator of reward to be an actor, and the recipients as observers; the allocator's actions affect the observing recipient. Specifically, Cohen contends that when the equity norm is salient, observers may set higher standards of deserving for actors than actors would set for themselves. For example, a worker may be expected to feel that he or she has performed adequately enough to merit a raise, although his or her supervisor may not agree. Both parties are operating out of tacit acceptance of the equity norm— reward in proportion to performance—but hold divergent opinions of the evaluation of the performance which determines the reward, hence, the extent to which the norm was met. The point is that agreement regarding the appropriate normative principle does not necessarily imply agreement about its implementation. The operation of the actor–observer divergence creates a potential source of conflict between claimants surrounding the implementation of justice principles.

It is an interesting possibility that self-serving views of justice (see Austin & Tobiasen, Chapter 7; Cohen, Chapter 4; Donnerstein & Hatfield, Chapter 9) may stem from self-serving biases attendant to the actor–observer divergence (Bradley, 1978). The caveat we wish to note in this regard is that the behavioral impact of a justice norm may be expected to be qualified by the perspective of the persons in situations in which a norm operates (see also Wegner, Chapter 3).

2. INDIVIDUAL CHARACTERISTICS

It has been either stated directly or implied many times in this volume that "justice is in the eyes of the beholder" (e.g., Austin & Tobiasen, Chapter 7). The implications of this suggestion for normative views of justice are that justice norms might not be universally: (1) understood; (2) internalized; or (3) acted on. This is apparent at many points in this volume where individual difference variables are discussed.

For example, the issue of age differences in adherence to various justice norms has been treated in detail by Major and Deaux (Chapter 2), and by Krebs (Chapter 8). These authors have noted that the distribution behavior of younger children tends to be guided primarily by the principle of equality, and that the equity principle operates as they get older. Explanations in terms of logico-mathematical abilities needed to adhere to the equity norm (Hook & Cook, 1979) and developmental changes in moral reasoning (Damon, 1977) have been offered. Hence, some allocation behavior may be guided by developmental limitations affecting ability to behave in accord with normative demands. Accordingly, justice norms may not be uniformly comprehended by all persons, and may not be expected to have uniform influences on behavior.

We also wish to make the point that justice norms may not be universally salient across cultures. As noted by several contributors to this volume (e.g., Allen, Chapter 6; Greenberg, Chapter 11; Major & Deaux, Chapter 2), there are well-documented differences in the tendencies of people to favor different justice norms in different cultures. These differences appear, to a large extent, to be due to differences in socialization practices followed in various societies that affect the acceptance and internalization of various moral standards (Gergen, Morse, & Gergen, 1980). Hence, it is suggested that various norms of justice may be differently incorporated into existing cultural values, and differentitally internalized by individuals.

There may also be an interesting parallel between individual development and societal development of justice norms. Weiner (1973) has pointed to striking similarities between stages in the development of individual moral evaluations of achievement performances (see also Gunzburger, Wegner, & Anooshian, 1977) and the development of normative standards appropriate to the development of different political–economic structures of society. The stage theories of development of both Piaget (1932) and Marx (1875/1978) suggest that changes in the moral norms internalized by individuals recapitulate changes in the historical development of the political and economic organization of societies and the moral norms associated with each stage.

In studies of other individual difference variables, such as sex differences, it has been observed that situationally defined justice norms may be understood and internalized equally by men and women, but not acted on with equal willingness. There is evidence to suggest that the demands of justice norms may sometimes conflict with the demands of sex-role requirements, resulting in behavior in violation of justice norms. For example, some research reviewed by Major and Deaux (Chapter 2) reveals that women are less likely than men are to reward themselves in accord with their performances, thereby less willing to behave in accord with the equity norm. One line of explanation that has been offered to account for this is that the requirements of the traditional female sex role dictate against risking the disruption of interpersonal harmony resulting from discriminating between people as may be required by the equity norm (Kidder, Bellettirie, & Cohn, 1977). Although there are many explanations for this finding, the possibility seems worth stressing

here that justice norm demands might fail to dictate anticipated behavioral patterns in instances in which they conflict with the demands
made by other normative systems, such as sex roles. Normative demands
may be understood and internalized, but not be acted on because they
conflict with other standards.

There is an important lesson to be learned from these lines of investigation that is applicable to our understanding of justice as normative.
Apparently not all persons are equally susceptible to influence by all
justice norms. This appears to be due to individual differences in ability
to comprehend a norm, to accept and internalize it, and *willingness* to act
on it. In addition to differences in willingness, however, there may be
important differences in individuals' *abilities* to act on a justice norm.
This suggests the importance of a third major limitation of the normative perspective on justice: the impact of the structure of power.

3. THE STRUCTURE OF POWER

The extent to which actual allocations or reallocations in a given situation are consistent with any justice norm will depend to a large extent on
the relative power of the individuals in that situation. If situational pressures are so prepotent that all actors agree on the appropriate justice
norm and how it is to be implemented, or if all actors are so similar in
personal and role characteristics that they agree as to the appropriateness of a particular norm, then *that* justice norm will have the predominant influence in the actual allocation of goods. However, to the extent
that there are differences in perspective, in roles, or in personal characteristics, there may be disagreements over what would constitute a "just"
allocation.

If there is a minimum degree of interdependence among individuals,
this disagreement must be resolved and a distribution produced. (Without this minimum degree of interdependence, anyone with a serious
disagreement could simply withdraw.) The distribution that results *might
be* the result of a compromise among the desires of all parties to it. The
literature reveals some evidence of distributions that appear to compromise between different norms, the strict implementation of either of
which would advantage one party more than another (e.g., Cohen,
1974). However, there is no reason for this necessarily to be the case.
Even where it is the case, it seems reasonable to suggest that a compromise reflects the power of each party to enforce a claim.

We have suggested that conflicts of interest are more likely to arise
where intimacy and interdependence are low (i.e., among strangers)
than where either or both are high (among bargainers, friends, or marrieds). This does not necessarily mean that conflicts of interest will *not*
arise in the latter cases. In fact, we might expect that when they do arise,

they arise with a great deal of intensity; for example, precisely among married couples, and precisely *because* of their high intimacy and inter-dependence. Conflicts of interest are resolved not only through appeals to norms (of justice), but also through direct conflict, conflict in which the relative power of the individuals may well be crucial. Thus, in any one of the four types of relationships we have tried to sketch here, individuals may have equal power over the allocation, or their power may be very unequal. The possibility of such conflicts of interest, re-solved through the exercise of power emerging because of differing perspectives and roles, is particularly acute between men and women today (see Scanzoni, 1972). And these conflicts take place between actors who possess very different amounts of power, often in the setting of marriage relationships, and usually in terms of the wider society. The relations among people in these situations are no less interdependent or intimate because they involve serious conflicts of interest likely to be resolved in accord with the distribution of power. Austin and Tobiasen (Chapter 7) discuss the abuse of children by parents, and we would add the all-too-prevalent examples of physical abuse of women by men in family settings, as instances of the effects of relative power in intimate settings.

Power is a very complex concept (see Wrong, 1980) which has several meanings relevant to our discussion. We can mention only a few here. At the simplest level, we might identify power as an input to an allocation decision. Clearly, those with no, or less, "voice" (see Folger, 1977; Hirschman, 1970) in this decision are less likely to have their normative demands met than are those with greater power. And the larger the disparity in power, the greater the likelihood that the allocation will reflect the interests, and the normative justification for them, of the stronger more than the interests of the weaker. At a slightly more com-plex level, we might identify the "legitimate" power accorded by the inferior performer to the superior performer (and claimed by the latter) even when each has equal "objective" voice in the allocation decision (cf. Schwinger, 1980).

There are, of course, limits to the exercise of such power. Some of these limits reflect the impact of internalized norms (e.g., social respon-sibility) that hint at a compensatory "power of dependence." Other limits reflect legal constraints. But there are other constraints, and these are represented by the ability of the weaker party to retaliate. Hatfield and her colleagues identify "retaliation distress" as one motive the powerful have for avoiding exploitation of the weaker (cf. Walster, Walster, & Berscheid, 1978). And there is research demonstrating that when an allocator can be later identified, or when he or she expects subsequently to reverse roles with the present recipient, the power to serve one's interests at the expense of the other is not exercised to its fullest extent (e.g., Greenberg, 1978; Shapiro, 1975). These constraints, both internal and external, prevent exploitation of the weak by the strong to a certain extent, but they do not ensure complete protection, and they most certainly do not eliminate the need to recognize the importance of distributions of power. On the contrary, their very existence underscores the importance of the power dimension.

In all cases, then, ostensibly prevailing justice norms *may* have no apparent effects on overt behavior. The popular research question of "Which norm will be followed when?" therefore may be answered in part by considerations of *who* its potential adherents may be.

III. JUSTICE AS INSTRUMENTAL

The normative approach to justice just discussed provides only one answer to the question of why people engage in justice behavior. It stresses that justice behavior results from prevailing social practices in various situations. An alternative solution specifies that justice behavior is derived from the belief that it provides a path toward attaining other goals. As such, it is motivated by instrumental ends.

This is not to imply that normatively motivated acts may not also be effective in attaining a goal. For example, adhering to a particular justice norm may be expected to enhance one's image as a conformist. However, for purposes of our analysis, we consider such an act instrumental only in instances in which behavior is guided by an intentional desire to attain a goal. Indeed, as we will note in this section, the desire to get another to view oneself in a particular way is one of the purposes to which fair behavior may be put. Quite simply, our point is that many enactments of fair behavior are motivated by the belief that these behaviors enhance goal attainment.

What, then, are the purposes to which justice behavior may be put? Why may behaving fairly actually be an effective means to other ends? Also, what are the limitations of "using" justice behavior in these ways? Before turning to each of these questions, we feel it will be useful to offer some historical perspective on the instrumental aspects of justice.

A. A Legacy of Instrumental Views of Justice Behavior

To readers who envision justice as an idealized moral state, one that guides our cherished tradition of legality, the proposal that justice may be merely a path toward attaining another goal may prove disquieting. Just as prosocial behavior is not always attributed to purely altruistic motives among helpers (see Krebs, Chapter 8, this volume; Schwartz, 1977), so too have many justice theorists chosen to deemphasize the possibility that behaviors ostensibly appearing to create justice are actually motivated by an interest in attaining an idealized state of justice for its own sake (e.g., Leventhal, 1976a; Walster *et al.*, 1973). Instead, our predominant theories are guided by what Lerner (1982) calls an "economic model of man," which sees people operating with a "market-place mentality" (Gergen, 1980) according to which justice behavior, in whatever form is appropriate, enhances one's self-interest. Indeed, as Walster *et al.* (1978) note, through the process of socialization people "soon learn that the most profitable way to be selfish is to be 'fair' [p. 15]." Accordingly, justice behavior may result when it is seen as instrumental to enhancing one's self-interest. As Walster *et al.* (1978) propose, "So long as individuals perceive they can maximize their outcomes by behaving equitably, they will do so [p. 16]."[4]

How is it that what is just may come to be what is also most profitable? Sociobiological theorists such as Wilson (1975) argue that justice may facilitate adaptation to the social environment and enhance preservation of the species. Similarly, Campbell (1975) has proposed that adaptation and survival depend on the balancing of altruistic and egoistic tendencies. Thus, to the extent that human existence depends on the smooth functioning of society, justice norms that help to minimize disputes over scarce resources may assist in reducing certain forms of societal conflict and preserve the social order.

Haphazard and chaotic claims over resources may be incompatible with the existence of any social structure, whether at the interpersonal or at the societal level of organization. Consider, for example, why more people do not become bank robbers. Are we deterred by the moral imperative against stealing? To some extent, yes. Another alternative is that most of us will find it more profitable to work (assuming jobs are available) and to be convinced that we have earned a fair day's pay for a fair day's work. The deterrents built into the social system make behavior consistent with moral and legal constraints more profitable, thereby reinforcing such behavior.

The link between equity and profitability has been stated explicitly by Leventhal (1976a): "it seems likely that an allocator who distributes re-

---

[4]They also proposed that inequitable behavior will be engaged in when its consequences are perceived to be profitable (Walster *et al.*, 1978). However, as we will subsequently point out (Section III. C. 1.), this may only occur in limited circumstances.

wards equitably does so more because he desires to maximize long-term productivity than because he desires to comply with an abstract standard of justice. His decisions are based on an expectancy that equitable distributions of reward will elicit and sustain high levels of motivation and performance [p. 96]." Leventhal (1980) makes this even more explicit by distinguishing between acts motivated by a concern for justice per se, which he calls "fair behavior," and ostensibly similar acts stemming from other motivational bases, which he refers to as "quasi-fair behavior."

Our suggestion is not only that justice may be simply a means to other goals, but that people internalize this fact and act justly because of it. It is an intriguing possibility that the justice-restoring effects of an action may be epiphenomenal (Leventhal, 1980), motivated apart from moral or ethical considerations. However, because few studies have probed into the motives behind subjects' behavior, it is difficult to determine the extent to which justice behavior is actually enacted as a precondition for another goal, or as an ultimate goal in itself.

Some experimental evidence collected by Greenberg (1978) suggests that subjects sometimes give different reasons for making similar allocation responses. Under some conditions, subjects even admitted to disguising the true motives for their allocations, and conspicuously engaged in allocation strategies intending to attain goals other than securing justice. In a condition in which subjects had unilateral control over reward, they took almost identically equitable shares whether the reward allocated was arbitrary points, or a more valuable raffle ticket worth 10 chances to win a monetary prize. However, despite their similar behaviors, subjects expressed greater interest in benefiting themselves in the later case. The point of this illustration is simply that justice behavior cannot always be taken as an indication of an underlying justice motive, and that such behavior may actually be used for purposes other than the attainment of justice per se.

Not only do ostensibly just allocations serve other purposes, but inferences about justice have often been drawn incorrectly from research that assumes implicitly that allocations are relevant only, or most importantly, to justice. Thus, if people believe that equitable allocations increase productivity, they may allocate equitably despite their feelings that equal allocations are most just. Without knowing the reasons people have for their allocations, we cannot know whether we have learned anything about their understandings of, or their adherence to, norms of justice (cf. Cohen, 1978).

Leventhal (1976a) has suggested that, "the impact of allocation norms probably stems from the benefits they produce [p. 95]" and that one's choice of an allocation norm may be seen as "an attempt to gain the unique pattern of instrumental benefits that is associated with following that norm [p. 95]." Accordingly, we suggest, following Sampson's (1975) lead, that the form distributive decisions take depends on the persons' interaction goals (cf. Jones & Thibaut, 1958; Mikula, 1980). Whatever form of justice is perceived as being effective in attaining one's goals will be the form of justice that is followed.

Certainly, to some degree, the extant normative standards have prevailed *because* of their instrumental value. As described earlier (Section II. B), the equity norm is adhered to by persons whose goal is to create economic productivity, and the equality norm is adhered to by persons whose goal is to create harmonious social relations. Why are these connections maintained? The answer appears to lie in the fact that justice in certain forms does indeed facilitate certain goals, and in the fact that allocators are socially rewarded for behaving fairly.

1. JUSTICE WORKS

a. Equity. The nature of the equity norm and the key to its success is based in part on the fact that it makes pay contingent upon certain types of performance. People get what they deserve as determined by their relative contributions to a particular task. To receive greater outcomes, a person has to create greater inputs, and a social system with such contingencies tends to reinforce productive behavior. Indeed, this appears to be the success behind many industrial incentive plans (see Greenberg, Chapter 11). Moreover, the creation of analogous social systems in the laboratory accounts for the considerable prevalence of equity responding in experimental research (see McClintock & Keil, Chapter 10). As societies differ in the extent to which they offer differential rewards based on performance, so too are concomitant differences observed in the use of equity as an incentive (see Allen, Chapter 6; Greenberg, Chapter 11; Major & Deaux, Chapter 2). Accordingly, when the rules of the organization, the laboratory situation, or the societal structure are such that they relate differences in pay to differences in performance, participants operating within that social system may be expected to favor a normative standard, such as equity, that specifies the "fair" relation between pay and performance.

Under such circumstances, the equitable solution to the distributive problem is a highly effective one from the perspective of economic rationality. To wit, people are differentially favored in terms of their ability to advance the goal of economic productivity. Equitable systems of reward distribution favor individuals who are the most economically useful, thereby maintaining their contributions to the system (cf. Dansereau, Cashman, & Graen, 1973; Deutsch, 1975; Diesing, 1962; Le-

458 JERALD GREENBERG AND RONALD L. COHEN

venthal, 1976a). Accordingly, in economically oriented systems equity is used because it works.

How else does it work? One requirement of the equity norm is that it must distinguish clearly among recipients, first with regard to their performance, and, assuming that it is possible, with regard to pay. These distinctions are thought to stimulate competition among recipients, and perhaps mutual antagonisms as well. These antagonisms may serve to prevent the emergence of a common identity among recipients, so that questions concerning the legitimacy of the allocator's role or the social structure encompassing it are less likely to arise.

Note that this is precisely what our normative model of social relations (Section II. C.) would suggest if recipients see relations among themselves in "bargaining" terms (that is, high interdependency and low intimacy). In such a case, the pursuit of individual self-interest is normatively appropriate. However, if they were to see relations among themselves as do friends (low interdependence and high intimacy) or marrieds (high intimacy and high interdependence), then equal distributions or distributions according to need would be seen as normatively appropriate. To the extent that the interests of recipients and allocators conflict, the distance in social relations among recipients produced by equitable distributions of pay reinforces the power of allocators by undermining the potential collective power of recipients. Such a goal may be as important to allocators as that of economic productivity.

This suggests that claims for the fundamental importance, in functional terms, of a particular norm of justice may be ideologically based. For example, the claims sometimes made on behalf of the equity norm (cf. Walster *et al.*, 1978) "would seem to have more of an ideological rather than a scientific explanatory function [Schwinger, 1980, p. 105]." Similar criticisms (e.g., Bowles & Gintis, 1976; Horan, 1978; Sampson, 1976) have been made of theoretical claims for the instrumentality of distributions according to performance, such as the claims made by sociologists in the functional theory of stratification (Davis & Moore, 1945) and by neoclassical economists in their marginal productivity theory of distribution.

b. Equality. The same kind of analysis can be applied to the effectiveness of equality. Where the goal is harmony and smooth social functioning, it may be considered disruptive to the social order to discriminate between people with unequal inputs as would be required by the equity norm. The equality standard, on the other hand, turns a blind eye to relative contributions and defines fairness as equality of outcomes regardless of inputs (Sampson, 1975). Some contributors to this volume have suggested that equality may help to foster social relationships because it helps create "we-feelings" and promotes a concern for the common good of the social group (e.g., Allen, Chapter 6; Greenberg, Chapter 11; Krebs, Chapter 8). In situations in which group identity is stressed over individuality, it is seen as "fair" to treat all persons equally, because doing so helps to avoid undermining the mutual respect that is necessary for accepting others and fostering friendships (Bales, 1955; Deutsch, 1975; Leventhal, 1976a; Sampson, 1975).

Several contributors to this volume have referred to a line of research showing that equality tends to be followed more than equity among allocators expecting to interact with recipients (e.g., Greenberg, Chapter 11; McClintock & Keil, Chapter 10; Wegner, Chapter 3). The suggestion is that the anticipation of meeting others makes subjects more concerned with ease of social interaction, rituals of politeness (cf. Schwinger, 1980), or possible retaliation (see Section II. D. 3) than with interest in economic productivity. Evidence is also cited herein (e.g., Austin & Tobiasen, Chapter 7) and elsewhere (e.g., Leventhal, 1976a) to suggest that equality may indeed be effective for avoiding interpersonal conflict.[5]

Analogous to our treatment of the equity norm, we should note that, because of its tendency to reduce conflict among recipients, attempts to introduce equal distributions may have clear ideological and political overtones. Again, to the extent that the interests of recipients and allocators are seen as antagonistic, recipients may try to "use" equal distributions among themselves to create a consciousness of kind, through emphasizing a similarity of fate. Note too, that one can describe these attempts as attempts to shift the understandings that recipients have of relations among themselves from that of bargainers to that of friends or intimates. Attempts to create and emphasize solidarity among union members may be understood in these terms.

c. Need. Although there has been much less research on the need norm, it seems reasonable to suggest that its use may promote increased amounts of intimacy and interdependence, or perceptions of such, among recipients or between recipients and allocators. In view of our earlier comments on the equity norm, it is only fair to point out that implementation of the need norm also requires distinctions among reci-

[5]This is not to imply that these harmonious interpersonal conditions may not also enhance indusrial productivity. Indeed, promoting social harmony as a key to productivity is one of the fundamental assumptions of the human relations orientation to management (e.g., McGregor, 1960), and has been popularly cited as one of the key determinants of contemporary Japan's industrial supremacy (Smith, 1980). However we must distinguish harmony among recipients from harmony between recipients and allocators.

pients. These distinctions may produce competition to demonstrate need, rather than ability to perform, potentially resulting in antagonism among recipients. At the same time, such distinctions seem likely to produce affection and obligation toward the allocator. Here, perhaps, we have some reasons for the apparent role of strong, even authoritarian, leaders in intentional communities (cf. Kanter, 1972) and a basis for understanding some aspects of sibling rivalry and parental affection (in this connection, see Austin & Tobiasen, Chapter 7).

2. JUSTICE IS SOCIALLY REWARDING

Not only may justice behavior facilitate the attainment of social system goals, task or interpersonal, but behaving fairly may also be personally rewarding. In fact, as one part of Proposition II. B. of Walster *et al.*'s (1978) equity theory states, "Groups will generally reward members who treat others equitably [p. 9]." There appear to be several sources of reward for the allocator who behaves fairly.

The fact that the allocator's justice behavior may have worked may ultimately prove rewarding to allocators. This may be the case because the allocator receives personal gratification for meeting goals; there is a sense of pride and accomplishment associated with doing the job well. Moreover, others may reward the successful allocator with social approval and financial rewards, such as bonuses, in exchange for their success. Any or all of these factors may motivate reward allocators to help attain system goals. Behaving fairly may be an effective strategy toward this end.

In addition, however, fair behavior may also be engaged in because of the extent to which it *directly* rewards allocators for what they actually do instead of the effects of what they do. What comes to mind here is Allen's discussion of conformity in justice contexts (Chapter 6). The point is made that confirmity to justice norms may sometimes be engaged in because of the allocator's desire to succumb to external social pressure. To conform to norms is rewarding; it makes interaction more predictable and less costly (Thibaut & Kelley, 1959).

Allocators may be rewarded for merely conforming to prevailing justice standards. Consider, for example, a new industrial supervisor who takes control over an existing group with a history of certain reward distribution practices. For the newcomer to change these practices abruptly to ones he or she sees as fair would certainly be disruptive, and may threaten the newcomer's acceptance by the group. In fact, as Allen notes, what is fair *is* what is normative. The newcomer's actions may not be seen as bringing about fairness, but as actually threatening existing standards of fairness. Continuing to distribute rewards in a manner that appears to be unfair by external standards may actually prove to be less costly.

The literature is full of examples of how allocators derive reward from others by intentionally giving the appearance that they are concerned with justice. Much of this work on manipulating self-presentation in reward allocation settings has been described in various places in this volume (e.g., Allen, Chapter 6; Cohen, Chapter 4; McClintock & Keil, Chapter 10; Wegner, Chapter 3) and elsewhere (see review by Reis, 1981). We see from this work that persons making fair allocation decisions, or making their reactions to injustice known to an external authority figure, such as an experimenter, tend to behave in accord with the equity standard (e.g., Morse, Gruzen, & Reis, 1976; Reis & Gruzen, 1976; Rivera & Tedeschi, 1976). Presumably, although persons in these experiments do not know the exact normative preferences of the experimenter, they may be able to assume that equitable behavior is expected on the basis of cues provided by the experimental situation (cf. Cohen, 1978; Leventhal, 1976a). The idea that favorable self-presentation may be rewarding has been well established (Arkin, 1980), and the related notion that such rewards appear to provide a basis for justice behavior helps to establish the instrumental character of such behavior.

C. Limitations of "Using" Justice

Despite the fact that behaving in accordance with justice norms may be an effective way of attaining one's goals, there are several factors that may limit the usefulness of justice as a means to other ends.

1. TEMPORARILY MOTIVATING WITH INJUSTICE

Both Allen (Chapter 6) and Greenberg (Chapter 11) have noted that unfair behaviors can also be used to help attain goals. Specifically, Allen describes how unjust distributions are sometimes justified in terms of the long-term advantages they may offer. He cites the religious belief that one will ultimately get what one deserves "in another world" as an example of this kind of temporary acceptance of injustice as an investment toward long-term gain (see also Moore, 1978).

However, it is unclear whether such an attitude actually stems from the belief that injustice now leads to advantages later, or is merely a post hoc cognitive justification for having to accept an unsatisfactory *fait accompli*. We suspect the latter. In fact, the basis of Lerner's (1975, 1977) notion of the "personal contract" is that individuals learn that fairness, not unfairness, is the key to long-term gratification.

Greenberg (Chapter 11) has noted that allocators may sometimes

purposely overpay workers to motivate them to improve their performance (see also Greenberg & Leventhal, 1976; Leventhal, 1976a). Presumably, overpayment would obligate workers to improve their future
performance in an attempt to earn the too generous pay they have
already received. However, such an action may only be used temporarily, and in emergency situations, as it would, over the long run, undermine the smooth functioning of work groups built upon adherence to
equity.

Victims of repeated injustice, those who *have to* accept unsatisfactory
states of affairs, by definition lack the power necessary to do anything
but accept them. Such victims can be expected to try to leave the field
(e.g., Finn & Lee, 1972) rather than accept the situation in the hopes that
it will ultimately prove advantageous. However, even their ability to
leave depends on the availability of alternative sources of satisfaction. If
these alternatives are not available (as would be the case if their high
dependence on the allocator is matched by the allocator's substantial
power over them), they may "sit and suffer" and perhaps redefine what
"is" as "what is just."

If victims of repeated injustices do not establish cognitive justifications
for their fate, nor accept the justifications offered to them by others, and
if they do not accept the explanation that current injustices are necessary
and will be righted in the future, they may well turn to forms of active
resistance and rebellion. Moore (1978) suggests that it is just such col-
lapses of legitimacy in the form of perceived collective injustice that can
produce social revolutions.

2. REACTANCE AND BOOMERANG EFFECTS

The point has also been made in this volume that, when persons
believe another's use of injustice represents a purposive attempt to control their behavior, they may intentionally avoid behaving as desired,
making the strategy backfire. Suggesting that attempts to use equity as a
tool of social influence may "boomerang," Ajzen (Chapter 5) warns as a
practical matter that such attempts should be avoided. Similarly, Krebs
(Chapter 8) notes that reactance (Brehm, 1966) may be expected to
follow from the feeling that one was intentionally manipulated—the
victim of another's influence attempt (Brehm & Cole, 1966; Schopler &
Thompson, 1968).

Such effects seem likely to occur when an allocator's behavior is made
particularly salient by his or her departure from usual practices. In an
organization in which equity is usually followed, an allocator who suddenly behaves generously but inequitably in an attempt to motivate calls
attention to his or her motives. In this case, the use of overreward may

fail to create obligations among workers to reciprocate the allocator's apparent generosity because they believe that it is really motivated by selfish interests. Research cited by Krebs (Chapter 8) suggests that the supervisor's role as an opponent rather than as an ally in the organizational structure may lead workers to suspect an ulterior motive behind the allocator's actions (cf., Nadler, Fisher, & Streufert, 1974), thereby leading workers to defend themselves against what appear to be blatant attempts at manipulation.

Surely then, the would-be user of justice as a mechanism of social influence would have to take suitable precautions. Interestingly, justice theorists (e.g., Adams & Freedman, 1976; Leventhal, 1980) have pointed to Jones's (1964) work on ingratiation as providing some potential insight into the instrumental uses of justice. One lesson to be learned from this line of research is that causing a person to perceive another's inputs or outcomes in certain ways may indeed be effective in creating obligations, but only when this is not recognized as the person's true motive (see also Gouldner, 1960).

Similarly, allocators cannot expect that recipients will be responsive to actions stemming from merely fulfilling role obligations (see M. Greenberg, 1980). As a result, for any allocation strategy to be effective, it seems essential for recipients to believe that the allocator's behavior was freely determined (cf. Krebs, Chapter 8). In organizations, it is frequently the case that allocation decisions are made by impersonal policies, suggesting that it is difficult to institute effective behavioral control, and not surprising to observe considerable amounts of distrust (Greenberg, Chapter 11; Kruglanski, 1970).

IV. SOME ADDITIONAL CONSIDERATIONS AND FUTURE DIRECTIONS

Before concluding our presentation, we feel that we would best serve the interests of the reader by pointing to some ways in which our analysis may be extended and qualified. To this end, we will address two separate issues: the existence of an additional motive for behaving fairly, and the interrelationships between the normative and instrumental interpretations of justice we have been discussing.

A. Justice as a Moral Ideal

By no means is the question of why people behave justly completely answered by pointing only to the normative and instrumental functions of justice. There is at least one other possibility that has been proposed, and indeed, it is in many respects the most morally basic and optimistic one. That is, that people behave fairly because they want to do what is right; they are motivated by a concern for justice as a moral and philosophical ideal.

In essence, this is what Lerner (1982) has recently argued. He asserts that justice behavior is guided primarily by a personal commitment to deserving, which makes justice the preeminent concern of human beings. Lerner's argument is that the quest for justice as a profit-maximizing scheme is a mythical illusion perpetrated by the historical legacy of legal and business ethics. Lerner contends that people are actually concerned about justice for its own sake, but often seek to disguise this interest to conform to the popular view that people are essentially selfish. This, he argues, provides a self-protecting element to the myth, one which encourages experimental subjects to display a "cynical bias" about human unfairness.

Although Lerner's analysis points to a more optimistic picture of human behavior, his is not the predominant view of the question of why people behave fairly. Indeed, he offers it as "a radical analysis" compared to the admittedly more popular view that people are motivated to act out of selfishness.

With the vast majority of the existing studies derived from the economic model of man, it is difficult to assess Lerner's arguments in an unbiased light. Yet, his analysis is intuitively appealing. Clearly, what is needed is research aimed at assessing justice motivations on an a priori rather than a post hoc basis. Under the assumption that the normative, instrumental, and moral views of justice are each correct to some extent, such efforts would be useful in determining the conditions that make various justice motivations salient.

B. Interrelationships between Normative and Instrumental Interpretations

At several points in our discussion we were careful to point out that the mere act of adhereing to a justice norm may, in itself, constitute a purpose for fair behavior. Was it a result of interest in doing what others do, or interest in bringing about the perceived results of fair behavior? Perhaps it was a mixture of both: Allocators seek the personal rewards associated with being normative. Existing research does not shed sufficient light on these questions.

In approaching these questions in the future, researchers need to be aware of the potential interplay between normative and instrumental concerns in justice research. The slippery nature of these motives derives from the idea that they may coexist, and that what appears to be either normative or instrumental behavior may actually be the other in disguise. For example, an industrial supervisor may ostensibly justify his decision to deny a raise to a poor worker on the grounds that it was not permitted by company policy (normative), although he may have actually been guided by an interest in stimulating performance (instrumental). Or, the same supervisor may justify his decision to maintain differential rates of pay for workers on the grounds that this stimulates productivity (normative), although he may have actually been guided by an interest in undermining the basis of solidarity among workers that may represent a threat to management (instrumental).

Which comes first? Do people recognize the existence of a norm that, in turn, makes their purposes salient, or is it that individuals with certain purposes call on certain norms to justify the fairness of their actions? We suspect that the answer to this question depends largely on the nature of our observations. In experimental situations, we typically either make the subjects' goals salient by manipulating them (e.g., Greenberg & Leventhal, 1976), or by creating experimental situations in which various normative cues are triggered (e.g., Shapiro, 1975). It is mostly because our research has been guided by interest in questions such as "which norm when?" that we typically create experimental situations that predispose us toward one or the other of these paradigms. A completely different line of investigation needs to be conducted to allow us to determine what people's motives are for behaving fairly or unfairly. Toward this end, it would appear that in-depth interviewing of people in naturalistic situations may prove to be useful. We recognize, of course, the potential problems of biased, socially desirable responses that may result. However, researchers need to work on overcoming them to enhance our understanding of the role that justice plays in social behavior.

V. SUMMARY

In an attempt to integrate the various themes emerging from this volume, we explored the question of when and why people behave justly. The normative and instrumental functions of justice were discussed.

It was noted that prevailing conceptualizations favor the view that there are several distinct norms of justice that are each associated with different types of social situations. For example, equity is normative in economically oriented situations, and equality is normative in interpersonally oriented situations. A model was presented to integrate and to summarize the various factors linking norms of justice to different types of social relationships. We then identified some limitations of the normative view suggested by the perspective of persons in the exchange system, their individual characteristics, and the structure of power in the system.

Instrumental views of justice, those emphasizing that fair behavior is used to facilitate goals, were presented as having a formidable contemporary tradition. We then noted that justice is often used to attain instrumental goals because it is effective toward that end, and because behaving fairly is often personally rewarding to the actor. This analysis was qualified by noting that persons sometimes attempt to meet goals by behaving unfairly, and that blatant use of justice as a technique of social influence may prove to be ineffective if the manipulation is suspected.

In closing, we noted that persons may also be motivated by a concern for justice for its own sake. Some problems of distinguishing between normative and instrumental motives were considered, with a call for research directed at ascertaining the motives behind justice behavior.

REFERENCES

Adams, J. S., & Freedman, S. Equity theory revisited: Comments and annotated bibliography. In L. Berkowitz, & E. Walster (Eds.). *Advances in experimental social psychology* (Vol. 9). New York: Academic Press, 1976.

Arkin, R. M. Self-presentation. In D. M. Wegner, & R. R. Vallacher (Eds.), *The self in social psychology*. New York: Oxford, 1980.

Austin, W. Friendship and fairness: Effects of type of relationship and task performance on choice of distribution rules. *Personality and Social Psychology Bulletin*, 1980, *6*, 402–408.

Austin, W., & Hatfield, E. Equity theory, power, and social justice. In G. Mikula (Ed.), *Justice and social interaction*. New York: Springer-Verlag, 1980.

Bales, R. F. Adaptive and integrative changes as a source of strain in social systems. In A. P. Hare, E. F. Borgatta, & R. F. Bales (Eds.), *Small groups: Studies in social interaction*. New York: Knopf, 1955.

Benton, A. A. Productivity, distributive justice, and bargaining among children. *Journal of Personality and Social Psychology*, 1971, *18*, 68–78.

Blau, P. *Exchange and power in social life*. New York: Wiley, 1964.

Bowles, S., & Gintis, H. *Schooling in capitalist America: Educational reform and the contradictions of economic life*. New York: Basic Books, 1976.

Bradley, G. W. Self-serving biases in the attribution process: A reexamination of the fact or fiction question. *Journal of Personality and Social Psychology*, 1978, *36*, 56–71.

Brehm, J. W. *A theory of psychological reactance*. New York: Academic Press, 1966.

Brehm, J. W., & Cole, A. H. Effect of a favor which reduces freedom. *Journal of Personality and Social Psychology*, 1966, *3*, 420–426.

Campbell, D. T. On the conflicts between biological and social evolution and between psychology and moral tradition. *American Psychologist*, 1975, *30*, 1103–1126.

Clark, M. S., & Mills, J. Interpersonal attraction in exchange and communal relationships. *Journal of Personality and Social Psychology,* 1979, *37,* 12–24.

Cohen, R. L. Mastery and justice in laboratory dyads: A revision and extension of equity theory. *Journal of Personality and Social Psychology,* 1974, *29,* 464–474.

Cohen, R. L. *A critique of reward allocation research on distributive justice.* Unpublished manuscript, Bennington College, 1978.

Dansereau, F., Cashman, J., & Graen, G. Instrumentality theory and equity theory as complementary approaches in predicting the relationship of leadership and turnover among managers. *Organizational Behavior and Human Performance,* 1973, *10,* 184–200.

Damon, W. *The social world of the child.* San Francisco: Jossey-Bass, 1977.

Davis, K., & Moore, W. Some principles of stratification. *American Sociological Review,* 1945, *10,* 242–249.

Deutsch, M. Equity, equality, and need: What determines which value will be used as the basis of distributive justice? *Journal of Social Issues,* 1975, *31,* 137–149.

Diesing, P. *Reason in society.* Urbana, Ill.: University of Illinois, 1962.

Finn, R. H., & Lee, S. M. Salary equity: Its determination, analysis, and correlates. *Journal of Applied Psychology,* 1972, *56,* 283–292.

Folger, R. Distributive and procedural justice: Combined impact of "voice" and improvement on experienced inequity. *Journal of Personality and Social Psychology,* 1977, *35,* 108–119.

Gergen, K. J. Exchange theory: The transient and the enduring. In K. J. Gergen, M. S. Greenberg, & R. H. Willis (Eds.), *Social exchange: Advances in theory and research.* New York: Plenum, 1980.

Gergen, K. J., Morse, S. J., & Gergen, M. M. Behavior exchange in cross-cultural perspective. In H. C. Triandis & R. W. Brislin (Eds.), *Handbook of cross-cultural psychology: Social psychology* (Vol. 5). Boston: Allyn & Bacon, 1980.

Goode, W. J. *The celebration of heroes: Prestige as a control system.* Berkeley, Calif.: University of California, 1978.

Gouldner, A. W. The norm of reciprocity: A preliminary statement. *American Sociological Review,* 1960, *25,* 161–178.

Greenberg, J. Effects of reward value and retaliative power on allocation decisions: Justice, generosity, or greed? *Journal of Personality and Social Psychology,* 1978, *36,* 367–379.

Greenberg, J., & Leventhal, G. S. Equity and the use of overreward to motivate performance. *Journal of Personality and Social Psychology,* 1976, *34,* 179–190.

Greenberg, M. S. A theory of indebtedness. In K. J. Gergen, M. S. Greenberg, & R. H. Willis (Eds.), *Social exchange: Advances in theory and research.* New York: Plenum, 1980.

Gunzburger, D. W., Wegner, D. M., & Anooshian, L. Moral judgment and distributive justice. *Human Development,* 1977, *20,* 160–170.

Hirschman, A. O. *Exit, voice, and loyalty: Responses to decline in firms, organizations, and states.* Cambridge, Mass.: Harvard University Press, 1970.

Hook, J. G., & Cook, T. D. Equity theory and the cognitive ability of children. *Psychological Bulletin,* 1979, *86,* 429–445.

Horan, P. M. Is status attainment research atheoretical? *American Sociological Review,* 1978, *43,* 534–541.

Jones, E. E. *Ingratiation: A social psychological analysis.* New York: Appleton-Century-Crofts, 1964.

Jones, E. E., & Thibaut, J. W. Interaction goals as bases of inference in interpersonal perception. In R. Tagiuri & L. Petrullo (Eds.), *Person perception and interpersonal behavior.* Palo Alto, Calif.: Stanford University Press, 1958.

Kanter, R. M *Commitment and community: Communes and utopias in sociological perspective.* Cambridge, Mass.: Harvard University Press, 1972.

Kidder, L.H., Bellettirie, G., & Cohn, E. S. Secret ambitions and public performances. The effects of anonymity of reward allocations made by men and women. *Journal of Experimental Social Psychology,* 1977, *13,* 70–80.

Komorita, S. S., & Kravitz, D. A. The effects of alternatives in bargaining. *Journal of Experimental Social Psychology,* 1979, *15,* 147–157.

Krebs, D. L. Altruism: An examination of the concept and a review of the literature. *Psychological Bulletin,* 1970, *73,* 258–302.

Kruglanski, A. J. Attributing trustworthiness in supervisor–worker relations. *Journal of Experimental Social Psychology,* 1970, *6,* 214–232.

Lamm, H., Kayser, E., & Schwinger, T. Justice norms and other determinants of allocation and negotiation behavior. In M. Irle (Ed.), *Decision making: Social-psychological and socioeconomic analyses.* New York: de Gruyter, 1981.

Lane, I. M., & Massé, L.A. Equity and the distribution of rewards. *Journal of Personality and Social Psychology,* 1971, *20,* 1–17.

Lerner, M. J. Justified self-interest and the responsibility for suffering: A replication and extension. *Journal of Human Relations,* 1971, *19,* 550–559.

Lerner, M. J. The justice motive in social behavior: An introduction. *Journal of Social Issues,* 1975, *31,* 1–20.

Lerner, M. J. The justice motive: Some hypotheses as to its origins and forms. *Journal of Personality,* 1977, *45,* 1–52.

Lerner, M. J. The justice motive in human relations and the economic model of man: A radical analysis of facts and fictions. In V. Derlega & J. Grzelak (Eds.), *Cooperation and Helping Behavior: Theories and research* New York: Academic Press, 1982.

Lerner, M. J., & Lichtman, R. R. Effects of perceived norms on attitudes and altruistic behavior toward a dependent other. *Journal of Personality and Social Psychology,* 1968, *9,* 226–232.

Lerner, M. J., Miller, D. T., & Holmes, J. G. Deserving and the emergence of forms of justice. In L. Berkowitz & E. Walster (Eds.), *Advances in experimental social psychology* (Vol. 9). New York: Academic Press, 1976.

Leventhal, G. S. The distribution of rewards and resources in groups and organizations. In L. Berkowitz & E. Walster (Eds.), *Advances in experimental social psychology* (Vol. 9). New York: Academic Press, 1976. (a)

Leventhal, G. S. Fairness in social relationships. In J. W. Thibaut, J. T. Spence, & R. C. Carson (Eds.), *Contemporary topics in social psychology.* Morristown, N.J.: General Learning Press, 1976. (b)

Leventhal, G. S. What should be done with equity theory? New approaches to the study of fairness in social relationships. In K. J. Gergen, M. S. Greenberg, & R. H. Willis (Eds.), *Social exchange: Advances in theory and research.* New York: Plenum, 1980.

Leventhal, G. S., & Anderson, D. Self-interest and the maintenance of equity. *Journal of Personality and Social Psychology,* 1970, *15,* 57–62.

Marx, K. [Critique of the Gotha Program]. In R. C. Tucker (Ed.), *The Marx-Engels reader* (2nd ed.). New York: Norton, 1978. (Article originally published, 1875).

McGregor, D. *The human side of enterprise.* New York: McGraw-Hill, 1960.

Mikula, G. On the role of justice in allocation decisions. In G. Mikula (Ed.), *Justice and social interaction.* New York: Springer-Verlag, 1980.

Mikula, G., & Schwinger, T. Intermember relations and reward allocation: Theoretical considerations of affects. In H. Brandstatter, J. H. Davis, & H. Schuler (Eds.), *Dynamics of group decisions.* Beverly Hills, Calif.: Sage, 1978.

Moore, B. *Injustice: The social bases of obedience and revolt.* White Plains, N.Y.: M. E. Sharpe, 1978.

Morgan, W. R., & Sawyer, J. Bargaining, expectations, and the preferences for equality over equity. *Journal of Personality and Social Psychology,* 1967, *6,* 139–149.

Morgan, W. R., & Sawyer, J. Equality, equity, and procedural justice in social exchange. *Social Psychology Quarterly,* 1979, *42,* 71–75.

Morse, S. J., Gruzen, J., & Reis, H. T. The nature of equity restoration: Some approval-seeking considerations. *Journal of Personality and Social Psychology,* 1976, *12,* 1–8.

Nadler, A., Fisher, J. D., & Streufert, S. The donor's dilemma: Recipient's reactions to and from a friend or foe. *Journal of Applied Social Psychology,* 1974, *4,* 275–285.

Piaget, J. [*The moral judgment of the child*]. New York: Free Press, 1965. (Originally published, 1932)

Reis, H. T. The multidimensionality of justice. In R. Folger (Ed.), *The sense of injustice: Social psychological perspectives.* New York: Plenum, in press.

Reis, H. T. Self-presentation and distributive justice. In J. T. Tedeschi (Ed.), *Impression management theory and social psychological research.* New York: Academic Press, 1981.

Reis, H. T., & Gruzen, J. On mediating equity, equality, and self-interest: The role of self-presentation in social exchange. *Journal of Experimental Social Psychology,* 1976, *12,* 487–503.

Rivera, A. N., & Tedeschi, J. T. Public versus private reactions to positive inequity. *Journal of Personality and Social Psychology,* 1976, *34,* 895–900.

Sampson, E. E. Studies of status congruence. In L. Berkowitz (Ed.), *Advances in experimental social psychology* (Vol. 4). New York: Academic Press, 1969.

Sampson, E. E. On justice as equality. *Journal of Social Issues,* 1975, *31,* 45–64.

Sampson, E. E. *Social psychology and contemporary society* (2nd ed.). New York: Wiley, 1976.

Scanzoni, J. *Sexual bargaining: Power politics in the American marriage.* Englewood Cliffs, N.J.: Prentice-Hall, 1972.

Schopler, J., & Thompson, V. D. Role of attribution processes in mediating amount of reciprocity for a favor. *Journal of Personality and Social Psychology,* 1968, *10,* 243–250.

Schwartz, S. Normative influences on altruism. In L. Berkowitz (Ed.), *Advances in experimental social psychology* (Vol. 10). New York: Academic Press, 1977.

Schwinger, T. Just allocations of goods: Decisions among three principles. In G. Mikula (Ed.), *Justice and social interaction.* New York: Springer-Verlag, 1980.

Shapiro, E. G. Effect of expectation of future interaction on reward allocation in dyads: Equity or equality. *Journal of Personality and Social Psychology,* 1975, *31,* 873–880.

Smith, A. The Japanese model. *Esquire,* October, 1980, pp. 22–23.

Thibaut, J. W., & Kelley, H. H. *The social psychology of groups.* New York: Wiley, 1959.

Walster, E., Berscheid, E., & Walster, G. W. New directions in equity research. *Journal of Personality and Social Psychology,* 1973, *25,* 151–156.

Walster, E., & Walster, G. W. Equity and social justice. *Journal of Social Issues,* 1975, *31,* 21–44.

Walster, E., Walster, G. W., & Berscheid, E. *Equity: Theory and research.* Boston: Allyn & Bacon, 1978.

Weiner, B. From each according to his abilities: The role of effort in a moral society. *Human Development,* 1973, *16,* 53–60.

Wilson, E. *Sociobiology.* Cambridge, Mass.: Harvard University Press, 1975.

Wrong, D. H. *Power: Its forms, bases, and uses.* New York: Harper Colophon, 1980.

Author Index

Numbers in italics refer to the pages on which the complete references are listed.

Subject Index

A

Actor–observer differences, *see* Attribution, divergent perspectives

Actual equity, 17–18, 300–301, 311, 318, 320–321

Adams, J. S., theoretical position, 14–15, *see also* Inequity, Adams, J. S., theory of

Age, *see* Developmental patterns of justice behavior

Aggression, 309–329, *see also* Victims, derogation of
  cues, 327–328
  defined, 312–313
  fear of retaliation, 322–323
  limitations of equity theory approach, 324–328
  reasons for, 325–328
  self-concept and, 321–322
  targets, 324–325

Allocation, *see* Distribution rules; Norms; Resource allocation

Altruism, *see* Prosocial behavior

Anomie, 23

Aristotle, philosophical position, 3–4, 232

Attitude-behavior correspondence, 179–181

Attitude formation and change, 161–186

Attribution, 119–152, 245–248
  biases, 140–150

cultural bias, 147–150
  ego-defensive bias, 144–146
  fundamental attribution error, 141–144
  role bias, 146–147
  cause and responsibility, 120–129
  conflict and, 134–135, 141, 245–248
  defensive, 123, 143–146
  divergent perspectives, 129–135, 142–143, 178n, 449–450
  in intimate relationships, 245–248
  self-serving, 133
  sex differences, 67–68
  single multiple cases, 135–140
  of social values, 346–347

Awareness
  of group, 100–108, 227, *see also* Conformity, in-group versus out-group categorization and
  of others, 85–91
  of self, 91–100
    focal self awareness, 94–96
    tacit self awareness, 92–94
    tacit-focal distinction, 77–85

B

Berger, J., *et al.*, theoretical position, 23–24, 373–374